Research Methods in Management

Research Methods in Management

2nd Edition

Edited by
MARION FRENZ, KLAUS NIELSEN and
GEOFF WALTERS

Los Angeles | London | New Delhi
Singapore | Washington DC

Editorial arrangement © Marion Frenz, Klaus Nielsen and Geoff Walters, 2011

Chapter 1 © David A. de Vaus, 2001
Chapter 2 © David A. de Vaus, 2001
Chapter 3 © David A. de Vaus, 2001
Chapter 4 © John Gill and Phil Johnson, 2010
Chapter 5 © John Gill and Phil Johnson, 2010
Chapter 6 © Michael D. Myers, 2008
Chapter 7 © David E. Gray, 2009
Chapter 8 © David E. Gray, 2009
Chapter 9 © David E. Gray, 2009
Chapter 10 © David E. Gray, 2009
Chapter 11 © Caroline Oates, 2000
Chapter 12 © Michael D. Myers, 2008
Chapter 13 © David Silverman, 2009

Chapter 14 © SAGE Publications, Inc., 2009
Chapter 15 © Peter K. Smith, 2000
Chapter 16 © The Open University, 1998
Chapter 17 © The Open University, 1998
Chapter 18 © Michael Crotty, 1998
Chapter 19 © Michael Crotty, 1998
Chapter 20 © John Gill and Phil Johnson, 2010
Chapter 21 © The Open University, 1998
Chapter 22 © John Gill and Phil Johnson, 2010
Chapter 23 © Ingeman Arbnor and Bjorn Bjerke, 2009
Chapter 24 © Ian Lings, 2008
Chapter 25 © David E. Gray, 2009

Reprinted 2012

SAGE Publications Ltd
1 Oliver's Yard
55 City Road
London EC1Y 1SP

SAGE Publications Inc.
2455 Teller Road
Thousand Oaks, California 91320

SAGE Publications India Pvt Ltd
B 1/I 1 Mohan Cooperative Industrial Area
Mathura Road
New Delhi 110 044

SAGE Publications Asia-Pacific Pte Ltd
3 Church Street
#10-04 Samsung Hub
Singapore 049483

Library of Congress Control Number: 2011938230

British Library Cataloguing in Publication data

A catalogue record for this book is available from the British Library

ISBN 978-1-4462-4884-3

Typeset by C&M Digitals (P) Ltd, Chennai, India
Printed and bound by CPI Group (UK) Ltd, Croydon, CR0 4YY
Printed on paper from sustainable resources

Contents

Research Methods in Management I

Marion Frenz, Klaus Nielsen and Geoff Walters

1.0 Introduction

Welcome to the main textbook accompanying the Research Methods in Management module taught at Birkbeck's Management Department. This textbook is customized by SAGE Publications to fit the unique purpose of our taught module. It is a compilation of individual chapters, or parts, taken from different teaching books, which, taken together, cover the entire range of topics relevant to the module as well as chapters which are meant to help students when they are working with their dissertation. It is packaged with another textbook which supports Lectures 4, 5 and 6.

This introductory chapter has two aims: to provide an introduction to Research Methods in Management; and to guide you through the individual chapters in this book and the accompanying text. It is structured in the following way. First, we start by summarizing the aims and main parts of Research Methods in Management. Second, specific elements of the module are discussed in more detail and with explicit reference to the specific chapters presented in this text. This part follows the sequence of lectures. The first section is a general introduction to research design followed by an introduction to qualitative methods. The next section is about case studies which is one of the most widely used methods in management research. Then follows an introduction to quantitative methods and finally there is a section on the philosophy of science.

1.1 Research Methods in Management

Research Methods in Management is core to all postgraduate degree programmes taught in the Department of Management. It is your *academic tool kit* which helps you to assess the quality of academic research, and, thus, bears relevance to all of your academic activities. The aims of the module are twofold: to provide you with the necessary knowledge and understanding to critically appraise published work in the area of management, and to provide you with the necessary skills to design and carry out your own research.

Research starts by defining a specific research question or a research problem. This involves theoretical/conceptual considerations concerned with the formulation of the relevant questions or development of specific hypotheses. Some research is concerned with uncovering causal relationships between two or more factors; for example, the impact lengths of revision time may have on exam performance. Other research attempts to uncover the meaning attached by individuals or groups to various social events and relationships, for example, students' perception of studying and learning.

Addressing research questions involves collecting and analysing evidence. The role of research design is generally to ensure that we collect appropriate evidence in an appropriate fashion and analyse the evidence in an appropriate way. It is crucial that the research is conducted in a rigorous way and that the findings are relevant. Some times rigour and relevance can be achieved simultaneously if the research is organized in a proper way. In other cases there may be a trade-off between rigour and relevance. These are issues covered in detail in the lectures.

When the purpose is to uncover causal relationships the role of research design is to ensure that the evidence used to analyze a relationship can sustain a causal claim and to assess the extent to which a causal relationship uncovered by the empirical evidence is applicable to a wider population, e.g., all firms; all individuals. When the purpose is to uncover the meaning of social events and relationships, the role of research design is to ensure that the evidence supports sensible interpretations of the phenomena in question.

The relevant research design is dependent on the research question. Some questions require a specific form of enquiry whereas other questions require another research design. However, the choice of research design is also dependent on the philosophical and theoretical assumptions of the student and the researcher. Some of the most important issues in this respect are touched on in Lecture 1, 7 and 8 whereas the lectures in-between introduce qualitative and quantitative methods in general and go into detail on some of the most relevant methods used in management studies.

1.1 Specific topics

Lecture 1: Introduction to research design and qualitative methods
Lecture 1 is primarily an introduction to research design. Chapters 1–5 of the book cover various issues related to research design and the variety of methods used in management research. The point of departure in Chapter 1 is the distinction between different types of research questions: what is going on (descriptive research) and; why is it going on (explanatory research). One could add exploratory research as a third type of research. The research design most suitable to address a specific research question is dependent on several factors, i.e. the prior knowledge about the phenomenon in question, the level of abstraction, and the complexity of causal linkages. Chapter 2 outlines the steps in the research design process and introduces a number of concepts used in efforts to assure good quality research such as validity and reliability. Chapter 3 briefly introduces the difference between co-variation and causal relationships which is crucial in the design of explanatory research. Chapter 4 compares and contrasts management research with management development. Different types of research (deductive and inductive) are presented, and some of the philosophical issues, which will be explored further in Lecture 7 and 8, are briefly presented. Chapter 5 is about the role of theory within various approaches in management research. The chapter also discusses the relationship between theory and management practice.

A proper understanding of design issues discussed in this text will underpin your further reading and understanding of the remaining materials of the course; starting with qualitative designs.

In addition to the general introduction, Lecture 1 also includes a brief introduction to qualitative methods. Chapter 6 outlines the main differences between qualitative and quantitative research, discusses what types of research questions can be answered by means of qualitative methods, and briefly introduces some of the most important quality issues related to qualitative research.

Lecture 2: Collection of data (questionnaires and interviews) and analysis of qualitative data
Lecture 2 is mainly about qualitative research methods. In addition to the fundamental issue of research design, the lecture gives a more detailed account of both collection and analysis of qualitative data. The lecture also includes a brief introduction to the collection of quantitative data by means of questionnaires. Whereas quantitative data are expressed in numbers, qualitative research is based on meanings expressed through words and other non-numerical symbols. The evidence consists of non-standardized data requiring classification into categories. Qualitative

methods are especially useful when the purpose of research is explorative, when rich or thick description of a phenomenon is required, and when focus is on the interpretation of phenomena by individuals and groups. They may also be used to uncover cause-effect relationships. Interviewing is a popular technique for collection of qualitative data. Other techniques include observation, focus groups and documentary sources.

Chapter 7 explores the issue of research design in relation to qualitative methods. The characteristics of qualitative data are identified. Sampling strategy and quality issues are also covered in the chapter. It also discusses which research questions fit with qualitative methods. Chapter 8 and 9 explore in detail the two main methods for collecting data in quantitative and qualitative research, respectively. Chapter 8 is about questionnaires. Data collection for quantitative surveys often takes the form of a questionnaire. The chapter discusses how questionnaire items (the questions in a questionnaire) are developed and assessed. Both overall design and writing of individual questions are covered as well as how to maintain validity and reliability. Chapter 9 is about interviewing. Different types of interviews are outlined and various issues in conducting high quality interviews are presented and discussed. Chapter 10 is about how to analyze the collected qualitative data. Some general principles of qualitative data analysis are presented, as well as the application of specific qualitative methodologies, such as grounded theory approaches. In addition, the readings for this part also include Chapter 11 which is a supplementary text that introduces focus group research.

Lecture 3: Case studies
The case study is one of the most popular approaches within social science research. This is the topic of Lecture 3. A case study can be defined as a research strategy with the objective of understanding the dynamics within a contemporary case setting, particularly where the researcher has little or no control. Within management studies the case study can be used to better understand an individual organization, a group of organizations, or a particular industry. A case study can draw on both qualitative and quantitative data and utilize different types of data collection methods. For this reason case study research can result in rich and detailed evidence from a range of sources, allowing for methodological triangulation in order to improve the internal validity of the research findings. However case study research cannot be used to make statistical generalizations where the results are used to make inferences about the broader population. Nevertheless, where case study research is grounded in a theoretical context the results can be related back to theory and used to make analytical generalizations.

These issues are explored in further detail within the lecture on case studies in week three. The objectives of the lecture are to introduce the case study as a research strategy; to understand the different types of case study and the different objectives that researchers might have for choosing this particular research approach; to consider the advantages and disadvantages of the case study strategy; and to consider the practicalities of undertaking case study research by introducing the key stages of which researchers should be aware. The case study readings in this collection to accompany the lecture intend to provide a broad introduction to case study research. Chapter 12 provides an introduction to case study research. It is useful in providing an overview of the objectives of case study research, and the different approaches to case study research, in addition to potential advantages and disadvantages. The text stresses that case study research is not an easy option, particularly for inexperienced researchers. To overcome this there is a need for a thorough case study design from the outset. Chapter 13 in this book addresses this point. Taken from the seminal text by Yin (2009) on case study research, it focuses on the components of case study design, considers the different types of case study, and the need to address validity and reliability in order to maximize the quality of case study research. The third reading about case study methodology is Chapter 14 which gives a good overview of selecting a case, sampling issues, and discusses how to generalize from a few or a single case.

> * Readings for Lectures 4, 5 and 6 are in the companion textbook, Burns and Burns (2008), *Business Research Methods and Statistics, Using SPSS*, SAGE: London, packaged with this text.

Lecture 4: Introduction to statistics

Lecture 4 is concerned with the following topics: presenting data; computing descriptive statistics, i.e. summarizing variables through measures of central location and measures of dispersion; and testing common assumptions in statistics, with an emphasis on issues around normal distribution. Chapter 1 (Burns and Burns) presents the rationale for the use of statistics in management research and distinguishes between descriptive and inferential statistics. Chapter 6 (Burns and Burns) introduces different levels of measurement and explains how to enter raw data into SPSS and how to use SPSS for initial data screening. Chapter 7 (Burns and Burns) introduces the most frequently used descriptive statistics and how to use SPSS to obtain them. The characteristics of frequency of occurrence, central location, spread and shape form major elements in making data sets intelligible. The central concepts of variance and standard deviation are defined. Chapter 8 (Burns and Burns) introduces other essential statistical concepts underlying all quantitative research such as normal distribution, probability and statistical significance.

Lecture 5: Inferential statistics based on the relationships between two variables

Lectures 5 and 6 explore the relationship between two variables, for example the relationship between advertising budgets and record sales. The relevant statistics are coupled with inferential statistics. It is the element of inference that contributes much to the popularity of statistical methods in social science research. Inferential statistics assess the probability that a relationship found in a sample holds in the wider population the sample is drawn from. Chapter 10 (Burns and Burns) integrates the concepts introduced in chapters 1, 6, 7 and 8, and demonstrates how this leads to the formulation and testing of hypotheses, using the concept of standard error and significance to estimate whether the effect is due to chance or a real one. Chapter 12 (Burns and Burns) is about hypothesis testing for differences between means and proportions. The lecture covers the most popular techniques, including the Chi-square test and correlation coefficients which are discussed in Chapter 14 (Burns and Burns), and Chapter 15 (Burns and Burns), respectively.

Lecture 6: Multiple regressions

In the business world the desired effect is typically driven by the impact of multiple independent variables working together rather than by a single variable. An example is the relationship of sales revenue to the amount of advertising expenditure and number of sales persons. The technique of regression allows the researcher to make predictions of the likely value of the dependent variable from known values of a number of independent variables (simple linear regression), or from known values of a combination of independent variables (multiple regression). Regression technique is the topic of Lecture 6. Chapter 16 (Burns and Burns) defines the purposes of the various regression techniques, presents the techniques, and explains how to use SPSS for simple and multiple regressions and how to interpret the printout.

Lecture 7: Philosophy of social sciences I

Enlightenment challenged theology as the hitherto only legitimate path to knowledge through the propagation of a methodology (nowadays called positivism) used by natural science. This methodology was then (without further questions) also employed by social sciences. Eventually, the question 'what are scientists really doing and what should they do when they conduct research?' was asked. Attempts to answer this question are what we call 'the philosophy of science'. It is important to have a proper understanding of the different philosophical assumptions hidden beneath management research in order to appreciate the strengths and weaknesses of each, in order to appreciate how different philosophical assumptions influence the criteria we use to judge research quality, and in order to be able to locate one's own philosophical position.

Lecture 7 introduces a set of basic concepts in the philosophy of science and discusses the philosophical rationale behind different research strategies. The readings cover these topics in different, and to some extent, overlapping ways. Chapter 15 is the most basic of the texts. The text clarifies what philosophy of science is about and provides a historical perspective. The chapter also includes a brief overview of most of the issues covered in more detail in the other readings for Lectures 7 and 8. Chapters 16 and 17 outline the main characteristics of positivism and idealism respectively. Idealism is in this context seen as the main alternative to positivism. In many other texts it is rather interpretivism which is presented as the main alternative whereas in these chapters interpretivism is considered a subset of idealist approaches. Chapter 16 outlines the main characteristics of positivism, its philosophical foundation and major traditions. The text explores the central debates on deduction versus induction. It outlines Popper's critique of inductivism and his falsificationist alternative. Chapter 17 identifies various strands of idealism which have epistemological assumptions that diverge radically from positivism. Human behaviour is unpredictable and is therefore seen as rule-governed rather than law-like. The role of consciousness and meaning is stressed as well as the unavoidable interaction between the researcher and the subject matter.

Chapters 18 and 19 can be seen as alternatives to Chapters 16 and 17. In these chapters, Crotty presents two main philosophical approaches: positivism (Chapter 18) and interpretivism (Chapter 19). In addition to a clear account of the main characteristics of positivism and post-positivism, Chapter 18 also briefly introduces the concept of paradigm which is explored in more detail in Lecture 8. Chapter 19 provides a slightly different understanding of the main alternative to positivism. It outlines the main features and the various strands of interpretivism. Chapter 20 provides a broader approach to philosophy of science than the outline of two major approaches in Chapters 16–19. More approaches are distinguished and all of them are discussed with reference to two crucial concepts in the philosophy of science: epistemology and ontology.

Lecture 8: Philosophy of social sciences II

Scientific progress was once seen as a continuous process where new knowledge is added to existing knowledge in an incremental way. This view has been challenged and substituted by the concepts of paradigm and paradigm shifts pioneered by Thomas Kuhn. Lecture 8 is about paradigms and similar discontinuous views of knowledge development. Paradigms are shared theoretical structures and methodological approaches about which there is high degree of consensus among a group of researchers. The truth of a scientific statement is only relevant to those who share the belief system upon which such 'truths' are based. Following Kuhn, scientific development is characterized by paradigm shifts and is accordingly far from continuous. In Chapter 21 the ideas behind the paradigm concept, the criticism of the concept and the alternative positions developed by Lakatos and Feyerabend are presented and discussed.

Lecture 8 also refers to the specific paradigms existing within management research and the issue of how to evaluate management research. In a sense, we return to the issues covered in Lecture 1 about the relation between theory, management research and management practice. Chapter 22 discusses the evaluation criteria for assessing management research. The chapter argues that the different methods have different strengths and weaknesses, and stresses that the relevant evaluation criteria depend on the philosophical assumptions at play in any given piece of research.

Chapters 23–25 are supplementary. They will not be referred to in the lectures. The chapters are included to assist the students when they are working with their dissertation. Chapter 23 presents the various philosophical issues, approaches and major contributions of relevance for management research in a 'handbook-like' fashion. Chapter 24 gives advice on how to conduct a literature review as part of a dissertation. Finally, Chapter 25 provides useful guidelines on how to write up the research, report structure and writing style.

1.3 Conclusion

We hope that this book will provide all postgraduate management students at Birkbeck with the methodological tool kit that makes it possible for them to conduct research of a high standard, as well as equip them with the knowledge and critical perspectives needed to critically assess research findings in books and journals as well as their own research.

Good luck with the book.

Lecture 1

Introduction to Research Design and Qualitative Methods

The Context of Design

DAVID DE VAUS

Before examining types of research designs it is important to be clear about the role and purpose of research design. We need to understand what research design is and what it is not. We need to know where design fits into the whole research process from framing a question to finally analysing and reporting data. This is the purpose of this chapter.

Description and explanation

Social researchers ask two fundamental types of research questions:

1 *What* is going on (descriptive research)?
2 *Why* is it going on (explanatory research)?

Descriptive research

Although some people dismiss descriptive research as 'mere description', good description is fundamental to the research enterprise and it has added immeasurably to our knowledge of the shape and nature of our society. Descriptive research encompasses much government sponsored research including the population census, the collection of a wide range of social indicators and economic information such as household expenditure patterns, time use studies, employment and crime statistics and the like.

Descriptions can be concrete or abstract. A relatively concrete description might describe the ethnic mix of a community, the changing age profile of a population or the gender mix of a workplace. Alternatively the description might ask more abstract questions such as 'Is the level of social inequality increasing or declining?', 'How secular is society?' or 'How much poverty is there in this community?'

Accurate descriptions of the level of unemployment or poverty have historically played a key role in social policy reforms (Marsh, 1982). By demonstrating the existence of social problems, competent description can challenge accepted assumptions about the way things are and can provoke action.

Good description provokes the 'why' questions of explanatory research. If we detect greater social polarization over the last 20 years (i.e. the rich are getting richer and the poor are getting poorer) we are forced to ask 'Why is this happening?' But before asking 'why?' we must be sure about the fact and dimensions of the phenomenon of increasing polarization. It is all very well to develop elaborate theories as to why society might be more polarized now than in the recent past, but if the basic premise is wrong (i.e. society is not becoming more polarized) then attempts to explain a non-existent phenomenon are silly.

Of course description can degenerate to mindless fact gathering or what C.W. Mills (1959) called 'abstracted empiricism'. There are plenty of examples of unfocused surveys and case studies that report trivial information and fail to provoke any 'why' questions or provide any basis for generalization. However, this is a function of inconsequential descriptions rather than an indictment of descriptive research itself.

Explanatory research

Explanatory research focuses on *why* questions. For example, it is one thing to describe the crime rate in a country, to examine trends over time or to compare the rates in different countries. It is quite a different thing to develop explanations about why the crime rate is as high as it is, why some types of crime are increasing or why the rate is higher in some countries than in others.

The way in which researchers develop research designs is fundamentally affected by whether the research question is descriptive or explanatory. It affects what information is collected. For example, if we want to explain why some people are more likely to be apprehended and convicted of crimes we need to have hunches about why this is so. We may have many possibly incompatible hunches and will need to collect information that enables us to see which hunches work best empirically.

Answering the 'why' questions involves developing *causal* explanations. Causal explanations argue that phenomenon Y (e.g. income level) is affected by factor X (e.g. gender). Some causal explanations will be simple while others will be more complex. For example, we might argue that there is a *direct* effect of gender on income (i.e. simple gender discrimination) (Figure 1.1a). We might argue for a causal chain, such as that gender affects choice of field of training which in turn affects

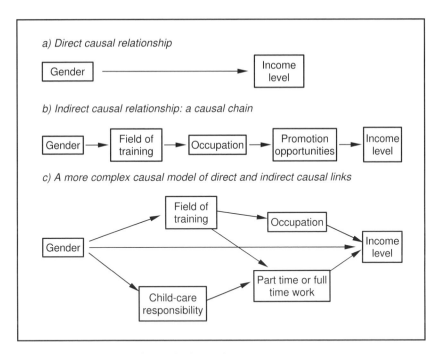

Figure 1.1   *Three types of causal relationships*

occupational options, which are linked to opportunities for promotion, which in turn affect income level (Figure 1.1b). Or we could posit a more complex model involving a number of interrelated causal chains (Figure 1.1c).

PREDICTION, CORRELATION AND CAUSATION

People often confuse correlation with causation. Simply because one event follows another, or two factors co-vary, does not mean that one causes the other. The link between two events may be coincidental rather than causal.

There is a correlation between the number of fire engines at a fire and the amount of damage caused by the fire (the more fire engines the more damage). Is it therefore reasonable to conclude that the number of fire engines causes the amount of damage? Clearly the number of fire engines and the amount of damage will *both* be due to some third factor – such as the seriousness of the fire.

Similarly, as the divorce rate changed over the twentieth century the crime rate increased a few years later. But this does not mean that divorce causes crime. Rather than divorce causing crime, divorce and crime rates might both be due to *other* social processes such as secularization, greater individualism or poverty.

Students at fee paying private schools typically perform better in their final year of schooling than those at government funded schools. But this need not be because private schools *produce* better performance. It may be that attending a private school and better final-year performance are *both* the outcome of some other cause (see later discussion).

Confusing causation with correlation also confuses prediction with causation and prediction with explanation. Where two events or characteristics are correlated we can predict one from the other. Knowing the type of school attended improves our capacity to predict academic achievement. But this does not mean that the school type affects academic achievement. Predicting performance on the basis of school type does not tell us *why* private school students do better. *Good prediction does not depend on causal relationships. Nor does the ability to predict accurately demonstrate anything about causality.*

Recognizing that causation is more than correlation highlights a problem. While we can observe correlation *we cannot observe cause.* We have to *infer* cause. These inferences however are 'necessarily fallible . . . [they] are only indirectly linked to observables' (Cook and Campbell, 1979: 10). Because our inferences are fallible we must minimize the chances of incorrectly saying that a relationship is causal when in fact it is not. *One of the fundamental purposes of research design in explanatory research is to avoid invalid inferences.*

DETERMINISTIC AND PROBABILISTIC CONCEPTS OF CAUSATION

There are two ways of thinking about causes: deterministically and probabilistically. The smoker who denies that tobacco causes cancer because he smokes heavily but has not contracted cancer illustrates deterministic causation. Probabilistic causation is illustrated by health authorities who point to the increased chances of cancer among smokers.

Deterministic causation is where variable X is said to cause Y if, and only if, X *invariably* produces Y. That is, when X is present then Y will 'necessarily, inevitably and infallibly' occur (Cook and Campbell, 1979: 14). This approach seeks to establish causal *laws* such as: whenever water is heated to 100 °C it always boils.

In reality laws are never this simple. They will always specify particular *conditions* under which that law operates. Indeed a great deal of scientific investigation involves specifying the conditions under which particular laws operate. Thus, we might say that *at sea level* heating *pure* water to 100 °C will always cause water to boil.

Alternatively, the law might be stated in the form of 'other things being equal' then X will always produce Y. A deterministic version of the relationship between race and income level would say that other things being equal (age, education, personality, experience etc.) then a white person will [always] earn a higher income than a black person. That is, race (X) causes income level (Y).

Stated like this the notion of deterministic causation in the social sciences sounds odd. It is hard to conceive of a characteristic or event that will invariably result in a given outcome even if a fairly tight set of conditions is specified. The *complexity* of human social behaviour and the *subjective, meaningful and voluntaristic* components of human behaviour mean that it will never be possible to arrive at causal statements of the type 'If X, and A and B, then Y will always follow.'

Most causal thinking in the social sciences is *probabilistic* rather than *deterministic* (Suppes, 1970). That is, we work at the level that a given factor increases (or decreases) the probability of a particular outcome, for example: being female increases the probability of working part time; race affects the probability of having a high status job.

We can improve probabilistic explanations by specifying conditions under which X is less likely and more likely to affect Y. But we will never achieve complete or deterministic explanations. Human behaviour is both *willed* and *caused*: there is a double-sided character to human social behaviour. People *construct* their social world and there are creative aspects to human action but this freedom and agency will always be constrained by the structures within which people live. Because behaviour is not simply determined we cannot achieve deterministic explanations. However, because behaviour is constrained we can achieve probabilistic explanations. We can say that a given factor will increase the likelihood of a given outcome but there will never be certainty about outcomes.

Despite the probabilistic nature of causal statements in the social sciences, much popular, ideological and political discourse translates these into deterministic statements. Findings about the causal effects of class, gender or ethnicity, for example, are often read as if these factors invariably and completely produce particular outcomes. One could be forgiven for thinking that social science has demonstrated that gender completely and invariably determines position in society, roles in families, values and ways of relating to other people.

Theory testing and theory construction

Attempts to answer the 'why' questions in social science are theories. These theories vary in their *complexity* (how many variables and links), *abstraction* and *scope*. To understand the role of theory in empirical research it is useful to distinguish between two different styles of research: theory testing and theory building (Figure 1.2).

Theory building

Theory building is a process in which research begins with observations and uses *inductive* reasoning to derive a theory from these observations.

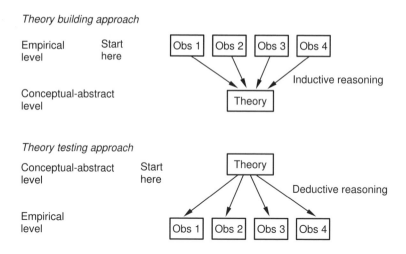

Figure 1.2 *Theory building and theory testing approaches to research*

These theories attempt to make sense of observations. Because the theory is produced *after* observations are made it is often called *post factum* theory (Merton, 1968) or *ex post facto* theorizing.

   This form of theory building entails asking whether the observation is *a particular case of a more general factor*, or how the observation *fits into a pattern or a story*. For example, Durkheim observed that the suicide rate was higher among Protestants than Catholics. But is religious affiliation a particular case of something more general? Of what more general phenomenon might it be an indicator? Are there other observations that shed light on this? He also observed that men were more suicidal than women, urban dwellers more than rural dwellers and the socially mobile more than the socially stable. He argued that the common factor behind all these observations was that those groups who were most suicidal were also less well socially integrated and experienced greater ambiguity about how to behave and what is right and wrong. He theorized that one of the explanations for suicidal behaviour was a sense of normlessness – a disconnectedness of individuals from their social world. Of course, there may have been other ways of accounting for these observations but at least Durkheim's explanation was consistent with the facts.

Theory testing

In contrast, a theory testing approach *begins* with a theory and uses theory to guide which observations to make: it moves from the general to the particular. The observations should provide a test of the worth of the theory. Using *deductive* reasoning to derive a set of propositions from the theory does this. We need to develop these propositions so that

Parents divorced?

		No	Yes
	Low	(a)	(b)
Parental conflict			
	High	(c)	(d)

Figure 1.3 *The relationship between divorce and parental conflict*

if the theory is true then certain things should follow in the real world. We then assess whether these predictions are correct. If they are correct the theory is supported. If they do not hold up then the theory needs to be either rejected or modified.

For example, we may wish to test the theory that it is not divorce itself that affects the wellbeing of children but the level of conflict between parents. To test this idea we can make predictions about the wellbeing of children under different family conditions. For the simple theory that it is parental conflict rather than divorce that affects a child's wellbeing there are four basic 'conditions' (see Figure 1.3). For each 'condition' the theory would make different predictions about the level of children's wellbeing that we can examine.

If the theory that it is parental conflict rather than parental divorce is correct the following propositions should be supported:

- *Proposition 1: children in situations (a) and (b) would be equally well off* That is, where parental conflict is low, children with divorced parents will do just as well as those whose parents are married.
- *Proposition 2: children in situations (c) and (d) should be equally poorly off* That is, children in conflictual couple families will do just as badly as children in post-divorce families where parents sustain high conflict.
- *Proposition 3: children in situation (c) will do worse than those in situation (a)* That is, those with married parents in high conflict will do worse than those who have married parents who are not in conflict.
- *Proposition 4: children in situation (d) will do worse than those in situation (b)* That is, those with divorced parents in high conflict will do worse than those who have divorced parents who are not in conflict.
- *Proposition 5: children in situation (b) will do better than those in situation (c)* That is, children with divorced parents who are not in conflict will do better than those with married parents who are in conflict.
- *Proposition 6: children in situation (a) will do better than those in situation (d)* That is, children with married parents who are not in conflict will do better than those with divorced parents who are in conflict.

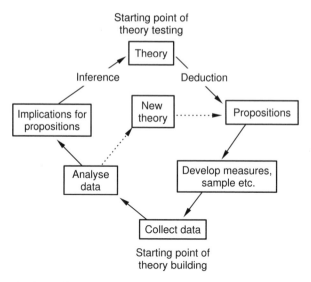

Figure 1.4   *The logic of the research process*

No single proposition would provide a compelling test of the original theory. Indeed, taken on its own proposition 3, for example, would reveal nothing about the impact of divorce. However, taken as a package, the *set* of propositions provides a stronger test of the theory than any single proposition.

Although theory testing and theory building are often presented as alternative modes of research they should be part of one ongoing process (Figure 1.4). Typically, theory building will produce a plausible account or explanation of a set of observations. However, such explanations are frequently just one of a number of possible explanations that fit the data. While plausible they are not necessarily compelling. They require systematic testing where data are collected to specifically evaluate how well the explanation holds when subjected to a range of crucial tests.

What is research design?

How is the term 'research design' to be used in this book? An analogy might help. When constructing a building there is no point ordering materials or setting critical dates for completion of project stages until we know what sort of building is being constructed. The first decision is whether we need a high rise office building, a factory for manufacturing machinery, a school, a residential home or an apartment block. Until this is done we cannot sketch a plan, obtain permits, work out a work schedule or order materials.

Similarly, social research needs a design or a structure before data collection or analysis can commence. A research design is *not* just a work plan. A work plan details what has to be done to complete the project but the work plan will flow from the project's research design. *The function of a research design is to ensure that the evidence obtained enables us to answer the initial question as unambiguously as possible.* Obtaining relevant evidence entails specifying the type of evidence needed to answer the research question, to test a theory, to evaluate a programme or to accurately describe some phenomenon. In other words, when designing research we need to ask: given this research question (or theory), what type of evidence is needed to answer the question (or test the theory) *in a convincing way*?

Research design 'deals with a *logical* problem and not a *logistical* problem' (Yin, 1989: 29). Before a builder or architect can develop a work plan or order materials they must first establish the type of building required, its uses and the needs of the occupants. The work plan flows from this. Similarly, in social research the issues of sampling, method of data collection (e.g. questionnaire, observation, document analysis), design of questions are all subsidiary to the matter of 'What evidence do I need to collect?'

Too often researchers design questionnaires or begin interviewing far too early – before thinking through what information they require to answer their research questions. Without attending to these research design matters at the beginning, the conclusions drawn will normally be weak and unconvincing and fail to answer the research question.

Design versus method

Research design is different from the method by which data are collected. Many research methods texts confuse research designs with methods. It is not uncommon to see research design treated as a mode of data collection rather than as a logical structure of the inquiry. But there is nothing intrinsic about any research design that requires a particular method of data collection. Although cross-sectional surveys are frequently equated with questionnaires and case studies are often equated with participant observation (e.g. Whyte's *Street Corner Society*, 1943), data for any design can be collected with any data collection method (Figure 1.5). How the data are collected is irrelevant to the *logic* of the design.

Failing to distinguish between design and method leads to poor evaluation of designs. Equating cross-sectional designs with questionnaires, or case studies with participant observation, means that the designs are often evaluated against the strengths and weaknesses of the method rather than their ability to draw relatively unambiguous conclusions or to select between rival plausible hypotheses.

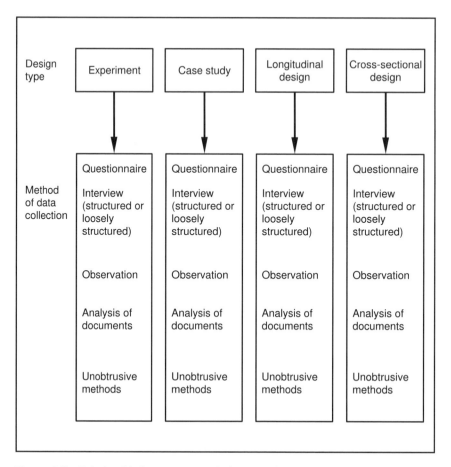

Figure 1.5   *Relationship between research design and particular data collection methods*

QUANTITATIVE AND QUALITATIVE RESEARCH

Similarly, designs are often equated with qualitative and quantitative research methods. Social surveys and experiments are frequently viewed as prime examples of quantitative research and are evaluated against the strengths and weaknesses of statistical, quantitative research methods and analysis. Case studies, on the other hand, are often seen as prime examples of qualitative research – which adopts an interpretive approach to data, studies 'things' within their context and considers the subjective meanings that people bring to their situation.

It is erroneous to equate a particular research design with either quantitative or qualitative methods. Yin (1993), a respected authority on case study design, has stressed the irrelevance of the quantitative/qualitative distinction for case studies. He points out that:

a point of confusion . . . has been the unfortunate linking between the case study method and certain types of data collection – for example those focusing on qualitative methods, ethnography, or participant observation. People have thought that the case study method required them to embrace these data collection methods . . . On the contrary, the method does not imply any particular form of data collection – which can be qualitative or quantitative. (1993: 32)

Similarly, Marsh (1982) argues that quantitative surveys can provide information and explanations that are 'adequate at the level of meaning'. While recognizing that survey research has not always been good at tapping the subjective dimension of behaviour, she argues that:

Making sense of social action . . . is . . . hard and surveys have not traditionally been very good at it. The earliest survey researchers started a tradition . . . of bringing the meaning from outside, either by making use of the researcher's stock of plausible explanations . . . or by bringing it from subsidiary in-depth interviews sprinkling quotes . . . liberally on the raw correlations derived from the survey. Survey research became much more exciting . . . when it began including meaningful dimensions in the study design. [This has been done in] two ways, firstly [by] asking the actor either for her reasons directly, or to supply information about the central values in her life around which we may assume she is orienting her life. [This] involves collecting a sufficiently complete picture of the context in which an actor finds herself that a team of outsiders may read off the meaningful dimensions. (1982: 123–4)

Adopting a sceptical approach to explanations

The need for research design stems from a sceptical approach to research and a view that scientific knowledge must always be provisional. The purpose of research design is to reduce the ambiguity of much research evidence.

We can always find some evidence consistent with almost any theory. However, we should be sceptical of the evidence, and rather than seeking evidence that is *consistent* with our theory we should seek evidence that provides a *compelling* test of the theory.

There are two related strategies for doing this: eliminating rival explanations of the evidence and deliberately seeking evidence that could *disprove* the theory.

PLAUSIBLE RIVAL HYPOTHESES

A fundamental strategy of social research involves evaluating 'plausible rival hypotheses'. We need to examine and evaluate alternative ways of explaining a particular phenomenon. This applies regardless of whether the data are quantitative or qualitative; regardless of the particular research design (experimental, cross-sectional, longitudinal or case

Causal relationship

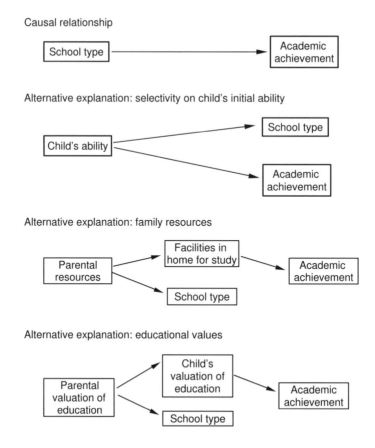

Figure 1.6   *Causal and non-causal explanations of the relationship between school type and academic achievement*

study); and regardless of the method of data collection (e.g. observation, questionnaire). Our mindset needs to anticipate alternative ways of interpreting findings and to regard any interpretation of these findings as provisional – subject to further testing.

The idea of evaluating plausible rival hypotheses can be illustrated using the example of the correlation between type of school attended and academic achievement. Many parents accept the causal proposition that attendance at fee paying private schools improves a child's academic performance (Figure 1.6). Schools themselves promote the same notion by prominently advertising their pass rates and comparing them with those of other schools or with national averages. By implication they propose a causal connection: 'Send your child to our school and they will pass (or get grades to gain entry into prestigious institutions, courses).' The data they provide are consistent with their proposition that these schools produce better results.

But these data are not compelling. There are at least three other ways of accounting for this correlation without accepting the causal link between school type and achievement (Figure 1.6). There is the *selectivity* explanation: the more able students may be sent to fee paying private schools in the first place. There is the *family resources* explanation: parents who can afford to send their children to fee paying private schools can also afford other help (e.g. books, private tutoring, quiet study space, computers). It is this help rather than the type of school that produces the better performance of private school students. Finally, there is the family *values* explanation: parents who value education most are prepared to send their children to fee paying private schools and it is this family emphasis on education, not the schools themselves, that produces the better academic performance. All these explanations are equally consistent with the observation that private school students do better than government school students. Without collecting further evidence we cannot choose between these explanations and therefore must remain open minded about which one makes most empirical sense.

There might also be methodological explanations for the finding that private school students perform better academically. These methodological issues might undermine any argument that a causal connection exists. Are the results due to questionable ways of measuring achievement? From what range and number of schools were the data obtained? On how many cases are the conclusions based? Could the pattern simply be a function of chance? These are all possible alternative explanations for the finding that private school students perform better.

Good research design will anticipate competing explanations *before* collecting data so that relevant information for evaluating the relative merits of these competing explanations is obtained. In this example of schools and academic achievement, thinking about alternative plausible hypotheses beforehand would lead us to find out about the parents' financial resources, the study resources available in the home, the parents' and child's attitudes about education and the child's academic abilities before entering the school.

The fallacy of affirming the consequent   Although evidence may be consistent with an initial proposition it might be equally consistent with a range of alternative propositions. Too often people do not even think of the alternative hypotheses and simply conclude that since the evidence is consistent with their theory then the theory is true. This form of reasoning commits the logical *fallacy of affirming the consequent*. This form of reasoning has the following logical structure:

- If A is true then B should follow.
- We observe B.
- Therefore A is true.

If we apply this logic to the type of school and achievement proposition, the logical structure of the school type and achievement argument becomes clearer.

Initial proposition:

- Private schools produce better students than do government schools.

The test:

- *If A then B*   If private schools produce better students (A) then their students should get better final marks than those from government funded schools (B).
- *B is true*   Private school students do achieve better final marks than government school students (observe B).
- *Therefore A is true*   Therefore private schools do produce better students (A is true).

But as I have already argued, the better performance of private school students might also reflect the effect of other factors. The problem here is that any number of explanations may be correct and the evidence does not help rule out many of these. For the social scientist this level of indeterminacy is quite unsatisfactory. In effect we are only in a position to say:

- If A [or C, or D, or E, or F, or . . .] then B.
- We observe B.
- Therefore A [or C, or D, or E, or F, or . . .] is true.

Although explanation (A) is still in the running because it is consistent with the observations, we cannot say that it is the most plausible explanation. We need to test our proposition more thoroughly by evaluating the worth of the alternative propositions.

FALSIFICATION: LOOKING FOR EVIDENCE TO DISPROVE THE THEORY

As well as evaluating and eliminating alternative explanations we should rigorously evaluate our own theories. Rather than asking 'What evidence would constitute support for the theory?', ask 'What evidence would convince me that the theory is *wrong*?' It is not difficult to find evidence consistent with a theory. It is much tougher for a theory to survive the test of people trying to disprove it.

Unfortunately some theories are closed systems in which any evidence can be interpreted as support for the theory. Such theories are said to be non-falsifiable. Many religions or belief systems can become closed systems whereby all evidence can be accommodated by the theory and nothing will change the mind of the true believer. Exchange theory (Homans, 1961; Blau, 1964) is largely non-falsifiable. It assumes that we always maximize our gains and avoid costs. But we can see almost anything as a gain. Great sacrifices to care for a disabled relative can be interpreted as a gain (satisfaction of helping) rather than a loss (income, time for self etc.). We need to frame our propositions and define our terms in such a way that they are capable of being disproven.

THE PROVISIONAL NATURE OF SUPPORT FOR THEORIES

Even where the theory is corroborated and has survived attempts to disprove it, the theory remains provisional:

> falsificationism stresses the ambiguity of confirmation . . . corroboration gives only the comfort that the theory has been tested and survived the test, that even after the most impressive corroborations of predictions it has only achieved the status of 'not yet disconfirmed'. This . . . is far from the status of 'being true'. (Cook and Campbell, 1979: 20)

There always may be an unthought-of explanation. We cannot anticipate or evaluate every possible explanation. The more alternative explanations that have been eliminated and the more we have tried to disprove our theory, the more confidence we will have in it, but we should avoid thinking that it is *proven*.

However we can *disprove* a theory. The logic of this is:

- If theory A is true then B should follow.
- B does *not* follow.
- Therefore A is not true.

So long as B is a valid test of A the absence of B should make us reject or revise the theory. In reality, we would not reject a theory simply because a single fact or observation does not fit. Before rejecting a plausible theory we would require multiple disconfirmations using different measures, different samples and different methods of data collection and analysis.

In summary, we should adopt a sceptical approach to explanations. We should anticipate rival interpretations and collect data to enable the winnowing out of the weaker explanations and the identification of which alternative theories make most empirical sense. We also need to ask what data would challenge the explanation and collect data to evaluate the theory from this more demanding perspective.

Summary

This chapter has outlined the purpose of research design in both descriptive and explanatory research. In explanatory research the purpose is to develop and evaluate causal theories. The probabilistic nature of causation in social sciences, as opposed to deterministic causation, was discussed.

Research design is not related to any particular method of collecting data or any particular type of data. Any research design can, in principle, use any type of data collection method and can use either quantitative or qualitative data. Research design refers to the *structure* of an enquiry: it is a logical matter rather than a logistical one.

It has been argued that the central role of research design is to minimize the chance of drawing incorrect causal inferences from data. Design is a logical task undertaken to ensure that the evidence collected enables us to answer questions or to test theories as unambiguously as possible. When designing research it is essential that we identify the type of evidence required to answer the research question in a convincing way. This means that we must not simply collect evidence that is consistent with a particular theory or explanation. Research needs to be structured in such a way that the evidence also bears on alternative rival explanations and enables us to identify which of the competing explanations is most compelling empirically. It also means that we must not simply look for evidence that supports our favourite theory: we should also look for evidence that has the potential to disprove our preferred explanations.

Tools for Research Design

DAVID DE VAUS

To achieve a reasonable research design we need to attend to a number of matters before we arrive at the final design. The first section of this chapter outlines these preliminary steps that precede design. It then expands on the idea of alternative rival hypotheses that was introduced in Chapter 1. The second section introduces a number of concepts that are fundamental to designing good research – internal validity, external validity and measurement error.

Before design

In the same way that an architect needs to know the purpose of the building before designing it (is it an office building, a factory or a home?) social researchers must be clear about their research question before developing a research design.

Focusing and clarifying the research question

The first question to ask is, 'What question am I trying to answer?' Specifying a question is more than identifying a topic. It's not enough to say, 'I'm interested in getting some answers about family breakdown.' What answers to what questions? Do you want to know the extent of family breakdown? Who is most vulnerable to family breakdown? Changing rates of breakdown? Over what period? Where? Or are you really looking at the causes of breakdown? The effects of family breakdown? All the effects or just particular ones?

FOCUSING DESCRIPTIVE RESEARCH QUESTIONS

To narrow the focus of descriptive research we need to specify the scope of what is to be described. The following guidelines, using family breakdown as an example, help narrow down a descriptive research topic into a researchable question.

1   What is the *scope of the core concepts*? What is to be included in the concept *family breakdown*? Do we mean divorce? What about

separation? Are we referring only to the breakdown in marital
relationships? Do we mean the *total* breakdown or simply poor relationships? What about relationships between parents and children or
between children? Until we specify what we mean by our core concepts it is going to be impossible to begin the description.

2 What is the *time frame* for the description? Is our interest in change
over time or just about *contemporary* levels of family breakdown? If it
is about change, over what period?

3 What is the *geographical* location for the description? Is the interest in
family breakdown in a particular community, in different regions or
the whole nation? Is it comparative, looking at breakdown in
different types of countries (e.g. highly industrialized versus rapidly
industrializing versus impoverished countries)?

4 How *general* is the description to be? Do you want to be able to
describe patterns for specific subgroups (e.g. among those who
married as teenagers, among those who are in *de facto* relationships,
second marriages etc.)?

5 What *aspect* of the topic are you interested in? Is the interest in rates of
breakdown? The experience? Laws? Attitudes and beliefs?

6 How *abstract* is your interest? Is your interest in family breakdown or
in family breakdown as a reflection of something more abstract (e.g.
social fragmentation, social conflict, individualism, the role of the
state in the private lives of citizens)?

7 What is the *unit of analysis*? The unit of analysis is the 'thing' about
which we collect information and from which we draw conclusions.
Often this is a person (e.g divorced person) but it may be 'things'
such as organizations (divorce courts), a family as a whole, events
(e.g. divorces), periods (divorce in different years), places (communities, countries).

The questions we can answer will depend on the unit of analysis.
We could compare divorced individuals with non-divorced individuals (individual as the unit of analysis). We could study a series of
divorces and examine what the process of becoming divorced was
(event as unit of analysis). We might use year as the unit of analysis
and track changes in divorce rates since 1945. Using countries we
might examine the different divorce rates in different types of countries with a view to comparing the patterns in different types of
countries. Alternatively families might be the units of analysis and we
may want to look at the characteristics of divorcing families (e.g. size,
family income, family type, nature of relationships in family)
compared with those of non-divorcing families.

Thinking beyond individuals as units of analysis broadens the
range of research questions we ask and broadens the range and
sources of data available. For example, if years were the unit of
analysis we would obtain statistics from the relevant national collection agencies regarding divorce for each year. We would also collect

other information about each year (e.g. unemployment level, inflation rate, changes to laws) that was relevant to the hypotheses.

FOCUSING EXPLANATORY RESEARCH QUESTIONS

In framing explanatory questions we need to further specify our focus. Explanatory research explores causes and/or consequences of a phenomenon, so the research question must be clear about the style of explanatory research and identify which causes or consequences it will investigate.

Before outlining some different types of explanatory research it is useful to introduce some terms.

- *Dependent variable* This is the variable that is treated as the *effect* in the causal model: it is dependent on the influence of some other factor. The dependent variable is also referred to as the outcome variable and in causal diagrams it is conventionally designated as the *Y* variable.
- *Independent variable* This is the variable that is the presumed *cause*. It is also called the predictor variable, the experimental variable or the explanatory variable and is designated in causal diagrams as the *X* variable (as in education $(X) \rightarrow$ income level (Y)).
- *Intervening variables* These variables come between the independent variable and the dependent variable in a causal chain. They are the *means* by which cause *X* produces effect *Y*. Intervening variables are represented in causal diagrams by the symbol *Z*, as illustrated in Figure 2.1.
- *Extraneous variables* Two variables can be correlated without being causally related. The correlation may be due to the two factors being outcomes of a third variable (see Chapter 1). This third variable is called an extraneous variable and is also symbolized as *Z* in causal diagrams, and the form of this relationship is illustrated in Figure 2.2.

Searching for causes or effects This is the least focused type of explanatory research. It involves identifying the core phenomenon (e.g. changes in divorce rate since World War II) and then searching for causes or consequences of this. Searching for causes would involve identifying possible causal factors (e.g. changing values, decline in religion, changing population mix, economic changes, legal reforms, changes in welfare support for lone parents). We would then design research to evaluate which of these causes helps explain changes in divorce rates. This form of research question is illustrated in Figure 2.3.

Alternatively we might focus on the consequences rather than causes of changes in divorce rate (Figure 2.4).

Figure 2.1   *An intervening variable*

Figure 2.2   *An extraneous variable*

Figure 2.3   *Searching for causes*

Figure 2.4   *Searching for effects*

Exploring a simple causal proposition   A more focused research question will specify a *particular* causal proposition to evaluate (Figure 2.5). It might propose an impact of a particular factor or examine a specific consequence. For example, we might propose that changes in government benefits to lone parents have led to an increase in divorce rates since World War II.

More complex causal models   Such propositions are simplistic in that they do not spell out the mechanisms by which the two factors might be related. We might develop more complex models that spell out some of the mechanisms in the causal chain. This fuller model then becomes the focus of the research and provides the framework within which the research design will be framed (Figure 2.6).

   When clarifying a research question it is helpful to draw diagrams like those in Figures 2.1–2.5. It is also helpful to ask four key questions:

1   What am I trying to explain (i.e. what is the dependent variable)?
2   What are the possible causes (what are the independent variables)?
3   Which causes will I explore?

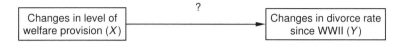

Figure 2.5 *A specific causal proposition*

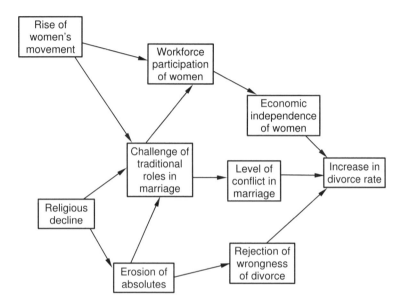

Figure 2.6 *A more complex causal model for increases in divorce*

4   What possible mechanisms connect the presumed causes to the presumed effects (what are the intervening variables)?

Another way of framing research questions is to formulate different ways of understanding a phenomenon and then compare which of these competing approaches best fits the facts. For example, we might compare three different ways of understanding changes in divorce rates: an economic approach, a social values approach and a legislative approach. The economic approach might argue that changes in divorce rates stem from economic factors such as the level of affluence, access of women to work and levels of welfare support for lone parents. The social values explanation might seek to explain the increased divorce rate in terms of increasing levels of individualism and greater social acceptance of divorce. A legislative approach might focus on the impact of legislative changes such as no-fault divorce or new rules regarding property division.

The above examples focus on particular causes and consequences and attempt to provide only a *partial* explanation of changes in divorce rates. These explanations are called *nomothetic* explanations – partial explanations of a class of cases rather than a 'full' explanation of a particular case. They involve an examination of relatively few causal factors and a larger number of cases. In contrast, *idiographic* explanations focus on particular cases and develop as complete an explanation of each case as possible. They involve examining as many factors as possible that contribute to the case including unique factors.

A nomothetic explanation of divorce might focus on the importance of a single contributing factor such as the intergenerational transmission of divorce. Are couples more likely to divorce if one of their parents have divorced? The study might involve comparing people who had divorced with those who had not to see if the divorcees were more likely to have a family history of divorce. In contrast, an idiographic approach might focus on a particular divorced couple and build a full explanation of why *this* couple divorced. The explanation would consider the family history of the couple and examine this along with many other contributing factors. The idiographic explanation would provide us with a good understanding of the *case* while the nomothetic explanation would provide an understanding of the influence of a *factor*.

Identifying plausible rival hypotheses

In Chapter 1 I stressed the importance of identifying plausible rival ways of accounting for the phenomenon being studied. Obviously it makes sense to anticipate these alternatives before carrying out the research. But how do we identify these alternative explanations? There are two main types of rival hypotheses and these suggest ways of anticipating alternative explanations.

THEORETICAL AND SUBSTANTIVE RIVALS

There is no magical way of producing a set of alternative substantive or theoretical explanations. In the end the researcher must formulate them. The more familiar the researcher is with the particular substantive topic and with social science models and theories, the more likely they are to anticipate different ways of interpreting a given set of results. The following provide sources of alternative explanations.

The theoretical literature Broad approaches in a discipline can present different ways of viewing any question. Suppose, for example, that we wanted to understand why some people seem to have happier marriages than other people do. An explanation could concentrate on the *personal attributes* of the couple – their personality, their values and beliefs and their interpersonal skills. It could focus on *economic* factors and interpret marital happiness in terms of the costs and benefits to each partner. Alternatively, the explanation could adopt a *life course perspective* that interprets differences in marital happiness according to where the couple is in the life course (e.g. newly married, before children, young children, adolescent children, empty nest, later life). A feminist approach might try to explain marital happiness in terms of gender roles, division of labour and power within the relationship. A demographer might focus on the birth cohorts (e.g. depression marriages, postwar marriages, 1990s marriages etc.). Other researchers might seek to explain marital happiness in structural terms such as the couple's level of social disadvantage. Social network theorists might concentrate on the extent to which a couple is integrated into the wider family and community and is able to receive support from these networks.

   This list is not exhaustive. The point is that different approaches (e.g. psychological, life course, exchange, structural, feminist) will have a particular 'angle' which alerts us to different ways of looking at an issue. When thinking about a problem, ask yourself questions such as 'How might a feminist account for this?', 'How might a Freudian psychologist explain this?', 'How would an exchange theorist account for this?', 'What might a conflict theorist say?'

Other researchers   Previous research on the topic can be a rich source of competing explanations. Read the literature in journals and search electronic databases. Review articles and introductory overviews can be extremely helpful.

Practitioners, key informants, policy makers, advocates   'Insiders' with practical knowledge of a field can be invaluable. In a study on divorce, marriage counsellors, married couples, divorced people and advocacy groups can provide valuable insights. Literature such as novels and plays can also provide keen ideas that can be tested systematically (e.g. Tolstoy's novel *Anna Karenina* provides one way of interpreting marital unhappiness).

Own experience, hunches, and intuitions   Do not ignore your own experience, your own intuitions and hunches. In the end all explanations start with hunches that spring from individuals who have ideas and observe things around them. Use these insights, experiences and observations and test them systematically.

There is no right way of developing ideas. Do not limit yourself to formal social science research or to research on the very specific topic you are working on. Use diverse sources of ideas. Brainstorm with a group and debate the topic. Think laterally: if your topic is marriage breakdown, look beyond the marriage and divorce literature.

If findings are likely to be due to poor measurement (see below) then any theoretical interpretation of these results will be unconvincing. Throughout this book I will identify many technical and methodological factors that can undermine the conclusions we draw from our research. Good research design will minimize the threat from these sources.

I will not at this point go into these methodological issues in detail. However, it will be helpful to highlight the types of methodological rivals that will be examined. These are outlined in Goldenberg (1992).

1 *Demand characteristics of the situation.*
2 *Transient personal characteristics* such as the respondent's mood, attention span, health etc.
3 *Situational factors* such as anonymity, people present when data were being collected, gender, age and class of investigator and respondent.
4 *Sampling of items*   Are the concepts well measured?
5 *Nature of the sample*   Can we generalize from the sample?
6 *Lack of clarity of the instrument*   Are the questions clear and unambiguous?
7 *Format of data collection*   Are the results an artifact of the data collection method? Would different patterns be found if a different method was used (e.g. observation rather than questionnaire)?
8 *Variation in the administration of the instrument* in studies tracking change over time.
9 *Processing/analysis errors.*

Operationalization

Most social science research involves making observations that we presume tap concepts. If we were conducting a study on the effect of marital breakdown on the wellbeing of children we would need first to work out what is meant by marriage breakdown, wellbeing and children. This involves defining these concepts, which in turn requires developing a *nominal definition* and an *operational definition* of each concept.

Concepts are, by their nature, not directly observable. We cannot see social class, marital happiness, intelligence etc. To use concepts in research we need to translate concepts into something observable – something we can measure. This involves defining and clarifying abstract concepts and developing indicators of them. This process of clarifying abstract concepts and translating them into specific, observable measures is called operationalization and involves *descending the ladder of abstraction.*

CLARIFYING CONCEPTS

Before developing indicators of concepts we must first clarify the concepts. This involves developing both nominal and operational definitions of the concept.

Nominal definitions   Concepts do not have a fixed or correct meaning. Marriage breakdown could be defined in terms of the law (such as whether the decree nisi has been granted), the quality of the relationship or practical arrangements (living apart). Similarly, we need to define children. Is a child defined by a blood relationship, a legal relationship (includes adopted), a social relationship (*de facto* parents), chronological age, level of dependency or some other criterion? By deciding on the type of definition we provide a *nominal definition*: it specifies the meaning of the concept but remains abstract.

Different definitions produce different findings. Consequently, defining concepts is a crucial stage of research. It needs to be done deliberately and to be systematically and carefully justified. There are three steps in developing and narrowing down a nominal definition.

First, *obtain a range of definitions*. Look at review articles, discipline dictionaries (e.g. a dictionary of sociology), encyclopaedias (e.g. an encyclopaedia of social sciences) and journal articles. Look for both explicit and implicit definitions.

Second, *decide on a definition*. From your list either select one definition or create a better definition from the common elements of several definitions. Explain and justify your approach.

Third, *delineate the dimensions of the concept*. Many concepts have a number of dimensions and it is helpful to spell these out as they can help to further refine your definition. This can be illustrated using the concept of the *child's wellbeing*. We can think of a number of dimensions of wellbeing: emotional, psychological, physical, educational, financial, social, environmental, legal etc. If we are arguing that marriage breakdown affects a child's wellbeing, what sort of wellbeing are we talking about? All of these? Just one or two? Having delineated various dimensions you will need to decide which are of interest in the present study. You may examine all aspects or limit yourself to one or two.

A concept may have *subdimensions*. Suppose we focused on *social* wellbeing. This broad concept could incorporate subdimensions such as the level of safety in the neighbourhood, the nature of the child's relationships and her experiences of social discrimination. The subdimension of 'relationships with others' could be further divided into relationships with particular people such as mother, father, peers, siblings and grandparents. Having settled on the particular relationships with which we are going to deal, we would need to identify what *aspects* of the relationships to measure and decide how to measure them (see below). In Figure 2.7 relationships are measured according to the level of

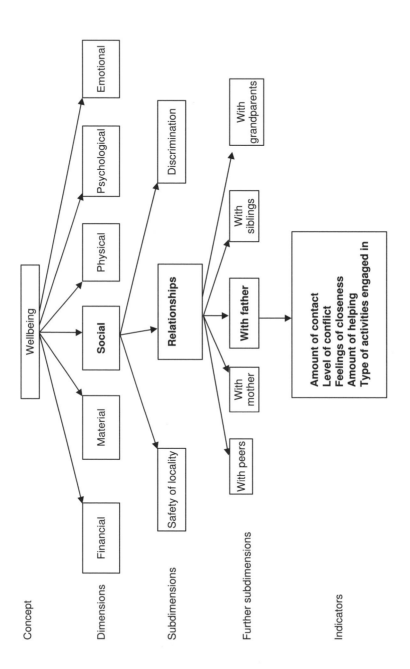

Figure 2.7 *Dimensionalizing the concept of child's wellbeing*

contact, conflict, closeness, helping and type of shared activities. These measures or indicators would then provide the core around which to frame specific questions or to focus an observational study.

In this example I have focused on one dimension at each level but I could have been exhaustive and developed measures for each conceivable dimension and subdimension. The decision of whether to adopt a focused or an exhaustive approach will depend on what you are interested in. The advantage of adopting a systematic approach as outlined in Figure 2.7 is that it helps focus and refine the research question and forces you to make deliberate decisions about how to measure a concept.

Operational definitions Having defined the concepts you will develop an *operational definition* – the observations to measure the concept. What *indicators* of marriage breakdown will you use? We might operationally define marriage breakdown according to the quality of the relationship. Using this definition we might measure breakdown according to level of conflict, type of communication, signs of lack of affection and level of cooperation or lack of cooperation.

How well such indicators tap the concept as defined will have a critical bearing on the value of the conclusions drawn from the study. If the indicators tap something other than what we claim they do then our conclusions can be easily challenged. For example, if our measures of marital breakdown simply tap social class differences in marital style rather than breakdown then our conclusions about marital breakdown will be suspect.

Once the operational definition of the concept has been developed we come to the final stage of operationalization. This entails the precise way in which the indicators will be measured. This might involve developing questions for a questionnaire or identifying what and how observations will be made. Articulating the mechanics of these strategies is beyond the scope of this book.

Concepts for research design

Two concepts, internal and external validity, are fundamental to developing research designs. Ideally research designs should be both internally and externally valid.

Internal validity

We need to be confident that the research design can sustain the causal conclusions that we claim for it. The capacity of a research design to do this reflects its internal validity.

Imagine a research project that compares the emotional adjustment of children from divorced families and intact families. It finds that children from divorced families are less well adjusted than children from intact families. Can we conclude that divorce caused emotional maladjustment? Not on the basis of these results. The design does not enable us to eliminate alternative explanations. The poorer adjustment of children with divorced parents might be due to adjustment differences that predated parental divorce.

A different research study may deal with this problem by tracking children before parents divorce and for some years afterwards. It may find that these children do show a significant decline in emotional adjustment after their parents' divorce. Does the research design show that divorce is producing this decline in adjustment? No. The decline in adjustment may simply reflect a general decline in emotional adjustment as children get older. The same decline may be evident among children from intact families.

Yet another study might try to overcome this problem by tracking changes in adjustment of children before and after their parents divorce and changes among children from intact families as well. If children from intact families show less deterioration in adjustment than children from divorcing families, this must surely demonstrate the effect of divorce. No. We would need to be sure that the two groups of children were comparable in other relevant respects (e.g. age). The different rates of change in adjustment could be because those from divorcing families were younger on average. Maybe younger children show greater changes in adjustment over a particular period than older children. It may be age differences rather than having divorced parents that account for the adjustment changes of the two groups of children.

Internal validity is the extent to which the structure of a research design enables us to draw unambiguous conclusions from our results. The way in which the study is set up (e.g. tracking changes over time, making comparisons between comparable groups) can eliminate alternative explanations for our findings. The more the structure of a study eliminates these alternative interpretations, the stronger the internal validity of the study. A central task of research design is to structure the study so that the ambiguities in the above examples are minimized. It is impossible to eliminate all ambiguities in social research but we can certainly reduce them.

External validity

External validity refers to the extent to which results from a study can be generalized beyond the particular study. A study may have good internal validity but its value is limited if the findings only apply to the people in that particular investigation. The critical question is whether the results are likely to apply more widely. The most common threat to our capacity to generalize more widely from a research study is the use of unrepresentative samples. This, and other threats to external validity, will be discussed more fully in Chapters 5, 8, 11 and 14.

Measurement error

A further threat to the conclusions that can be drawn from any study is measurement error. This occurs when we use flawed indicators to tap concepts (see Chapter 1).

TYPES OF MEASUREMENT ERROR

Indicators must meet two fundamental criteria. They must be both valid and reliable. A valid indicator in this context means that the indicator measures the concept we say it does. For example an IQ test is used to measure intelligence. If it really measures intelligence the test would be valid. If the IQ test measured something else instead, such as education level or cultural background, then it would be an invalid measure of intelligence.

Reliability means that the indicator *consistently* comes up with the same measurement. For example, if people consistently obtain the same IQ score on repeated IQ tests, then the test would be reliable. If their results fluctuate wildly depending on when they take the test, then it would be unreliable.

Validity The earlier discussion of internal validity related to the validity of the *research design*. It addressed the question: is the research design delivering the conclusions that we claim it delivers? In addition we need to examine the validity of the *measures* used in any piece of research.

The validity of a measure depends both on the use to which it is put and on the sample for which it is used. For example, the validity of using frequency of arguments between partners to measure marital happiness turns on what we mean by marital happiness. The validity of this measure may vary for different cultural groups and for the same cultural group in different historical periods. Measures of children's emotional adjustment will vary according to their age and their cultural group.

There are three basic ways of assessing validity. *Criterion validity* is best suited to situations where there are well-established measures of a concept that need adapting, shortening or updating. It involves comparing the way people rate on the new measure with how they rate on well-established measures of the concept. If ratings on the new measure match those of an established measure we can be confident of its validity.

Criterion validity has two limitations. First, it requires that the established benchmark is valid. If the benchmark is invalid then it is of little value in assessing the new measure. Second, there are no established measures for many social science concepts.

Sometimes criterion groups can be used to assess criterion validity. Instead of comparing a measure against an existing benchmark measure, the new measure can be trialled. For example, a new measure of marital happiness could be trialled on couples who seek marital counselling. We would expect that this group of couples would normally obtain low scores on a valid measure of marital happiness. If these couples actually obtain high scores on the marital happiness measure we would probably want to question whether the measure was really tapping marital happiness.

Content validity evaluates how well the measures tap the different aspects of the concept as we have defined it. A test of arithmetic skills that only tested subtraction skills would clearly not be a valid measure of arithmetic skills. Similarly a measure of marital happiness that only asked about the frequency of arguments between partners would probably lack content validity unless we had defined marital happiness simply as the absence of arguments. Measures of marital happiness could also include the nature of the arguments, leisure activities shared by partners, communication, methods of resolving conflict, the quality of the sexual relationship etc.

Given disagreement about the 'content' of many social science concepts it can be difficult to develop measures that have agreed validity. Even if we can agree on the concept and measure it using a whole battery of questions, we then face the problem of the *relative importance* of the various components of the measure. For example, should measures of the frequency of arguments be as important as the nature of the arguments, the method of conflict resolution, the style of communication or statements about level of subjective marital satisfaction?

Construct validity relies on seeing how well the results we obtain when using the measure fit with theoretical expectations. To validate a measure of marital happiness we might anticipate, on the basis of theory, that happiness will vary in predictable ways according to stage in the life cycle. If the results of a study provide confirmation, this could reflect the validity of our measure of marital happiness. However, this approach to assessing validity relies on the correctness of our expectations. If our theory is not supported this could be for one of two reasons: the measure of marital happiness could be wrong or the theory against which the measure is being benchmarked may be wrong.

There is no ideal way of assessing validity. If a measure passes all three tests it is more likely to be valid but we cannot be certain. In the final analysis we will need to *argue* for the validity of our measures.

Reliability   A reliable measure is one that gives the same 'reading' when used on repeated occasions. For example, *assuming there was no actual change*, a reliable measure of marital happiness should yield the same 'reading' if it is used on different occasions. A thermometer that measured body temperature as 97.4 °F one minute and 105 °F the next would be useless. Which measurement is right? Does the change reflect real change or just measurement 'noise'?

Unreliability can stem from many sources. Poor question wording may cause a respondent to understand the question differently on different occasions. Different interviewers can elicit different answers from a person: the match of age, gender, class and ethnicity of an interviewer and interviewee can influence responses. Asking questions about which people have no opinion, have insufficient information or require too precise an answer can lead to unreliable data. The answers to some questions can be affected by mood and by the particular context in which they are asked.

Measures need to be both valid and reliable. Although these two concepts are related they are not the same. A measure can be reliable without being valid. That is, a measure can be consistently wrong. For example, people consistently underestimate their level of alcohol consumption in questionnaire surveys. Alcohol consumption measures are reliable but do not accurately tell us about the true level of alcohol consumed.

Measures will never be perfectly reliable and perfectly valid. These are not all or nothing concepts and the goal is to maximize the reliability and validity. If these aspects of measurement are weak then the results of the study that uses them might plausibly be attributed to poor measurement rather than telling us anything about social reality.

FORMS OF MEASUREMENT ERROR

Error can take different forms and the consequences of error will vary depending on its form. These forms of error are *random, constant* and *correlated.*

Random error is that which has no systematic form. It means that in some cases a measurement for a variable might be too low while in others it is too high. The measurement of someone's weight might display random error. Sometimes people underestimate their weight while others may overestimate it, but if these errors are random there will be the same number of over- and underestimates and the size of the overestimates will be the same on average as the underestimates. When the average (mean) is calculated for the whole group it will be accurate because the overestimates and the underestimates cancel each other out. Furthermore, these mis-estimates are not correlated with any other characteristic (e.g. gender, age) but are truly random. Because random error does not distort means and is uncorrelated with other factors, it is less serious than other forms of error.

Constant error occurs where there is the same error for every case. For example, if everyone underreported their weight by 5 kilograms we would have constant error. Such error is uncorrelated with other characteristics. Although purely constant error will be rare there will be variables for which there will typically be a component of constant error (e.g. overstatements of frequency of sexual intercourse and understatements about the amount of alcohol consumed). Because such error is constant it does not cancel out but has an effect on sample estimates. Thus the average weight of the sample would be an underestimate to the extent of the constant error.

Correlated error takes place when the amount and direction of error vary systematically according to other characteristics of respondents. For example, if women tend to overestimate their weight while men underestimate theirs then this error would be correlated with gender. If the format or language in a questionnaire is difficult then mistakes in answering questions may well be correlated with education. This would produce results that make it appear that people with different levels of education behave or think differently while in fact it is only their capacity to understand the question that differs.

A crucial goal of the design and administration of survey instruments is the minimization of the various forms of measurement error. Achieving this entails paying careful attention to question wording, indicator quality, interviewer and observer training, and to ways of identifying social desirability responses and other forms of deliberate misrepresentation by respondents. In many cases it is difficult to identify the extent to which such errors actually occur. However, this does not reduce the need to do all that one can to minimize their likelihood and to have built-in checks to identify some sources of error. Such checks include looking for inconsistencies in answers, using multiple questions rather than single questions to tap concepts, identifying social desirability response sets, making inter-interviewer checks and careful fieldwork supervision.

Summary

This chapter has emphasized the importance of clarifying research questions and concepts before developing a research design. Lack of clarity regarding the research question and the central research concepts will severely compromise any research design. Guidelines were provided to help focus both descriptive and explanatory research questions and to clarify the concepts they employ.

It is also unwise to develop a research design unless alternative ways of understanding the matter at the heart of the research question have been identified. Since one of the purposes of research design is to help identify which of a range of alternative explanations work best it is desirable that these alternative explanations be identified before the research design is developed. The design can then be structured in such a way that relevant data are collected to enable us to choose between these alternatives. Guidelines were provided to assist in identifying these alternative explanations.

Finally, three core concepts that are at the heart of good design were discussed. These were the concepts of internal validity, external validity and measurement error. Later chapters will evaluate the various designs using these concepts.

Causation and the Logic of Research Design

DAVID DE VAUS

Establishing causal relationships is at the heart of explanatory research design. However, it is not a simple matter to establish that one event causes another (Blalock, 1964; Hage and Meeker, 1988). The main reason why it is difficult to establish causal relationships is because we cannot actually *observe* one phenomenon producing change in another. Even though one event might always follow another we do not know that this is because one event causes the other. Causal relationships must therefore be inferred rather than observed. *The purpose of research design in explanatory research is to improve the quality of our causal inferences.*

Inferring causal relationships

Criteria for inferring cause

In Chapter 1 I distinguished between probabilistic and deterministic concepts of causation. Probabilistic approaches to causation are those that argue that a given factor increases (or decreases) the probability of a particular outcome. For example we may argue that there is a causal relationship between gender and working part time – that gender affects the probability of working part time.

In order to infer that a probabilistic causal relationship exists between two variables, two basic criteria must be met. First, there must be co-variation of causal and outcome variables (e.g. between gender and being a full time or part time worker); and second, the assertion that one variable affects the other must make sense.

Co-variation

If two factors are causally related they must *at least* be correlated: they must co-vary. If X causes Y then people who differ from one another on X should tend to differ from one another on Y. For example, if we were to argue that working in the private sector rather than the public sector makes people more achievement oriented at work we would, *at the very*

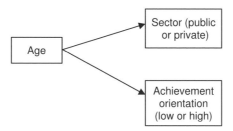

Figure 3.1 *A spurious relationship*

least, need to demonstrate that private sector workers had a higher achievement orientation than public sector workers. If two factors did not co-vary – that is public and private sector workers had identical levels of work achievement – then we would be hard pressed to argue that they are causally related.[1]

However, while co-variation is a precondition it is not enough for us to assert that the variables are causally related. Correlations can also reflect non-causal relationships. When two variables or events are correlated but not causally related the relationship between the two variables is said to be spurious (see Chapter 1). For example, the correlation between sector of employment and employment orientation might be due entirely to a third variable such as age (Figure 3.1). Younger people might be more likely than older people to work in the private sector and younger people might also have a higher achievement orientation than older people. These two patterns will mean that sector and achievement orientation are correlated (more young people in the private sector, so therefore the private sector is associated with achievement orientation). However the link between sector and achievement orientation is coincidental rather than causal.

It must make sense

Any assertion that co-variation reflects a causal relationship must be plausible. It must make sense at three levels.

Time order   If two variables are correlated the cause must come *before* the effect. Causal reasoning has no time for the assertion that a future event can have a present effect (teleological explanation). Our causal proposition must be such that the causal variable occurs before the presumed effect. The time gap between cause and effect can be minutes or may be years (e.g. the effect of education on income can take many years to show itself).

Even though two variables might be causally related it can sometimes be difficult to work out which variable comes first and therefore to establish which variable is the cause and which is the effect. For example, does sector of employment affect achievement orientation or is it the other way around? Even where we assert that one variable comes first the causal relationship may be two-way. That is, sector of employment may affect achievement orientation which in turn influences future decisions about the sector of employment in which one works. Causal relationships can be reciprocal (two-way) rather than one-way.

Dependent variable must be capable of change   If we say that a correlation between two variables is because one is causing the other, we must make sure that the dependent variable (the effect) is *capable* of being changed. If it cannot be changed then a causal account of the relationship makes no sense. For example, any causal relationship between sex and income could only be in the direction of sex affecting income. The opposite proposition (income→sex) makes no sense.

Theoretical plausibility   The causal assertion must make sense. We should be able to tell a story of how X affects Y if we wish to infer a causal relationship between X and Y. Even if we cannot empirically demonstrate *how* X affects Y we need to provide a plausible account of the connection (plausible in terms of other research, current theory etc.). For example, to support the assertion that sector of employment affects achievement orientation we might argue that the private sector fosters the development of an achievement orientation by strategies such as paying performance bonuses, developing a culture of higher expectations, providing better resources and creating less job security. When backed up by this type of reasoning, any correlation between employment sector and achievement orientation can be plausibly interpreted in causal terms.

Types of causal patterns

DIRECT AND INDIRECT CAUSAL RELATIONSHIPS

Causal relationships can be either *direct* or *indirect*. A direct relationship is one where we assert that the cause affects the outcome directly rather than via other variables. An indirect causal relationship is one where the cause has its effect by operating via its influence on another variable that, in turn, produces the effect. The variable through which the two variables are related is called the *intervening* variable: it comes in time and in a causal sequence between the initial cause and the effect. For example, we might argue that the way the private sector produces higher achievement orientation is by making employees fear for their jobs (the intervening variable) (Figure 3.2).

Indirect causal relationships may be simple (as in Figure 3.2) or consist of an extended causal chain or a number of different causal paths (Figure 3.3).

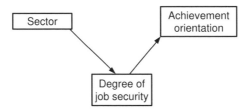

Figure 3.2 *An indirect causal relationship*

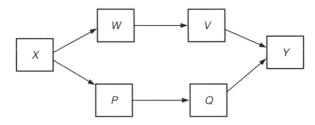

Figure 3.3 *More complex indirect causal relationships*

TYPES OF RELATIONSHIPS IN A THREE-VARIABLE MODEL

Any relationship between two variables will consist of two components – a causal component and a non-causal (spurious) component. The causal component can consist of a direct component, an indirect component or both.

It follows then that any relationship between two variables can be interpreted as:

- a direct causal relationship
- an indirect causal relationship
- a spurious relationship
- any combination of these.

Figure 3.4 illustrates the possibilities where we have three variables which, for the purpose of the example, I will call X, Y and Z. The relationship between X and Y could be any of the following:

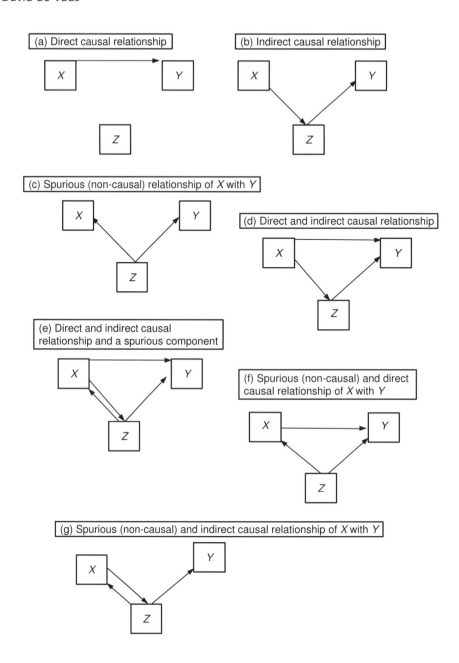

Figure 3.4   *Types of relationships between three variables*

(a) *Direct causal*   Y follows X in time, Y is capable of being changed, and it is plausible that X could produce changes in Y. In the absence of finding any other variable that is responsible for this relationship we may continue to argue that the observed correlation is direct and is causal (Figure 3.4a).

(b) *Indirect causal*   Y follows X in time, Y is capable of being changed, and it is plausible that X could produce changes in Y. However, in this case we are spelling out the mechanism by which X affects Y. We may think of Z as a single mechanism or a whole lot of intervening variables (Figure 3.4b).

(c) *Spurious*   X and Y are not causally related to one another. Even though Y might follow X in time and be capable of being changed, both X and Y are joint effects of some third variable Z. X and Y co-vary purely because Z has a simultaneous effect on both X and Y (Figure 3.4c).

(d) *Both direct and indirect*   The effect of X may be partly via its effect on an intervening variable and partly direct (Figure 3.4d).

(e) *Direct and indirect causal and spurious*   The relationship between X and Y could consist of three components: a direct causal part ($X{\rightarrow}Y$), an indirect causal part ($X{\rightarrow}Z{\rightarrow}Y$) and a spurious part ($X{\leftarrow}Z{\rightarrow}Y$) (Figure 3.4e).

(f) *Direct causal relationship combined with a spurious component*   (Figure 3.4f).

(g) *Indirect causal relationship combined with a spurious component*   (Figure 3.4g).

This set of possibilities results from situations in which we have only three variables. The more variables we take into account, the more complex matters become.

When we collect and analyse data it can be helpful to draw diagrams to spell out the ways in which we propose variables are interrelated. We need to specify:

1   whether relationships are presumed to be causal or spurious
2   whether causal relationships are expected to be direct or indirect
3   the mechanisms (intervening variables) underlying any indirect causal relationships.

Resolving these matters allows us to articulate our research question and the most plausible line of explanation.

Introduction to Research Methods for Managers

JOHN GILL and PHIL JOHNSON

Learning outcomes At the end of this chapter the reader should be able to:

- appreciate the complexity of management research and some of the controversies and developments that are encouraging methodological diversity;

- begin to understand the impact of the researcher's philosophical commitments upon the choice of methodological approach;

- understand the difference between deduction and induction in research methodology;

- appreciate the relationship between management research and management development;

- understand the aims, structure and content of this book.

In this chapter preliminary consideration is given to the complexities of management as a field of study and its increasing methodological diversity. Within this context, management research is clarified as a process by comparing and contrasting it with management development. The chapter also introduces the two main, yet often competing, approaches to management research that articulate competing philosophies – induction and deduction. The philosophical rationales underpinning these alternatives are further explored throughout the book, especially so in Chapter 3, and their varying methodological expressions give a framework for our examination of different research methods throughout subsequent chapters. Chapter 1 concludes by providing an outline of the structure of the rest of the book and the content of those chapters.

Innovation and diversity in management research

Management research is a complex and changing field which demonstrates several interrelated tendencies. In order to understand these developments it is initially helpful to place management research in some historical context. Some 25 years ago, in a discussion of the historical development of management studies, Whitley (1984a, b) described it as being in a fragmented state; as a field characterized by a high degree of task uncertainty and a low degree of co-ordination of research procedures and strategies between researchers who undertake research in an ad hoc and opportunistic manner. This apparent situation led Pfeffer (1993, 1995) to argue, by using economics as an exemplar to be copied, that management research must develop consensus through the enforcement of theoretical and methodological conformity. As he argued, such a paradigmatic convergence may increase the social standing of the discipline and thus should assure more access to scarce resources, whilst easing its methodological development. However, in a reply to Pfeffer, Van Maanen (1995a) argued that if management research followed Pfeffer's recommendations the resultant enforced conformity would create what amounted to a 'technocratic unimaginativeness' which could drive out tolerance of the unorthodox and significantly reduce our learning from one another. During the intervening years, management students have been confronted by much controversy about the most appropriate approaches to the study of management as an academic discipline. Of course, it is debatable how far these controversies have actually reconfigured management research practice as it may be argued that there is a dominant orthodoxy within management research which is maintained by very powerful institutional pressures. Nevertheless, the dominance of this mainstream in management research is being resisted by numerous management researchers and indeed has been under attack on a number of fronts (see Symon et al., 2008). To some extent the development of these controversies has been due not only to the emergence of different schools of management thought but also to the development of different approaches to research methodology, especially so in the social sciences. Indeed, since the first edition of this book in 1991, there seems to have been an increasing methodological diversity amongst those who undertake what can be broadly classified as management research – although it is important to note that quantitative methods still dominate much of what is published in prestigious academic journals.

Whilst it remains accurate to say that the diversity in management research has been exacerbated due to its multi-disciplinary (Brown, 1997) and inter-disciplinary (Watson, 1997) nature and its position at the confluence of numerous social science disciplines (e.g. sociology, psychology, economics, politics, accounting, finance and so on), other forces are clearly at play which have promoted methodological innovation and change. For instance, this increasing diversity might also be explained by the 'coming of age' of qualitative and interpretive methods (see Prasad and Prasad, 2002) which may be seen as arising in response to certain perceived limitations in conventional management research and thereby presents a significant challenge to, and critique of, the quantitative mainstream of management research. However, qualitative management research is itself characterized by an expanding array of methodologies that articulate different, competing, philosophical assumptions which have significant implications for how management research should be (Johnson et al., 2006), and is (Johnson et al., 2007), evaluated by interested parties. Simultaneously, there has been the development of an array of critical approaches to the study of management usually going under the umbrella term 'critical management studies'. This influential development, in part, arises out of a philosophical and methodological critique of the assumed objectivity and neutrality of the quantitative mainstream but also aims to generate what are presented as emancipatory forms of research that challenge the status quo in contemporary organizations by exposing and undermining dominant managerial discourses whose content is often just taken-for-granted by organizational members and thereby assumed to be natural and unchallengeable (see Fournier and Grey, 2000; Grey and Willmott, 2005; Kelemen and Rumens, 2008). Of course such developments open questions about who is the intended audience for management research. For instance, is management research about:

1 addressing the presumed pragmatic concerns and presumed business needs of practising managers, or,
2 is it about investigating and understanding the structures and processes of oppression and injustice, that are taken to be part of organizing in a capitalist society, whose main beneficiaries and victims are often these social actors labelled managers?

Any cursory inspection of management research would suggest that a great deal of it published in prestigious academic journals adopts, often by default, the first orientation noted above. Unlike our second orientation above, it adopts the view that management research must be relevant in the sense that it helps managers to manage more efficiently and effectively by enhancing their ability to cope with the problems that assail contemporary organizations by improving the technical content of managerial practice based upon rigorous analysis using social scientific theory rather than common sense. However, many commentators (e.g. Tranfield and Starkey, 1998; Keleman and Bansal, 2002) have noted some irony here in the sense that the channels by which this research is disseminated, and often the language used, all tend to reflect the institutional incentives, intellectual requirements, interests, and concerns of academia rather than the needs of management practitioners, whoever they might be. Nevertheless, many management researchers (e.g. Heckscher, 1994; Osbourne and Plastrik, 1998; Kalleberg, 2001; Johnson et al., 2009) have pointed to how the nature of managerial work, and the roles available to managers, may indeed be fundamentally changing under the impact of the organizational changes driven by a possible shift from bureaucratic forms of command and control to post-bureaucratic forms of organizational governance. The latter are usually characterized as flatter, less hierarchical, more networked and flexible organizations wherein employees are necessarily empowered to use their discretion to cope with a more volatile and uncertain workplace and requires managers capable of facilitating the participation of self-directed employees in decision-making (Tucker, 1999): something which further requires the evolution and deployment of managers' research skills at work (Hendry, 2006).

Of course the second orientation noted above is much more associated with critical management studies, which often overtly rejects a managerially orientated approach partially on the basis of a desire to enhance the democratic rights and responsibilities of the relatively disempowered majorities of members of work organizations: an approach that has significant methodological implications but which also is an outcome of a philosophical challenge to mainstream management research (which we shall consider later in this book) which seems to reflect Whitley's (1984b: 387) criticism that management research had adopted 'a naïve and unreflecting empiricism'. For Whitley, the solution to this problem required freeing researchers from lay concepts and problem formulations and by providing them with a more sophisticated understanding of the epistemological and sociological sciences.

In sum, there are a range of forces at play which have created a trajectory in management research that seems to be one of increasing methodological diversity and innovation, much of which uses varying philosophical critiques of the quantitative mainstream as a starting point to legitimate the methodological changes that are deemed to be necessary.

One of the major themes of this book is that there is no one best methodological approach but rather that the approach most appropriate for the investigation of a given research question depends on a large number of variables, not least the nature of the research question itself and how the researcher constitutes and interprets that question. Research methodology is always a compromise between options in the light of tacit philosophical assumptions, and choices are also frequently influenced by practical issues such as the availability of resources and the ability to get access to organizations and their memberships in order to undertake research.

Making methodological choices

In this book we will advance criteria for choice of methodology by reviewing the major approaches to management research and, through examples, their appropriateness to finding answers to particular research questions. Therefore, one key aim of this work is to illustrate the different means by which business and management research is undertaken by presenting some of the variety of methodologies that are potentially available to any researcher. In attempting to meet our key aim we are also concerned to illustrate that the research methods available to the management researcher are not merely neutral devices or techniques that we can just 'take off shelf' to undertake a particular task for which they are most suited. Such a perspective implies that it is the nature of the research question, and what phenomenon is under investigation, which should pragmatically dictate the correct research method to use since different kinds of information about management are most comprehensively and economically gathered in different ways. Whilst at first sight this stance seems to have much to offer, and of course the nature of the research question being investigated is methodologically important, it can simultaneously deflect our attention from what we see to be a key issue: that the different research methods available to the management researcher also bring with them a great deal of philosophical baggage which can remain unnoticed when they are classified as constituting merely different data collection tools that can be chosen to do different jobs. Therefore, management researchers need to be aware of the philosophical commitments they make through their methodological choices, since that baggage has a significant impact not only upon what they do, but also upon how they understand whatever it is that they think they are investigating in the first place.

For instance (see Figure 1.1), the decision to use deductive research methods (for example, experiments, analytical surveys, etc.) that are designed to test, and indeed falsify, previously formulated theory through confronting its causal predictions about human behaviour with empirical data gathered through the neutral observation of social reality, tacitly draws upon an array of philosophical assumptions and commitments that are contestable yet so often remain taken-for-granted. Even a cursory inspection of the management field would show that such methodological choices are common place yet, by default, also involve the decision not to engage through alternative means: alternatives that in themselves articulate different philosophical commitments, e.g. to build theory inductively out of observation of the empirical world that focuses upon the operation actors' everyday culturally derived subjective interpretations of their situations in order to explain their behaviour theoretically. As we will see in Chapter 3, there are significant philosophical differences between these

Figure 1.1 | Deduction vs induction

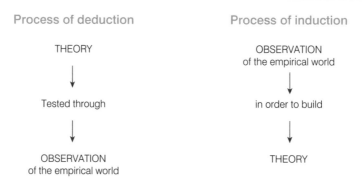

two approaches, to a degree initially centred upon what each assumes to be the key influences upon human behaviour and the forms that it takes as well as how those influences are best investigated by researchers.

The point is that whilst we cannot avoid making philosophical commitments in undertaking any research, a problem lies in the issue that any philosophical commitment can be simultaneously contested because they are merely assumptions that we have to make. This is because the philosophical commitments which are inevitably made in undertaking research always entail commitment to various knowledge-constituting assumptions about the nature of truth, human behaviour, representation and the accessibility of social reality. In other words there are always tacit answers to questions encoded into what is called the researcher's pre-understanding. These answers are:

- about ontology (what are we studying?)
- about epistemology (how can we have warranted knowledge about our chosen domains?)
- and about axiology (why study them?).

Those answers always have a formative impact upon any methodological engagement. Quite simply we cannot engage with our areas of interest without having answers already to those questions. The philosophical assumptions we make in dealing with these questions implicitly present different normative specifications, justified by particular rationales, for management research regarding what it is and how it should be done. But significantly these assumptions also impinge upon a further crucial area – how should we judge, or evaluate, the findings and quality of any management research? Here there is the persistent danger that particular evaluative criteria, deriving from particular philosophical traditions within management research, are inadvertently applied to all management research regardless of its particular philosophical stance. This is a particularly important issue as it could mean that the outcomes of some management research may be inappropriately and unfairly evaluated: an issue we shall explore in the later chapters of this book.

The notion that methodological choices regarding how to do research always involve philosophical choices that need to be excavated is supported by some recent developments in management research. For instance, since the early 1990s, there has been much discussion of the notion that in order to understand ourselves as social science researchers we must reflexively engage (see Holland, 1999; Newton, 1999; Weick, 1999; Alvesson and Deetz, 2000; Johnson and Duberley, 2003) with ourselves through thinking about our own thinking and how those beliefs have repercussions for our engagements with our areas of interest. According to Chia and Morgan such vigilance must also embrace management education through the inculcation of 'an intimate understanding of the way ... management knowledge ... is organized, produced and legitimized' (1996: 58) – an agenda which has become all the more important with the increasing 'managerialization of the world' (Alvesson and Deetz, 2000: 209). Although this 'new sensibility' (Willmott, 1998) has many implications for management research, several commentators have emphasized how it entails noticing, and being suspicious of, the relationship between the researcher and the substantive focus of his/her research. This involves reflecting upon how those often tacit, unacknowledged, pre-understandings impact upon:

- how those 'objects' of research are conceptually negotiated and constituted by the researcher;
- what kinds of research question are then asked by the researcher;
- how the results of research are methodologically arrived at, justified and presented to audiences for consumption;
- how those results are then, or should be, evaluated by interested parties.

Such increased awareness regarding the philosophical choices made by management researchers, either consciously or by default, might serve to broaden the philosophical repertoire available to both management researchers and practitioners so that alternatives to the current mainstream are also understood and appreciated rather than being just discounted as outlandish eccentricities not worthy of serious contemplation, never mind use. The choices we always have to make in doing research can then be based upon a fuller consideration of the ever present alternatives rather than inadvertently limiting the focus of these decisions, by default, to that which is conventionally seem as 'normal' and thus incontrovertible. Mutual understanding is paramount here.

This book attempts to support this 'new sensibility' and, simultaneously, to bridge the gap between academic and managerial views of what constitutes appropriate research by offering challenges to both the academic community and the practising manager.

The management research process and management development

Harvey-Jones (1989: 240), in his bestselling book *Making it Happen*, advised managers when setting about tasks to distinguish content from process. What he meant by this is that it is helpful conceptually to separate the content of the task from the way the task is accomplished; that is, to separate the content (what) from the process (how). Research methods on this analysis are then primarily concerned with how (process) to tackle tasks (content).

Despite the variety of approaches to management research they all, in essence, share a problem-solving sequence that may serve as a systematic check for anyone undertaking research at whatever level. At this point we introduce a cautionary note in qualification. An idealized representation of the research sequence will help the naïve researcher at this stage to review the research process as a whole and make a start; however it rarely accords with actuality. It should be borne in mind that 'the research process is not a clear-cut sequence of procedures following a neat pattern but a messy interaction between the conceptual and empirical world, deduction and induction occurring at the same time' (Bechhofer, 1974: 73).

Nevertheless, the seven-step sequence proposed by Howard and Sharp (1983) which builds on earlier work by Rummel and Ballaine (1963), may be found particularly useful (see Figure 1.2), and is referred to again in the next chapter.

Figure 1.2 | The research sequence (adapted from Howard and Sharp, 1983) © The Management of a Student Research Project, by John A. Sharp, John Peters and Keith Howard (1983), Gower Publications Ltd.

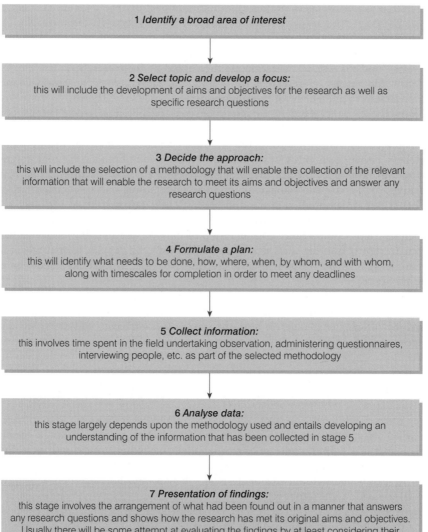

1 *Identify a broad area of interest*

2 *Select topic and develop a focus:*
this will include the development of aims and objectives for the research as well as specific research questions

3 *Decide the approach:*
this will include the selection of a methodology that will enable the collection of the relevant information that will enable the research to meet its aims and objectives and answer any research questions

4 *Formulate a plan:*
this will identify what needs to be done, how, where, when, by whom, and with whom, along with timescales for completion in order to meet any deadlines

5 *Collect information:*
this involves time spent in the field undertaking observation, administering questionnaires, interviewing people, etc. as part of the selected methodology

6 *Analyse data:*
this stage largely depends upon the methodology used and entails developing an understanding of the information that has been collected in stage 5

7 *Presentation of findings:*
this stage involves the arrangement of what had been found out in a manner that answers any research questions and shows how the research has met its original aims and objectives. Usually there will be some attempt at evaluating the findings by at least considering their strengths and weaknesses, limitations and areas of applicability, etc

These seven steps should be useful to all students at whatever level they are under-taking project work, from diploma to doctorate. It is recommended that each step in the sequence be given equal attention if time is to be saved in the longer term. For example, it is commonplace for people to be able to identify a broad area of interest but find it difficult to select a topic within that area that is researchable and often give insufficient attention to defining clearly the focus of research. Unless it is dealt with early in the development of the research, this issue can completely hamstring further progress down the seven-step sequence. However, sometimes a lack of clarity may only become apparent at later stages of the process, either when planning the project or deciding on methods of collecting data. As a consequence time may be lost recycling to earlier stages of the sequence or the work may fail to meet its objectives. Nevertheless, there will inevitably be some iteration between the seven stages – particularly between 2, 3, and 4 – as ideas and how to pursue them are explored and the practicality and viability of the intended research becomes clearer. These issues will also be explored in more detail in the following chapter, concerned with starting research projects.

It should of course be clear that in essence many managerial activities and the research process outlined in Figure 1.2 are similar. Notwithstanding the point made earlier about the need for reflexivity when it comes to conceptualizing 'problems' in the first place, managers need to be competent in investigative approaches to decision-making and problem-solving and this has been recognized in practically all management development programmes and business education by the inclusion of project work involving problem-solving as part of taught courses. The research process, while being the means of developing knowledge and understanding, also serves as a disciplined and systematic procedure of help in solving any managerial problem.

Both management and research activities require a decision as to what to do; this is followed by a planning stage concerned with making judgements about ways of collecting valid information to tackle the issue. Finally, the information gathered will need to be analysed and assessed, and action taken. Both managerial and research processes are uncertain and risky, and necessarily entail considerable self-initiated endeavour involving co-operation with others and skill in managing all the factors inherent in finding and implementing solutions to complex problems. Not only are the findings of the research important, then, but it is suggested that the processes of systematic discovery have clear benefits to the manager's self-development as a manager or problem-solver.

These parallels between the research and managerial processes as action sciences are implicitly and explicitly recognized both in project work and dissertations as a significant part of most taught programmes, and also in the merits of research train-ing as a component of higher degree programmes in management.

At the undergraduate level in business and management a research project or disser-tation usually forms a significant part of the final assessment demanding independent inquiry and judgement. Taught master's programmes in management vary widely in their dissertation requirements. Some relatively uncommon programmes are guided by an action learning philosophy pioneered by Revans (1971) and are taught solely around project work based in the student's own organization. More usually a wide variety of MBA, MSc and MA programmes exist where the requirement is generally for the dissertation to be completed, through independent research usually guided by a supervisor, in about six to eight months part time or around 4 months full-time as part of a largely taught programme of study. Nevertheless, in most cases the dissertation forms a significant part of the assessment and is almost invariably preceded by a taught research methods component.

Typically a postgraduate master's level dissertation aims to allow the student to develop and demonstrate powers of rigorous analysis, critical inquiry, clear expression and independent judgement in relation to an area of business and management activity. Simultaneously there will always be an emphasis upon the student demonstrating methodological competence in the sense that the student can:

- systematically justify the choice of approach to collecting data deployed;
- competently undertake any data collection;
- be able to analyse that data and make sense of its implications for the dissertation's aims, objectives and research questions;
- demonstrate an understanding of the strengths and weaknesses of the approach used with reference to findings;
- demonstrate an appreciation of the applicability of any findings, often with particular reference to any managerial implications either within the organization studied or more generally – and very often both.

Many postgraduate dissertations are based on an in-depth investigation into a managerial problem within the student's own organization or a client organization where the student is not a direct employee. However, the most usual requirement is for more than just problem-solving typical of management consultancy since it requires the student to stand back from the problem, conceptualize it and explore its wider implications for other managers outside the particular case.

Some taught master's programmes designed for specialists, such as operations researchers, HRM and organization development practitioners, may make even greater demands on students in terms of the dissertation requirement. The time devoted to the dissertation may be as much as one third of that spent on the taught programme accounting for as much as 60 out a total of 180 credits. Commonly such dissertations are concerned with the student's management of a consultancy project where the student is required not only to find a solution to a particular problem but also to reflect on the consulting approach and the problems of implementation with regard to any identified remedial changes to the organization. For instance, the philosophy supporting the research methods component of such a master's programme in organization development is outlined by a colleague who advocates respect for data, the appropriateness of the research strategy to the problem confronted and the use of a hermeneutic approach to encourage a more reflexive understanding of the theories and philosophies of management held by both managers themselves and by self-aware researchers in order to comprehend organizational change-management issues and cope with the consulting process more effectively (McAuley, 1985; see also Darwin et al., 2002).

On other types of postgraduate programme students may have the choice to undertake more issue-centred research. This is where an issue relevant to management practice is investigated in order to determine its incidence and/or its causes across a number of different social and organizational contexts in order to answer specific research questions determined from the relevant literature rather than resolve a particular client's organizational problems.

The requirements for master's degrees undertaken solely by research (e.g. M.Phil.) and doctoral projects are similar except that the doctorate is a much more demanding piece of work requiring an independent and original contribution to knowledge.

In both degrees, however, there is a heavier emphasis upon demonstrating method-ological competence and most significantly a need to demonstrate an understanding of research methods appropriate to the chosen field and a requirement for students to defend their final theses by oral examination. At this final stage attention is given to the quality of the methodology; the thoroughness of the bibliographic search; the depth of the analysis and conclusions; and the standard of the presentation of the thesis. Finally, the extent of the contribution to knowledge is assessed: clearly, the contribution made by the master's thesis will be of some importance and will probably at least serve as a reference work. Work at master's level is, however, to be distinguished from the doctorate by the requirement placed on the latter to provide a distinct and original contribution to knowledge.

We now turn to the broad approaches or strategies to management research cov-ered in this book. It is clear that methodological choices are determined not only by the nature of the topic being investigated and the resources available but also by the particular training and socialization processes to which the researcher has been exposed which have a significant formative impact upon any pre-understanding thereby sometimes severely limiting any decision-making process regarding meth-odological choice. It will therefore be helpful at this point to diagnose your own predispositions towards particular research approaches, by doing Stop and Think Exercise 1.1.

Stop and Think Exercise 1.1   Self-diagnose your research approach

Say whether you agree or disagree with the following statements by placing a tick (agree) or a cross (disagree) in the box against each statement.

1   Quantitative data are more objective and scientific than qualitative data.   ☐
2   It is always necessary to define precisely the research topic before data   ☐
    collection.
3   Of all methods the questionnaire is probably the best by which to collect   ☐
    objective data on management topics.
4   Field experiments such as the Hawthorne Studies effectively determine   ☐
    cause and effect relationships.
5   A good knowledge of statistics is essential for competence in all   ☐
    approaches to management research.
6   A case study is an inappropriate way to undertake management research   ☐
    as it cannot be generalized.
7   Anthropological methods are obviously fine as a means of studying exotic   ☐
    tribes but have little utility in management research.
8   Laboratory experiments, such as studies of decision-making in groups,   ☐
    should be used more widely in management research as they can be
    closely controlled by the researcher.
9   Research into management issues is best achieved through the   ☐
    accumulation of quantitative data.
10 As a management research method, participant observation is too prone   ☐
    to researcher bias to be valid.

Method of scoring: For the method of scoring, see the instructions at the end of this chapter.

Approaches to management research

It has been suggested that a common stereotype firmly held by managers is to regard researchers as remote, ivory-tower individuals working on issues of little practical relevance. This stereotype, by analogy with the 'boffin' scientist, may of course be partly defensive and serve to preserve managers from the study of difficult philosophical concepts necessary for a comprehensive understanding of research methodology (Gill, 1986; Gill et al., 1989; Grey and Mitev, 1995; Johnson and Duberley, 2000).

Managers are not alone in this, for most people associate the word 'research' with activities that are substantially removed from daily life and which, it is assumed, usually take place in a laboratory. Further, research – and its connection in many minds with 'science' – is often understood to refer to the study of problems by scientific methods or principles deriving from the natural or physical sciences. Management is no exception and there is an influential body of writers who all apparently believe that science is basically a way of producing and validating knowledge which can be applied to managerial problems without too much difficulty. For example, House (1970), in discussing 'scientific' investigation in management, suggests that in order to be objective there is a requirement of public demonstration to prevent the construction of theories and the formulation of general laws on the basis of inadequately tested hypotheses (see also Donaldson, 1996; Hogan and Sinclair, 1996). The requirement of demonstration is satisfied, he believes, when the research design includes:

1 a priori hypotheses that specify causal predictions of relationships between variables that may be then tested empirically through data collection;
2 a priori criteria that can be used to measure the acceptability of those hypotheses;
3 isolation and control of the variables under investigation so as to enable testing; and
4 methods of quantitatively measuring and verifying the variables in the investigation.

Whilst we shall explore the logic underpinning this deductive approach to research, and how it has been criticized in much more detail in Chapters 3 and 9, it is worth stating here that this is also a 'positivist' approach which remains predominant in management research (see Alvesson and Willmott, 1996; Alvesson and Deetz, 2000; Symon et al., 2008). Whilst there are many important aspects to positivism, for the time being it is worth noting that positivists usually suggest that management research methodology has to be essentially similar to that used in the natural and physical sciences in order to emulate its evident successes. As Hogan and Sinclair (1996) also argue, positivist methods allow the checking of the validity of their findings through replication. The findings are therefore pivotal to promoting organizational effectiveness and efficiency by providing verified guides to managers' interventions into their organizations. However, the assumptions on which this normative view is based have been challenged on at least three main grounds:

1 That there is no single method which generates scientific knowledge in all cases.
2 That what may be an appropriate method for researching the natural or physical world may be inappropriate in the social world given the inherent

meaningfulness, and subjective or cultural basis, of all human behaviour including management action.

3 That knowledge generated is not objective or neutral but is affected by, amongst others things, the goals of managers and the pressuppositions of researchers themselves.

Key methodological concept

Performativity

Positivist methodology emphasizes objectivity and the importance of unbiased data collection in order to test hypotheses and protect against 'fanciful theorizing in management research' (Donaldson, 1996: 164). It is widely agreed that positivism is pivotal to management for two reasons. First, as Thomas (1997: 693) notes, positivism promises to enable control – something which managers expect to be provided by relevant knowledge. Second, if managers appear to deploy objective scientific knowledge, their subsequent practices are more likely to be justified as merely technical activities in which their superior knowledge of things is merely being deployed on behalf of others to improve organizational efficiency and effectiveness (Grey and Mitev, 1995; Grey 1997). Whilst we shall explore the largely philosophical criticisms of the positivistic approach to management research in subsequent chapters, it is worth considering criticism number 3 (see pp. 193–200) above in more detail. For instance, Grey and Willmott (2005: 5–6) draw attention to the issue of performativity. They argue that much management research presupposes the need to try to develop knowledge that is useful to managers (whether or not it actually does this is another question) with the acid test being whether or not the knowledge developed may be applied to enhance the efficient achievement of management sanctioned ends, or goals, that in effect become taken-for-granted by the researcher. In other words, knowledge only has value if it aids the means by which pre-established ends are achieved (i.e. it is performative). The problem for Grey and Willmott is that the findings of such research may at first sight appear neutral, but the point is that this is a masquerade because it pays little attention to the nature of the ends being pursued and aided by the research: in effect they are naturalized, by being assumed to be normal and thus unchallengeable. As they argue the result is that, 'ethical and political questions are unacknowledged or assumed to be resolved. It follows that issues of a fundamentally ethical and political character – such as the distribution of life chances within and by corporations – are ignored ... Efforts are then directed at the matter of how limitations and "dysfunctions" within the established system can be ameliorated without significantly changing or disrupting the prevailing order of privilege and advantage' (ibid.: 6).

Stop and Think Exercise 1.2   From the point of view of Grey and Willmott, what steps could the management researcher take to be more 'ethical' in their approach to undertaking management research?

The distinction between science ('normal science') and non-science ('pseudo-science') is essentially blurred. In the West, for some people, this line of demarcation is relatively clear; for something to be scientific it must use the agreed set of conventions, that is to say, it must use the scientific method. In other cultures, by contrast, alternative forms of inquiry are acceptable, for example meditation, and it seems inappropriate to reject them simply because those cultures are different from ours.

Moreover, the conventions we agree to are simply those which have proved useful in the past. If these conventions, and so our scientific process, cease to be successful, however, it would be time to re-evaluate them. An exponent of this view, from 'management science' or operations research, believes that the extreme complexity of managerial problems, and attempts to apply natural scientific methodology to real-world, essentially social problems, have been responsible for the limited success of management science (Checkland, 1981, 1991).

Similarly, Bygrave (1989) endeavoured to account for what he regards as the unhelpful tendency for researchers to use the methods of the physical sciences in the context of research into entrepreneurship. He pointed out that many of the key contributors to business strategy have educational backgrounds in engineering, natural science and mathematics and are steeped in Newtonian mechanics at a very impressionable age. Amusingly he makes a plea for less 'physics envy' in approaches to research into the emerging field of entrepreneurship. As Van Maanen has more recently commented in his critique of positivism, 'we display more than a little physics envy when we reach for covering laws, causes, operational definitions, testable hypotheses and so forth' (1995a: 133–43). In relation to this issue of 'physics envy', now undertake Stop and Think Exercise 1.3.

Stop and Think Exercise 1.3 What are the main characteristics of the behaviour of the phenomena studied by physicists (i.e. physical things) as opposed to the behaviour of the phenomena studied by management researchers (i.e. human beings)? How are they different and if so what may be the implications for how we might study them? How does this relate to what you found out about yourself during Exercise 1.1? How do these differences relate to the issue of performativity in the natural and social sciences?

The main contemporary criticisms of positivism have been well summarized by Burrell and Morgan (1979: 255) as follows:

Science is based on 'taken for granted' assumptions, and thus, like any other social practice, must be understood within a specific context. Traced to their source all activities which pose as science can be traced to fundamental assumptions relating to everyday life and can in no way be regarded as generating knowledge with an 'objective', value-free status, as is sometimes claimed. What passes for scientific knowledge can be shown to be founded upon a set of unstated conventions, beliefs and assumptions, just as every day, common-sense knowledge is. The difference between them lies largely in the nature of rules and the community which recognises and subscribes to them. The knowledge in both cases is not so much 'objective' as shared.

Accordingly, we may need to change our conception of science to one of problem-or puzzle-solving, where science is simply regarded as a problem-solving process which uses certain conventions in that process (Kuhn, 1970; Morgan, 1993). In this respect Pettigrew's (1985a) view of problem-solving as a craft may be inadvertently misleading because if researchers are regarded as 'tool users rather than as tool builders then we may run the risk of distorted knowledge acquisition techniques' (Hirschheim, 1985: 15). An old proverb says 'for he who has but one tool, the hammer, the whole world looks like a nail'. For the most part, the way we currently practise much research in management leads directly to that view, but times are changing and increasing awareness of, and sensitivity to, the various assumptions we inevitably make in undertaking any research should further facilitate these challenges to the positivist mainstream of management research.

In view of these concerns it is unsurprising that there are a number of approaches to management research and several ways of classifying them as a means to clarify the available approaches to research. This book aims to present and discuss certain key methodological approaches to management research and their underlying philosophical rationales.

5 The Role of Theory in Management Research

JOHN GILL and PHIL JOHNSON

Learning outcomes At the end of this chapter the reader should be able to:

● understand what is meant by the term theory and identify what theories are and what they enable us to do;

● understand the relationship between theory and management practice;

● differentiate deductive approaches to management research from inductive approaches;

● appreciate the variety of methods used in management research;

● understand the rationale for the rest of this book.

In this chapter we introduce a series of debates about philosophical issues pertinent to the role of theory in management research. The different positions and competing rationales articulated in these debates implicitly underpin the only too evident variation in how management research is undertaken. Hence, an understanding of these debates is pivotal to enabling an understanding of how management research is variably undertaken in practice. First, this chapter identifies what theories are and then briefly explores the interrelationship between theory and management practice, making the point that there is nothing so practical as a good theory. Second, it then covers the philosophical foundations of inductive and deductive methodological approaches to research, wherein the relationship of the research to theory varies, and compares their competing underlying rationales. Third, using the inductive–deductive frame of reference, the chapter concludes by initially describing and explaining the variety of research methods used in management research; methods which form the foci for subsequent chapters.

The methodological importance of theory

Key methodological concept

Theory

A scheme or system of ideas or statements held to explain a group of facts or phenomena; a statement of general laws, principles, or causes of something known or observed (Oxford English Dictionary).

Trying to understand the relationship between theory and management research methods is a very complicated task which we are going to undertake in stages starting with this chapter. Here we shall argue that the varying role of theory in management research is of fundamental significance in understanding why management researchers approach their research in very different ways. By collecting data in different ways, some management researchers are trying to test theory through observation whilst others are trying to create, or discover, theory through observation. In other words, these different theoretical aims lead directly to the deployment of different methods by which management research is undertaken. Largely these different theoretical aims express deeply held philosophical assumptions about how it is best to explain the various aspects of human behaviour which management researchers are interested in. However, the importance of theory to us goes beyond an initial understanding of such methodological variation. For instance, although we might not be immediately aware of it, our everyday lives are fundamentally interwoven with our use of theory. Here we shall argue that theories influence how we understand and explain what is going on around us and how we practically do things. One important aspect of this 'theory-dependent' character relates to the way in which the various practical activities in which we routinely engage might be seen as involving regular attempts at creating, applying and evaluating theory – even though we might not necessarily usually notice this aspect of our practices.

Here it is important to emphasize that our use of the term 'theory-dependent' must not be confused with the term 'theory-laden'. Although the two are intimately related, the latter specifically refers to the way in which the prior theories of the observer are taken to influence how he or she engages with, and makes sense of, the world. That is, as Norwood Hanson (1958: 7) famously claimed, 'there is more to seeing than meets the eyeball'. Thus, the issue of how observation may be 'theory-laden' raises the problem that perhaps there is no independent or neutral point from which an observer might occupy and objectively observe the 'facts' of the world and thus all knowledge is knowledge from particular points of view or even paradigms (see Burrell and Morgan, 1979; Schultz and Hatch, 1996) or schools of thought (Ofori-Dankwa and Julian, 2005). The methodological implications of the possibly 'theory-laden' nature of observation are considered in later chapters of this book, especially Chapter 8. Meanwhile, we shall use the term 'theory-dependent' to specifically refer to the way in which practical activities which human beings undertake, in all circumstances, involve the use of theory in various ways. This everyday variation in the use of theory, which we all deploy, has a direct relevance to the kinds of research methods used by social scientists generally and management researchers specifically.

Theory and practice

To many readers, particularly those who might perceive themselves as 'practical people', the claim that all our everyday practical activities are theory-dependent might seem an absurd assertion. Often such a view is expressed in the lament of vocationally orientated management and business students that particular courses are too 'theoretical', or 'academic', and hence irrelevant to the 'real' world of their chosen careers. By implication, academics are seen to occupy 'ivory towers' that are far removed from the professional activities of practising managers. Intriguingly this lament resonates with the archaic Platonic–Aristotelian view that theoretical knowledge was knowledge acquired for its own sake, rather than for some practical use.

Indeed, both Plato and Aristotle had severed theory from practice in the sense that they distinguished between episteme (genuine theoretical knowledge that was an end in itself) and doxa (opinions or beliefs suitable only for the conduct of practical affairs). However, for many commentators such a view tended to endow a submissiveness on the part of people to nature's vagaries because it divorced knowledge from practice and hence stymied our ability to develop and use our knowledge to intervene and assert practical control over our natural environments. Episteme, which had a higher social status and perceived value, was more about passive contemplation of the world rather than about directing interventions to promote desirable change. To some extent this view of knowledge and science eventually lost its dominance during the seventeenth and eighteenth centuries with the arrival of a new version of the scientific enterprise articulated by people such as Francis Bacon (Tiles, 1987; Johnson and Duberley, 2000). This alternative philosophical stance emphasized the necessity for science to provide knowledge and theory for the control of nature through the discovery of regularities or patterns which allowed for the prediction of, intervention into, and manipulation of, nature to meet human needs. Moreover, as we shall try to demonstrate, the conception of theory as being divorced from practice is grounded in a misunderstanding of what theories are and what they enable us to do. We shall now try to illustrate the fundamental importance of theory in relation to practice.

During our everyday lives we all regularly attempt to understand the events that occur around us. For instance, in regard to the social behaviour of the people with whom we have regular contact, whether colleagues at work or friends and neighbours, we routinely have expectations (i.e. predictions) about the way they will behave in particular circumstances. These expectations are closely tied to explanations of why they behave in the ways that they do. These expectations and explanations might concern rather mundane events such as a friend's change in mood, or the behaviour of particular groups of colleagues at work, or even more personally distant events such as the performance of the national football team or the apparent nationwide increase in the incidence of particular types of criminal behaviour. Regardless of the particular focus of these expectations and explanations, when the former are not fulfilled or when the latter appear to be wrong, we will often reflect upon recent events and experiences and thereby begin to generate new webs of explanations and expectations that help us understand and cope with the events that impact upon us (Law and Lodge, 1984: 125). This process might result in our changing the way in which we do things, such as how we relate to friends or communicate with colleagues at work in particular circumstances. It might also lead us to suggest remedial strategies for dealing with perceived social problems which, for instance, we think the government ought to implement. It also involves our creation, application and evaluation of theory.

Figure 3.1 | Kolb's experiential learning cycle. Adapted from Kolb et al., 1979: 38. Kolb, David A., Osland, Joyce S., Rubin, Irwin M., *Organizational Behaviour: An Experimental Approach*, 6th edition © 1995, p. 49. Reprinted by permission of Pearson Education Inc., Upper Saddle River, NJ.

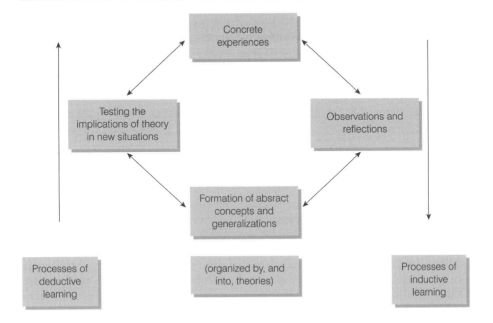

For Kolb et al. (1979), although their terminology is somewhat different, the above processes are linked to how human beings learn and can be diagrammatically represented by the model in Figure 3.1. According to Kolb, learning might start *inductively* with the experience of an event or stimulus, which the individual then reflects upon in trying to make sense of it. This might lead to the generation of explanations of how or why what was observed actually happened in the way it did – explanations that can then be used to form an abstract rule or guiding principle that can be extrapolated (or generalized) to new situations similar to that already experienced. Alternatively, for Kolb, learning can start *deductively* at this point where such an abstract rule is merely inherited from other people by the learner, along with its web of explanations and expectations, and is subsequently applied by that learner and thereby practically tested out. In either case, whether the rule is received from others or generated out of the prior personal experience and reflection, its testing in new situations creates a source of new experiences which enable consequent reflection, observation and ultimately new rules.

Kolb et al. (1979) also suggest that particular individuals might emphasize particular elements of the learning cycle to the neglect of others due to the presence of particular predilections into which they have been previously socialized: for example, the emphasis may be a product prior to education and/or professional training.

For our purposes here, what is very significant about the processes described in Figure 3.1 is that they might be seen as attempts at constructing, using and testing or evaluating explanatory statements, or theories, about what is going on around us. As Friedman (1953) puts it, such theories might be seen as 'filing systems' which allow observations to be used for explaining past and predicting (i.e. they create expectations about) future events. For instance, consider the following statements/views:

1 The notion that a friend's evident irritability is due to his or her inability to get sufficient sleep the previous night.
2 The claim that the relative demise of the Scottish National Football team is due to too few indigenous Scottish players gaining experience of playing in the Scottish Premier League due to a large number of foreign imports.
3 The idea that improved training provision will create a more productive, reliable and satisfied workforce.

These three statements are all theories. They are all characterized by an attempt at explaining observations and, from those explanations, predictions or expectations might be generated. In this they reveal an important aspect of a theory – that it can be used to guide our practical actions, e.g. if we do A then B will happen, if we don't do A then C will happen. In other words, the formulation and application of theory is at the heart of our attempts at understanding, influencing, or controlling, what goes on around us. Taking the third theory above, we could thus claim that if we improve a workforce's training we should expect an increase in employee productivity, reliability and satisfaction: an important issue for any manager attempting to get things done through other people. By actually attempting to do this, and then by observing what happens, we can evaluate the accuracy of that theory. An outcome of that evaluation may be a retrospective change in the nature of the third theory so as to make it more accurately fit our observations. Alternatively we might reject the theory because its predictions have not been borne out by experience and observation. Conversely the theory might be supported by what is observed as happening and therefore considered to be useable in other organizational situations. For instance, if the second theory was correct it could give the English Football Association forewarning about what could be happening to its own international team and provide an indication of what might be done to mitigate the effects of the problem.

Indeed, it is this latter process of evaluating and changing theory which is so often haphazard and imprecise, that for some commentators (for example, Kidder and Judd, 1986: 5) separates science from common sense. Basically, it is claimed that 'science' entails deliberate and rigorous searches for bias and invalidity through systematically testing theory – research processes which a range of commentators have noted to be remarkably lacking when it comes to management's appropriation of organizational recipes often deriving from 'management gurus' (Huczynski, 1993) or copied from the apparent practices of other institutions (Scott and Meyer, 1994; Cappelli et al., 1997).

Stop and Think Exercise 3.1   Dr Snow and the Broad Street Pump
In Soho, London, 1854. There was a devastating outbreak of cholera. By 10 September, 500 people had died, increasing to 616 people by the end of that month. Dr John Snow was investigating the causes of the outbreak in a desperate attempt to prevent further deaths. However, at first he could see no pattern in the trajectory of the cholera epidemic's incidence that might indicate its source. For instance, who was dying came from diverse social and economic backgrounds and seemed to live all over the Soho area. However, upon further investigation, he noticed that of the 70 workers at the Broad Street Brewery none had died, neither had any

of their families been infected with cholera. The fact that the workers at the brewery received a free ration of beer which they took home and shared with their families and hence did not drink the local water made Dr Snow suspect that contaminated water may have been at fault. This was a controversial explanation at the time. His suspicions began to centre on the Broad Street Pump which supplied most of the people in Soho with water. An exception to this was the Poland Street Workhouse which had its own supply of water and therefore inmates did not drink water from the Broad Street Pump. At the time of his investigation no one had suffered from cholera at the Poland Street Workhouse. His suspicions were further confirmed when he discovered that some wealthy people who lived outside the Soho area had also died from cholera but they had got their servants to fetch water from the Broad Street Pump, rather than locally, because they believed the water tasted better. Despite considerable local opposition, Dr Snow eventually managed to get the Broad Street Pump shut down. The outbreak of cholera promptly ceased. It was later discovered that a nearby sewer had been leaking into the groundwater accessed by the Broad Street Pump.

In relation to Kolb's learning cycle, what was Dr Snow doing in his analysis and subsequent intervention?

Theories and hypotheses

*Theory is to be judged by its predictive power for the class of phenomena which it is intended to 'explain'.... the only test of the **validity** of a hypothesis is comparison of its predictions with experience. Friedman, 1953: 8, emphasis in original*

Now, to elaborate upon the above examples, it is necessary to consider more closely what a theory is and attempts to do. Although the terms 'theory' and 'hypothesis' are often used interchangeably, in its narrowest sense the term theory usually refers to a linguistic framework that is advanced so as to conceptualize and explain the occurrence, or non-occurrence, of a particular social or natural phenomenon. In other words:

1 a theory is an abstract conceptual framework which allows us to explain why specific observed regularities happen;
2 in doing, a theory defines or categorizes aspects of the world and relates these phenomena together in terms of cause and effect relationships which explain why what we have observed has actually happened;
3 usually a theory will also specify situations in which it does, or does not, apply, thereby setting boundaries to where it is applicable as an explanation;
4 in contrast a hypothesis is more specific yet also speculative: a hypothesis makes a precise prediction about what should happen, in particular conditions, if the underlying theory is an accurate representation and explanation of the phenomena in question – predictions that are testable through observation (i.e. the collection of specific data).

Stop and Think Exercise 3.2   In relation to Dr Snow's work in Soho – what was his theory and what was his hypothesis that allowed him to test his theory?

So any hypothesis presents an assertion about the relationship between two or more concepts in an explanatory fashion. Concepts are the building blocks of theories and hypotheses in that they are 'abstract ideas which are used to classify together things sharing one or more common properties' (Krausz and Miller, 1974: 4).

For instance, in the third theory above (see p. 42), 'improved training', 'productive', 'reliable' and 'satisfied' are all concepts. Moreover, we can see that this third theory links together these concepts in an explanatory way. Such explanations are usually causal – that is, they state that one aspect of our world causes, or leads to, another (see Pratt, 1978: 65–7, for an elaboration of what is meant by 'cause' and its importance); that the action or behaviour of phenomenon A causes, or leads to, specific responses in the behaviour of phenomenon B (i.e. in the third theory, improved training causes or leads to a more productive, reliable and satisfied workforce); from this we can predict that if we were to improve training for certain people in the workforce we should observe that they become more productive, reliable and satisfied either in comparison to what they were before and/or in comparison to other employees who have not experienced the provision of enhanced training.

An alternative example might be a hypothetical assertion that:

1 the adoption of a participative management style causes or leads to increased job satisfaction among the manager's subordinates; and
2 increased job satisfaction causes or leads to increased productivity.

From 1 and 2 we might infer that:

3 the adoption of a participative management style should cause, or lead to, increased productivity amongst the manager's subordinates.

Obviously any theory would normally state the underlying reasoning behind the postulated associations between management style, job satisfaction and productivity by locating its assertions in a critical review of the relevant literature. Although this example seems deceptively simple, hypotheses can be much more complex, not only in terms of being interlinked with other hypotheses but also by bringing in qualifying concepts that limit the causal relationship to particular classes of phenomena, e.g. A causes B only in conditions of C. For instance, we could rewrite our initial hypothesis that the adoption of a participative management style causes increased productivity among subordinates by limiting its applicability to conditions where subordinates are motivated primarily by the desire for intrinsic rewards. By implication, where those conditions do not apply, neither do the hypothetical assertions put forward by, or deduced from, the theory.

In trying to understand and explain the social and natural phenomena that surround us, and in our attempts at making decisions about what to do in particular circumstances, nobody escapes making or assuming these kinds of theoretical linkages. Every intentional act, every regularly undertaken practice, can be seen as an attempt to attain or create some desired state of affairs or conversely avoid the undesired. This implies the belief on the part of the actor that a causal relationship exists between his or her decision, or act, and the state of affairs he or she desires. In this sense, much of our everyday social lives and our work activities are in essence theory-dependent activities. Now this clearly illustrates the conjectural and practical aspects of theory, since people act in accordance with their expectations about, or indeed their prejudices about, what will, might, or should, happen in particular circumstances. Such conjectures are often derived from, and hence generalized from, our

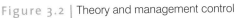
Figure 3.2 | Theory and management control

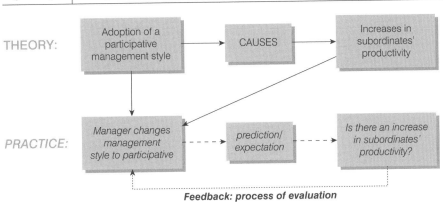

Feedback: process of evaluation

impressions regarding what has previously happened in what we take to be similar circumstances. Thus, even the most mundane activity, such as walking down a street, might be considered in terms of an actor applying theoretical assertions, virtually without thinking about them in a conscious fashion, that are usually borne out by being able to accomplish that activity. Often it is only when we become aware that our expectations, that are grounded in such tacit or taken-for-granted knowledge, have not been met (perhaps due to the intervention of some capricious circumstances) that we begin consciously to re-evaluate the webs of causal relationships that have previously been used to orientate and enable our practical actions. Out of this re-evaluation we may begin to generate a new theory to account for the previously unconsidered, or unencountered, anomalies. So, to paraphrase Douglas (1970: 80–103), such tacit knowledge is ordered and reordered according to the ebb and flow of situations. In Kolb et al.'s (1979) terms we are inductively and deductively learning.

Theory and management control

So it is evident that theories are a means by which we generate expectations about the world; often they are derived from what we have perceived to have happened before and thus they influence (tacitly or otherwise) how we set about future interactions with our world(s). Moreover, it is also evident that if we have the expectation that by doing A, B will happen, then by manipulating the occurrence of A we can begin to predict and influence the occurrence of B. In other words, theory is clearly enmeshed in practice since explanation enables prediction which in turn enables us to assert control over what happens or does nor happen (see Figure 3.2 above) – or at least it proffers the potential for doing such things.

In recent years many commentators, from an array of different perspectives, have all argued that there is an inextricable relationship between management and the control of the behaviour of subordinates so as to ensure that the latter accomplish particular tasks (e.g. Braverman,1974; Mant, 1977; Kunda, 1992; Johnson and Gill, 1993; Du Gay, 2000). If this is so, the importance of theory so as to enable such a control process is only too evident. Indeed, as Pugh (1971: 9) has claimed, every managerial act rests upon 'assumptions about what has happened and conjectures about what will happen; that is to say it rests on theory'.

As we have implied above, managers in their everyday activities rely upon both theories deriving from their 'common sense' and theories deriving from social science research. Although, as we shall see, the differences between the two are subtle and complex, many social scientists would ostensibly claim that the differences relate primarily to the extent to which social science research incorporates the overt and rigorous search for bias (Cook, 1983: 82), while common sense is much more imprecise and haphazard. In a similar vein, Kidder and Judd claim that

> social scientists look for biases and pitfalls in the processes used to support and validate hypotheses and submit their conclusions to the scrutiny of other scientists who attempt to find biases that were overlooked. The casual observer or ordinary knower often gathers evidence in support of hypotheses without being aware of or worried about the biases inherent in the process. (1986: 18)

As we have already noted, the danger in uncritically and unreflectively acting upon common-sense theories and hypotheses of the casual observer may be that one entraps oneself in the current 'traditions' or 'fads' dominant among the social groups to which we belong or defer to, at work or elsewhere. Although these traditions and fads may at first sight appear plausible as they 'create order out of disorder' (Huczynski, 1993: 198) with regard to the complex problems with which any manager has to cope, the potential for creating the problems associated with 'groupthink', so vividly described by Janis (1972), whereby decision-makers (amongst other things) fail to identify and evaluate options and information which might threaten to undermine the prevailing group consensus, is only too evident.

These issues provide a very useful starting point for considering the processes by which social science theories are constructed, evaluated and justified. In other words, what are the sources of such theories and hypotheses, and how do we set about judging rigorously whether or not these theories and hypotheses are 'true' and hence appropriate for our use? Different answers to these questions enable us to distinguish between different social science research methods. Pivotal to understanding these issues is the need to differentiate between those research methods that are deductive and those that are inductive.

Deduction

As illustrated by Figure 3.3, deduction entails the development of a conceptual and theoretical structure prior to its testing through empirical observation of the facts 'out there' in the world through data collection. As the reader may realize, deduction in this sense corresponds to the left-hand side of Kolb's experiential learning cycle (see Figure 3.1) since it begins with abstract conceptualization and then moves on to testing through the application of theory so as to create new experiences or observations. As we shall show later in this book, certain research methods, such as the various forms the experiment takes, certain types of survey and some forms of action research, all follow deductive logic – however, how they do this varies considerably.

To some researchers working within the deductive tradition, the source of one's theory is of little significance. Popper (1967: 130–43), for example, claims that it is the creative element in the process of science that is essentially unanalysable. Obviously we would not recommend this stance – usually it is very important to be able to justify why you think a particular theory, or hypothesis, is worth testing by

Figure 3.3 | Processes of deductive logic

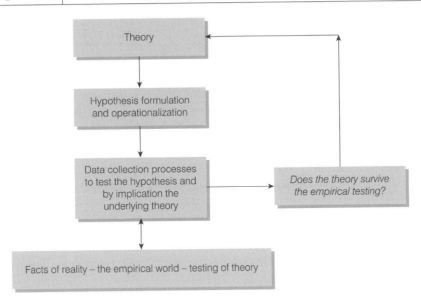

undertaking a critical review of the relevant literature that legitimizes your research (see Chapter 2). Nevertheless, according to Popper, what is most important here is the logic of deduction and the operationalization process, and how this enables the subsequent testing of the theory through its confrontation with the empirical world. Essentially the process of deduction might be divided into the following stages.

The use of concepts and hypotheses

First, the researcher must decide which concepts represent important aspects of the theory or problem under investigation. As we have already implied, concepts are abstractions that allow us to select and order our impressions of the world by enabling us to identify similarities and differences, e.g. 'efficient', 'social class', 'authoritarian', 'satisfied', 'manager', and so on. Concepts are linguistic devices that people regularly use to make sense of their worlds by signifying a particular phenomenon in terms of its perceived common features and its differences with other phenomena thereby allowing users to convey a sense of meaning during communication with others. In other words, a concept is an abstraction that enables us to give order to our otherwise chaotic sensory impressions by enabling the categorization of certain aspects of our experience. Everyone regularly does this in making sense of what is going on around us and in articulating those impressions to other people. However, how an abstract concept is construed and used in everyday sense making may vary because the definitions in-use are often implicit, tacit, and emergent, rather than explicitly formulated. This may create confusion during everyday debate and discussion since different people may be talking about different phenomena and not realize this because the same conceptual label is being deployed – yet it actually refers to different things. In social science research such abstractions, and the potential dissensus they can create, are problems that need to be resolved through what is called operationalization.

Operationalization is the process whereby precise and accessible definitions of phenomena are created.

Operationalization

As we have seen, hypotheses link two or more concepts together in a causal chain – a set of untested assertions about the relationship between the concepts which entails precise predictions about what should happen if the underlying theory, from which the hypothesis have been deduced, holds. However, since concepts are abstract they are not readily observable, and therefore the asserted relationships between concepts provided by the theory are not open to empirical testing until these abstractions are translated into specific observables, or indicators, which also ideally measure variation in the phenomenon of interest. That is, they have to be operationalized.

Through the operationalization of an abstract concept it becomes defined in such a way that rules are laid down for making observations and determining when an instance of the concept has empirically occurred. For instance, take the concept 'managerial level or status' – something that is regularly used by some researchers to identify similarities and differences between the people with whom we come into contact, e.g. line managers, middle managers, senior managers and so on. But when people use this concept to categorize others, they often do so in vague and varied ways. For instance, the term 'middle manager' used by one person may mean something very different when used by another. They may appear to be talking about the same things when in fact they are not: for example, one person might mean people in a certain income bracket, someone else may identify 'middle manager' with accent or educational background, but not income, others may be referring to a particular hierarchical level and span of control within organizational arrangements. Essentially, what these people are doing is operationalizing a concept in different ways and hence creating different meanings which cause confusion because people do not have an overt agreement about what they refering to in their use of particular concepts.

Therefore, by creating rules for making observations we are making a clear definition of what it is we are going to observe and how we are going to observe it. In this we create indicators, or measures, which represent empirically observable instances of, and variations in, the concept(s) under investigation. That is, we overtly link the abstract concept to something that is observable and whose variation is measurable.

Management research example Defining and operationalizing the concept of empowerment

During the last two decades, the use of the concept empowerment has permeated the language of business leaders and the remedial prescriptions of popular business press commentaries upon contemporary organizational issues (e.g. Block, 1987; Clutterbuck, 1994; Robinson, 1997; Cloke and Goldsmith, 2002).

However, the concept is replete with ambiguity and amenable to a variety of interpretations in practice. Spreitzer (1995) noted this growing interest but observed that the lack of a measure of empowerment had deterred substantive research on empowerment and its causes – a gap she attempted to fill by operationalizing the concept. Through an exhaustive review of the literature available at the time she then argues that organizational researchers in the past had focused upon empowering managerial practices but had not grappled with the effects of those practices upon employees. Hence, her focus was upon employees' psychological experience of empowerment in developing a systematic definition of empowerment. By drawing upon a sparse literature she then defines psychological empowerment in terms of a set of four cognitions (1995: 1443–4):

Meaning: the value of a work goal or purpose judged in relation to an individual's own ideals or standards;

Competence: the individual's belief in his or her capability to perform activities with skill;

Self-determination: an individual's sense of having choice in initiating and regulating actions such as making decisions about working methods, pace and effort;

Impact: the degree to which an individual can influence strategic, administrative or operating outcomes at work.

Spreitzer then notes that '[t]he four dimensions … combine additively to create an overall construct of psychological empowerment. In other words, the lack of any single dimension will deflate, though not completely eliminate, the overall degree of felt empowerment … empowerment is a continuous variable; people can be viewed as more or less empowered, rather than empowered or not empowered' (1995: 1444). In her research she then used a separate scale to measure each of the four dimensions of empowerment which were administered to respondents in her sample of middle managers. Each dimension was further operationalized via three statements (illustrated below, 1995: 1994–5) and the extent of respondents' agreement with each

statement was measured and recorded using a seven-point Lickert Scale.

Meaning
The work I do is very important to me.
My job activities are personally meaningful to me.
The work I do is meaningful to me.

Competence
I am competent about my ability to do my job.
I am self-assured about my capabilities to perform my work activities.
I have mastered the skills necessary for my job.

Self-determination
I have significant autonomy in determining how I do my job.
I can decide on my own how to go about doing my work.
I have considerable opportunity for independence and freedom in how I do my job.

Impact
My impact on what happens in my department is large.
I have a great deal of control over what happens in my department.
I have significant influence over what happens in my department.

Consider the way in which Spreitzer has defined and operationalized the concept empowerment – are there any problems with conceiving empowerment in terms of how people subjectively feel with regard to their own experiences at work? What are the assumptions Spreitzer is making about the phenomenon empowerment? Are these assumptions viable?

The linking rules, that is, the rules about when and where an observable instance of the concept has empirically occurred, are called operationalizations (see Figure 3.4). The point of these rules is that, by using the same indicators of a concept, and by standardizing the recording of the results of any observation, it should be possible to have a 'reliable', or consistent, measure of the relevant concept.

Figure 3.4 | Operationalizing abstract concepts

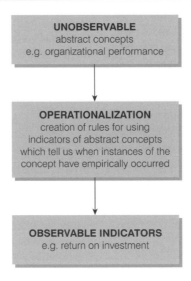

So at the heart of deductive approaches to management research is the process of operationalization because it enables the construction of clear and specific instructions about what and how to observe which in a sense can establish a consensus about what it is we are investigating. This enables the testing of hypotheses and theories by confronting them with the empirical data, which is then collected. In this testing, priority is given to what are considered directly observable phenomena and behaviour: things, events or activities which are publicly observable and hence can be corroborated and agreed upon by other observers. This emphasis upon the control of potential bias through replication by others has thus led to attempts to create standardized procedures for undertaking observation that can be followed exactly by those other researchers. This has in turn created the tendency in this approach to dismiss the analysis of the subjective or intangible since these kinds of phenomena, it is often claimed, cannot be directly observed in an unproblematic fashion and hence any findings cannot be corroborated through the replication of the research by other researchers. However, there is a great deal of choice regarding how we operationalize concepts such as 'organizational performance' and it may be instructive at this point to try Stop and Think Exercise 3.3.

Key methodological concept

Empiricism

Empiricism is a philosophical position which has a long history which does not directly concern us here (see Johnson and Duberley, 2000 for a description of empiricism's historical development). It has been the basis of much scientific thinking and practice in that empiricism articulates an important commitment: if a phenomena cannot be directly observed using our senses (i.e. touch, sight, hearing, smell) we must question whether or not it exists. Phenomena which cannot be directly observed through our senses probably do not exist and are most likely the result of myth, superstition or fantasy (e.g. gods, ghosts, demons, extraterrestrials, the paranormal, etc.). The point is, according to empiricism, the social and natural science must be limited to explaining phenomena that are directly observable whilst avoiding bias on the part of the scientist through the deployment of the most appropriate research methodology. Empiricism assumes, therefore, that provided the correct methodology is rigorously deployed it is possible to objectively observe the real world 'out-there' without contaminating what we find during the act of observation.

Stop and Think Exercise 3.3   In Figure 3.4 the abstract concept that we have attempted to operationalize is organizational performance. Obviously this is a very important concept for both management researchers and practitioners and has been the focus of much research especially when evaluating the impact of various changes and developments in management practices. Here we have operationalized organizational performance in terms of return on investment.

1 What assumptions have been made about business organizations, and the different groups of people who make them up, in how organizational performance has been operationalized in Figure 3.4?
2 Identify some alternative ways of operationalizing organizational performance.
3 How might these alternative indicators affect what is found in management research which for instance explores the relationship between certain management practices and organizational performance?
4 What does your answer to question 3 tell you about the objectivity of deductive research methodology and how it controls potential bias?
5 What does your answer to question 4 tell you about the strengths and weaknesses of empiricist philosophical commitments in practice?

Testing theory

The outcome of the above operationalization process is the ability to test: where the assertions or predictions put forward by the hypothesis are compared with the 'facts' collected by observation. Often, within the deductive tradition, once tested and if corroborated the theory is assumed to be established as a valid explanation. Those explanations are often termed 'covering-law explanations' in that the observations or variables to be explained are covered by the assertions about those phenomena contained within the theory. However, since these covering-law explanations posit regular relationships between those variables, which hold across all specified circumstances, they not only explain past observations but also predict what future observations ought to be like. Take the example: 'water boils when heated to 100° centigrade, at sea level, in an open vessel'. This covering-law not only explains what has happened when water is heated to 100° centigrade in such circumstances but it also predicts what will happen if water is subjected to those conditions. They also help us practically by providing a guide for our activities. However, it is usually the statistical version of the covering-law, whereby the relationships asserted by the theory have only some degree of probability of obtaining across all circumstances, which has generally been adopted by social scientists working within this deductive tradition.

So far we have used the term 'corroboration' in a fairly unproblematic fashion; but what is possible in, and what is meant by, corroboration, has been open to considerable dispute. Here we must turn to some of the debates that have taken place, and are continuing, in that branch of philosophy that has a concern with science: the 'philosophy of science'. As we shall show many of the methods used in management research articulate a particular stance within the philosophy of science so without some understanding of these debates it is difficult to fully understand why some researchers do the things that they do when conducting management research.

What we are alluding to here has often been generally called 'Hume's problem of induction' (Hume, 1739–40/1965). This problem arises because the testing of a theory inevitably involves a finite number of observations undertaken by researchers. Even if every observation that is made confirms the assertions put forward by a theory, logically we can never be certain whether some future observations might demonstrate instances in which the theory does not hold. In other words, we can never verify a theory and say that it applies everywhere, or prove it to be true in a universal sense, because we cannot extrapolate what we have observed so far to unobserved instances without contradicting the empiricist scientific commitment of limiting our claims about the world to what is observable. Future instances, by definition, have not been observed. This problem plagued scientific research until Sir Karl Popper, a famous philosopher, appeared to provide a viable solution. This philosophical solution is important because it is directly articulated by many of the research methods used today by management researchers, how they report their findings and the kinds of claim they make. Moreover, it also has a direct bearing upon management practice.

Popper's hypothetico-deductive approach

Popper, in perhaps one of his most famous contributions to the philosophy of science (1967, 1972a, 1972b), attempted to avoid the difficulties apparent in attempting to inductively verify, or prove, a theory built up from a finite number of observations. Popper cleverly avoids the philosophical problems he associated with 'verificationism', in which scientists attempt to prove their theories, by proposing the alternative maxim of 'falsificationism'. As the term falsificationsim implies, Popper argued that scientists should attempt to refute, or disprove, their theories rather than prove them. At the risk of oversimplifying, what Popper proposes is that no theory can ever be proven by a finite number of observations. No matter how many confirmatory instances have been observed that support the theory, we can never be certain whether or not future observations might demonstrate the falsity of the theory. In other words he is questioning the viability of the right-hand, or inductive, side of Kolb's Learning Cycle, as a model for scientific practice, because we can never be certain that our experiences are exhaustive of all possible instances of the phenomena we are interested in. He is also posing significant issues for what we can claim from following the left-hand, or deductive, side of the Learning Cycle.

Let us use an illustrative example used by Popper – the statement that 'all swans are white'. In the past, to Europeans, this seemed self-evident as it seemed to have been confirmed (i.e. inductively verified) by countless observations that all swans had white feathers regardless of breed. This appeared to be a universally true statement to Europeans until they explored the Australian continent where they discovered black swans. A further example of the potential problems created by 'induction' is provided by the statement 'one plus one equals two'. Again this appears self-evident, something that has been verified or confirmed by so many observations it would be impossible to count them. But according to the maxim of Popperian falsificationism, despite these numerous (but finite) confirmatory observations, we cannot be sure that some future instance might demonstrate its falsity, or limit its applicability. Indeed, such a consideration is to some extent borne out by the observations made in subatomic physics, that when two subatomic particles collide, their resultant fusion creates a mass that is sometimes more, or less, than their combined masses (Capra, 1975).

So, to summarize, Popper argues that while theories can never be proven to be true, they can be falsified, since only one contradictory observation is required. For Popper, therefore, the defining features of scientific theories are that:

1 they must be capable of empirical testing;
2 scientists should not try to find confirming instances of their theories but, rather, should make rigorous attempts at falsifying them using deduction (this is called the hypothetico-deductive method);
3 science advances as falsified propositions and theories fall away leaving a core of theory which has not, as yet, been disproved and which can be taken to approximate the truth (Popper called this verisimilitude, or truth-like);
4 theories which have not been falsified can be used to guide practice but we have to be cautious because future observations might disprove them – therefore such theory-driven practice should only be undertaken carefully, on a small scale, and continuously evaluated in terms of its affects (Popper, 1957: 44–5).

So for Popper, knowledge grows through the above processes whereby error is detected and removed. It follows that a critical attitude is a fundamental distinguishing feature of both science and rationality. Indeed, for Popper (1967: 50)

a dogmatic attitude is clearly related to the tendency to verify our laws and schemata by seeking to apply them and confirm them, even to the point of neglecting refutations, whereas the critical attitude is one of readiness to change them – to test them; to refute them; to falsify them, if possible.

What Popper calls the 'hypothetico-deductive' approach is summarized in Figure 3.5.

Stop and Think Exercise 3.4   To what extent do you think that Popper's critical attitude has penetrated actual management practice? What might be the barriers to its adoption by managers in practice?

The deductive tradition in the social sciences (although, as we shall show later, in Chapter 8, it is by no means unproblematic) clearly specifies what is involved in the development of 'scientific knowledge'. The 'hypothetico-deductive method' illustrated in Figure 3.5 emphasizes that what is important in 'science' is not the sources of the theories and hypotheses that the scientist starts out with, rather it is the process by which those ideas are tested that is crucial. Generally, the hypothetico-deductive approach to research is intimately bound up with what is often termed 'positivist' philosophy. Three of the main characteristics of positivism (there are others, which we shall consider later) are elaborated by Keat and Urry (1975: Ch. 4).

Figure 3.5 | The hypothetico-deductive method

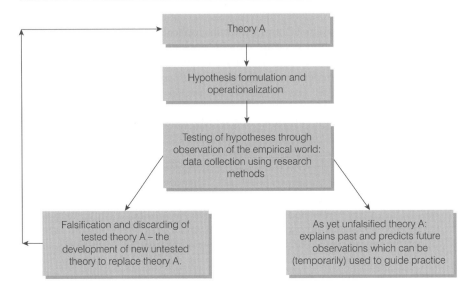

1 The view that, for the social sciences to advance, they must follow the hypothetico-deductive methodology used, with such evident success, by natural scientists (e.g. physicists) – in a nutshell, the experimental method and its derivatives;

2 The knowledge produced by, and the explanations used in, social science should be the same as those proffered by the natural sciences – e.g. that A causes B in specific circumstances;

3 The above entails social scientists treating their subject matter, the social world, as if it were the same as the natural world of the natural scientist.

Indeed, one could argue that the natural (or physical) sciences have to some degree enabled the explanation and prediction of many aspects of our natural environments and thereby has allowed for human beings to exercise increasing control over nature's vagaries – such as the occurrence of cholera. The advances in medicine, engineering and agriculture, for example, can all be considered in this light. This has led some social scientists, such as Hogan and Sinclair (1996), to argue that scientific inquiry based upon the methods of the natural sciences are the proper means for examining what happens in organizations. These methods, they claim, enable replicable and generalizable empirical validation to determine whether or not any theoretical description, explanation and prediction of members' organizational behaviour is accurate. The findings are therefore pivotal in promoting organizational efficiency and effectiveness through guiding management's interventions into organizations, affairs.

As Whitley (1984b: 369–71) has pointed out, the above belief that research methods derived from natural sciences can be applied to management in a straightforward way is based upon three crucial assumptions:

- there is a single set of procedures which generates scientific knowledge in all circumstances – a universally applicable method;
- this universal method, although developed in the natural sciences, is directly applicable to the social world which can be studied in the same way as the natural world;
- the knowledge generated is directly useful to management and this is neither affected by the nature of the problems management might deal with nor by the power relations between managers and those whose behaviour they are trying to influence through their knowledge-guided interventions.

With regard to the third set of assumptions above, Whitley gives us a stark warning ...

> ... *changing existing practices ... is premised upon the judgement that present patterns of social organization could be improved with respect to some general goal which is derived from a set of value judgements. The nature of such judgements affects the sort of situations which are seen as in need of improvement and the criteria by which solutions are evaluated as leading to desired improvements. In other words, what is seen as a problem and how knowledge about it is assessed are dependent upon the values adopted. (1984b: 373)*

Thus, Whitley alludes to how the use of theory in management practice is not merely a technical issue of applying neutral scientific knowledge – rather it is also an issue of who defines what is a 'problem' and and who defines 'improvement'. This raises important ethical questions about whose values are at play here and whose are by default being excluded by the form and use of such partial definitions?

However, it is Whitley's first and second set of assumptions above, which we are going to be most concerned with below in our initial exploration of management research methods. This is because it is only too apparent that with management studies, we are concerned with the application of social science theory (see Lupton, 1971; Griseri, 2002) to understand and explain human conduct in organizational and/or business settings. But this raises a question, which has direct methodological relevance, regarding whether or not we can study the social world in the same way as the natural world (see Stop and Think Exercise 3.5).

Stop and Think Exercise 3.5

1. Given the incredible successes of the natural science (e.g. physics) in enabling us to both explain and exert control over the natural world, should the social sciences in general, and management science in particular, copy the research methods used by natural scientists and thereby hope to emulate their successes?

2. Is there a difference between the subject matter of the natural sciences (e.g. the behaviour of physical objects) and that of the social sciences (e.g. the behaviour of human beings) which means that for the latter to adopt the research methods used in the former would be therefore a mistake? If you see there to be differences between the subject matters, what are they?

As we shall see, disputes over questions 1 and 2, and different answers to these questions, have pervaded debates about research methodology and what is deemed appropriate in the social sciences.

Figure 3.6 | The inductive development of theory

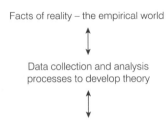

Facts of reality – the empirical world

Data collection and analysis
processes to develop theory

Theory developed that is already tested and verified because it
fits, and is grounded in, the observed facts

It is from objections to some of the implications and assumptions of such a positivist conception of social science that particular inductive approaches to management research arise. However, there is a need for some caution here for these objections, at first sight, seem to pose a significant break with positivism. However, as we shall see in later chapters, this is not necessarily the case because there are some further characteristics of positivism, which are underplayed by Keat and Urry's definition above, which are shared by some inductive approaches. So the break with positivism might not be so great as it first appears.

Induction

The logical ordering of induction is the reverse of deduction as it involves moving from the 'plane' of observation of the empirical world to the construction of explanations and theories about what has been observed. In this sense, induction relates to the right-hand side of Kolb's learning cycle (Figure 3.1): learning by reflecting upon particular past experiences and through the formulation of categories that class observed phenomena together and/or differentiate them; identifying patterns of association between those phenomena to produce theories and generalizations that explain past, and predict future, experience. In sharp contrast to the deductive tradition, in which a conceptual and theoretical structure is developed prior to empirical research, theory grounded in observation is the outcome of induction.

The debates and rivalry between supporters of induction and supporters of deduction, in both the natural and social sciences, have a long history (Ryan, 1970): debates which continue today amongst management researchers (see Johnson and Duberley, 2000; Johnson and Clark, 2006). However, contemporary justification for taking an inductive approach in the social sciences tends to revolve around two closely related arguments.

First, for many researchers working within the inductive tradition, explanations of social phenomena are relatively worthless unless they are grounded in observation and experience. Perhaps the most famous rendition of this view is provided by Glaser and Strauss (1967) in their much referenced book *The Discovery of Grounded Theory*. In this they argue that in contrast to the speculative and a priori nature of deductive theory, theory that inductively develops out of systematic empirical research is more likely to fit the data and thus is more likely to be useful, plausible and accessible especially to practising managers (see Tenbrunsel et al., 1996; Partington, 2000).

Key methodological concept

Grounded theory

'… theory that was derived from data systematically gathered and analysed through the research process' (Strauss and Corbin, 1998: 12).

As the above quotation implies, grounded theory is theory that is inductively generated out of the systematic analysis of data gathered by the researcher. Here the collected data is organized by the researcher (through what is often called coding) to conceptually categorize variations in the data in terms of observed patterns (i.e. similarities and differences) thereby creating indicators of particular phenomena the researcher in interested in. This involves the careful scrutinization of data to generate initial descriptive categories of the phenomena of interest that share particular distinguishing characteristics by constructing the uniformities and differences underlying and defining emergent categories. Successive categorical schemes are usually generated through a series of re-readings and re-codings of data where the properties of, the connections and differences between, emergent conceptual categories are reconfigured through elaboration, consolidation or division to further generate and develop those categories. Whilst these iterative processes inevitably entail some 'data reduction' since they involve 'selecting, focusing, simplifying, abstracting and transforming the raw data' (Miles and Huberman, 1994: 10) the overriding aim is to develop a scheme of 'saturated' categories that are exhaustive of all the data available in the sense that all variance identified in the data is eventually covered without any exceptions (see Glaser and Strauss, 1967: 106). Having conceptually categorized the data, the researcher then looks for patterns in the data that suggest causal relationships between different categories which enable the generation of hypothetical explanations regarding the phenomena of interest. Such hypotheses are revised and reformulated until all the collected data are explained by the emergent theory. Hence, data collection and analysis continue simultaneously throughout the research process until there are no observed exceptions to both the categorical scheme created to organize the observed data and their theoretical explanation – this involves numerous iterations between data collection and analysis which systematically refer to each other and should be mutually reinforcing.

The second, and related, rationale articulated in support of an inductive approach arises more overtly out of a critique of some of the philosophical assumptions embraced by positivism as initially, for our purposes here, defined above by Keat and Urry (1975). It is to this particular critique of positivism that we shall now turn. As we have seen, one of the main themes of positivism and of much of the deductive tradition in the social sciences is a conception of scientific method constructed from what is assumed to be the approach in the natural sciences, particularly physics. This positivist requirement is often called *methodological monism* (see Ross, 1991: 350). It involves the idea that only natural science methodology can provide certain knowledge and enable prediction and control. This necessarily entails the development of theory that successfully explains past and predicts future observations, through causal analysis and deductive-hypothesis testing. The format of this explanation and prediction is illustrated by Figure 3.7 below.

The use of methodological monism in the social sciences usually involves conceptualizing and explaining human behaviour deterministically: as necessary responses to the action of empirically observable, measurable and manipulable stimuli, causal variables or antecedent conditions. This form of explanation is often called *erklaren* (see Outhwaite, 1975). It is the various problems associated with using *erklaren* in

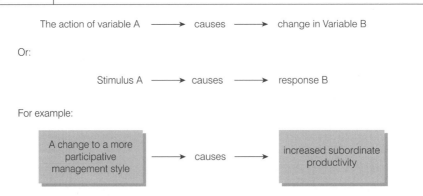

Figure 3.7 | Methodological monism

the social sciences as an organizing frame of reference for research, that provide the initial point of departure for the second critique that justifies the use of induction in the social sciences.

Stop and Think Exercise 3.6   Lift a pen few centimetres in the air and drop it. You can understand the subsequent behaviour of the pen in terms of necessary responses to the action of external stimuli (e.g. the action of gravity, the friction of the pen against the air as it falls, the impact of atmospheric disturbances, and so on). You do not have to refer to the pen's subjective comprehension and evaluation of the situation in order to explain its choice of behaviour. This is because, as far as we know, the pen does not have any subjective apprehension of itself as an entity in particular social circumstances, etc. However, in contrast to the pen, human beings clearly do have subjective capacities, both emotional and cognitive, which influence how we consciously make choices about how to behave, where, and when. Hence, it may be argued that to ignore these subjective processes when explaining human behaviour is a mistake. It is precisely because the stimulus-response model of behaviour illustrated in Figure 3.7 ignores how human beings are agents who interpret and attach meaning to what is going on around them that leads to the model's rejection: active sense making that influences their generation, evaluation, selection and enactment of different courses of action. In other words, we are sentient beings not inanimate objects (like our pen) and therefore research methods originally developed to investigate the latter should not be used to investigate the former.

However, one tactic that is widely used to deal with the above issue is to assume that everyone subjectively apprehends the world in the same way and therefore there is no need to investigate it thereby preserving a stimulus-response model of behaviour because all stimuli will be interpreted by people in the same way. For instance, Game Theory in Economics homogenizes human subjectivity and presents a particularly pessimistic view of human 'rationality' that allows the theorist to model and predict human behaviour without further investigation of this subjective domain. In this, it assumes that all human interaction entails individuals attempting to 'rationally' calculate what behaviour best serves their own interests. Based on those calculations, individuals will always pursue courses of action that maximizes those interests even to the detriment of other people. Indeed, Game Theory assumes that individuals in seeking to maximize their personal advantage presume that other individuals are simultaneously undertaking the same kind of self-interested analyses to plot what they should also do. Essentially society is assumed by Game Theorists to be characterized by a war of all against all as it is constituted by the actions of self-serving individuals continuously strategizing about what they should do based upon their low-trust apprehension of other people. Of course what one could also argue is that perhaps the only people who believe that all people are like this are some economists and all psychopaths!

At the risk of oversimplifying, many supporters of induction in the social sciences reject the causal model illustrated in Figure 3.7 above because they consider that this kind of explanation is inappropriate. For instance, Guba and Lincoln (1994: 106) have argued that *erklaren*, with the quantitative measures of phenomena and the statistical reasoning it uses to investigate causation, imposes an external researcher-derived logic upon its subject matter which excludes, or at best distorts rather than accesses, actors' subjective sense making from the data that is collected. So although *erklaren* may be adequate for the subject matter of the natural sciences, it is not adequate for the social sciences. Hence, supporters of induction in the social sciences take a particular philosophical position regarding human behaviour which sees there to be fundamental differences between the subject matter of the social sciences (thinking, sentient, human beings) and the subject matter of the natural sciences (animals and physical objects). This differentiation directly leads to the use of what are generally labelled qualitative research methods which are primarily inductive.

This philosophical position is illustrated by Laing (1967: 53), who points out the error of blindly following the approach of the natural sciences in the study of the social world. 'The error fundamentally is the failure to realise that there is an ontological discontinuity between human beings and it-beings . . . Persons are distinguished from things in that persons experience the world, whereas things behave in the world.' By implication Laing is drawing our attention to the following issues:

1 Human action has an internal logic of its own which must be understood in order for researchers to be able to make that action intelligible and explicable. It is the rightful aim of social science to access and describe this internal logic through a methodological approach which is generally called *verstehen* (see Outhwaite, 1975) – a German word meaning 'to understand'. This has significant methodological implications for how researchers can and should investigate human activities.

2 The subject matter of the natural sciences does not have this subjective comprehension of its own behaviour – it does not have an internal logic which the scientist must tap in order to understand its behaviour. Therefore, the natural scientist can legitimately, and indeed has to, impose an external causal logic upon the behaviour of his or her subject matter in order to explain it. But such methodology is inappropriate and does not explain the actions of human beings, due to their subjectivity. For example, the behaviour of a pool or snooker ball might be adequately understood in terms of necessary responses caused by particular sets of stimuli in certain conditions: the amount of force delivered to the cue ball propelling it in a particular direction; the angle at which the cue ball strikes the object ball and the amount of momentum it delivers; the

friction of the balls in play against the cloth of the table and the friction of air of a specific humidity upon the moving balls, and so on. At no point do we have to refer to the subjective apprehension of the balls of what is going on around them in order to explain their behaviour. In comparison, to describe and explain the behaviour of the pool or snooker players in terms of stimulus-response would seem bizarre. For surely their behaviour can be only adequately explained through reference to their subjective motives and intentions, their strategic and tactical interpretation of the situation, their knowledge of the rules of the game, their expectations about the articulation, monitoring and enforcement of those rules by other people present during the playing of the game.

3 Therefore, the social world cannot be understood in terms of causal relationships that do not take account of the situation that human actions are based upon the actor's interpretation of events, his or her social meanings, intentions, motives, attitudes and beliefs; i.e. human action is only explainable only by understanding these subjective dimensions and their operation in specific social contexts. Therefore, human action is seen as purposive and becomes intelligible only when we gain access to that subjective dimension which is usually taken to be socially, or culturally, derived. In other words, the norms, beliefs and values that we deploy in making sense of our worlds, which play a crucial role in our construction of meaningful action, derive from our social interactions with other people during the course of our everyday lives, and therefore are to varying degrees shared with them in specific social contexts. Hence, it is more appropriate to talk about an *inter-subjective* dimension to human behaviour rather than a purely subjective.

4 It follows that research in the social sciences must entail what are called emic analyses, in which explanations of human action derive from the meanings and interpretations of those conscious actors who are being studied. This approach is usually generically called *interpretivism*. With an interpretivist approach the etic analyses embraced by deduction, in which an external frame of reference is imposed upon the behaviour of phenomena, are deemed to be inappropriate where the phenomena in question have subjective capabilities – it is this internal yet socially derived dimension that is the key to explanation in the social sciences. Moreover, one cannot make a priori assumptions about the nature of this subjective world – the researcher has to go out and discover it by observation and data collection, in other words through induction. This interpretive and inductive approach is therefore based upon a rejection of the stimulus-response model of human behaviour that is built into the methodological arguments of many positivists. 'Stimulus causes response' is rejected in favour of one of the two approaches represented in Figure 3.8 below.

As is evident from Figure 3.8, modes 1 and 2 are very closely related. Indeed, it may be a short step from initially accepting 1 to then accepting 2. In (1) above, the actor's subjectivity is taken to be an 'intervening variable' that mediates between the stimuli coming from the external world and subsequent human responses expressed as behaviour or action. In (2), however, the actor's subjectivity is accorded greater 'formative or creative' power in its own right. Here the interpretation of reality, upon which actions are based, is not a mere medium through which external stimuli act (as in (1)). Rather, interpretation has a projective quality in the sense that such inter-subjective processes create, or socially construct, the reality in which action arises

Figure 3.8 | Two modes of interpretive, or emic, analysis using *verstehen*

Mode (1)

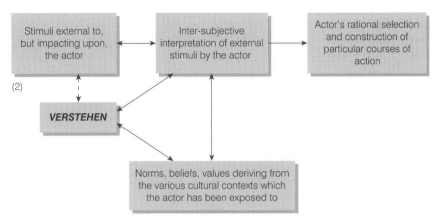

Mode (2)

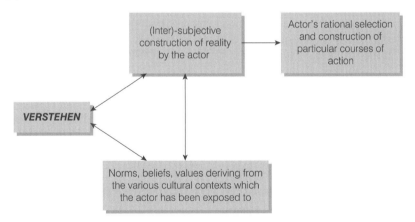

(see Berger and Luckmann, 1967; Burr, 1995), and hence the idea that (inter)-subjectivity mediates the action of external stimuli becomes rather meaningless: all that there is for us to research is human inter-subjective processes, through which their sense of reality is created, in order to explain behaviour.

Although these differences have resulted in somewhat different methodological approaches, both (1) and (2) above share a commitment to conceiving human action as arising out of actors' inter-subjectivity and hence the need in research methodology to undertake *verstehen*. Thus, both (1) and (2) entail the initial philosophical agreement that the possession by human beings of a mind has freed them from the stimulus-response relationships that dominate the behaviour of 'natural phenomena' (see Mead, 1934). As we have indicated, this perceived need drives particular methodological commitments but it also opens up some sources of debate and dispute within these more interpretive approaches as well as with mainstream positivism. These are summarized below.

Debates and disputes

1 The model of human behaviour underpinning *verstehen* creates serious objections to the contention of some positivists that social phenomena might be treated as being analogous to the 'it-beings' or 'things' of nature and thereby are amenable to a similar type of causal analysis in which the subjective or intentional dimension is ignored and effectively lost. Instead, it is postulated that the difference between the social and the natural world is …

> … that the latter does not constitute itself as 'meaningful': the meanings it has are produced by men (sic) in the course of their practical life, and as a consequence of their endeavours to explain it for themselves. Social life – of which these endeavours are part – on the one hand, is produced by its component actors, precisely in terms of their active constitution and reconstitution of frames of meaning whereby they organise their experience. (Giddens, 1976: 79)

2 These considerations create the need for social scientists to explain human behaviour adequately, to develop a sympathetic understanding of the frames of reference and meaning out of which that behaviour arises. But of course this poses significant methodological questions around how this accessing of other's subjective interpretations of their experiences may be achieved. We will need to turn to this issue in much detail in later chapters. However, for the time being it is important to point out that these methods are generically called qualitative methods and they are usually recognized as having a direct concern with enabling *verstehen*. Through *verstehen*, qualitative methods are seen to be (see Van Maanen 1998; Alvesson and Deetz, 2000; Denzin and Lincoln, 2000) aimed at enabling a sympathetic understanding of others' experience by inductively accessing the actual meanings and interpretations they subjectively deploy in making sense of their worlds and which influence their ongoing social construction and accomplishment of meaningful action. Hence, explanation of behaviour is in terms of describing these cultural processes and elements. Thus, through 'fidelity to the phenomena under study' (Hammersley and Atkinson, 1995: 7) an array of qualitative methods have been developed in order to investigate how actors construct, sustain, articulate and transmit socially derived versions of reality in order to describe and explain their behaviour in specific social contexts.

3 Generally the methodological implications of *verstehen* usually entail the avoidance of the highly structured methodological approaches of deduction; these, it is usually argued, prevent and ignore the access to actors' subjectivity – or at best they distort our access to that subjective domain. This happens because the deductive researcher, prior to conducting empirical research, formulates a theoretical model of the behaviour of interest, which is then tested through data collection. Hence, they impose an external logic upon a phenomenon which has an internal logic of its own. It is precisely the discovery of this internal logic, through empirical research, that is the concern of many supporters of induction in the social sciences. To achieve

this, what is recommended are relatively less structured approaches usually using qualitative methods to research that ostensibly allow for access to human subjectivity, without creating distortion, in its natural or everyday settings. However, this claim to objectivity in exploring others' subjective worlds has become increasingly controversial amongst qualitative researchers and has led to considerable variability in how and why qualitative research is undertaken – something we shall return to in later chapters. Nevertheless, for the time being, the most important issue for us here is that an interpretivist view of human behaviour undermines methodological monism since a clear implication is that different methods are appropriate for investigating social and natural phenomena – not the same method.

4 Because interpretivism, in its various forms, undermines methodological monism this has provoked the response that if it was followed in the social sciences the latter would be unable to emulate the envied operational successes of the natural sciences. Moreover, the interpretive prescriptions described above have also encouraged the positivist counter-argument that because this kind of inductive research is relatively unstructured, it is unreliable since it is not easily replicable and therefore bias cannot be ruled out nor even investigated through the replication of research, by other social scientists, to cross check findings. This point is made forcefully by Behling (1980: 489) where he argues that research methods similar to those used in the natural sciences, whilst not immune to systematic bias do have built into them 'extensive means for protecting the researcher against personal biases' – unlike those qualitative methods which attempt to enable *verstehen*.

5 According to Giddens (1976: 19), many positivists regard the 'intuitive or empathic grasp of consciousness' as merely a possible source of hypotheses about human conduct and not a method for social science research in its own right. Moreover, some philosophers (e.g. Neurath, 1959) have argued that to attempt such grasping of others' culturally derived consciousness is inappropriate for science. This is because it is presumed that human subjectivity, and related inter-subjective processes, cannot be empirically observed in a direct, objective, manner. Therefore, social science theory based upon such attempts is inadmissible as genuinely scientific explanations. Indeed, trying to investigate actors' subjective processes, because they are considered to be unobservable in an objective fashion, might introduce into social science the very guess work and dogma (what Neurath calls 'the residues of theology' (1959: 295)) that science has been trying to eradicate since the Enlightenment. In other words, some positivists see that any genuine social science should limit itself to what they see as directly observable stimulus-response (or cause and effect) relationships preferably, and usually, using quantitative measures of such phenomena which are taken to be more objective and enable rigorous testing of hypotheses. Simultaneously, some interpretive researchers would reject such a dismissal by arguing that it is indeed possible to objectively access human subjective processes provided that the correct methodological steps are undertaken. However, such a claim to objectivity is simultaneously questioned by other interpretive researchers – another philosophical dispute, as we shall show in later chapters, that has led to an increasing diversity in how qualitative management research is undertaken.

Key methodological concept

Reliability

For many management researchers a key methodological requirement is to ensure distance between the researcher and the researched so that research processes and findings are not contaminated by the actions or idiosyncrasies of the researcher. Hence, a key way of evaluating the findings of research pertains to the reliability of findings in the sense that different researchers, or the same researcher on different occasions, would 'discover the same phenomena or generate the same constructs in the same or similar settings' (Lecompte and Goetz, 1982: 32). In other words, reliability refers to 'the extent to which studies can be replicated' (ibid.: 35). Therefore, the assessment of reliability requires the use of clear methodological procedures and protocols so that regulation by peers, through replication would be, in principle, possible. However, reliability becomes a contentious issue in qualitative research because the commitments to *verstehen* and induction usually mean that research design and fieldwork emerges out of, and is largely limited to and dependent upon, specific research settings. This lack of structure makes the possibility of replication problematic and hence makes the policing of findings by the wider scientific community difficult if not impossible.

Conclusions

In this chapter we have initially confronted some of the key philosophical debates that have a bearing upon the diverse ways in which management research is conducted in practice. As we shall see there are other philosophical issues relevant here which we have already hinted at and which we shall develop as we proceed in the book. A key point here is that research methods are not merely neutral tools or techniques that we can just take off the shelf and use to undertake management research. Rather different research methods come with considerable philosophical baggages which in part influence how you perceive and understand the management issue or problem that you hoping to investigate by using particular methodological approaches. This is an issue that we will repeatedly return to in the rest of the book.

For the time being, and as a way of summarizing much of that has been covered so far, it is possible to construct a continuum of research methods, as a heuristic device, that initially allows us to differentiate between different methods in terms of the various philosophical stances and logics they bring to bear in conducting research. That is, we can discriminate between different methods in terms of their relative emphasis upon deduction or induction, their degree of structure, the kinds of data they generate and the forms of explanation they create. At each extreme of the proposed continuum we can distinguish what are known as nomothetic and ideographic methodologies.

As Burrell and Morgan (1979: 6–7) note, nomothetic methodologies have an emphasis on the importance of basing management research upon the rigorous use of systematic protocols and technique. This is epitomized in the approach and methods employed in the natural sciences, which focus upon the process of testing hypotheses in accordance with particular standards of scientific rigour. Standardized research instruments of all kinds are prominent among these methodologies which articulate a set of rules that the researcher should follow. Emphasis is therefore placed upon covering-law explanations and deduction, using quantified operationalizations of concepts in which the element of motive/purpose/meaning is lost, partially because of the need for precise models and hypotheses for testing but also because of the particular philosophical assumptions about human behaviour that are being tacitly deployed that often render the subjective domain as non-researchable or even irrelevant.

On the other hand, according to Burrell and Morgan (1979: 6–7), ideographic methodologies emphasize the analysis of subjective accounts that one generates by 'getting inside' situations and involving oneself in, or accessing in various ways, the everyday flow of life without disrupting it. This usually involves the deployment of qualitative methods in management research. Here there is an emphasis upon theory inductively grounded in such empirical observations which takes account of subjects' meaning and interpretational systems in order to gain explanation by understanding (i.e. *verstehen*). However, it is important to note at this point that this shared commitment to *verstehen* does

Table 3.1 A comparison of nomothetic and ideographic research methods – a continuum

Nomothetic methods emphasize		Ideographic methods emphasize
1 Deductive testing of theory	vs	1 Inductive development of theory
2 Explanation via analysis of causal relationships and explanation by covering-laws (called etic or *erklaren*)	vs	2 Access to, and description of, subjective meaning systems and explanation of behaviour through understanding (called emic or *verstehen*)
3 Generation and use of quantitative data	vs	3 Generation and use of qualitative data
4 Use of various controls, physical or statistical, so as to allow the rigorous testing of hypotheses	vs	4 Commitment to research in, or access to, everyday settings, whilst minimizing the disruption caused by the research to those being investigated so as to preserve the natural context in which their behaviour arises
5 Highly structured research methodology to ensure replicability by other scientists and as a result of 1, 2, 3, and 4	vs	5 Minimum structure to ensure 2, 3 and 4 (and partially as a result of 1)

◄──────────────── A methodological continuum ────────────────►	
Laboratory experiments, quasi experiments, some action research, surveys,	Mixed methods, some action research, qualitative methods e.g. ethnography

(Cont'd)

not explain the considerable heterogeneity evident in qualitative management research. This heterogeneity suggests that considerable differences underlie the initial appearance of similarity usually invoked by the term 'qualitative' and it is something that we will turn to in much more detail when we come to consider qualitative management research.

For the time being, and as a heuristic device, it is useful as a way in to considering management research methods to propose that any method adopts a position on a continuum according to its relative emphasis upon the characteristics summarized by Table 3.1.

It is to the various different methods (e.g. laboratory experiments, quasi-experiments, surveys, various forms of action research and various forms of qualitative management research such as ethnography), their various commitments and characteristics, together with their use in management research, that we turn in the following chapters. It is important to remember that the above continuum is only an initial snapshot of some complex issues. Indeed, as we try to represent in Table 3.1 certain approaches, such as action research, do themselves vary in terms of our comparative criteria – something we shall consider in detail in Chapter 5. Notwithstanding this issue we shall begin this methodological journey with what many social scientists consider to be the gold standard of sciences: experimental research design.

Further reading

Lupton's (1971) classical work provides an interesting and important starting point for the consideration of the role and nature of theory in social science generally and with specific regard to management. For an interesting analysis of the interplay between management theory and practice the reader should see Tranfield and Starkey (1998). However, their account might be gainfully compared with an incisive critique of technicism in management education provided by Grey and Mitev (1995). Also useful for its focus on the world of the manager is Checkland (1981). Checkland, himself trained as a physical scientist, reviews the systems movement as a scientific endeavour to tackle the ill-structured problems of the managerial world. He comes to the conclusion that 'hard systems' engineering needs to be modified to something more appropriate which he calls 'soft systems' methodology. We have found the book to be particularly useful in helping students from a background in the physical or natural sciences to bridge the gap between deductive and inductive approaches to management research.

With regard to the issues around philosophy of science that have emerged in this chapter, Lessnoff (1974) provides a detailed survey of many of the philosophical issues important in social science research, with an interesting focus upon the relevance of a natural science 'model' for research in the social sciences. More recently Johnson and Duberley (2000) provide an overview of the key philosophical debates which influence management and organizational research. For an interesting and increasingly important perspective on the relationship between theory and data the reader could also turn to Ragin's (1994) discussion of how all social research constructs representations of social life through a dialogue between ideas (theory) and evidence (data).

Meanwhile, for those who wish to explore the assumptions that underpin different approaches to research and theory in further depth, they should turn to Slife and Williams (1995) who provide a thorough overview of psychoanalysis, behaviourism, humanism, cognitivism, eclecticism, structuralism and postmodernism. Assumptions specifically about human behaviour are investigated by Ashworth (2000) where he examines the major contributors to the development of our thinking about consciousness, selfhood, culture and the effects of the physical world on genetic inheritance.

For an important outline of the characteristics of positivist management research and its continuing relevance to managerial practice the reader should turn to Hogan and Sinclair (1996). Their argument is that scientific inquiry based upon the methods of the natural sciences is the proper means for examining what happens in organizations. These methods, they claim, enable replicable and generalizable empirical validation to determine whether or not any theoretical description, explanation and prediction of organizational behaviour is accurate. The resulting tested theory is directly helpful to management as it is pivotal in promoting organizational effectiveness through guiding their organizational interventions. Likewise Behling (1980) explores five major objections to using research methods that derive from the natural sciences in the study of organizations – objections which he feels are not insurmountable. Whilst he concludes that using such methods does have its problems, and hence requires more thoughtful application, a key advantage of this approach, he argues, is that it has built in an extensive means for protecting the researcher against personal biases.

The ambiguous relationship between the concepts researchers might use to direct the focus of their fieldwork and the role theory is explored by Blumer (1954) in a famous article. Here the target of Blumer's attack is the use of what he calls 'definitive' concepts that are used in quantitative research and which once developed, and operationalized into sets of indicators, become fixed benchmarks which guide data collection. In contrast Blumer advises researchers to use what he calls 'sensitizing concepts' which suggest directions in which the research must look. This idea is of particular importance to researchers setting out to undertake inductive research because it clarifies the relationship between prior literature searches and subsequent inductive data collection. For Blumer sensitizing concepts taken from existing theory and literature are used in a way that only gives a sense of direction in which to look and can thereby act merely as a guide for uncovering the variety of ways in which a phenomena can empirically assume, rather than imposing prior conceptualized format for engaging with, and recording variation in, phenomena of interest.

Morgan and Smircich (1980) take a very different approach to understanding qualitative research to that of Behling, or Hogan and Sinclair. They draw upon the concept of paradigm as previously used by Burrell and Morgan (1979). Here they directly relate the choices researchers make between quantitative and qualitative methods to varying philosophical assumptions about ontology, epistemology and human nature. In doing so they call for a more reflexive approach to understanding the nature of social research that admits how the choice of particular methodological techniques is contingent upon our philosophical assumptions about the nature of the phenomena under investigation.

However, the view put forward by the above writers of what natural science methodology entails, although widely accepted, is quite different to that presented by Whitley (1984b) who reviews a number of writers who claim that science is essentially a method of producing and validating knowledge that is directly useful to management. In his critique of this stance, Whitley exposes the tacit and uncritical adoption of positivistic philosophical assumptions that underpin such an approach and points to the substantial difficulties that render these assumptions, and their prescriptions for management research, as increasingly untenable. He proceeds to explore how management research can be understood as a practically orientated science in terms of its similarities to, and differences from, other social sciences as well as the natural sciences. Whilst Whitley feels that there are substantial differences between the subject matters of the natural and social sciences, he does not consider that these differences rule out the possibility of a social science that is broadly comparable with what he presents as a more sophisticated version of the natural sciences to that presented by Behling (1980) or Hogan and Sinclair (1996).

These journal articles are freely available on the companion website (www.sagepub.co.uk/gillandjohnson):

Hassard, J. (1991) Multiple paradigms and organizational analysis: a case study, *Organization Studies*, 12(2): 275–99.
Prasad, A. and Prasad, P. (2002) The coming age of interpretive organizational research, *Organizational Research Methods*, 5(1): 4–11.

Overview of Qualitative Research

MICHAEL D. MYERS

Objectives

By the end of this chapter, you will be able to:

- Understand the purpose of qualitative research
- Appreciate the benefits of qualitative research
- Recognize what counts as research and what does not
- Distinguish between quantitative and qualitative research
- Decide whether or not to use triangulation
- See how qualitative research can contribute to the rigour and relevance of research

WHY DO QUALITATIVE RESEARCH?

Qualitative research methods are designed to help researchers understand people and what they say and do. They are designed to help researchers understand the social and cultural contexts within which people live.

One of the key benefits of qualitative research is that it allows a researcher to see and understand the *context* within which decisions and actions take place. It is often the case that human decisions and actions can only be understood in context – it is the context that helps to 'explain' why someone acted as they did. And this context (or multiple contexts) is best understood by talking to people.

Qualitative researchers contend that it is virtually impossible to understand why someone did something or why something happened in an organization without talking to people about it. Imagine if the police tried to solve a serious crime without being able to talk to the suspects or witnesses. If the police were restricted to using only quantitative data, almost no crimes would be solved. Imagine if lawyers and judges were not allowed to question or cross-examine witnesses in court. The validity and reliability of any court decision would be thrown into serious doubt. So, likewise, qualitative researchers argue that if you want to understand people's motivations, their reasons, their actions, and the context for their beliefs and actions in an in-depth way, qualitative research is best. Kaplan and Maxwell (1994) say that the goal of understanding a phenomenon from the point of view of the participants and its particular social and institutional context is largely lost when textual data are quantified.

One of the primary motivations for doing qualitative research, as opposed to quantitative research, comes from the observation that, if there is one thing which distinguishes humans from the natural world, it is their ability to talk. It is only by talking to people, or reading what they have written, that we can find out what they are thinking, and understanding their thoughts goes a long way towards explaining their actions.

TYPES OF QUESTIONS USING QUALITATIVE RESEARCH

The questions that a qualitative researcher might typically ask are what, why, how, and when questions:

- **What** is happening here?
- **Why** is it happening?
- **How** has it come to happen this way?
- **When** did it happen?

WHAT IS RESEARCH?

In a university setting, research is defined as an *original investigation* undertaken in order to contribute to knowledge and understanding in a particular field. Research is a creative activity leading to the production of *new* knowledge. The knowledge produced is new in the sense that the facts, the interpretation of those facts, or the theories used to explain them might not have been used in a particular way before in that specific discipline.

Research typically involves enquiry of an empirical or conceptual nature and is conducted by people with specialist knowledge about the subject matter, theories, and methods in a specific field. Research may involve contributing to the intellectual infrastructure of a subject or discipline (e.g. by publishing a dictionary). In some fields, such as engineering, computer science, or information systems, research can also include the experimental design of new artefacts. Engineers often try to develop new or substantially improved materials, devices, products, or processes.

Of course, as more research is published, the subject matter, theories, and methods used in a particular field may change over time. For this reason, scholars in many disciplines will write a literature review of previous relevant research to show that they understand and are up-to-date with the latest thinking.

But how do we know that the research results are new? How do we know that the findings are original? How do we know that the research was conducted in a rigorous manner?

The only way to tell if the research findings are both sound and original is if those findings are open to scrutiny and formal evaluation by experts in a particular field. That is, the findings must be evaluated by those who are experienced and 'qualified' to do so. If these experts, in evaluating the research, find that the results are sound, and that the findings are new *to them*, then we can say that the research project represents an original contribution to knowledge.

This way of evaluating the quality of research in science is called the peer review system. The peer review system exists in all scientific disciplines and is in effect a system of quality assurance. Of course, the peer review system is a social system, and as such it has its drawbacks, but it does ensure that only research of a certain standard is published. I discuss the peer review system and the publication process in more detail in Part VI.

It should be clear from the above discussion that some activities do not count as research in a university setting (Tertiary Education Commission, 2005). Some of these activities are as follows:

- The preparation of teaching materials. Teaching materials are excluded since they are not normally formally evaluated by experts in the field as a whole. For example, case study books written for teaching purposes are written primarily for students, not researchers. As Yin describes, 'For teaching purposes, a case study need not contain a complete or accurate rendition of actual events; rather, its purpose is to establish a framework for discussion and debate among students'(2003: 2). The distinction between producing case studies for teaching and research is discussed more fully in Chapter 7.
- The provision of advice or opinion, e.g. consulting work.
- Feasibility studies (where the output is a recommendation to a client).
- Routine data collection (where there is no attempt to contribute to new knowledge in the field as a whole).
- Routine information systems development (where the output is a new or improved product for a client, not the experimental design of a new product or service).
- Any other routine professional practice.

QUANTITATIVE AND QUALITATIVE RESEARCH COMPARED

There are many different ways to classify and characterize different types of research. However, one of the most common distinctions is between qualitative and quantitative research methods (Table 2.1).

Table 2.1 Examples of qualitative and quantitative research

Qualitative research A focus on text	Quantitative research A focus on numbers
Action research	Surveys
Case study research	Laboratory experiments
Ethnography	Simulation
Grounded theory	Mathematical modelling
Semiotics	Structured equation modelling
Discourse analysis	Statistical analysis
Hermeneutics	Econometrics
Narrative and metaphor	

Quantitative research methods were originally developed in the natural sciences to study natural phenomena. Examples of quantitative methods now well accepted in the social sciences include survey methods, laboratory experiments, formal methods (e.g. econometrics), and numerical methods such as mathematical modelling. All quantitative researchers emphasize numbers more than anything else. That is, the numbers 'come to represent values and levels of theoretical constructs and concepts and the interpretation of the numbers is viewed as strong scientific evidence of how a phenomenon works' (Straub, Gefen, & Boudreau, 2004). Most quantitative researchers use statistical tools and packages to analyse their data.

Qualitative research methods were developed in the social sciences to enable researchers to study social and cultural phenomena. Examples of qualitative methods are action research, case study research, and grounded theory. Qualitative data sources include observation and participant observation (fieldwork), interviews and questionnaires, documents and texts, and the researcher's impressions and reactions. Qualitative data are mostly a record of what people have said. For example, interviews (the most common technique for collecting qualitative data) record what one of your informants said about a particular topic; field notes record what the researcher experienced or thought about a particular topic or event; and documents record what the author of the document wrote at the time. In all cases, these qualitative data can help us to understand people, their motivations and actions, and the broader context within which they work and live.

In the 1980s most business disciplines favoured quantitative research. In the 1990s, however, there was an increased interest in qualitative research in almost every business discipline. The quality of this research improved over time such that many articles using qualitative research have now been published in the top peer-reviewed journals of virtually every business discipline.

My view is that both quantitative and qualitative research approaches are useful and needed in researching business organizations. Both kinds of research are important, and both kinds of research can be rigorous. Most of the resources and readings cited in this book have been peer reviewed by leading experts and published in the top journals in the various business disciplines. However, there are advantages and disadvantages in each approach.

Generally speaking, quantitative research is best if you want to have a large sample size and you want to generalize to a large population. In this case the objective is to study a particular topic across many people or many organizations. You want to find out trends or patterns that apply in many different situations. Various statistical techniques can be used to analyse your data.

A major disadvantage of quantitative research is that, as a general rule, many of the social and cultural aspects of organizations are lost or are treated in a superficial manner. The 'context' is usually treated as 'noise' or as something that gets in the way. The quantitative researcher trades context for the ability to generalize across a population.

Qualitative research is best if you want to study a particular subject in depth (e.g. in one or a few organizations). It is good for exploratory research, when the particular topic is new and there is not much previously published research on that topic. It is also ideal for studying the social, cultural, and political aspects of people and organizations.

A major disadvantage of qualitative research, however, is that it is often difficult to generalize to a larger population. You can generalize from qualitative research, but not by using sampling logic. For instance, if you conduct three in-depth case studies of three organizations, a sample size of three does not count for much in statistical terms. Three cases are no better than one. Therefore it is normally impossible for qualitative researchers to make generalizations from a sample to a population.

However, you can generalize from qualitative research to theory, and you can generalize from just one case study or one ethnography (Klein & Myers, 1999; Lee & Baskerville, 2003; Yin, 2003). How you can use qualitative research to make generalizations and how the contributions and quality of qualitative research studies can be evaluated is discussed in each of the chapters in Part III.

Although the qualitative/quantitative distinction in research methods is by far the most common, there are other distinctions which can be made. Research methods have variously been classified as objective versus subjective (Burrell & Morgan, 1979), as being concerned with the discovery of general laws (nomothetic) versus being concerned with the uniqueness of each particular situation (idiographic), as aimed at prediction and control versus aimed at explanation and understanding, as taking an outsider (etic) versus taking an insider (emic) perspective, and so on. Considerable controversy continues to surround the use of these terms (Myers & Avison, 2002). However, a discussion of these distinctions is beyond the scope of this book. For a fuller discussion see Luthans and Davis (1982) and Morey and Luthans (1984). See also Chapter 3 which discusses the various philosophical perspectives that can inform research.

TRIANGULATION

Triangulation is the idea that you should do more than just one thing in a study. That is, you should use more than one research method, use two or more techniques to gather data, or combine qualitative and quantitative research methods in the one study. Triangulation is an excellent idea if you want to look at the same topic from different angles. It allows you to gain a 'fuller' picture of what is happening. It allows you to triangulate data from interviews with data from documents, or data from two different research methods (e.g. a qualitative case study with quantitative data from a survey).

TRIANGULATING CASE STUDY DATA

Doing marketing research, Fournier (1998) conducted three in-depth case studies looking at the relationships consumers form with brands. She triangulated data within her case studies.

She used multiple stories from the same person, interviews conducted with the same persons at multiple points in time, and information from other data sources such as grocery lists, shelf contents, stories of other household members, and so forth. In addition, researchers who had multiple encounters with informants in previous stages were employed. Thus interpretations were triangulated across researchers and authors as well.

It is relatively common for qualitative researchers to triangulate data within a study using just one research method. For example, a researcher conducting a case study of one organization might triangulate interview data with data from published or unpublished documents; or an ethnographer might triangulate data from interviews with data from observation. Many qualitative research methods require the triangulation of data in some way or other.

Much less common, however, and much more difficult, is when researchers try to combine two or more research methods in the one study. The idea is to triangulate data and findings on the same topic, but to use different methods. Triangulation is especially challenging if the research methods are substantially different in their underlying philosophy or approach, e.g. when researchers try to combine qualitative and quantitative research methods.

TRIANGULATING QUALITATIVE AND QUANTITATIVE DATA

An excellent example of triangulating data obtained from the use of qualitative and quantitative research methods is Markus' (1994a) study of how and why managers use email. Her study questioned the assumptions of media richness theory (that 'richness is better') and demonstrated how a 'lean' medium such as email could be used for complex communication.

To answer her research question, 'how and why do managers use email?', Markus used two research methods. First, she used a quantitative method, a statistically analysed survey. The survey was sent to a large sample of managers. Second, she used a qualitative method called analytic induction. The data were purely textual – mostly she used email messages that were sent by managers. She also obtained data from interviews.

Using both quantitative and qualitative research methods meant that Markus had quantitative data (e.g. frequency of email use) and qualitative data (transcripts of email message exchanges). Her findings and conclusions are rigorous and convincing.

I believe it can be difficult for most people to do this kind of triangulation well. This is because you need to be well trained and become an expert in multiple research methods, not just one. Also, each method has its own underlying perspective and involves the use of certain techniques. It can take months, if not years, for someone to become proficient in the use of just one particular method, e.g. ethnography. However, if you have the inclination, enthusiasm, and time, this is certainly a worthwhile and viable option. It is something that can be done (Mingers, 2001).

A slightly easier way to achieve the triangulation of research methods is for a single study to include multiple researchers. In this case, each researcher brings to the table his or her own method of expertise and experience. Having multiple researchers and multiple perspectives on any research topic can be positive. A key requirement for the project to be successful, however, is for the researchers concerned to respect each other's expertise and method. There must be mutual respect for any real dialogue to take place. In such cases, the research findings can be truly outstanding.

RESEARCH IN BUSINESS AND MANAGEMENT

All research in business and management focuses on a topic that is of relevance to one or more of the business and management disciplines. This disciplinary area is actually very broad and depending upon your background and institution may include the following: accounting and finance; commercial law; economics; human resource management; logistics and supply chain management; organizational behaviour and organizational development; information systems; management strategy and international business; marketing; and operations management. Of course, these business and management disciplines often build on research from other disciplines, such as statistics, psychology, or sociology. The list of potentially relevant disciplines is very large.

A key feature of a qualitative or quantitative study, as opposed to a purely conceptual study, is that it is an empirical investigation, i.e. it relies on empirical data from the natural or social world. The empirical investigation seeks to contribute to the body of knowledge in a particular field. A simple model of the process of empirical research in business and management is represented in Figure 2.1.

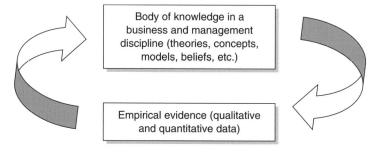

Figure 2.1   A model of research in business and management

As can be seen in the figure, a researcher finds a topic or a research problem that is relevant to the body of knowledge in a particular discipline. Normally the research questions are derived from the research literature, but they could come from current business practice or your own intuitive hunches (Marshall & Rossman, 1989). In order to answer the questions raised by the problem, the researcher subsequently uses a research method to find some empirical evidence. These findings are hopefully significant enough such that they are published and hence add to the body of knowledge. A new researcher then comes along and starts the process once more.

RIGOUR AND RELEVANCE IN RESEARCH

A perennial issue for researchers in business and management is the apparent trade-off between rigour and relevance (Table 2.2). It has become a common complaint over the past decade that research in business schools has become more rigorous at the expense of relevance.

Table 2.2 Rigour and relevance

Rigorous research	Relevant research
'Scientific research'	Relevant to business practitioners
Emphasis on meeting scientific standards such as validity and reliability	Emphasis on being immediately relevant to practice
Subject to academic peer review	Published in consulting reports or industry magazines
Published in academic journals	
Theoretical contribution	Practical contribution

Rigorous research is usually defined as research that meets the standards of 'scientific' research; it is research that has been conducted according to the scientific model of research, subject to peer review, and published in an academic journal. Unfortunately, much of the research that is published in academic business journals is often seen as being too theoretical and of little practical relevance to business professionals.

Relevant research is usually defined as research that is of immediate relevance to business professionals. The research results can be used right away. This kind of research is usually seen as more akin to consulting. Unfortunately, much of this kind of research is difficult if not impossible to get published in academic journals in business and management. The lack of a theoretical contribution almost guarantees rejection.

In my own field of information systems, the issue of rigour versus relevance seems to be discussed at almost every conference. Most academics tend to agree with the notion that research in information systems and business schools more generally should be more relevant to business professionals. In practice, however, they are faced with the need to gain tenure and promotion. In order to gain tenure, most business schools in research universities require faculty members to have a record of publication in reputable academic journals. This job requirement means that most faculty members end up postponing indefinitely their desire (if they have one) to conduct 'relevant' research.

As an example of this debate in the management literature more generally, Bennis and O'Toole (2005) argue that business schools focus far too much on what they call 'scientific' research. Writing in the *Harvard Business Review*, they claim that business management is not a scientific discipline, but a profession. They lament the fact that business schools have followed a scientific model of research rather than a professional model (as found, for example, in medicine and law). They say that graduating business students are ill equipped to wrangle with the complex, unquantifiable issues that are the reality of business. As most decisions in business are made on the basis of messy and incomplete data, they are particularly critical of statistical and quantitative research which they believe can blind rather than illuminate (Bennis & O'Toole, 2005).

I must admit that I do not entirely agree with Bennis and O'Toole's argument. In my view, the focus on research in business schools has transformed them from having a mostly vocational focus to being proper scholarly institutions. Faculty members have become scholars rather than consultants. Also, while most academic research may not be immediately relevant to business professionals, it may become relevant over the longer term. In fact, I would argue that one of the failings of contemporary management is the predilection to seek 'silver bullets', i.e. quick fixes, or magic solutions to more deep-seated problems. Few silver bullets turn out to be of any long-lasting value.

However, I do agree with them that research in business and management could be much more relevant than it is right now, and that it should be able to deal with 'complex, unquantifiable issues that are the reality of business'. And this is where the value of qualitative research lies.

It is my view that qualitative research is perhaps the best way for research in business and management to become both rigorous and relevant at the same time. It allows scholarship and practice to come together. Qualitative researchers study real situations, not artificial ones (as, for example, in a laboratory experiment). To do a good qualitative study, qualitative researchers need to engage actively with people in real organizations. An in-depth field study, in particular, needs to look at the complexity of organizations including the 'complex, unquantifiable issues' that are the reality of business. A case study researcher or an ethnographer may well study the social, cultural, and political aspects of a company.

Hence, if you are trying to decide whether to do qualitative or quantitative research in a business discipline, the choice should not be made on the basis of whether one approach is more rigorous than the other. This would have been a valid question in the 1980s and early 1990s, but it is no longer a valid question today. Rather, the choice should be more on the topic, on the research question you want to ask, on the basis of your own interest and experience, and how relevant you want to be to practice. It is also important to consider the expertise of your supervisor or faculty members in your institution. If you want to use qualitative research but there is no one with the qualifications, interest, or experience to supervise you at your university, then it is probably best to choose a different topic and method, or change university.

Exercises

1   Conduct a brief literature search using Google Scholar or some other bibliographic database and see if you can find both qualitative and quantitative articles in your chosen field. What kinds of topics appear?
2   Looking at some of the articles you found in more detail, can you describe the research problem and the research questions? Can you describe the research method(s) that the author(s) used? Did any of them use triangulation?
3   Looking at these same articles, would you describe some of them as more rigorous or relevant than the others? Why?

Further Reading

 ### Books

There are two books which I recommend for anyone wanting to do qualitative research at PhD level; both these books are required or recommended texts in many doctoral-level courses in business.

First, *The Sage Handbook for Qualitative Research* (Denzin & Lincoln, 2005) provides a collection of readings with authors selected from many disciplines. It examines the various paradigms for doing qualitative work, the strategies developed for studying people in their natural setting, and a variety of techniques for collecting, analysing, interpreting, and reporting findings.

Second, *Qualitative Data Analysis: An Expanded Sourcebook* (2nd edn) (Miles & Huberman, 1994) is also very useful.

A third book that is an excellent primer for novice researchers is *Doing Qualitative Research* (Silverman, 2005).

Websites on the Internet

There are quite a few useful websites on qualitative research:

- The ISWorld Section on Qualitative Research is at http://www.qual.
auckland.ac.nz/
- The Qualitative Report is an online journal dedicated to qualitative research
and critical enquiry at http://www.nova.edu/ssss/QR/index.html
- Sage Publications is arguably the leading publisher of qualitative methodology
texts at http://www.sagepublications.com
- Narrative Psychology is an excellent resource on narrative and related areas at
http://narrativepsych.com
- The Association for Qualitative Research has useful information at
http://www.latrobe.edu.au/www/aqr/
- QualPage includes calls for papers, conferences, discussion forums, and
publishers at http://www.qualitativeresearch.uga.edu/QuaiPage
- The International Journal of Social Research Methodology is a new cross-
disciplinary journal designed to foster discussion and debate in social research
methodology at http://tandf.co.uk/journals
- Forum: Qualitative Social Research is a bilingual (English/German) online
journal for qualitative research edited by Katja Mruck. The main aim of
the forum is to promote discussion and cooperation between qualitative
researchers from different nations and social science disciplines at http://
qualitative-research.net/fqs/fqs-eng.htm
- Evaluation and Social Research Methods has links to books, manuals, and articles on how to do evaluation and social research at http://gsociology.icaap.
org/methods

Lecture 2

Collection of Data (Questionnaires and Interviews) and Analysis of Qualitative Data

7 Research Design: Qualitative Methods

DAVID E. GRAY

CHAPTER OBJECTIVES

After reading this chapter you will be able to:

- Identify the characteristics of qualitative data.
- Formulate qualitative research questions.
- Develop a robust qualitative design, including an appropriate sampling strategy.
- Select and apply the criteria that make for a rigorous qualitative research study.

We saw in the previous chapter that there are well established and generally accepted approaches to quantitative design. As we shall see in this chapter, however, qualitative design is different in a number of ways. Firstly, within qualitative research, the role of the researcher is to gain a deep, intense and 'holistic' overview of the context under study, often involving interacting within the everyday lives of individuals, groups, communities and organizations. It is a naturalistic approach that seeks to understand phenomena within their own context-specific settings. Capturing data on the perceptions of actors in the field of study, means being attentive, suspending (often called 'bracketing') preconceptions about a subject and being empathetic to those being studied. The focus of study becomes not just the field setting, but also the researcher's role within it.

Secondly, qualitative researchers often differ in the kinds of claims they make for their research. Some seek to emulate 'traditional science' in attempting, for example, to make generalizations from their results. Others, however, reject this approach, selecting instead to conduct a study which is 'authentic', and providing results that are dependable and trustworthy within a specific context. The types of data gathering tools and resources used by qualitative researchers also tend to be different, including the use of semi-structured interviews, observation, focus groups and the analysis of materials such as documents, photographs, video recordings and other media. This chapter deals primarily, with the **design** of qualitative studies. Principles and processes in the analysis of qualitative data are covered later in Chapter 18.

SOME CRITICISMS OF QUANTITATIVE RESEARCH

Before we look in detail at qualitative research design, let us pause for a moment to examine some of the most common criticisms of quantitative research often made by qualitative researchers. Exploring these criticisms helps us to understand the kinds of concerns held by qualitative researchers and how they view the world. As the list in Table 7.1 suggests, quantitative research can often involve designs that disengage the researcher from the people and field they are researching. While quantitative researchers would regard this positively (as a means of generating objectivity and detachment), qualitative researchers would see it as failing to gain access to people's social and cultural constructions of their 'reality' (Guba and Lincoln, 1994; Silverman, 2000). According to qualitative critics, quantitative researchers claim objectivity, but end up arbitrarily defining the variables in their research, or trying to explain away correlations using common-sense reasoning. All research is selective and depends on collecting particular sorts of evidence through the prism of particular methods (Mays, 1995). For example, in a quantitative survey, the categories and questions selected by the researcher may not be shared or understood by respondents. Similarly, even if two respondents give the same reply, their interpretation of the response may have different meanings. As Flick (2006) also points out, despite methodological controls in quantitative research, the researcher's personal interests, and the influence of their social and cultural backgrounds are difficult to avoid.

Table 7.1
Some typical criticisms of quantitative research by qualitative researchers

1.	Quantitative research can involve little or no contact with people or field settings.
2.	Statistical correlations may be based upon 'variables' that are arbitrarily defined by the researchers themselves.
3.	After-the-fact analysis about the meaning of correlations may involve some very common-sense reasoning or even speculation that science claims to avoid.
4.	The pursuit of 'measurable' phenomena mean that difficult concepts such as 'criminality' or 'intelligence' are treated unproblematically.

Beyond these practical complaints, quantitative research has also come under attack from critical epistemological positions. As Snape and Spencer (2003) relate, postmodern arguments have questioned the very notion of objectivity, and also maintain that the notions of meaning and reality are problematic. There can be no overarching meanings, because meanings are a product of time and context. Other criticism has come from neo-Marxism, feminism and race researchers who have called for a greater equality between the researcher and those they research. Indeed, for some, research should be a collaborative process involving the subjects of the study in formulating the focus of research and the ways in which it is conducted (Reason, 1994). A logical extension of this belief has been the development of action research methods (see Chapter 12), involving the active engagement of participants in the research process.

CHARACTERISTICS OF QUALITATIVE RESEARCH

Qualitative research is not built upon a unified theory or methodological approach (Flick, 2006) and can adopt various theoretical stances and methods, the latter including the use of observations, interviews, questionnaires and document analysis. While, even today, qualitative research is often regarded in some quarters as less valid and reliable than its quantitative cousin, qualitative data can be a powerful source for analysis. First, qualitative research is highly contextual, being collected in a natural 'real life' setting, often over long periods of time. Hence, it goes beyond giving a mere snapshot or cross-section of events and can show how and why things happen – also incorporating people's own motivation, emotions, prejudices and incidents of interpersonal cooperation and conflict (Charmaz, 1995). Far from lacking scientific rigour, qualitative research can (in certain circumstances) even be used for testing hypotheses to see if theoretical **propositions** can be supported by the evidence. Qualitative studies can be used in circumstances where relatively little is known about the phenomenon, or to gain new perspectives on issues where much is already known (Strauss and Corbin, 1990). Qualitative research can also be used to identify the kinds of concepts or variables that might later be tested quantitatively (as in a mixed methods research design – see Chapter 8).

As Miles and Huberman (1994) show, most qualitative research involves a number of characteristics:

- It is conducted through intense contact within a 'field' or real life setting.

- The researcher's role is to gain a 'holistic' or integrated overview of the study, including the perceptions of participants.

- Themes that emerge from the data are often reviewed with informants for **verification**.

- The main focus of research is to understand the ways in which people act and account for their actions.

Qualitative data are open to multiple interpretations (but some are more compelling than others either on theoretical grounds or because of internal consistency). As Flick (2006) points out, these interpretations can include the voices of those being studied as well as that of the researcher. Indeed, **reflexivity**, the researchers own reflections on their actions and observations in the field and their feelings, become part of the data themselves. We will see what kinds of factors influence these interpretations in Chapter 18.

PARADIGMS AND STRATEGIES FOR QUALITATIVE RESEARCH

Qualitative research comes with a confusing array of different categories and descriptive headings, which tend to be used interchangeably by different scholars. So, for example, grounded theory can be seen as both a 'school of thought' but also as a particular research design or strategy. Qualitative research is also influenced by the kind of research paradigm adopted by the researcher. At the outset, however, it needs to be stressed that in qualitative research the adoption of strategies and data collection methods tends to be highly flexible. Indeed, it is not a case of adopting one strategy rather than another, but often the combining of several strategies and methods within a research design. Taking strategies of enquiry in Table 7.2, for example, it is both feasible and legitimate (depending on the kinds of research questions asked), to adopt a case study strategy, which also includes the use of **participatory action research** within a case site (for example, a workplace). In using these combined strategies, the researcher may select interviews, focus groups and observations as the prime data collection methods. However, how this is done will partly depend on the research paradigm adopted. For example, if the researcher holds to a naturalistic tradition, the research design will probably require the collection of data from representative, multiple case sites using a variety of sources to achieve substantiation of the findings. Substantiation is gained by minimal interference and bias by the researcher through objective coding of verbatim accounts of participants and non-participant observation. If committed to a progressive paradigm, the researcher will be less concerned with replicating finds (across sites) than with achieving deep engagement with participants to achieve authentic accounts of how they construct their social reality. This also includes how the researcher constructs social reality through their interpretation of their findings. Hence, the views and feelings of the researcher (including critical self-reflections) themselves become part of the research data. Table 7.2 provides an overview of paradigms, strategies and methods.

Table 7.2
An overview
of qualitative
paradigms,
strategies and
methods

Source: Adapted
from Holliday (2002)

PARADIGMS AND PERSPECTIVES	STRATEGIES OF ENQUIRY	DATA COLLECTION METHODS
All items usable by all items in other columns		
NATURALISTIC	**Case study**: studies a specific 'bounded system', e.g., a person or institution (Stake, 1994).	Interviewing
Postpositivism		Observation
Realism		Focus groups
Reality is 'out there'.		Documents
Deeper social reality needs qualitative enquiry.	**Ethnography**: explores the nature of a specific social phenomenon, often using a small number of cases (Atkinson and Hammersley, 2004).	Video and photographs
Probably truth is supported by extensive recording in real settings.		Unobtrusive measures
		Research diary
Researchers must remain detached from real settings.	**Ethnomethodology**: investigates people's everyday procedures for creating, and managing a sense of objective reality (Holstein and Gubrium, 2008).	
PROGRESSIVE		
Critical theory		
Constructivism		
Postmodernism	**Phenomenology**: explores how people's taken for granted world is experienced and how structures of consciousness apprehend the world (Holstein and Gubrium, 1994).	
Feminism		
Reality and science are socially constructed.		
Researchers are part of the research setting.	**Grounded theory**: uses the interplay between analysis and data collection to produce theory (Strauss and Corbin, 1994).	
Research must engage in reflexive and self-critical dialogue.		
Purpose of research is to problematize, reveal hidden realities.	**Participatory action research**: implies an effort on the part of people to understand the role of knowledge as a significant instrument of power and control (Reason, 1994).	

(Cont'd)

Table 7.2

PARADIGMS AND PERSPECTIVES	STRATEGIES OF ENQUIRY	DATA COLLECTION METHODS
	Narrative analysis: the analysis of a chronologically told story, exploring how various elements are sequenced.	
	Cultural studies: the study of a complex web of social customs, values and expectations that affect our ways of working (Frow and Morris, 2003).	
	Gender studies: explores the process of constructing and differentiating gender and particularly gender inequalities (Cranny-Francis, et al., 2003).	

Activity 7.1

Examine the naturalistic and progressive paradigms outlined in Table 7.2. What major differences do you see between them?

Now let us examine the strategies of enquiry described in Table 7.2 in more detail, noting that a qualitative research design may utilize a number of them at the same time.

CASE STUDIES

The term case study is strongly associated with qualitative research (indeed, the two are sometimes used synonymously), partly because case studies allow for the generation of multiple perspectives either through multiple data collection methods, or through the creation of multiple accounts from a single method (Lewis, 2003). The integration and contrasting of different perspectives can build up rich and detailed understanding of a context. As Punch (2005) asserts, a case is not easy to define since almost anything can serve as a case. But typical examples include: individuals, a role or occupation, organizations, a community or even a country. It could even be a policy, process, crisis or event.

Case study designs are generally flexible, but at the design stage, a number of issues arise that require addressing.

* What is the 'unit of analysis' for the case, e.g. individuals, organizations, local communities, etc.?

* What criteria are to be used in selecting cases for study?

* Who are the key participants?

* How many cases are there and how many participants within each case?

The design of case studies is discussed in more detail in Chapter 10.

ETHNOGRAPHY

Although first associated with anthropological studies, around the 1970s the term ethnography came to be used for describing participant observation studies in social and organizational settings. Ethnography seeks to understand social processes less by making reports of these events (for example, through using an interview), than by participating within them, often for long periods of time. Overt or **covert participant** observation, then, would be a typical approach to data collection in ethnographic research (see Chapter 15). While ethnography generally involves 'immersion' in the field for long periods, micro-ethnography adopts a more focused approach on, say, one aspect or element of a work or social setting, allowing for observation over a few weeks or months.

ETHNOMETHODOLOGY

Ethnomethodology, founded in the 1960s by the American sociologist Harold Garfinkel, studies the ways in which people make sense of their social world, and accomplish their daily lives. Ethnomethodologists start with the assumption that social order is an illusion. While social life appears ordered, it is, in fact, chaotic. Social order is constructed in the minds of actors as a series of impressions which they seek to organize into a coherent pattern. While ethnography seeks to answer questions about *what* is happening, ethnomethodology seeks answers on *how* realities in everyday life are accomplished (Seale, 1999). So, by carefully observing and analysing the processes used in actors' actions, researchers will uncover the processes by which these actors constantly interpret social reality (Coulon, 1995).

PHENOMENOLOGY

Phenomenoligists argue that the relation between perception and objects is not passive – human consciousness actively constructs the world as well as perceiving it. Phenomenological ideas were first applied to social science research by the German philosopher Alfred Schutz (1899–1959), who argued that social reality has a specific meaning and relevance structure for people who are living, thinking and experiencing it. And it is these thought structures (objects) that determine their behaviour by motivating it. It also follows that the thought objects constructed by researchers who are trying to grasp reality, have to be founded upon the thought objects of ordinary men and women living their daily lives in the social world. It is necessary, then, for researchers to gain access to people's common-sense thinking in order to interpret and understand their actions. In other words, phenomenology seeks to understand the world from the participant's point of view. This can only be achieved if the researcher 'brackets out' their own preconceptions.

GROUNDED THEORY

First developed by Glaser and Strauss (1967), grounded theory has been highly influential in qualitative research in terms of its inductive but systematic approach to design and data analysis, and the important principle that qualitative research is capable of generating theory. Theories are not applied to the subject being studied, but emerge or are discovered from the empirical data themselves. Unlike quantitative approaches which seek simplicity by breaking down constructs into variables, grounded theory seeks to build complexity by including context (Flick, 2006). Grounded theory is discussed in greater detail in Chapter 18.

PARTICIPATORY ACTION RESEARCH

Participatory Action Research (PAR) builds upon the action research model first developed by Lewin (1946) particularly incorporating an understanding of the power of group dynamics and the relationships between individuals, groups and communities. Some approaches to PAR have also adopted a critical pedagogy espoused by Freire (2000), which seeks to empower learners to take responsibility for their learning. In essence, PAR follows the cyclical processes of planning, taking action, observing and reflecting. But PAR distinguishes itself from other action research approaches in that participants will also critically reflect on the political and cultural context in which the action is taking place.

NARRATIVE ANALYSIS AND BIOGRAPHICAL RESEARCH

Narrative analysis is the analysis of a chronologically told story, with a focus on how the various elements of the story are sequenced. Key elements in narrative analysis include 'scripts', predictive frames that people use to interpret events, and stories that expand on scripts, adding evaluative elements that reveal the narrator's viewpoints. Narrative analysis tends to use the narrative interview as the primary method of data collection, with a focus on the biographical experiences of the respondent. The research focus of narrative analysis often includes issues that deal with ethical, moral and cultural ambiguities. An important focus of feminism is the study of lives from the narrator's experience, emphasizing the role of these narratives in empowering persons through a more subtle understanding of their life situation. Using a small number of stories, narrative analysis can be used to cast a light on the culture, complexities and contradictions in organizations.

CULTURAL STUDIES

For nineteenth century social theorists, culture was regarded as merely a by-product of wider social, economic and political forces underpinning society. The everyday life of individuals was seen as a product of the structural forces acting beyond the consciousness of social actors. From the late nineteenth century, however, new theoretical perspectives began to emerge which started to take into account the individual's capacity for agency (self-motivated action) in their everyday lives. During the late twentieth and early twenty-first centuries, social and cultural theorists have begun to conceptualize the 'everyday' as dynamic, pluralistic and contested (Bennett, 2005). At the root of this transformation are several interrelated factors. Firstly, there is the rupturing of modernity and the decreasing importance of modernist notions such as social class, gender, race and occupation. Secondly, witness the increasing prevalence of media and cultural industries which have helped to form new kinds of social identity based around patterns of consumption and leisure. Cultural studies has often been concerned with focusing on those who are marginalized and at the edges of modern culture, using sources drawn from anthropology, textual analysis, social and cultural history and psychoanalysis. Studies are centred on analysis of texts, images, observational notes or transcripts of everyday talk.

GENDER STUDIES

Gender studies explore the processes of constructing and differentiating gender and gender inequalities, particularly in areas such as literary theory, film studies, drama, anthropology, sociology, psychology and psychoanalysis. Gender is not simply what one is, but rather a set of meanings that sexes assume in particular societies. Gender, then, is seen as a social construct (Cranny-Francis et al., 2003). The school is, not surprisingly, strongly influenced by feminist theory. Gender studies have been associated with qualitative methods, largely because such methods allow the voices of women to be 'heard', in contrast to quantitative methods, which feminists have criticized for being value-neutral and turning women into objects rather than the subjects of research.

> Activity 7.2
>
> Taking each of the qualitative strategies above, what similarities can you identify amongst them? What important differences do you notice?

APPROACHES TO QUALITATIVE DESIGN

Research design sits between a set of research questions and the data, and shows how the research questions will be addressed (Punch, 2005). It is strongly influenced by the epistemological stance adopted by the researcher. A further, and connected, influence will occur if the researcher is an adherent of any of the qualitative strategies discussed above. For example, adherents of the ethnographic school will, obviously, adopt ethnographic design methods, usually involving observation and participation. It is important, however, to distinguish between qualitative data gathering methods (such as observation or focus groups) and the holistic framework of a research design. Data gathering methods are incorporated, and are sometimes intrinsically associated, with a particular design. Observation, for example, is often associated with ethnographic research design. For other qualitative research designs, such as case studies or grounded theory, a wide variety of data gathering instruments are valid.

An important feature of qualitative design is that it is 'emergent'. Although a researcher may set off with some provisional ideas about design, these may change during the research process – often as a result of the analysis of data providing new directions (Patton, 2002). Qualitative research design, then, should be seen less as a linear, sequential pathway, but rather as a series of iterations involving design, data collection, preliminary analysis and re-design.

> TOP TIP 7.1
>
> Student researchers who adopt a qualitative approach sometimes confine themselves to describing a set of research questions, a sampling strategy and one or more data gathering methods and leave it at that. It is important, however, that these are positioned within an overarching qualitative design strategy, discussed in this section. An overarching design provides a framework through which both the practical but also the theoretical and philosophical traditions of the design can be presented.

Figure 7.1
Conceptual
framework for a
research project on
drug liberalization
and policing

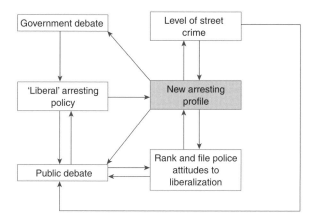

According to Eisner (1991: 169) there is a 'paucity of methodological pre-scriptions' as to how to formulate a qualitative design. However, bringing together recommendations from a range of scholars provides a quite detailed design outline, the main elements of which are discussed next.

DETERMINING THE FOCUS OF THE INQUIRY

The purpose of making clear, unambiguous statements about the focus of the study helps to establish a boundary for the research. Above all, it makes clear what is 'in' and what is 'out' and the kinds of criteria for judging the inclusion/exclusion criteria for new information. These boundaries, however, are not fixed and may alter during the research process. Miles and Huberman (1994) provide an approach which helps in formulating this focus by construct-ing what they refer to as a conceptual framework. This describes in narrative, and often in graphical format, the key factors, constructs and variables being studied – and the presumed relationship between them. Of course, whether this relationship really exists is one of the elements of the study.

Miles and Huberman conceive of this conceptual framework as a series of intellectual 'bins' containing key events and behaviours. Hence, Figure 7.1 shows a study of new 'liberal' policing policies which have de-criminalized pos-session of 'soft' drugs, and a hypothesized conceptual framework containing interrelated bins. For example, it is believed that the new policy will change the profile of arrests, with fewer people being arrested for possession of soft drugs (that is, if the policy is being effectively implemented by officers on the street) and that this will reduce the level of street crime. Producing a conceptual frame-work forces the researcher to specify what it is that is going to be studied and what is going to be omitted, and hypothesized relationships between key vari-ables. This, of course, is not a hypothesis in the positivistic sense, but a way of alerting the researcher to the possible relationships that exist and which can be explored through the formulation of research questions.

Activity 7.3

Examine Figure 7.1. Do you agree with its hypotheses? Draw an alternative conceptual framework adding new bins and relationships.

FORMULATING RESEARCH QUESTIONS

We saw in Chapter 1 that qualitative research is often associated with inductive research designs. If the research design is entirely inductive, there may be no formulation of a priori questions for study. But it would be wrong to assume that qualitative researchers always enter a field of study with no prior theoretical assumptions or research questions. For highly ethnographic studies this may be the case, but, often, qualitative researchers will wish to impose at least some structure on the study in terms of the kinds of questions that are being asked, the focus of the research and the selection of field sites. The amount of structure required will depend on factors such as the time available and how much is already known about the phenomenon. Other decisions then have to be made about what is going to be researched (including the units of analysis and the sampling frame). Again using Figure 7.1 as an illustration, we might ask about the actual impact of policy changes on practice (the number and profile of drug-related arrests), and how rank and file police attitudes have mediated between policy and practice. Like the conceptual framework, research questions allow the researcher to see where the boundaries of the study lie. Of course, having established the research questions, the researcher still has to remain open to new and perhaps unexpected results (Flick, 2006). Research questions can be orientated towards describing states or describing processes, as Table 7.3 shows.

Table 7.3
Orientation of
research questions

ORIENTATION	RESULTING QUESTIONS
States	Which type of object, event or behaviour is this?
	How often does this event occur?
	What caused it?
	How is it maintained?
Processes	How is the object, event or behaviour changing over time?
	What are the consequences of this process?
	What strategies are being used?

Figure 7.2
Inductive and
deductive
approaches and
research questions

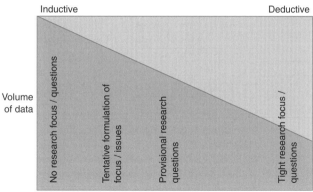

As Flick (2006) notes, the less clearly research questions are formulated, the greater the chance that researchers will find themselves confronted with mountains of data. As Figure 7.2 shows, starting with a purely inductive approach (which implies relatively little focus and no research questions) usually leads to the accumulation of large volumes of data, which then have to be analysed.

Activity 7.4

Return to Table 3.1 in Chapter 3 and review the types of research question that can be formulated. Do any of these lend themselves more naturally to qualitative research?

Suggested answer at end of chapter.

DETERMINING THE UNITS OF ANALYSIS

As in any research approach, in qualitative research decisions have to be taken at the design stage on the unit of analysis to be used. Typically, this might include: individuals, groups, organizations or communities. Using healthcare as an example, the research might focus on individuals (patients, doctors, nurses and other healthcare professionals), groups (the hospital management board), organizations (hospitals or professional bodies) and communities (a town and its hospitals and local surgeries). Alternatively, the unit of analysis might be the government's policy on, say, reducing HIV infection. As Mason (2002) points out, identifying the unit of analysis is important, especially when it comes to analysing the data. Using the healthcare example, we might study the level of care given by nurses. The data gathered are for individual nurses (in which case, the unit of analysis is the individual). If, however, we wanted to compare the level of care given across a group of hospital wards (say, to identify inefficiencies), results for individuals would be aggregated for each ward – hence the unit of analysis is the ward rather than the individual.

DETERMINING THE TYPES OF QUALITATIVE DATA

In quantitative research the purpose is to collect quantitative data in the form of numbers measuring occurrences and to fragment or delimit phenomena into measurable categories. In qualitative research, however, the types of data to be collected are much more diverse. While, generally, most qualitative studies tend to depend on the assimilation of data in the form of words (interview transcripts, diary entries, observational notes), qualitative design is quite flexible in terms of the variety of data types applicable. Table 7.4 provides a brief summary of the types of data collected, their characteristics and how they are collected, including an imaginary example for illustration. It is also worth noting that, even though plans may have been made at the outset to collect one type of data, these plans may change at any time due to the evolving nature of qualitative research. Gathering data using a variety of these types will contribute to the construction of the kind of 'thick descriptions' upon which qualitative research depends.

CASE STUDY 7.1   EXAMPLES OF OBSERVATIONAL DATA GATHERING TECHNIQUES

A qualitative researcher is conducting a study on power relationships within the health service. One data gathering process in the study is a two-day non-participation observation, involving the 'shadowing' of a hospital consultant. Table 7.4 provides an outline of the types of data collected, their characteristics, data collection methods and some examples from each data type. The Case Study illustrates the use of observational data gathering techniques, but also the use of a reflective diary, documentary evidence and video recordings.

Activity 7.5

Review Case Study 7.1. What does this tell you about the richness of data collected in a qualitative study? What does it tell you about the time and resources needed?

Table 7.4
Types of data, their
characteristics and
collection
approaches
Source: Adapted
from Holliday, 2002

TYPE	CHARACTERISTICS	COLLECTION METHOD	EXAMPLES
Description of behaviour	What people are doing or saying	Observation notes, research diary, etc.	The consultant moved closer to the patient's bed, but continued talking to the nurse in a low voice (observational notes).
Description of event	Behaviour within in an event – e.g., meeting, car journey, argument, training session	Observation notes, research diary, maps, etc.	The consultant's 'bleeper' went off. He looked at it, frowned, and rushed from the ward, muttering the word, 'Problem'. The doctors and nurses around the bed looked surprised and unsure as to what to do (observational notes).
Description of institution	How the organization 'works' in terms of its rules, rituals, culture, etc.	Observation notes, research diary, maps, etc.	As a private hospital, the use of every resource (drugs, bandages, even meals) is logged and added to the patient's bill. This looks very much to me like a profit-led culture (extract from researcher's diary).
Description of appearance	What the setting and/or people look like (e.g., buildings, spaces, clothing, arrangement of office furniture, etc.)	Observation notes, research diary, photographs, drawings, diagrams, maps, etc.	The consultant's office was larger than those of lower rank doctors, but its walls were painted the same faded, pale green. On his desk was a laptop computer, a photograph of his family, and a half finished cup of coffee. A set of golf clubs stood in a corner (observational notes).

(Cont'd)

Table 7.4

TYPE	CHARACTERISTICS	COLLECTION METHOD	EXAMPLES
Description of research event	What people say or do in interview or focus group, etc.	Observation notes, research diary, etc.	I noticed that the consultant looked nervous during the interview. He shuffled about in his seat, particularly when talking about the recent complaint made against him (extract from researcher's diary).
Account	What people say or write to the researcher – verbatim	Interview, audio recording, questionnaire, participant's diary, transcription, verbatim notes	The whole thing was a complete misunderstanding. My words were taken out of context (transcript from interview with consultant).
Talk	The actual words that people are heard saying	Audio recording, transcription, verbatim notes	Mr Giles is one of the politest people I know. I've never seen him lose his temper (verbatim notes from overheard conversation between two nurses).
Behaviour in setting	What is seen happening	Film, video recording	Digital recordings of 'life on the ward' taken by two nurses and one hospital manager using a camcorder
Document	Piece of writing belonging or relevant to the setting	Photocopy	I absolutely refute the accusations made against me. I wish you to note that I have already taken legal advice (letter from consultant to hospital board).

DECIDING ON A SAMPLING STRATEGY

We saw in Chapter 6 that experimental and quasi-experimental research designs are concerned to use samples that are as representative as possible of the population under study – hence the use of random **probability sampling**. In qualitative research this approach is usually impractical or rejected by researchers on epistemological grounds. However, as Mays (1995) argues, there are no a priori reasons for supposing that qualitative research will never use random sampling. For example, in a study investigating the quality of health and safety training in sports centres, a random sample of such centres could be taken to discover its prevalence and impact. Onwuegbuzie and Leech (2007) refer to this as external statistical generalization and compare it to external statistical sampling in quantitative research. If this is the preferred route, then the authors recommend the use of simple random sampling, stratified random sampling, cluster sampling, or systematic random sampling.

However, qualitative research usually works with purposive non-probability samples because it seeks to obtain insights into particular practices that exist within a specific location, context and time. Informants are therefore identified because they are known to enable the exploration of a particular behaviour or characteristic relevant to the research. Purposive sampling seeks to identify information-rich cases which can then be studied in depth (Patton, 2002). Qualitative research, then, often works with small samples of people, cases or phenomena nested in particular contexts. Again, in contrast to more quantitative approaches, samples may not always be pre-planned in advance, but may evolve once **fieldwork** has begun. So an initial choice of informants may lead to a decision to select a more contrasting set of deviant subjects (cases) as a comparison (Lincoln and Guba, 1994). A wide range of qualitative sampling strategies suggested by Patton (2002) is presented in Table 7.5.

Activity 7.6

Examine the sampling strategies in Table 7.5. Which of them can be most easily defended for potentially yielding valid results? Which are most susceptible to accusations of invalidity?

Suggested answers are provided at the end of the chapter.

Very often it is not a case of selecting between the various approaches illustrated in Table 7.5 but combining some of them into multiple case sampling. By using a number of cases that yield similar findings we can show replication (see Figure 10.4 in Chapter 10) hence strengthening claims for the validity of findings and the grounds for their generalizability. What is needed, however, is

Table 7.5
Sampling strategies
in qualitative
research
Source: Adapted
from Patton, 2002

SAMPLING STRATEGY	DESCRIPTION
Comprehensive sampling	Examines every case or instance in a given population (e.g., suicides amongst insurance salespeople).
Intensity sampling	Looks for information-rich cases, and ones that are more typical than those at the extremes.
Deviant case sampling	Selects at two extremes (e.g., punctual and unpunctual staff) and tries to identify factors that influence these predispositions. Can yield focused information but poses dangers in generalizing from extreme cases.
Maximum variation sampling	Seeks to look for a wide range of variations and patterns across the sample. Includes examining outlier cases to see if the main pattern still holds.
Homogenous sampling	The opposite of maximum variation, seeks homogenous groups of people to be studied in depth. Focus group interviews are typically conducted with such homogenous groups.
Typical case sampling	Highlights what is 'normal' or average in order to illuminate the whole population. Since generalizing is involved, it becomes important to substantiate that the sample is typical, using other sources (e.g., statistical data or other findings).
Stratified purposeful sampling	Selecting a strata (e.g., infant schools, secondary schools and colleges) and purposefully choosing cases (schools/colleges) within each.
Critical case sampling	Similar to intensity sampling, but the focus is on one case or site that is deemed to be critical or crucial.
Snowball sampling	A first group of participants is used to nominate subsequent individuals or groups for study.
Criterion sampling	The sample is selected on the basis of the prime focus of the study (e.g. early retirement); hence, all cases would be chosen to meet this criterion.
Theory-based sampling	A more formal type of criterion sampling, cases are chosen on the basis that they represent a theoretical construct.
Confirming and disconfirming cases	Often a second-stage sampling strategy, where cases are chosen on the basis that they can confirm or disconfirm emerging patterns from the first stage.

(Cont'd)

Table 7.5

SAMPLING STRATEGY	DESCRIPTION
Purposeful random sampling	From a large possible set of choices, a limited number are selected randomly.
Comparable case selection	Individuals, sites and groups representing the same relevant characteristic are chosen over a time period.
Politically important cases	A focus on key, politically important cases because these are more likely to be noticed by policy makers and the results of the study more likely to be implemented.

an explicit sampling frame where, between them, the cases cover the various issues and variables detailed in the study's research questions. Miles and Huberman (1994) advise that the best strategy is to initially target those cases that are most likely to yield the richest data, leaving more peripheral cases until later. But peripheral sampling is still important because it may often yield negative or exceptional cases (those that contradict the initial case findings or the findings of previous empirical studies). Similarly, Lincoln and Guba (1994) recommend maximum variation sampling as a way of identifying common themes that cut across samples that vary when measured across key criteria.

An important but often neglected consideration in qualitative sampling is selecting the size of the sample. Onwuegbuzie and Leech (2007) suggest that sample sizes in qualitative research should not be so large that it becomes difficult to extract thick, rich data. At the same time, the sample should not be too small so that it becomes difficult to achieve data saturation (Flick, 2006), theoretical saturation (Strauss and Corbin, 1990) or information redundancy (Lincoln and Guba, 1994).

PLAN DATA ANALYSIS PROCESSES

The data analysis processes should be planned for at the design stage, not as an afterthought just before the data analysis processes is due to start. One of the classic mistakes made by novice qualitative researchers is to think about approaches to data analysis far too late. Approaches to the analysis of qualitative data are discussed in Chapter 18.

THE ROLE OF THE RESEARCHER

As we saw in Chapter 6, in quantitative research the role of the researcher is to try to maintain objectivity and detachment from the research process. In qualitative research, the researcher's role is very different. According to Glaser and Strauss (1967) and Strauss and Corbin (1990), researchers need to adopt a stance of **'theoretical sensitivity'**, which means being 'insightful', demonstrating the capacity to understand and the ability to differentiate between what is important and what is not. They must be able to perceive of situations holistically and be responsive to environmental cues in the field. For example, they need to be sensitive to situations where they risk biasing the responses of people they are interviewing. In addition, they usually adopt a reflexive stance, reflecting on the subtle ways in which bias might creep into their research practice through the influence of their personal background and belief systems.

USING THE LITERATURE IN QUALITATIVE RESEARCH

We saw, briefly, in Chapter 3, that qualitative research differs from quantitative research in its approach to positioning the literature review. While, in quantitative studies, the literature review normally comes at the beginning of the research process, in qualitative research the issue of where to position the literature is less predetermined. This issue has been heavily influenced by Glaser and Strauss (1967) who, in their description of grounded theory, argued that research should start with data collection without any reference to the literature, which should come later. Strauss later modified this position, but some qualitative researchers have stubbornly retained this approach. Flick (2006) suggests that, in qualitative research, there are several types of literature that play a part in the development of a qualitative study, namely: the theoretical literature; the literature from empirical studies; and the methodological literature on how the study is to be conducted.

THE THEORETICAL LITERATURE

The purpose of exploring the theoretical literature around a research topic is to gain an insight and contextual knowledge about the subject in order to raise questions such as:

- What is already known about the subject?
- Which theories or models are accepted or influential?
- Which concepts or theories are disputed?
- What can be said critically about what is already known?
- What are the main theoretical or methodological debates in the field?
- What new research is worth doing?

The theoretical literature, then, provides a detailed description and critical analysis of the current state of knowledge.

THE EMPIRICAL LITERATURE

Previous empirical studies in the field, illustrate what has been studied and help in providing concrete evidence in support of, or in opposition to, an argument. They also provide evidence on the kinds of methodological approaches or traditions used in studying the field. A critical evaluation of these studies might suggest the adoption of similar methodological approaches, or, indeed, the need to adopt alternative ones. Empirical studies might also highlight contradictory findings or ambiguities that are worthy of further research. Both the empirical and theoretical literature can be used to identify current gaps in knowledge, and therefore in the formulation of research questions.

THE METHODOLOGICAL LITERATURE

Reviewing the methodological literature allows the researcher to identify the kinds of methodological approaches that have, typically, been used to address the subject they are interested in. This includes issues of qualitative research design and also the choices made for approaches to qualitative data analysis. Having reviewed the methodological literature it will also be necessary to study qualitative research methods textbooks and academic articles in order to gain a deeper understanding of the kinds of issues involved (Silverman, 2000).

> ## TOP TIP 7.2
>
> Inexperienced researchers often believe that conducting a literature review on qualitative methodology means developing an unfocused discourse on qualitative methods in general. Nothing could be further from the truth. As this chapter suggests, qualitative methods comprise a wide and diverse set of methods. So, you should try to give some focus to the qualitative methodology you are actually using. For example, if using grounded theory, do not waste time telling the reader about the wonders of ethnomethodology or ethnography. Describe, briefly, the history of grounded theory, some of the changes in the views of its originators and discuss the grounded theory stages in data collection and analysis.

COLLECTING QUALITATIVE DATA

Qualitative data emerge from a wide spectrum of sources. One of the most common is field studies where the researcher enters a selected setting to gather data, often through the use of observations or interviews. While observation is likely to elicit qualitative data (such as **field notes** and analysis), interviews may be used to collect both qualitative and quantitative information. Similarly, case studies might involve the use of research instruments such as questionnaires, interview schedules and observations, all of which might yield data that is qualitative in nature.

CONDUCTING INTERVIEWS

Qualitative interviews can be used as either the main instrument of data collection, or in conjunction with observation, document analysis or some other type of data gathering technique. Qualitative interviews utilize open-ended questions using either informal, conversational interviews, semi-structured interviews (where additional probing questions can be used) or standardized interviews, where they are not. Chapter 14 discusses approaches to interviewing in more detail.

OBSERVATIONS

Observations are one of the prime data collection methods for naturalistic or fieldwork settings. Observational data is primarily descriptive of settings, people, events and the meanings that participants ascribe to them. As we will see in Chapter 15, observation may be conducted with the knowledge of those being observed (overt observation) or without their knowledge (covert). Researchers may also remain detached from the field setting as a non-participant or become a member of a group or setting.

Field notes remain one of the mainstays of qualitative data collection methods through observations. Accurate, detailed and extensive field notes are difficult to write, especially when the researcher is busy observing in the field (and particularly if that research has to be covert). This is why it is important that field notes are written up on the same day as the observation and not after this point. Field notes can be supplemented by diaries written by researchers, and also by participants, so that triangulation can be performed. Photographs, drawings, maps and other visual material can also be added (see next section). Lofland and Lofland (1984) recommend that if field notes are supplemented by tape recordings, these should be transcribed as quickly as possible, and that at least as much time should be spent studying and analysing the materials as spent in the interview itself. Flick (2006) also recommends the use of documentation sheets that provide useful summary information on the context within which the data were collected (see Figure 7.3). Document sheets allow for an overview of the data and can provide a guide as to which files and transcripts to consult at the analysis stage.

USING PHOTOGRAPHS AND OTHER SOURCES

In addition to text, photographs or other visual data such as video or film recordings are also sources of qualitative data. Photographs in particular have a

Figure 7.3
Example of
document sheet

Interviewee data summary	
Date of interview	_____
Place of interview	_____
Duration of interview	_____
Interviewer	_____
Identifier number for interviewee	_____
Gender of interviewee	_____
Age of interviewee	_____
Job role of interviewee	_____
Qualifications of interviewee	_____
Professional training of interviewee undertaken in the past 3 years	_____

long history in ethnography and anthropology (Flick, 2006). Photographs allow the detailed recording of facts, including the presentation of lifestyles and living and working conditions. They can also capture processes that are too rapid for the human eye. Sometimes, the subjects of research can be encouraged to take on the role of the photographer, documenting either a subject of their choice, or a theme that the researcher wants them to record. If desired, these photographs can subsequently be used to stimulate an interview or encourage a participant to produce a narrative to accompany and expand upon the photographic evidence. This can be seen as a concretization of the focused interview (Flick, 2006). But do photographs tell the truth? Of course, what the camera focuses on, and what it leaves out, is selective. There may also be problems of **reactivity**, with the subjects altering their behaviour in the presence of the photographer. Hence, there are always dangers of bias, and questions about the extent to which photographs help in the social construction of reality. It may be best to use visual data alongside other sources such as observational and interview data and documents.

USING UNOBTRUSIVE DATA

As we shall see in Chapter 16, organizations contain a rich array of unobtrusive data in the form of documents such as company reports, business plans, written statements by members of staff, accounts and contracts. Most medium-sized and large organizations also have dedicated websites that present a 'public' image to the world. Analysis of such a site may reveal not only the organization's perception of itself and the image it wants to present, but also what it does not wish to reveal. The organization's intranet site and evidence from email interactions may also prove of interest (if accessible as part of a study).

Atkinson and Coffey (2004) warn that it is not only the content of documents that should be of concern to researchers, but also the way in which they are produced, circulated, read, stored and used for a variety of purposes. This means that they are not necessarily a description of 'reality' nor are they necessarily 'transparent representations of organizational routines, decision-making processes or professional diagnoses' (Atkinson and Coffey, 2004: 47). Although they should be treated seriously, documents should not be taken as factual evidence of what they report. Rather, they should be examined for their place within the organizational setting, and the cultural values attached to them. But conversely, the temptation should be avoided to use only observational or oral data as the primary source and downgrade documentary evidence to a validating role. Atkinson and Coffey (2004) urge that documents should be regarded as valid sources in their own right.

KEEPING A RESEARCH DIARY

Given that, particularly in progressive qualitative research, the researcher is considered a valid part of the research setting, then the ideas, feelings and perceptions of the researcher become part of the data. But there is a danger in qualitative research that the reader is presented with what Silverman (2000: 193) calls a 'seamless web' of ideas that conceals the researcher's complex experience of the research process including false leads, inspirational hunches, triumphs and disappointments. Keeping a diary maintains a proper record of the researcher's thinking and helps to develop a reflexive stance (Miles and Huberman, 1994). For example, there is a tendency in qualitative research to present the 'voices' of respondents as though these voices speak on their own. Yet it is the researcher who makes choices about how to interpret these voices and which quotations to use as evidence (Mauthner and Doucet, 2003).

Hence, the kinds of issues noted in a research diary could include:

- The processes involved in approaching the field and making contact (in the terms often used by participatory action research – 'getting in').
- Experiences (positive and negative) in getting access to respondents and in using data gathering instruments.
- Details of literature sources read (and ordered).
- Reflections on the interpretation and presentation of results, including important changes in direction.

As Silverman (2000) points out, there is no single correct method for keeping a diary. What is important is that researchers are meticulous in record keeping and reflective about their data.

Table 7.6
Checklist of ethical
commitments and
responsibilities
during qualitative
research

Source: Adapted
from Mason, 2002

- Have I honoured my commitments about confidentiality and privacy?
- Have I acted in the spirit of informed consent?
- Have I used my research effectively and morally?
- Have I generalized appropriately?
- Do I have a responsibility to anticipate how others might use my research and explanations?

ETHICS AND QUALITATIVE RESEARCH

As we saw in Chapter 4, all researchers need to take into account ethical princi-ples when conducting their research. Ethics, however, can pose a particular prob-lem for qualitative researchers who often work so closely and for longer periods of time with research participants, and deal with the most sensitive and intimate matters in people's lives (Punch, 2005). Indeed, with some qualitative research methods such as, say, ethnography using **participant observation**, the researcher may develop close relationships with those they are studying. This has important implications for issues such as respecting the privacy of participants and avoid-ing deception (especially if the observation is covert). Furthermore, as we have seen earlier, the flexibility of qualitative research design, means that questions and focus may change during the research process. Since this may mean that the samples used and the kinds of question asked may have to change, this implies that, in qualitative studies, ethical consent may have to be renegotiated on an ongoing basis.

Mason (2002) agrees that, for qualitative research, the issue of informed consent needs to be revisited regularly. Some research methods, for example interviews, can promote a high degree of trust amongst research subjects, which imposes a special responsibility on researchers to avoid reneging on commitments, acting deceitfully or producing explanations that in some way cause harm to the interests of those subjects. For example, the uses of visual data such as photographs can make confidentiality impossible to maintain. Table 7.6 provides a brief checklist of issues qualitative researchers would do well to reflect on during the research process.

According to Bell and Bryman (2007), many ethical frameworks are based upon a model of research processes that is insensitive to the kinds of open-ended research strategies associated with qualitative methods. Lincoln and Tierney (2004: 222), for example, note that some institutional review boards (IRBs) have rejected qualitative research projects on the grounds that they are 'unscientific' and incapable of generalization – a judgement based upon a 'realist' ontology and 'objectivist' epistemology that underpins conventional science (Lincoln and Guba, 1989). One result is a series of endless revisions as IRBs seek to make such projects appear more conventional.

One approach to qualitative research, ethnography, has difficulties in meeting ethical protocols because the research questions can rarely be specified in advance and it can be difficult to specify when projects start and when they end (Bosk, 2004). Similarly, grounded theory promotes an open-ended approach that allows new lines of enquiry to emerge during the research process, making it difficult to determine an exact set of research questions in advance of the project. In these circumstances, the best approach is probably to recognize that informed consent is a fluid process requiring constant monitoring rather than a pre-research agreement which precludes further thought.

Activity 7.7

Given the fluid nature of qualitative research, what kinds of processes should researchers put in place to ensure that ethical principles are followed throughout the project?

ENSURING RIGOUR IN QUALITATIVE RESEARCH

One of the criticisms levelled at qualitative research is that it is 'unscientific', anecdotal and based upon subjective impressions. It is also claimed that qualitative research lacks reproducibility – the research is so based in or confined to one context that it lacks **generalizability**. In addition, it is argued that the research is so personal to the researcher that another researcher might use the same data to come to radically different conclusions (Mays, 1995). These contentions are countered by qualitative researchers who seek to show, through a range of strategies, how qualitative research can, indeed, demonstrate rigour. We will look at how rigour is preserved in the analysis of qualitative data in Chapter 18, confining ourselves here largely to the issue of rigour in qualitative design and data collection.

In discussing the issue of quality in qualitative research, some commentators resist the temptation to even address such matters as validity and reliability, because, they argue, these concepts were originally developed in a quantitative tradition and are rooted in a positivist paradigm (Bryman, 1988; Golafshani, 2003). Lincoln (1985) also asserts that naturalistic researchers, for example, tend anyway to be more modest and reluctant about making generalizations from their findings. Issues of external validity, then, are not high on their agendas. However, as we shall see, even some of the most enthusiastic adherents to the qualitative approach see the need to address validity and reliability as inescapable, although some do suggest additional quality criteria, some of which they see as having more importance.

DESIGNING FOR VALIDITY IN QUALITATIVE RESEARCH

Validity has traditionally been a concept used in quantitative research (Campbell and Stanley, 1963). The word, however, has been adopted in qualitative research, resulting in 17 different terms associated with it, with no generally agreed definition (Dellinger and Leech, 2007). Despite this caution, we will explore validity in qualitative research from two perspectives – internal validity and external validity.

Internal validity

The issue of internal validity revolves around the question of how far the constructions of the researcher are grounded in the constructions of those being researched (Flick, 2006). Hall and Callery (2001) criticize grounded theory in particular for assuming that the data collected reflect reality, and are independent of, and not influenced by, the subjective interpretations of researchers. What is needed, they argue, is for researchers to adopt a reflexive stance, through which they critically reflect on their influence on the research process. Self-reflective criticality is strengthened through repetitive checks of the researcher's interpretations (Whittemore et al., 2001). Of course, another approach is to involve those being researched in checking the data for accuracy and in the analysis for the faithfulness of interpretation.

Data can be fabricated, discounted or misinterpreted. One way of avoiding such problems is where research can be validated through replication, but as Dey (1993) cautions, qualitative research is notoriously difficult to replicate. In place of external validation, 'internal' replication may be adopted, whereby other researchers can inspect the procedures through which the research has been conducted. This is much easier, of course, where two researchers collaborate on the same project. Another approach might be to split the data and analyse them in two stages to see if the results are similar.

Establishing principles for validity is all very well, but how do researchers achieve them in practice? Whittemore et al. (2001) present a useful checklist (see Table 7.7) but warn that selection depends upon contextual factors and the purpose of the research.

External validity

One important aspect of external validity is the extent to which it is possible to generalize from the data to other cases or situations. Generalizations can be

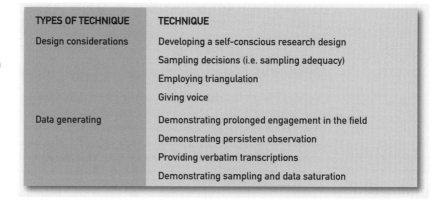

TYPES OF TECHNIQUE	TECHNIQUE
Design considerations	Developing a self-conscious research design
	Sampling decisions (i.e. sampling adequacy)
	Employing triangulation
	Giving voice
Data generating	Demonstrating prolonged engagement in the field
	Demonstrating persistent observation
	Providing verbatim transcriptions
	Demonstrating sampling and data saturation

defined as assertions of enduring value that are context-free (Lincoln and Guba, 1994). Since sampling in qualitative research tends to be purposive rather than random, and data gathered from a limited number of cases (sometimes one), can we generalize? Lincoln and Guba (1994) distinguish between two kinds of generalization. The first is nomothetic, based upon a rationalistic, law-like stance, as in the positivist paradigm. The second they term 'naturalistic generalization', which is a more intuitive, ideographic but none the less, an empirical approach based upon personal, direct experience. The authors then dismiss the notion of nomothetic generalizations that are truly universal to all times and situations. Local conditions, they contend, make it impossible to generalize. 'If there is a "true" generalization, it is that there can be no generalization' (Lincoln and Guba, 1994: 124). At best, the results from individual cases allow us to build working hypotheses that can be tested in subsequent cases. As Miles and Huberman (1994) point out, through the use of multiple case studies, attempts are made to match on the basis of underlying theories. As more similar or contrasting cases are used, we can justify, through replication, the stability of the findings. Even then, as Dey (1993) asserts, as a basis for generalization, qualitative analysis is more likely to be suggestive than conclusive. At best, rather than generalize, we can see if the findings from Context A can be transferred to Context B.

If qualitative researchers decide that generalizing is essential, then this entails treating it as an integral element of the research design. In particular, it means taking extra care over sample selection (of both people and sites). Efforts then need to be made to demonstrate the similarities between the sample and the target population or research sites to which generalization is to be made. Hence, if generalization is an aim of the research, care with sample selection has to be built into the research design, and not considered as an afterthought. Payne and Williams (2005) suggest that in attempting to formulate generalizations, qualitative researchers will achieve more **plausibility** if they are:

- Cautious, moderating the range of generalizing conclusions. Being too ambitious in conclusions merely undermines the credibility of otherwise competent research. If the sample is specialized in some way, be clear that the results may only be applicable to a limited type of site or categories of person – and say what they are.

- Careful in recognizing the limitations of time periods. So, claims are more believable if made for current conditions than about some period in the future.

- Meticulous in demonstrating clear linkages between generalizing conclusions and the specific data that provide its foundation.

- Honest and transparent about findings from sub-groups, the views or behaviours of which differ or are similar to those of the population being reported.

- Modest by making claims for basic patterns or tendencies, so that other studies may find similar but not identical findings.

- Diligent in reporting alternative explanations or the constraints on generalizations. The constraints on generalizations need to become a standard element of the analysis.

CASE STUDY 7.2   THE LIMITS OF GENERALIZATION

A group of researchers are conducting an observational study of an international supermarket chain based in the UK, France and Germany. To what extent should they attempt to generalize their findings to other supermarkets in Europe? They decide that this will depend on the features being explored. As far as products or brands are concerned, generalization is quite feasible because many products and brands are sold all over Europe. Similarly, features such as management structures may be quite similar across many countries, particularly in Western Europe. However, the researchers decide that they would be unwise to generalize to Eastern European supermarkets, because forms of management structure and culture are still emerging from a post-communist society and still tend to be hierarchical. The ability to generalize, then, is influenced by arguments about the similarities or otherwise between the research (sending) site and sites to which generalizations are being made (receiving site).

TOP TIP 7.3

Decide at the research planning stage on your attitude towards generalization. If rejecting the necessity of generalizing, explore the qualitative research methods literature for what alternative measures of rigour you may use to justify the quality of your research. If generalizing, follow the advice of Payne and Williams (2005) to acknowledge the modesty of your findings.

DESIGNING FOR RELIABILITY IN QUALITATIVE RESEARCH

Reliability refers to the stability of findings. A reliable observation, for example, is one that could have been made by any similarly situated observer (Denzin, 1989). For most qualitative approaches, reliability is improved, if not guaranteed, by triangulation, gathering information, for example, from multiple sources or by using multiple data gathering tools. Denzin (1989) offers four kinds of triangulation:

- *Data triangulation* – where data are gathered using multiple sampling strategies. This can include: time triangulation, when data are collected on the same phenomenon over a period of time; space triangulation, when data are collected from multiple sites and; person triangulation, where data are collected at three levels in an organization – for example, individuals, groups and departments.

- *Investigator triangulation* – using more than one observer in field situations so that observer bias can be reduced (and inter-judge reliability improved). Thus, a training programme would teach observers to keep an 'open mind' and not to become obsessed with their hypothesis (if they start with one). They should not jump towards 'solutions' to a problem as this will tend to make them ignore facts that do not confirm their expectations. In making a study, they are trained to notice all aspects of a situation and to deliberately search for unexpected facts, and to seek alternative interpretations. The data will then be checked by other trained colleagues (and even informants) who will, if possible, repeat the observation to see if they get the same results.

- *Multiple triangulation* – in which a combination of multiple methods, data types, observers and theories are combined in the same investigation. While it is often a practical difficulty to achieve a combination of all of these, it is more common to at least use multiple data levels and methods.

- *Methodological triangulation* – of which there are two kinds: within-method, where the researcher employs varieties of data gathering techniques within the same method; and between method, where a variety of different methods are used – for example, quantitative data from a survey, with qualitative data from observations (see Chapter 8 on using mixed methods).

It should be noted, however, that the significance of reliability is not universally accepted. Glaser (1992), for example, asserts that verification has no place in grounded theory, the task of which is to generate hypotheses, not to test them. This is in sharp contrast to the views of Strauss and Corbin (1994), who suggest that within the data collection and analysis process there is an in-built mandate to strive towards the verification of any resulting hypotheses. For interview data, reliability can be increased through the training of interviewers and through the use of standardized interview schedules. For observations, researchers also need to be trained before they enter the field. Reliability can also be improved through the use of pre-designed observation schedules.

OTHER APPROACHES TO RIGOUR

Some researchers, particularly those from the naturalistic tradition, argue that *trustworthiness* is more important than concerns over the validity or reliability checks that have just been outlined. Skrtic (1985), for example, suggests that this is addressed through a focus on:

- Transferability, with purposive sampling to illustrate pertinent issues and factors when comparing two contexts for similarity, and thick descriptions to provide evidence for making judgements about similarities between cases.

- Dependability, through the use of **audit trails** through the data.

- Confirmability, with the audit showing the connections between data and the researcher's interpretations.

- **Credibility**, the use of persistent observations; triangulation (of data, methods, theories and investigations); and member checks (where data and interpretations are tested with research participants).

Lincoln and Guba (1994) argue that credibility can be strengthened through the researcher making a conscious effort to establish confidence in the accuracy of interpretation, and the fit between description and explanation.

To these we can add *authenticity*, which relates analysis and interpretation to the meanings and experiences that are lived and perceived by the subjects of the research. This means the research being aware of the multiple voices contained within the data, and the subtle, sometimes conflicting realities within it. Do the interpretations ring true? Have rival explanations been considered? Davies and Dodd (2002) also suggest that just as important are practices that are honest, open, empathetic, sensitive, respectful and engaging. Perhaps these

Table 7.8
Comparison of
criteria for judging
the trustworthiness
of quantitative and
qualitative research

Source: Adapted
from Hoepfl, 1997
and Lincoln and
Guba, 1994

CONVENTIONAL TERMS	NATURALISTIC TERMS	NATURALISTIC TERMS DEVELOPED THROUGH…
Internal validity	Credibility	Examining the study design and methods used to derive findings.
External validity	Transferability	Exploring the degree to which findings are context bound, so assessed by examining the characteristics of sample.
Reliability	Dependability	Evaluating reliability of study's conclusions.
Objectivity	Confirmability	Addressing the degree to which the steps of the study can be audited, confirmed or replicated.

concepts should also be seen as essential ingredients of research quality. Table 7.8 offers a brief comparison of criteria used by quantitative and qualitative approaches, and the measures suggested by Lincoln and Guba (1994) for developing the trustworthiness of qualitative data.

However, as Johnson and Harris (2002) comment, one problem with qualitative research is that a standard practice for achieving validity, reliability or any other quality indicator has yet to be established. This is because of the variable nature of qualitative research and the relative novelty of many research studies.

SUMMARY

- Qualitative research has advantages over quantitative research in that researchers are closer to the fields or settings they are trying to research – it is highly contextual.

- Qualitative research is not built upon a unified theory or methodological approach – hence its variety and flexibility.

- In qualitative research, data analysis does not necessarily follow data gathering – there can be a number of iterations between the two.

- Even though there are various schools of qualitative research including grounded theory, ethnomethodology, narrative analysis and ethnography, they all have one element in common – generally, an inductive approach (although deduction or prior questions cannot be ruled out).

- Methods of collecting qualitative data include interview transcripts, field notes from observations, photographs, video and unobtrusive data.

- Decisions on whether to attempt generalization need to be built into the research design paying particular attention to sampling strategies.

- Qualitative approaches to achieving rigour include building trustworthiness, authenticity, credibility, transferability, dependability and confirmability.

FURTHER READING

Berg, B.L. (2006) *Qualitative Research Methods for the Social Sciences*, 6th edn. Needham Heights, MA: Allyn & Bacon. Shows inexperienced researchers how to design, collect and analyse data. Discusses seven different qualitative data collecting strategies in detail, including a guide to conducting focus groups.

Flick, U. (2006) *An Introduction to Qualitative Research*, 3rd edn. London: Sage. Provides a systematic framework for doing qualitative research, as well as a guide to research design. Each chapter concludes with a helpful overview.

Denzin, N.K. and Lincoln, Y.S. (2005) *The Sage Handbook of Qualitative Research*, 3rd edn. Thousand Oaks, CA: Sage. Includes 14 topics not touched by previous editions, including institutional review boards, critical and performance ethnography, narrative enquiry and strategies of online research. Previous authors have all updated their chapters.

SUGGESTED ANSWERS FOR ACTIVITY 7.2

There might tend to be more confidence in the validity of results from a comprehensive sample since this covers every case in a given population. Similarly, intensity samples focus on cases that are typical of the population rather than outliers or atypical examples. Deviant case sampling, which looks at extreme cases, may be accused of producing invalid results, but may, in fact, yield illuminating and unexpected data that allow new avenues of exploration. Critical case sampling, with its focus on one case or site, can only provide a strong case for validity if evidence is provided that the case is, indeed, typical of the trait, characteristic or phenomenon under investigation.

SUGGESTED ANSWER TO ACTIVITY 7.4

Question	Type of question	Comments
What changes in alcohol consumption have taken place over the last 10 years?	Descriptive	A question that deals with national aggregates – a quantitative question.

Do high levels of alcohol consumption lead to absenteeism at work?	Explanatory	At one level this is a quantitative question exploring a relationship between two variables. But if a relationship is identified, a follow-up qualitative study could seek to understand why.
Why is alcohol consumption on the increase?	Explanatory	A quantitative study would attempt to identify variables (such as demographic changes, income levels, etc.) that might explain the increase. But a qualitative study could delve into people's attitudes to alcohol and explore changing personal and cultural values.
What is the scale and cause of alcohol abuse amongst the under 16s?	Exploratory	The scale of alcohol consumption is a quantitative question, but the cause could adopt a qualitative approach to establish reasons for this change, including changing social attitudes.
What is the impact of rising alcohol consumption on family life?	Interpretive	Seeks to uncover people's views and perspectives. A valid question for exploratory, largely qualitative studies.

SUGGESTED ANSWER TO ACTIVITY 7.6

Qualitative sampling strategies that are probably most easily defended as yielding valid results include comprehensive sampling and typical case sampling. Those that might sometimes struggle in achieving valid results include deviant case sampling, critical case sampling and snowball sampling simply because the selected cases may not be representative of the population being studied. Note, however, that these strategies might be adopted by qualitative researchers because they offer other benefits, as highlighted in Table 7.5.

Collecting Primary Data: Questionnaires

DAVID E. GRAY

CHAPTER OBJECTIVES

After reading this chapter you will be able to:

● Plan and design valid and reliable questionnaires.

● Describe the processes involved in collecting primary data, including piloting.

● Demonstrate the skills for writing appropriate individual questions and designing questionnaires.

● Write appropriate documentation to accompany questionnaires.

As an important data gathering tool, questionnaires are used as part of many of the research methodologies described in Part B of this book. Indeed, it is difficult to imagine a large-scale survey (Chapter 9), for example, without the use of a carefully constructed questionnaire. Similarly, case studies (Chapter 10) can use a combination of data gathering tools, with the use of questionnaires, sometimes in the form of an interview schedule (see Chapter 14).

Questionnaires are research tools through which people are asked to respond to the same set of questions in a predetermined order. Since questionnaires are one of the most widely used primary data gathering techniques, considerable space will be devoted here to their design and construction. Many people in the business and educational worlds have had experience in data gathering using questionnaires, but fewer are knowledgeable about how difficult it is to construct questionnaires that are valid, reliable and objective. It is thus relatively easy to produce reports and recommendations based upon the most spurious of data. Hopefully, after reading this chapter you will understand many of the pitfalls of questionnaire design so that you can avoid them.

Questionnaires should be used when they fit the objectives of the research. Hence, in a case study that involves seeking the in-depth opinions and perspectives of a small number of respondents, a highly structured questionnaire might be completely inappropriate. Here you might want to construct an interview schedule containing open-ended questions, adopting a descriptive approach. But where the audience is relatively large, and where standardized questions are needed, the questionnaire is ideal, and will allow, if this is required, an analytical approach exploring relationships between variables. Of course, in many cases questionnaires will be only one tool used in the general research effort. The research design may plan for a wide-scale survey using questionnaires, to be followed up by in-depth structured interviews or observations with a target sample, identified to be of interest by the survey.

In this chapter we will explore some of the essential principles in questionnaire design, including how to write appropriate questions, whether to use open or **closed questions**, how to sequence questions and questionnaire layout. We also look at some of the more specific principles behind designing Web or Internet questionnaires, and how questionnaires of any kind should be administered.

WHY USE QUESTIONNAIRES?

Questionnaires are perhaps one of the most popular data gathering tools, probably because they are thought by many researchers to be easy to design. This belief, as we shall see, is not necessarily supported by the evidence. As Gillham (2000) points out, the popularity of questionnaires is also probably based on some of their inherent advantages. For example:

- They are low cost in terms of both time and money. In contrast to, say, interviews, questionnaires can be sent to hundreds or even thousands of respondents at relatively little cost.

- The inflow of data is quick and from many people.

- Respondents can complete the questionnaire at a time and place that suits them. Contrast this with interviews, when it can be difficult to find convenient times to meet the respondent.

- Data analysis of closed questions is relatively simple, and questions can be coded quickly.

- Respondents' anonymity can be assured. But Gillham (2000) rightly notes that in small-scale surveys, this can be largely nominal in character – it may not be difficult for the researcher to recognize the responses of individuals. But real anonymity can also be double-edged. If you do not know who has not responded, to whom do you send reminders?

• These is a lack of interviewer bias. There is evidence that different interviewers get different answers – because of the way in which they place different emphasis on individual words in questions and because of the different probes (additional questions) that they follow up with.

Of course, not surprisingly, using questionnaires also has its drawbacks. Unless we can make completing the questionnaire intrinsically rewarding, the response rate can be depressingly low. This is even more of a danger if questionnaires are too long. Gillham (2000) advises that questionnaires should be limited in length to four to six pages, otherwise the return rate may be adversely affected. Few people greet receiving a questionnaire with unbounded enthusiasm, particularly long ones. Most people find verbal communication easier than using the written word, yet questionnaires demand a certain level of literacy. But there is no opportunity to ask questions or clear up ambiguous or ill-conceived answers. Respondents may give flippant, inaccurate or misleading answers, but the researcher is not in a position to detect this. In contrast, the face-to-face interview might reveal underlying problems through observing body language or the verbal tones of the respondent.

> **Activity 13.1**
>
> Take a questionnaire that you have designed, preferably quite recently. Was it less than six sides in length? Was it well designed and easy for respondents to complete? Were the answers, in your view, honestly given? Overall, how successful was the questionnaire in eliciting the required data and how could you explain its success or failure?

DESIGNING QUESTIONNAIRES

Questionnaires reflect the designer's view of the world, no matter how objective a researcher tries to be. This is true not only for the design of individual questions, but often about the very choice of research subject. Furthermore, what we choose *not* to ask about, may just as easily reflect our world view as what we include in the questionnaire. It is important, then, that, as a researcher, you are aware of this and try, as far as possible, to be objective. Indeed, it is the values, perceptions and interests of the respondent that you should be attempting to capture, and the questionnaire should reflect this as much as possible. In this section, we will look at the design of individual questions, including open and closed questions, the sequencing of questions and questionnaire layout.

WRITING INDIVIDUAL QUESTIONS

Piloting a questionnaire usually helps to eliminate or at least reduce questions that are likely to mislead. But it needs to be understood that people may read and interpret questions in quite distinct ways. It is naive to believe that standardized questions will always receive standardized, rational, responses. Nevertheless, it helps if questions are phrased in ways that are clear, concise and unambiguous (to everyone in the sample), and free from jargon and abbreviations. While the overall content, style and structure of the questionnaire must satisfy the respondent, each individual question must stand on its own merits. Arksey and Knight (1999) provide a useful list of what to avoid when constructing individual questions.

Prejudicial language: Try to avoid language that is prejudicial or contains sexist, disablist or racist stereotyping. A question that annoys, irritates or insults a respondent may affect the way they respond to questions that follow – if they decide to complete them at all! For example, the question: 'What is your marital status?' may annoy those who live with partners or who are not living in a heterosexual relationship (assuming that the society allows only heterosexual marriages).

Imprecision: Avoid vague phrases such as 'average', 'regularly' and 'a great deal' since they are likely to be interpreted in different ways by different respondents.

Leading questions: These suggest a possible answer and hence promote bias. Questions such as 'Why do you think the organization has been successful in the past three years?' are leading because they are making an assumption with which the respondent may not necessarily agree.

Double questions: These should be avoided because they are impossible to answer. For example, if the question: 'Do you like chocolate and strawberry ice-cream?' receives a reply of 'Yes' you would be unclear as to whether this relates to both of the ice-cream flavours or just one of them.

Assumptive questions: Avoid questions that make assumptions about people's beliefs or behaviours. For example, 'How often do you drink alcohol?' makes an assumption about the respondent's drinking habits which may be entirely false (and even hurtful – see prejudicial language, above).

Hypothetical questions: Try to avoid hypothetical questions such as: 'Suppose you were asked to …' since these have been shown to be poor predictors of people's actual subsequent behaviour. A useful check on whether the content and structure of a question is right is to ask whether a respondent would understand why the question was being asked within the overall context of the study. Arksey and Knight (1999) also argue that such questions can generate insightful data when people have some direct knowledge or experience of the subject being discussed.

Knowledge: Make sure that the group that has been targeted to answer the questions has the knowledge actually to do so. Sometimes it may be necessary to provide people with some background information if the subject is quite technical.

Memory recall: People may have difficulty recalling what has occurred even quite recently. If, say, you are constructing some questions around recent newsworthy events, then it would be appropriate to present respondents with a list of such events before asking them questions about them.

In determining how to ask individual questions consider the following:

- Can the question be misunderstood? Does it contain difficult or unclear phraseology?

- Is the question misleading because of unstated assumptions or unseen implications?

- Is the wording biased? Is it emotionally loaded or slanted towards a particular kind of answer?

- Is the question wording likely to be objectionable to the respondent in any way?

- Can the question be asked in a more direct or a more indirect form?

- Are double questions avoided?

- Are **leading questions** avoided?

- Is attention paid to detail – e.g. overlapping categories such as 'age 30–35, 35–40'

- Do questions avoid taxing respondents' memories?

- Can the questions be shortened?

- Are categories such as 'Don't Know' and 'Not Applicable' provided?

- Will the words used have the same meaning for all respondents, regardless of nationality, language, culture, etc.?

- Is the frame of reference clear – e.g. if asking how often, is the range of possible responses made obvious?

- Do questions artificially create opinions on subjects where respondents really do not have any?

- Is personal wording preferable (e.g. 'How do *you* feel?'), or impersonal (e.g. 'How do you think people feel'). The first is a measure of attitudes, the second a measure of respondents' perceptions of other people's attitudes.

DEVELOPING QUESTIONS TO MEASURE A CONSTRUCT

As indicated above, the development of individual questions is a skilful process. However, as we shall see later, to increase reliability we normally have to use more than one question to measure a construct accurately. This might be relatively straightforward when eliciting customers' views on the quality of a physical entity such as a can of baked beans. Here we can ask questions about the aesthetic design of the can, the taste and texture of the beans and their 'value for money'. But what about more service-related subjects such as service efficiency, staff friendliness, hospital cleanliness, etc? How do we go about measuring a construct when even the very definition of the construct itself may be vague or even unknown to us? Ekinci and Riley (1999) suggest that using the Q-sort methodology can be of considerable assistance here. The Q-sort approach falls into three stages:

- Stage 1: Create construct definitions. It is important that these should have a high degree of face validity so they need to be derived from previous studies or from expert opinion.

- Stage 2: Create sets of statements that are designed to represent the definition.

- Stage 3: Test the statements against the definitions by getting participants to combine the statements with the definitions on a 'free sort' basis, with the option 'don't know' or 'no opinion'.

CASE STUDY 13.1   APPLYING THE Q-SORT METHODOLOGY

A hotel chain wishes to conduct a customer survey on the quality of staff behaviour and attitudes to customers and the reliability of services. Using some well known articles in the field of hospitality management, definitions of appropriate staff behaviour and attitudes were developed, followed by a definition for reliability of hotel services. Each definition was written onto a card – but without any title. For example, a card contained a definition of reliability but the card did not have 'Reliability' as a title. This card read: *It is the hotel's regularity and consistency in performing services which inspires confidence and trust to customers. In operational terms this means keeping promises, trustworthiness in transaction and efficiency of recovery process if anything goes wrong.* Another card was created for the response 'don't know'. Five positive and five negative statements were then developed for each of the two categories, making 20 statements in all.

Thirty participants took part in Stage 3 of the process. All the cards were shuffled to create a random order and each participant was then asked to place the statement cards against one of the two definition cards or the 'don't know' option. The results of each participant's choice was noted. From these data it was possible to calculate what proportion of respondents agreed that a statement described the definition.

Table 13.1   The frequency of staff behaviour/attitude and reliability statements (acceptable statements appear with an asterisk)

STAFF BEHAVIOUR AND ATTITUDE STATEMENTS	FREQUENCY (%)
*Staff don't know what they were doing	82
*Staff displayed effortless expertise	82
*Staff seemed to anticipate what I needed	76
*Staff recognized you	73
*Staff didn't care whether you were pleased or not	73
*Staff were willing to explain things when I asked	70
Staff seemed to want to get rid of me when I asked questions	68
If they didn't like you it was hard to get service	68
Staff were committed to pleasing customers	65
You were always treated like a stranger	46
You were always treated the same	41
If you wanted something you had to ask twice	31
Reliability statements	
*The hotel did not deliver any of its promises	80
*The hotel always delivered what it promised	78
*You had to constantly dispute items on the bill	71
The billing was always clear and accurate	66
They apologized for the mistakes and rectified the problems	59
They neither apologized nor made any attempt to rectify the problem or offered compensation	56
I always expected a screw-up with room reservations	49
When they told me how long it was going to be, I left it to fate and forgot about waiting	46
I didn't expect any problem with room reservation	44
When they told me how long it was going to be, I believed them	17

Source: Adapted from Ekinci and Riley, 1999

(Cont'd)

In interpreting the results, a definition is only deemed to be legitimate if at least two statements are accepted as describing it. Secondly, for a statement to be legitimate, at least 70 per cent of the sample must allocate it to the same definition. Ideally, a minimum of four to six statements should be obtained for each definition (construct) in order to obtain internal consistency for the scale. Table 13.1 illustrates the results for each statement. We can see that for the construct 'Staff behaviour and attitude' there are six statements that yield a recognition rate about 70 per cent. For the reliability construct three statements are deemed satisfactory. Hence, the Q-sort process has helped in the development of 9 statements that are deemed adequate for measuring two constructs used to measure customer satisfaction within the hotel industry.

USING CLASSIFICATION QUESTIONS

One type of question often required by a survey is the classification question, dealing with, for example, the name, sex, age, status, etc. of the respondent. These are important for providing the basis for analysing associations between variables (for example, a respondent's gender and attitude towards sexual harassment issues in the workplace). These questions should be introduced by a gentle 'It will help us in further analysis if you would tell us a little about yourself'. Take care not to run the risk of alienating the respondent by prying for information that is not, subsequently, needed. For example, is it necessary to know the respondent's exact age, or would a response within a range of ages suffice? People may also be reluctant to reveal details of their salary, particularly to a stranger within their own organization. It may be easier to obtain their response to a question on job grade that may provide an indirect indication of salary.

TOP TIP 13.1

Response rates will be maximized if the curiosity and interest of respondents is 'grabbed' on the first page of the questionnaire. Hence, it is usually best to place the important, but less than exciting, classification questions at the end of the questionnaire. People may be pleased to complete them because they have already invested time in responding to the questionnaire's main themes.

Activity 13.2

Anyone can write a questionnaire? Evaluate the questions in the short questionnaire shown in Figure 13.1.

Suggested answers are provided at the end of the chapter.

1 State your age

            Under 20   20–25   25–30   Over 30

2 What are your views on appraisal?

3 Do you consider appraisal to be vital for organizational development or a way of wasting time?

    Yes   No

4 Do you consider that appraisal should be:

- Integrated with training plans so people are better trained?   1
- Linked to the reward system so everyone earns more money?   2 Please tick one

5 Without effective 'best practice' appraisal the organization cannot prosper

  Yes
  No

6 Give details on the number of appraisals conducted within the organization over the recent time period

7 How many of your appraisals have you failed?

8 How often do you think that people should be appraised: (a) once a year (as now); (b) twice a year; (c) once every two years; (d) never (the scheme should be abandoned); (e) other (please specify)

Name:

Department:

Salary:

Complete and return

Figure 13.1 **Example questionnaire**

DRAFTING THE QUESTION CONTENT

Clearly, in writing questions issues such as validity need to be borne in mind. Hence, the content of the questionnaire needs to cover the research issues that have been specified. But Foddy (1993) points out that this is by no means a simple matter. A series of precise steps must be followed:

- The researcher has to be clear about the information required and encode this accurately into a question.

- The respondent must interpret the question in a way that the researcher intended.

- The respondent must construct an answer that contains information that the researcher has requested.

- The researcher must interpret the answer as the respondent had intended it to be interpreted.

Unfortunately, as Foddy (1993) comments, there is ample opportunity for the process to break down at any stage, with resulting threats to validity. Even if the respondent understands the question, there also needs to be some confidence that he or she will know the answer, and that they will be willing to provide it. In deliberating about question content ask yourself the following questions:

- Is the question necessary? Just how will it be useful?

- Are several questions needed on the subject matter of this question?

- Do respondents have the information necessary to answer the question?

- Does the question need to be more concrete, specific and closely related to the respondent's personal experience?

- Is the question content sufficiently general and free from spurious concreteness and specificity?

- Is the question content biased and loaded in one direction, without accompanying questions to balance the emphasis?

- Will the respondents give the information that is asked for?

Cannell (1985) deals with the issue of how to ask difficult or embarrassing questions. Referring to the work of Barton, he illustrates a number of ways in which the cooperation of respondents can be maintained. The possible approaches are illustrated in Table 13.1, in which, by means of illustration, a set of hypothetical questions are asked about whether a respondent sabotaged the organization's intranet.

DRAFTING THE ANSWER

Decide on how you want people to respond and stick with it. So, if you require respondents to *tick* their responses, get them to do this throughout the

APPROACH	QUESTION
Casual approach	Do you happen to have sabotaged the intranet?
Give a numbered card	Would you please read off the number on this card which corresponds to what became of the intranet [*Hand card to respondent*]: (a) It went down of its own accord (as usual) (b) I hacked into it and programmed a bug to make it self-destruct (c) Other (what?)
The Everybody approach	As you know, many people are tempted to sabotage the intranet these days. Do you happen to have done it recently?
The Other People approach	(a) Do you know any people who have sabotaged the intranet? (b) How about yourself?
Sealed Ballot technique	We respect your right to anonymity. Please complete this form, indicating whether, or not, you sabotaged the intranet, seal it in the envelope and place it in the box marked 'Secret Ballot'

questionnaire, rather than to also incorporate *underlining* and *circling*. In general, people seem to be used to box-ticking. The golden rule is that it should be absolutely clear how the respondent is to complete the questionnaire.

TYPES OF QUESTION

With the above warnings in mind, we can now move on to look at the types of questions that can be posed in a questionnaire. Oppenheim (1992) suggests that a funnel approach can often be used, whereby the questionnaire starts off with a broad set of questions and then progressively narrows down the questions to target specific areas. This is sometimes achieved by **filter questions** that are designed to exclude some respondents. So, for example, in a survey of employee commuting experiences, a question might be posed: Have you ever had difficulty in getting to work? If the answer is 'Yes', then more market research questions follow; if the answer is 'No' then the respondent is routed to a later part of the questionnaire on different transport issues. The main body of the questionnaire, however, will comprise either open or closed questions. It should be noted that different formats can be used for questions. Cannell (1985) argues that using a variety of such formats adds interest and can even help increase questionnaire response rates. Let us look at some now.

Open questions

Open questions have no definitive response and contain answers that are recorded in full. Hence, the questionnaire must be designed in such a way that respondents are able to provide such a response without the restriction of lack of space. Open questions often begin with words such as 'How', 'Why', 'What', etc.

The advantage of open questions is the potential for richness of responses, some of which may not have been anticipated by the researchers. But the downside of open questions is that while they are easy to answer they are also difficult to analyse. At first sight much of the information gathered may seem varied and difficult to categorize. Generally, the solution to this is the use of **coding** and the adoption of a **coding frame**.

Open questions may lead to interesting or unexpected responses, so, as we saw in Chapter 5, follow-up questions called probes or probing questions can be used (if the questionnaire is administered by an interviewer). These probes should be general in nature, and should not try to lead the respondent – for example, 'Could you say a little more about that accident report'; 'How do you feel about those new operational procedures'. Probing questions can also be used to add some clarity where the interviewer has not understood a response. Clearly, it is easier to ask probing questions when conducting a structured interview than when using a postal questionnaire.

The simplest form of open question is the specified response, as illustrated in Question 1.

QUESTION 1 SPECIFIED RESPONSE QUESTION

What aspects of the government's healthy living campaign do you find the most useful?
Please write in. _____

What aspects of the government's healthy living campaign do you find the least useful?
Please write in. _____

(You could follow up each response with a 'Why?' question.)

TOP TIP 13.2

In making use of open questions, give careful consideration to how you intend to analyse the qualitative data that results from them. How much qualitative data do you expect to generate? Do you have the time and resources to handle it? What approach to qualitative data analysis do you intend to adopt?

Closed questions

A closed question is one to which the respondent is offered a set of pre-designed replies such as 'Yes/No', 'True or False', multiple-choice responses, or is given the opportunity to choose from a selection of numbers representing strength of feeling or attitude. In contrast to open questions, closed questions may restrict the richness of alternative responses, but are easier to analyse. They also make it easier to compare the views of one group with another. Closed questions can be useful in providing respondents with some structure to their answers. There are a number of approaches to asking closed questions.

List questions: These provide the respondent with a list of responses, any of which they can select. This approach avoids making the answering of a questionnaire a test of memory. If list questions are being presented as part of a structured interview, then prompt cards can be used which list responses and which are shown to respondents. So, rather than read out Question 2 and rely on respondents to remember each item accurately, a card is given to them that reproduces the question and the possible responses.

QUESTION 2 LIST QUESTION

What do you think is the most important influence on the success of the organization in the next two years? Please ✓ as many responses as you think accurate.

Changes in government policy affecting the legal regulation of the market	☐
The entry of new competitors to the market	☐
The impact of the company's current reorganization strategy	☐
Foreign exchange rates	☐

While the list will, clearly, influence the direction of people's responses, this does not make the approach invalid. If the questionnaire is concerned with issues that require recall of information, the list might act as a useful memory-jogger. But it must be recognized that influencing respondents in this way may affect their response to any later open questions.

Category questions: These are designed so that only *one* response is possible. For structured interviews there can be any number of categories, provided a prompt card is used. But for self-administered questionnaires and telephone questionnaires Fink (2003) suggests a maximum of no more than five alternative responses (see Question 3).

QUESTION 3 CATEGORY QUESTION

How often in an average week do you use our e-banking facilities? Please ✓ one response.

Never	☐
Once	☐
2–3 times	☐
4–5 times	☐
6 times or more	☐

Ranking questions: This requires the respondent to **rank** responses in order. With this kind of question it is important to make the instructions for completing the question clear and explicit. Be aware that more than seven or eight items in the list may make it too complex for many respondents to complete. For face-to-face interviews use will have to be made of prompt cards and for telephone interviews, items should be limited to no more than three or four. Note that an 'other' category is also provided to catch any features not mentioned in the list (see Question 4).

QUESTION 4 RANKING QUESTION

Please indicate in the boxes provided which features you believe are the most important when visiting our superstore (1 indicating the most important, 2 the next most important, etc.) Please leave blank those features that have no importance at all.

Ease of car parking	☐
Low prices	☐
Friendly staff	☐
Store loyalty card	☐
Variety of goods	☐
Other (please specify)	☐

Scale questions: Scale or rating questions are used to measure a variable, and comprise four types of scale: **nominal, ordinal, interval** and **ratio**. A common type is the Likert scale on which respondents are asked to indicate how strongly they agree or disagree with a series of statements (see Question 5). This is an example of an ordinal scale. Further details of all these scales are presented in Chapter 17. Most Likert scales use either a four- or five-point scale.

QUESTION 5   SCALE QUESTION (ORDINAL)

As a loyal electricity customer we would like to know your views on the service we provide. Please put one ✓ for each of the following statements

	Strongly Agree	Agree	Disagree	Strongly Disagree
I have been pleased with the emergency 24-hour call out service	☐	☐	☐	☐
Electricity prices have been competitive with gas prices	☐	☐	☐	☐

Other forms of scaling can also be used. The number of response categories, for example, can be changed. Common formats are 'True/False', 'Yes/No'. Another approach would be to get respondents to mark a point on a continuum. Question 6 seeks responses on the quality of helpline support. Czaja and Blair (2005) warn, however, that this approach can lead to complexities at the data analysis stage. For example, do we calculate the average rating; combine parts of the scale into high, medium and low categories; or use a threshold that indicates a trend in one direction or another?

QUESTION 6   CONTINUUM SCALE

Please circle one number that reflects your opinion of our helpline support

Quick	1 2 3 4 5 6 7 8 9 10	Slow
Friendly	1 2 3 4 5 6 7 8 9 10	Discourteous
Informative	1 2 3 4 5 6 7 8 9 10	Confusing

Oppenheim (1992) provides a useful table comparing the advantages and disadvantages of open and closed questions, reproduced in Table 13.3. Note that often a questionnaire will use a mixture of both open and closed questions. Indeed, it is often useful to follow up a closed question with an invitation to add comments.

SEQUENCING QUESTIONS

There should be a logical flow to the sequence of questions, just as you would expect in a formal written text. Such a flow will aid the respondent in understanding

Table 13.3
The advantages
and disadvantages
of open and closed
questions

Source: Adapted
from Oppenheim,
1992

ADVANTAGES	DISADVANTAGES
Open questions	
Freedom and spontaneity of the answers	Time-consuming
Opportunity to probe	In interviews: costly of interviewer time
Useful for testing hypotheses about ideas or awareness	Demand more effort from respondents
Closed questions	
Require little time	Loss of spontaneous response
No extended writing	Bias in answer categories
Low cost	Sometimes too crude
Easy to process	May irritate respondents
Make group comparison easy	
Useful for testing specific hypotheses	

individual questions and the overall purpose of the questionnaire. One way of designing the flow of questions is to use a flowchart, as shown in Figure 13.2.

Oppenheim (1992) points out that after reading the accompanying documentation that tells them all about the survey, respondents may be quite eager to answer some of the questions. Therefore, the last sort of question they want

Figure 13.2
Flowchart for
planning of question
sequences

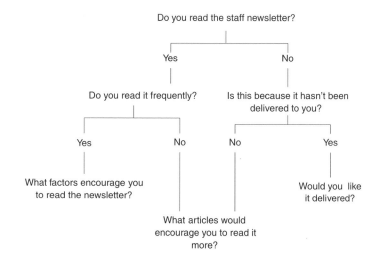

to see is what is presented in many surveys – a list of personal questions about age, gender, rank, status (work and marital, etc.). These types of questions should be kept to nearer the end of the questionnaire, and should be preceded by a short statement explaining that this data is needed for making statistical comparisons, so the respondent's help would be appreciated. De Vaus (2002) argues that questions that should come first include those that are easily answered, factual questions and those that are obviously key to the purposes of the survey. Indeed, as Dillman (2007) points out, if the covering documentation has highlighted the key themes of the questionnaire, it is sensible to start with questions that deal directly with the theme. He also suggests that special attention be given to the first question since this will help determine whether the questionnaire is answered or put in the wastepaper bin.

Other useful advice includes going from easy to more difficult questions and from more concrete to abstract. Any sensitive questions should be left until the end. Where possible, a variety of answering formats should be used to provide interest, some additional advice on the sequencing of questions being:

- Is the answer to the question likely to be influenced by the content of preceding questions?

- Is the question led up to in a natural way? Is it in correct psychological order?

- Does the question come too early or too late from the point of view of arousing interest and receiving sufficient attention, avoiding resistance, etc?

> ## Activity 13.3
>
> Take a questionnaire that has been designed either by yourself or a colleague (it could be the one you used for Activity 13.1). Evaluate individual questions. Are they clear, concise and unambiguous? Would the intended audience be able to answer them? Are instructions on answering the questions clear? Is the sequencing of questions appropriate?

PROVIDING RESPONSE CATEGORIES

Asking a question like 'What employment sector did you work in before your present job?' is asking for trouble. It might both confuse the respondent ('What do they mean – sector?') or the respondent might be uncertain as to whether their classification is acceptable. So, for the question cited, it would be appropriate to provide a list of categories such as: Finance, Retailing, Education, Commerce, Agriculture, Other (please specify), etc. Providing these categories also yields a standardized set of responses that will make the data easier to analyse. Note that we have been careful to provide an 'Other' category, just in case. Some common

Table 13.4
Common response
category quantifiers
Source: Adapted
from Czaja and
Blair, 2005

CATEGORY	QUANTIFIERS
Opinions	Very satisfied/Somewhat satisfied/Somewhat dissatisfied/Very dissatisfied
	Very important/Somewhat important/Not too important/Not at all important
	Oppose/Support
Knowledge	Very familiar/Somewhat familiar/Not too familiar/Not at all familiar
	True/False
Frequency of events or behaviour	Always/Frequently/Seldom/Never
	Often/Sometimes/Rarely/Never
	Per day/Per week/Per month/Per year/Never
Ratings	Excellent/Good/Fair/Poor
	Got better/Got worse/Stayed the same
	Very fair/Fair/Unfair/Very unfair
	High/Medium/Low

response category statements are provided by Czaja and Blair (2005) and are summarized in Table 13.4.

QUESTIONNAIRE LAYOUT

One way of improving the rate of response to a questionnaire is by making it as attractive as possible. Hence, factors such as the general layout, choice of paper, line spacing and answering directions should be considered. So, the way of answering multiple-choice questions should be consistent throughout – for example, ticking boxes or circling numbers. Boxes or lines should be provided for open question responses. It is best to avoid making the questionnaire too cramped as this can be off-putting to respondents.

Dillman (2007) warns against unconventional designs, such as printing on both sides of paper with a staple to bind the pages together, or using landscape (horizontal) orientation. He argues strongly for a booklet format which, he says, is understood automatically by respondents. With this format, people start on page 1 and turn over to page 2 which is to the left of page 3. If the budget is tight, then it is legitimate to print on one side only and to staple sheets together. Carroll (1994) suggests that other typographical issues require careful consideration such as:

- Putting boxes around groups of questions.

- Shading multiple-choice questions.

- Selecting clean, clear typefaces.

- Using lines to take the respondent's eye from question to response.

- Numbering all questions and sections.

WRITING A SET OF INSTRUCTIONS

Most questionnaires will also contain, probably at the start, a set of instructions for completing them. This is important, and it should not be assumed that respondents will all know that they should, say, only tick one choice for each question. Unless instructions are made absolutely specific, it is almost certain that questionnaires will be returned completed incorrectly resulting in a loss of data. Cohen and Manion (2000) even suggest that with postal questionnaires it is advisable to repeat the instructions. Carroll (1994) supports this idea, arguing that providing additional instructions for groups of questions will help the response rate.

One of the problems with instructions is that they are either not read or are misread. Dillman (2007) suggests that respondents can be helped by careful use of typography and design. De Vaus (2002) suggests that, to improve the flow of a questionnaire, the following instructions should be considered:

- General instructions, dealing with the purpose of the questionnaire, assurances of confidentiality, how and when to return the questionnaire.

- Section introductions when the questionnaire is divided into subsections.

- Question instructions (e.g. tick only one response).

- 'Go to' instructions.

Dillman (2007) refers to these 'go to' instructions as 'skip instructions' and argues that they are important because they avoid respondents reading or completing questions that do not apply to them. But in self-administered questionnaires the problem is getting people to read the skip instructions correctly. Figure 13.3 illustrates a poorly constructed skip question and an improved version. Note that in the improved version, the 'No' response is presented first and respondents re-routed if necessary. Instructions are in bold and a pointed finger used for emphasis.

Similarly, the use of spacing can help to improve the understanding of a question, as illustrated in Figure 13.4. See how a quite densely packed question is laid out so that different elements are separated.

Figure 13.3
Uses of typography
and emphasis to aid
the functionality of
skip instructions
(adapted from
Dillman, 2007)

A problem skip question

12   Do you use public transport to get to work?

  ❑   Yes (Go to 13)
  ❑   No (Go to 18)

13   How long does your journey take you (in minutes)?

An improved skip question

12   Do you use public transport to get to work?

  ❑   No ☞ (**Skip to 18**)
  ❑   Yes

13   How long does your journey take you (in minutes)?

Figure 13.4
The uses of spacing
to help identify
groups of elements

A problem question

1   When you joined the company, what was your major ambition (a) promotion; (b) job satisfaction; (c) a rise in salary; (d) learning a new skill; (e) None of these? Mark.

2   How long have you now worked for the company? _____ Years

An improved question

❶   When you joined the company, what was your major ambition? Mark one answer.

  ❑   Promotion
  ❑   Job satisfaction
  ❑   A rise in salary
  ❑   Learning a new skill
  ❑   None of these

❷   How long have you now worked for the company?
    _____ Years

TOP TIP 13.3

Researchers who are new to questionnaire design tend to give little thought to helping respondents in completing the questionnaire. Re-read your questionnaire. Is it clear how a respondent should complete it? If, say, you want just one response from a list of five choices, have you stated this? Ask for feedback on the quality of instructions at the piloting stage.

DESIGNING INTERNET AND WEB-BASED QUESTIONNAIRES

As we saw in Chapter 9, the advent of the Internet and World Wide Web has transformed the way in which many surveys are conducted. Given that many organizations, particularly larger ones, have good connections to the Internet, the use of online surveys is especially advantageous in terms of convenience and access to large samples and populations.

EMAIL QUESTIONNAIRES

Email questionnaires (often used as part of surveys) are relatively easy to compose but offer fewer opportunities to provide visual stimulation or interactivity. It is difficult, for example, to use the kind of skip patterns discussed in the previous section. On the whole, the principles of email questionnaire design are very similar to many of those concerned with paper-based design. Dillman (2007) suggests the following strategies:

- Use multiple contacts (e.g. preliminary email, questionnaire email, 'thank-you' email, etc.)

- Personalize all email contacts, do not send them via a listserv. One reason for this is that a response would be sent to all others on the list – so much for confidentiality!

- Keep the covering (introductory) text brief, avoiding the need for the respondent to scroll down the page.

- Suggest alternative ways to respond, such as printing out the questionnaire and completing it by hand. Some respondents may feel insecure about email responses, which can always be checked by an employer.

- Limit column width to 70 characters to decrease the likelihood of text wrapping around to the next line.

- Start with an easy but interesting question.

- Provide instructions on completing questions, such as putting an X inside the brackets.

- In the case of non-response, include a replacement questionnaire with the reminder message.

WEB-BASED QUESTIONNAIRES

Web-based questionnaires offer many facilities for questionnaire design that are not available in traditional, paper-based formats, such as the use of drop-down menus, pop-up instruction boxes and sophisticated skip patterns. One of the more popular Web-based survey tools, SurveyMonkey, for example, offers the following functionality:

- A range of question types (including multiple choice, rating scales, drop-down menus).
- Question forcing (requiring the respondent to answer a question before they can proceed).
- Choices of colour, size and style of font.
- Tracking facilities to see who responds and follow-up messages to those who do not.
- Data downloaded into either spreadsheet or database format ready for analysis.

ON THE WEB 13.1

Go to the SurveyMonkey website at:

http://www.surveymonkey.com/

To understand more about how the software works, take a look at one of the video tutorials.

However, the very flexibility of the Web makes the opportunities for making design errors all the greater, which may, in turn, affect response rates. It is extremely easy to get 'lost' in a website, at which point many users exit the site quickly. Hence, following some simple design instructions is all the more important. Dillman (2007) makes a number of recommendations:

- Introduce the Web questionnaire with a welcome screen that is motivational, that emphasizes the ease of responding, and shows how to proceed.
- Provide a login to limit access to the site to the selected sample.
- Choose a first question that is easy and stimulating to answer.
- Present questions in a similar format to that used in a conventional questionnaire.
- Use colour appropriately and not just for the sake of it.
- Unless you are sure that all respondents have the same screen configuration, test the Web pages on different screen resolutions and Web browsers to ensure that the appearance is always the same.
- Use drop-down boxes sparingly and identify each with a 'click here' instruction.

All questionnaires, whether paper-based, email or Web-based need careful piloting before dissemination to a wider audience. In the case of Web-based questionnaires, it is best if a paper-based version is piloted first to produce a final version ready for putting online. But once online this Internet version should also be piloted to see if respondents find it easy to use. Note that while your questionnaire may appear neat and tidy on your own screen, words may appear out of place on some users' screens if they are using a Web browser different to your own. Piloting using a variety of Web browsers is therefore a sensible step.

ON THE WEB 13.2

Take a look at the following website, which contains a wide variety of Web-based questionnaires:

http://www.accesscable.net/~infopoll/Library.htm

Now find examples of:

* Accompanying documentation, including information letters.
* Different question formats (open/closed; listing questions; category questions; ranking questions; scale questions).
* The use of skip questions.
* Face sheet information.
* The use of response category quantifiers.

Also take a look at Sample Web Questionnaires at:

http://www.surveysystem.com/websurveys.htm

PILOTING QUESTIONNAIRES

Research instruments such as interview schedules can be modified if certain questions appear to be ineffective, but questionnaires, particularly if used for large surveys, are a 'one-shot' attempt at data gathering. It is therefore essential that they are accurate, unambiguous and simple to complete. As we saw in Chapter 9, piloting is vital. Judicious piloting will reduce the incidence of non-response to the questionnaire. Gillham (2000) suggests that it is wise to pilot at least 50 per cent more questions than you need so that confusing or unreliable questions can be thrown out at this stage. What else should be piloted? Well, basically, anything and everything! But you could consider the:

* Instructions given to respondents.
* Style and wording of any accompanying letter.

- Content of face-sheet data, that is, respondents' names, addresses, etc.

- Formality or informality of the questionnaire in terms of tone, presentation, etc.

- Length of the questionnaire – if too long, is the response rate likely to be reduced?

- Sequence of questions.

- Quality of individual questions in terms of whether they are understood and answered in a way that was intended.

- Scales and question format used, for example, Likert scales, Yes/No responses, etc.

Oppenheim (1992) even suggests that the tables for the data analysis phase of the final report should be piloted (that is, dummy tables written) before the questionnaire is issued. This might highlight new issues or problems that could require consideration and inclusion in the questionnaire itself.

De Vaus (2002) suggests that evaluation is important in a number of design areas, including checking for:

- The ability of a question to discriminate. If everyone responds with the same answer to a question this is often not very useful, since one purpose of using a questionnaire is to examine the diversity of views on a subject.

- The validity and reliability of questions.

- Redundancy, so if it is found that two questions measure the same thing, one of them can be dropped.

- The response set. With some respondents, a pattern of answering Likert-type questions quickly sets in. So, if they tick 'Strongly agree' for, say, the first three questions, this response becomes habitual and they tick all remaining questions with this response. To avoid this happening, it is wise to alternate responses, for example, by using a negative statement on which the respondent will have to disagree.

Who can help you with piloting? Gillham (2000) advises trying out your initial list of questions with one or two people who are not part of the target group. Explain that you are trying to get the questions right, and that they should indicate where a question is unclear. Even sit with them as they look through the questions, noting their comments and your own observations on a spare questionnaire. Once you have amended the questionnaire, re-trial it with another two or three people who are similar to, but not part of, the target group. The procedure is the same, but this time also ask for improvements, deletions and additions. You are now ready to start designing the layout of the questionnaire.

Of course, if the survey is delivered via the Web, in addition to the issues raised above a whole new set of problems have to be faced. As we saw earlier, the design of Web-based surveys offers both flexibility but also opportunities to get things spectacularly wrong. As in any software development, it is sensible to design and pilot a prototype of the final site, so that user problems can be identified. Issues to look at here include the use of colour, on-screen instructions, navigational routes (especially for skip questions) and how respondents handle inputting their responses to questions (do they know what to do?). Observation at the piloting stage with respondents actually using the website questionnaire may also reveal some entirely unanticipated problems. Case Study 13.2 provides an example of how piloting can help to improve a questionnaire.

CASE STUDY 13.2   QUESTIONNAIRE PILOTING TO GET IT RIGHT

A research project is set up to study public attitudes towards the decriminalization of certain categories of drugs. The study starts with the question:

Would you say that most people think that certain 'soft' drugs should be decriminalized?

1. Yes
2. No
3. Don't know/not sure

Piloting the questions reveals that:

• Most respondents cannot report in general what 'most people' think, they only know what they, personally, think.
• Some people did not understand the concept 'decriminalize'.
• Some could not differentiate between 'soft' and 'hard' drugs.
• Respondents resisted selecting between just 'Yes' and 'No' and wanted an opportunity to express their feelings between alternatives.

The question then was modified to read:

Do you think that people arrested for the possession of drugs such as cannabis are sentenced fairly: (a) almost always; (b) most of the time; (c) some of the time; (d) never?

Piloting shows that this is an improvement because it asks people what they themselves think, and it is more specific about the type of drugs being discussed. It also provides a range of categories. Its disadvantage is that it has become too specific and shifted away from the central theme of the original question, decriminalization.

The third and final version becomes:

(Cont'd)

Please indicate your view on each of the following statements:

Fining someone for possession of cannabis is: Very fair, Fair, Unfair, Very unfair.

Imprisoning someone for possession of cannabis is: Very fair, Fair, Unfair, Very unfair.

Fining someone for dealing in cannabis is: Very fair, Fair, Unfair, Very unfair.

Imprisoning someone for dealing in cannabis is: Very fair, Fair, Unfair, Very unfair.

Activity 13.4

Take one or a small number of questions from a questionnaire you are designing and pilot it/them with a sample audience. Amend the question(s) on the basis of the responses and advice given. Pilot the amended question(s). Amend them again. How similar is the third version of the question(s) to what you started with?

MAINTAINING QUALITY: VALIDITY AND RELIABILITY

Since questionnaires are one of the most popular instruments for data gathering, you will not be surprised that we pause yet again to discuss the issues of validity and reliability.

VALIDITY

We saw earlier in this chapter that the validity of a questionnaire can be affected by the wording of the questions it contains. But even if individual questions are valid, a poor sequencing of questions or confusing structure or design of the questionnaire can all threaten its validity.

The questionnaire must cover the research issues both in terms of content and detail. Recall Figure 6.6 in Chapter 6 which shows the dangers of a questionnaire not covering the research area (Zone of Neglect) and some questions being asked that are irrelevant to the study (Zone of Invalidity). It should be noted that asking spurious, irrelevant questions increases the length of a questionnaire, which in turn, may reduce the number of responses. If the response rate becomes too low, this may limit the generalizability of the findings, and hence external validity.

As we saw in Chapter 9, two threats to the validity of postal questionnaires are the extent to which respondents complete the questionnaires accurately, and the problem of non-response. Accuracy can be checked by interviewing a sample of respondents, and probing for how carefully they have answered the questionnaire. For non-response, again follow-up interviews can be used for those who did not reply, and their responses compared with those who did answer the questionnaire to see if the two sets of responses are similar. If they are, it suggests that the responding and non-responding populations are the same, and there is no threat from this source to the validity of data collected.

TOP TIP 13.4

The validity of questionnaires is greatly assisted if you start from the basis of a set of clear and concise research questions. You can then formulate, say, three or four questions in the questionnaire that seek to gather data for each research question. In this way, you are achieving a tight match between your questionnaire and what you are attempting to research. If you find a question within the questionnaire that does not address one of your research question themes, ask yourself: should this question be here? Do I need it? If the answer is, 'No', eliminate the question. But if the answer is, 'Yes', you will need to return to your research questions and modify or add to them so that your new question is addressed.

RELIABILITY

In terms of questionnaire design, a high reliability means that if you measured something today, you should get the same results at some other time, assuming that what is being measured has not changed (Black, 1993). As we discussed in Chapter 6, reliability is a measure of consistency and can include measures of

- Stability (over time).
- Equivalence (administering two versions of a test instrument to the same people on the same day).
- Inter-judge reliability.

The extent of this consistency is measured by a reliability coefficient using a scale from 0.00 (very unreliable) to 1.00 (perfectly reliable). In practice, a score of 0.9 is generally deemed to be acceptable. There are several ways in which this coefficient can be calculated. One of the most common is Cronback's alpha, which presents the average of all possible split-half correlations, and so measures the consistency of all items, both globally and individually.

QUESTIONNAIRE ADMINISTRATION

Even the best-designed questionnaire will not create an impact if care is not taken with its administration, one of the fundamental objectives of which is to maximize the return rate. We examine next some of the techniques associated with different kinds of survey methods that were discussed in Chapter 9.

SELF-ADMINISTERED QUESTIONNAIRES

Postal questionnaires

It is usual for a questionnaire to be accompanied by a letter. Getting the content, style and tone of this letter right is just as important as achieving the quality of these elements in the questionnaire. Indeed, since respondents will probably read the letter first, it could be argued that it is even more important. It is essential that you get the respondent's name, initials and preferred title absolutely right. Documentation sent to women should usually be titled Ms unless you know that they prefer another form.

The letter should cover issues such as the aims of the research, its importance (particularly its importance to the respondent's company or organization, if applicable), how long it will take to complete, and an assurance of confidentiality. The name of the sponsor or researcher should appear on the letterhead, and details of where to return the questionnaire should appear both on the letter as well as the questionnaire itself. Above all, the letter should be as brief and concise as possible, and should contain a note of thanks for the questionnaire's completion. If there are instructions that you particularly need to emphasize, state them as part of a postscript as people often notice these below the main text.

Saunders et al. (2007) list six further techniques that researchers will find useful:

- Ensure that questionnaires and letters are printed and envelopes properly addressed.

- Make a pre-survey contact with recipients either by email, post or phone to warn them that the questionnaire is on its way.

- Post the questionnaire and covering letter to arrive at a convenient time.

- One week after the initial posting, send out the first follow-up reminder letters to all recipients.

- Send the second follow-up reminder to those who have not responded after three weeks.

- Post out a third follow-up if the response rate is low.

Table 13.5
Likely timing of
responses for
postal survey

DISTRIBUTION	TIMING (P-DAY)*	RESPONSES
First posting	P-day + 10 days	50 per cent of final return
First reminder	P-day + 17 days	80 per cent of final return
Second reminder	P-day + 27 days	A few more

* P-day = Postal-day, i.e. the initial posting.

Of course, before reminders can be sent, it is necessary to know who has not responded. A useful technique is to number the questionnaires, but this will not work if anonymity has been promised to respondents. In this situation, a 'scatter-gun' approach may be necessary, reminding all respondents but apologizing in advance to those who have already responded.

When sending reminders, emphasize the importance of the study and do not imply that the initial response has been poor – imply the contrary, if anything (providing this is truthful). When prompting, it is important not to be apologetic. Enclose another copy of the questionnaire and another stamped addressed envelope in case people had not received or had 'mislaid the original'. In terms of responses and timings, Table 13.5 suggests a typical pattern. It can be seen that after just over two weeks you will have received about 80 per cent of what will prove to be your final total. You will know by this point whether your final return rate is going to be successful, or not.

Postal questionnaires should be sent by first-class post and include a stamped addressed envelope. If the questionnaire is going to an individual in their home, Gillham (2000) suggests Thursday as the best day for posting as people have more time at weekends. Letters to organizations should be sent on Mondays or Tuesdays so that they can be completed at work.

Delivery and collection questionnaires

Since questionnaires are to be collected, clearly one of the prime factors is to ensure that respondents know exactly when this will occur. Saunders et al. (2007) advise that, when conducting research in an organization, response rates can be dramatically improved by calling all respondents to a meeting in the organization's time, explaining the purpose of the questionnaire, and getting it completed before people leave the meeting. A box near the exit to the room for collecting questionnaires may help to assure confidentiality.

Online questionnaires

As we saw earlier, online questionnaires can be administered either by email or via the Web. For emails, it is relatively easy to obtain people's email addresses, but to contact a sample of respondents 'cold' would risk the accusation of 'spamming', that is, sending unsolicited messages. Another danger is that anonymity will be lost as respondents can be identified by their email addresses.

Nevertheless, emails can be used effectively for surveys either by including the questions in the main body of the email or sending the questionnaire as an attached document. Including questions in the body of an email message makes the questionnaire simple to return, but there is little opportunity for using the kind of layout and design that encourages the completion of a questionnaire.

If you are, say, conducting a survey within an organization that uses one software application standard, then you may be able to attach the document in a word processed application version that can be read by all. If the survey is cross-organization there will be risks that not everyone will be able to read the attachment, so including questions in an email is the safest approach. After this, procedures for sending reminders are the same as for postal questionnaires.

INTERVIEWER-ADMINISTERED QUESTIONNAIRES

Structured interview

Since structured interviews involve face-to-face contact, one of the essential administrative factors is arranging meetings with respondents, and improving the chances of respondents turning up for the interview. This chance will be increased if respondents are contacted in advance of the meeting and advised of dates, times and location, etc. If the structured interview involves some open as well as closed questions, it might be advisable to tape record the interview since transcribing verbal dialogue is difficult unless you are skilled at shorthand. The use of tape recorders involves ethical issues including confidentiality, so you must ask permission before using one. Once interviews are completed, times for any return visits should be arranged.

Telephone questionnaire

For telephone questionnaires it is important that respondents know when they are to be interviewed, so they must be contacted by post and given clear details of dates and times (including the likely length of the interview). When calls are unsuccessful, the reasons should be noted, such as the fact that the respondent has moved or did not pick up the telephone. In the latter case, call three more times at different times of the day.

SUMMARY

- Designing individual questions involves a rigorous process of analysis to avoid ambiguity, leading questions, double questions and simply misleading questions.

- Questions must be clearly linked to the purpose of the research (as specified in the accompanying letter or documentation).

- Questionnaires should start with questions that are easy to answer, interesting and transparently linked to the purpose of the research.

- Questionnaire layout and the use of typography can make a questionnaire easier to complete and more appealing to respondents, enhancing the response rate.

- Clear, well set out instructions on completing the questionnaire can also boost the response rate.

- Web and email questionnaires offer a new and potentially powerful tool, but also require additional design skills.

- All questionnaires, whether paper-based, email or Web-based, require thorough piloting which will include evaluation of accompanying documentation, instructions, individual questions, types of question, question sequencing, the use of scales and skip instructions – basically, everything!

∷// SUMMARY OF WEB LINKS /

http://www.accesscable.net/~infopoll/library.htm

http://www.surveysystem.com/websurveys.htm

FURTHER READING

Colton, D. and Covert, R.W. (2007) *Designing and Constructing Instruments for Social Research and Evaluation*. San Fransisco, CA: Jossey-Bass. An easy-to-read and accessible book for students who are new to questionnaire design as well as the more experienced. Contains guidelines for reviewing and revising questionnaires to enhance their validity and reliability.

Gillham, B. (2000) *Developing a Questionnaire*. London: Continuum. A small and simply written book that provides an excellent introduction to the subject. Includes chapters on questionnaire design, distribution, data presentation and the analysis of open and closed questions.

De Vaus, D.A. (2002) *Surveys in Social Research*, 5th edn. London: George Allen & Unwin. See specifically Chapter 7 on constructing questionnaires and Chapter 8 on administering questionnaires.

SUGGESTED ANSWERS FOR ACTIVITY 13.2

1. An *ambiguous* question since the categories overlap. Also *impertinent* in two ways – the fact that age is asked for (why is this necessary?) and the curt way in which this is demanded.

2. *Vague* and therefore probably unreliable.

3. *Double question* and therefore also ambiguous.

4. *Loaded question*.

5. *Double negative*. It also contains the phrase 'best practice' – what does this mean?

6. Demands either *memory recall* (if the person is in a position to know the answer) or an expectation that they have the *knowledge*, which may not be the case.

7. *Impertinent*.

8. *No instructions*. It is unclear how to complete an answer – ticking or circling? The fact that only one answer can be given is assumed, but should be made explicit.

Finally, the questionnaire contains no introductory paragraph nor explanation of its purpose. It asks for respondents to give their name, which does not appear necessary, and asks for their salary, which is both unnecessary and impertinent. It offers no assurances of confidentiality, does not explain what is going to be done with the information and is unclear as to where it can be returned (and when).

Collecting Primary Data: Interviewing

DAVID E. GRAY

CHAPTER OBJECTIVES

After reading this chapter you will be able to:

● Describe and choose between structured, semi-structured, non-directive, focused and informal interviews on the basis of the objectives of the research.

● Select between using interviews and self-completed questionnaires.

● Produce valid and reliable interview schedules.

● Conduct an interview skilfully, tactfully, safely and ethically.

An interview is a conversation between people in which one person has the role of researcher. Very often, the interviewer will have on hand a set of written questions which are posed in a structured and methodical fashion (a structured interview). Alternatively, these questions might only be used as an *aide-mémoire*, to remind the researcher of the key areas that need probing. In either case, interviews often make use of questionnaires, so this chapter has much in common with Chapter 13. However, whereas the previous chapter focused on the design of questionnaires, this chapter looks at one way, the interview, in which they can be used. Hence, we are shifting from product (the questionnaire) to process.

Interviewing may pose challenges because of the human interaction between the interviewer and respondent. The interviewer has to pose questions (in either a structured, semi-structured or unstructured format), listen to (and data capture) the responses and pose new questions. If the interview format is relatively unstructured, then these questions have to be constructed 'on the fly'. The interviewer may also not only be listening to the verbal responses, but be noting other elements of the interview process such as the body language of the interviewee. However, despite the challenges involved, the well-conducted interview is a powerful tool for eliciting rich data on people's views, attitudes and the meanings that underpin their lives and behaviours.

In this chapter, we will examine some of the different interview approaches, and look at some of the essential interviewing skills you will need to acquire. We will also look, briefly, at telephone interviews, and conclude with some thoughts on ethical issues in interviewing.

WHY USE INTERVIEWS?

There are a number of situations in which the interview is the most logical research technique. If the objective of the research, for example, is largely exploratory, involving, say, the examination of feelings or attitudes, then interviews may be the best approach. The use of semi-structured interviews also allows the researcher to 'probe' for more detailed responses where the respondent is asked to clarify what they have said. This phenomenological approach, then, is concerned with the *meanings* that people ascribe to phenomena. As Arksey and Knight (1999) comment:

> Interviewing is a powerful way of helping people to make explicit things that have hitherto been implicit – to articulate their tacit perceptions, feelings and understandings. (Arksey and Knight, 1999: 32)

Interviews are also useful where it is likely that people may enjoy talking about their work rather than filling in questionnaires. An interview allows them an opportunity to reflect on events without having to commit themselves in writing, often because they feel the information may be confidential. They may never have met the researcher and may feel concerned about some of the uses to which the information may be put. Also, with questionnaires the concise meaning of a question may not always be clear, whereas with an interview meanings can be immediately clarified. Potentially, at least, interviews can produce a greater response rate for these reasons.

As Cohen and Manion (2000) point out, the interview can serve a number of distinct purposes. First, it can be used as the means of gathering information about a person's knowledge, values, preferences and attitudes. Secondly, it can be used to test out a hypothesis or to identify variables and their relationships. Thirdly, it can be used in conjunction with other research techniques, such as surveys, to follow up issues. For example, a survey by a clothing company might find a relationship between age and the tendency to purchase certain kinds of clothes. The company might then follow this up with structured interviews among a sample of people from the original survey to explore in more depth the values and motivation behind these buying patterns.

Interviews are also preferable to questionnaires where questions are either open-ended or complex, or where the logical order of questions is difficult to predetermine. But whether an interview is successful in eliciting the range and depth of answers required will depend in large part on the skills of the interviewer.

Essentially, the interview is the favoured approach where:

- There is a need to attain highly personalized data.
- Opportunities for probing are required.
- A good return rate is important.
- Respondents are not fluent in the native language of the country, or where they have difficulties with written language.

In contrast, standardized questionnaires are more powerful where:

- Large numbers of respondents must be reached.
- Better reliability of data is desired.

A summary of some of the pros and cons of interviews and self-administered questionnaires is presented in Table 14.1.

SELECTING INTERVIEW APPROACHES

There are several different types of interview, so the choice of interview technique will depend in large part on the aims and objectives of your research. Indeed, one of the purposes of the interview may be to determine these research objectives themselves. There may also be occasions when more than one interview type is used for a research project.

Interviews may be divided into five categories:

- Structured interviews.
- Semi-structured interviews.
- Non-directive interviews.
- Focused interviews.
- Informal conversational interviews.

We will look at each of the five interview approaches in turn.

Table 14.1
Comparison of
interviews and
self-administered
questionnaires
Source: Adapted
from Arksey and
Knight, 1999

CHARACTERISTICS	INTERVIEWS	SELF-ADMINISTERED QUESTIONNAIRES
Provide information about	As for questionnaires, but potential for exploring in more depth.	Attitudes, motivation, opinions, events.
Best at	Exploring stories and perspectives of informants.	Testing the validity of a hypothesis.
Richness of responses	Dialogue between interviewer and respondent allows for nuances to be captured and for questions to be clarified and adapted or improvised. Long interviews common.	Questions cannot be modified once printed, and nuances of respondent's voice cannot be heard. Long questionnaires rarely acceptable.
Ethics	Interviewers know whom they have interviewed, although transcripts can be anonymized.	Anonymous questionnaire responses can be assured.
Sample size	With the exception of telephone interviews, less suitable for wide coverage.	If generalizing to a population, samples often have to be large.
Time cost Planning and design	Devising interview guide, piloting, etc., may be less of an issue.	Devising questionnaire (checking validity and reliability), piloting, etc. may be very time-consuming.
Operation	Arranging interviews, travelling, establishing rapport – all time-consuming.	Distributing questionnaire.
Data transcription	Typically 7–10 hours for 1 hour interview.	Usually swift, especially where optical readers are used.
Data analysis	Time needed usually underestimated.	Usually swift (unless there are many open-ended questions).
Money costs	High if includes interviewers, travel costs, tapes, batteries, transcription of tapes.	Mainly costs of printing, distributing and receiving questionnaires. Looks cheap per questionnaire, but looks more expensive if return rate low.

STRUCTURED INTERVIEWS

Structured interviews are used to collect data for quantitative analysis, and use pre-prepared questionnaires and standardized questions, that is, the same questions are posed to all respondents. Responses are recorded by the interviewer on a standardized schedule, and, while there is some interaction between interviewer and respondent, this is kept to a minimum. Ideally, questions are read out in the same tone of voice so as not to influence answers. Structured interviews are often used as a precursor for more open-ended discussions such as non-directive interviews.

SEMI-STRUCTURED INTERVIEWS

Semi-structured interviews are non-standardized, and are often used in qualitative analysis. The interviewer has a list of issues and questions to be covered, but may not deal with all of them in each interview. The order of questions may also change depending on what direction the interview takes. Indeed, additional questions may be asked, including some which were not anticipated at the start of the interview, as new issues arise. Responses will be documented by note-taking or possibly by tape-recording the interview.

The semi-structured interview allows for probing of views and opinions where it is desirable for respondents to expand on their answers. This is vital when a phenomenological approach is being taken where the objective is to explore subjective meanings that respondents ascribe to concepts or events. Such probing may also allow for the diversion of the interview into new pathways which, while not originally considered as part of the interview, help towards meeting the research objectives.

NON-DIRECTIVE INTERVIEWS

Non-directive interviews are used to explore an issue or topic in depth and questions are not, generally, pre-planned. Clearly, though, the researcher must have a notion of the objectives of the research and, therefore, what issues are going to be addressed in the interview. The format of the interview will be such that the respondents are allowed to talk freely around the subject. The input of the interviewer is mainly confined to checking on any doubtful points and rephrasing answers to check for accuracy of understanding. Like semi-structured interviews, non-directive interviews tend to collect data for qualitative analysis.

FOCUSED INTERVIEWS

The focused interview is based upon the respondent's subjective responses to a known situation in which they have been involved. The interviewer has prior knowledge of this situation and is, thus, able to re-focus respondents if they drift

Table 14.2
Characteristics
of structured,
semi-structured
and unstructured
interviews

Source: Adapted
from Arksey and
Knight, 1999

STRUCTURED	SEMI-STRUCTURED	UNSTRUCTURED (NON-DIRECTIVE, FOCUSED AND INFORMAL CONVERSATION)
Quick to data capture	Slow and time-consuming to data capture and analyse.	As for semi-structured.
Use of random sampling	The longer the interview, the more advisable it is to use random sampling.	Opportunity and snowball sampling often used. In organizations, targeting of 'key informants'.
Interview schedule followed exactly	Interviewer refers to a guide containing mixture of open and closed questions. Interviewer improvises using own judgement.	Interviewer uses *aide-mémoire* of topics for discussion and improvises.
Interviewer-led	Sometimes interviewer-led, sometimes informant-led.	Non-directive interviewing.
Easy to analyse	Quantitative parts easy to analyse.	Usually hard to analyse.
Tends to positivist view of knowledge	Mixture of positivist and non-positivist.	Non-positivist view of knowledge.
Respondents' anonymity easily guaranteed	Harder to ensure anonymity.	Researcher tends to know the informant.

away from the theme. An analogy would be the celebrity television interview in which the interviewer has already analysed the interviewee's autobiography and wishes to probe certain issues in more depth.

INFORMAL CONVERSATIONAL INTERVIEWS

The informal conversational interview relies on the spontaneous generation of questions as the interview progresses. This is the most open-ended form of interview technique. One of the advantages of this approach is the flexibility it offers in terms of what path the interview takes. Indeed, the interviewee may not even know an interview is taking place. This, though, will rule out the taking of notes during the interview. In cases where the fact that an interview is taking place *is* known, it is appropriate to take notes or to use a tape recorder.

One of the drawbacks of the conversational interview is the danger of the 'interviewer effect', that is, the interviewer may begin to influence the course and direction of the interview. Another disadvantage is that it may take some time before the interviewer has posed similar questions to the set of people being interviewed. Finally, the data collected through conversational interviews may be difficult to analyse because different questions have been asked of different people. As a result, the researcher will have to sift through the data to find emerging patterns.

A summary of the characteristics of the different types of interview is provided in Table 14.2.

> ## TOP TIP 14.1
>
> Non-directive, focused, and informal conversational interviews are great for collecting a large amount of qualitative data. However, before you decide on one of these approaches, make sure that you have decided on what approach you intend to adopt for data analysis.

DESIGNING CREDIBLE INTERVIEWS

One of the prime driving forces behind the design of interviews is the search for credibility by ensuring that the findings can be trusted, which includes issues of validity and reliability. But since interviews often come from a more qualitative perspective, it would be a mistake to apply these concepts rigidly. Instead, we might want to also make use of other indicators of credibility. We also need to ask some familiar questions about the extent to which the findings from the interview study can be generalized to a wider population.

VALIDITY

As we saw in Chapter 6, validity means that an instrument must measure what it was intended to measure. In the case of structured and semi-structured interviews, the issue of validity can be directly addressed by attempting to ensure that the question content directly concentrates on the research objectives. For informal conversational, focused and non-directive interviews, the issue of validity is more problematic because, by their very nature, the direction questions take will depend, in large part, on the responses of the interviewee. In a sense, instead of these approaches commencing with a rigid set of objectives, the subject matter emerges inductively from the interview itself. But the research will need to ensure that, if any research questions require addressing, this is achieved by the end of the interview.

According to Arksey and Knight (1999), validity is strengthened by:

- Using interview techniques that build rapport and trust, thus giving informants the scope to express themselves.

- Prompting informants to illustrate and expand on their initial responses.

- Ensuring that the interview process is sufficiently long for subjects to be explored in depth.

- Constructing interviewing schedules that contain questions drawn from the literature and from pilot work with respondents.

Another important issue of interview design is that of external validity, as we have seen, the extent to which findings from a study can be generalized. As we saw in Table 14.1, interviews are best used when the study is relatively small scale, since interviewing very large samples can be both expensive and time-consuming. Hence, external validity may be restricted. Arksey and Knight (1999), however, offer two practical principles that can be adopted in making a more plausible case for generalizing from interview findings:

- Try to select a sample that allows for a subject to be viewed from all relevant perspectives.

- Keep increasing the sample size, or sub-samples that represent different perspectives, until no new viewpoints are emerging from the data. A sample size of eight is often sufficient, although a survey should then be used to verify the data.

In a practical sense, this means that interview data need to be studied and analysed as they are collected, until it is clear that perspectives are being repeated and data saturation reached.

RELIABILITY AND BIAS

For a research instrument to be reliable it must *consistently* measure what it set out to measure. There is, at least, some potential for such consistency when an interview is standardized, with the same questions being asked of each respondent. However, even with standardized questions the issue of interviewer bias comes into play – does the interviewer ask the questions in the same way and with the same tone of voice with all respondents? In other words, what must be avoided is the 'interviewer effect'.

Interviewer bias can creep into the interview situation in many subtle, and not so subtle, ways. An interviewer, for example, might (unconsciously) give less time to shopfloor workers when conducting an interview than to supervisory and management grade employees. Similarly, prompt cards might be issued to shopfloor workers but not to 'more intelligent-looking' office workers. The only way to avoid this kind of systematic error is to standardize not only the interview schedule, but the behaviour of the interviewer. This is especially important if interviews are being conducted by more than one person. This does not mean that all interviews will be identical, since sometimes an interviewer will have to depart from a script to provide guidance or clarification. The skill of the interviewer is to provide such explanation without influencing the answer of the respondent.

Oppenheim (1992) suggests a number of ways in which bias occurs, namely:

- Departures from the interviewing instructions.
- Poor maintenance of rapport with the respondent.
- Altering factual questions.
- Rephrasing of attitude questions.
- Careless prompting.
- Biased probes.
- Asking questions out of sequence.
- Biased recording of verbatim answers.

One way of avoiding, or at least minimizing, interviewer bias is to require all interviewers to follow the same protocol. Hence, a set of guidelines might be drawn up which ask the interviewer to read the questions *exactly* as they are written, to repeat a question if asked, to accept a respondent's refusal to answer a question without any sign of irritation, and to probe in a non-directive manner. The following Case Study gives a practical example of how bias can occur if guidelines such as these are not followed.

CASE STUDY 14.1   INTERVIEWER BIAS – IT CAN DRIVE YOU TO DRINK!

In 1929, during the Great Depression, a New York researcher hired several interviewers to ask destitute people about their situation. Several years later the researcher reviewed some of the interviews. He noticed that the responses of one interviewer attributed most of the causes of destitution to economic factors such as unemployment, while the responses of another interviewer focused on problems with alcohol abuse. The researcher located the two interviewers and talked to them. He found that the first one was a socialist and the second, a prohibitionist. There was, thus, a strong suggestion that the causes of bias were located in the behaviour of the interviewers.

Source: Adapted from Beed and Stimson, 1985

Activity 14.1

Record a 'serious' television interview. From the content of the interview look for evidence of interviewer bias in the content of the questions, the way in which they are expressed, or the non-verbal behaviour of the interviewer. Political interviews, of course, are not necessarily intended to exemplify the degree of objectivity of a research interview, but they may illustrate the issue of bias more clearly.

MORE QUALITY INDICATORS

We have looked so far at validity and reliability as factors that enhance the credibility of an interview study. We need, however, to find some alternative, or at least additional, sources of quality. One important indicator is *consistency*, showing how the research has been conducted and the plausibility of the researcher's actions and analysis. The study should also provide evidence of *accuracy*, showing that the data is a fair representation of what informants have actually said. This might mean checking with interviewees that they have not been misinterpreted. Finally, the study must attempt to demonstrate *neutrality*, showing that the researcher is aware of the possible confounding effects of their own actions and perceptions and that these, as far as possible, have been accounted for.

INTERVIEWING SKILLS

Interviewing is a skill that must be learned through experience and practice. Of course, the respondent must first of all agree to be interviewed, and this might depend on a number of factors. Arksey and Knight (1999) suggest that getting an interview might depend upon:

- *Your status*: Are you 'internal' to the organization, or, say, someone completing a research project for an external client? If you are an internal researcher, how senior are you in the organization – and particularly, how senior compared to the interviewee?

- *The project*: Is the project of interest to the potential respondent? Is there a potential pay-off?

- *Yourself*: Do you seem trustworthy, personable and professional?

Once agreement is obtained, there is some preparatory work to be done, after which there is a number of techniques that help in the interviewing process.

GETTING STARTED

Preparing for the interview

Interviews cannot be rushed. Wengraf (2001) advises that you should arrive at least 30 minutes before the scheduled interview to make the necessary preparations and put aside at least an hour after the interview to make field notes. So, a 45-minute interview, for example, could take up to 2–3 hours to complete. Only by allowing yourself a clear stretch of time will you be assured that the interview will be conducted in a stress-free and unhurried fashion.

Wengraf sets out a schedule that should be followed, even before the day of the interview. About three weeks before, it is sometimes useful to get respondents to complete a pre-interview questionnaire dealing with demographic issues (for example, age, occupation and other details) so that the interview can focus on more substantive matters. Or you may have requested material from the respondent, and you will need time to read and reflect on it. About 7–10 days before the interview, you need to contact the respondent to make sure that they are still available, provide final confirmation about the exact location of the interview, and respond to any last-minute queries or concerns. The day before the interview you need to check that you have all the material you need at your disposal, and especially that you have an up-to-date version of your interview schedule. Obviously, make sure that any equipment, such as tape recorders, is working and that you have spare batteries, plenty of blank tapes, cables to the electricity supply and extension leads, note paper, pens and perhaps two bottles of mineral water in case you or the interviewee gets thirsty.

Preliminaries at the start of the interview

The first task of the interviewer is to explain the purpose of the interview, who the information is for, how the information is going to be handled (including issues of confidentiality), why the information is being collected and how it will be used. This should not require a long speech, but should be done quickly and simply. Above all, the importance of the information should be stressed. If the research has been commissioned by a particular division or department of the organization this should be made clear.

Also ensure that the seating arrangements are acceptable to both parties. Sitting closely and face-to-face can feel confrontational and threatening. It is usually best to face each other but at a slight angle. Having some furniture such as a table between the interviewer and respondent also provides something on which to place note-paper and creates safe 'distance' between the parties. The seating should also be arranged so that the interviewee cannot read forthcoming questions or any notes that are being made.

Building rapport with the respondent

Rapport means an understanding, one established on a basis of respect and trust between the interviewer and respondent. To establish a rapport it is particularly important to make the respondent relaxed and to get the interview off to a good start. This means you should:

- Describe how the interview will be conducted, how long it should last and the general subjects that are to be covered.

- Ask for permission to audio-tape the interview (and listen attentively for responses and note body language).

- Make guarantees of confidentiality.

- Ask if the respondent has any questions.

Rapport is described by Oppenheim (1992) as an elusive quality, and one that often only experienced and skilled interviewers possess. If an interviewer has little rapport, the respondent may be unwilling to answer questions or may cut the interview short. If the interviewer has too much rapport he or she may soon find themselves cast in the role of social worker or counsellor. The secret is to remain objective, professional and detached yet relaxed and friendly (who said that interviewing was easy?!)

TOP TIP 14.2

Before commencing an interview, it is very important to get your interviewee as relaxed as possible. When relaxed, they are more likely to provide you with rich, honest and illuminating data. Smile and be relaxed yourself. Make sure that the respondent knows about the purpose of the interview so that they are put at ease. Start off with easy questions or questions that the respondent is more likely to enjoy answering.

CONDUCTING THE INTERVIEW

Impression management

Oppenheim (1992) warns that an interviewer creates an impression on the respondent, even before he or she opens their mouth. Features such as general appearance, mode of dress, accent (see next section), hairstyle, ethnicity and social background may all play a part. Different respondents will be affected in different ways. If an interviewer wears an expensive business suit and interviews top management, this might be acceptable, but would it receive the same reaction in the machine shop? As Oppenheim warns, however, there are no hard and fast rules here. Production line workers might be quite intrigued about being interviewed by someone in a suit and tie.

The key is that the interviewer should be aware of the process of impression management, and should try to avoid giving expression to her or his own distinctive style. The aim is for bland, social neutrality.

Use of language

One problem that needs to be borne in mind is that words can have different meanings to different people. In the UK, especially, there are difficulties stemming from the way different social classes use vocabulary. The word 'dinner', for example, has a meaning that is different in middle- and working-class language. In a business setting, the word 'management' may have different connotations. Managers themselves, for example, may see it as a way of steering the company (in the interests of *all* employees) towards profit and efficiency. Some employees, however, may view the word more negatively in terms of interference and control from 'above'. The key is making use of language that is accessible to your audience.

Maintaining control of the interview

Since time is usually of the essence, it is important that the interviewer keeps control of the interview, minimizing long-winded responses and digressions. Patton (2002) argues that control is maintained by:

- Knowing what the interview is seeking to find out.
- Asking the right questions.
- Giving appropriate verbal and non-verbal feedback.

This means listening carefully to responses and channelling the interview back onto the right tracks if necessary. As Patton (2002) warns, it is not enough to have an excellent list of questions if the respondent is permitted to stray from the point.

Activity 14.2

Consider the following exchange:
Interviewer: Could you tell me something about your feelings when voluntary redundancies were called for.

Respondent: The request for redundancies came in a letter to all of us just before Christmas last year. They were asking for 200 people to go, out of a workforce of just 850. Quite a few people I know were very interested in the package on offer from day one.

Is the response an acceptable reply to the question?

Suggested answers are provided at the end of the chapter.

Verbal and non-verbal communication should be used to provide appropriate feedback. If, for example, the respondent is on-track, head nodding, the active taking of notes and the occasional verbal acknowledgement, should all help. Similarly, the use of a silent probe, remaining quiet when further elaboration of a point is desired, is quite valid. If the respondent is straying off the point, then the usual cues such as head nodding should cease, and a new question interjected as soon as the respondent hesitates. As Patton (2002) warns, it may sometimes become necessary to actively intervene with a statement such as: 'Can we stop there. I just want to check that I fully understanding something you just said'. Then ask a question aimed at a more targeted response. Do not be embarrassed about interrupting the interviewee if this means getting the interview back on track. But one of the skills of interviewing is knowing what is relevant and irrelevant as the interview progresses (so think back to your research objectives or general theme!).

Improvising when necessary

In semi-structured or unstructured interviews, improvisation may be the key to success. Arksey and Knight (1999) offer the following tips:

- Vary the question order to fit the flow of the interview.

- Vary the phrasing of the questions to help the conversation seem natural.

- Let the interview seem to go off track.

- Build trust and rapport by putting something of the interviewer's self into the interview, possibly by raising similar or different experiences.

Improvising, of course, is a skill that needs to be built through experience.

Activity 14.3

Having used a semi-structured or unstructured approach, go through the transcripts and note where you improvised. What was the result? How else could the question or comment have been phrased to improve the response? Was the eventual outcome a success? Should you continue with this approach, or adopt a more structured one?

Questioning techniques

As with the case of questionnaires, interview questions should be phrased so that their meaning is unambiguous, and they should be delivered in as neutral a tone of voice as possible. As we saw in Chapter 13, there are also certain ways of formulating questions that must be avoided. These include questions that:

- Contain jargon.

- Use prejudicial language.

- Are ambiguous.

- Lead the respondent.

- Include double questions.

- Contain hypothetical statements.

- Probe personal or sensitive issues.

- Require memory recall or knowledge the respondent does not possess.

Cluster groups of questions that deal with similar issues, and then sequence these blocks of questions in a logical order.

TOP TIP 14.3

The type and quality of questions you ask are at the core of a successful interview. So, having drafted a set of questions, try them out on friends or peers to see if they 'work'. Do they avoid the kinds of problems identified above? Are they clear and unambiguous?

Active listening skills

Active listening involves attentive listening, that is, not just listening to the words that are being said, but also to the tone and emphasis. Attentive listening also means that the respondent should be doing most of the talking! If attentive listening is achieved, it should be possible to pick up new or significant themes that can be probed with new questions. Sometimes silences or incomplete statements can reveal more than what is actually said. Attentive listening involves identifying these incomplete replies and following them up.

It should be remembered that an interview is not a normal conversation and therefore the usual norms of human interaction do not necessarily apply. Where in normal conversation it might be acceptable to occasionally glance at one's watch or look away, in interviews a far greater degree of attentiveness is required. This means listening to and interpreting the meaning of what is being said, but also noting the tone and delivery of the dialogue to pick up any traces of irritation, confusion or boredom.

Observing and reflecting

Like listening, careful observing helps to detect information on how the interview is progressing. Observation of the respondent's body language, for example, is important, to detect important clues on the respondent's concentration level, motivation to continue with the interview and whether she or he is at ease. If negative signs are detected, it may mean changing the sequencing of questions, bringing easier or less controversial ones up the order.

Of course, self-observation (reflection) is just as important. Self-understanding helps us to make our questioning and probing more sensitive. If, for example, the interviewer knows that he tends to dominate most natural conversations, he might make a conscious effort to hold back and leave spaces for the respondent to fill.

Testing and summarizing understanding

A useful approach is occasionally to repeat back to the interviewee what you believe they have just told you. This is particularly important if there are statements or issues that are not fully understood.

Closing the interview

It is at this point that you should check that you have asked all the questions that you intended. It is worthwhile asking the interviewee if they have any questions or final comments that they would like to make.

It is important that both you and the respondent leave the interview with a positive sense of achievement. Even if you feel less than elated by the data you have gathered, thank the interviewee for their help and their valuable observations. Then describe what happens next, particularly in terms of whether the respondents will be needed for checking the accuracy of transcripts, and the reporting process and follow-up work. It is worth noting that interviewees often make some of their most interesting and valuable points once they think that the interview is over. Interviewers should not then suddenly scramble for note-paper, but should remember and note these remarks once the respondent has left the interview setting.

RECORDING AND TRANSCRIBING DATA

There should be no short cuts when it comes to recording data. The analysis stage is made redundant if the data have not been collected carefully. Patton (2002) suggests that, no matter what the kind of interviewing style used, and no matter how carefully interview questions are worded, all is wasted unless the words of the interviewee are captured accurately.

Taking notes may be useful for a number of reasons, since it:

* Can help in the formulation of new questions.

* Provides a means for locating important quotations during later analysis.

* Is a non-verbal behaviour that helps pace the interview, providing the interviewee with a cue that they have said something significant.

Note taking, however, is much harder than it sounds, particularly because making handwritten notes is a slow and often inaccurate process. You will also be observing the respondent and thinking of the next question. It is probably best to jot down key words and occasional verbatim comments. It is usually better to make notes in conjunction with an audio or video recording. Particularly in the case of the former, it should be possible to note the tape recorder counter number where a key statement has been made.

The use of a tape recorder is vital for conducting interviews. Not only does it record the essential data, it permits the interviewer to concentrate on the process of listening, interpreting and re-focusing the interview. Using a tape recorder, though, is not always without its problems. In the workplace, respondents may, initially, feel uneasy about being tape-recorded. They will need reassurance as to confidentiality. In terms of the ethics of research, they should also be given the right to turn off the tape recorder at any time.

Give some careful consideration to the recording equipment you will need. Ensure you have enough tapes for the length of interview. Always make use of an external microphone rather than relying on the tape recorder's internal microphone, as this will give you superior sound reproduction.

Activity 14.4

Test out the quality of reproduction of your tape recorder by making practice recordings at different distances from the microphone. What is the furthest distance that gives you a quality of recording from which you can comfortably transcribe? If you are doing group interviews, will you need two microphones?

Patton (2002) suggests that the ideal objective is to achieve a full transcription of the interview. This process, however, is both expensive and time-consuming, with perhaps each hour of live interview requiring between 7 and 10 hours of transcribing. Nevertheless, there is really no substitute for being able to see all the transcribed data at a glance during the analysis stage of the research. If it is simply impractical to achieve full transcription, one option is to use notes taken at the interview to locate key quotations or passages that can be accessed on the tape for transcription.

DEALING WITH PROBLEM RESPONDENTS

Interviewing presents a wide variety of potential difficulties. Within the workplace, people may be very reluctant to answer questions connected with their job responsibilities because they may feel vulnerable. Why am I being asked about my job? Why have *I* been picked out? What are they going to do with the information? Similarly, they may be nervous about expressing their views about issues and subjects connected with the company, and may be tempted to provide answers they think are wanted (socially desirable responses) rather than what they actually believe. Also, unless the research is seen to be officially sponsored by the organization in some way, it might be viewed as irrelevant snooping. If the research *is* sponsored, the level of this sponsorship within the organization hierarchy may prove a factor in eliciting cooperation.

Knowledge questions can also prove to be an embarrassment if people do not know the answer. The interviewer must never show surprise at a wrong answer or hint what the correct answer should be. Keep a look out for body language that signals discomfort, anger or irritation, and be prepared to switch questions or even to curtail the interview. Table 14.3 provides a simple summary checklist of do's and don'ts of conducting interviews.

CONDUCTING MULTICULTURAL INTERVIEWS

It is worth considering the implications of conducting interviews with people who are of a different ethnic, social or cultural group to that of the interviewer. We have seen the importance of building rapport between the two parties, and the significance of impression management and the use of language. It is extremely easy for any of these elements to go wrong unless the interviewer is aware of, and prepared for, the kinds of problems that can arise. Vazquez-Montilla et al. (2000) talk about the need for *culturally responsive* interviewing that is more sensitive to and aware of multi-ethnic cultural perspectives, and they introduce the notion of 'Triple A' (AAA) practices: authenticity, affinity and accuracy.

Working with Hispanic families in Florida, USA, the researchers found that their own Hispanic backgrounds were vital in establishing authenticity since the researchers were able to 'validate their ethnic match and cultural backgrounds' (Vazquez-Montilla et al., 2000: 4). To accomplish this task they were able to make reference to specific cities, events, characteristics of their native country, foods, etc. Since respondents were made aware of the interviewer's shared cultural perspectives, they became more confident that their message

Table 14.3
Checklist of do's
and don'ts of
interviewing
Source: Adapted
from Arksey and
Knight, 1999

DO	DON'T
Establish clearly what the interviewee thinks.	Do not give an indication to the interviewee of *your* meanings and understandings or appear to judge their responses.
Provide a balance between open and closed questions.	Do not ask leading questions or questions to which it is easy for interviewees to simply agree with all you say.
Listen carefully to all responses and follow up points that are not clear.	Do not rush on to the next question before *thinking* about the last response.
If necessary, either to gain interviewer thinking time or for the clarity of the audio recording, repeat the response.	Do not respond with a modified version of the response, but repeat exactly what was said.
Give the interviewee plenty of time to respond.	Do not rush, but do not allow embarrassing silences.
Where interviewees express doubts or hesitate, probe them to share their thinking.	Avoid creating the impression that you would prefer some kinds of answers rather than others.
Be sensitive to possible misunderstandings about questions, and if appropriate repeat the question.	Do not make any assumptions about the ways in which the interviewee might be thinking.
Be aware that the respondent may make self-contradictory statements.	Do not forget earlier responses in the interview.
Try to establish an informal atmosphere.	Do not interrogate the interviewee.
Be prepared to abandon the interview if it is not working.	Do not continue if the respondent appears agitated, angry or withdrawn.

would not be misunderstood. Affinity was established through the interviewer spending time building up a knowledge of the community, often through community agencies and groups. During the interviews, the interviewer attempted to match the respondent's conversational and interaction style, terminology and gestures (although stopping short of mirroring exaggerated mannerisms which would probably appear mocking and offensive). To enhance accuracy, interviewers made themselves aware of basic language terms used by participants by keeping a list of words and idiomatic expressions commonly used by the group. A second researcher always validated the analysis so that cultural stereotyping was avoided.

Keats (2000) suggests that some cultures would find the following actions unacceptable:

- Sending a woman to interview a man.

- Sending a man to interview a woman.

- Sending a person of one religion to interview a person of a different religion when factions from each are in conflict.

- Making direct rather than circuitous replies.

- Looking directly into a person's face when speaking.

Clearly, when conducting interviews with people of a different cultural or ethnic background to yourself, you need to be sensitive to these kinds of issues.

GROUP INTERVIEWS

So far we have assumed a one-to-one situation between an interviewer and single respondent, but, of course, other combinations are possible. Group interviews can comprise a number of different formats, including multiple interviewers, joint interviews and focus groups. An advantage of using group interviews is that costs can be drastically reduced, while the chance of non-response is reduced to about zero. But a drawback is that the social nature of responding may have an influence. Furthermore, as Dillman (2007) reports, group interviews using a questionnaire may invoke test-taking behaviour. He observed respondents checking through questions after completing them and even changing their answers.

MULTIPLE INTERVIEWERS

It can be very useful to have more than one interviewer present since different roles can be performed. For example, one interviewer can act as chairperson, controlling the pace and direction of the interview, while the other takes notes. At the end of the interview, each researcher can compare thoughts and observations to ensure that nothing has been missed.

JOINT INTERVIEWS

Joint interviews involve one researcher talking with two people simultaneously about one phenomenon. This can facilitate collecting differing or corroborating perspectives of the one event. Having both parties present can also allow for them to fill in details that the other has omitted. Against this must be set the danger of interviewees diverting each other's attention, or one respondent dominating the interview.

FOCUS GROUPS

Focus groups originated in market research in the 1950s when people were brought together so that their attitudes to new products could be tested. Today, focus groups are still used for this purpose, but their popularity has spread to wider aspects of research. They can be a low-cost way of collecting data, but require a considerable amount of cooperation and enthusiasm from participants. Logistical problems can also arise. If the focus group contains only six or seven participants, then tape recording may not pose a major problem. But if the group size is 20 or more, you may need two good quality tape recorders strategically placed to pick up usable recordings.

So far we have assumed that interviews can be successfully conducted either in an unstructured manner or through the use of various types of questionnaires or interview schedules, however, there may be some special groups for which these techniques will either be inappropriate or entirely ineffective. The next Case Study provides an illustration of some more creative and imaginative approaches.

TOP TIP 14.4

When running a focus group, be prepared for unexpected comments and even the expression of views you find unhelpful or even distasteful. Do not get drawn into expressing your own opinion. You are there to facilitate the session and elicit the views of others. Remain as calm and as neutral as possible. Welcome the expression of all opinions and keep the tape recorder running!

CASE STUDY 14.2   SECRET BOXES, SOAP OPERAS AND SPIDERS

Punch (2002) reports on a research study she carried out that explored young people's perceptions of their problems, coping strategies and help-seeking behaviour. The sample was drawn from young people both living at home and in residential care. The interviews were conducted using single-sex friendship groups of five people. Clearly, because of the private nature of

(Cont'd)

their problems and often their difficulty or unwillingness to articulate their worries, some innovative approaches were required. These included:

- A *'secret box'*: The young people were asked to write down any current or recent problem and to post their anonymous response into a box. This was then sealed with sticky tape with the assurance that responses would only be read by the researcher after the completion of the last interview with each sample. It was also shaken up to ensure that the last response would not be on the top. Respondents were also permitted either to write a response or to post a blank piece of paper. This process both assured anonymity but also that questions would not be asked about the responses. Typical concerns to emerge concerned puberty, grief at the death of a close relative and illegal activities (drinking, drug taking and stealing). However, one of the limitations of this technique is that, because of anonymity, it is impossible to probe any of the responses.
- *Stimulus material – video clips from soap operas*: Three short clips from recent soap operas were recorded onto one video tape, each one depicting a typical problem that young people have to cope with. During a group interview, each of the clips was discussed in relation to young people's coping strategies. They were firstly asked how the people in the clip had coped. Secondly, they were asked how they would cope in similar circumstances. Punch describes these video clips as visual vignettes. The clips were highly effective in sparking off memories of personal experiences and provided a stimulus for discussions. One of the drawbacks was the time it took to locate appropriate clips and the time taken up by the clips in the interview sessions.
- *Stimulus material – problem letter pages*: These were used in a similar way as video clips to discuss issues such as eating disorders, sexual activity and depression.
- *Stimulus material – task-based activities*: A grouping and ranking exercise was used where the young people grouped 20 different problems written on plain index cards and placed them into three piles: big, middle and small worries. Then each pile was ranked from the most to the least worry. This was then used to provoke a group discussion about the nature of different problems. Spider diagrams were also used. Using a large sheet of paper, 'coping with problems' was circled in the middle and each person was asked to add a 'leg' indicating how they dealt with problems. Thus, the diagrams were used to build information and allow for issues to be probed in greater depth.

Source: Adapted from Punch, 2002

Activity 14.5

Consider the following questions in relation to Case Study 14.2:

1. Why were the interviews conducted with single-sex friendship groups?
2. In developing a simple protocol that you could use for each of the above activities, how would you explain each activity, and how would you provide the necessary reassurances?

Suggested answers are provided at the end of the chapter.

USING TELEPHONE INTERVIEWS

We looked briefly at telephone interviews in Chapter 9 in the context of conducting telephone surveys. One of the main advantages of conducting interviews by telephone is the low cost. They also tend to be conducted more quickly, another important benefit. A potential disadvantage of telephone interviews is the fear that the refusal rate may be higher. Oppenheim (1992), however, provides some comfort here, suggesting that refusals are sometimes actually lower because of 'interviewer invisibility' for some respondents. But interviewers will need to adopt a professional telephone manner, especially to strike up a rapport. For a long interview, though, it is usually best to make a preliminary call to set up a time for the interview.

In terms of questions, all but the most complex kinds can be asked over the telephone. Indeed, as Arksey and Knight (1999) point out, one of the strengths of telephone interviews over questionnaires is that the interviewer can help respondents with any misunderstandings or difficulties they have. Response rates can also be raised if the interviewer has a slick, persuasive manner and can give encouragement. Table 14.4 provides a summary of the kinds of responses commonly given.

ETHICAL ISSUES

The central ethical issue surrounding data collection through interviews is that participants should not be harmed or damaged in any way by the research. If a respondent becomes anxious or upset during the course of an interview, the session should be immediately abandoned. We have already seen that confidentiality should be offered to respondents when completing questionnaires, so, clearly, the same respect should be afforded those participating in interviews. Furthermore, interviewees have the right not to answer individual questions or to terminate the interview before its completion. It is also important that interviews are not used as a devious means of selling something to the respondent.

Table 14.4
Example of
explanations given
by telephone
interviewers

Source: Adapted
from Arksey and
Knight, 1999

RESPONDENT'S COMMENTS	TYPICAL INTERVIEWER'S REPLIES
What's the purpose of the survey?	The questions are about your attitude to [*give name of topic*]. It will give us a better idea of [*what to do/how to improve things/what the firm, department, etc.should concentrate on in the future*]. I'm doing this as part of my work for [*name your institution*]. All your replies will be treated in confidence.
How will the survey be used?	A summary of the findings will go to [*add name of sponsor*]. A short version of the survey will be available to our respondents at [*give Web address*].
How did you get my number?	Your number was chosen by a computer which randomly generates a list of numbers. Your name was provided by a professional association/club [*name association/club*].
Why don't you want to talk to [*someone of the opposite sex, someone older or younger*] rather than me?	I need to make sure I have a good mix of men and women, younger and older people. You have been chosen because this helps us to achieve this mix.
Hmm. I'm still not sure	If you want to check [*our/my*] credentials, why not call [*give name and number of sponsor*] and I'll call back later.

One of the problems is that, as Patton (2002) comments, effective interviewing opens up the interviewees' thoughts, knowledge and experience to both the interviewer, but also the interviewees themselves. Hence, after a good interview, the interviewees know more about themselves and their situation than they did before. This, in itself, may be quite therapeutic (or not as the case may be), but the purpose of research is to collect data, not to change people or opinions. A key ethical consideration is that of **informed consent**. In some countries, for example the USA, written consent is required even when the research is small-scale or only involves structured, closed-question interviews. An example of an informed consent form is given in Figure 14.1.

Having taken steps to ensure informed consent, what are the practical considerations that help to ensure that an interview is ethically conducted? Table 14.5 sets out some issues and suggested ethical solutions.

Figure 14.1
Example of an
informed consent
form (adapted from
Arksey and Knight,
1999)

CONSENT FORM		
Beechwood Academy		
Evaluation of anti-bullying policy		
This consent form is designed to check that you understand the purposes of the study, that you are aware of your rights as a participant and to confirm that you are willing to take part		
Please tick as appropriate		
	YES	NO
1 I have read the leaflet describing the study.		
2 I have received sufficient information about the study for me to decide whether to take part.		
3 I understand that I am free to refuse to take part if I wish.		
4 I understand that I may withdraw from the study at any time without having to provide a reason.		
5. I know that I can ask for further information about the study from the research team.		
6 I understand that all information arising from the study will be treated as confidential.		
7 I know that it will not be possible to identify any individual respondent in the study report, including myself.		
8 I agree to take part in the study.		
Signature:	Date:	
Name in block letters, please:		
I confirm that quotations from the interview can be used in the final research report and other publications. I understand that these will be used anonymously and that no individual respondent will be identified in such report.		
Signature:	Date:	
Name in block letters, please:		

Ethical issues might arise in any number of unexpected ways. For example, in dealing with particularly difficult or sensitive topics, the respondent might ask for practical guidance or advice. It should be noted that the interviewer is not a counsellor, and should avoid being drawn into this type of discussion. The proper course of action would be to offer contact details for those kinds of organization that could provide help. These would include advice bureaux, voluntary organizations, support networks and telephone helplines.

Table 14.5
Action that can be
taken for conducting
an ethical interview

Source: Adapted from
Patton, 1990

ETHICAL ISSUE	ACTIONS
Promises and guarantees	State what the interviewee will gain. Ensure that if a copy of the report is promised, it is delivered.
Risk assessment	Consider in what ways might the interview put people at risk in terms of: • Stress • Hostility from line-managers, peers, etc.
Confidentiality	Reflect on the extent to which promises of confidentiality can *actually* be met.
Organizational permissions	Consider whether you have the 'right' to interview respondents. Are permissions necessary?
Data access and ownership	Evaluate who has the right to access data and for what purpose. Who 'owns' the final report in terms of intellectual property rights?
Mental health	Consider how the mental health of the interviewer and interviewee may be affected by conducting the interview.
Advice	Appoint an adviser on ethical matters during the course of the study.

SUMMARY

- Interviews can be divided into five categories ranging from the informal conversational to the completely structured.

- The choice of approach will depend on the objectives of the research, with structured interviews eliciting more quantitative data and unstructured or focused interviews, qualitative.

- The danger of bias in interviews stems not only from the type of questions asked but the way in which they are articulated by the interviewer.

- Interviewing is a skill and includes the ability to build rapport with respondents while maintaining detachment, and observing and listening in order to keep control of the interview.

- Ethical issues are of paramount importance since confidentiality may be more difficult to maintain than in other forms of data gathering, such as postal questionnaires.

FURTHER READING

Seidman, I. (2006) *Interviewing as Qualitative Research: A Guide for Researchers in Education and the Social Sciences*, 3rd edn. New York: Teachers College Press. Covers interviewing from a phenomenological perspective, the ethics of qualitative interviewing and the relationship between data gathering and analysis.

Keats, D.M. (2000) *Interviewing: A Practical Guide for Students and Professionals*. Buckingham: Open University Press. A simple but practical guide to interviewing skills that includes the structure of interviews, interpreting responses, and chapters on interviewing children, adolescents, the aged and people with disabilities.

Arksey, H. and Knight, P. (1999) *Interviewing for Social Scientists*. London: Sage. Easy to read, but detailed and comprehensive. This book shows how to design an interview study and provides essential advice on how to conduct a successful interview.

SUGGESTED ANSWERS FOR ACTIVITY 14.2

While the response does offer factual information, the question is probing for the respondent's feelings, and so the response received is inappropriate.

SUGGESTED ANSWERS FOR ACTIVITY 14.5

1. Clearly, because of the often personal nature of some of the discussions, single-sex groups are more appropriate for the interviews.

2. Any research protocol should be simple and easy to use. It could, perhaps, take the form of a single side of A4 paper to be given to the respondent, containing the purpose of the research and a short list of instructions. Assurances of confidentiality could be given at the top of the pro forma and at the end (as reinforcement). The researcher could repeat these assurances orally.

Analysing and Presenting Qualitative Data

DAVID E. GRAY

CHAPTER OBJECTIVES

After reading this chapter you will be able to:

● Describe some of the principles of qualitative data analysis.

● Select appropriate qualitative analytical methods, including grounded theory approaches.

● Apply qualitative methods to produce valid, reliable and trustworthy data.

● Make use of the 'voice' of the researcher.

We saw in Chapter 2 that while some research methodologies tend to utilize either quantitative *or* qualitative methods, very often both are used. This is because qualitative data can provide rich descriptions and explanations that demonstrate the chronological flow of events as well as often leading to serendipitous (chance) findings. According to Miles and Huberman (1994) qualitative studies have a quality of 'undeniability' because words have a more concrete and vivid flavour that is more convincing to the reader than pages of numbers. However, qualitative analysis has been criticized for being lacking in methodological rigour, prone to researcher subjectivity and based on small cases or limited evidence. We will explore how qualitative analysis addresses such problems later in this chapter.

Qualitative analysis is (or should be) a rigorous and logical process through which data are given meaning. Through analysis, we can progress through an initial description of the data then, through a process of disaggregating the data into smaller parts, see how these connect into new concepts, providing the basis for a fresh description. As we saw in Chapter 2, there are different approaches to qualitative research, including grounded theory, ethnography and phenomenology, researchers often using a combination of approaches in a research project. One of the challenges of qualitative research is that there are no widely accepted rules about how qualitative data should be analysed, other than that the approach is generally inductive and involves the coding of data.

Another major issue is the extent to which data should be analysed. As Strauss and Corbin (1998) point out, some researchers believe that the data should not be analysed at all, but should merely be presented. This allows the data to 'speak for themselves', untainted by the potential subjective interpretations of the researcher. Other qualitative researchers are concerned, however, with accurate selection, synthesis and description of the data, but in as detached and objective a way as possible. Other researchers are more concerned with theory building, interpreting the data to build concepts and categories that can be brought together into theoretical frameworks. In contrast, some researchers see qualitative research as primarily being about storytelling and description (Wolcott, 1994).

In this chapter we will look at approaches to how data can be analysed, looking particularly at content analysis and grounded theory methods and also including some increasingly influential approaches such as the use of narratives, conversational analysis and discourse analysis. The important issues of reliability and validity will also be addressed, particularly from the stance of those who favour interpretivist and naturalistic approaches.

TOP TIP 18.1

Many people who are new to qualitative research collect their data and then wonder how to analyse it. This is too late in the day! Plan for the qualitative data analysis method you intend to use at the design phase of the research process. This is essential, because some approaches to data analysis will influence the ways in which data are collected and the phases in which they are analysed.

ELEMENTS OF QUALITATIVE DATA ANALYSIS

There is what may seem at first sight, a quite bewildering number of approaches to the analysis of qualitative data (some of which will be discussed in this chapter) and no clear rules on which approach to adopt in different circumstances. Thankfully, however, there are a few general principles to qualitative data analysis that should be understood and applied, whatever the qualitative data analysis approach being adopted. These include analytic induction, the principles and practices of coding, the place of **secondary data analysis** and the reflexivity of the researcher. We will look at each of these in turn.

Figure 18.1
The process of
analytic induction
(adapted from
Bryman and Bell,
2007)

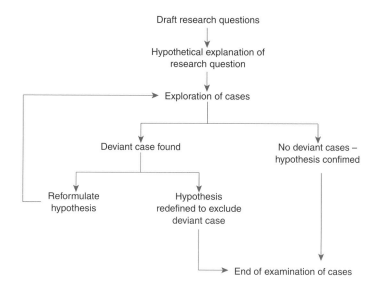

Figure 18.1
The process of
analytic induction
(adapted from
Bryman and Bell,
2007)

ANALYTIC INDUCTION

As we saw in Chapters 2 and 3, induction involves the collection and analysis of data from a range of individual cases in order to identify patterns from them for the development of conceptual categories. As Figure 18.1 illustrates, the process of analytic induction involves a number of defined stages. Essentially, starting from at least an approximate definition of a research question, cases are examined to see if they are consistent with a hypothetical explanation of the research question. If no deviant cases are found, then the hypothesis can be confirmed. If, however, cases emerge that are inconsistent with the hypothesis, then either the hypothesis has to be rewritten (and new cases examined), or the hypothesis itself is redefined to exclude the deviant case.

As Bryman and Bell (2007) contend, analytical induction is an extremely rigorous method of data analysis because if a single case is inconsistent with the hypothesis, then either further data have to be collected, or the hypothesis has to be reformulated. The selection of cases also needs to be sufficiently diverse for the theory that emerges to be adequately tested. So while **theoretical sampling** makes use of cases that add weight to the development of a concept, analytical induction deliberately chooses negative or deviant cases to disconfirm a hypothesis (Flick, 2006).

STEPS IN THE CODING PROCESS

Unlike quantitative data analysis where the statistical tools are well understood, in qualitative analysis there are no hard and fast rules for how data should be coded. There are, however, a number of useful principles that should be applied, irrespective of whether you are using grounded theory, content analysis or any other method.

Transcribe the data: Field notes from observations or reflective diaries should be written up into a format that can be easily read. Hastily written field notes, for example, should be typed into a document. Assuming that interviews have been tape recorded, these should be transcribed. Whether you do this yourself, or pay for the service, may partly be determined by your budget. While typing up the transcript yourself may be time-consuming and laborious, it does develop a familiarization with the data at an early stage.

Collect/code/collect: Avoid waiting until all data are collected before starting the coding process, start as soon as possible. Coding allows you to become familiar at an early stage with the issues emerging from the data. Identifying these themes also helps with theoretical sampling (selecting new cases on the basis of theories and concepts emerging from the analysis).

Familiarization: Read through all field notes, documents and transcripts but suspend the temptation to interpret. Get a general flavour of what is happening. Perhaps at this point make some general notes as an *aide-mémoire* in your research diary on what seemed interesting, unusual or perhaps significant.

Focused reading: Next comes a more focused reading of the data, this time underlining key words or phrases and making notes in the margins. The underlined words/phrases are the beginning of the coding process. You might also allot a word or phrase (code) that summarizes or seems pertinent to a particular passage. Notes might include reminders to yourself or reflective thoughts on puzzles or passages that throw up the unexpected.

Review/amend codes: On the second reading, begin to modify your codes. If two or more codes seem to apply to the same phenomenon, then remove one of them. If a code relates to a concept in the literature, then make use of the literature category or description. Are some of the codes hierarchical? In other words, is one concept a sub-category of another? Generate as many codes as seem logical. These can always be amended or rationalized at a later stage.

Generating theory: Look for connections between categories and concepts that are emerging from the data. Do they amount to a set of theoretical principles? Do they relate to any theoretical models in the literature? Develop hypotheses about some of these connections and return to the literature to see if they can be confirmed by the evidence. Some of the principles outlined here will be demonstrated when we look at the use of grounded theory in qualitative data analysis.

However, even when these principles are applied consistently and with care, a common accusation levelled at qualitative data analysis is that the coding tends to fragment the data, losing the connection between the text and its context. For example, in presenting a quote from a respondent, the reader loses the context within which it appeared. The narrative flow of what people say is lost. This is one of the reasons why narrative analysis as a form of qualitative data analysis has gained in popularity in recent years.

> ## TOP TIP 18.2
>
> In analysing qualitative data, make sure that you don't end up merely using isolated quotations from a number of respondents as if they contained some significant meaning. You have to move beyond description to include an analysis and interpretation of the data. Any verbatim quotations should be used as a way of supporting this analysis.

SECONDARY DATA ANALYSIS

While most of this chapter is concerned with the analysis of primary data gathered in field settings (for example, through observations or interviews) it is important to also recognize that researchers can have access to data in the form of documents and other resources where the data has been collected (and in some cases analysed) by others. For quantitative researchers, secondary analysis can involve the use of both documents and official statistics. For qualitative researchers, secondary data analysis primarily involves the analysis of another researcher's qualitative data or documents. While the re-analysis of quantitative data sets has been common in policy analysis and in the interpretation of key business decisions, its use in qualitative analysis has been much more modest (Fielding, 2004). The purpose, however, remains similar – to perform additional, in-depth analysis of a sub-set of the original data; or to apply a new perspective or conceptual focus to the data.

Bryman and Bell (2007) suggest a checklist that researchers should use when making use of documents (for both quantitative and qualitative secondary analysis). The criteria include:

- Who produced the document?

- Why was it produced?

- Is the material genuine and produced by someone who could write authoritatively and objectively on the subject?

- Can the events or accounts presented in the document be corroborated by other evidence?

To these we can add a concern about ethics. Are safeguards in place to honour any commitments made by the original researchers to the research subject? Whatever promises were made about confidentiality need to be followed during the secondary data analysis.

Secondary data analysis offers the researcher a number of advantages, particularly in terms of saving cost and time. Furthermore, where a subject is particularly sensitive, researchers can make use of previously gathered secondary data, rather than having to re-interview participants. Secondary analysis is not, however, without its detractors. One major criticism is epistemological, arguing that the context in which the data were collected cannot be replicated. Mauthner et al. (1998) contend that since qualitative data are the result of a reflexive relationship between the researcher and the researched (see the following section), the conditions under which the data were collected are inescapable. This means that secondary data analysis can only be valid if limited to methodological exploration. Attempts to go beyond this by attempting, say, to establish new analytical themes from the data are inappropriate. Fielding (2004), however, sees this as less of an epistemological than a practical problem since qualitative researchers have always had to monitor the effects of contextual features whether performing primary or secondary analysis. Vital evidence for judging the validity of an analytical point may well be sometimes missing from archived data – but the same can be said of primary data too.

REFLEXIVITY – THE VOICE OF THE RESEARCHER

Reflexivity is a concept used to describe the relationship between the researcher and the object of research (Brannick and Coghlan, 2007), and has been discussed by social scientists for over 30 years, influenced in the main by feminist researchers and those from hermeneutic and critical theory traditions. It has mainly been applied to the collection of qualitative data, usually through interviewing (Ryan and Golden, 2006). Reflexivity involves the realization that the researcher is not a neutral observer, and is implicated in the construction of knowledge. Far from being a disinterested bystander, the researcher is seen as someone whose observations are by their very nature, selective, and whose interpretations of results are partial. Coffey (1999), for example, argues that researchers need to be aware of how fieldwork data gathering and ethnographic writing construct, reproduce and implicate selves, relationships and personal identities. The problem is that many researchers fail to recognize this. In the words of Mauthner and Doucet, in many research accounts, the researcher is 'rendered invisible as are the interpersonal, social and institutional contexts' (2003: 415). This process, they contend, has been made even worse by the growth in the use of computer-assisted qualitative data analysis programs which have given an air of scientific objectivity to what remains a fundamentally subjective and interpretive process.

There are, essentially, at least two forms of reflexivity. Through epistemological reflexivity the researchers reflect on their assumptions about the world and about the nature of knowledge. So they will ask themselves questions such as: how has the research question limited or distorted what was found? How could the study have been conducted differently? Then there is personal reflexivity, where the researcher reflects upon how their personal values, attitudes, beliefs and aims have served to shape the research. This might also involve a personal reflection on how the research process impacted and changed the stance taken by the researcher. It involves honesty and openness and locates the researcher firmly within the dynamic of the research process, or in the words of Dupuis (1999) a continuous, intentional and systematic self-introspection.

Mauthner and Doucet (2003) note that, while reflexivity has been increasingly seen as important, the research methods literature has been relatively silent on practical steps for achieving it. However, some practical approaches could include:

- Designing research that involves multiple investigators. This can encourage dialogue and the critical interchanges of ideas – pushing researchers to make transparent their epistemological positions and personally held beliefs.

- Writing a reflexive journal. Lincoln and Guba (1994) recommend that this should include writing: (1) a daily schedule describing the logistics of the study; (2) a log of methodological decisions and changes; and (3) a personal diary recording reflections with particular reference to one's values and interests.

- Reporting research perspectives, values and beliefs in any research report. Dupuis (1999) recommends that this is done pre and post data collection so that changes in personal feelings can be made explicit.

Weber (2003), however, notes some of the potential dangers of reflexivity. One is narcism. We become so wrapped up in self-introspection, that it becomes the actual focus of the study. Another is self-righteousness. We start to denigrate the work of other researchers who, for whatever reason, do not engage in reflexivity. Next, there is the danger of nihilism. We see that our research is limited in more and more ways. We become so conscious of the constraints on our research, the indeterminacy of theory, the limitations of research methods and the assumptions and biases that underlie our work that we become paralysed. Finally, there is the arrogance that dismisses any work that can be generalised, arguing that every research context (including, or even particularly, our own) is unique. While apposite, these warnings are perhaps aimed at those researchers at the more extreme wings of the reflexivity movement. For the rest of us, we should embrace reflexivity to the extent that it is in line with our attitudes towards epistemology and our principles of research design and practice.

ANALYSING QUALITATIVE DATA

Analysis involves the process of breaking data down into smaller units to reveal their characteristic elements and structure (Dey, 1993: 30). Descriptions can lay the basis for analysis, but we need to go beyond description: we want to interpret, to understand and to explain. Through analysis, however, we can also gain new insights into our data. Data can be broken down into their constituent parts, and connections made between these concepts, providing the basis for new descriptions (see Figure 18.2).

Figure 18.2
Qualitative analysis
as a circular
process (Dey, 1993)

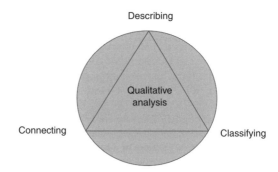

As we have seen, there are a wide range of approaches to qualitative analysis, some being more deductive in approach (such as content analysis) and others heavily inductive. Inevitably, the various approaches also differ in the mechanics of data analysis, including the attitude taken to the fragmentation of data.

CONTENT ANALYSIS

One of the most common approaches to analysing qualitative data is through content analysis. Essentially, this involves the making of inferences about data (usually text) by systematically and objectively identifying special characteristics (classes or categories) within them. The attempt to achieve a measure of objectivity in this process is addressed by the creation of specific rules called *criteria of selection* which have to be established before the data can be analysed. In contrast to this, with grounded theory (see the following section) no a priori criteria are assumed, with these emerging through the process of data collection and analysis itself. Hence, at the risk of over-simplification, grounded theory is more inductive in character, and content analysis more deductive.

In using content analysis, there are three procedures for identifying classes and categories. First, *common classes*, comprising categories in everyday thinking such as age, gender, boss, worker are identified. These common classes can be useful in linking or finding associations between the data and important demographic characteristics. Secondly, *special classes* are identified, comprising the kind of labels particular groups or communities use to distinguish amongst things, persons or events. This can include specialist types of language (including slang, the use of acronyms, specialist professional terms, etc.). Thirdly, *theoretical classes*, or those classes that arise in the process of analysing the data, are identified, providing the key linkages and patterns. As Flick (2006) points out, however, these categories are themselves often derived from theoretical models. So categories are brought to the empirical data, and not necessarily derived from them. Of course, they will be repeatedly evaluated against the data and modified if necessary.

Having identified categories within the text, the next step is the analysis itself. The key here is to reduce the volume of textual material. Using the work of Mayring (1983), Flick (2006) distinguishes three steps in the analysis process:

- *Summarizing content analysis*, where the material is paraphrased, with similar paraphrases bundled together and less relevant passages eliminated.

- *Explicating content analysis*, which clarifies ambiguous or contradictory passages by introducing context material into the analysis. This could include dictionary definitions of terms, statements from the text or outside the text (for example, contextual information, theoretical propositions) that illustrate the passages being analysed. Through this process a clarifying paraphrase is formulated and tested.

- *Structuring content analysis* seeks to identify types of formal structures in the materials. Hence, the analysis might extricate key features in the material and describe them in more detail. Alternatively, the material might be rated according to dimensions on a scale. So, in a passage dealing with, say, 'motivation', the concept could be given a rating scale from 'Highly motivated' to 'Completely demotivated'. The passage is then searched for examples of motivational feelings against the scale, resulting in a frequency count for each of the motivational levels.

Berg (2006) argues that content analysis can also be used with hypothesis testing, that is, a more experimental or quasi-experimental design. With hypothesis testing, he suggests going through the following stages:

- Make a rough hypothesis based upon observations from the data.

- Search the data to find cases that do not fit with the hypothesis.

- If negative cases are found, discard or reformulate the hypothesis to account for the negative cases (recall the process of analytical induction, above).

Hence, it is necessary to develop research questions in advance that are linked to previous research (Mayring, 1983 in Flick, 2006). It is because of this insistence on measurement and hypothesis testing that Locke (2001) places content analysis within the modernist, objectivist paradigm.

Content analysis is potentially a very important weapon in the researcher's armoury because it can be highly cost-effective. There may be no need to design and issue costly questionnaires – existing documentation such as company reports, memoranda or emails may provide the basis for the data (as in secondary data analysis, above). This, however, could also be construed as a disadvantage since the approach has to rely on 'old' data, rather than gathering fresh information. Another weakness is that it is incapable of exploring associations and causal relationships between variables. As Flick (2006) also points out, the very conceptual structures that content analysis imposes on the data may obscure some of the interpretations that may have emerged inductively from within it.

GROUNDED THEORY

One of the most influential qualitative approaches is that of grounded theory, defined as a theory that is: 'discovered, developed and provisionally verified through systematic data collection and analysis of data pertaining to that phenomenon' (Strauss and Corbin, 1998: 23). Locke (2001) suggests that locating grounded theory in a particular research paradigm is difficult because it has been used in both modernist (objectivist) and interpretivist approaches. There is, however, a clear influence of symbolic interactionism, and this interpretivist paradigm's commitment to studying the social world and the rejection of a priori theorizing.

Grounded theory methods have been extensively used in education, evaluation research, nursing and organizational studies (Charmaz, 1995). Unlike the deductive approach, grounded theory does not begin with prior assumptions about hypotheses, research questions or what literature should underpin the study. This is not to say that grounded theorists embark on a study with no theoretical position. They will have a competent level of knowledge about the area. But, as Strauss and Corbin (1998) warn, grounded researchers should not be so steeped in the literature that their creative efforts become impeded or constrained. The research should commence with a defined purpose, but also with the realization that this purpose may become modified or even radically altered during the research process itself. Through data analysis new theoretical positions or understandings may emerge.

The grounded theory researcher works with his or her participants to actively construct the data, to get beyond static analysis to multiple layers of meaning. According to Charmaz (1995), these layers could include the participant's:

* Stated explanations of her or his actions.

* Unstated assumptions about these actions.

* Intentions and motivation for engaging in the actions.

* The effects of the actions on others.

* The consequences of these actions for interpersonal relations and for further individual actions.

What about the data analysis process itself? Strauss and Corbin (1998) lay down a structured process and one that has become a highly influential way of analysing data comprising:

* Open coding: the disaggregation of the data into units.

* Axial coding: recognizing relationships between categories.

* Selective coding: the integration of categories to produce a theory.

These are pulled together into a framework that is called a conditional matrix, a 'complex web of interrelated conditions, action/interaction, and consequences pertaining to a particular phenomenon' (Strauss and Corbin, 1998: 181). These coding processes, however, are not necessarily completely distinct, and do not need to take place in sequence. In a single coding session, the researcher might move quickly from one coding method to another, particularly from open to axial coding. Another point to stress is that data collection and analysis should be an interwoven process with analysis, prompting the sampling of new data. Charmaz (1995) provides advice on the timing of the analysis, also suggesting that the data should be studied as they emerge, making it easier to identify respondents' implicit meanings and taken-for-granted assumptions. Hence, for the novice grounded researcher, it is best to transcribe your own tapes as this gets you into contact with the data at an early stage.

Before we begin to look at these coding categories in detail, a word of warning. As Dey (1999) discusses, not all advocates of grounded theory agree with Strauss and Corbin's approach. Glaser (1992), for example, accuses their later work of abandoning their earlier, influential ideas, suggesting that it has evolved into a quite different methodology (the coding paradigm, dealt with next). For Glaser, this smacks too much of rules and structure being imposed upon the data. However, despite these criticisms, the Strauss and Corbin approach is widely used and recognized as a valuable methodology. Given that the methodological advice coming from the grounded theory literature can be 'bewilderingly complex' (Partington, 2002: 138), an attempt is made here to supplement procedural descriptions with illustrative graphics. It must be stressed that this is just one interpretation of how grounded theory can be applied in practice.

Open coding

Open coding is defined as 'the naming and categorizing of phenomena through close examination of the data' (Strauss and Corbin, 1998: 62). Two analytical procedures are involved in the open coding process: the making of comparisons and the asking of questions, both of which help towards the labelling of phenomena in terms of concepts or categories (see Table 18.1). According to Strauss (1987), there are four essential guidelines to follow in the data analysis process:

- Ask the data a specific and consistent set of questions, keeping in mind the original objectives of the research study. The intention here is to uncover whether the data fit with these objectives. There may be occasions when new or unanticipated results emerge from the data, an outcome that is entirely valid.

- Analyse the data minutely, but also include as many categories, examples and incidents as possible.

- Frequently interrupt the coding to write a theoretical account. As the data are being coded, ideas or theoretical perspectives may arise. It is essential that these are noted immediately otherwise they may well be forgotten.

- Do not assume the analytical relevance of any traditional variable such as age, gender, social class, etc. until its relevance emerges from the data. This is particularly so if the impact of an expected variable does not emerge – this result must be accepted.

Table 18.1
Open coding:
definition of
terms

Source: Adapted
from Strauss and
Corbin, 1998

TERM	DEFINITION
Concept	Conceptual labels placed on discrete happenings, events and other instances of phenomena
Category	A classification of concepts
Coding	The process of analysing data
Code notes	The products of coding
Open coding	The process of breaking down, examining, comparing, conceptualizing and categorizing data
Properties	Attributes or characteristics pertaining to a category
Dimensions	Location of properties along a continuum
Dimensionalization	The process of breaking a property down into its dimensions

Open coding works through a process of making constant comparisons. Each time an instance of a category is found, it is compared with previous instances. If the new instance does not fit the original definition, then either the definition must be modified, or a new category created. Case Study 18.1 provides a practical example of how the process of asking questions and making comparisons can lead to the generation of concepts and categories.

CASE STUDY 18.1   DEVELOPING GROUNDED THEORY – OPEN CODING

A researcher is asked to observe customer behaviour in a large department store. She positions herself in an unobtrusive way, where she can see customers entering and leaving the store, walking down the aisles, looking at merchandise and buying goods, etc. Although the store is very busy and the activity at first appears chaotic, some tentative patterns begin to emerge which she begins to label. Some customers, for example, seem content with examining goods (picking them up, looking at them, putting them down) but then just moving on. She asks herself: why are they doing this? This behaviour she labels *exploring*. Other customers approach counter staff or supervisors walking around and ask them questions. This she labels *questioning*. Still other customers approach the busy tills and seem content to stand in line to be served. The label attached to this is simply *queuing*. Once at the till, they are, of course, *buying*. It is clear, however, that a minority of customers queue for a short time and grow impatient. They can be observed to put the merchandise down on a counter or shelf before leaving the store. This behaviour is labelled as *deserting*. One customer, however, is seen to be arguing with a supervisor. This behaviour is called *remonstrating*.

   Later she notices that some customers not only pick up and look at goods they even rub them between their fingers and in some cases smell them! Hence under the category of exploring, she is able to identify three sub-categories: looking, feeling and smelling.

   After the observation session our researcher begins the process of *categorizing* the data. In doing this, she is careful to choose categories that are more abstract in nature than the concepts they describe. Hence, she groups exploring and questioning to form the category *information seeking* while queuing and buying are grouped together as *intentional purchasing*.

Activity 18.1

Conduct a detailed observation of an event or phenomenon within a field setting. Analyse your data using open coding, providing your own set of descriptive labels.

Note that the labels given in Case Study 18.1 are original and specific to the researcher. This is important because if she had taken already existing and 'borrowed' categories, these can come with pre-existing meanings that can bias the research. Once categories are produced they still have to be developed so that they can be used in further data collection and analysis. Categories are developed in two ways: by their *properties* and by their *dimensions*. Using Case Study 18.1, we could take the category 'information seeking' and examine it for its properties and dimensions. Table 18.2 illustrates the results, showing that properties are the characteristics or attributes of a category. Dimensions represent the location of a property along a continuum. The development of properties and dimensions is crucially important because they are central in making relationships between categories and sub-categories and later between major categories. They thus provide the basis of the analytical processes of grounded theory.

Table 18.2
The properties
and dimensions
of the category
'information
seeking'

Source: Adapted
from Strauss and
Corbin, 1998

CATEGORY	PROPERTY	DIMENSIONAL RANGE	
Information-seeking	Questioning	Often	Never
	Looking	Up close	From a distance
	Smelling	Repeatedly	Once
	Feeling	Vigorously	Gently

Table 18.2
The properties
and dimensions
of the category
'information
seeking'

Source: Adapted
from Strauss and
Corbin, 1998

Axial coding

As we saw in the previous section, open coding disaggregates data so that categories can be located. **Axial coding** then takes these categories and tries to make connections between categories and sub-categories. Essentially, this means specifying:

* A *category* (phenomenon) in terms of the conditions that helped to give rise to it.

* The *context* in which it arises.

* The *actions* and *interactions* that stem from it.

* Its *consequences*.

We are also interested in what caused the phenomenon. Figure 18.3 provides a highly simplified illustration of the relationships between a phenomenon and its causes, context, actions and consequences. Note that Strauss and Corbin (1998),

Figure 18.3
Making connections
between categories
and sub-categories
by examining a
phenomenon in
terms of its
properties,
dimensions and
causal conditions

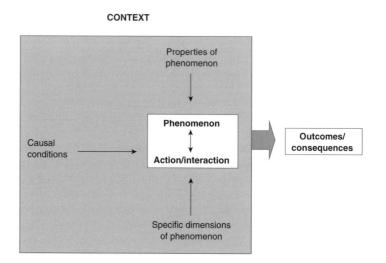

referring to the work of Dewey, caution that an initial condition rarely leads to an action/interaction and then a consequence in a direct manner.

> Rather, action/interaction may be taken in response to multiple conditions, some of which occurred in the past, some of which are happening in the present, and/or some of which are anticipated in the future. (Strauss and Corbin, 1998: 184)

Hence, in Figure 18.3, causal conditions may occur in a variety of different temporal states.

To illustrate the process of linking sub-categories to categories, let us take the example of our retail store in the previous Case Study. We have seen a customer remonstrating (phenomenon) with a supervisor. We observe that the reason (causal condition) for this is the fact that the queues for the tills were very long and that she could not get served. But the description of this phenomenon, 'remonstration', does little to fully describe the event. We need more detail. So we are also interested in the specific dimensions of the phenomenon, and discover that this was an angry remonstration (in terms of volume/language) that lasted 10 minutes (time) in the middle of the store (location). But we also need to know something about the properties of the causal condition (the queuing) and discover that the customer queued for eight minutes at a till that was shut seconds before she was about to be served. Next, we take a look at the context in which the phenomenon occurred, examining issues such as when, how and the type of cause. We discover that some tills are not operational due to staff shortages and that the till closure happened suddenly because the member of staff was due her lunchbreak.

Figure 18.4
Making connections between categories and sub-categories: the impact of intervening conditions

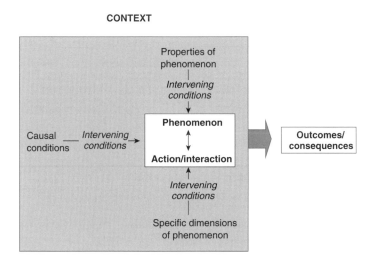

Yet, there are also *intervening conditions*, or what could be called a 'broader structural context' (Strauss and Corbin, 1998: 103), which act either to constrain or facilitate the actions being taken (see Figure 18.4). For example, again using our illustration, we find that during the angry remonstration, the store manager happens to be passing and intervenes to help. She uses her cellphone to call for more staff and opens a till herself and serves the irate customer. But in general terms, intervening conditions within a context can include a wide range of conditions, including the influence of culture, time, economic status, hierarchical position in an organization, technological status, individual biography, etc. For example, the remonstration is a long one, not just because of the scale of the inconvenience, but because only the previous week the company that owns the store had announced record profits so the customer may be reasoning 'Why haven't they employed more staff?'

We can see from the above analysis that grounded theory is an action/interaction method of theory building which is concerned with the ways in which people manage and respond to phenomena, existing within a specific context or conditions. Recalling the discussion of symbolic interactionism in Chapter 2, people assign meaning to phenomena and then act upon these interpretations, these actions bringing forth fresh interpretations and actions amongst participants. But this action and interaction also has *consequences* that may be predictable or unanticipated. Indeed, the failure to take action also has its consequences. Yet, while axial coding can help us to identify relationships between categories, we still need to see how these categories or classes can be integrated to build theories. This is achieved through selective coding.

Selective coding

This is the process of selecting **core categories** from the data in order to form the grounded theory. In terms of processes, this is not too different to axial coding, the main difference being that it is completed at a much higher level of abstraction. Through axial coding you will have derived a set of phenomena or categories that have been defined in terms of their properties, dimensions, etc. Through selective coding, core categories are sought through which a 'story' can be told. The selective coding process involves a number of stages that illuminate the social processes going on unconsciously among a group of people comprising:

- Finding a story line formulated around core categories.
- Relating sub-categories to the core categories.
- Validating these relationships against the data.
- Filling in categories that need further refinement.

Table 18.3 provides a brief summary of some of these terms, after which we will discuss them in more detail.

Table 18.3
Selective coding:
definition of terms

Source: Adapted from
Strauss and Corbin,
1998

TERM	DEFINITION
Story	A descriptive narrative about the central phenomenon of the study
Story line	The conceptualization of the story around the core category
Selective coding	The process of selecting the core category, systematically relating it to other categories, and validating these relationships
Core category	The central phenomenon around which all the other categories are integrated

One of the key features of grounded theory is *theoretical sampling*, which helps to make the emerging theory more generalizable. This is achieved by seeking to minimize and maximize the selected differences and similarities between core categories and the relationships between them across cases. Hence, finding strong similarities across cases (and minimum differences) helps to build confidence in the validity of the emerging theory. Attempting to find cases that contradict the theory may help to locate unexpected data and perhaps the emergence of new perspectives.

Identifying the story
The best way to start is to describe in a few short sentences the essence of the story to produce a general, descriptive overview. What are the most salient features? What are the main problems being scrutinized? It might be useful to return to the axial coding stage and find an abstract category that in some way summarizes the story. If such a category does not exist, then one will have to be formulated that encapsulates the categories in the study. If more than one category exists, it is necessary to make a choice between them so that only one core category is used. Taking our example of the observation in the retail store, the main story here could be construed as intentional shopping behaviour. Whether customers are asking questions, examining goods, leaving the store impatiently or patiently queuing, they behave, or attempt to behave, intentionally – that is, with a specific aim.

Relating sub-categories to the core categories
This involves relating subsidiary categories around the core category by means of the paradigm so that they fit and provide an analytical version of the story. This may mean writing or re-writing the story and rearranging categories until they achieve a better fit with the story. Within these conceptual categories there will be relationships and networks of patterns. Strauss and Corbin (1994) stress how important it is to identify these patterns because it is these that give

the theory specificity. Hence, it becomes possible to say that under one set of conditions *this* happens, whereas under another set of conditions *that* happens. Case Study 18.2 takes our retailing research a little further.

CASE STUDY 18.2   DEVELOPING GROUNDED THEORY – SELECTIVE CODING

Although the store is crowded and presents the appearance of chaos, in fact, thanks to the highly intentional behaviour of most customers, there are distinctive patterns of behaviour that become predictable. People do not simply rush into the store, grab the first item they see and then run out with it! They look around (touring) the isles, sometimes leaving this department, but returning later. Our researcher notices that those who examine merchandise closely tend to be with someone else rather than being alone – hence, exploratory behaviour is usually collaborative. Opinions are being shared (the 'second opinion'). People queue, because the alternative, pushing and shoving one's way to the counter, will lead to even more stress. Queuing is a time-consuming activity that is undertaken to save time. Customers who approach store staff for information are also attempting to save themselves time by gaining quicker access to information.

Activity 18.2

Returning to your data in Activity 18.1, take your open coding categories through the axial coding process, making connections between categories. Then, using selective coding, identify core categories and formulate a story line.

Validating these relationships against the data

Having found a story and related various categories to it, the relationships uncovered can be validated (grounding the theory) by returning to the data and asking whether the story fits for all those observed in the study. We may find, for example, that a minority of customers do not appear to behave intentionally at all. We noted in Case Study 18.1 that some customers spent some time queuing before losing patience and leaving the store. If their intention was to buy goods, they failed. Yet their behaviour may perhaps still be construed as intentional because leaving the store in this way has saved them time from not queuing. They valued their time more highly than the satisfaction to be gained from the purchased commodities. However, for instances that cannot be analysed as intentional, we need to fill in more detail. The researcher needs to trace back to the data to uncover the conditions that might be causing this variation.

Filling in categories that need further refinement

This is necessary to give 'conceptual density' to the theory as well as developing more conceptual specificity. This filling in phase may continue even up to the process of writing up the project, since report writing itself may reveal gaps and inconsistencies that require attention. If this occurs, the researcher may have to return to the field to collect more data (for example, by interviewing some of the shoppers). This illustrates that the task of data collection and analysis is not necessarily sequential but can be an iterative process.

The grounded theory approach just described should be a dynamic one when *process* is built into the analysis. Process means showing the evolving nature of events by noting why and how action/interaction (in the form of events, doings, or happenings) will change, stay the same, or regress (Strauss and Corbin, 1998). In other words, it is a case of not only noticing changes in phenomena but also of explaining why they occur. As Strauss and Corbin (1998) concede, however, explanations may not always be obvious, even after additional data have been collected. They suggest, therefore, that a more deductive approach is adopted, in terms of a hypothesis, after which the researcher should return to the data to see if this hypothesis can be supported, modified or rejected.

But how and where do changes occur? There are three potential sources:

- Changes can occur in the causal conditions that led to the phenomenon.

- There may be a change in the intervening conditions.

- The outcomes or consequences of the action/interaction may in turn feed back into new causal conditions (see Figure 18.5).

Maintaining theoretical sensitivity

Strauss and Corbin (1998) argue that theoretical sensitivity, keeping an awareness of the subtleties of meaning in data, is an important element of grounded theory. Accordingly, they argue that theoretical sensitivity implies:

> the ability to give meaning to data, the capacity to understand, and capability to separate the pertinent from that which isn't. (Strauss and Corbin, 1998: 42)

Figure 18.5
The impact of
outcomes and
consequences on
the original causal
conditions

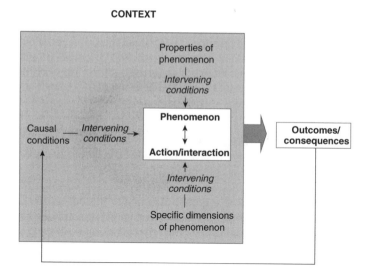

Glaser (1992) links this sensitivity more overtly with theory building, arguing that it is the ability to generate concepts from the data and to relate them,
according to normal models of theory. This sensitivity stems from a number of
sources.

- The literature, which helps highlight issues and what might be important and
  unimportant.

- The professional experience of the researcher, showing what is important in the field
  of research chosen, and how things work, allowing events to be more clearly understood and interpreted.

- Personal experience, including experience in research, which can facilitate the making
  of comparisons.

- The analytical process itself, which can provide insights into the meaning of the data.

Theoretical sensitivity is a way of ensuring that the creativity involved in
qualitative research is harnessed in such a way that the interests of science are
not impeded. The process of scientific inquiry is further facilitated if the
researcher is willing to 'step back from the data' and ask basic questions such
as: do the data really fit the hypothesis? This is part of the process of maintaining a healthy scepticism and realizing that all elements of a study –
hypotheses, concepts, questions, theories, etc. – are provisional. Strauss and
Corbin (1998) advise that a sound approach is to alternate between collecting
and analysing data. Through this approach, analysis can allow for further

questions to emerge, for sample selection and data collection, and the verification of hypotheses as they are being developed.

Concluding grounded research

As we have seen, grounded theory research can involve a fairly continuous iteration between data collection and analysis and between the different levels of coding. So, when is the research completed? When is it time to stop? Glaser and Strauss (1967) suggest that this is when the level of 'theoretical saturation' is reached. By this they mean the non-emergence of new properties, classes, categories or relationships from the data. Knowing when this point is reached, of course, is a matter of experience and judgement. This decision is helped if the research has moved towards the clear identification of core categories (around which the main story line is woven) and peripheral categories of less central significance. Hence, once the analysis has been integrated around the core categories and an adequate theory has emerged, the research could be said to be complete. Note that Bryman (2007a) cautions that grounded theory may be effective in the generation of concepts, but he questions whether it actually produces theory itself.

Before finishing this section, it might be useful to look at grounded theory in relation to other research approaches. Locke (2001), for example, suggests that grounded theory has much in common with:

- Ethnography, in that data collection and theory building are woven together as the researcher progresses (although grounded theorists are less interested in the cultural aspects of contexts).

- Case studies, in that grounded theory may be incorporated into a case study as a means of handling and interpreting data.

- Action research (see Chapter 12), in that both seek to develop theoretical elements that are useful to practitioners within the research setting (although grounded theorists are less concerned with organizational transformation).

OTHER APPROACHES TO QUALITATIVE ANALYSIS

In a sense, having discussed two of the main analytical approaches, content analysis and grounded theory, we are left with the category of 'other' in which there are a considerable number of competing approaches. Three of the most significant, the use of narratives, conversational analysis and discourse analysis, are discussed, briefly, here.

NARRATIVE ANALYSIS

One of the criticisms of content analysis, and particularly of grounded theory approaches, is that they lead to the fragmentation and decontextualization of data away from the social processes they are meant to represent. However, research that encourages the use of oral or life histories, or uses unstructured interviews, often elicits qualitative data in the form of narratives or stories that lead to more holistic data right from the start. Using narratives is an ideal way of capturing the lived experiences of participants and has been used extensively in settings such as research into medical illness, the study of traumatic events, in education, and studies in the life of organizations. Musson (1998), for example, shows how people's narratives can be used to explain the contradictions, confusions and complexities of working within a modern organization, and how this can illuminate how both individuals and their organizations function. The analysis of narrative data is also sensitive to the temporal sequence that people inject into the accounts of their lives or events that surround them (Bryman and Bell, 2007).

While different approaches to the analysis of narratives have been put forward, all have a number of common characteristics. First, the text is viewed in the gestalt, that is, within the context and social situation in which it is created. Next comes the formal analysis of the text, including making distinctions between text that constitute narrative passages, and other forms of text. Where researchers generally differ is in their attitude to the status of the text itself. While some take the 'truth' of the narrative at face value, others see narratives as a special way of constructing events, that is, they are 'social constructions located within power structures and social milieux' (Punch, 2005: 223). In the context of research within organizational settings, narratives bring forth a variety of perspectives and viewpoints, some of which may contradict and contest each other. From a postmodern perspective, the analysis and interpretation of these narratives itself constitutes a narrative, which may be more or less compelling than other interpretations.

CONVERSATIONAL ANALYSIS

Conversational analysis is interested in the formal analysis of everyday conversations (Flick, 2006). Primarily, this includes the analysis of natural texts (often the results of transcribed tape recordings) and seeks to specify the formal principles and mechanisms with which participants express themselves in social interactions, or what Hutchby and Wooffitt (1998) term talk-in-interaction. Research in conversational analysis was originally limited to the study of everyday conversations such as telephone calls or family conversations, but has been extended to institutional-based conversations such as courtrooms, meetings and various kinds of interviews.

Conversational analysis is less concerned with the formal analysis of language per se, than with elements of social interaction such as 'turn taking' or 'opening

up closings', interruptions and the distribution of speaking rights, often in relation to various aspects of an institution's functions (Have, 1999). Hence, conversational analysis is very much focused on the issue of context. Meaning or
order in conversation can only be understood within the context of local practices and are embedded within concrete contexts. Through turn by turn analysis
and the description of conversations, the researcher is able to sense how social
order among participants is accomplished (Samra-Fredericks, 2004).

DISCOURSE ANALYSIS

The focus of discourse analysis is on how both spoken and written language is
used in social contexts. Attention is given to the structure and organization of
language with an emphasis on how participants' versions of events are constructed. In contrast to content analysis, discourse analysis rejects the view that
language is a transparent medium which merely reflects 'reality'. Analysis
becomes focused on recognizing the regularities in language in terms of patterns
and repertoires. These repertoires (constructs) do not emanate from the individual as such, but are embedded in culturally and socially constructed situations.

QUALITY IN QUALITATIVE ANALYSIS

In Chapter 7 we explored how rigour can be enhanced at the design stage. Here
we examine how quality can be improved at the data analysis and data presentation stages, looking once more at the themes of validity and reliability.

VALIDITY

Validity refers to whether a researcher is observing, identifying or measuring
what they claim they are (Mason, 2002). External validity refers to the degree to
which findings can be generalized to other social or organizational settings. As
was noted in Chapter 7, this is difficult to achieve in qualitative research due, in
large part, to the tendency to use case studies and small samples. Internal validity refers to whether there is compelling evidence that the researcher has
achieved a strong link between their evidence and the theoretical ideas they
develop from it. Table 18.4 summarizes a range of techniques through which the
researchers can seek to enhance the internal validity of their results.

Member checking can involve getting respondents to review transcripts of
their interviews both for accuracy and to see if there are any comments they
would like to add. This can even include getting participants to comment on
coding schemes. Expert checking, as the name implies, involves obtaining the
collaboration of research or other experts in validating and approving the
analysis. Does the expert, for example, using the same data, come to the same

TYPE OF TECHNIQUE	TECHNIQUE
Analytic	Member checking
	Expert checking
	Exploring rival explanations
	Writing memos
	Testing hypotheses in data analysis
	Analysing negative cases
	Performing a literature review
Presentation	Providing an audit trail
	Providing evidence that supports interpretations
	Acknowledging the researcher perspective
	Providing thick descriptions

or similar conclusions? Are there rival explanations that have been over-looked? Writing memos both for themselves and for others to review, helps in the generation and checking of concepts and categories. As we saw earlier in this chapter, analytic induction makes use of hypotheses as part of the process. Deciding whether the weight of evidence supports or requires us to reject a hypothesis is a useful way of determining whether claims made for the data analysis are valid or not. Analysing negative or deviant cases can be important here, as they may require the hypothesis to be reformulated and more evidence collected, or the hypothesis to be reformulated so as to exclude the deviant case (as in analytical induction, above). Finally, performing a literature review, allows for the findings of the research study to be compared and contrasted with what previous studies or experts have found.

Validity can be catered for at the data presentation stage through providing an audit trail from the analysis back to the concepts, constructs or data sets from which they were generated. In this way, other researchers can confirm that the analysis is based upon appropriate evidence. If, before this is done, the original researchers make explicit their own philosophical perspectives and intentions, then the task of validators is made much easier. The same goes for 'thick descriptions' through which we not only describe a phenomenon but the context in which it occurs. Providing context encourages more confidence that the interpretations that have been made are valid.

> **Activity 18.3**
>
> Examine the list in Table 18.4. Which of them would you find useful to implement to aid the validity of your own qualitative research?

RELIABILITY

External reliability is the extent to which the findings of a study can be replicated, frequently a challenge in qualitative research which often deals with unique social settings or cases. It is both for epistemological as well as practical reasons that some adherents of qualitative research regard external reliability as either unattainable, unnecessary, or both. Internal reliability is improved by the use of more than one observer in the field, or at the analysis stage when multiple researchers are used in the interpretation of the findings. This often starts with researchers sharing and comparing coding schemes to determine the extent of agreement and consistency. The use of computer-assisted programs for qualitative data analysis (see the following section) often help here. Also recall the discussion in Chapter 7 where some researchers reject this approach to rigour, arguing for criteria such as transferability, dependability, confirmability and credibility.

One element of qualitative analysis, conversational analysis, brings with it some different reliability issues. Since conversational analysis is often based on tapes and transcripts of conversations, in terms of reliability, it is fairly obvious that taped conversations will tend to present more reliable evidence than hastily written field notes. But as Peräkylä (2004) warns, video- or audio-recording of events may lose some important aspects of social interaction. These reliability problems include:

- Time: A single recording of events taking place in an organization may be either unenlightening or completely misleading if those events do not represent what typically happens most of the time. Hence, reliability will be improved with a more longitudinal research design, with multiple visits and recordings.

- 'Ambulatory events': That is, the movements of people that simply do not show up on video or audio recordings. One solution is the setting up of multiple cameras to catch these movements.

- Documentary realities: Some conversations (for example, professional people such as doctors or lawyers talking to their clients) may be influenced by the documents (such as forms) they are discussing. Researchers must have access to these documents and include them in the analysis process.

USING COMPUTER-ASSISTED PROGRAMS

Before the arrival of computer-assisted qualitative analysis programs, researchers had to perform a quite laborious process of writing marginal codes on field notes or transcripts, making photocopies of these documents and physically cutting chunks of text associated with a particular code and pasting them together. Over the last 20 years, or so, computer-assisted qualitative data analysis software (CAQDAS) has made this redundant. Typically, CAQDAS software allows the researcher to:

- Import transcripts or other computer-generated documents directly into the program.

- Work through the data, marking words, phrases or sections of text with codes.

- For each code, collect together all the chunks of text associated with that code.

It is important to note what CAQDAS programs do not do. They do not generate codes for you – this, obviously is the task of the researcher. The researcher still also has to interpret the data. But CAQDAS software does cut out much of the drudgery of manipulating qualitative data. Yet in doing this, there can be drawbacks. Richards, for example, warns of the danger of 'coding fetishism' (2002: 269). Since computers can code so easily, the novice researcher can easily get 'hooked' on coding so that it becomes an end in itself. Coding, then, comes to drive out the need for interpretation. What is essential is that researchers move beyond the 'search-and-retrieve' functionality of CAQDAS programs. Certainly, such programs are very effective at doing this and it is an important function. But, as Richards (2002) points out, CAQDAS also provides you with the opportunity to retrieve all the data on a coded theme, to browse the data, and, if necessary, to recode it, or explore it against new dimensions. Hence, coding becomes an iterative, creative processes, not something that is just done once and halted. The following case study provides an illustration of how one CAQDAS market leader, NVivo, was used in the analysis of qualitative data. Note that the intention here is not to provide you with a tutorial on how to use NVivo itself (there are many of these available on the Web and elsewhere), but to demonstrate the process of using a CAQDAS program in analysing raw data.

CASE STUDY 18.3   CODING WITH NVIVO

A study was undertaken which explored the kinds of criteria business leaders apply when choosing the people they employ as executive coaches. A literature review had identified the possibility that male and female executives might employ different criteria when making this choice. Thirty interviews were conducted, the tapes transcribed and the Word files imported into NVivo.

The first stage in the analysis process was the construction of *nodes*. A node in NVivo is used to represent a code, theme or idea about the data. NVivo offers a number of different nodes, including *free nodes*, *tree nodes* and *case nodes*. Free nodes are free-standing and are not associated with a framework of themes or concepts. At the start of the coding process free nodes were used because it was not clear how codes related to each other. However, later this became clearer and free nodes were converted into tree nodes. Tree nodes are codes that are organized in a hierarchical structure of related themes. Case nodes are used to store information about a case, which might include data from interviews, field notes or focus groups. Codes can be a priori, based upon themes that have emerged from the literature search, or in vivo, emerging from a reading of the text. For this project, the nodes created from previous reading comprised a number of attributes that other research studies had revealed as potentially important: qualifications, experience, career development and coaching skills (including sub-themes such as empathy, ability to set objectives and career development skills). However, on reading the text, several respondents (both men and women) mentioned that they had deliberately chosen female coaches. Hence, gender was added as a node.

An interactive and iterative process then took place, applying existing nodes to the data and creating new nodes from the data. For example, several respondents mentioned either a strong like or strong dislike for coaches who were experts in Neuro-linguistic programming techniques – NLP was therefore added as a node. Further exploration of the data then led to some nodes being modified or even eliminated. For example, the node 'career development' which came from the mentoring literature was not mentioned by these beneficiaries of coaching and was abandoned. As each node was created, a memo was written which described and explained the node and added some preliminary thoughts or ideas about the node and relationships within the data. These memos became part of the data analysis. A series of attributes (variables) were then added to each case node, including the gender of each respondent, their age and the industry sector they worked in.

The next stage in the process involved querying the data. Since it was suspected that male and female coaches may have different attitudes towards the selection of coaches, a coding query was run on the attribute 'male' and then on 'female'. A more sophisticated query was then used

(Cont'd)

which added a second attribute, age, making it possible to explore the data for the views of young and older women and then young and older men. Queries were then run on attitudes towards coaches with expertise in NLP. Two nodes had previously been created, 'Likes NLP' and 'Dislikes NLP'. The results of each query were then saved as nodes. Following this creative process of creating nodes and running (and saving) queries on the data, allowed for the testing out of ideas about the potential relationship between variables and for the development of at least provisional theories.

Activity 18.4

Explore some of the tutorials on NVivo at the following websites:

- www.sagepub.co.uk/richards/pdf/Tutorial_1.pdf
- www.qsrinternational.com/support_tutorials.aspx?productid=7

TOP TIP 18.3

Should you use a CAQDAS program or not? The answer probably rests on the amount of qualitative data you are trying to analyse. All software programs come with a built-in overhead – the amount of time and effort you need to learn them to a sufficient level of proficiency. If, say, you have conducted 10 one-hour interviews, generating about 60 pages of transcripts, you could probably conduct a manual analysis, using the approach discussed in 'Elements of qualitative data analysis', above. If, however, you feel that the amount of data generated is substantial and fairly overwhelming, then by all means make use of NVivo or a similar program. Learning a CAQDAS program will also give you a useful research skill for the future.

ON THE WEB 18.1

Evaluate the wide range of software packages for qualitative analysis at the following websites:

http://caqdas.soc.surrey.ac.uk/index.htm

http://www.scolari.co.uk/

SUMMARY

- Qualitative data can have a quality of 'undeniability' because they are rooted in the natural context of field settings.

- The main focus of qualitative analysis is to understand the ways in which people act and the accounts that people give for these actions.

- Approaches to qualitative data analysis include content analysis and grounded theory. Content analysis involves locating classes or categories within the data. These categories are usually derived from theoretical models. In contrast, grounded theory uses a process of open, axial and selective coding to develop categories and theories inductively from the data.

- Due to the lack of non-probability sampling methods, qualitative analysis is open to accusations of invalidity. However, claims for the validity of results can be strengthened, for example, by eliciting the views of research participants.

- The reliability of qualitative research can be strengthened by using multiple cases, or by supporting assertions using numerous examples, or by verifying the analysis using other researchers. Concepts such as credibility, authenticity, honesty and openness are also important in qualitative research.

- CAQDAS programs provide useful functionality for qualitative data coding and analysis. But before embarking on the process of learning a program, make sure that the quantity of data requiring analysis justifies the expenditure of time.

⋮// SUMMARY OF WEB LINKS /

http://caqdas.soc.surrey.ac.uk/index.htm

http://www.scolari.co.uk/

FURTHER READING

Bazaley, P. (2007) *Qualitative Data Analysis with NVivo*. London: Sage. Provides a step-by-step guide to using NVivo, plus a set of data files that the tutorials show you how to manipulate and analyse.

Symon, G. and Cassell, C. (2004) (eds) *Qualitative Methods and Analysis in Organizational Research*, 2nd edn. London: Sage. Presents a refreshing array of qualitative techniques that are dealt with only sparingly by many of the standard texts. Subjects include: life histories, critical incident techniques, qualitative research diaries and pictorial representation.

Etherington, K. (2004) *Becoming a Reflexive Researcher*. London: Jessica Kingsley. A book in which the author uses a range of personal narratives to show how reflexive research works in practice.

Locke, K. (2001) *Grounded Theory in Management Research*. London: Sage. Provides a detailed summary of the evolution of grounded theory, and illustrates how it can be applied in a management and organizational context.

Flick, U. (1998) *An Introduction to Qualitative Research*. London: Sage. Deals with all the major theories and methods of qualitative research design, including some less well known approaches such as the use of personal narratives.

Fielding, N. and Lee, R.M. (1998) *Computer Analysis and Qualitative Research*. London: Sage. A valuable introduction to some of the principles of using computers in qualitative research as well as a practical guide to managing data and coding categories.

Miles, M.B. and Huberman, A.M. (1994) *Qualitative Data Analysis*, 2nd edn. Thousand Oaks, CA: Sage. Still an outstanding source of many and varied qualitative analysis methods.

The Use of Focus Groups in Social Science Research

CAROLINE OATES

In the social sciences, the focus group is becoming an increasingly frequent technique for interviewing research participants, but despite this recent popularity, there is some uncertainty about what the term 'focus group' actually means. There are several books devoted to the definition, use and analysis of focus groups (Morgan, 1988, 1993; Stewart and Shamdasani, 1990), yet the term remains vague and is often used interchangeably with others such as 'group discussions' or 'group depth interviews'. This chapter will identify the key characteristics of focus groups, consider their appropriate uses and illustrate their application with an example from research on readers of women's magazines in the UK. The chapter will then conclude with a discussion of the advantages and disadvantages of using focus groups.

What is a Focus Group?

Focus groups have been used by market researchers since the 1920s (Basch, 1987) and by social scientists since the 1940s. Merton was the first to use this technique in his research on the public's reaction to morale films during World War II and he coined the phrase 'the focussed interview' (Merton and Kendall, 1955). Since their original use by Merton, focus groups have become widely used. Thus, there is some confusion as to the nature of a focus group and how it is distinguished from other methods of group interviewing. Kitzinger (1994: 103) has defined focus groups as 'group discussions organised to explore a specific set of issues such as people's views and experiences of contraception, drink driving, nutrition or mental illness'. The group is focused in the sense that it involves some kind of collective activity such as viewing a film (as in Merton's original research), examining a health education message or reading magazines. But what distinguishes the focus group technique from the wider range of group interviews is 'the explicit use of the group interaction as research data' (Kitzinger, 1994: 103). Thus, although focus groups can provide insight into the experiences of individual participants, their value lies in the opportunity to analyse the interaction between participants (Catterall and Maclaran, 1997). This is the key to focus group research and what makes it such an insightful technique. As Morgan suggests, 'focus groups are useful when it comes to investigating *what* participants think, but they excel at uncovering *why* participants think as they do' (Morgan, 1988: 25). Focus groups can achieve this because the participants not only articulate their views and experiences about a particular topic, but also explain to the other members of the group why they hold those views. Such interaction occurs as participants question each other, or challenge views which might differ from their own. Participants are obliged to expose the reasoning behind their own opinions, allowing the researcher to explore and record such interaction. As participants think and reason out loud, their changing attitudes within the context of the group can be documented (Catterall and Maclaran, 1997). Not only do focus groups provide space for interaction between participants, but they also allow the researcher to access sites of 'collective remembering' (Kitzinger, 1994: 105). By using preformed groups (a practice discouraged by market research manuals but common in academic research), Kitzinger explored how people talked about AIDS within the various overlapping groups in which they normally operate. The advantage of using participants who knew each other meant that friends or colleagues were able to relate comments made in the focus group to events in their everyday, shared lives. Thus, Kitzinger was able to tap into fragments of interactions which resembled naturally occurring data. Further, using pre-existing groups is appropriate because groups form a social context in which ideas are nurtured and decisions made. However, it must be remembered that focus groups are artificial situations and therefore the data is not completely natural – the groups are deliberately constructed for the purpose of gathering data. A focus group is more than a group interview or discussion because of the *community of interest* shared by the group and the use of *participants' interaction* as research data.

When Should Focus Groups be Used?

Although focus groups can be used to produce quantitative data (for example, they can be systematically coded via content analysis; see Stewart and Shamdasani, 1990; Lunt and Livingstone, 1996), they are almost always used to collect qualitative data. This is one of the strengths of focus groups – their production of rich data in the participants' own words. But this can also be seen as a failing of focus groups in their inability to yield hard data. There are also concerns over representativeness. However, all techniques of data collection have their limitations and the key to using focus groups successfully is to ensure they are consistent with the objectives and purpose of the research. According to Kitzinger (1994), focus groups are invaluable for grounded theory development, that is focusing on the generation rather than the testing of theory and exploring the categories which participants use to order their experiences. Focus groups put the emphasis on the participants' ways of understanding, their language and what they feel is important. Focus groups can also be used with sensitive topics, although not all writers would agree. Kitzinger (1994) suggests focus groups are appropriate for discussing issues like AIDS because they provide safety in numbers and the company of others who share similar experiences. Schlesinger *et al.* (1992) used focus groups with women to explore issues around films and violence. Focus groups can also be used with populations that may be seen as particularly sensitive: for example, Buckingham (1987) held focus groups with children to explore the meanings in the television soap opera *EastEnders*. Therefore, they can be used for a variety of purposes and with different populations.

Focus groups can be used alone or combined with other methods. Lunt and Livingstone (1996) suggest that the use of focus groups as a self-contained method is becoming more frequent in the social sciences. However, focus groups can be combined with other sources of data in the triangulation method, where different forms of data on the same topic are collected. For example, Radway (1987) used focus groups and individual interviews together in a wider research study to inform her of how women read and use romantic fiction. Jackson and Holbrook

(1995) utilized a number of different methods in their research design, including focus groups, and discuss how these methods worked in their study of shopping and identity. Thus, focus groups can be used without additional methods or can be part of a wider research study. Stewart and Shamdasani (1990) sum up the more common uses of focus groups:

1   Learning how respondents talk about the topic of interest.
2   Generating research hypotheses that can be submitted to further research and testing.
3   Stimulating new ideas.
4   Diagnosing the potential for problems with a new service or programme.
5   Obtaining general background information about a topic of interest.
6   Interpreting previously obtained quantitative results.

Focus Groups in Practice

In this section, I shall discuss my own research using focus groups. This will raise several questions about the practical issues involved in the focus group method and how they might be resolved in relation to other research. This section should also enable readers to judge whether the focus group approach is appropriate for their own research projects.

Background

The focus groups used in my study were part of a research project investigating women's use of certain weekly magazines. During the 1980s the previously staid domestic women's magazine market had been transformed by the launch of three new titles, *Prima*, *Best* and *Bella*, all owned by German publishers. A fourth title was added to the list in 1990 when *Take a Break* was launched. These four magazines were an immediate success and spurred British publishers like International Publishing Corporation (IPC) to respond by creating new magazines to compete. In addition, existing titles were given an overhaul to bring them up to date and the tactics used by the German publishers were imitated by the British. As a result, the weekly women's magazine market became more homogeneous as other titles copied the style and content of *Best*, *Bella* and *Take a Break*.

At the same time as the revolution in the magazine market, the academic approach to popular culture was undergoing change. Notions of the audience were beginning to be problematized. Rather than investigating the content of media forms and then inferring an ideal reader, writers like Morley (1980) had begun to explore the audience itself, looking at how readers/viewers responded to media messages. From the idea of a passive audience, which had been the accepted paradigm, came the idea of an active, critical, knowing audience, opening the way for studies on how people watched *Nationwide* (Morley, 1980) or read teenage magazines like *Jackie* (Frazer, 1992). This change in audience perception, combined with the new magazines and the changing role of women in society, prompted a sociological analysis of how women were reading and using *Best*, *Bella* and *Take a Break*, and whether the magazines could be identified in any way with the backlash against feminism concept (Faludi, 1991).

Given my research topic, it was appropriate to consider focus groups as a means of gathering data. Women read magazines in various social locations, as well as at home and because they discuss magazines with friends or colleagues, interviewing in a group situation seemed particularly suitable. Previous research on women's magazines had focused on the content. My intention was to explore the reading of magazines and how women made sense of them. The interaction between participants would be valuable and the research would take a different approach from previous studies.

Access

One of the main problems in choosing the focus group method is the question of access – and this brings further associated problems:

- Where do you find your target population?
- How many groups do you need?
- How many people should be in each group?
- Should you use new or preformed groups?
- Does the composition of the groups matter?
- What location would be best for the group?
- Should you tape-record the group?
- Should you use questionnaires in conjunction with the focus group?

Having gradually realized that all these issues needed to be dealt with, it became clear why nobody had used focus groups in an academic research project with magazine readers before (although the magazines do have their own, very thorough research agendas which are conducted by market researchers using focus groups). The chief obstacle was access. Although millions of women read *Best*, *Bella* and *Take a Break*, there were no obvious means of contacting any of them. My uncertainty about how to access and then use focus groups was by no means unusual. Because previous researchers have rarely described their methodology, it was difficult to find others' experiences of using focus groups. Recently, there has been recognition of this omission and writers such as Holbrook and Jackson (1996) have detailed their own difficulties and uncertainties about using focus groups.

After having worked my way through several possible options, I decided to approach women I knew from my previous jobs in schools and a bank. This would mean using pre-existing groups, but I felt this would be an advantage when discussing magazines, because the intention was to access the everyday and taken-for-granted uses of magazines between readers. Using existing friendship networks seemed to be an ideal way to tap into the normal routines and uses of women's magazine reading. In her recent book on magazine readers, Hermes (1995) used not only friends but family for her interviews. Therefore, previous studies have used people known to the researcher, but this should not be allowed to restrict the sample if diversity is required. A recognized option is to start with friends or colleagues and then snowball to unknown others. (Snowball sampling is discussed more fully by Burton in Chapter 21.) Once all my existing networks had been utilized I snowballed to related groups, for example, playgroups and mother and toddler groups, via my original contacts.

Size and number of focus groups

When the access issue had been resolved, the number of focus groups required and how many people should be in each had to be arranged. In a sense, the latter question was already decided. Although it is suggested that the ideal number for a group is between eight and twelve (Stewart and Shamdasani, 1990), there may be little choice for the researcher. Given that I was returning to old workplaces, I really had to accept however many women happened to be in the staffroom at the time. Fortunately, there always seemed to be an appropriate number, and if there were too many it was possible to split them into two groups. For example, a local playgroup held their meetings in a small room which was adjacent to the church hall, so it was feasible to carry out two focus groups in succession. Carrying out the focus groups led to the conclusion that the recommended size of between eight and twelve members for each group is too high – a more manageable number is between six and ten.

The number of focus groups needed depends on the required amount of diversity among participants and the use of different locations. Knowing that women's magazines are read in a variety of situations, I felt it would be informative to conduct focus groups both at work and at leisure, and also with readers of different ages and backgrounds. It was a case of covering a wide range of readers with different characteristics. Knodel (1993) has formalized this process of difference by suggesting that groups be organized according to *break* and *control* characteristics. Control characteristics are common to all groups, and break characteristics differentiate groups from each other. Thus, for my research, all group members had the common characteristic of being women and also readers of women's magazines, but break characteristics included age and family position. Incorporating break characteristics into the research design is necessary for contrasting views between subgroups and also for establishing common views.

A useful means of deciding how many focus groups to run is suggested by Lunt and Livingstone (1996) who advise that the researcher should continue to run new groups until the last group has nothing to add, but simply repeats previous contributions. For my own study, I found that fourteen focus groups were appropriate.

Researcher as interviewer
Before returning to the schools and bank, I had written to or contacted colleagues to explain my research and ask permission to carry out a focus group. Having received permission, I prepared a schedule of questions or topic areas to ask in the group. This schedule needs careful preparation and the role of the researcher in leading the discussion has to be acknowledged. The researcher provides the agenda for discussion by virtue of her role in the group. Participants look to the researcher (or moderator) for direction, particularly at the beginning of the focus group. When the researcher suggests a new topic or area by asking a certain question, the group tends to comply. It is up to the researcher to decide how much she wants to direct the group and she needs to be flexible with the interview schedule. Some groups need little direction after the discussion has started, while others need frequent questions. It depends on whether the researcher has specific information needs or whether the aim is to learn about what the group thinks is important. These issues will be determined by the broader research agenda and the information required. At the very least a list of topic areas is recommended, which serves two purposes: it helps to reduce the researcher's nervousness, particularly in the first few groups; and it gives a broad outline to the discussion, preventing it from straying into unrelated areas.

Location of the focus group
Choosing the location for focus groups can be quite a problem. In many of the books about focus groups, it is assumed that there will be money to pay for the hire of a room which is specially designed for hosting focus groups. This is unrealistic for many researchers and there may be little choice in location. The focus groups I carried out in the workplace usually took place in the staffroom of the bank or schools, and those in leisure situations had to be in any available room. Sometimes shortage of quiet space posed problems, particularly in the mother and toddler groups. The lack of a quiet, separate room meant that the women were constantly interrupted by their children and the noise level was high. The focus groups carried out in these groups tended to be much shorter than any of the other focus groups. The average time is usually between one hour and an hour and a half, but the shorter ones lasted for thirty minutes only. Therefore, it is important to check before finalizing a potential focus group that there will be a suitable space which is quiet. Otherwise the level of recording may be too poor to allow for the tape to be transcribed.

Use of materials

As suggested earlier, one of the defining characteristics of a focus group is its use of materials to facilitate discussion and interaction between participants. I used *Bella*, *Best* and *Take a Break* for this purpose, with a number of similar weeklies included for comparison and articulation of difference between titles. The same magazine issues were used for every focus group, thus allowing potential analysis of both similarities and differences between groups in relation to the same stories or articles. Having the magazines there served further purposes in addition to facilitating interactive discussion. At the beginning of the group, members sometimes felt self-conscious about voicing their opinions and so the magazines 'broke the ice' as the women looked through them together or recalled certain issues they had already seen. If some women were familiar with only one or two of the titles, it was an opportunity for other members of the group to explain why they liked the magazines. At any awkward moments when conversation tailed off or began to drift into other unrelated topics, the magazines could be used to draw attention back to the relevant topic. Kitzinger (1994) noted that use of card games or vignettes served to 'warm up' participants, encouraging them to engage with one another, but this has the disadvantage that some people do not like such games and might be made to feel uncomfortable. The advantage of using magazines was the familiarity of them to participants and the instant shared reference points of being a *Take a Breakie* or a *Best* or *Bella* fan.

Group dynamics

Each focus group has its own dynamics and it is difficult to predict how the members will interact. Carrying out two focus groups, one after the other, at a mother and toddler group, illustrated how similar groups may differ. The first group was vocal, interested and lively, with many new points about magazines I had not considered. Yet the second group was quiet, unenthusiastic and not very interested in the magazines they read. Both kinds of groups can present problems to the researcher: the first kind because there is often a dominant member who tries to take over the conversation, or because the conversation is so fast and loud that it is difficult to keep track of people's comments and explore interesting points which may arise; the second because the researcher has to work that much harder, and impose more of her own agenda onto the discussion.

   Reading theoretical books about focus groups gives the novice researcher the impression that all groups run smoothly, with well-modulated conversations and polite members taking it in turns to speak. The reality is very different. There will be times when the tape is untranscribable because of the number of people talking at the same time, or because two people at the other end of the table are having their own private conversation. Running a focus group takes practice. There is a fine line between letting people have their say, allowing the discussion to degenerate into an incomprehensible noise, or being so in control that there is no interaction whatsoever between the participants. It is advisable to have one or two practice sessions first with friends, just to get the feel of knowing when to speak or how to prevent one person from dominating the discussion.

Recording the focus group

The use of tape recorders in recording the focus group discussions has already been mentioned and I suggest that these are essential (but see Chapter 22 for an alternative view of recording). All my focus groups were taped as it is impossible to take notes as well as moderate a group, and this is also distracting for the participants. A small recorder, placed discreetly in the middle of the table, is soon forgotten after the first few nervous comments and it leaves the researcher free to concentrate on the interaction. It also means the researcher can quote verbatim from participants when writing up the research.

This latter point introduces the issue of confidentiality. Permission has to be obtained from the group before taping and it has to be explained that the outcome of the research might be published. The use of pseudonyms for group members is essential, but to ensure the participants can be identified on the tape when transcribing, it is useful to get each person to state their name at the beginning of the discussion. This also helps the moderator in addressing participants and gets the conversation going. It is helpful to transcribe the tapes as quickly as possible after doing each focus group and also to write brief notes after the groups about the discussion or any particular comments which were unusual. Morgan (1988: 63) calls these 'field notes' and suggests they are an essential element of focus groups because they are both part of the data collection and a preliminary form of analysis.

Use of questionnaires
In my research project, I designed a questionnaire to elicit both personal details and details about the participants' reading habits and use of other media in addition to women's magazines. The purpose of this information was to allow comparisons between participants according to their different characteristics (for example, to see if women without children read magazines differently to those with a family). Where possible, these were given out before the focus groups were held so that participants would have time to think a little about the magazines they read. The use of these questionnaires became rather haphazard. Sometimes they were administered before the focus group, sometimes afterwards and in one group some of the women had reading and writing difficulties and the questionnaires had to be abandoned altogether. Thus, use of questionnaires to acquire background details, while useful for identifying participants' age, occupation and marital status, needs to be organized within the research design, where the relevance of participants' characteristics should be decided. Being consistent and always distributing the questionnaires before the focus group begins is the most advantageous strategy, as this helps the participants to start thinking about the topic (although the questionnaires should not be too long as participants may lose interest). For a discussion of the most appropriate way to use questionnaires in focus group research, see Morgan (1988).

Summary of Advantages and Disadvantages of Focus Groups

Advantages

1   Participants can react to and build on the responses of other group members.
2   Focus groups allow the researcher to interact directly with respondents.
3   They allow the researcher to obtain rich data in the participants' own words.
4   They provide data from a group of people more quickly than interviewing individuals.
5   Focus groups are flexible in their suitability for investigating a wide range of topics.
6   They are suitable for use with children.
7   The results of a focus group are accessible and understandable.

Disadvantages

1   The small number of respondents limit generalization to the wider population.
2   The results may be biased by a particularly dominant group member.
3   The open-ended nature of responses may make interpreting results difficult.
4   The researcher as interviewer may influence the responses of the group members.

(Adapted from Stewart and Shamdasani, 1990)

Conclusion

Focus groups are a rich source of qualitative data for the social science researcher and as such are an attractive and popular method of data collection. But they are not particularly easy to use. The researcher needs to have means of access to willing participants and also to have the skills to interview and moderate those participants. This chapter has raised some of the issues involved in using focus groups as a research method and has discussed some of the main advantages and disadvantages. As with any issues in social sciences, there are no right or wrong ways of doing focus groups. It is up to the individual researcher to design their own study and to use focus groups appropriately. Clearly, they are better suited to certain kinds of research questions than others. This chapter should have helped to explain when focus groups are most useful and whether they should be incorporated into the researcher's own design.

Lecture 3

Case Studies

12 Case Study Research

MICHAEL D. MYERS

Objectives

By the end of this chapter, you will be able to:

- Understand the purpose of case study research
- Appreciate the difference between teaching cases and research cases
- Distinguish between different approaches to conducting case study research
- Be more confident in doing case study research
- Identify the advantages and disadvantages of case study research
- Evaluate case study research
- See how case study research has been used in business and management

INTRODUCTION

In all of the business disciplines, case studies are used in many different ways. The two most popular uses of case studies in business schools are, first, in teaching, and, second, in research.

In teaching, case studies are tremendously helpful to students in allowing them to understand better the theory and principles that are relevant to business. Case studies illustrate a principle or a particular point that the instructor wishes to make. They show that the theory has a practical application and bring the subject matter to life. Probably the most famous case studies of this type – in business schools at least – are the Harvard cases published by the Harvard Business School. These cases describe actual situations that the instructor and students explore together. The idea is for the students to figure out by themselves the 'correct' answer or answers to the discussion

Table 7.1   A comparison of teaching and research cases

Teaching cases	Research cases
Written primarily for students	Written primarily for researchers
Designed to illustrate an existing theory or principle	Designed to contribute to a new theory or explore/test an existing theory
Published on its own as a teaching case, often with notes for the instructor	Published as part of a research article in a journal, conference, or book

questions. As students study more cases, hopefully they get better at identifying current business problems and solutions, and how such solutions might be implemented.

Teaching case studies are thus written for students of business. They are designed to illustrate a more general point or a theory that is already well known to most, if not all, instructors in the subject. The purpose of teaching cases is to help students learn. The cases themselves may be based on real life or they may be fictional.

By contrast, research case studies are written primarily for researchers, not students. Research cases are used as empirical evidence to convince other researchers of the applicability (or inapplicability) of a particular theory or proposition. If the case is first published as part of a research article, the particular point that the research article makes is likely to be new to those reviewing the paper (i.e. other experts in the same field). The purpose of research cases is thus to contribute to knowledge in a particular field. Teaching and research cases are compared in Table 7.1.

This chapter is concerned with the use of case studies in research, but does not deal with the use of case studies in teaching. Although the writing of teaching cases for business students is a very worthwhile activity and one that I fully support, the preparation and writing of case studies for teaching purposes is outside the scope of this book. Instead, this book focuses on the use of case studies for research in business, hence the name of this chapter.

Writing a research case requires different skills and knowledge than when writing a teaching case. To write a teaching case, an author needs to be familiar with the subject matter of the course being taught: for example, the textbook and readings that are used in that course. The author also needs to gain access to or to create an interesting scenario that illustrates the point to be made. However, the theory or the guidelines that the case is designed to illustrate may or may not be explicitly mentioned in the write-up of the case itself. As a general rule, the write-up will include few, if any, citations of the relevant research literature. This is because the very idea of a teaching case is often for students to 'discover' the applicable theory or principles for themselves. One of the key things about creating teaching cases is that the case needs to be written in an engaging manner such that students are inspired and encouraged to learn.

To write a research case, the author needs to have a much higher and more detailed knowledge of the subject matter. The author needs to be familiar with, and cite, the latest research on the particular topic in question. The author also needs to write up a case that directly relates to that research topic. The case needs to be written in such a way that the story is plausible and convinces other researchers that the research article is indeed a new contribution to knowledge in the field. The case also needs to be written in an engaging manner, such that fellow researchers will find the story interesting.

THEORY BUILDING FROM CASE STUDIES IN MANAGEMENT

Following the logic of inductive case study methods, Dutta, Zbaracki, and Bergen (2003) analysed the data collected from a study of the pricing process of a large manufacturing firm in an iterative manner: first, they analysed the data and compared the data with existing theory; second, they developed a new theory; third, they returned to the data to see how the emergent theory matched the data; lastly, they returned to the theory for yet another revision (Dutta et al., 2003).

Research case studies can be used in the exploratory phase of a research topic, to discover the relevant features, factors, or issues that might apply in other similar situations. In this way, case studies are used in the early stages of research on a particular topic. Research cases can also be used in explanatory research, when there is already a large body of literature on the subject. In this way, case studies can be used to test theory, to develop causal explanations, or even to compare theories. It is mistake to suggest, as some do, that research cases can only be used in an exploratory way.

RESEARCH CASES CAN BE USED:

- In exploratory research – to discover.
- In explanatory research – to test, to explain, or to compare.

Case study research is thus applicable at any stage of the research on a particular topic. The key defining feature of case study research is not *when* in the research process it should be used, but *what* is studied. The 'what' are contemporary real-life situations where there is no control on the part of the researcher and where everything might happen all at once. Real life is sometimes messy, but then business theories that are unable to deal with messy real-life situations are probably of little value.

In a business discipline, case study research uses empirical evidence from real people in contemporary real-life organizations. The specific topics vary widely, from current marketing practices in marketing through to the implementation of enterprise resource planning (ERP) systems in the field of information systems. But a defining feature of case study research is its focus on asking 'how' and 'why' questions. The case study researcher seeks to understand how and why a particular business decision was made, or how and why a business process works the way it does. Unlike action research, the case study researcher does not deliberately intervene in a situation but seeks, at least in the first instance, simply to describe it. And as was mentioned earlier, as distinct from teaching cases, the primary audience for the case study write-up is fellow researchers in a particular discipline, not students. The case study write-up has to convince these fellow researchers that the case study is an original contribution to knowledge. These fellow researchers might be the examiners of your Masters or PhD thesis, or reviewers from a peer-reviewed research conference or journal.

> The purpose of case study research in business and management is to use empirical evidence from real people in real organizations to make an original contribution to knowledge.

A CLASSIC THEORY-TESTING CASE STUDY

One of the most cited articles in the field of information systems is a theory-testing case study written by Markus (1983). Markus compared three theories of resistance with the implementation of computer-based information systems (IS), using an in-depth case study to test the predictions of each theory.

The first theory of IS implementation is what she calls a 'people-determined' theory. This theory assumes that people resist IS because of factors internal to the person or group. An example of this is when it is said that 'people resist change'.

(Cont'd)

The second theory of IS implementation is what she calls a 'system-determined' theory. This theory assumes that people resist IS because of factors inherent in the system itself. In this second theory, resistance is determined externally by the environment or the technology.

The first theory thus suggests that 'people' are the primary cases of resistance, whereas the second theory suggests that 'systems' or the technology are the primary cases of resistance.

Markus suggested a third theory – a theory of interaction. The third theory holds that people resist IS because of an interaction between characteristics related to the people and characteristics related to the system.

Using empirical data from a case study of the implementation of a financial information system, Markus showed that the interaction theory has superior explanatory and predictive power (Markus, 1983).

Defining Case Study Research

The word 'case study' has multiple meanings. The simplest idea of 'a case' is that the phenomenon described is of a more general category. That is, the description of a particular case or situation is used to draw some conclusions about the phenomenon more generally. For example, a medical journal might describe the case of an asthma patient who showed certain symptoms after taking a particular medication. The particular case might be new and unique, but the case is still an example of a more general phenomenon (e.g. asthma).

A somewhat narrower definition of a case study, one that is more applicable for the social sciences, is that it is a detailed study of a single social unit: 'The social unit is usually located in one physical place, the people making up the unit being differentiated from others who are not part of it. In short, the unit has clear boundaries which make it easy to identify' (Payne & Payne, 2004: 31). A case study can be of a social process, an organization, or any collective social unit.

Along similar lines, Yin (2003) defines a case study in two parts, as follows:

1 A case study is an empirical inquiry that

   - Investigates a contemporary phenomenon within its real-life context, especially when
   - The boundaries between phenomenon and context are not clearly evident

2 The case study inquiry

- Copes with the technically distinctive situation in which there will be many more variables of interest than data points, and as one result
- Relies on multiple sources of evidence, with data needing to converge in a triangulating fashion, and as another result
- Benefits from the prior development of theoretical propositions to guide data collection and analysis. (pp. 13–14)

The first part of Yin's definition specifies the scope of a case study. The real-life context of a case means that the phenomenon of interest is not studied divorced from its context. In case study research, it is in fact very difficult to separate the phenomenon of interest from the context, because the context itself is part and parcel of the story. Also, in a case study the researcher has no control over the situation. This contrasts with the use of some other research methods such as a laboratory experiment, where the whole idea is for the researcher to maintain control of certain specified variables and to separate clearly the context from the phenomenon.

The second part of Yin's definition specifies the data collection and data analysis strategies. Yin advocates using multiple sources of evidence, triangulating these data, and using theoretical propositions from the research literature to guide the research.

Although Yin's definition of a case study is very helpful – and I thoroughly recommend his book as one of the best books available on case study research – the definition does not necessarily fit all case studies within the business disciplines. In one respect it is too broad, in another it is too narrow.

Yin's definition is too broad in the sense that case studies in business are usually restricted to studies of one or more business organizations. A 'case study' in business is almost always synonymous with a study of some business aspect of an organization. This organizational focus is an important identifying feature of most case studies in the business disciplines, and distinguishes case study research in business from case study research in other fields. In other fields, there can be case studies of educational programmes, or case studies of communities in a local neighbourhood. But as these are not studies of a business-related issue in an organization, they would not qualify as being called case study research in business.

Yin's definition is too narrow in the sense that he advocates just one type of case study research. This is perhaps best described as a positivist approach to case study research. Like most positivist researchers, Yin recommends the prior development of theoretical propositions or hypotheses. He also suggests that the quality of case study research designs can be judged by paying attention to four design tests, namely, construct validity, internal validity, external validity, and reliability. However, there are other types of case studies such as interpretive and critical case study research that do not require or recommend the use of propositions or hypotheses in research. Also, these other types of case study research do not use the words 'validity' or 'reliability' as part of their quality assessment.

The aim of Buxey's (2005) research project was to document how the Australian textiles, clothing, and footwear industry has responded to the forces of globalization. Given the high level of competition within the industry, the objective of the study was to discover what strategies the survivors employed.

Buxey conducted three representative cases of firms in the industry. He describes the strategy that each firm employed in responding to the forces of globalization (Buxey, 2005).

Hence, while Yin's (2003) book can be regarded as one of the most useful books on case study research – and it is widely cited by researchers in most business disciplines – his definition of case study research is not entirely appropriate for all qualitative researchers in business. Therefore I propose my own definition of case study research as follows:

Case study research in business uses empirical evidence from one or more organizations where an attempt is made to study the subject matter in context. Multiple sources of evidence are used, although most of the evidence comes from interviews and documents.

There are three important points to note about this definition:

1 This definition draws attention to the fact that case study research in business *almost always involves a firm or organization,* even if the main issue, topic, or subject matter being studied is something else. For example, a case study of a joint venture might focus primarily on the joint venture – its governance, its financial or marketing success – but the researcher would still use empirical evidence from one or more of the organizations concerned; a case study in information systems might focus on an information systems development project, but the project will be situated within one or more organizations; or a case study in marketing might focus primarily on the development of brands, but these brands would still involve one or more firms. The most common

research cases in business, therefore, have an explicit organizational focus and tell the story of that organization.

2   This definition also distinguishes case study research from ethnographic research. Case study research, even in-depth case study research, *does not normally involve participant observation or fieldwork*. Most of the empirical evidence in case study research in business comes from interviews and documents. Ethnographic research, on the other hand, relies extensively on data from fieldwork. Fieldwork is the defining feature of ethnography.

3   Lastly, this definition of case study research is philosophically neutral. That is, it allows for the fact that *case study research can be conducted according to positivist, interpretive, or critical tenets* of what is considered to be 'good' research. These different types of case study research are discussed next.

APPROACHES TO CASE STUDY RESEARCH

Just like action research, case study research can take positivist, interpretive, or critical forms. These three types correspond to the three main philosophical approaches to research discussed in Chapter 3.

Positivist case study research was the norm in business schools some 10 or 15 years ago. However, interpretive case studies have become more accepted over the past decade and now appear on a reasonably regular basis in the top journals and conferences of most business disciplines. There are still very few critical case studies, but I predict that these will increase over the next decade.

The first type of case study research, positivist case study research, attempts to meet the requirements of positivist social science. Work of this kind is often justified in positivistic terms – case study research is seen as a method for testing and refining hypotheses or propositions in the real world. An example of this approach is Yin (2003), who discusses the importance of propositions and emphasizes construct validity, internal validity, external validity, and reliability. The concern with 'validity' and 'reliability' represents an attempt to ensure that the case meets the quality standards expected of a positivistic study. Another example of a positivistic approach to case study research is Benbasat, Goldstein, and Mead's (1987) approach to case study research in information systems. Essentially, they apply Yin's approach to the field of information systems and advocate case study research along positivistic lines.

The second type of case study research is of an interpretive nature. Interpretive case study research relies on an underlying interpretive and constructivist epistemology, i.e. social reality is socially constructed. Interpretive case studies generally attempt to understand phenomena through the meanings that people assign to them. Unlike positivist case studies, which define quality in terms of validity and reliability, interpretive case studies define quality in terms of the plausibility of the story and the overall argument. An example of an interpretive case study in business is Corley and Gioia's study of organizational identity change in the spin-off of a Fortune 100 company's top-performing organizational unit into an independent organization (Corley & Gioia, 2004). Another example is Walsham and Waema's study of information systems strategy development in a building society in the United Kingdom (Walsham & Waema, 1994). Both case studies focus on the social construction of reality – how and why people see the world the way they do. Both cases are plausible, and the authors do not justify their research in positivistic terms.

The third type of case study research, critical case study research, involves critical reflection on current practices, questions taken-for-granted assumptions, and critiques the status quo based on the theories of one or more critical theorists. An example of a critical case study is Myers' study of the failed implementation of an information system in the health sector. Myers (1994) used the critical hermeneutics of Gadamer and Ricoeur to help explain the findings. Like interpretive case studies, the author does not justify the quality of the research in positivist terms. Words such as 'validity' and 'reliability', which imply an objective reality independent of social reality, are not normally used in interpretive or critical studies.

Some Practical Suggestions

One of the most important things in doing case study research is finding an 'interesting' case in the first place. If your case is boring, then it does not matter how well you do the research, or how meticulous you are in recording your interviews, or how well you write it up; a boring case is really just a waste of everyone's time. So what makes an interesting case?

An interesting case study is one which tells us something new. That is, it tells researchers in a particular field something that they did not know before. For example, if it is an exploratory case, then it provides the vehicle for exploring a new subject area. If it is a theory-testing case, then perhaps it is a critical case which disconfirms existing theory and suggests an alternative. At the very least both you and your supervisors should find the story and the implications of the case interesting.

One of the biggest challenges in doing case study research is to find a company in which you can do the research. Some of my students have found that it can take a good few attempts before permission is obtained.

One way of finding a suitable company is to read the local newspaper or business magazines. If the story in a magazine includes quotations from some of the people in a relevant organization, then you already have one or more contact names. Another way is to explore existing personal or corporate friendships. For example, if you have already worked for a company or have friends or relatives working there, they might be more likely to be receptive to the idea of case study research. In particular I have found that previous graduates of the university are much more likely to be receptive to case study research than complete strangers. I suspect this is because they feel some obligation to the university which educated them, and because they are more open to the idea of research being done on them. Also they may be less threatened by the idea of the researcher finding out some bad news about the organization. In fact, they may well welcome such findings and treat them as an opportunity to learn and improve.

Once you have been given access to an organization, then you need to gather as much evidence as possible that is relevant to your topic. There are various techniques for gathering data (these are discussed in more detail in Part IV); however, the most common technique – and probably the most important – used for gathering data in business is the interview. Interviews are an excellent 'window' into an organization, and can help you to find out what people are thinking. They are particularly useful for finding out people's motivations, and their rationale as to why they did certain things.

Of course, there is a need for those doing interviews to have good people skills. If you are not good at relating to people or empathizing with them, then it is highly unlikely that you will learn much. Not everyone is suited to doing case study research. Although people skills can be taught, it might be easier and less time consuming for some budding researchers to choose another research method altogether, one that does not rely so heavily on people interaction. Case study research is not a soft option, particularly for those who are socially challenged.

It is possible to conduct a case study that is based almost entirely on a few interviews with key people. However, a more in-depth case study will rely on interviews with many people in the organization, and these people will represent diverse perspectives.

Either way, it is extremely important to identify and interview 'key' informants. Key informants are those who know the most about a particular topic in the organization and have decision-making authority for the general area in which you are interested. For example, if you are doing a case study about the marketing strategy of a particular company, then you will definitely want to interview the marketing manager. The marketing manager is the one who is likely to know the most about the whys and wherefores of the company's approach.

A more in-depth case study will use other sources of evidence besides interviews. Written documents can be extremely valuable as they often provide evidence for things which people sometimes have difficulty remembering, e.g. exact dates of a particular event, or the attendee list at a particular meeting, and so forth. Documentary evidence includes items such as annual reports, newspaper clippings, reports, memos, organization charts, and minutes of meetings. In some cases, physical artefacts such as devices, tools, or systems might provide additional sources of evidence.

TIPS FOR SUCCESS IN DOING CASE STUDY RESEARCH

- Find an interesting case.
- Make sure you have good people skills.
- Gather rich data and try to establish the context.

CRITIQUE OF CASE STUDY RESEARCH

Advantages and Disadvantages of Case Study Research

Case study research is the most popular qualitative research method used in the business disciplines. It is popular because one of the main advantages of case study research is what I would call its 'face validity'. By 'face validity', I mean that a well-written case study based on empirical research in an organization represents a real story that most researchers can identify with. This is especially the case with well-known organizations, where everyone is already familiar with the company or its products. Most cases are also contemporary stories, which means that the case documents one or more firms' attempt to deal with issues of current importance to other firms, many of which are likely to be in the same boat.

Another advantage of case study research is that it allows researchers to explore or test theories within the context of messy real-life situations. These situations are never as neat and tidy as our theories. For example, there may be multiple, equally valid interpretations of the same situation, or a chief executive officer (CEO) may have many reasons for doing a particular action, some personal, some professional, and some based on rational business principles (this is not to say that personal reasons are not rational reasons). These kinds of complexities can only be brought out in a research method that allows a researcher to get 'close to the action', as the case study research method does.

IMPLEMENTING ACTIVITY-BASED COSTING: A CASE STUDY IN MANAGEMENT ACCOUNTING

Consultants, business schools, and the business media have promoted activity-based account-ing (ABC), claiming that it gives more accurate product costs and helps managers understand cost causation. However, there have been few empirical studies of the implementation of ABC. Doubts about the benefits and impact of ABC remain.

Therefore Major and Hopper (2005) decided to conduct an in-depth, interpretive case study of Marconi, a Portuguese telecommunications company, investigating ABC implemen-tation and usage. They decided they wanted to identify and explore issues from the perspec-tive of the actors involved, cast light on previous findings, and aid theory development. Like most case study research, they focused on exploring 'how' and 'why' research questions.

The data were obtained mostly from interviews and documents. Semi-structured interviews were conducted with managers and employees of Marconi, its parent company, the consul-tants that implemented ABC, the Portuguese telecommunications regulator, and managers from other telecommunication companies in Portugal. Their aim was to gain a rich description of Marconi's ABC system, its implementation, and managers' usage and evaluation of ABC.

Their research case makes three important contributions to the management accounting literature on ABC implementation:

1 Technical issues arose, in that there were technical problems associated with joint and common costs. These are significant in telecommunications. The ABC system did not meet the stringent conditions for providing valid data.
2 Implementing ABC in firms beset by conflict is difficult. As it turned out, only parts of the company used ABC. The production engineers resisted using ABC. They saw ABC as threatening their autonomy, threatening their employment prospects, and increasing their work load. Generally, they regarded it as a confusing and meaningless exercise.
3 Outside production the ABC implementation was judged a 'success' (in terms of eval-uations and usage). This was associated with top management support, adequate resources, clear goals, and employee commitment. The implementer tried to give employees ownership of the project (Major & Hopper, 2005).

One of the main disadvantages of doing case study research, particularly in business settings, is that it can be difficult to gain access to the particular company or group of companies that you want to study. This is because firms may be sceptical of the value of the research for themselves. In fact they may worry that not only will the researcher take up too much of their valuable time in interviews, but also that the findings may be unflattering and lead to some unwelcome publicity. The last thing a company wants is bad PR. For these reasons it can sometimes take you months to find a suitable company and one that gives you the required permissions.

Another disadvantage of case study research is that the researcher has no control over the situation. In practice, this means that if the company you are studying is suddenly taken over by another company halfway through your study, there is very little that you can do about it. Alternatively, if your key sponsor (e.g. the chief operating officer) resigns just as you are starting to conduct your interviews, you may find that you have too few friends within the firm to continue your research.

Yet another disadvantage of case study research is that it can be difficult, particularly for younger, inexperienced researchers, to focus on the most important issues. As the context of the study can be as large or as small as you want, a real danger is that an inexperienced researcher will think everything is relevant. Therefore such a person ends up with a huge amount of data, most of which turns out to be irrelevant in the final analysis.

The last disadvantage of case study research is that it takes a long time, even for experienced researchers. It takes time to gain access, it takes time to do the empirical research, and it takes even more time to do the write-up. From start to finish, case study research is time consuming.

If we put all these disadvantages together, it means that only those who are enthusiastic and committed, and only those who have the required people skills, should consider doing case study research. It is a serious mistake to think that case study research is an easy or a soft option. It is not easy at all.

However, for those who are keen, case study research can be very rewarding. It gives you the opportunity to find out at first hand whether or not your concepts or theories have any value in the business world.

How to Evaluate Case Study Research

Like all qualitative research methods, it is important that case study research should be evaluated in an appropriate way. In other words, it is important to evaluate case study research according to its fundamental tenets, and not by the assumptions or tenets of some other method. It would be inappropriate to evaluate case study research by criteria used in evaluating survey research, just as it would be inappropriate to evaluate survey research by criteria used in evaluating a case study.

Keeping this comment in mind, it is important to note that conducting just one case study is fine. Many budding qualitative researchers make the mistake of thinking that one case study is not enough. They think that if only they had three or more cases, then this would increase the 'validity' of the findings.

However, this way of thinking confuses things. Researchers who think this way are making the common mistake, of using sampling logic to judge the validity of the case method. But case study research does not use sampling logic. Sampling logic is based on statistics. Sampling logic and statistical theory are what are used when you conduct a survey.

In a survey, the larger your sample size, the better. The larger the sample, the more sure you can be that the results truly reflect the population as a whole. Most statistical concepts such as significance tests and confidence intervals assume you have a truly random sample.

But in case study research, statistical concepts such as confidence levels and confidence intervals are meaningless. Using three or four cases is no better than using one case when it comes to increasing the confidence in your findings. First of all, the sample size is still far too small; second, you do not have a truly random sample in the first place. A case study is not one instance of a much larger random sample!

Instead of using sampling logic to justify case study research, which generalizes from a sample to a population, it is much better to generalize one or more cases to theory, as Yin (2003) points out. Just as it is possible to generalize from a single experiment, so it is possible to generalize from a single case (Lee, 1989; Yin, 2003).

So what makes an exemplary case study? The following criteria are offered as general guidelines for evaluating a research case in business:

1 The case study must be 'interesting'.
2 The case study must display sufficient evidence.
3 The case study should be 'complete'.
4 The case study must consider alternative perspectives.
5 The case study should be written in an engaging manner.
6 The case study should contribute to knowledge.

First of all, the case study must be 'interesting'. As was mentioned earlier, this means that the case study should tell the researchers in a particular field something new that they did not know before. At the very least both you and your supervisors should find the story of the case interesting.

Second, the case study must display sufficient evidence. If you are writing a research article for a journal, this means that it is usually a good idea to include some supporting quotations from those who were interviewed. Quotes that are verbatim bring the case to life. The general idea is that you need to include sufficient evidence such that your argument makes sense and is plausible.

Third, the case study should be 'complete'. By complete, I do not mean that everything that it is possible to say about the case has been said. Rather,

I mean that all the relevant evidence to prove or disprove a particular theoretical point has been collected.

Fourth, the case study must consider alternative perspectives. This may mean considering different theories, alternative cultural views, or disagreements among the subjects. The key point here is that cases that document real-life situations should reflect real life. Since real life is never neat and tidy, the story that is presented in your case study should not be so neat and tidy either. A 'perfect story' where there is a hero or heroine and everyone lives happily ever after is a fairy story, not a research case. Hence it may be advisable to include evidence which does not necessarily support your own theory.

Fifth, the case study should be written in an engaging manner. The key test here is whether you are enthusiastic about it. If you are not captivated by the story, then it is almost guaranteed that others will not be enthusiastic either. The write-up requires some creative energy.

Sixth, the case study should contribute to knowledge. This is fairly similar to the first criterion, except that it emphasizes the contribution to scientific knowledge rather than the case's intrinsic interest value. As a general rule, this means that a research case will be generalized to one or more theories or concepts.

These six criteria for evaluating a research case apply to all kinds of case study research. However, it is also possible to add additional quality criteria for evaluating case study research depending upon the type of such research that is conducted. These quality criteria will vary depending upon whether this research is positivist, interpretive, or critical.

For positivist research, good case study design is vital (Dubé & Paré, 2003; Yin, 2003). Yin (2003) suggests five components of good case study design:

1   A study's questions.
2   Its propositions, if any.
3   Its unit(s) of analysis.
4   The logic linking the data to the propositions.
5   The criteria for interpreting the findings.

For interpretive research, the plausibility of the case is far more important than its design. That is, fellow researchers in a particular field will need some confidence in the case, and its story should be believable. The plausibility of a case is improved by many things, such as using multiple sources of evidence, and having a clear description of what you did and how.

Klein and Myers (1999) suggest seven principles for evaluating interpretive case studies (although these principles also apply to interpretive ethnographies):

1 The Fundamental Principle of the Hermeneutic Circle
2 The Principle of Contextualization
3 The Principle of Interaction between the Researchers and Subjects
4 The Principle of Abstraction and Generalization
5 The Principle of Dialogical Reasoning
6 The Principle of Multiple Interpretations
7 The Principle of Suspicion.

These seven principles are summarized in Figure 7.1. They apply to interpretive work that is of a hermeneutic nature, but other criteria or principles might be more applicable to interpretive work that takes a different approach.

For critical research, the case should question taken-for-granted assumptions, and open to scrutiny possible hidden agendas, power centres, and assumptions that inhibit, repress, and constrain (cf. Thomas, 1993). Most critical case studies will use one or more critical theories such as from Habermas or Foucault.

EXAMPLES OF CASE STUDY RESEARCH

Open-Book Accounting in Networks: A Case Study in Management Accounting

Many manufacturing companies have developed close cooperative relationships with their key suppliers and buyers in recent years. This has led to the emergence of manufacturing networks, where there is a more comprehensive sharing of information among supply chain members.

In their research, Kajuter and Kulmala (2005) looked at the issue of manufacturing networks providing a platform for inter-organizational cost management. Compared with traditional cost management in single companies, they say that additional opportunities for cost reduction arise through collaborative efforts of network members. However, in order to reveal such opportunities, transparency of cost structures is essential. Open-book accounting can play a key role in inter-organizational cost management.

The authors, using an interpretive type of case study research, investigated the reasons why open-book accounting is successful in some cases and often fails in others. They examined the main obstacles hindering firms from exchanging cost data in networks.

This interpretive study consisted of two parts. First, a single case study of a German car manufacturing network – the Eurocar case – was conducted. Second, a multi-site case study of three Finnish manufacturing networks was

---

1 **The Fundamental Principle of the Hermeneutic Circle**

Suggests that all human understanding is achieved by iterating between considering the interdependent meaning of parts and the whole that they form. This principle of human understanding is fundamental to all the other principles.
Example: Lee's (1994) study of information richness in email communications. It iterates between the separate message fragments of individual email participants as parts and the global context which determines the full meanings of the separate messages to interpret the message exchange as a whole.

2 **The Principle of Contextualization**

Requires critical reflection on the social and historical background of the research setting, so that the intended audience can see how the current situation under investigation emerged.
Example: After discussing the historical forces which led to Fiat establishing a new assembly plant, Ciborra, Patriotta, and Erlicher (1996) show how old Fordist production concepts still had a significant influence despite radical changes in work organization and operations.

3 **The Principle of Interaction Between the Researchers and the Subjects**

Requires critical reflection on how the research materials (or "data") were socially constructed through the interaction between the researchers and participants.
Example: Trauth (1997) explains how her understanding improved as she became self-conscious and started to question her own assumptions.

4 **The Principle of Abstraction and Generalization**

Requires relating the idiographic details revealed by the data interpretation through the application of Principles 1 and 2 to theoretical, general concepts that describe the nature of human understanding and social action.
Example: Monteiro and Hanseth's (1996) findings are discussed in relation to Latour's actor–network theory.

5 **The Principle of Dialogical Reasoning**

Requires sensitivity to possible contradictions between the theoretical preconceptions guiding the research design and actual findings ("the story which the data tell") with subsequent cycles of revision.
Example: Lee (1991) describes how Nardulli (1978) came several times to revise his preconceptions of the role of case load pressure as a central concept in the study of criminal courts.

6 **The Principle of Multiple Interpretations**

Requires sensitivity to possible differences in interpretations among the participants as are typically expressed in multiple narratives or stories of the same sequence of events under study. Similar to multiple witness accounts even if all tell it as they saw it.
Example: Levine and Rossmore's (1993) account of the conflicting expectations for the Threshold system in the Bremerton Inc. case.

7 **The Principle of Suspicion**

Requires sensitivity to possible 'biases' and systematic 'distortions' in the narratives collected from the participants.
Example: Forester (1992) looks at the facetious figures of speech used by city planning staff to negotiate the problem of data acquisition.

Figure 7.1 The seven principles of interpretive research as suggested by Klein and Myers (1999)

conducted. In these studies the contextual factors influencing the implementation, utilization, and outcome of open-book accounting in networks were analysed.

Most of the data were obtained by conducting 61 semi-structured interviews with key personnel. At Eurocar and at the Finnish main contractors, manager-level personnel responsible for product development, purchasing, production, and accounting were interviewed. In the Finnish networks, at least one person from each supplier's top management, either the managing director or the entrepreneur, was interviewed. These people were assumed to have a good overview of their entire company and its relationships to network partners.

The interviews included mainly open questions. Due to the confidential nature of some of the issues discussed, the interviews were not recorded on tape. Non-recording was expected to encourage the respondents to answer as freely and openly as possible. The interviews took from 1.5 to 3 hours each.

All firms were visited at least once in order to gain an understanding of the operations and business environment. In addition, content analysis was used for both official and internal documents.

The authors' analysis was based upon the contingency theory of management accounting. As this theory suggests, many, or even most, of the changes and improvements in management accounting can be explained through contingencies in the external environment and internal structure, strategy, and culture of companies.

On the basis of a contingency model, the authors found that open-book accounting is most likely to work in long-term hierarchical networks that manufacture functional products, provide a sound infrastructure for open-book practice, and comprise trust-based network relationships (Kajuter & Kulmala, 2005).

Mergers and Acquisitions: Multiple Interpretive Cases Telling the Seller's Side of the Story

Graebner and Eisenhardt (2004) say that most of the research literature in the area of corporate governance in management has taken the buyer's perspective. Most acquisition studies have focused on the acquirer as the decision maker of importance and have ignored the seller.

Therefore, the authors chose to explore acquisition from the seller's perspective. Specifically, they wanted to know when and to whom company leaders sell their firms. Given that this research was exploratory, they decided to conduct 12 case studies of entrepreneurial firms. They chose entrepreneurial firms because they say these firms 'are a primary engine of growth' whose acquisition has emerged as central to the corporate strategy of many corporations.

The research design they chose to use was a multiple case, inductive study involving 12 entrepreneurial firms in the United States. Four firms (three acquired, one not acquired) were chosen in each of three industries: networking hardware, infrastructure software, and online commerce. These industries have significant entrepreneurial activity and yet differ along key dimensions such as cost structure, sales and distribution channels, and customer characteristics. The time period was 1999–2000.

Most of the data were obtained from semi-structured interviews with key acquisition decision makers from both sellers and buyers. The authors also used emails and phone calls to follow up interviews and track real-time acquisition processes, and used archival data, including company websites, business publications, and materials provided by informants. Lastly, the authors used quantitative data on financing rounds. This study illustrates that interpretive case study research can use quantitative as well as qualitative data.

More than 80 interviews were conducted over 14 months. The interviews were 60–90 minutes long. All interviews were tape recorded and transcribed.

The first phase included 15 pilot interviews with managers who had sold their companies, managers who had purchased companies, investors in companies that were sold, and acquisition intermediaries. The pilot interviews indicated that the selling firm's acquisition decisions are usually made by a very small set of people, typically the CEO and two or three key executives and/or board members. Other individuals at the selling firm will have limited, if any, awareness of the events taking place. This pattern reflects the sensitive nature of acquisition decisions and is consistent with prior evidence that awareness of a firm's strategy declines rapidly below the top management team.

In the second phase, multiple senior-level informants in the selling and buying firms were interviewed. The pilot interviews provided guidance in identifying the most influential informants in the acquisition process. To ensure further that the sample included the most important individuals, 'snowball sampling' was used. The initial entry was made through either the CEO of the selling firm or the head of business development at the buying firm, if applicable. This contact then identified other individuals who had been actively involved in the acquisition with both the buyer and seller. These individuals then identified others, as appropriate.

As is typical in inductive research, the data were analysed by first building individual case studies synthesizing the interview transcripts and archival data. A central aspect of case writing was 'triangulation' between each interview and archival sources to create a richer, more reliable account.

The case histories were used for two analyses: within-case and cross-case. The within-case analysis focused on developing constructs and relationships to describe the process experienced by a single focal firm. A core aspect of the inductive process was that it allowed constructs to emerge from the data during this process, rather than being guided by specific hypotheses.

Cross-case analysis began after all cases were finished. Using standard cross-case analysis techniques, similar constructs and relationships across multiple cases were looked for. Tentative propositions were developed by grouping the firms according to the potential variables of interest. Case pairs were compared to identify similarities and differences. Emerging relationships were refined through replication logic, revisiting the data often to see if each separate case demonstrated the same pattern, using charts and tables to facilitate comparisons. The analysis process was iterative and lasted six months. From this process a framework emerged describing when acquisitions occur from the seller's perspective.

The key contribution of this study was to propose an emergent framework of when acquisition occurs from the seller's perspective. The authors framed acquisition as a courtship, emphasizing that acquisition is a process of mutual agreement between buyer and seller, and encompasses timing and strategic and emotional factors, not just price (Graebner & Eisenhardt, 2004).

Responding to Schedule Changes in Supply Chains: Multiple Case Studies in Operations Management

A supply chain is a network of plants and logistical resources producing the materials, components, assemblies, and final product for various customers. With the trend of mass customization and personalization, more and more products – from personal computers and customized bicycles to automobiles – are being made through build-to-order (BTO) supply chains. Krajewski, Wei, and Tang (2005) say that, unlike a typical assembly-to-order environment where customers can only choose from a small set of pre-configured end products, a BTO supply chain allows each customer to configure a final product from a personalized subset of components.

In this study, the authors focused on the short-term dynamics in BTO supply chains brought on by changes in the replenishment shipping schedules of members in the chain. They explored the reaction strategies that suppliers use to respond to short-term dynamics in BTO supply chains, and also looked at the power relations between a buyer and supplier.

The authors studied five firms in the microcomputer industry involved in the production of notebook computers and their components in Taiwan. The microcomputer industry was selected because of the prevalent use of BTO supply chains and because short-term dynamics in this industry create a challenging environment.

As can be seen, the authors decided to use multiple cases to address the research question. In this multiple case study design, the cases were treated as a series of experiments that confirm or disconfirm the emerging conceptual insights. Data were obtained primarily via structured interviews.

With regard to their data analysis, the authors first of all conducted within-case analysis, where members of the research team discussed the elements of reaction strategies and the short-term process flexibility and supplier power relationships. Then a cross-case analysis was conducted to denote the differences and similarities between the cases. The cross-case analysis provided the basis for developing the study's propositions.

In their research article, the authors describe the various reaction strategies of the various firms in the BTO supply chain and make some recommendations for best practice. In summary, the study shows that high short-term process flexibility can be used to competitive advantage by offering flexible supply contracts and supporting that linkage with frequent schedule revisions, even though finished goods inventories must be maintained (Krajewski et al., 2005).

EXERCISES

1 Look in the business pages of your local newspaper and find an interesting story about a new company, product, or service. Try to find other related articles in the paper and obtain as much publicly available information related to your story as you can (e.g. the latest annual report of the company). Are there one or more theories that you think might be relevant to the story? Write up a mini-case that attempts to explain your data in the light of your chosen theory.

2 Conduct a brief literature search using Google Scholar or some other bibliographic database and see if you can find some case study research articles in your chosen field. What kinds of topics appear?

3 Now narrow your search to one of the top journals in your field that has a reputation for publishing qualitative research (e.g. *Academy of Management Review, Accounting, Organizations and Society, Journal of Consumer Research, MIS Quarterly,* etc.). How many articles using case study research can you find over the past 2–3 years?

4 Evaluate some of the articles you found earlier. Do the articles adopt a positivist, interpretive, or critical approach?

5 Evaluate some of these same articles. Did the authors rely mostly on data from interviews? Did the authors use data from the use of other data-gathering techniques? What approach to data analysis did they use?

> 6   Brainstorm to come up with a list of three or four possible practical research topics. How could these topics be studied using case study research?
>
> 7   Find one or more faculty members at your institution or at a conference who conducts case study research. Ask them what topics they are working on right now, and why.

Further Reading

 Articles

An article by Walsham (1995) discusses how interpretive case studies can be evaluated. The article by Klein and Myers (1999), as mentioned earlier, suggests a set of principles by which interpretive field studies (both case studies and ethnographies) can be evaluated.

 Books

One of the best books on case study research is the classic book entitled *Case Study Research: Design and Methods* by Yin (2003). This book provides an excellent introduction to the case study research method. However, you should keep in mind that Yin, by and large, adopts a positivistic approach to case study research.

Another book by Yin entitled *Applications of Case Study Research* provides a companion to the first (Yin, 2002). This book discusses numerous completed case studies on a variety of topics and includes examples using specific case study techniques and principles.

 Websites on the Internet

- The Qualitative Report includes a few useful articles on case study research. This resource is freely available at http://www.nova.edu/ssss/QR/index.html
- More references are available at www.qual.auckland.ac.nz

13   Selecting a Case

DAVID SILVERMAN

Chapter Objectives

By the end of this chapter, you will be able to:

- Understand what a case study is.
- Know the main types of case study.
- Understand how to generalize from a single case.

Introduction

9.1 I concluded the previous chapter with my favourite research maxim: 'make a lot out of a little'. If you take me seriously, you will have every chance of producing a thorough, analytically interesting research study. However, at least three nagging doubts may well remain. I list them below together with some soothing words about each.

- *My case may not be important.* Here you are worried that the case you are studying may be seen by others as 'trivial' or 'not a real problem'. The famous ethnographer Howard Becker (1998) remarks that such criticisms have been made of his own work on several occasions. As he puts it: 'Just as some people think tragedy is more important than comedy … some problems are seen as inherently serious and worthy of grownup attention, others as trivial, flyspecks on the wallpaper of life … mere exotica' (1998: 92). There is a very good response to this kind of complaint, namely: what seems to be important is usually governed by little more than current fashions; who knows what might become important? Apparently trivial cases may, through, good analysis, turn out to have far-reaching implications.

- *I can only study the (part of the) case to which I have access.* This is a more serious issue. When we are studying an organization, we are dependent on the whims of gatekeepers. Such people will usually seek to limit what we can study, assuring us that, if we need to know more, they can tell us about it (1998: 90). How do we get round this problem? Becker suggests two answers: first, 'doubt everything anyone in power tells you'; second, look for other opinions (1998: 91). Like Dalton (1959), in his classic study of middle managers, case study researchers should system-atically attempt to assess the likely linkages between opinions, activities and interests.

- *I have so little data, just one case.* This is a more serious problem. As we shall see below, even in qualitative research it is important to consider what kind of generalizations can be made from a single case.

The rest of this chapter will be devoted to the issue of **generalizability** in case study research. First, however, we need to define both 'case study' and 'generalizability'.

What Is a Case Study?

9.2
This question has a relatively simple answer. As Keith Punch puts it:

The basic idea is that one case (or perhaps a small number of cases) will be studied in detail, using whatever methods seem appropriate. While there may be a variety of specific purposes and research questions, the general objective is to develop as full an understanding of that case as possible. (1998: 150)

There are, of course, an endless variety of possible 'cases'. If, like Becker, we are interested in occupations, cases to study may range from dancehall musicians to student physicians. By contrast, if you are interested in childhood, a case may be a single child, a classroom or clinic, or a charity or other organization concerned with the welfare of children. So, as Stake suggests: 'A case may be simple or complex ... [but] it is one among others. In any given study, we will concentrate on the one' (2000: 436).

All this is purely descriptive. Table 9.1 identifies three analytic features of case study research.

TABLE 9.1   Case study research

1 Each case has boundaries which must be identified at an early stage of the research (e.g. if you are studying a school, whether this includes classroom behaviour, staff meetings, parent–teacher meetings, etc.)
2 Each case will be a case of something in which the researcher is interested. So the unit of analysis must be defined at the outset in order to clarify the research strategy
3 Case studies seek to preserve the wholeness and integrity of the case. However, in order to achieve some focus, a limited research problem must be established that is geared to specific features of the case

Source: adapted from K. Punch, 1998: 153

Generalizing from Cases

9.3 Generalizability is a standard aim in quantitative research and is normally achieved by statistical sampling procedures. Such sampling has two functions. First, it allows you to feel confident about the representativeness of your sample: 'If the population characteristics are known, the degree of representativeness of a sample can be checked' (Arber, 1993: 70). Second, such representativeness allows you to make broader inferences: 'The purpose of sampling is usually to study a representative subsection of a precisely defined population in order to make inferences about the whole population' (1993: 38).

Such sampling procedures are, however, usually unavailable in qualitative research. In such studies, our data are often derived from one or more cases and it is unlikely that these cases will have been selected on a random basis. Very often a case will be chosen simply because it allows access. Moreover, even if you were able to construct a representative sample of cases, the sample size would be likely to be so large as to preclude the kind of intensive analysis usually preferred in qualitative research (Mason, 1996: 91).

This gives rise to a problem, familiar to users of quantitative methods: 'How do we know ... how representative case study findings are of all members of the population from which the case was selected?' (Bryman, 1988: 88).

Types of Case Studies

9.4 Robert Stake (2000: 437–8) has identified three different types of case study:

1 The *intrinsic case study* where 'this case is of interest ... in all its particularity and ordinariness'. In the intrinsic case study, according to Stake, no attempt is made to generalize beyond the single case or even to build theories.
2 The *instrumental case study* in which a case is examined mainly to provide insight into an issue or to revise a generalization. Although the case selected is studied in depth, the main focus is on something else.
3 The *collective case study* where a number of cases are studied in order to investigate some general phenomenon.

The idea of a purely *intrinsic case study* is resisted by many qualitative researchers. If all you aim to do is simply to 'describe a case', you may rightly get the response: 'So what?' Such scepticism arises from the following concerns:

- Description is a tricky activity which is inevitably theoretically laden (if you doubt this, you might look back at Table 7.1).

- To call something a 'case' implies that it is a case of 'something'; so we can only understand the distinctiveness of a case by making theoretical assumptions about what is typical for a certain population.

- Given how behaviour varies in different contexts, we need to understand how any one setting may be different from others (see Gobo, 2008: 97–8).

In this context, most supervisors of student qualitative research would expect your study of a case to be based upon some concept(s) which are developed as a result of your study. For examples of concept development through case study research, see Chapter 3.

Furthermore, empirical issues arise in case studies just as much as theoretical concerns. It is reasonable to ask what knowledge your case study has produced. If you are to answer this question, you must consider the degree of generalizability of your research. As Jennifer Mason puts it:

> I do not think qualitative researchers should be satisfied with producing explanations which are idiosyncratic or particular to the limited empirical parameters of their study ... Qualitative research should [therefore] produce explanations which are *generalizable* in some way, or which have a wider resonance. (1996: 6)

So description of a case for description's sake (the *intrinsic* case study) is a weak position. Quite rightly, the problem of 'representativeness' is a perennial worry of many qualitative or case study researchers. How do they attempt to address it? Can we generalize from cases to populations without following a purely statistical logic?

In the rest of this chapter, I will discuss four different but positive answers to this question of how we can obtain generalizability:

- combining qualitative research with quantitative measures of populations
- purposive sampling guided by time and resources
- theoretical sampling
- using an analytic model which assumes that generalizability is present in the existence of *any* case.

Combining Qualitative Research with Quantitative Measures of Populations

9.5 Quantitative measures may sometimes be used to infer from one case to a larger population. Hammersley (1992) suggests three methods through which we can attempt to generalize from the analysis of a single case:

- obtaining information about relevant aspects of the population of cases and comparing our case to them
- using survey research on a random sample of cases
- coordinating several ethnographic studies.

Hammersley argues that such comparisons with a larger sample may allow us to establish some sense of the representativeness of our single case.

However, two of Hammersley's methods are very ambitious for the student researcher. For instance, you are unlikely to have the funds for even a small piece of survey research, while the coordination of several ethnographic studies requires substantial resources of time and personnel as well as good contacts with other researchers. Such contacts allowed Miller and Silverman (1995) to apply the comparative approach in describing talk about troubles in two counselling settings: a British haemophilia centre counselling patients who are HIV-positive, and a family therapy centre in the US. In this study, we focused on similarities in three types of discursive practices in these settings: those concerned with trouble definitions, trouble remedies, and the social contexts of the clients' troubles (see also Gubrium, 1992).

Without such contacts and resources, the student researcher is left with Hammersley's first method: obtaining information about relevant aspects of the population of cases and comparing our case to them. This is more useful because, at its simplest, this method only involves reading about other cognate studies and comparing our case to them. For instance, in my study of HIV counselling (Silverman, 1997) I compared my counsellor–client interviews to Heritage and Sefi's (1992) data on interviews between health visitors and first-time mothers. Although this had little to do with establishing the representativeness of my sample, it gave a firmer basis to my generalizations about advice sequences in my data (1997: 124–8). The comparative method used here allows you to make larger claims about your analysis without leaving your library. As Peräkylä puts it:

> The comparative approach directly tackles the question of generalizability by demonstrating the similarities and differences across a number of settings. (2004: 296)

In this sense, your literature review (see Chapter 18) has as much to do with the issue of generalizability as with displaying your academic credentials.

Purposive Sampling

9.6 Before we can contemplate comparing our case to others, we need to have selected our case. Are there any grounds other than convenience or accessibility to guide us in this selection?

Purposive sampling allows us to choose a case because it illustrates some feature or process in which we are interested. However, this does not provide a simple approval to any case we happen to choose. Rather, purposive sampling demands that we think critically about the parameters of the population we are studying and choose our sample case carefully on this basis. As Denzin and Lincoln put it: 'Many qualitative researchers employ ... purposive, and not random, sampling methods. They seek out groups, settings and individuals where ... the processes being studied are most likely to occur' (1994: 202).

TABLE 9.2 A typology of children's museums

Programme type	Type of museum		
	Art	Science	History
Exhibitory	1	2	3
Participative	4	5	6

Source: adapted from Stake, 2000: 446–7

Stake (2000: 446–7) gives the example of a study of interactive displays in children's museums. He assumes that you only have resources to study four such museums. How should you proceed? He suggests setting up a *typology* which would establish a matrix of museum types as in Table 9.2. The typology yields six cases which could be increased further by, say, distinguishing between museums located in small and big cities – bringing up the cases to 12. Which cases should you select?

You will be constrained by two main factors. First, there may not be examples to fit every cell. Second, your resources will not allow you to research every existing unit. So you have to make a practical decision. For instance, if you can cover only two cases, do you choose two participatory museums in different locations or in different subjects? Or do you compare such a museum with a more conventional exhibit-based museum?

As a student researcher, your limited time and resources will usually determine how you settle these questions. However, the very fact that you have asked yourself these questions will satisfy most examiners.

> **TIP**
>
> **When designing your research, resist the assumption that qualitative research merely describes a single case. Then adopt the simplest design that will allow you properly to address your research question(s).**

Take the case of the mathematics teacher I met in Tanzania who was trying to design a qualitative study to discover what made maths lessons 'effective'. We came up with two factors that might be important here:

* the teaching style used (loosely 'traditional' or 'non-traditional')
* background features (school resources, staff turnover, parental support) which were likely to make maths lessons more or less 'effective'.

This suggested a simple 2 × 2 purposive sample as set out in Table 9.3. The simplicity of the research design set out in the table made for a study that showed the necessary critical thinking about the research problem and was achievable within the constraints of time and resources.

TABLE 9.3 A typology of mathematics lessons

		Teaching methods	
		Traditional	**Non-traditional**
Background	Favourable	1	2
	Unfavourable	3	4

However, in thinking through issues of sampling, we are following our quantitative colleagues. Before reading on, think what this student might gain from using a qualitative perspective on each of his 'cells'.

My answer to this question arises from the way in which the analytical models we use in qualitative research allow us to problematize matters that our quantitative colleagues may be compelled to take for granted or to settle prior to the commencement of research. In the context of this study, although our sample will be based upon prior assumptions, we can problematize:

• whether the categories 'traditional' and 'non-traditional' do justice to the variety of lessons we observe in the classroom

• what 'effective' education looks like in different contexts, so that we can go beyond scoring examination performance in each cell to considering how 'effectiveness' may be used as a rhetoric in settings as diverse as parent–teacher meetings, teacher promotion reviews and government documents.

In both cases, the beauty of qualitative research design is that it allows us to put 'scare marks' around apparently 'objective' concepts such as 'effectiveness'.

This shows that how you set up your typology and make your choice between cases should be grounded in the theoretical apparatus you are using. Sampling in qualitative research is neither statistical nor purely personal: it is, or should be, theoretically grounded.

 **Attempt Exercise 9.1**

To improve your understanding of this point, you could now attempt Exercise 9.1.

Theoretical Sampling

9.7
Theoretical and purposive sampling are often treated as synonyms. Indeed, the only difference between the two procedures applies when the 'purpose' behind 'purposive' sampling is not theoretically defined.

Bryman argues that qualitative research follows a theoretical, rather than a statistical, logic: 'The issue should be couched in terms of the generalizability of cases to *theoretical* propositions rather than to *populations* or universes' (1988: 90, my emphasis).[1]

The nature of this link between sampling and theory is set out by Jennifer Mason:

> theoretical sampling means selecting groups or categories to study on the basis of their relevance to your research questions, your theoretical position ... and most importantly the explanation or account which you are developing. Theoretical sampling is concerned with constructing a sample ... which is meaningful theoretically, because it builds in certain characteristics or criteria which help to develop and test your theory and explanation. (1996: 93–4)

Theoretical sampling has three features which I discuss below:

- choosing cases in terms of your theory
- choosing 'deviant' cases
- changing the size of your sample during the research.

Choosing cases in terms of your theory

9.7.1 Mason writes about 'the wider universe of social explanations in relation to which you have constructed your research questions' (1996: 85). This theoretically defined universe 'will make some sampling choices more sensible and meaningful than others'. Mason describes choosing a kind of sample which can represent a wider population. Here we select a sample of particular 'processes, types, categories or examples which are relevant to or appear within the wider universe' (1996: 92). Mason suggests that examples of these would include single units such as 'an organization, a location, a document ... [or] a conversation'.

Mason gives the example of a **discourse analysis** of gender relation as discourses which construct subjects of gender relations. In this approach, as she puts it, 'You are ... unlikely to perceive the social world in terms of a large set of gender relations from which you can simply draw a representative sample of people by gender' (1996: 85).

So in qualitative research the relevant or 'sampleable' units are often seen as theoretically defined. This means that it is inappropriate to sample populations by such attributes as 'gender', 'ethnicity' or even age because how such attributes are routinely defined is itself the *topic* of your research.

As an example of theoretically defined sampling, Bryman uses Glaser and Strauss's discussion of 'awareness contexts' in relation to dying in hospital:

> The issue of whether the particular hospital studied is 'typical' is not the critical issue; what is important is whether the experiences of dying patients are typical of the broad class of phenomena ... to which the theory refers. Subsequent research would then focus on the validity of the proposition in other milieux (e.g. doctors' surgeries). (1988: 91)

We can understand better the theoretical logic behind choice of a sample in a further example of a study of policework. Say you are interested in the arrest and booking of suspects (see Miles and Huberman, 1984: 37–8). You are now confronted with a series of choices which relate to:

- the particular setting to be studied
- the elements or processes on which you will focus
- how you might generalize further.

Let us look at each of these in turn.

Settings

In independent, unfunded research, you are likely to choose any setting which, while demonstrating the phenomenon in which you are interested, is accessible and will provide appropriate data reasonably readily and quickly. In the police study, this might well lead you to study the police station rather than a squad car, the scene of the crime, the suspect's residence or hangout. In the police station, at the very least, you will keep warm and dry, you will be safe and you can expect several arrests and bookings on any visit. However, so far you are being guided by quite practical influences.

The research focus

In focusing your research, you necessarily are making a theoretically guided choice. By opting to focus on particular individuals, events or processes, you are electing particular theoretical frameworks. For instance, a focus on differential behaviour between police officers and suspects with different characteristics may draw on some version of the structural determinants of action. Conversely, a focus on how laws are interpreted in practice (cf. Sudnow, 1968b) may derive from a concern with the creative power of common-sense interpretive procedures.

Generalizing further

When wedded to other studies which share your theoretical orientation, your research on a single police station may provide enough data to develop all the generalizations you want about, say, how common-sense reasoning works. However, if you have a more 'structural' bent, it may now be necessary to widen your sample in two ways: first, to add more observations of arrests in this police station; and second, to compare it with other stations, perhaps in a range of areas.

In all these cases, the sample is not random but theoretical. It is 'designed to provide a close-up, detailed or meticulous view of particular units which may constitute ... cases which are relevant to or appear within the wider universe' (Mason, 1996: 92).

As Kathy Charmaz argues, this kind of 'theoretical sampling directs you where to go' (2006: 100) when you need to make further generalizations from the cases you have already selected.

Choosing 'deviant' cases

9.7.2 Mason notes that you must overcome any tendency to select a case which is likely to support your argument. Instead, it makes sense to seek out negative instances as defined by the theory with which you are working.

TIP

When designing your research, it is useful to contemplate the kind of experiences or situations that you initially think are most unlikely. One of Howard Becker's 'tricks of the trade' is: 'Just to insist that nothing that can be imagined is impossible, so we should look for the most unlikely things that we can think of and incorporate their existence, or the possibility of their existence, into our thinking' (1998: 85–6).

For instance, in a study of the forces that may make trade unions undemocratic, Lipset et al. (1962) deliberately chose to study a US printing union. Because this union had unusually strong democratic institutions, it constituted a vital deviant case compared to most American unions of the period. Lipset et al.'s union was also deviant in terms of a highly respected theory which postulated an irresistible tendency towards 'oligarchy' in all formal organizations.

So Lipset et al. chose a deviant case because it offered a crucial test of a theory. As our understanding of social processes improves, we are increasingly able to choose cases on such theoretical grounds.

Changing the size of your sample during the research

9.7.3 So far we have been discussing theoretical sampling as an issue at the *start* of a research study. However, we can also apply such sampling during the course of a piece of research. Indeed, one of the strengths of qualitative research design is that it often allows for far greater (theoretically informed) flexibility than do most quantitative research designs. As Mason puts it:

Theoretical or purposive sampling is a set of procedures where the researcher manipulates their analysis, theory, and sampling activities *interactively* during the research process, to a much greater extent than in statistical sampling. (1996: 100)

Such flexibility may be appropriate in the following cases:

- As new factors emerge you may want to increase your sample in order to say more about them (for instance, a gatekeeper has given you an explanation that you doubt on principle).

- You may want to focus on a small part of your sample in the early stages, using the wider sample for later tests of emerging generalizations.

- Unexpected generalizations in the course of data analysis lead you to seek out new deviant cases.

Alasuutari has described this process using the analogy of an hourglass:

> A narrow case-analysis is broadened ... through the search for contrary and parallel cases, into an example of a broader entity. Thus the research process advances, in its final stages, towards a discussion of broader entities. We end up on the bottom of the hourglass. (1995: 156)

Alasuutari (1995: 155) illustrates this hourglass metaphor through his own study of the social consequences of Finnish urbanization in the 1970s. He chose local pubs as a site to observe these effects and eventually focused upon male 'regulars'. This led to a second study even more narrowly focused on a group where drinking was heavier and where many of the men were divorced. As he puts it: 'Ethnographic research of this kind is not so much generalization as extrapolation ... the results are related to broader entities' (1995: 155).

Generalizability Is Present in a Single Case

9.8 The fourth and final way of thinking about how we generalize in qualitative research is far more radical than our earlier alternatives. According to this approach, since the basic structures of social order are to be found anywhere, it does not matter where we begin our research. Look at *any* case and you will find the same order.

For this linguistically inspired approach, the possibility something exists is enough. As Peräkylä suggests:

> Social practices that are possible, i.e., *possibilities of language use*, are the central objects of all conversation analytical case studies on interaction in partic-ular institutional settings. The possibility of various practices can be considered generalizable even if the practices are not actualized in similar ways across different settings. (2004: 297)

Peräkylä illustrates his argument by the example of his own study of AIDS counselling in a London teaching hospital (Peräkylä, 1995). This study focused on specific questioning practices used by counsellors and their clients. As he puts it:

> As possibilities, the practices that I analyzed are very likely to be generalizable. There is no reason to think that they could not be made possible by any competent member of (at least any Western) society. In this sense, this study produced generalizable results. The results were not generalizable as descriptions of what other counsellors or other professionals do with their clients; but they were generalizable as descriptions of what any counsellor or other professional, with his or her clients, *can* do, given that he or she has the same array of interactional competencies as the participants of the AIDS counselling sessions have. (2004: 297)

As the most cogent proponent of this view once put it: 'tap into whomsoever, wheresoever and we get much the same things' (Sacks, 1984b: 22).

Sacks had a strategy of working with any data that crossed his path. This clearly conflicts both with the standard approach of quantitative social scientists, who usually work with random samples from particular populations, and with the common defensiveness of their qualitative brethren about the representativess of the cases that they study.

Sacks's lack of defensiveness on this issue stems from his argument about the obvious pervasiveness of the social forms (or what he calls the 'machinery') with which he is concerned. For example, Sacks notes the ability of a child to learn a culture from very limited contacts and of the sociolinguist Whorf to build a Navajo grammar from talking to just one person (1992, Vol. 1: 485).

For Sacks, the pervasiveness of structures which these examples suggest carry the implication that it does not matter what data you select. As he argues:

> Now if one figures that that's the way things are ... then it really wouldn't matter very much what it is you look at – if you look at it carefully enough. And you may well find that you [have] got an enormous generalizability because things are so arranged that you *could* get them; given that for a **member** encountering a very limited environment, he has to be able to do that, and things are so arranged as to permit him to. (1992, Vol. 1: 485, bold added)

However, apprentice researchers have to be very cautious about simply parroting Sacks's 'solution' to the problem of the generalizability of research findings. This solution is really only appropriate to the most basic research on social order guided by theoretically sophisticated positions like Sacks's own **conversation analytic** (CA) approach (or, perhaps, French **structuralism**).

 **■ Attempt Exercise 9.2** ▬▬▬▬▬▬▬▬▬▬▬▬▬▬▬▬

If you are interested in this sort of research, you should now attempt Exercise 9.2.

Within CA, following Sacks: 'The baseline assumption is that the results are or should be generalizable to the whole domain of ordinary conversations, and to a certain extent even across linguistic and cultural boundaries' (Peräkylä, 1995: 214). However, Peräkylä notes that even this depends on the type of CA research:

> Even though the most primordial conversational practices and structures – such as **turn-taking** or **adjacency pairs** – are almost universal, there are others, such as openings of telephone calls (see Schegloff, 1986; Houtkoop-Steenstra, 1991; Lindström, 1994), which show considerable variation in different cultures. This variation can only be tackled through gradual accumulation of studies on ordinary conversation in different cultures and social milieux. (1995: 156–7)

Peräkylä's observation about the need for comparative work shows that even the most potentially radical approach, like CA, has to take seriously the issue of the empirical generalizability of its findings. Sometimes, an appeal to 'possibilities' will be sufficient. Often, however, other examples will be required.

Attempt Exercise 9.3

LINK

For an excellent discussion of generalization from case study research, see Giampietro Gobo's *Doing Ethnography* (2008) Chapters 5 and 14 and the associated website at:

http://www.sagepub.co.uk/gobo/resources.htm

Concluding Remarks

9.9 In this chapter, I have set out various strategies which you can use to defend your research against the charge that it 'merely' depends upon a single case. My overall message is that there is usually no need to be defensive about the claims of qualitative research. As Howard Becker argues:

> Sampling is a major problem for any kind of research. We can't study every case of whatever we're interested in, nor should we want to. Every scientific enterprise tries to find out something that will apply to *everything* of a certain kind by studying *a few examples*, the results of the study being, as we say 'generalizable' to all members of that class of stuff. We need the sample to persuade people that we know something about the whole class. (1998: 67)

Following Becker, sampling is not a simple matter even for quantitative researchers. Indeed, as we have seen, the relative flexibility of qualitative research can improve the generalizability of our findings by allowing us to include new cases after initial findings are established.

The crucial issue here seems to be thinking through one's theoretical priorities. Providing that you have done that and can demonstrate a research design driven by those priorities, nobody should have cause for complaint.

So the secret seems to be to substitute theoretical cogency for the statistical language of quantitative research. In this sense, as Alasuutari (1995) has suggested, perhaps 'generalizability' is the wrong word to describe what we attempt to achieve in qualitative research. As he puts it:

> Generalization is ... [a] word ... that should be reserved for surveys only. What can be analyzed instead is how the researcher demonstrates that the analysis relates to things beyond the material at hand ... *extrapolation* better captures the typical procedure in qualitative research. (1995: 156–7)

KEY POINTS

There are four positive answers to the question of how we can generalize from qualitative data:

- combining qualitative research with quantitative measures of populations
- purposive sampling guided by time and resources
- theoretical sampling
- using an analytic model which assumes that generalizability is present in the existence of *any* case.

Note

1   As Clive Seale (personal correspondence) has pointed out, theoretical sampling may have more to do with generating theories than with empirical generalization. I take up Seale's point at the end of this chapter in relation to Alasuutari's argument that the idea of empirical generalization 'should be reserved for surveys only' (1995: 156).

Further Reading

Seale, Gobo, Gubrium and Silverman's edited book *Qualitative Research Practice* (Sage, 2004: 420–72) contains three very useful chapters on case studies by Flyvberg, Gobo and Emerson. The most thorough book on this topic is Clive Seale's *The Quality of Qualitative Research* (Sage, 1999). For chapter length treatments of this topic, see Kathy Charmaz's excellent *Constructing Grounded Theory: A Practical Guide through Qualitative Analysis* (2006: 96–122). Other useful discussions are: Jennifer Mason's *Qualitative Researching* (second edition, Sage, 2002); Pertti Alasuutari's *Researching Culture* (Sage, 1995: Ch. 12); and Howard

Becker's *Tricks of the Trade* (University of Chicago Press, 1998: Ch. 3). Robert Stake's chapter 'Case studies' is a good account of the conventional qualitative methods position on generalizability (in N. Denzin and Y. Lincoln (eds), *Handbook of Qualitative Research*, Sage, 2000) and Anssi Peräkylä's chapter 'Reliability and validity in research based upon transcripts' is an excellent, more specialist treatment (in David Silverman (ed.), *Qualitative Research*, second edition, Sage, 2004).

 ■ Exercise 9.1

Assume that you are studying a single case. On what basis do you think you might generalize from your findings? Distinguish your possible empirical contribution from any potential development of concepts.

 ■ Exercise 9.2

Imagine that you have the resources to study *four* cases of the phenomenon in which you are interested. Following my discussion of Stake (Table 9.2), draw up a typology to indicate the universe of cases potentially available. This typology should include between six and 12 possible cases.

  Now explain why you propose to select your four cases in terms of the logic of purposive sampling.

 ■ Exercise 9.3

Using conversation analysis, Harvey Sacks has argued: 'tap into whomsoever, wheresoever and we get much the same things' (1984b: 22).

  Consider how far your own theoretical model might allow you to use Sacks's argument to justify working with a very small dataset.

Designing Case Studies: Identifying Your Case(s) and Establishing the Logic of Your Case Study

ROBERT YIN

In identifying the method for your research project, Chapter 1 has shown when you might choose to use the case study method, as opposed to other methods. The next task is to design your case study. For this purpose, as in designing any other type of research investigation, you need a plan or *research design.*

The development of this research design is a difficult part of doing case studies. Unlike other research methods, a comprehensive "catalog" of research designs for case studies has yet to be developed. There are no textbooks, like those in the biological and psychological sciences, covering such design considerations as the assignment of subjects to different "groups," the selection of different stimuli or experimental conditions, or the identification of various response measures (see Cochran & Cox, 1957; Fisher, 1935, cited in Cochran & Cox, 1957; Sidowski, 1966). In a laboratory experiment, each of these choices reflects an important logical connection to the issues being studied. Similarly, there are not even textbooks like the well-known volumes by Campbell and Stanley (1966) or by Cook and Campbell (1979) that summarize the various research designs for quasi-experimental situations. Nor have there emerged any common designs—for example, "panel" studies—such as those recognized in doing survey research (see L. Kidder & Judd, 1986, chap. 6).

One pitfall to be avoided, however, is to consider case study designs to be a subset or variant of the research designs used for other methods, such as experiments. For the longest time, scholars incorrectly thought that the case study was but one type of quasi-experimental design (the "one-shot post-test-only" design). This misperception has finally been corrected, with the following statement appearing in a revision on quasi-experimental designs (Cook & Campbell, 1979): "Certainly the case study as normally practiced should not be demeaned by identification with the one-group post-test-only design" (p. 96). In other

---

Tip: *How should I select the case(s) for my case study?*

You need sufficient access to the potential data, whether to interview people, review documents or records, or make observations in the "field." Given such access to more than a single candidate case, you should choose the case(s) that will most likely illuminate your research questions. Absent such access, you should consider changing your research questions, hopefully leading to new candidates to which you do have access.

Do you think access should be so important?

---

words, the one-shot, post-test-only design as a quasi-experimental design still may be considered flawed, but the case study has now been recognized as something different. In fact, the case study is a separate research method that has its own research designs.

Unfortunately, case study research designs have not been codified. The following chapter therefore expands on the new methodological ground broken by earlier editions of this book and describes a basic set of research designs for doing single- and multiple-case studies. Although these designs will need to be continually modified and improved in the future, in their present form they will nevertheless help you to design more rigorous and methodologically sound case studies.

Definition of Research Designs

Every type of empirical research has an implicit, if not explicit, research design. In the most elementary sense, the design is the logical sequence that connects the empirical data to a study's initial research questions and, ultimately, to its conclusions. Colloquially, a research design is *a logical plan for getting from here to there,* where *here* may be defined as the initial set of questions to be answered, and *there* is some set of conclusions (answers) about these questions. Between "here" and "there" may be found a number of major steps, including the collection and analysis of relevant data. As a summary definition, another textbook has described a research design as a plan that

> guides the investigator in the process of collecting, analyzing, and interpreting observations. It is a *logical model of proof* that allows the researcher to draw inferences concerning causal relations among the variables under investigation. (Nachmias & Nachmias, 1992, pp. 77-78, emphasis added)

Another way of thinking about a research design is as a "blueprint" for your research, dealing with at least four problems: what questions to study, what data are relevant, what data to collect, and how to analyze the results (Philliber, Schwab, & Samsloss, 1980).

Note that a research design is much more than a work plan. The main purpose of the design is to help to avoid the situation in which the evidence does not address the initial research questions. In this sense, a research design deals with a *logical* problem and not a *logistical* problem. As a simple example, suppose you want to study a single organization. Your research questions, however, have to do with the organization's relationships with other organizations—their competitive or collaborative nature, for example. Such questions can be answered only if you collect information directly from the other organizations and not merely from the one you started with. If you complete your study by examining only one organization, you cannot draw unbiased conclusions about interorganizational partnerships. This is a flaw in your research design, not in your work plan. The outcome could have been avoided if you had developed an appropriate research design in the first place.

Components of Research Designs

For case studies, five components of a research design are especially important:

1. a study's questions;
2. its propositions, if any;
3. its unit(s) of analysis;
4. the logic linking the data to the propositions; and
5. the criteria for interpreting the findings.

Study questions. This first component has already been described in Chapter 1, which suggested that the *form* of the question—in terms of "who," "what," "where," "how," and "why"—provides an important clue regarding the most relevant research method to be used. The case study method is most likely to be appropriate for "how" and "why" questions, so your initial task is to clarify precisely the nature of your study questions in this regard.

More troublesome may be coming up with the substance of the questions. Many students take an initial stab, only to be discouraged when they find the same question(s) already well covered by previous research. Other less desirable questions focus on too trivial or minor parts of an issue. A helpful hint is to move in three stages. In the first, try to use the literature to narrow your interest to a key topic or two, not worrying about any specific research questions. In the second, examine closely—even dissect—a few key studies on your topic of interest. Identify the questions in those few studies and whether they conclude with new questions or loose ends for future research. These may then stimulate your own thinking and imagination, and you may find yourself articulating some potential questions of your own. In the third stage, examine another set of studies on the same topic. They may provide support for your potential questions or even suggest ways of sharpening them.

EXERCISE 2.1   Defining the Boundaries of a Case Study

Select a topic for a case study you would like to do. Identify some research questions to be answered or propositions to be examined by your case study. How does the naming of these questions or propositions clarify the boundaries of your case study with regard to the time period covered by the case study; the relevant social group, organization, or geographic area; the type of evidence to be collected; and the priorities for data collection and analysis?

Study propositions. As for the second component, each proposition directs attention to something that should be examined within the scope of study. For instance, assume that your research, on the topic of interorganizational partnerships, began with the following question: How and why do organizations collaborate with one another to provide joint services (for example, a manufacturer and a retail outlet collaborating to sell certain computer products)? These "how" and "why" questions, capturing what you are really interested in answering, led you to the case study as the appropriate method in the first place. Nevertheless, these "how" and "why" questions do not point to what you should study.

Only if you are forced to state some propositions will you move in the right direction. For instance, you might think that organizations collaborate because they derive mutual benefits. This proposition, besides reflecting an important theoretical issue (that other incentives for collaboration do not exist or are unimportant), also begins to tell you where to look for relevant evidence (to define and ascertain the extent of specific benefits to each organization).

At the same time, some studies may have a legitimate reason for not having any propositions. This is the condition—which exists in experiments, surveys, and the other research methods alike—in which a topic is the subject of "exploration." Every exploration, however, should still have some purpose. Instead of propositions, the design for an exploratory study should state this purpose, as well as the criteria by which an exploration will be judged successful. Consider the analogy in BOX 4 for exploratory case studies. Can you imagine how you would ask for support from Queen Isabella to do your exploratory study?

> **BOX 4**
> **"Exploration" as an Analogy for an Exploratory Case Study**
>
> When Christopher Columbus went to Queen Isabella to ask for support for his "exploration" of the New World, he had to have some reasons for asking for three ships (Why not one? Why not five?), and he had some rationale for going westward (Why not south? Why not south and then east?). He also had some (mistaken) criteria for recognizing the Indies when he actually encountered it. In short, his exploration began with some rationale and direction, even if his initial assumptions might later have been proved wrong (Wilford, 1992). This same degree of rationale and direction should underlie even an exploratory case study.

Unit of analysis. This third component is related to the fundamental problem of defining what the "case" is—a problem that has plagued many investigators at the outset of case studies (e.g., Ragin & Becker, 1992). For instance, in the classic case study, a "case" may be an individual. Jennifer Platt (1992) has noted how the early case studies in the Chicago school of sociology were life histories of such persons as juvenile delinquents or derelict men. You also can imagine case studies of clinical patients, of exemplary students, or of certain types of leaders. In each situation, an individual person is the case being studied, and the individual is the primary unit of analysis. Information about the relevant individual would be collected, and several such individuals or "cases" might be included in a multiple-case study.

You would still need study questions and study propositions to help identify the relevant information to be collected about this individual or individuals. Without such questions and propositions, you might be tempted to cover "everything" about the individual(s), which is impossible to do. For example, the propositions in studying these individuals might involve the influence of early childhood or the role of peer relationships. Such seemingly general topics nevertheless represent a vast narrowing of the relevant data. The more a case study contains specific questions and propositions, the more it will stay within feasible limits.

Of course, the "case" also can be some event or entity other than a single individual. Case studies have been done about decisions, programs, the implementation process, and organizational change. Feagin et al. (1991) contains some classic examples of these single cases in sociology and political science. Beware of these types of cases—none is easily defined in terms of the beginning or end points of the "case." For example, a case study of a specific program may reveal (a) variations in program definition, depending upon the perspective of different actors, and (b) program components that preexisted the formal designation of the program. Any case study of such a program would therefore have to confront these conditions in delineating the unit of analysis.

As a general guide, your tentative definition of the unit of analysis (which is the same as the definition of the "case") is related to the way you have defined your initial research questions. Suppose, for example, you want to study the role of the United States in the global economy. Years ago, Peter Drucker (1986) wrote a provocative essay (not a case study) about fundamental changes in the world economy, including the importance of "capital movements" independent of the flow of goods and services. Using Drucker's work or some similar theoretical framework, the unit of analysis (or "case") for your case study might be a country's economy, an industry in the world marketplace, an economic policy, or the trade or capital flow between countries. Each unit of analysis and its related questions and propositions would call for a slightly different research design and data collection strategy.

Selection of the appropriate unit of analysis will start to occur when you accurately specify your primary research questions. If your questions do not lead to the favoring of one unit of analysis over another, your questions are probably either too vague or too numerous—and you may have trouble doing a case study. However, when you do eventually arrive at a definition of the unit of analysis, do not consider closure permanent. Your choice of the unit of analysis, as with other facets of your research design, can be revisited as a result of discoveries during your data collection (see discussion and cautions about flexibility throughout this book and at the end of this chapter).

Sometimes, the unit of analysis may have been defined one way, even though the phenomenon being studied actually follows a different definition. Most frequently, investigators have confused case studies of neighborhoods with case studies of small groups (as another example, confusing a new technology with the workings of an engineering team in an organization; see BOX 5A). How a geographic *area* such as a neighborhood copes with racial transition, upgrading, and other phenomena can be quite different from how a small *group* copes with these same phenomena. For instance, *Street Corner Society* (Whyte, 1943/1955; see BOX 2A in Chapter 1 of this book) and *Tally's Corner* (Liebow, 1967; see BOX 9, this chapter) often have been mistaken for being case studies of neighborhoods when in fact they are case studies of small groups (note that in neither book is the neighborhood geography described, even though the small groups lived in a small area with clear neighborhood implications). BOX 5B, however, presents a good example of how units of analyses can be defined in a more discriminating manner—in the field of world trade.

BOX 5
Defining the Unit of Analysis

5A. What Is the Unit of Analysis?

The Soul of a New Machine (1981) was a Pulitzer Prize–winning book by Tracy Kidder. The book, also a best seller, is about the development of a new minicomputer, produced by Data General Corporation, intended to compete with one produced by a direct competitor, Digital Equipment Corporation (also see BOX 28, Chapter 5, p. 142).

This easy-to-read book describes how Data General's engineering team invented and developed the new computer. The book begins with the initial conceptualization of the computer and ends when the engineering team relinquishes control of the machine to Data General's marketing staff.

The book is an excellent example of a case study. However, the book also illustrates a fundamental problem in doing case studies—that of defining the unit of analysis. Is the "case" being studied the minicomputer, or is it about the dynamics of a small group—the engineering team? The answer is critical for understanding how the case study might relate to any broader body of knowledge—that is, whether to generalize to a technology topic or to a group dynamics topic. Because the book is not an academic study, it does not need to, nor does it, provide an answer.

5B. A Clearer Choice among Units of Analysis

Ira Magaziner and Mark Patinkin's (1989) book, *The Silent War: Inside the Global Business Battles Shaping America's Future*, presents nine individual case studies (also see BOX 35, Chapter 5, p. 161). Each case helps the reader to understand a real-life situation of international economic competition.

Two of the cases appear similar but in fact have different main units of analysis. One case, about the Korean firm Samsung, is a case study of the critical policies that make the firm competitive. Understanding Korean economic development is part of the context, and the case study also contains an embedded unit—Samsung's development of the microwave oven as an illustrative product. The other case, about the development of an Apple computer factory in Singapore, is in fact a case study of Singapore's critical policies that make the country competitive. The Apple computer factory experience—an embedded unit of analysis—is actually an illustrative example of how the national policies affected foreign investments.

These two cases show how the definition of the main and embedded units of analyses, as well as the definition of the contextual events surrounding these units, depends on the level of inquiry. The main unit of analysis is likely to be at the level being addressed by the main study questions.

Most investigators will encounter this type of confusion in defining the unit of analysis or "case." To reduce the confusion, one recommended practice is to discuss the potential case with a colleague. Try to explain to that person what questions you are trying to answer and why you have chosen a specific case or group of cases as a way of answering those questions. This may help you to avoid incorrectly identifying the unit of analysis.

Once the general definition of the case has been established, other clarifications in the unit of analysis become important. If the unit of analysis is a small group, for instance, the persons to be included within the group (the immediate topic of the case study) must be distinguished from those who are outside it (the context for the case study). Similarly, if the case is about local services in a specific geographic area, you need to decide which services to cover. Also desirable, for almost any topic that might be chosen, are specific time boundaries to define the beginning and end of the case (e.g., whether to include the entire or only some part of the life cycle of the entity that is to be the case). Answering all of these types of questions will help to determine the scope of your data collection and, in particular, how you will distinguish data about the subject of your case study (the "phenomenon") from data external to the case (the "context").

These latter cautions regarding the need for spatial, temporal, and other concrete boundaries underlie a key but subtle aspect in defining your case. The desired case should be some real-life phenomenon, not an abstraction such as a topic, an argument, or even a hypothesis. These abstractions, absent the identification of specific examples or cases, would rightfully serve as the subjects of research studies using other kinds of methods but not case studies. To justify using the case study method, you need to go one step further: You need to define a specific, real-life "case" to represent the abstraction. (For examples of more concrete and less concrete case study topics, see Figure 2.1.)

Take the concept of "neighboring." Alone, it could be the subject of research studies using methods other than the case study method. The other methods might include a survey of the relationships among neighbors, a history of the evolution of the sense of neighboring and the setting of boundaries, or an experiment in which young children do tasks next to each other to determine the distracting effects, if any, of their neighbors. These examples show how the abstract concept of "neighboring" does not alone produce the grounds for a case study. However, the concept could readily become a case study topic if it were accompanied by your selecting a specific neighborhood ("case") to be studied and posing study questions and propositions about the neighborhood in relation to the concept of "neighboring."

One final point pertains to the role of the available research literature and needs to be made about defining the case and the unit of analysis. Most researchers will want to compare their findings with previous research. For

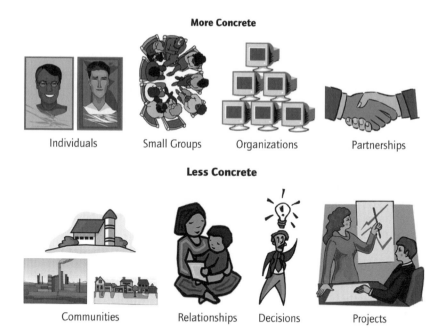

Figure 2.1   Illustrative Case Study Topics

this reason, the key definitions used in your study should not be idiosyncratic. Rather, each case study and unit of analysis either should be similar to those previously studied by others or should innovate in clear, operationally defined ways. In this manner, the previous literature also can become a guide for defining the case and unit of analysis.

> **EXERCISE 2.2   Defining the Unit of Analysis (and the "Case") for a Case Study**
>
> Examine Figure 2.1. Discuss each subject, which illustrates a different unit of analysis. Find a published case study on at least one of these subjects, indicating the actual "case" that was being studied. Understanding that each subject illustrates a different unit of analysis and involves the selection of different cases to be studied, do you think that the more concrete units might be easier to define than the less concrete ones? Why?

Linking data to propositions and criteria for interpreting the findings. The fourth and fifth components have been increasingly better developed in doing case studies. These components foreshadow the data analysis steps in case study research. Because the analytic techniques and choices are covered in detail in Chapter 5, your main concern during the design phase is to be aware of the main choices and how they might suit your case study. In this way, your research design can create a more solid foundation for the later analysis.

All of the analytic techniques in Chapter 5 represent ways of *linking data to propositions:* pattern matching, explanation building, time-series analysis, logic models, and cross-case synthesis. The actual analyses will require that you combine or calculate your case study data as a direct reflection of your initial study propositions. For instance, knowing that some or all of your propositions cover a temporal sequence would mean that you might eventually use some type of time-series analysis. Noting this strong likelihood during the design phase would call your attention to the need to be sure you had sufficient procedures to collect time markers as part of your data collection plans.

If you have had limited experience in conducting empirical studies, you will not easily identify the likely analytic technique(s) or anticipate the needed data to use the techniques to their full advantage. More experienced researchers will note how often they have either (a) collected too much data that were not later used in any analysis or (b) collected too little data that prevented the proper use of a desired analytic technique. Sometimes, the latter situation even may force researchers to return to their data collection phase (if they can), to supplement the original data. The more you can avoid any of these situations, the better off you will be.

Criteria for interpreting a study's findings. Statistical analyses offer some explicit criteria for such interpretations. For instance, by convention, social science considers a p level of less than .05 to demonstrate that observed differences were "statistically significant." However, much case study analysis will not rely on the use of statistics and therefore calls attention to other ways of thinking about such criteria.

A major and important alternative strategy is to identify and address rival explanations for your findings. Again, Chapter 5 discusses this strategy and how it works more fully. At the design stage of your work, the challenge is to anticipate and enumerate the important rivals, so you will include information about them as part of your data collection. If you only think of rival explanations after data collection has been completed, you will be starting to justify and design a *future* study, but you will not be helping to complete your *current* case study. For this reason, specifying important rival explanations is a part of a case study's research design work.

Summary. A research design should include five components. Although the current state of the art does not provide detailed guidance on the last two, the complete research design should indicate what data are to be collected—as indicated by a study's questions, its propositions, and its units of analysis. The design also should tell you what is to be done after the data have been collected—as indicated by the logic linking the data to the propositions and the criteria for interpreting the findings.

The Role of Theory in Design Work

Covering these preceding five components of research designs will effectively force you to begin constructing a preliminary theory related to your topic of study. This role of theory development, prior to the conduct of any data collection, is one point of difference between case studies and related methods such as ethnography (Lincoln & Guba, 1985; Van Maanen, 1988) and "grounded theory" (Corbin & Strauss, 2007). Typically, these related methods deliberately avoid specifying any theoretical propositions at the outset of an inquiry. As a result, students confusing these methods with case studies wrongly think that, by having selected the case study method, they can proceed quickly into the data collection phase of their work, and they may have been encouraged to make their "field contacts" as quickly as possible. No guidance could be more misleading. Among other considerations, the relevant field contacts depend upon an understanding—or theory—of what is being studied.

Theory development. For case studies, theory development as part of the design phase is essential, whether the ensuing case study's purpose is to develop or to test theory. Using a case study on the implementation of a new management information system (MIS) as an example (Markus, 1983), the simplest ingredient of a theory is a statement such as the following:

> The case study will show why implementation only succeeded when the organization was able to re-structure itself, and not just overlay the new MIS on the old organizational structure. (Markus, 1983)

The statement presents the nutshell of a theory of MIS implementation—that is, that organizational restructuring is needed to make MIS implementation work.

Using the same case, an additional ingredient might be the following statement:

> The case study will also show why the simple replacement of key persons was not sufficient for successful implementation. (Markus, 1983)

This second statement presents the nutshell of a *rival* theory—that is, that MIS implementation fails because of the resistance to change on the part of

individual people and that the replacement of such people is the main requirement for implementation to succeed.

You can see that as these two initial ingredients are elaborated, the stated
ideas will increasingly cover the questions, propositions, units of analysis,
logic connecting data to propositions, and criteria for interpreting the
findings—that is, the five components of the needed research design. In this sense,
the complete research design embodies a "theory" of what is being studied.

This theory should by no means be considered with the formality of grand
theory in social science, nor are you being asked to be a masterful theoretician.
Rather, the simple goal is to have a sufficient blueprint for your study, and this
requires theoretical propositions, usefully noted by Sutton and Staw (1995) as
"a [hypothetical] story about why acts, events, structure, and thoughts occur"
(p. 378). Then, the complete research design will provide surprisingly strong
guidance in determining what data to collect and the strategies for analyzing
the data. For this reason, theory development prior to the collection of any case
study data is an essential step in doing case studies. As noted for nonexperi-
mental studies more generally, a more elaborate theory desirably points to a
more complex pattern of expected results (P. R. Rosenbaum, 2002, pp. 5–6 and
277–279). The benefit is a stronger design and a heightened ability to interpret
your eventual data.

However, theory development takes time and can be difficult (Eisenhardt,
1989). For some topics, existing works may provide a rich theoretical framework for designing a specific case study. If you are interested in international
economic development, for instance, Peter Drucker's (1986) "The Changed
World Economy" is an exceptional source of theories and hypotheses. Drucker
claims that the world economy has changed significantly from the past. He
points to the "uncoupling" between the primary products (raw materials) economy and the industrial economy, a similar uncoupling between low labor costs
and manufacturing production, and the uncoupling between financial markets
and the real economy of goods and services. To test these propositions might
require different studies, some focusing on the different uncouplings, others
focusing on specific industries, and yet others explaining the plight of specific
countries. Each different study would likely call for a different unit of analysis. Drucker's theoretical framework would provide guidance for designing
these studies and even for collecting relevant data.

In other situations, the appropriate theory may be a descriptive theory (see
BOX 2A in Chapter 1 for another example), and your concern should focus on
such issues as (a) the purpose of the descriptive effort, (b) the full but realistic
range of topics that might be considered a "complete" description of what is
to be studied, and (c) the likely topic(s) that will be the essence of the description. Good answers to these questions, including the rationales underlying the

answers, will help you go a long way toward developing the needed theoretical base—and research design—for your study.

For yet other topics, the existing knowledge base may be poor, and the available literature will provide no conceptual framework or hypotheses of note. Such a knowledge base does not lend itself to the development of good theoretical statements, and any new empirical study is likely to assume the characteristic of an "exploratory" study. Nevertheless, as noted earlier with the illustrative case in BOX 4, even an exploratory case study should be preceded by statements about what is to be explored, the purpose of the exploration, and the criteria by which the exploration will be judged successful.

Overall, you may want to gain a richer understanding of how theory is used in case studies by reviewing specific case studies that have been successfully completed. For instance, Yin (2003, chap. 1) shows how theory was used in exploratory, descriptive, and explanatory situations by discussing five actual case studies.

Illustrative types of theories. In general, to overcome the barriers to theory development, you should try to prepare for your case study by doing such things as reviewing the literature related to what you would like to study (also see Cooper, 1984), discussing your topic and ideas with colleagues or teachers, and asking yourself challenging questions about what you are studying, why you are proposing to do the study, and what you hope to learn as a result of the study.

As a further reminder, you should be aware of the full range of theories that might be relevant to your study. For instance, note that the MIS example illustrates MIS "implementation" theory and that this is but one type of theory that can be the subject of study. Other types of theories for you to consider include

- ◆ individual theories—for example, theories of individual development, cognitive behavior, personality, learning and disability, individual perception, and interpersonal interactions;
- ◆ group theories—for example, theories of family functioning, informal groups, work teams, supervisory-employee relations, and interpersonal networks;
- ◆ organizational theories—for example, theories of bureaucracies, organizational structure and functions, excellence in organizational performance, and interorganizational partnerships; and
- ◆ societal theories—for example, theories of urban development, international behavior, cultural institutions, technological development, and marketplace functions.

Other examples cut across these illustrative types. Decision-making theory (Carroll & Johnson, 1992), for instance, can involve individuals, organizations, or social groups. As another example, a common topic of case studies is the evaluation of publicly supported programs, such as federal, state, or local programs. In this situation, the development of a theory of how a program is supposed to work is essential to the design of the evaluation. In this situation, Bickman (1987) reminds us that the theory needs to distinguish between the substance of the program (e.g., how to make education more effective) and the process of program implementation (e.g., how to install an effective program). The distinction would avoid situations where policy makers might want to know the desired substantive remedies (e.g., findings about a newly effective curriculum) but where an evaluation unfortunately focused on managerial issues (e.g., the need to hire a good project director). Such a mismatch can be avoided by giving closer attention to the substantive theory.

Generalizing from case study to theory. Theory development does not only facilitate the data collection phase of the ensuing case study. The appropriately developed theory also is the level at which the generalization of the case study results will occur. This role of theory has been characterized throughout this book as "analytic generalization" and has been contrasted with another way of generalizing results, known as "statistical generalization." Understanding the distinction between these two types of generalization may be your most important challenge in doing case studies.

Let us first take the more commonly recognized way of generalizing—*statistical* generalization—although it is the less relevant one for doing case studies. In statistical generalization, an inference is made about a population (or universe) on the basis of empirical data collected about a sample from that universe. This is shown as a Level One inference in Figure 2.2.[1] This method of generalizing is commonly recognized because research investigators have ready access to quantitative formulas for determining the confidence with which generalizations can be made, depending mostly upon the size and internal variation within the universe and sample. Moreover, this is the most common way of generalizing when doing surveys (e.g., Fowler, 1988; Lavrakas, 1987) or analyzing archival data.

A fatal flaw in doing case studies is to conceive of statistical generalization as the method of generalizing the results of your case study. This is because your cases are not "sampling units" and should not be chosen for this reason. Rather, individual case studies are to be selected as a laboratory investigator selects the topic of a new experiment. Multiple cases, in this sense, resemble multiple experiments. Under these circumstances, the mode of generalization is *analytic* generalization, in which a previously developed theory is used as a template with which to compare the empirical results of the case study.[2] If two or more cases are shown to support the same theory, replication may be

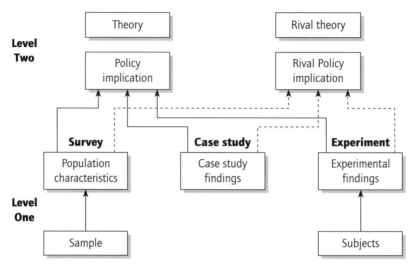

Figure 2.2   Making Inferences: Two Levels

claimed. The empirical results may be considered yet more potent if two or more cases support the same theory but do not support an equally plausible, *rival* theory. Graphically, this type of generalization is shown as a Level Two inference in Figure 2.2.

Analytic generalization can be used whether your case study involves one or several cases, which shall be later referenced as single-case or multiple-case studies. Furthermore, the logic of replication and the distinction between statistical and analytic generalization will be covered in greater detail in the discussion of multiple-case study designs. The main point at this juncture is that you should try to aim toward analytic generalization in doing case studies, and you should avoid thinking in such confusing terms as "the sample of cases" or the "small sample size of cases," as if a single-case study were like a single respondent in a survey or a single subject in an experiment. In other words, in terms of Figure 2.2, you should aim for Level Two inferences when doing case studies.

Because of the importance of this distinction between the two ways of generalizing, you will find repeated examples and discussion throughout the remainder of this chapter as well as in Chapter 5.

Summary. This subsection has suggested that a complete research design, covering the four components described earlier, in fact requires the development of a theoretical framework for the case study that is to be conducted. Rather than resisting such a requirement, a good case study investigator should make the effort to develop this theoretical framework, no matter whether the study is to be explanatory, descriptive, or exploratory. The use of theory, in doing case studies, is an immense aid in defining the appropriate research design and data collection. The same theoretical orientation also becomes the main vehicle for generalizing the results of the case study.

CRITERIA FOR JUDGING THE QUALITY OF RESEARCH DESIGNS

Because a research design is supposed to represent a logical set of statements, you also can judge the quality of any given design according to certain logical tests. Concepts that have been offered for these tests include trustworthiness, credibility, confirmability, and data dependability (U.S. Government Accountability Office, 1990).

Four tests, however, have been commonly used to establish the quality of any empirical social research. Because case studies are one form of such research, the four tests also are relevant to case studies. An important innovation of this book is the identification of several tactics for dealing with these four tests when doing case studies. Figure 2.3 lists the four widely used tests and the recommended case study tactics, as well as a cross-reference to the phase of research when the tactic is to be used. (Each tactic is described in detail in the referenced chapter of this book.)

Because the four tests are common to all social science methods, the tests have been summarized in numerous textbooks (see L. Kidder & Judd, 1986, pp. 26–29):

♦ *Construct validity:* identifying correct operational measures for the concepts being studied

♦ *Internal validity* (for explanatory or causal studies only and not for descriptive or exploratory studies): seeking to establish a causal relationship, whereby certain conditions are believed to lead to other conditions, as distinguished from spurious relationships

♦ *External validity:* defining the domain to which a study's findings can be generalized

♦ *Reliability:* demonstrating that the operations of a study—such as the data collection procedures—can be repeated, with the same results

Each item on this list deserves explicit attention. For case studies, an important revelation is that the several tactics to be used in dealing with these tests

TESTS	Case Study Tactic	Phase of research in which tactic occurs
Construct validity	◆ use multiple sources of evidence ◆ establish chain of evidence ◆ have key informants review draft case study report	data collection data collection composition
Internal validity	◆ do pattern matching ◆ do explanation building ◆ address rival explanations ◆ use logic models	data analysis data analysis data analysis data analysis
External validity	◆ use theory in single-case studies ◆ use replication logic in multiple-case studies	research design research design
Reliability	◆ use case study protocol ◆ develop case study database	data collection data collection

Figure 2.3   Case Study Tactics for Four Design Tests

should be applied throughout the subsequent conduct of the case study, not just at its beginning. Thus, the "design work" for case studies may actually continue beyond the initial design plans.

Construct Validity

This first test is especially challenging in case study research. People who have been critical of case studies often point to the fact that a case study investigator fails to develop a sufficiently operational set of measures and that "subjective" judgments are used to collect the data.[3] Take an example such as studying "neighborhood change"—a common case study topic (e.g., Bradshaw, 1999; Keating & Krumholz, 1999).

Over the years, concerns have arisen over how certain urban neighborhoods have changed their character. Any number of case studies has examined the types of changes and their consequences. However, without any prior specification of the significant, operational events that constitute "change," a reader cannot tell whether the claimed changes in a case study genuinely reflect the events in a neighborhood or whether they happen to be based on an investigator's impressions only.

Neighborhood change can cover a wide variety of phenomena: racial turnover, housing deterioration and abandonment, changes in the pattern of urban services, shifts in a neighborhood's economic institutions, or the turnover from low- to middle-income residents in revitalizing neighborhoods. The choice of whether to aggregate blocks, census tracts, or larger areas also can produce different results (Hipp, 2007).

To meet the test of construct validity, an investigator must be sure to cover two steps:

1. define neighborhood change in terms of specific concepts (and relate them to the original objectives of the study) and
2. identify operational measures that match the concepts (preferably citing published studies that make the same matches).

For example, suppose you satisfy the first step by stating that you plan to study neighborhood change by focusing on trends in neighborhood crime. The second step now demands that you select a specific measure, such as police-reported crime (which happens to be the standard measure used in the FBI Uniform Crime Reports) as your measure of crime. The literature will indicate certain known shortcomings in this measure, mainly that unknown proportions of crimes are not reported to the police. You will then need to discuss how the shortcomings nevertheless will not bias your study of neighborhood crime and hence neighborhood change.

As Figure 2.3 shows, three tactics are available to increase construct validity when doing case studies. The first is the use of *multiple sources of evidence,* in a manner encouraging convergent lines of inquiry, and this tactic is relevant during data collection (see Chapter 4). A second tactic is to establish a *chain of evidence,* also relevant during data collection (also Chapter 4). The third tactic is to have the draft case study report reviewed by key informants (a procedure described further in Chapter 6).

Internal Validity

This second test has been given the greatest attention in experimental and quasi-experimental research (see Campbell & Stanley, 1966; Cook & Campbell, 1979). Numerous "threats" to validity have been identified, mainly dealing with spurious effects. However, because so many textbooks already cover this topic, only two points need to be made here.

First, internal validity is mainly a concern for explanatory case studies, when an investigator is trying to explain how and why event x led to event y. If the investigator incorrectly concludes that there is a causal relationship between x and y without knowing that some third factor—z—may actually have caused y, the research design has failed to deal with some threat to internal validity. Note that this logic is inapplicable to descriptive or exploratory studies (whether the studies are case studies, surveys, or experiments), which are not concerned with this kind of causal situation.

Second, the concern over internal validity, for case study research, extends to the broader problem of making inferences. Basically, a case study involves an inference every time an event cannot be directly observed. An investigator will "infer" that a particular event resulted from some earlier occurrence, based on interview and documentary evidence collected as part of the case study. Is the inference correct? Have all the rival explanations and possibilities been considered? Is the evidence convergent? Does it appear to be airtight? A research design that has anticipated these questions has begun to deal with the overall problem of making inferences and therefore the specific problem of internal validity.

However, the specific tactics for achieving this result are difficult to identify. This is especially true in doing case studies. As one set of suggestions, Figure 2.3 shows that the analytic tactic of *pattern matching,* described further in Chapter 5, is one way of addressing internal validity. Three other analytic tactics, *explanation building, addressing rival explanations,* and *using logic models,* also are described in Chapter 5.

External Validity

The third test deals with the problem of knowing whether a study's findings are generalizable beyond the immediate case study. In the simplest example, if a study of neighborhood change focused on one neighborhood, are the results applicable to another neighborhood? The external validity problem has been a major barrier in doing case studies. Critics typically state that single cases offer a poor basis for generalizing. However, such critics are implicitly contrasting the situation to survey research, in which a sample is intended to generalize to a larger universe. *This analogy to samples and universes is incorrect when dealing with case studies.* Survey research relies on *statistical* generalization, whereas case studies (as with experiments) rely on *analytic* generalization. In analytical generalization, the investigator is striving to generalize a particular set of results to some broader theory (see three examples in BOX 6).

For example, the theory of neighborhood change that led to a case study in the first place is the same theory that will help to identify the other cases to which the results are generalizable. If a study had focused on population transition in an urban neighborhood (e.g., Flippen, 2001), the procedure for selecting a neighborhood for study would have begun with identifying a neighborhood within which the hypothesized transitions were occurring. Theories about transition would then be the domain to which the results could later be generalized.

BOX 6
How Case Studies Can Be Generalized to Theory: Three Examples

6A. The Origins of Social Class Theory

The first example is about the uncovering and labeling of a social class structure based on a case study of a typical American city, *Yankee City* (Warner & Lunt, 1941). This classic case study in sociology made a critical contribution to social stratification theory and an understanding of social differences among "upper," "upper-middle," "middle-middle," "upper-lower," and "lower" classes.

6B. Contributions to Urban Planning Theory

The second example is Jane Jacobs and her famous book, *The Death and Life of Great American Cities* (1961). The book is based mostly on experiences from a single case, New York City. However, the chapter topics, rather than reflecting the single experiences of New York, cover broader theoretical issues in urban planning, such as the role of sidewalks, the role of neighborhood parks, the need for primary mixed uses, the need for small blocks, and the processes of slumming and unslumming. In the aggregate, these issues in fact represent Jacobs's building of a theory of urban planning.

Jacobs's book created heated controversy in the planning profession. As a partial result, new empirical inquiries were made in other locales, to examine one or another facet of her rich and provocative ideas. Her theory, in essence, became the vehicle for examining other cases, and the theory still stands as a significant contribution to the field of urban planning.

6C. A More Contemporary Example

A third example covers a 5-year ethnographic study of a single neighborhood at the edge of Chicago (Carr, 2003). The study shows how the neighborhood successfully thwarted undesirable youth-related crime. The experience, in the author's view, challenged existing theories claiming that strong social ties are crucial to effective neighborhood control. Instead, the author offers newer theories of informal social control that he believes may be especially pertinent to youth crime prevention in contemporary suburban neighborhoods.

The generalization is not automatic, however. A theory must be tested by replicating the findings in a second or even a third neighborhood, where the theory has specified that the same results should occur. Once such direct replications have been made, the results might be accepted as providing strong support for the theory, even though further replications had not been performed. This *replication logic* is the same that underlies the use of experiments (and allows scientists to cumulate knowledge across experiments). The logic will be discussed further in this chapter in the section on multiple-case designs.

Reliability

Most people are probably already familiar with this final test. The objective is to be sure that, if a later investigator followed the same procedures as described by an earlier investigator and conducted the same case study all over again, the later investigator should arrive at the same findings and conclusions. (Note that the emphasis is on doing the *same* case over again, not on "replicating" the results of one case by doing another case study.) The goal of reliability is to minimize the errors and biases in a study.

One prerequisite for allowing this other investigator to repeat an earlier case study is the need to document the procedures followed in the earlier case. Without such documentation, you could not even repeat your own work (which is another way of dealing with reliability). In the past, case study research procedures have been poorly documented, making external reviewers suspicious of the reliability of the case study method.[4] Figure 2.3 indicates two specific tactics to overcome these shortcomings—the use of a *case study protocol* to deal with the documentation problem in detail (discussed in Chapter 3) and the development of a *case study database* (discussed in Chapter 4).

The general way of approaching the reliability problem is to make as many steps as operational as possible and to conduct research as if someone were always looking over your shoulder. Accountants and bookkeepers always are aware that any calculations must be capable of being audited. In this sense, an auditor also is performing a reliability check and must be able to produce the same results if the same procedures are followed. A good guideline for doing case studies is therefore to conduct the research so that an auditor could in principle repeat the procedures and arrive at the same results.

Summary

Four tests may be considered relevant in judging the quality of a research design. In designing and doing case studies, various tactics are available to deal with these tests, though not all of the tactics occur at the formal stage of designing a case study. Some of the tactics occur during the data collection, data analysis, or compositional phases of the research and are therefore described in greater detail in subsequent chapters of this book.

EXERCISE 2.3   Defining the Criteria for Judging the Quality of Research Designs

Define the four criteria for judging the quality of research designs: (a) construct validity, (b) internal validity, (c) external validity, and (d) reliability. Give an example of each type of criterion in a case study you might want to do.

CASE STUDY DESIGNS

These general characteristics of research designs serve as a background for considering the specific designs for case studies. Four types of designs will be discussed, based on a 2×2 matrix (see Figure 2.4). The matrix first shows that every type of design will include the desire to analyze contextual conditions in relation to the "case," with the dotted lines between the two signaling that the boundaries between the case and the context are not likely to be sharp. The matrix then shows that single- and multiple-case studies reflect different design situations and that, within these two variants, there also can be unitary or multiple units of analysis. The resulting four types of designs for case studies are (Type 1) single-case (holistic) designs, (Type 2) single-case (embedded)

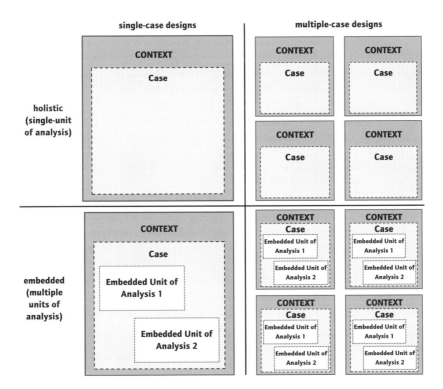

Figure 2.4   Basic Types of Designs for Case Studies
SOURCE: COSMOS Corporation.

designs, (Type 3) multiple-case (holistic) designs, and (Type 4) multiple-case (embedded) designs. The rationale for these four types of designs is as follows.

What Are the Potential Single-Case Designs (Types 1 and 2)?

Rationale for single-case designs. A primary distinction in designing case studies is between *single-* and *multiple-*case designs. This means the need for a decision, prior to any data collection, on whether a single case or multiple cases are going to be used to address the research questions. The single-case study is an appropriate design under several circumstances, and five rationales are given below. Recall that a single-case study is analogous to a single experiment, and many of the same conditions that justify a single experiment also justify a single-case study.

One rationale for a single case is when it represents the *critical case* in testing a well-formulated theory (again, note the analogy to the critical *experiment*). The theory has specified a clear set of propositions as well as the circumstances within which the propositions are believed to be true. A single case, meeting all of the conditions for testing the theory, can confirm, challenge, or extend the theory. The single case can then be used to determine whether a theory's propositions are correct or whether some alternative set of explanations might be more relevant. In this manner, like Graham Allison's comparison of three theories and the Cuban missile crisis (described in Chapter 1, BOX 2), the single case can represent a significant contribution to knowledge and theory building. Such a study can even help to refocus future investigations in an entire field. (See BOX 7 for another example, in the field of organizational innovation.)

A second rationale for a single case is where the case represents an *extreme* case or a *unique* case. Either of these situations commonly occurs in clinical psychology, where a specific injury or disorder may be so rare that any single case is worth documenting and analyzing. For instance, one rare clinical syndrome is the inability of certain clinical patients to recognize familiar faces. Given visual cues alone, such patients are unable to recognize loved ones, friends, pictures of famous people, or (in some cases) their own image in a mirror. This syndrome appears to be due to some physical injury to the brain. Yet the syndrome occurs so rarely that scientists have been unable to establish any common patterns (Yin, 1970, 1978). In such circumstances, the single-case study is an appropriate research design whenever a new person with this syndrome—known as prosopagnosia—is encountered. The case study would document the person's abilities and disabilities, determine the precise nature of the face recognition deficit, but also ascertain whether related disorders exist.

BOX 7
The Critical Case as a Single-Case Study

One rationale for selecting a single-case rather than a multiple-case design is that the single case can represent the critical test of a significant theory. Gross, Bernstein, and Giacquinta (1971) used such a design by focusing on a single school in their book, *Implementing Organizational Innovations* (also see BOX 19B, Chapter 3, p. 110).

   The school was selected because it had a prior history of innovation and could not be claimed to suffer from "barriers to innovation." In the prevailing theories, such barriers had been prominently cited as the major reason that innovations failed. Gross et al. (1971) showed that, in this school, an innovation also failed but that the failure could not be attributed to any barriers. Implementation processes, rather than barriers, appeared to account for the failure.

   In this manner, the book, though limited to a single case, represented a watershed in organizational innovation theory. Prior to the study, analysts had focused on the identification of barriers to innovation; since the study, the literature has been much more dominated by studies of the implementation process.

Conversely, a third rationale for a single case is the *representative* or *typical* case. Here, the objective is to capture the circumstances and conditions of an everyday or commonplace situation (see BOX 8; also see BOX 14, p. 75). The case study may represent a typical "project" among many different projects, a manufacturing firm believed to be typical of many other manufacturing firms in the same industry, a typical urban neighborhood, or a representative school, as examples. The lessons learned from these cases are assumed to be informative about the experiences of the average person or institution.

   A fourth rationale for a single-case study is the *revelatory* case. This situation exists when an investigator has an opportunity to observe and analyze a phenomenon previously inaccessible to social science inquiry, such as Whyte's

---

BOX 8
The Average Case as a Single-Case Study

A famous community case study in sociology, *Middletown*, is about an average American city. The investigators, Robert and Helen Lynd (1929), deliberately chose to study a small town in middle America during the early 20th century (also see BOX 14, p. 75). Their purpose was to show how the transition from an agricultural to an industrial economy occurred in the average town—and thereby to provide a case study about a significant development in all of American history.

(1943/1955) *Street Corner Society,* previously described in Chapter 1, BOX 2A. Another example is Elliot Liebow's (1967) famous case study of unemployed men, *Tally's Corner* (see BOX 9). Liebow had the opportunity to meet the men in an African American neighborhood in Washington, D.C. and to learn about their everyday lives. His observations of and insights into the problems of unemployment formed a significant case study, because few social scientists had previously had the opportunity to investigate these problems, even though the problems were common across the country. When other investigators have similar types of opportunities and can uncover some prevalent phenomenon previously inaccessible to social scientists, such conditions justify the use of a single-case study on the grounds of its revelatory nature.

BOX 9

The Revelatory Case as a Single-Case Study

Another rationale for selecting a single-case rather than a multiple-case design is that the investigator has access to a situation previously inaccessible to scientific observation. The case study is therefore worth conducting because the descriptive information alone will be revelatory.

Such was the situation in Elliot Liebow's (1967) sociological classic, *Tally's Corner.* The book is about a single group of African American men living in a poor, inner-city neighborhood. By befriending these men, the author was able to learn about their lifestyles, their coping behavior, and in particular their sensitivity to unemployment and failure. The book provided insights into a subculture that has prevailed in many U.S. cities for a long period of time, but one that had been only obscurely understood. The single case showed how investigations of such topics could be done, thus stimulating much further research and eventually the development of policy actions.

A fifth rationale for a single-case study is the *longitudinal* case: studying the same single case at two or more different points in time. The theory of interest would likely specify how certain conditions change over time, and the desired time intervals would presumably reflect the anticipated stages at which the changes should reveal themselves.

These five serve as major reasons for conducting a single-case study. There are other situations in which the single-case study may be used as a pilot case that is the first of a multiple-case study. However, in these latter instances, the single-case study cannot be regarded as a complete study on its own.

Whatever the rationale for doing single-case studies (and there may be more than the five mentioned here), a potential vulnerability of the single-case design is that a case may later turn out not to be the case it was thought to be at the outset. Single-case designs therefore require careful investigation of the potential case to minimize the chances of misrepresentation and to maximize the access needed to collect the case study evidence. A fair warning is not to commit yourself to any single-case study until all of these major concerns have been covered.

Holistic versus embedded case studies. The same single-case study may involve *more than one unit of analysis.* This occurs when, within a single case, attention is also given to a subunit or subunits (see BOX 10). For instance, even though a case study might be about a single organization, such as a hospital, the analysis might include outcomes about the clinical services and staff employed by the hospital (and possibly even some quantitative analyses based on the employee records of the staff). In an evaluation study, the single case might be a public program that involves large numbers of funded projects— which would then be the embedded units. In either situation, these embedded units can be selected through sampling or cluster techniques (McClintock, 1985). No matter how the units are selected, the resulting design would be called an *embedded case study design* (see Figure 2.4, Type 2). In contrast, if the case study examined only the global nature of an organization or of a program, a *holistic design* would have been used (see Figure 2.4, Type 1).

These two variants of single-case studies both have their strengths and weaknesses. The holistic design is advantageous when no logical subunits can be identified or when the relevant theory underlying the case study is itself of a holistic nature. Potential problems arise, however, when a global approach allows an investigator to avoid examining any specific phenomenon in operational detail. Thus, a typical problem with the holistic design is that the entire case study may be conducted at an unduly abstract level, lacking sufficiently clear measures or data.

BOX 10
An Embedded, Single-Case Design

Union Democracy (1956) is a highly regarded case study by three eminent academicians— Seymour Martin Lipset, Martin Trow, and James Coleman. The case study is about the inside politics of the International Typographical Union and involves several units of analysis (see "Kinds of Data" table). The main unit was the organization as a whole, the smallest unit was the individual member, and several intermediary units also were important. At each level of analysis, different data collection techniques were used, ranging from historical to survey analysis.

Kinds of Data (BOX 10 Continued)

Unit Being Characterized	Total System: Issues, Data on Occupation; Union Laws; Policies; Historical Data; Convention Reports	Intermediate Units: Locals' Histories and Voting records; Issues on Local Level; size of Locals	Shops' Voting Records; Shop Size	Individuals: Interviews with Leaders	Interviews of the Sample of Men
ITU as a whole	Structural, environmental, behavioral properties	By inference, communication network (structural)			
Locals	Behavioral properties (militancy, etc.)	Behavioral properties, size	By inference, communication network (structural)	Structural, environmental, behavioral properties	
Shops			Behavioral properties, size		Distributions of individual properties
Other immediate social environment of men	The social climate, by inference from dominant issues and election outcome	The social climate, by inference from dominant issues and election outcome			Chapel chairman's attributes; friends' attributes
Men	By inference, dominant values and interests	By inference: values, interests, and loyalties (e.g., local over international)	By inference: values, interests, loyalties (e.g., to shop over local)	By inference: values	Behavior, background, values, attitudes

SOURCE: Lipset, Trow, & Coleman (1956, p. 422). Reprinted by permission.

A further problem with the holistic design is that the entire nature of the case study may shift, unbeknownst to the researcher, during the course of study. The initial study questions may have reflected one orientation, but as the case study proceeds, a different orientation may emerge, and the evidence begins to address different research questions. Although some people have claimed such flexibility to be a strength of the case study approach, in fact the largest criticism of case studies is based on this type of shift—in which the implemented research design is no longer appropriate for the research questions being asked (see COSMOS Corporation, 1983). Because of this problem, you need to avoid such unsuspected slippage; if the relevant research questions really do change, you should simply start over again, with a new research design. One way to increase the sensitivity to such slippage is to have a set of subunits. Thus, an embedded design can serve as an important device for focusing a case study inquiry.

An embedded design, however, also has its pitfalls. A major one occurs when the case study focuses only on the subunit level and fails to return to the larger unit of analysis. For instance, an evaluation of a program consisting of multiple projects may include project characteristics as a subunit of analysis. The project-level data may even be highly quantitative if there are many projects. However, the original evaluation becomes a project study (i.e., a multiple-case study of different projects) if no investigating is done at the level of the original case—that is, the program. Similarly, a study of organizational climate may involve individual employees as a subunit of study. However, if the data focus only on individual employees, the study will in fact become an employee and not an organizational study. In both examples, what has happened is that the original phenomenon of interest (a program or organizational climate) has become the context and not the target of study.

Summary. Single cases are a common design for doing case studies, and two variants have been described: those using holistic designs and those using embedded units of analysis. Overall, the single-case design is eminently justifiable under certain conditions—where the case represents (a) a critical test of existing theory, (b) a rare or unique circumstance, or (c) a representative or typical case, or where the case serves a (d) revelatory or (e) longitudinal purpose.

A major step in designing and conducting a single case is defining the unit of analysis (or the case itself). An operational definition is needed, and some caution must be exercised—before a total commitment to the whole case study is made—to ensure that the case in fact is relevant to the issues and questions of interest.

Within the single case may still be incorporated subunits of analyses, so that a more complex—or embedded—design is developed. The subunits can often add significant opportunities for extensive analysis, enhancing the insights into the single case. However, if too much attention is given to these subunits, and if the larger, holistic aspects of the case begin to be ignored, the case study itself will have shifted its orientation and changed its nature. If the shift is justifiable, you need to address it explicitly and indicate its relationship to the original inquiry.

What Are the Potential Multiple-Case Designs (Types 3 and 4)?

The same study may contain more than a single case. When this occurs, the study has used a multiple-case design, and such designs have increased in frequency in recent years. A common example is a study of school innovations (such as the use of new curricula, rearranged school schedules, or a new educational technology), in which individual schools adopt some innovation. Each school might be the subject of an individual case study, but the study as a whole covers several schools and in this way uses a multiple-case design.

Multiple- versus single-case designs. In some fields, multiple-case studies have been considered a different "methodology" from single-case studies. For example, both anthropology and political science have developed one set of rationales for doing single-case studies and a second set for doing what have been considered "comparative" (or multiple-case) studies (see Eckstein, 1975; Lijphart, 1975). This book, however, considers single- and multiple-case designs to be variants within the same methodological framework—and no broad distinction is made between the so-called classic (that is, single) case study and multiple-case studies. The choice is considered one of research design, with both being included under the case study method.

Multiple-case designs have distinct advantages and disadvantages in comparison to single-case designs. The evidence from multiple cases is often considered more compelling, and the overall study is therefore regarded as being more robust (Herriott & Firestone, 1983). At the same time, the rationale for single-case designs cannot usually be satisfied by multiple cases. By definition, the unusual or rare case, the critical case, and the revelatory case all are likely to involve only single cases. Moreover, the conduct of a multiple-case study can require extensive resources and time beyond the means of a single student or independent research investigator. Therefore, the decision to undertake multiple-case studies cannot be taken lightly.

Selecting the multiple cases also raises a new set of questions. Here, *a major insight is to consider multiple cases as one would consider multiple experiments*—that is, to follow a "replication" design. This is far different from a mistaken analogy in the past, which incorrectly considered multiple cases to be similar to the multiple respondents in a survey (or to the multiple subjects within an experiment)—that is, to follow a "sampling" design. The methodological differences between these two views are revealed by the different rationales underlying the replication as opposed to sampling designs.

Replication, not sampling logic, for multiple-case studies. The replication logic is analogous to that used in multiple experiments (see Hersen & Barlow, 1976). For example, upon uncovering a significant finding from a single experiment, an ensuing and pressing priority would be to replicate this finding by conducting a second, third, and even more experiments. Some of the replications might attempt to duplicate the exact conditions of the original experiment. Other replications might alter one or two experimental conditions considered unimportant to the original finding, to see whether the finding could still be duplicated. Only with such replications would the original finding be considered robust.

The logic underlying the use of multiple-case studies is the same. Each case must be carefully selected so that it either (a) predicts similar results (a *literal replication*) or (b) predicts contrasting results but for anticipatable reasons (a *theoretical replication*). The ability to conduct 6 or 10 case studies, arranged effectively within a multiple-case design, is analogous to the ability to conduct 6 to 10 experiments on related topics; a few cases (2 or 3) would be literal replications, whereas a few other cases (4 to 6) might be designed to pursue two different patterns of theoretical replications. If all the cases turn out as predicted, these 6 to 10 cases, in the aggregate, would have provided compelling support for the initial set of propositions. If the cases are in some way contradictory, the initial propositions must be revised and retested with another set of cases. Again, this logic is similar to the way scientists deal with conflicting experimental findings.

An important step in all of these replication procedures is the development of a rich, theoretical framework. The framework needs to state the conditions under which a particular phenomenon is likely to be found (a literal replication) as well as the conditions when it is not likely to be found (a theoretical replication). The theoretical framework later becomes the vehicle for generalizing to new cases, again similar to the role played in cross-experiment designs. Furthermore, just as with experimental science, if some of the empirical cases do not work as predicted, modification must be made to the theory. Remember, too, that theories can be practical and not just academic.

For example, one might consider the initial proposition that an increase in using a new technology in school districts will occur when the technology is used for both administrative and instructional applications, but not either alone. To pursue this proposition in a multiple-case study design, 3 or 4 cases might be selected in which both types of applications are present, to determine whether, in fact, technology use did increase over a period of time (the investigation would be predicting a literal replication in these 3 or 4 cases). Three or

4 additional cases might be selected in which only administrative applications are present, with the prediction being little increase in use (predicting a theoretical replication). Finally, 3 or 4 other cases would be selected in which only instructional applications are present, with the same prediction of little increase in use, but for different reasons than the administrative-only cases (another theoretical replication). If this entire pattern of results across these multiple cases is indeed found, the 9 to 12 cases, in the aggregate, would provide substantial support for the initial proposition.

Another example of a multiple-case replication design comes from the field of urban studies (see BOX 11). You also can find examples of three entire case studies, all following a replication design but covering HIV/AIDS prevention, university administration, and the transformation of business firms, in the companion text (Yin, 2003, chaps. 8–10).

This replication logic, whether applied to experiments or to case studies, must be distinguished from the sampling logic commonly used in surveys. The sampling logic requires an operational enumeration of the entire universe or pool of potential respondents and then a statistical procedure for selecting a

---

BOX 11
A Multiple-Case, Replication Design

A common problem in the 1960s and 1970s was how to get good advice to city governments. Peter Szanton's (1981) book, *Not Well Advised*, reviewed the experiences of numerous attempts by university and research groups to collaborate with city officials.

The book is an excellent example of a multiple-case, replication design. Szanton starts with eight case studies, showing how different university groups all failed to help cities. The eight cases are sufficient "replications" to convince the reader of a general phenomenon. Szanton then provides five more case studies, in which nonuniversity groups also failed, concluding that failure was therefore not necessarily inherent in the academic enterprise. Yet a third group of cases shows how university groups have successfully helped business, engineering firms, and sectors other than city government. A final set of three cases shows that those few groups able to help city government were concerned with implementation and not just with the production of new ideas, leading to the major conclusion that city governments may have peculiar needs in receiving but also then putting advice into practice.

Within each of the four groups of case studies, Szanton has illustrated the principle of literal replication. Across the four groups, he has illustrated theoretical replication. This potent case study design can and should be applied to many other topics.

specific subset of respondents to be surveyed. The resulting data from the sample that is actually surveyed are assumed to reflect the entire universe or pool, with inferential statistics used to establish the confidence intervals for which this representation is presumed accurate. The entire procedure is commonly used when an investigator wishes to determine the prevalence or frequency of a particular phenomenon.

Any application of this sampling logic to case studies would be misplaced. First, case studies are not the best method for assessing the prevalence of phenomena. Second, a case study would have to cover both the phenomenon of interest and its context, yielding a large number of potentially relevant variables. In turn, this would require an impossibly large number of cases—too large to allow any statistical consideration of the relevant variables.

Third, if a sampling logic had to be applied to all types of research, many important topics could not be empirically investigated, such as the following problem: Your investigation deals with the role of the presidency of the United States, and you are interested in doing a multiple-case study of a (few) presidents to test your theory about presidential leadership. However, the complexity of your topic means that your choice of a small number of cases could not adequately represent all the 44 presidents since the beginning of the Republic. Critics using a sampling logic might therefore deny the acceptability of your study. In contrast, if you use a replication logic, the study is eminently feasible.

The replication approach to multiple-case studies is illustrated in Figure 2.5. The figure indicates that the initial step in designing the study must consist of theory development, and then shows that case selection and the definition of specific measures are important steps in the design and data collection process. Each individual case study consists of a "whole" study, in which convergent evidence is sought regarding the facts and conclusions for the case; each case's conclusions are then considered to be the information needing replication by other individual cases. Both the individual cases and the multiple-case results can and should be the focus of a summary report. For each individual case, the report should indicate how and why a particular proposition was demonstrated (or not demonstrated). Across cases, the report should indicate the extent of the replication logic and why certain cases were predicted to have certain results, whereas other cases, if any, were predicted to have contrasting results.

An important part of Figure 2.5 is the dashed-line feedback loop. The loop represents the situation where important discovery occurs during the conduct of one of the individual case studies (e.g., one of the cases did not in fact suit the original design). Such a discovery even may require you to reconsider one or more of the study's original theoretical propositions. At this point,

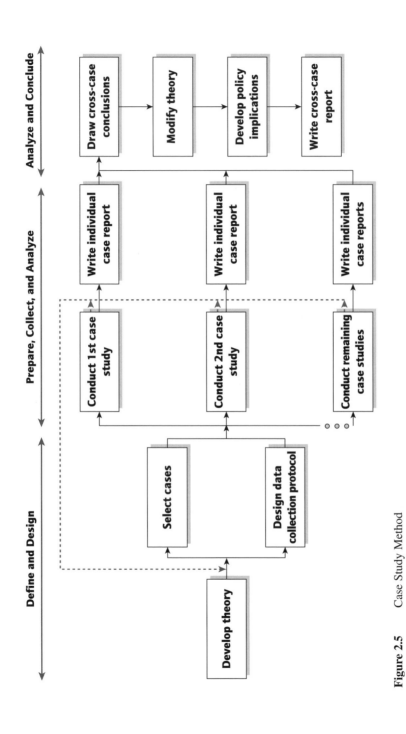

Figure 2.5 Case Study Method

SOURCE: COSMOS Corporation.

"redesign" should take place before proceeding further. Such redesign might involve the selection of alternative cases or changes in the case study (i.e., data collection) protocol (see Chapter 3). Without such redesign, you risk being accused of distorting or ignoring the discovery, just to accommodate the original design. This condition leads quickly to a further accusation—that you have been selective in reporting your data, to suit your preconceived ideas (i.e., the original theoretical propositions).

Overall, Figure 2.5 depicts a very different logic from that of a sampling design. The logic as well as its contrast with a sampling design may be difficult to follow and is worth extensive discussion with colleagues before proceeding with any multiple case study.

When using a multiple-case design, a further question you will encounter has to do with the *number* of cases deemed necessary or sufficient for your study. However, because a sampling logic should not be used, the typical criteria regarding sample size also are irrelevant. Instead, you should think of this decision as a reflection of the number of case replications—both literal and theoretical—that you need or would like to have in your study.

For the number of literal replications, an appropriate analogy from statistics is the selection of the criterion for establishing the sample size desired to detect an "effect." Designating a "$p < .05$" or "$p < .01$" likelihood of detection as part of a power analysis is not based on any formula but is a matter of discretionary, judgmental choice. Analogously, designating the number of replications depends upon the certainty you want to have about your multiple-case results (as with the higher criterion for establishing the likelihood of detection, the greater certainty lies with the larger number of cases). For example, you may want to settle for two or three literal replications when your theory is straightforward and the issue at hand does not demand an excessive degree of certainty. However, if your theory is subtle or if you want a high degree of certainty, you may press for five, six, or more replications.

For the number of theoretical replications, the important consideration is related to your sense of the importance of rival explanations. The stronger the rivals, the more additional cases you might want, each case showing a different result when some rival explanation had been taken into account. For example, your original hypothesis might be that summer reading programs improve students' reading scores, and you already might have shown this result through several cases that served as literal replications. A rival explanation might be that parents also work more closely with their children during the summer and that this circumstance can account for improved reading scores. You would then find another case, with parent participation but no summer reading program, and in this theoretical replication you would predict that the scores would not improve.

Rationale for multiple-case designs. In short, the rationale for multiple-case designs derives directly from your understanding of literal and theoretical replications. The simplest multiple-case design would be the selection of two or more cases that are believed to be literal replications, such as a set of cases with exemplary outcomes in relation to some evaluation questions, such as "how and why a particular intervention has been implemented smoothly." Selecting such cases requires prior knowledge of the outcomes, with the multiple-case inquiry focusing on how and why the exemplary outcomes might have occurred and hoping for literal (or direct) replications of these conditions from case to case.[5]

More complicated multiple-case designs would likely result from the number and types of theoretical replications you might want to cover. For example, investigators have used a "two-tail" design in which cases from both extremes (of some important theoretical condition, such as good and bad outcomes) have been deliberately chosen. Multiple-case rationales also can derive from the prior hypothesizing of different types of conditions and the desire to have subgroups of cases covering each type. These and other similar designs are more complicated because the study should still have at least two individual cases within each of the subgroups, so that the theoretical replications across subgroups are complemented by literal replications within each subgroup.

Multiple-case studies: Holistic or embedded. The fact that a design calls for multiple-case studies does not eliminate the variation identified earlier with single cases: Each individual case may still be holistic or embedded. In other words, a multiple-case study may consist of multiple holistic cases (see Figure 2.4, Type 3) or of multiple embedded cases (see Figure 2.4, Type 4).

The difference between these two variants depends upon the type of phenomenon being studied and your research questions. In an embedded design, a study even may call for the conduct of a survey at each case study site. For instance, suppose a study is concerned with the impact of the same type of curriculum adopted by different schools. Each school may be the topic of a case study, with the theoretical framework dictating that nine such schools be included as case studies, three to replicate a direct result (literal replication) and six others to deal with contrasting conditions (theoretical replications).

For all nine schools, an embedded design is used because surveys of the students (or, alternatively, examination of students' archival records) are needed to address research questions about the performance of the schools. However, the results of each survey will *not* be pooled across schools. Rather, the survey data will be part of the findings for each individual school, or case. These data may be highly quantitative, focusing on the attitudes and behavior of individual students, and the data will be used along with archival information to interpret the success and operations at the given school. If, in contrast, the survey data are pooled across schools, a replication design is no longer being used. In fact, the study has now become a single-case study, in which all nine schools and their students have now become part of some larger, main unit of analysis. Such a new case study would then require a complete redefinition of the main unit of analysis, with extensive revisions to the original theories and propositions of interest also a likely need.

Summary. This section has dealt with situations in which the same investigation may call for multiple-case studies. These types of designs are becoming more prevalent, but they are more expensive and time-consuming to conduct.

Any use of multiple-case designs should follow a replication, not a sampling logic, and an investigator must choose each case carefully. The cases should serve in a manner similar to multiple experiments, with similar results (a literal replication) or contrasting results (a theoretical replication) predicted explicitly at the outset of the investigation.

The individual cases within a multiple-case study design may be either holistic or embedded. When an embedded design is used, each individual case study may in fact include the collection and analysis of quantitative data, including the use of surveys within each case.

EXERCISE 2.4 Defining a Case Study Research Design

Select one of the case studies described in the BOXES of this book, reviewing the entire case study (not just the material in the BOX). Describe the research design of this case study. How did it justify the relevant evidence to be sought, given the basic research questions to be answered? What methods were used to draw conclusions, based on the evidence? Is the design a single- or multiple-case design? Is it holistic or does it have embedded units of analysis?

MODEST ADVICE IN SELECTING CASE STUDY DESIGNS

Now that you know how to define case study designs and are prepared to carry out design work, three pieces of advice may be offered.

Single- or Multiple-Case Designs?

The first word of advice is that, although all designs can lead to successful case studies, when you have the choice (and resources), multiple-case designs may be preferred over single-case designs. Even if you can do a "two-case"

case study, your chances of doing a good case study will be better than using a single-case design. Single-case designs are vulnerable if only because you will have put "all your eggs in one basket." More important, the analytic benefits from having two (or more) cases may be substantial.

To begin with, even with two cases, you have the possibility of direct replication. Analytic conclusions independently arising from two cases, as with two experiments, will be more powerful than those coming from a single case (or single experiment) alone. Alternatively you may have deliberately selected your two cases because they offered contrasting situations, and you were not seeking a direct replication. In this design, if the subsequent findings support the hypothesized contrast, the results represent a strong start toward theoretical replication—again vastly strengthening your findings compared to those from a single case alone (e.g., Eilbert & Lafronza, 2005; Hanna, 2005; also see BOX 12).

BOX 12
Two, "Two-Case" Case Studies

12A. Contrasting Cases for Community Building

Chaskin (2001) used two case studies to illustrate contrasting strategies for capacity building at the neighborhood level. The author's overall conceptual framework, which was the main topic of inquiry, claimed that there could be two approaches to building community capacity—using a collaborative organization to (a) reinforce existing networks of community organizations or (b) initiate a new organization in the neighborhood. After thoroughly airing the framework on theoretical grounds, the author presents the two case studies, showing the viability of each approach.

12B. Contrasting Strategies for Educational Accountability

In a directly complementary manner, Elmore, Abelmann, and Fuhrman (1997) chose two case studies to illustrate contrasting strategies for designing and implementing educational accountability (i.e., holding schools accountable for the academic performance of their students). One case represented a lower cost, basic version of an accountability system. The other represented a higher cost, more complex version.

In general, criticisms about single-case studies usually reflect fears about the uniqueness or artifactual conditions surrounding the case (e.g., special access to a key informant). As a result, the criticisms may turn into skepticism about your ability to do empirical work beyond having done a single-case study. Having two cases can begin to blunt such criticism and skepticism. Having more than two cases will produce an even stronger effect. In the face of these benefits, having at least two cases should be your goal. If you do use a single-case design, you should be prepared to make an extremely strong argument in justifying your choice for the case.

> ### EXERCISE 2.5   Establishing the Rationale for a Multiple-Case Study
>
> Develop some preliminary ideas about a "case" for your case study. Alternatively, focus on one of the single-case studies presented in the BOXES in this book. In either situation, now think of a companion "case" that might augment the single case. In what ways might the companion case's findings supplement those of the first case? Could the data from the second case fill a gap left by the first case or respond better to some obvious shortcoming or criticism of the first case? Would the two cases together comprise a stronger case study? Could yet a third case make the findings even more compelling?

Closed Designs or Flexible Designs?

Another word of advice is that, despite this chapter's details about design choices, you should not think that a case study's design cannot be modified by new information or discovery during data collection. Such revelations can be enormously important, leading to your altering or modifying your original design.

As examples, in a single-case study, what was thought to be a critical or unique case might have turned out not to be so, after initial data collection had started; ditto a multiple-case study, where what was thought to be parallel cases for literal replication turn out not to be so. With these revelations, you have every right to conclude that your initial design needs to be modified. However, you should undertake any alterations only given a serious caution. The caution is to understand precisely the nature of the alteration: Are you merely selecting different cases, or are you also changing your original theoretical concerns and objectives? The point is that the needed flexibility should not lessen the rigor with which case study procedures are followed.

Mixed Methods Designs: Mixing Case Studies with Other Methods?

Researchers have given increasing attention to "mixed methods research"— a "class of research where the researcher mixes or combines quantitative and qualitative research techniques, methods, approaches, concepts or language into a *single* study" (Johnson & Onwuegbuzie, 2004, p. 17, emphasis added). Confinement to a single study forces the methods being mixed into an integrated mode. The mode differs from the conventional situation whereby different methods are used in *separate* studies that may later be synthesized.

Mixed methods research forces the methods to share the same research questions, to collect complementary data, and to conduct counterpart analyses (e.g., Yin, 2006b)—in short, to follow a mixed methods design. As such, mixed methods research can permit investigators to address more complicated research questions and collect a richer and stronger array of evidence than can be accomplished by any single method alone. Depending upon the nature of your research questions and your ability to use different methods, mixed methods research opens a class of research designs that deserve your consideration.

The earlier discussion of embedded case study designs in fact points to the fact that certain kinds of case studies already represent a form of mixed methods research. The embedded case studies rely on more holistic data collection strategies for studying the main case but then call upon surveys or other more quantitative techniques to collect data about the embedded unit(s) of analysis. In this situation, other research methods are embedded within your case study.

The opposite relationship also can occur. Your case study may be part of a larger, mixed methods study. The main investigation may rely on a survey or other quantitative techniques, and your case study may help to investigate the conditions within one of the entities being surveyed. The contrasting relationships (survey within case or case within survey) are illustrated in Figure 2.6.

At the same time, mixed methods research need not include the use of the case study strategy at all. For instance, much historical work embraces the quantitative analysis of archival records, such as newspapers and other file material. And, in an even broader sense, mixed methods research need not be limited to combinations of quantitative and qualitative methods. For instance, a study could employ a survey to describe certain conditions, complemented by an experiment that tried to manipulate some of those conditions (e.g., Berends & Garet, 2002).

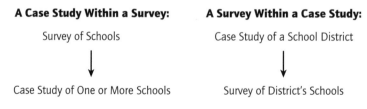

A Case Study Within a Survey:

Survey of Schools

↓

Case Study of One or More Schools

A Survey Within a Case Study:

Case Study of a School District

↓

Survey of District's Schools

Figure 2.6   Mixed Methods: Two Nested Arrangements

By definition, studies using mixed methods research are more difficult to execute than studies limited to single methods. However, mixed methods research can enable you to address broader or more complicated research questions than case studies alone. As a result, mixing case studies with other methods should be among the possibilities meriting your consideration.

NOTES

1. Figure 2.2 focuses only on the formal research design process, not on data collection activities. For all three types of research (survey, case study, and experiment), data collection techniques might be depicted as the level below Level One in the figure. For example, for case studies, this might include using multiple sources of evidence, as described further in Chapter 4. Similar data collection techniques can be described for surveys or experiments—for example, questionnaire design for surveys or stimulus presentation strategies for experiments.

2. See Gomm, Hammersley, and Foster (2000) for more explanation of *analytic* generalization, though their work uses different labels for the same concept.

3. One of the anonymous reviewers of the third edition of this book pointed out that construct validity also has to do with whether interviewees understand what is being asked of them.

4. For other suggested guidelines for reviewers of case study proposals or manuscripts, see Yin (1999).

5. Strictly quantitative studies that select cases with known outcomes follow the same design and have alternatively been called "case-control," "retrospective," or "case referent" studies (see P. R. Rosenbaum, 2002, p. 7).

REFERENCE TO EXPANDED CASE STUDY
MATERIALS FOR CHAPTER 2

For selected case studies cited in the text of this chapter, two anthologies contain either a more extensive excerpt or the full case study. The table on the next page crosswalks the reference in this book to the location of the excerpt or full rendition.

Chapter 2 Chapter Topic and Page Number	Topics of Illustrative Case Studies	Reference to Lengthier Material
General Approach to Designing Case Studies		
BOX 4, p. 2-6	Exploratory study	None
BOX 5A, p. 2-9	Computers and technology	None
BOX 5B, p. 2-9	Business and industry	CSA-6
p. 2-15 text	Five different case studies	ACSR-1
Criteria for Judging the Quality of Research Designs		
BOX 6A, p. 2-23	Cities and towns	CSA-4
BOX 6B, p. 2-23	Urban planning	None
BOX 6C, p. 2-23	Neighborhoods	None
Case Study Designs		
BOX 7, p. 2-27	Schools	CSA-9
BOX 8, p. 2-28	Cities and towns	CSA-3
BOX 9, p. 2-28	Neighborhoods	None
BOX 10, p. 2-29	Business and industry	CSA-10
BOX 11, p. 2-35	Government agencies	None
p. 2-35 text	Health (HIV/AIDS) care	ACSR-8
p. 2-35 text	University administration	ACSR-9
p. 2-35 text	Business and industry	ASCR-10
Modest Advice in Selecting Case Study Designs		
BOX 12A, p. 2-41	Community organizations	None
BOX 12B, p. 2-41	Schools	None

NOTE: CSA = *Case Study Anthology* (Yin, 2004). ACSR = *Applications of Case Study Research* (Yin, 2003). The number denotes the chapter number in the book.

Lecture 7

Philosophy of Social Sciences I

Philosophy of Science and its Relevance for the Social Sciences

PETER K. SMITH

Are the social sciences really sciences, or is this a misnomer? In the UK, the Social Science Research Council (SSRC) had to change its name to the Economic and Social Research Council (ESRC), in part because of a belief in government at the time that the social sciences were not sciences. And academics also debate these issues. This is not just a matter of a name – it affects how we carry out our research and what we think is the status of 'facts', 'evidence' and 'theories'. These are issues which confront all researchers. At times, we may get by unthinkingly, doing as colleagues have done previously; but we may also be challenged – by new ideas or by other disciplines – and these issues will come to the forefront.

As part of such considerations, it is important for social scientists to understand something of the 'philosophy of science' even as it applies to the traditional 'hard' sciences, the physical sciences especially, and the biological and earth sciences. After all, a significant part of the debate about procedures in the social sciences is whether we can profitably apply – or whether instead we routinely misapply – methods and procedures from the physical sciences. Often, too, the procedures of the physical sciences are misunderstood. So, it is very relevant to know how the traditional sciences work, or are thought to work, whether we as social scientists then imitate these methods, modify them, or reject them.

In this chapter I will define what is meant by Philosophy of Science and give a brief historical survey of the main issues. I will review the traditional 'inductivist' view of science, the hypothetico-deductive view of Popper, and the alternative views of Kuhn and Lakatos, including more recent critiques and ideas (see also Chalmers, 1982; Hacking, 1981; Losee, 1980).

What is Meant by Philosophy of Science?

The philosophy of science is concerned with questions such as:

1 What characteristics distinguish science from non-science?
2 What procedures should scientists follow?
3 What conditions must be satisfied for a scientific explanation to be correct?
4 What is the cognitive status of scientific laws and principles? (See Losee, 1980: 2.)

These are fundamental questions: (1) and (2) are definitional for the scientific method; (3) and (4) may seem more abstract, but they too are fundamental.

Question (4) was a matter of life and death in the case of Galileo. Traditionally (and follow-ing obvious perceptual information) people believed that the sun revolved round the earth. Following the work of Copernicus, Galileo (1564–1642) argued that in fact the earth revolved round the sun. This brought him into conflict with the Catholic Church at the time. In 1615 Cardinal Bellarmine corresponded with Galileo about this. It is permissible, he said to Galileo, for you to argue that the earth revolving around the sun is a possible mathematical model; in fact, it is even permissible for you to argue that it is the best model at the moment; but you must not say that it is actually, physically, true. Despite this warning, Galileo continued to assert that it was true. In 1633 the Inquisition condemned Galileo's views, which he subse-quently recanted. Only in 1992, after 359 years, did the Catholic Church admit it was wrong to condemn him. This was a debate about the status of a scientific law. Interestingly, most modern philosophers of science would accept the 'best model' compromise without qualms, rather than insisting on an actual physical truth which, ultimately, is provisional rather than certain.

As a discipline, the philosophy of science is related to other areas, notably:

- *the history of science* – how science has actually developed, whatever the 'ideal' science might do;
- *the sociology of knowledge* – how social structures and institutions, scientific societies and journals and the social networks of individual scientists affect the growth of science;
- *the psychology of research* – how individual scientists develop ways of thinking about and interpreting the world; pressures for conformity and bursts of creativity.

Of twentieth-century philosophers of science, Kuhn has reached out to the history of science and the sociology of knowledge. However, the origins of the philosophy of science go back long before the twentieth century.

Historical Origins of the Philosophy of Science

Systematic writing about the philosophy of science can be dated back to the ancient Greeks. Aristotle (384–322 BC) provided a foundation for speculating about 'the nature of things' which had an enduring influence. In particular, he had an 'inductive-deductive' view of how we obtained systematic knowledge. According to this, we first 'induce' certain regularities in the world around us. For example, we might notice the regularity of flowering plants in springtime; we 'deduce' that next spring the plants will flower again. This very simple example could be made more sophisticated by induced explanatory principles such as the effects of rain and sun on plants. We could then deduce that a drought or lack of sunshine will prevent or delay plant growth in the spring.

Aristotle also started the consideration of what is meant by causality. Looking at the regularities or 'correlations' in observed phenomena, he clearly distinguished between accidental correlations and causal correlations. As an example of an accidental correlation, at the time of year when plants start blossoming, birds start singing (plant blossom does not cause birds to sing; bird song does not cause plants to blossom; both are caused by the increase in temperature and hours of daylight during spring). As an example of a causal correlation, when we feel the wind blowing strongly, we see clouds scudding across the sky (the same wind which blows on us also causes the clouds to move). However, Aristotle was not an experimentalist. As we shall see, the role of experiments was a gradual, later development in the philosophy of science, linked to the greater importance given to deductivism.

The works of Aristotle and other Greek philosophers from the classical period were translated from Greek into Latin and Arabic (since Arab philosophers kept these works alive during the European 'dark ages'). Latin translations of Aristotle's writings on science became available to European philosophers as learning revived during the twelfth and thirteenth centuries.

Roger Bacon (1214–1292), for example, affirmed Aristotle's 'inductive-deductive' pattern of scientific inquiry, but took it one stage further. Bacon argued that the factual base available for induction to operate on could be augmented by active experimentation on the world. At the time there was much interest in magnetism (and its possible uses in compasses and for navigation). What happens if you break a magnetic bar or needle? You get two magnets, each with its own N and S poles. These simple kinds of 'experimentation' would be useful, Bacon argued. Note, however, that Bacon was not testing any theory here; rather, this was experimentation to 'see what happens'. Bacon and a few other philosophers at the time did begin to point to the need to test exploratory principles arrived at by induction, but this did not proceed very far.

In fact, another tradition from classical Greek writings laid the foundation for hypothesis testing and experimentation. Euclid (c.300 BC) and Archimedes (287–212 BC) developed the idea of axioms, or hypotheses, in mathematics and geometry. Given certain axioms, then certain consequences follow – hypothesis and deduction. But this approach was used in the abstract realm of mathematics. In the seventeeth century, Descartes (1596–1650) elaborated this hypothetico-deductive method and laid the groundwork for its application in science. But it was not until the twentieth century that this hypothetico-deductive approach became central in the understanding of science, together with a full appreciation of the role of experimentation in actively testing hypotheses.

The Traditional 'Inductivist' View of Science

Aristotle's view came under more critical scrutiny as the philosophy of science developed in modem Europe. By and large, the inductivist view of science held sway and was further augmented. Among many contributions, we can take John Stuart Mill (1806–1873) as a prominent example from the nineteenth century. Mill argued that there were four primary inductive methods which could be used (for example, to distinguish accidental and causal correlations). These were agreement, difference, concomitant variations and residues.

As a fictional illustration of this in the social sciences, suppose we have induced a correlation between having the death penalty for murder and a reduced number of homicides. According to Mill, we could infer causation – that hanging deters homicides: if there are few homicides at times/places where the death penalty is enforced (*agreement*); there are many homicides at times/places where the death penalty is not enforced (*difference*); there are fewer homicides when the death penalty is enforced strictly and more when it is interpreted more leniently (*concomitant variations*); and presence/ absence or variation in other possible causes (e.g. unemployment, marital instability) do not affect the number of homicides (*residues*).

Mill argued that the processes of inference and induction, could lead us to deduce causal relations. If these were verified – if they explained observations and other causal relations did not – then we could regard the hypothesis as verified. Mill cited Newton's inverse square law of force (that the gravitational attraction between two bodies reduces as the square of the distance between them – a crucial part of explaining planetary motion) as an example of a completely verified law. This law could then be considered 'true' in some absolute sense.

Mill's work epitomizes the 'traditional' or 'inductivist' view of the scientific method. In brief, this holds that science proceeds by collecting factual data through observation and by experimentation which serves to increase the observational data base. By inductive methods, generalizations and causal laws could be arrived at. In principle, induced laws could be completely verified if all the deductions from them were correct. This view held sway in many quarters well into the twentieth century. For example, Karl Pearson (who developed the well-known product–moment correlation coefficient) wrote: 'the classification of facts and the formation of absolute judgments upon the basis of this classification . . . *essentially sum up the aim and method of modern science*' (1892: 6; author emphasis).

A crucial part of the traditional view is that *hypothesis follows observation* (this refers to procedures, question 2 of our four questions at the start of the chapter). It also argues that *we can achieve completely verifiable, 'true' theories* (this refers to questions 3 and 4). Yet few modern philosophers of science accept either of these conclusions. In fact, most would argue that *hypothesis precedes observation* and that *we cannot achieve completely verifiable, 'true' theories*. Thus, the 'traditional' view has come to be radically overthrown.

The Hypothetico-Deductive View of Popper

Karl Popper (1902–1994) has been one of the most well-known philosophers of science to attack the traditional view and to establish an alternative, hypothetico-deductive view (Popper, 1959, 1963, 1976, 1979, 1986; see Magee, 1982). Another well-known figure who has propounded similar views to Popper, is Peter Medawar (1915–1988). This hypothetico-deductive view also has a long intellectual history and as an example we can consider statements by Charles Darwin in the 1860s (quoted in Medawar, 1969: 11): 'I have an old belief that a good observer really means a good theorist' and 'how odd it is that anyone should not see that all observations must be for or against some view if it is to be of any service'.

From Darwin's notebooks we know that he was formulating ideas about evolution well before the publication of *The Origin of Species* in 1859. Even during the voyage of HMS *Beagle* (1831–6) he may have been directing his observations towards testing ideas that were fermenting in his mind. As Medawar (1969) put it, 'we cannot browse over the field of nature like cows at pasture'. If Darwin had gathered data randomly, this would not have provided nearly such good evidence for natural selection as the systematic data he did collect – on where fossils were found, on how the beaks of finches varied in different habitats, and so forth – which allowed him to confirm or disconfirm his hypotheses.

Popper holds that science and knowledge progress by advancing hypotheses, making deductions from them and using observations and experiments continually to test these deductions until they are falsified; then revising or changing the hypothesis to cope with this. (Note the increased role of experiments here explicitly to test hypotheses.) Hence, the hypothetico-deductive method: Hypotheses come first and observations follow; 'observations are interpretations ... in the light of theories'. It is easy to underestimate the importance of this view, which is fundamentally different from the traditional view and itself leads to other differences. Essentially, it is saying that we do not collect facts, as Pearson had implied; we do not gather unbiased observations. Rather, we interpret our observations in the light of biases, preconceptions, hypotheses and theories. We choose which aspects of incoming stimuli to attend to and what interpretation to put on them. This view relates to some modern ideas on the psychology of perception and the psychology of development.

Psychology of perception
The study of ambiguous figures, as in Escher drawings and visual illusions, or the interpretation of minimal sketches or cartoons shows that the human brain actively interprets visual (and other sensory) stimuli. Depending on our expectations and previous experiences, different people may experience a certain stimulus in different ways – as an old lady or a young lady in Figure 1.1, for example. Thus, preconceptions are biasing our observation.

FIGURE 1.1 Ambiguous figures: old lady or young lady?

Psychology of development

There is a developmental history to our preconceptions. Ultimately, there is an evolutionary history in that our sensory systems themselves are 'biased' to respond to certain kinds of external signals (e.g. wavelengths in the visible light range; sounds in our audible range) because the 'hypotheses' that such signals were important were successful in the natural selection of our ancestors. Looking at individual development, a human baby has biases about which kinds of stimuli to attend to and readily develops hypotheses about human faces, about depth and about causal relationships. Jean Piaget's theory of cognitive development views the developing child as trying out hypotheses in the world. This is very explicit in his 'formal operational thinking' stage of adolescence, which is itself very similar to a Popperian view of scientific method in its testing of hypotheses. The individual scientist can be viewed as someone who carries out formal operational thinking systematically and consistently in his or her scientific domain.

Thus, Popper is saying that observation is 'theory laden'; that is, there are always hypotheses implicit or explicit in observation (even, ultimately, back to innate perceptual hypotheses in the newborn infant). However, this implies a different status to 'facts' than Pearson and the traditional thinkers had in mind. Facts or observations are open to reinterpretation in the light of a different theory. Also, a theory may fit the observations now, but future observations may disprove it – the deductions from a theory, even if satisfied now, may not always be satisfied. This leads to two related points:

1 A theory can never be verified in the sense of proved correct, but it can be falsified.
2 All knowledge is provisional, there is no absolute truth, but we can prefer one theory over another.

In forming these views, it is very likely that Popper was influenced by developments in physics at the beginning of the twentith century. For a long time, Newtonian physics held sway and seemed to provide a perfect explanation of force and motion and, via the inverse square law of gravitational attraction, of the motion of the planets and comets in the solar system. The predictions of this theory seemed very well confirmed. Yet there were a few anomalies, for example, the detailed orbit of Mercury, the innermost planet, was not exactly as predicted. Other difficulties were discussed. Physics entered a period of ferment at the turn of the twentieth century, which was resolved when Einstein's theories of special and general relativity (as well as the theories of quantum mechanics developed by Schrodinger, Heisenberg, and others) provided a totally new and different basis for understanding physical reality. In particular, Einstein's theories replaced Newton's as a basis for predicting planetary motion and did so better, for example, correctly predicting the orbit of Mercury.

If a theory as apparently well established as Newton's could be overthrown, what theory was safe? This was a dramatic example of how many prior confirmations do not safeguard a theory against future refutation. Effectively, Einstein had falsified Newton's theory. This did not mean that Einstein had achieved absolute truth – perhaps his theories will be overthrown in the future – but he had provided a better explanation than Newton.

This illustrates the final crucial point about Popper's view – that theories cannot be proved, but can be falsified, and that falsifiability is the criterion separating science from non-science. Using this criterion, Popper addressed directly the first of our questions at the start of the chapter, providing a 'demarcation criterion' which he claims can be used to separate (or demarcate) the sciences from the non-sciences. One can falsify Newton's theory, but one cannot falsify a painting. Paintings can be beautiful and valuable, but they are not science.

Popper placed much (scientific) value on falsifiability. He argued that highly falsifiable theories should be preferred to less falsifiable ones – provided, of course, that they had not actually been falsified. Also, scientists should try to falsify their theories, rather than confirm them: 'the wrong view of science betrays itself in the craving to be right'. Planned experiments have a crucial role in attempts at falsification, potentially deciding whether one theory or perhaps another can be disproved. Using his falsifiability criterion, he also attacked two prominent theories in the social sciences – psychoanalysis and Marxism.

Popper and psychoanalysis

Popper regarded psychoanalysis as non-science by the falsifiability criterion. (In fact, he regarded psychology generally as 'riddled with fashions, and with uncontrolled dogmas'.) He argued that psychoanalytic ideas could be used to explain any example of human behaviour; thus, they could not be falsified; therefore, psychoanalysis was not science. Grünbaum (1979) argued that, in fact, Freud's theories could make predictions which were in principle falsifiable; for example, that early severe toilet training would lead to an anal personality; and that some of these predictions were confirmed (not falsified) by cross-cultural studies.

However, Popper (1986) reiterated that 'every conceivable case [of human behaviour] could be interpreted in the light of Freud's theory'. He gave as example an argument attributed to Grünbaum, that a Freudian prediction is that 'if people do not repress traumatic experiences, then they will not become victims of neurosis'. Popper argues that this is untestable since who decides what is traumatic, and what is repressed: 'Who has never been hurt, never suffered a trauma? And who has not tried to get over it by forgetting about it – which means 'trying to repress it'? But if so ... all [such] so-called predictions are untestable.'

Popper and Marxism

Popper attacked Marxism, or Marx's theories, not for being unfalsifiable but because Marxists ignored the falsifications which had happened. In *The Open Society and its Enemies* (1945),

Popper argued that Marxism predicted that only fully developed capitalist economies would become Communist (falsified: the principal Communist countries such as Russia and China were pre-industrial); Communist revolutions would be based on the industrial proletariat (falsified: Mao Zedong's revolution in China relied on the peasantry); capitalism should, through its own contradictions, lead to increased inequality, crisis and revolution (falsified: many capitalist countries have achieved less inequality through social democratic governments). Marxists ignore these falsifications and find 'excuses' to preserve the theory. Thus, according to Popper, Marxists abandon pretensions to be scientific. Popper more fundamentally criticized 'historicism' in the sense of any preordained prediction of history, given what he saw as our ability and responsibility to control our own destiny.

Popper's views have become very influential, not only in the physical sciences but in some areas of the social sciences. His views are a radical alternative to the traditional view and the emphasis on requiring prior hypotheses and then attempting to falsify them may seem a refreshing antidote to a lot of psuedo-science. However, it is worth noting that some traditions in science and in social science are not too compatible with this. In science, consider the work of Konrad Lorenz and Niko Tinbergen, Nobel prize winners in ethology (the study of animal behaviour). Ethologists emphasized the importance of getting rid of preconceptions when studying a species of animal. In order to enter the animals own experienced environment, or *umwelt*, one should try to discard (so far as possible) one's anthropomorphic expectations. Ethologists would acknowledge that prior hypotheses bias our perceptions, as Popper does, but unlike Popper they would see this as a hindrance rather than an advantage. They would argue that theories should emerge later, from immersion in the data.

This view shows correspondences to that of grounded theory in the social sciences. This is one way of treating qualitative data obtained from people through observation and/or interview. Again, a considered aim of this approach is that concepts, and subsequently theories, should emerge from an (as far as possible) unbiased immersion in what the environment or setting throws up in the way of data. Hypothesis testing is not rejected, but the intention is to go some way to the induction-deduction-testing cycle rather than the straightforward deduction-testing cycle which Popper espouses.

Alternative Views of Kuhn

Popper's views have also been criticized more directly within the philosophy of science literature. A major protagonist to Popper has been Thomas Kuhn (1922–98), especially in his key work *The Structure of Scientific Revolutions* (1970). Kuhn agreed with Popper (and most other recent philosophers of science) in seeing observation as 'theory laden', and science as a problem-solving activity which cannot arrive at an absolutely verifiable truth. However, he disagreed about the role of falsifiability and about the criteria demarcating science and non-science. The main thrust of his view of science is summarized in Figure 1.2.

In his work, Kuhn paid much more attention than Popper to the history of science and the way in which scientists have actually worked. For example, he drew particularly on the development of modem chemistry from the earlier work of alchemists, as well as the development of physics. Kuhn characterized a mature branch of science as having an accepted 'paradigm' (a basic set of assumptions, or ways of problem solving). In a very early stage, a discipline might be pre-paradigmatic, characterized by many schools which quarrel about fundamental issues, and by rather random fact gathering. With maturity, one paradigm is accepted and directs observation and experiment.

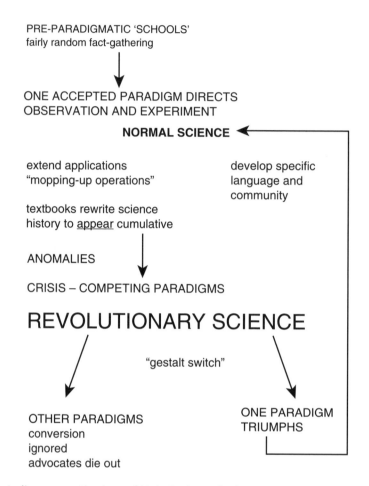

PRE-PARADIGMATIC 'SCHOOLS'
fairly random fact-gathering

ONE ACCEPTED PARADIGM DIRECTS
OBSERVATION AND EXPERIMENT

NORMAL SCIENCE

extend applications
"mopping-up operations"

develop specific
language and
community

textbooks rewrite science
history to <u>appear</u> cumulative

ANOMALIES

CRISIS – COMPETING PARADIGMS

REVOLUTIONARY SCIENCE

"gestalt switch"

OTHER PARADIGMS
conversion
ignored
advocates die out

ONE PARADIGM
TRIUMPHS

FIGURE 1.2   A diagrammatic view of Kuhn's view of science

As an example of this shift, Kuhn pointed to the alchemists as being pre-paradigmatic. With the vague aim of seeking life-enhancing elixirs, or turning base metals to gold, they mixed anything to see what happened. Chemistry only became a science when Dalton proposed his atomic theory, and the concepts of particular elements made up of atoms of different atomic numbers and weights (which could not be transmuted). This provided a basic set of assumptions which could guide future work – the identification of missing elements, the examination of how particular elements combined, etc.

Kuhn here has advanced a demarcation criterion between science and non-science (question 2, at the start of the chapter), but one different from Popper's: a field is a science if it has a paradigm. Science is distinguished from non-science by being a problem-solving activity with an accepted paradigm.

This period of chemistry (or any other area where a paradigm becomes accepted, for example, Newtonian theories in physics, plate tectonics in geology) would be an example of what Kuhn calls 'normal science' (see Figure 1.2). This is a period of 'mopping-up operations' in which paradigm applications are extended. 'Mopping-up operations are what engage most scientists throughout their careers' (Kuhn, 1970: 22). Methodologies are developed and characteristic jargon appears which is accessible to those in the paradigm but not to others (in chemistry such terminology would be 'element', 'atom', atomic weight', 'atomic number', etc.).

Interestingly, Kuhn also looked at how normal science is transmitted to the wider community and taught to the next generation. He argued that textbooks characteristically reinterpret past history as leading to the current paradigm. For example, chemistry textbooks may portray the work of alchemists as leading to modern chemistry. Physics textbooks may portray Newtonian physics as leading on to Einstein's theories. In fact, Kuhn argued, these transition points are much more chaotic and unfocused than such simplified accounts would suggest.

Normal science continues, despite the existence of anomalies or falsifying instances. Kuhn argued that scientists are quite content to ignore difficulties while developing a new paradigm (for example, early chemists had to ignore the problem that certain elements had varying atomic weights which were not whole numbers – an anomaly only solved by recognizing the existence of isotopes, elements of the same atomic number but different atomic weight, itself only fully explicable by nuclear theory, much later). The paradigm is doing well generally, so why reject it because it temporarily fails in some areas?

The paradigm is not rejected unless, apart from anomalies accumulating, a potentially superior paradigm appears. 'To be accepted as a paradigm, a theory must seem better than its competitors, but it need not, and in fact never does, explain all the facts with which it can be confronted' (Kuhn, 1970: 17–18). This view is different from Popper's; rather than trying to falsify their theory, Kuhn suggested not only that scientists avoid falsifying their theories, but that this is a necessary part of normal science.

As can be seen, the role of falsifiability is limited in Kuhn's approach. All paradigms always have anomalies. But Kuhn obviously had to recognize that theories are sometimes falsified, or disproved; like Popper, he was very aware of Einstein's overthrowing of Newton's ideas. However, Kuhn described such events as a period of 'revolutionary science' (see Figure 1.2). Such a period comes about when an accepted paradigm, despite a period of development, has not dealt with anomalies, and indeed anomalies have begun to accumulate to an embarassing extent. At this point, competing paradigms may appear. There will be a period of some confusion or chaos, as the previous paradigm loses adherents, but no one new paradigm predominates. Eventually, one paradigm triumphs, in part through resolving some anomalies, but also perhaps through making some new successful predictions or appearing more precise or elegant. This new, triumphant paradigm then becomes 'normal science' in its turn (Figure 1.2). Adherents of the older, or alternative, paradigms are converted, ignored, or eventually die out.

Kuhn argued that each paradigm embodies such different assumptions that a 'gestalt switch' in perception is needed to move from one to the other. Just as in Figure 1.1 the switch from 'old woman' to 'young woman' requires a sudden, complete reinterpretation of the same stimulus information, so (Kuhn argued) a paradigm shift (for example, from Newtonian to Einsteinian theory) requires a complete reconceptualization, in new language, of information previously interpreted in the old paradigm. Kuhn also stated that competing paradigms are 'not only incompatible but often actually incommensurable' (1970: 103), that is, only partially comparable in logical terms. Proponents of different paradigms characteristically 'argue past each other', employing such different language and different basic assumptions that meaningful dialogue is difficult if not impossible.

Kuhn's work has inspired many thinkers in the social sciences who have taken up the idea of 'paradigm' enthusiastically, claiming that their area represents a new paradigm for their discipline (see Lambie, 1991; Peterson, 1981). However, Kuhn saw 'controversies over fundamentals' as 'endemic among, say, psychologists and sociologists' (1970: viii). He seems to have viewed the social sciences as at an early, pre-paradigmatic stage in science, though this was not discussed in depth in his writings.

In fact, the nature of a 'paradigm' has been one of the two major criticisms made of Kuhn's work (e.g. Lakatos, 1970). Kuhn defined paradigms as 'universally recognised scientific achievements that for a time provide model problems and solutions to a community of practitioners' (1970: viii). Besides the circularity of including 'scientific' in this definition of science, it has been pointed out that Kuhn provides many other explanations of 'paradigm' in his 1962 book, which vary appreciably (some 111 different definitions, according to Masterman, in Lakatos and Musgrave, 1970). Is it a grand theory, a localized hypothesis, a new tool or technique? Kuhn recognized the force of this criticism and in the Postscript to the second edition of his book (1970) distinguished between a more global meaning as 'disciplinary matrix', or network of shared conceptual assumptions; and a more localized meaning as 'exemplar' or useful problem-solving methodology.

The other main criticism of Kuhn's work related to the nature of paradigm change. Was Kuhn saying that such change was rational, or was it more due to fashion and social pressure? For Popper (as for more traditional philosophers of science), scientific change was seen as progress. New theories were more powerful than old ones, encompassing more known observations and successfully predicting new findings. For Kuhn, it was not so clear cut. Certainly, a paradigm gets into trouble when anomalies accumulate. But Kuhn stated that all paradigms have anomalies and falsification is in reality not used as a primary criterion for paradigm rejection. He states (1970: 8) that 'competition between segments of the scientific community is the only historical process that ever actually results in the rejection of one previously accepted theory or in the adoption of another'. This, together with the incommensurable nature of different paradigms, leaves open the door to suggestions that a paradigm shift occurs because one group of scientists is just more powerful or has more social influence than another.

Clearly science is influenced by social pressures. The history of Lysenkoism in the former Soviet Union (in which Lysenko, through his influence, promulgated what are widely held to be false ideas of effects of plant breeding) is one example. This and other examples could be dismissed as aberrations in science. Kuhn's work, however, has opened up a debate as to whether even normal science and the competition between paradigms is strongly influenced by such social forces. This debate has obvious relevance to the social sciences. So far as the philosophy of science is concerned, this debate has led to a defence of rationality in science (e.g. Lakatos, Bunge) and to further attacks (e.g. Feyerabend, Collins, and recent sociologists of science).

Views of Lakatos and Others

A compromise between the positions of Popper and Kuhn was advanced by Imre Lakatos (1922–74). Lakatos agreed with Kuhn that Popper was wrong in emphasizing falsification as the demarcation criterion between science and non-science; but he wished to reject the relativism that Kuhn was near to espousing. Lakatos sought for ways to keep Popper's ideas of scientific progress, while retaining Kuhn's insights into how science actually changes (Lakatos, 1970).

Lakatos distinguished three kinds of falsificationism in science:

1   *Dogmatic falsificationism*: this would be the repeated overthrow of theories by 'facts'; a single disconfirmation would lead to a theory being discarded. (This would clearly be pointless as a disconfirmation might later be shown to be due to some mistake, such as measurement error or faulty procedure. Popper in fact recognized this and was not as guilty of it as some of his critics imply.)

2   *Naive methodological falsificationism*: to safeguard premature rejection of theories, Popper says that 'criteria of refutation have to be laid down beforehand'. But Lakatos (like Kuhn) does not believe that science actually progresses this way.

3   *Sophisticated methodological falsificationism*: according to Lakatos 'there is no falsification before the emergence of a better theory'. A theory T is falsified only if a new theory T' explains all the unrefuted content of T and makes further predictions, some of which are corroborated.

Lakatos's key concept was that of a a 'scientific research programme' (see Figure 1.3). A research programme encompasses a set of theories and methods which can change over time. However, there is a 'hard core' of very basic theoretical assumptions which do not change (for example, in chemistry, this could be atomic theory). This hard core would not be questioned by adherents of the research programme; indeed, they would defend them vigorously ('negative heuristics'). However, the hard core would have generated a range of 'auxiliary hypotheses'. These are much more open to question. They are the frontiers of the research programme, ideas

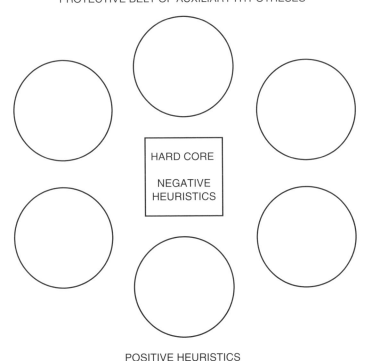

SCIENTIFIC RESEARCH PROGRAMME

PROTECTIVE BELT OF AUXILIARY HYPOTHESES

HARD CORE

NEGATIVE HEURISTICS

POSITIVE HEURISTICS

FIGURE 1.3   A schematic view of Lakatos's concept of a scientific research programme

which are being tried out and tested for their range and explanatory power. If they prove successful, well and good. If they do not, they will be jettisoned, or changed to accommodate anomalies or falsifications, without threatening the 'hard core'. These 'positive heuristics' of active testing and questioning complement the 'negative heuristics' used to protect the hard core assumptions.

Lakatos then saw mature science as a history of competing research programmes. His is a sophisticated conception of science which seems to advance beyond what Lakatos saw as the naive methodological falsificationism of Popper, retaining the insights of Kuhn into historical processes of competing programmes (similar to Kuhn's 'global' paradigms). Kuhn had empha-sized the revolutionary nature of scientific change – to the extent that his approach was carica-tured as seeing science as 'a series of widely spaced upheavals separated by lengthy dogmatic intervals' (Watkins, in Lakatos and Musgrave, 1970). Lakatos showed the extent to which each research programme also embodied positive heuristics of testing and debate.

Unlike Kuhn, Lakatos rescued the idea of rational progress, at least in part, by describing research programmes as 'progressive', or 'degenerating'. Rational criteria are available to decide whether a particular research programme is 'progressive' or 'degenerating'. A 'progressive' programme anticipates novel facts and produces novel theories, which have 'heuristic power'; changes in the auxiliary hypotheses are productive. A 'degenerating' programme, by contrast, patches up anomalies in ad hoc ways which do not generalize to other situations; changes in the auxiliary hypotheses are unproductive. Nevertheless, Lakatos concedes that there is necessarily some subjectivity in these judgments and also that, over time, what had seemed a degenerating programme may become progressive again (or vice versa).

These ideas have been applied to the social sciences (Friman et al., 1993; Rowell, 1983). For example, Gholsen and Barker (1985) described traditional learning theory in psychology as a degenerating research programme. One could mount a similar argument for psychoanalysis or Marxism.

Similar ideas have been proposed by Larry Laudan (b. 1941), who argues that even the 'hard core' of a research programme can be modified over time. He also postulates a close and recip-rocal influence between the philosophy of science and the history of science (Laudan, 1977).

By contrast, Paul Feyerabend (b. 1924) emphasizes the non-rational aspect of Kuhn's ideas of paradigm conflict. In this relativist position there are no logical grounds for preferring one theory over another one (Feyerabend, 1975). Kuhn's relativist views are developed further in recent trends in the sociology and history of scientific knowledge (e.g. Collins, 1985). This holds that 'the results of scientific experiments are more ambiguous than they are usually taken to be, while theory is more flexible than most people imagine. This means that science can progress only within communities that can reach consensus about what counts as plausible. Plausibility is a matter of social context so science is "a social construct"' and that 'in a sociological or his-torical investigation, act as though the world does not constrain what scientists believe about it' (Collins, 1994).

The view that science is (just) a social construct is of course vigorously debated; for a critique of these views, see Bunge (1991, 1992). As Richard Dawkins put it:

> When you take a 747 to an international convention of sociologists or literary critics, the reason you will arrive in one piece is that a lot of western-trained scientists and engineers got their sums right. If it gives you satisfaction to say that the theory of aerodynamics is a social construct that is your privilege, but why do you then entrust travel plans to a Boeing rather than a magic carpet? As I have put it before, show me a cultural relativist at 30,000 feet and I will show you a hypocrite. (Dawkins, 1994: 17–18)

16 The Emergence of the Social Sciences

MARK J. SMITH

1 Introduction

As you saw in Chapters 1 and 2, the creation of objective knowledge has been a central goal of science for quite a while. This chapter explores attempts by social scientists to create 'objective knowledge' about the social world. A special emphasis is placed upon the way in which our assumptions about the construction of knowledge have implications for the collection and interpretation of empirical evidence. There are seven sections in this chapter. The first two examine the ideas associated with positivism, particularly the six general assumptions which underpin this approach. We see how positivism played an important role in generating claims about objective knowledge in the social sciences. Most significantly, the positivist approach draws a great deal from the Enlightenment thinkers outlined in Chapter 2, especially in the way in which they placed a stress upon the search for certainty and universal explanations. Section 3 focuses upon how the construction of objective knowledge or 'hard science' has been, and can be, misleading. Two case studies, on scientific racism and positivist criminology, are used to demonstrate how the values and prejudices of social scientists can masquerade as social facts in scientific accounts of social differences and in the relationship between normal and abnormal behaviour.

In sections 4 and 5 we see how important it is to distinguish positivism from the broader approach of empiricism, by focusing upon the differences between the positivist approaches in the twentieth century and the falsificationist method developed by Karl Popper. Section 6 explores one social science discipline, economics, in order to demonstrate how the empiricist approaches identified in this chapter appear within a particular field of human knowledge. Economics is a good example; first, because of its associations with objective accounts of social relations and, second, because of the clearly identifiable positions which exist within economic methodology. Finally, in section 7 we return briefly to the six general assumptions of positivism to highlight the differences between empiricism and positivism.

Positivism develops ideas established during the Enlightenment, but ...

In Chapter 2 we looked at the origins of scientific thinking and the ways in which these ideas were applied to the study of social phenomena during the Enlightenment. In this chapter we consider the legacy of the Enlightenment in explaining and understanding social life. The most significant feature of social science in the last two centuries has been the rise to dominance and the subsequent fall of the positivist tradition. Positivism has been increasingly questioned since the middle of the twentieth century. Even if positivism is something that many social researchers would like to forget, it is hard to imagine any social scientific approach which does not, even now, draw from or develop its ideas in opposition to the positivist approach. The label of positivism has been applied to a wide variety of approaches in the social sciences, all of which claimed to offer a 'scientific' or **objective** picture of the social world and its constituent parts. As a result, the term 'positivism' has become very ambiguous and often contains different assumptions for different people. To make matters worse, 'positivism' is often used as a synonymous term for 'empiricism', but it is important to recognize that empiricism is a broad church and that it is possible to be empiricist without being positivist.

... take care, positivism means different things to different social scientists.

	Definition	Implication
Naturalism	Positivists are committed to naturalism, the idea that it is possible to transfer the assumptions and methods of natural sciences to the study of social objects, often referred to as the 'unification of method'.	This means that you would study behaviour, institutions and society in much the same way as studying, for example, chemical processes, hydraulic systems, geological structures. The closed system of a scientific experiment is often taken as a model for knowledge production in the social sciences.
Phenomenalism	Phenomenalism is the assumption that only knowledge gained through observed experience can be taken seriously. If something cannot be directly experienced it is said to be **metaphysical** – beyond our physical senses.	If we cannot touch it, see it, hear it, taste it or smell it, then an object cannot be said to exist except in so far as it is an idea of something. For example, 'happiness' is something which exists only in people's minds and cannot be directly physically experienced.
Nominalism	Nominalism shares with phenomenalism the argument that concepts must be based upon experience, but it also asserts that concepts have no use other than as names. Words are seen as pure reflections of things. It is, of course, very difficult to do this because the words we use are usually far more than simple descriptions.	All concepts or ideas which are not directly experienced through the senses are meaningless. In a strict sense, concepts such as the 'unconscious' and 'capitalism' are all names for things which we can't directly experience through our senses. Therefore, by this criteria, such concepts are meaningless.
Atomism	Atomism is a particular approach to the definition of objects. Atomism states that the objects of scientific study are discrete, that is, the objects cannot be broken down into any smaller parts. These objects act as the foundations of a scientific study. Collective objects are thus the sum total of their smaller atomic components.	When approaching any field of study, atomists look for the smallest observable units which cannot be broken down any further. When studying a society the most discrete unit is often taken as the individual. Atomistic explanations of society would start with the individual and regard society as no more than a collection of individuals.
Scientific Laws	The purpose of science is to develop laws. To develop a scientific law you start from the observation of a particular set of objects and look for regularities. The regular appearance of two or more things together, or in some kind of sequence, can be called an **empirical regularity.** This is sometimes described as a constant conjunction of events. You then explore whether the same regularities occur in other similar circumstances. A scientific law is a general statement which describes and explains empirical regularities which occur in different places and at different times.	The search for scientific laws involves finding empirical regularities, such as the well known example of smoking tobacco and developing lung cancer. Social scientists adopting this assumption would look for empirical regularities between, say, • poverty and crime, • the money supply and price inflation, • school class sizes and literacy levels, • gender and earnings, and so on. In practice, one is usually taken as the cause of the other. For instance, high levels of poverty are seen as a causal factor in crime levels.
Facts/Values	Facts and values are seen as distinct. Only facts can be regarded as scientific. Facts can be empirically verified, that is, observed, measured and explained by reference to observational evidence. Values involve subjective assessments and claims about what ought to be. Thus values cannot be observed, measured or explained.	Social scientists accepting these assumptions would distinguish scientific statements, which describe what is the case, from unscientific value-laden statements. For example, a measure of the number of homeless is often viewed as a fact whereas the statement that homelessness is a social evil is a value statement.

assumptions
of
positivism

naturalism
phenomenalism
nominalism
atomism
scientific laws
facts/values

When this box appears, the shaded portions will indicate which assumptions are at work.

Figure 3.1   The six general assumptions of positivism.
The terms in bold are also defined in the glossary.

As a result, the potential for conceptual confusion is very large, so this chapter offers a guide to the issues raised by the positivist and empiricist approaches within the social sciences.

1.1 Defining positivism

In Chapter 2 you discovered that the idea of science is closely associated with authoritative knowledge. Positivism is, perhaps, the most important attempt to generate authoritative knowledge about the social world. Actually, it is possible to define 'positivism' in many different ways. Nevertheless, it can be argued that there are three generations of positivists within the social sciences, as the social theorist William Outhwaite has usefully suggested:

See sections 2 and 3.

- the positivist traditions established in the nineteenth century (Auguste Comte, Herbert Spencer and some interpretations of Émile Durkheim);

See section 4.

- the logical positivism of the Vienna Circle (A.J. Ayer and Rudolf Carnap) in the early twentieth century;

- the 'standard positivist account', developed in the post-war period in the West, (associated with Carl Hempel) which emphasized the importance of value freedom, hard facts and prediction as a basis for offering policy proposals for governments, businesses and other private institutions.

(adapted from Outhwaite, 1987, pp.5–8)

Although there are three generations of positivist thinkers, it is important to establish what they hold in common. Norman Blaikie in *Approaches to Social Enquiry* (1993) suggests that certain shared assumptions can be identified without overlooking the significant differences between them. These six general assumptions, presented in Figure 3.1, are not solely associated with positivism but only positivism puts them together in this unique way. In particular, positivist science has a preference for empirical data which can be observed and measured so that the various component parts can be compared for their relative frequency. On the basis of such quantitative evidence, it is possible to generate law-like regularities which may then be generalized to other situations. Each of the six assumptions is explored in the sections that follow by reference to different forms of positivism.

Summary

Positivist approaches to the social sciences claim the label scientific, for they assume things can be studied as hard facts and the relationships between these facts established as scientific laws. For positivists, such laws have the status of truth and social objects can be studied in much the same way as natural objects.

2 Positivism and the foundations of the social sciences

As you will be aware from Chapter 2, the Enlightenment introduced new ways of thinking about the natural and social worlds, and that, after the Enlightenment, the world could no longer be explained as a manifestation of some divine plan in which the Church provided an authoritative account of both the natural and the social worlds in the name of God. Human beings were seen increasingly as the originators of knowledge. This means that instead of simply describing and clarifying what God had created, knowledge was seen as human-made and constantly open to question. Critical inquiry came to be seen as essential to human progress. The social transformations of the seventeenth and eighteenth centuries also produced a whole series of new objects of analysis, including 'society', the 'economy', the 'mind', the 'modern state', the 'individual' and the 'realm of ideas', and these objects have become the focus of analysis for the social sciences.

Post-Enlightenment knowledge is increasingly seen as human-made, rather than divine in origin.

The commitment to science as a means of promoting human progress is evident in the writings of Antoine Destutt de Tracy, a French rationalist philosopher working in the midst of the French Revolution. De Tracy proposed the foundation of the discipline of 'ideology' as the 'scientific study of ideas' as early as 1797. In this way, it was argued, science could reveal how society worked and, with this in mind, a rational social order could be sketched out, planned and implemented. Science, defined as the pursuit of truth, offered a means of social engineering so that social evils, such as conflict and war, could be eliminated and human progress achieved. Thus the choice of progress or catastrophe was seen as resting in human hands. In the context of the maelstrom of changes accompanying the emergence of the modern world, it was not altogether surprising that the certainties of religious faith were replaced by the belief in the certainties of science.

Rational scientific knowledge of human societies raises the possibility of improving the human condition.

This section highlights three approaches from the nineteenth century (Outhwaite's first generation of positivists) which have had an impact on contemporary social science. The positivism of Auguste Comte, the evolutionary utilitarianism of Herbert Spencer and the study of the social facts advocated by Émile Durkheim, each in their different ways, linked science to progress. You should bear in mind that each of these earlier positivist approaches illustrates some, but not all, of the six general assumptions of positivism identified in Figure 3.1.

naturalism

phenomenalism

nominalism

atomism

scientific laws

facts/values

4.3 The standard positivist approach

In response to these problems some positivist philosophers, such as Carl Hempel (1905–1997), place a greater stress on the deductive process to explain the steps involved in theory construction. Hempel's work modifies the arguments of the logical positivists to take account of the way in which scientists usually start with a set of general laws and theories before directly engaging in empirical research. His emphasis upon deduction came to be regarded as the model for the post-war standard positivist account of the scientific method. **Deduction** refers to the mental process through which valid conclusions can be logically deduced from valid premises, that is, a generalization or universal law. Deduction is used to establish a series of logical steps in the process of forming a theoretical statement about the world. Usually, a general claim is made and this is applied to a particular case or instance with a definite set of conditions. Finally, a conclusion is posed and the scientist engages in research to establish whether the predicted outcome is indeed the case. The truth value of the premise acts as a guarantor of the truth value of the conclusions, for the conclusions do not go beyond what is already contained within the premises. Let's look at two examples of deductive reasoning to illustrate the relationship between premises and conclusions.

Example A	Example B
1 Heavy people leave deep footprints.	1 All children are cruel.
2 This person makes deep footprints.	2 This person is a child.
3 This person is heavy.	3 This person is cruel.

The starting-point in deductive reasoning is theoretical (although the theory may have been established through induction at some point) and then observation serves as a basis for testing statements (regardless of how the statements are derived). In this general sense, deductive reasoning is compatible with all kinds of approaches to **knowledge construction** and does not of itself stand or fall as a logical technique, even if the initial premises are false, as Example B demonstrates, for not all children are cruel. In this case, logical consistency (alongside predictive success) is an important feature of a scientific explanation. It is important to recognize, as did Hempel, that the strict limits placed upon the scientific method developed by the Vienna Circle were too restrictive for science to be an innovative process.

The logical positivists had argued that a statement is either cognitively significant (in describing the world as it is) or it is simply meaningless. However, Hempel recognized that the empirical content of a theoretical statement could only be considered to be meaningful when the theory is placed within its 'interpretive system'. As with the logical positivist approach, Hempel is concerned to identify the empirical regularities which are significant in definite situations. Empirical regularities are not only seen as necessary for establishing a causal law, they are sufficient; that is, all you need for a law statement is 'if A then B'.

So, within the standard positivist approach, scientific explanations involve a particular way of developing a logical argument. We can see this when we look at how deduction was viewed as a process through which valid conclusions are deduced from valid premises in order to ensure logical consistency, as in Examples A and B above. In this model of scientific inquiry, one proceeds from general law statements (within specific conditions) to explain and predict particular cases. The combination of the laws and specified conditions (the premises) are often defined as the explanans statement and the conclusion is described as the explanandum statement (Hempel, 1965; but for a quick introduction see: Keat and Urry, 1982, pp.12–13; Hacking, 1983, pp.2–6). With this approach, providing that it is possible to identify the operating laws at work and the conditions within which these laws operate, then it should be feasible to predict the outcome accurately. The emphasis on the role of prediction implies that there should be complete symmetry between predicting something and explaining it. Successful prediction in this model is the same as providing a satisfactory explanation. So, in practice, if a scientific theory appears to predict an outcome accurately, then it must be true.

Standard positivists put a special emphasis on the symmetrical relationship between explanation and prediction.

An example of this way of thinking can be seen in the study of human behaviour, developed by the psychologists B.F. Skinner and J.B. Watson, in the development of the concept of 'operant conditioning'. This approach, which became known as **behaviourism**, focuses upon the ways in which individuals respond to various stimuli and/or conditions in ways that maximize rewards and minimize punishments. One of the theoretical premises of this approach is the assumption that human beings are passive recipients of external pushes or pulls and that they modify their behaviour accordingly. The behaviourist approach also rests upon the assumption that it is misleading to speculate about the inner states or human creativity in explaining social life. In this way, it is plausible to construct a scientific statement, starting from a series of principles or laws (for example, operant conditioning) which are accepted as the motivation for certain forms of human behaviour, and examine an activity which demonstrates these laws in specific conditions, such as obedience or disobedience in schools. By establishing the conditions in which obedience is reinforced and/or disobedience deterred, it is possible to explain the level of order or disorder in certain schools. The success of this explanation would be measured in terms of its ability to produce the predicted results in the conditions of an experiment (to remove the possible influence of other variables in the empirical evidence); that is, a **closed system**. Of course, this whole approach rests upon the implicit assumption that the organization of school life can only be studied through the observation of the actual behaviour of the individuals involved – teachers, head, pupils, governors and so on.

Behaviourism is covered in more detail in Chapter 5.

4.4 Practical implications of standard positivism

Standard positivism was committed to value freedom, that scientific explanations could be constructed without reference to the value positions of scientists. This was partly possible because of the emergence of a dominant set of assumptions within post-war Western societies. These assumptions reflected growing agreement about what sort of society should exist, and hence also about the purpose and focus of social science. The liberal social theorist Raymond Aron expressed this well when he suggested that 'in both East and West, debate was suppressed', while others were led to proclaim the 'end of ideology' and the emergence of 'consensus politics'. In this period of consensus in the 1950s, social scientists worked within a relatively solid framework with well established social goals. The main effect upon social science was the growth of empirical research with a relatively low level of theoretical sophistication and a fairly clear set of policy applications. This meant that values appeared to be less important, because there were relatively few fundamental disputes among social scientists until the later 1960s. Debate and disagreement focused upon how problems were resolved, rather than questioning which problems existed in society. Broadly speaking, social science was geared towards the primary goals of the post-war welfare state and the managed economy.

Standard positivism served as a useful framework for policy-oriented research where there was broad agreement on the character and form of social problems in the post-war consensus.

This suited the needs of post-war governments and large corporations, who were concerned with identifying problems, finding solutions and anticipating the practical difficulties or unintended consequences of various courses of action. Empirical research following the guidelines established by Hempel and the positivist assumptions of this scientific method went largely unquestioned. A great deal of research that you might encounter on social problems in sociology, human geography, economics and psychology can seen as policy oriented in this way. For instance, social research conducted by both psychologists and sociologists on the educational performance of different groups in society (largely in terms of class and, later, in terms of gender and ethnicity) assumed that low attaining groups suffered from 'cultural deprivation'. The main differences among researchers lay in their recommendations for resolving the problem, rather than questioning whose culture is referred to in the concept of 'cultural deprivation'. Broadly speaking, this research did not consider whether it was the form of knowledge which was responsible for low levels of educational attainment by working-class children. Instead, 'educational failure' was attributed to some flaw or defect in the child, the family structure and patterns of child-rearing, the characteristics of the neighbourhood and culture, and so on. In this way, the relationship between normality and pathology which characterized earlier forms of positivism resurfaced in the use of categories such as 'educational subnormality'.

Social researchers simply assumed that the criteria for success or failure in education should be the extent to which the working-class pupils displayed conventional signs of attainment within an educational system which favoured the standards and forms of knowledge associated with the already successful middle classes. They did not question whether these standards themselves were part of the problem. The 'causes' of educational success or failure were identified as parental interest, poverty in cultural and material terms, the ways in which teachers labelled pupils and/or the presence or absence of a positive school ethos. Few of these social scientists made their positivist credentials explicit, because they did not feel the need to proclaim what was obvious to them as good practice. In examining the existing sources of any field of human knowledge, it is important for you to inquire about what kind of questions are being asked as much as the nature of the evidence which social researchers produce. In the next section we examine an approach which challenged this uncritical use of a model of scientific inquiry, and which cast doubt upon the aspirations of science to attain the 'truth'.

Summary

Positivists in the twentieth century attempted to use careful analysis of language to distinguish between scientific knowledge and speculative metaphysics. The aim was to produce a body of knowledge composed of observation statements and tautologies, with theory playing no creative role except as a reflection of empirical evidence.

The logical positivist approach placed a greater emphasis upon induction and verification, while exponents of the post-war standard positivist view (such as Hempel) stressed the importance of deduction, although within strict empirical constraints. In all approaches, it was assumed that there was a clear separation of facts from values and that it was possible to 'discover' general laws.

Imagination and Complexity in the Social Sciences

MARK J. SMITH

1 Introduction

In the earlier chapters we focused upon empiricist approaches in social research and considered how they applied natural scientific methods to the study of social objects. All of these accounts were primarily geared towards providing scientific explanations of distinct social objects rather than attempting to understand the meaning of social relationships and processes. As you will recall from Chapter 3, in the empiricist approach, theory and observation are treated as distinct things. Chapter 4 now challenges this assumption by arguing that it is not possible to separate theory and observation in this way and by examining the important role played by the human mind in the organization and interpretation of these observational experiences. While you will find that the approaches to social research covered here disagree about the precise role of imaginative interpretation of experience, they all agree that it is impossible to separate observation from the mental constructs we use to organize and understand our perceptions. Without such constructs in place, it is suggested, we simply cannot make sense of the complex world around us. For the sake of convenience, and to distinguish them clearly from empiricism, from this point onwards these approaches are labelled 'idealism'. There are many definitions of idealism, but in this chapter we are using the label to identify approaches which see knowledge as the use of ideas to organize experience.

Let's explore how different idealist approaches are from those of empiricism. For a start, they suggest that we should pay closer attention to the concepts and constructions which we invent and use as social scientists and recognize that we only come into contact with the 'real world' through these constructions. Moreover, as idealists reject the idea that observation is theory free, the clear separation of facts and values, which characterized empiricist social science, no longer holds so much weight as a key assumption of social science. Idealist approaches attempt to find a way of resolving the relationship between the development of scientific explanations and the role of interpretative understanding and cultural values. It is these very issues and problems that led empiricists to reject the formative role of values in scientific research in the first place. So, while empiricism tried to sidestep the issue, idealism takes this bull by the horns.

You may want to have a glance back at both Figure 3.1 and section 6 in Chapter 3.

We know from Chapter 3 that all empiricists are committed to **phenomenalism**. This assumes that the validity of a statement derives from the way it refers to empirical evidence. In short, empiricists assert that observations are the raw material from which we fashion theory. Positivist and empiricist approaches to the scientific method treat the role of interpretations, constructs, models and the human imagination as secondary factors in, if not irrelevant to, the study of empirical evidence. For instance, in logical positivism theoretical statements about observable evidence are treated as pictures of a definite state of affairs or, if they attempt to do more than this, they are seen as flawed by metaphysical assumptions. For empiricists, interpretative skills are seen, at best, as a necessary evil which must be constantly constrained by reference to empirical evidence. In Popper's case, scientific guesswork and hunches are constrained through repeated attempts at falsification. In the pursuit of **objective knowledge**, whereby facts and values are seen to be distinct, any attempt to bring subjective

assessment into scientific research is regarded as a suspicious and potentially dangerous practice which tends to give rise to bias, distortion and
prejudice.

In this chapter we also examine the problems involved in understanding
the relationship between explanations and predictions. Idealist approaches
enable us to account for **complexity** in social scientific research, as well as
the simpler relationships established within the experimental setting. This
means we will be considering accounts of social life which attempt to generate explanations which do not depend upon a **closed system** of variables
that can be clearly observed and measured. If it is recognized that social life
is too complex to reproduce through experimental, theoretical and statistical closure, then we should consider the role of the imagination of social
scientists in putting together meaningful and plausible accounts of social
relations and processes. In the following sections we look at four ways in
which the role of imaginative thinking within natural and social scientific
research is taken much more seriously.

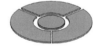

*See Chapter 2,
section 2.2.*

Each section addresses one of the four approaches (see Figure 4.1) which
attempt to integrate the human imagination with scientific research, but
reach different conclusions on how this should be done. In section 2, on
the conceptual organization of experience, we briefly revisit the contribution of the Enlightenment thinker Immanuel Kant. In particular, we
trace the role of interpretation and imagination in the organization of impressions and perceptions in both the natural and social sciences.
Understanding Kant's position will enable you to gain a better sense of the
three approaches in contemporary social science which are considered in
the subsequent sections.

*Idealism questions
the assumption
that only closed
systems offer a
basis for scientific
laws and raises
the possibility of
social science using
open systems –
see Chapter 2,
section 2.2.*

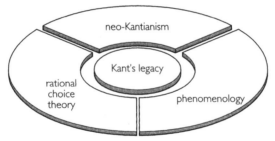

Figure 4.1 Imaginative approaches in the social sciences: the chapter structure.

*As in Chapter 1,
this sign helps you
to keep track of
your progress
through the
approaches.*

In section 3 we explore the neo-Kantian approaches which have had a significant role in defining the problems familiar to the disciplines of the social
sciences today. Here, we look at the use of 'ideal types' as a way of simplifying complex evidence. Ideal types are concepts which exaggerate aspects
of social life in order to demonstrate the mechanisms through which social
existence is produced. For instance, Max Weber developed three ideal types
to characterize the dynamic patterns of behaviour in any interaction
situation – habitual action, emotional action and rational action. None of
these types actually exists in a pure state, but they serve as useful devices
for organizing evidence and building a useful account of empirical reality.
At this point, you will find the first of two sections on geographical models.
Geographical Models 1 demonstrates how the neo-Kantian approach has
been developed in one social scientific discipline.

Section 4 examines rational choice theory, a standpoint which differs, in some respects, from the other approaches considered in this chapter. Rational choice theory regards human beings as purposive rational actors and explores the ways in which the treatment of individuals as purely rational and self-interested can generate insights into human behaviour. This rational calculating individual is often characterized as a 'minimaxing' actor (for making decisions which minimize costs and maximize benefits). In addition, this approach is often portrayed as one which offers the possibility of general laws. You will be expected to consider whether this characterization of human action is an accurate one and to identify some of the problems in making unrealistic assumptions about human actors and the organization of social relations.

See Chapter 3, section 2.2, on Bentham.

See Chapter 1, section 4.1.

Finally, in section 5 we return to some of the themes raised briefly in Chapter 1 by considering the meaningful construction of social life. This section explores approaches developed by phenomenological or interpretive accounts of natural and social science. As you saw in Chapter 1 in Schütz's story of the person on the street, the cartographer and the stranger, this approach attempts to bridge the gap between subjective everyday experiences and objective explanations in social science. At the close of section 5, you will find the second part of the disciplinary case study. Geographical Models 2 explores how these phenomenological approaches can be applied in a particular social science. At any point in this chapter, to help you build a picture of the range of contemporary approaches in social research considered here, you may find it useful to refer to Table 4.1, which

Table 4.1   A quick guide to idealist approaches to knowledge construction.

	Varieties of Idealism			Empiricism
	Neo-Kantian Idealism	**Rational Choice Theory**	**Hermeneutics and Phenomenology**	**Empiricism**
Theory and Observation	The complex empirical world is 'organized' through the use of mental constructs for comparing and contrasting evidence.	Theoretical work involves the reconstruction of rational decisions within definite constraints on the basis of calculations of costs and benefits of various courses of action.	The problem facing social science is the gulf between the everyday experiences of social actors and the detached accounts of social life produced by social scientists.	The scientific method involves a clear separation of theory and observation.
Facts and Values	The social sciences should be relevant to the problems of a particular society in question at a specific time.	Facts can only be identified through the subjective values and the intentional choices of individuals.	Scientific facts are the commonsense assumptions of the social scientists, for values remain unacknowledged in concept formation.	Facts and values are treated as separate to eliminate from scientific knowledge the researchers' subjective biases.
Explanation and Prediction	An empirical regularity between variables is necessary but not sufficient for establishing a causal law. The complexity of causal factors in any empirical situation makes it difficult to make accurate predictions. Rational choice theory applies the same formal model across different situations.		Social settings only exist through the intersubjective relations of the actors involved as the product of meaningful communication.	For empiricists, successful predictions are effective explanations. Empirical regularities have the status of scientific laws.

provides a quick guide to the key assumptions, similarities and differences between idealist approaches, as well as a comparison with empiricism. A more detailed version of this table can be found in the conclusion to this chapter, once you have become more familiar with these approaches and what they mean in practice.

Before we look at these approaches more closely, we should consider what it is they attempt to address. All of these approaches consider the problems of thinking about experience and argue that the human imagination is a powerful tool which enables us to sift and sort the mass of sensory perceptions, impressions and experiences we constantly encounter. This enables us to establish patterns and formulate guidelines for our own choices and actions. In the study of natural objects, the role of the human imagination can be seen in the tendency to read social qualities or human sentiments into natural processes, that is, **anthropomorphism**. For instance, it is common to read what Western societies conventionally regard as feminine qualities into the forces of nature. Weather systems can be described as tempestuous and unpredictable, the product of mysterious forces. Within Western culture, this involves an implicit contrast to scientific attempts to observe, measure, dismantle and tame nature. For feminist interpretations of science, this is another reflection of the androcentric (male-centred) assumptions of the dominant culture of Western societies.

Let's explore the way in which the human imagination can lead us astray by taking a clear-cut example, that of media representations of animal behaviour. You may have noticed in natural history programmes that studies of primates reveal strongly subjective currents by identifying human qualities in the behaviour of various species of apes and monkeys. The popular science of Desmond Morris in *The Naked Ape* (1969) and *The Human Zoo* (1970) provides a good example of the problems of thinking about instinctive drives in human behaviour. Morris uses social qualities (such as 'male promiscuity') to define animal behaviour. Then, when explaining human courtship and sexual behaviour, the human male role is portrayed as a product of natural tendencies demonstrated by primates. For Morris, these natural tendencies always resurface in human behaviour when moral norms do not keep such 'animal passions' under control. In short, Morris has attributed social characteristics to animals, only to read them back into human behaviour as instinctual, in the process implying that male promiscuity is natural.

Even when describing natural things we need to take care – the words we use are always packed full of meaning.

You may have also noticed how such representations ignore the way that concepts such as 'promiscuity' can only be understood within a cultural setting. In this case, 'promiscuity' makes sense where there are moral and legal limitations on the number of sexual partners – something which cannot be identified in animal behaviour. Such imaginings, far from being neutral pictures of the world, are loaded with culturally specific values which involve complex sets of assumptions about permissible and impermissible behaviour. If such problems arise in the exploration of the relationship of society and nature, it should not be surprising that similar issues exist in the study of social objects. The remainder of this chapter provides you with some tools for unpacking the kinds of problem associated with thinking through the relationship between interpretation and observation, as well as continuing to explore the role of cultural values in social scientific practice.

2 The conceptual organization of experience: Kant's legacy

This section considers imaginative thinking in scientific knowledge. In Chapter 2 we saw how Immanuel Kant characterized the Enlightenment as a process containing the ethos of the critical spirit, that we should question all assumptions. To achieve this, he established a compromise position between **rationalism** (reason will lead us to the truth) and **empiricism** (observation and experimentation will lead us to the truth). Kant's approach emerged as a response to the inadequacies of both of these positions, although each approach had strengths as well as weaknesses (see Caygill, 1995). Empiricism, you will remember, had a solid foundation in sensory experience; however, it oversimplifies the relationship between theory and observation, for it treats the mind as a blank slate as if it is empty before receiving physical sensations. Rationalism, on the other hand, emphasized the important role of human reason in developing theories about the empirical world, but it also tended to neglect the role of observational evidence as a way of testing the validity of theoretical statements. Kant's compromise between these two positions sought to emphasize the strengths of each. For Kant, it is only through a 'synthesis' of both rational thinking and observable experiences that we can comprehend the world. In short, without reason we cannot make sense of our experiences and without observation we have nothing on which to employ our capacity for rational thought. It should be stressed that this is a synthesis, not a way of fitting the evidence conveniently within one's own theoretical model. This compromise became the basis of the range of approaches which attempted to place human imagination more clearly at the centre of social scientific inquiry.

Kant found a compromise between reason and observation by claiming that it is impossible to have one without the other – they should be seen as a synthesis.

It is useful to reconsider empiricism in a little more detail to gain a better sense of what Kant had in mind. This will help us to understand how he challenged the distinction between **analytic** and **synthetic** statements which came to be so central for the logical positivists. For the positivists, only analytic statements (that is, those that are true by definition) can be known through reason alone rather than through human experience. Such analytic statements are logically true by virtue of the meanings of the words they contain. Consider the statement 'Roses are flowers'. If we already understand what roses are, then this statement has the same logical status as 'A short man is a man'. It does not tell us anything new, for we already know this to be true by definition. The truth of all other statements rests upon observation, such as 'These roses are yellow and fragrant'. Statements like this are synthetic, for they express in ideas the textures, colours, sounds, odours, tastes and motions of the objects of our experiences. Kant was inspired by the clear thinking and conceptual tools developed by empiricists like David Hume, but he argued that empiricists were not asking the most appropriate questions.

It is often said that before we can recognize the right answers we have to ask the right questions. Empiricism asks us to consider the question, 'What objects do we experience?' – and consequently finds answers to human problems in the observable relations of human life.

Empiricists ask the question: what can we experience?

3 Understanding complexity

Empiricists tend to see the observation of variables as the basis for
establishing causal explanations. For idealists, the empiricist starting-point
is deficient in two respects. First, the social world is much more complex
than the use of **closed systems** can allow for. Second, observations only
make sense through the use of prior concepts. In this section we explore
the relationship between causal explanations and interpretative understanding. Explanations are more often associated with the natural sciences,
while understanding is usually seen as characteristic of the arts and
humanities. The natural sciences are said to be able to generate universal
law statements which apply across space and time, while the arts and
humanities only represent unique events in a particular time and place.
The social sciences carved out their own space between these two traditions

and have had to straddle these two modes of inquiry. Over the last century and a half, an intellectual and scientific movement has emerged which explicitly attempted to use Kant's ideas in order to study social relations and historical change. This approach came to be labelled neo-Kantianism. Although there remained considerable variation within this movement, there has always been a common concern to resolve the dilemmas raised by attempting to reconcile the tensions between hard facts and cultural values, between theoretical constructs and empirical observations and between explanation and understanding. Neo-Kantian debates about what would be the most appropriate methods for social science originated in economics, but they also had important implications for the subsequent development of sociology, psychology, geography and political studies. These approaches are so influential that they often remain unacknowledged. They have become such an integral part of social scientific inquiry that few feel the need to acknowledge them. They are simply part of the conceptual landscape of social science.

3.1 The emergence of neo-Kantianism

The neo-Kantian approach attempts to do two things. First, it attempts to resolve the dilemmas posed by accommodating both objective truth and subjective values in the same approach. Second, it attempts to find a way of addressing the thorny question of cultural values and their relationship to the generation of cultural and historical knowledge. Two key figures in this school, Wilhelm Windelband and Heinrich Rickert, both criticized positivism in the study of social life. Windelband's work provided us with a way of thinking about our methodological options, while Rickert (considered in more detail in section 3.2) raised interesting issues about the relationship between facts and values. In this section we focus upon Wilhelm Windelband, whose *History and Natural Science* (1894) regarded both the natural sciences and the human sciences as the study of empirical reality. Nevertheless, he distinguished between studying natural things and studying people and their institutions. For Windelband, there was a methodological difference between two forms of scientific thought:

Elsewhere this sign *g* will direct you to the glossary, but revisit this section if you need to.

- **nomothetic** – involving the construction of generalizing models and the identification of general laws;

- **idiographic** – the individualizing method of the cultural sciences concerned with the detailed depiction of particular circumstances.

This made it possible to distinguish between the study of natural objects in establishing objective knowledge and the important role played by the values and interests of the researcher in the study of social life. In the social sciences the objects are other subjects – thinking, creative and communicative beings. Scientists have different interests in their objects of analysis and define them in different ways. In the natural sciences, Windelband argued, the objects (physical matter) remain constant, allowing for the development of a 'science of laws', whereas in the social sciences the objects involved are 'unique configurations of events'. He argued that history and the humanities involve the use of individualizing or 'idiographic' method, while the natural sciences aim to produce general laws, the 'nomothetic' method. Within the nomothetic framework, values are seen as the product of an evaluative procedure and as such are subjective and cannot serve as the objective basis for establishing general laws. The social sciences are thus caught between two approaches to the study of social life, with one approach emphasizing the importance of scientific general laws and the other treating each set of social circumstances as unique. This helps to explain the competing options faced by social scientists.

For neo-Kantians, social scientific explanations offer a choice between developing general laws and attempts to understand unique events.

In the remainder of this section we explore how this innovative distinction had an impact on the emergence of economics and psychology. The relationship between nomothetic and idiographic positions can be illustrated by briefly considering the *Methodenstreit* (the debate over method), which originated in Germany in the late nineteenth century. This was primarily focused upon which key organizing principles should act as a foundation for economic research and for social research in general. It had become widely accepted that it was appropriate to study the economy idiographically, understanding the complexities of each economic system rather than in terms of discovering general universal laws. By focusing upon actual economic conditions, it was hoped that the social scientific knowledge produced would deliver human progress and the social improvement of the condition of the working classes through the actions of the state. This established the idea that state policy and social scientific research could work hand in hand. One of these early economists, Carl Menger, was concerned that this focus on social problem solving would lead to 'economics without thinking'. So, in *Problems of Economics and Sociology* (1883/1981), Menger developed a nomothetic account of the general relations of economic phenomena rather than describing economic processes in a particular time and place. He suggested that it was possible to

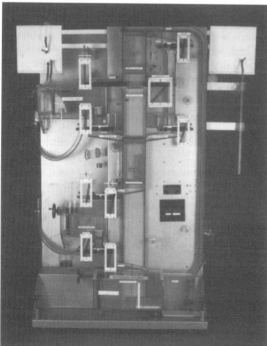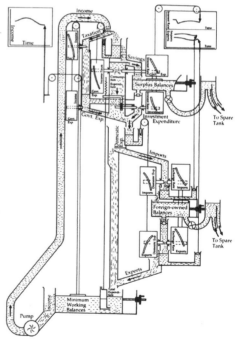

Figure 4.5   Representation of macroeconomics – the economy as a machine.

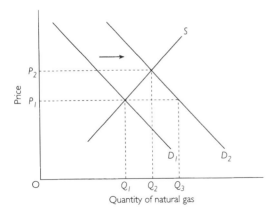

Figure 4.6   Representation of microeconomics. Alterations in the price of a particular commodity, in this case natural gas, relate to the quantity consumed. This is a fairly typical example of the way economists see the relationship in a market between price and the level of supply and demand for goods and services.

view the branches of economics (economic history, economic theory, economic policy and public finance) as each having its own distinctive forms of theory and method.

This was to have a profound effect on twentieth-century economics. For Menger, the appropriate method for economic theory involved two steps: first, break down phenomena into their smallest elements and, second, use these to deduce the development of more complex social phenomena. Thus a 'market' was no more than the sum total of consumer choices and the relations between them operating as a function of the individual actions which produced them. This approach to studying social life was to become known as **methodological individualism**. Menger was to establish a line of argument which rejected the aggregate concepts of macroeconomics in favour of microeconomics, which focused upon individuals, households and firms as decision makers (see examples in Figures 4.5 and 4.6).

In many social sciences, the difference between nomethetic and idiographic approaches came to be institutionalized in the branches of disciplines, such as the difference between theory and applied research work.

There was clear disagreement about which scientific method (nomothetic or idiographic) the discipline of economics should follow. In psychology, we find examples of both idiographic and nomothetic approaches living side by side. The emergence of experimental psychology enabled psychologists to develop a clearly nomothetic approach to scientific method. In particular, the technique of experimental closure was developed by the physiological psychologist Wilhelm Wundt, who established the first psychological laboratory in Leipzig in 1879 in order to demonstrate the interrelationships between sensory physiology and the 'mind'. Wundt, like all neo-Kantians, rejected the empiricist treatment of the mind (as a blank page for impressions) in favour of an active consciousness which could be selective in making discriminating judgements about our experiences. For Wundt:

> scientific investigation has three problems to be solved. ... The first is the analysis of composite processes; the second is the demonstration of combinations into which the elements discovered in the analysis enter; the third is the investigation of the laws that are operative in the formation of such combinations.

> (Wundt, 1897, p.25, cited in Manicas, 1987, p.183)

In this way, by clearly defining an object of analysis, psychologists began to carve out a space for their discipline, although the way in which the object of analysis, the mind, was defined in psychology was to change again with the emerging dominance of positivism. In particular, by focusing upon closed systems in the positivist way, the discipline of psychology was to lose its sense of the empirical complexity of social relations. However, in both psychology and economics the neo-Kantian framework came to be widely accepted. One of the legacies of this approach is the establishment of the distinction between theoretical and applied study in economics, psychology, geography, sociology and social policy.

Summary

The debate on method centred on what form social scientific inquiry should take – idiographic approaches study concrete social processes in a particular time and place, whereas nomothetic approaches attempt to construct accounts of general laws in some branches of the social sciences along the lines of the assumptions and methods of the natural sciences (especially physics).

Differences remained unresolved among the various alternative models emerging in the social science disciplines. Nevertheless, the debate triggered an increased awareness of the distinctive problems of social science posed by the role of cultural values in social research.

3.2 Facts, values and relevance in social science

The relationship between facts and values has generated a huge amount of heated discussion in the social sciences. As you saw in Chapter 3, taking their cue from logical positivism, many social scientists have been concerned to keep values out of scientific research. The contribution by the German philosopher Heinrich Rickert on the relationship between values and social science is the key starting-point for all the debates since. Rickert distinguished between the logical methods of the natural and the social sciences but also raised the possibility of differences between them because of the way in which the objects of analysis in each science are related to the values of those engaged in research. In the natural sciences, physics is formally nomothetic for it attempts to identify general laws and the objects concerned (atoms, neutrons, etc.) are not related to values. However, Rickert argued that some forms of natural science were formally idiographic (that is, concerned with unique situations), rather than nomothetic. For instance, in some areas of biology attempts have been made to establish the unique characteristics of earth-bound species, even though biologists have the same relationship to their objects as physicists.

In the social sciences, the objects of analysis are defined as value laden and culturally meaningful. Nevertheless, economics still concentrates upon developing general laws from the identification of recurrent patterns of events (as do many branches of sociology, psychology and political science). Rickert suggested that other approaches in the social sciences, influenced by history, are concerned much more with unique events and particular conditions. This helps to explain the variety of approaches in the social sciences.

Nomothetic and idiographic approaches coexist in both the natural sciences and the social sciences.

Sociology has often been described as containing two traditions, with one attempting to generate causal explanations in general terms and the other concerned with interpreting and understanding social life. These differences have also been developed into the methodological criteria of reliability and validity. **Reliable knowledge** can be defined as evidence which is supported through repeated testing under the same conditions, while **valid knowledge** (if difficult to replicate) is often defined as being true to life in a particular place and time. Nevertheless, in each case there is a clear attempt to represent reality even if there is considerable disagreement about what should be done. Both criteria claim to produce authentic knowledge, although they do so in different ways.

Identifying the values and purposes of social scientists raised problems which were to become known as the value judgement debate. Neither the nomothetic method nor the idiographic method provide us with clear criteria for deciding *what* we should actually study. Rickert suggested that it is possible to define objects and form concepts about them by following the criteria of **value relevance**. This means that, for a social scientist, the objects of analysis would be defined in such a way that they would already connect with the cultural values of the society in question and hold some meaning for the members of that culture. Therefore, it was argued, we should treat all social scientific concepts as expressions of the values of a given community and the conventional standards of morality considered to be universal within that community. The principle of value relevance means that concepts should be relevant to the problems of a particular society at a particular time. This also means that value judgements are the concern of philosophers in that time and place and cannot be established for all time.

Values are always involved in social research – this should be acknowledged so that social scientific knowledge is related to specific social and historical conditions.

Earlier in this chapter, we explored some of the problems involved in studying crime. In terms of the issues raised by value relevance, it is possible to identify important shifts in the study of criminality over the last forty years. The study of crime can be said to have moved through three stages:

- an attempt to establish the objective cause of criminality;
- a period concerned with processes through which crime was viewed as constructed by the criminal justice system itself;
- more recently, greater attention focused on the consequences of crime in terms of the experiences of victims and the development of crime prevention strategies.

Each phase of empirical research and theorizing can be related to the prevailing social issues at the time that the research took place. In the first phase, crime was attributed to definite causes, with some types of individuals identified as having criminal dispositions. This is often referred to as the positivist approach to crime. In the second phase, it was seen as a product of decisions by people in the criminal justice system. This phase emerged in the 1960s and 1970s when many social scientists were concerned with the ways that the police and courts constructed criminality. In the last phase, crime has been understood as something all rational individuals are capable of doing unless there is the possibility of being caught. This phase has been influential since the 1980s, with a move to more crime prevention measures. Each phase connects to a different set of concerns within Western societies.

3.3 Using ideal types

We noted previously, in the introduction, the use of ideal types in social science. This technique was popularized in social scientific research by Max Weber, who adopted an explicitly interdisciplinary approach using sources from economics, sociology, psychology, political studies and history. He was not concerned to demarcate the different forms of scientific method but, instead, wanted to bring them together in a coherent and unified approach. For Weber, this would provide a bridge between the interpretative understanding of human action and the scientific explanation of the causes and consequences of a particular relationship. To do this, Weber used the ideal type, a device which had been developed by Menger's economic theory. An **ideal type** is a theoretical device for generalizing beyond a particular situation, but one which accepts the complexity of social relations. It does not have the status that empiricists attribute to general laws for, in idealist approaches, it is assumed that closed systems are inappropriate for studying people. Ideal types are simplistic and exaggerated categories providing a yardstick against which it is possible to compare and contrast empirical evidence.

An important pair of ideal types in economics is the 'command economy' and the 'free market'. In terms of these 'ideal types', free markets are largely self-regulating systems for distributing goods and services, with a minimal state involvement ensuring that grievances are resolved and trust is maintained. Command economies have extensive state involvement in both producing and distributing goods and services as well as in fixing prices. They are portrayed as polar opposites in terms of the level of competition and degree of free choice displayed by the actors involved. In the free market these actors are assumed to be completely rational creatures operating according to opportunity cost (that we make purchasing decisions in markets fully aware that our choices always mean that we have to deny ourselves something else). In fact, although each ideal type is often used to describe empirical reality, neither can be said to actually exist. In practice there is no such thing as a perfectly free economy or a command economy for, as Figure 4.7 indicates, all actual economies can be located in between these types. In some cases, we can use these ideal types to identify how economies change, as in the transformation in post-communist Russia. For these reasons, Weber saw ideal types above all as useful devices for simplifying and identifying patterns in a concrete and complex empirical reality.

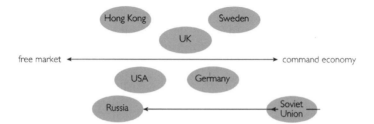

Figure 4.7
A use of ideal types in economics.

So, we can use the ideal type as an organizing device through which it is possible to establish the patterns of activity involved across social and economic institutions. By focusing upon patterns, these devices offer no final answers but allow for the development of useful models of human activity. Weber used them throughout his own research; for example, the

Ideal types simplify and allow for the identification of patterns of social relations within complex empirical evidence.

ideal types of traditional authority, charismatic authority and rational-legal authority. Authority relations are defined as ways of making power relations legitimate. Each of these, in turn, derives from Weber's more abstract ideal types of human action (that is, idealized in three ways: habitual, emotional and/or rational).

In order to understand the usefulness of this approach, imagine that Weber was alive in the 1980s in the UK and was faced with the social and political phenomenon of 'Thatcherism'. Using Weber's authority types, it is possible to develop a coherent and suggestive, if incomplete, picture of the Thatcher administrations in the UK which serves as a useful foundation for further research. The Conservative administrations in the 1980s consistently drew upon and reinvented 'traditional national' values as well as engaging in debates about the decline of moral values. Thatcher, as a 'charismatic' political figure, cultivated a populist appeal whereby she was able to draw upon the support of individuals within groups, such as trade unionists, whose interests are often seen as opposed to the Conservative agenda. The programmes for privatization, for taxation reforms and for the reform of the Civil Service can be seen as a return to a conception of bureaucratic administration that could be regarded as closer to the ideal type of 'bureaucracy as an efficient and rational machine for getting things done' which Weber would have seen as most suitable for a liberal democracy. In this way, the use of such ideal types provides a means of organizing the mass of empirical evidence about politics in the 1980s. This enables us to make sense of a more complex reality and even to deal with the evidence that appears to be contradictory. For instance, Thatcherism involved a 'strong state' (less freedom) in many areas of moral concern such as law and order, but also a considerable increase in personal freedom in the economy. By considering the 'strong state' as a strategy for maintaining traditional authority and the 'free market' (minimal state) policy as a means of generating popular support (through tax cuts and council house sales), we can see both as attempts to legitimate power in the way that Weber suggests. Of course, such an account only provides a partial picture of one brief period in British history. Nevertheless, it is a useful demonstration of neo-Kantian research practice.

4 Rational choices and human action

In this section we explore one of the most influential idealist approaches in recent social science, rational choice theory. This approach sees all social phenomena as the sum total of individual choices involved, no more and no less. All forms of interaction are portrayed as exchange relations in the manner of a marketplace and all human choices are seen as the product of rational decision making. The attempt to develop models of social relationships and intentional actions based upon rational choice calculations has been a strong current in social sciences since the 1960s. This arose as a response to dissatisfaction with the attempts by positivist economists to establish general laws simply through the testing of predictions.

The problems within empiricism prompted a re-evaluation of the relationship between explanation and prediction.

Economists had discovered that, because their predictions were rarely accurate, they faced the choice of either rejecting reasonably solid theories without a clear idea of what could replace them or introducing a *ceteris paribus* rule. This rule requires 'holding other things constant' in order to ensure that it is possible to identify testable relationships between a limited number of variables. This involves placing the particular relationship within a closed system. However, in practice, this also means that empirical evidence which is contrary to that which is expected can be interpreted as either a refutation of the statement or as a failure of the *ceteris paribus* conditions used in the test. Consequently, statements which would have been shelved if Popper's criteria had been adopted can survive empirical falsification when the *ceteris paribus* rule is used.

Rational choice explanations start from the premise that all social phenomena are the products of intentional decision making.

One response to these problems was developed by Austrian economist Ludwig von Mises, whose influence on contemporary social science has generally been indirect but important. Mises attempted to establish a purely **nomothetic** science of human action which he labelled praxeology. He was concerned with establishing universally valid knowledge which could be taken to exist prior to experience and which could be identified through reason. The focus upon the intentional and purposeful nature of human action within economic life prepared the way for contemporary rational choice theory. In *Theory and History,* Mises argued, 'There are no judgements of values other than those asserting I prefer, I like better, I wish' (Mises, 1957, p.22). Therefore, the value of all things can only be identified through the subjective preferences of the actors involved, in this case, actors involved in the processes of economic calculation based on money prices within the conditions of market exchange.

Once social complexity is acknowledged, social scientists should limit their aspirations to identifying the prediction of patterns rather than specific outcomes.

By questioning the foundations of economics, Mises identified how the relationship between explanation and prediction needs to be rethought. In situations of social complexity, where scientific theories cannot be taken as simple pictures of the processes they attempt to represent, the empiricist assumption that explanations and predictions are the same thing becomes an ineffective tool of inquiry. Mises distinguished between the role of 'quantitative predictions' within the natural sciences and 'qualitative predictions' in sociology and economics. He argued that it is impossible to predict specific outcomes in social science with any degree of accuracy and that, instead, social science should concern itself only with the prediction of patterns. Praxeology, therefore, develops 'imaginary constructions' through which all human beings can comprehend these patterns. The main difference between everyday life and science, he argued, is that whereas commonsense constructions are 'more or less confused and muddled, economics is intent upon elaborating them with utmost care, scrupulousness, and precision' (Mises, 1957, p.237).

4.1 Game theory

The rational principles of the praxeological method were developed for more general use in the social sciences by Oscar Morgenstern (a student of Mises) and John von Neumann, in *The Theory of Games and Economic Behaviour* (1944). This approach has only become popular as a research approach across the social sciences since the 1960s. Game theory provides a means of describing and explaining social relationships in contexts where actors make rational choices in rule-governed situations. It is assumed that all participants in a 'game' understand the possible choices or 'moves' open to all players and their likely outcomes. Applications of this analogy have been very wide ranging – from decisions on family planning, criminal behaviour, voting behaviour and electoral campaigning, to the Cuban missile crisis and the environmental impact of overgrazing on commonly owned land. The actors in this approach are assumed to have certain characteristics; in particular, they are considered to be 'minimaxers' in their behaviour (a label for describing the tendencies of rational actors to minimize their perceived costs and maximize their perceived benefits).

Game theory enables social scientists to identify rule-governed patterns of behaviour within which all choices are made by purely rational and self-interested players.

This can be illustrated by focusing upon two of the well known games applied to non-economic situations. In the game of 'chicken' (an American teenage dare game with cars), two actors race their cars towards each other in the certain knowledge that, unless one of them moves out of the way, both may be seriously injured or worse. The object of the game is to test the nerve of participants and the likely outcome is that one of the vehicles will veer away, leaving both unscathed but one of the actors shamed in the process. Allison (1971) has applied this game to the superpower confrontation in 1962 between Khrushchev and Kennedy following the deployment of Soviet nuclear missiles in Cuba within easy range of the American mainland. As the confrontation intensified, Kennedy called the bluff of the Soviet leadership by threatening nuclear confrontation, and as a result the Russian navy withdrew. Allison argues that these events can be explained as a complex game of chicken involving very high stakes, with the ultimate victors being the Americans, especially because of the increase in prestige for Kennedy, and the recognition by the Soviet leadership that they had severely underestimated the resolve of the American leadership.

In a more complex game, prisoners' dilemma, the capacity of actors to make rational choices which generate unanticipated consequences is addressed. This game is most often illustrated through an imaginary sketch in which two partners in crime have been taken for questioning by the police. The police inspector is well aware that there is very little substantive evidence with which to take the case to court and that a successful prosecution depends upon the statements of the two suspects to provide the necessary evidence of wrongdoing. The suspects are faced with a choice of either telling the truth about the crime, in the anticipation of receiving a lenient penalty, or keeping quiet, without knowing whether the partner will do the same and not confess. Since the two suspects are separated from each other, this game is based upon each one's trust in the other partner and their perceptions of which choice would serve their self-interest. In terms of the consequences of their actions, if both refuse to confess they are unlikely to receive a harsh punishment and may avoid any penalty. If one confesses and the other does not, then the suspect who remains silent is likely to receive a harsh punishment and the confessor a suspended sentence for cooperating with the authorities. If both confess, then both are likely to receive a moderate to harsh punishment. The scores involved in such choices are represented in Figure 4.13.

Figure 4.13   One variation of the prisoners' dilemma game. The lowest score produces the best outcome; the highest score produces the worst outcome.

When we examine the aggregate consequences of these choices in numerical terms, it is clear that the combined choices of both not to confess would produce the best outcome, a score of 2. The worst outcome of 8 follows from both confessing. A minimaxing individual in this situation would resolve to choose the outcome which minimized the risk of a harsh punishment and which took into account the lack of trust in the other partner. From the point of view of each individual the minimax decision would be to confess in the hope that the other partner did not, and so escape harsh punishment. However, if both actors in this situation applied this rational decision to their situation and opted to confess, the aggregate outcome would be the worst outcome. In this way, game theorists argue, it is possible for rational individuals to act in ways which appear to be the best in the light of the circumstances and yet the unintended consequence of their individual actions is to produce the worst outcome for all involved.

In prisoners' dilemma, the rational decisions of the actors produce the worst possible outcomes for all the players involved.

This rational choice framework has been adapted for the study of electoral politics by James Buchanan and others in developing public choice theory (see Buchanan et al., 1978; Buchanan and Tullock, 1981; Green, 1987). The focus on public or political choices as rational decisions has led to it being labelled the 'economics of politics'. Buchanan's approach is interesting in its attempts to examine the interrelationship between the rational choices of voters and of political leaders, and how their combined decisions had effects on public policy (Buchanan et al., 1978). For Buchanan, the electorate is composed of individuals who behave like consumers in the marketplace and the votes they cast in elections are the same as purchases. Consequently, voters are seen to vote for the party which offers them the most in terms of their perceived self-interest. This approach to voters in the 1960s and 1970s seemed to provide a means of explaining the decline of voting according to party loyalty and class background and the rise of issue-based voting alongside the increase in electoral volatility more generally. It is assumed that voters overall would prefer to have lower taxes at the same time as greater public spending on services such as health, education and social services. For political leaders who, as rational actors, attempt to bid for votes in order to win power, these apparently contradictory demands by the electorate lead them into a situation where they can only keep themselves in power by increasing state intervention without passing on the costs to the taxpayer.

The consequence of such a policy, according to Buchanan, is increased public debt and the undermining of wealth creation sectors (private business) by state regulation and higher corporate taxation. Buchanan was associated with New Right or neo-liberal demands for 'rolling back the frontier of the state' under Thatcher in the UK and Reagan in the USA. He adds that the rational choices of members of the bureaucracy also lead to an expansion of the state, supposedly in the interests of the citizen, but really to serve the self-interest of the administrators in expanding their own power and rewards. In this case, as in prisoners' dilemma, the rational self-interested choices of those involved lead to a situation where everyone suffers in the long term. Buchanan argues that the expansion of the state undermines the economic growth upon which the social programmes depend because the tax base shrinks.

Activity 4.4

Now turn to Reading C, an extract from Garrett Hardin's *The Tragedy of the Commons* (1968), and Reading D, 'When rationality fails' (1989), by Jon Elster.

- Identify how Hardin follows the game of prisoners' dilemma identified above.
- Make a list of what you consider to be the strengths and weaknesses of Hardin's extract.
- Identify the main themes of Elster's account of the limits of rational choice explanations.

As you read through the extract by Hardin you may be struck by the way that certain premises and assumptions can lead you to certain conclusions. As you read through Elster, you should think about whether Hardin's assumptions about people are really true.

4.2 Problems in rational choice theory

The assumptions of game theory are open to criticism on a number of grounds, which all hinge on the extent to which the models used are realistic. In particular, a great deal of doubt can be cast upon the definition of the concept of rationality in rational choice theory; this has, in turn, raised questions about when the model can usefully be applied and when it would be inappropriate. To address these problems it is worthwhile to consider what it means for behaviour to be rational or irrational.

The relationship between our choices and desires is often less clear-cut than the advocates of rational choice theory suggest for, in some situations, human beings act against their desires or experience conflicting desires. Since all decisions in the market involve these sorts of choices, it may not be accurate to characterize economic choices as rational calculations of costs and benefits. The characterization of rationality also depends upon the situation in which it takes place. What appears to be rational behaviour in one context may seem irrational in another situation, so that a universal principle of rational choice is unlikely to be established. Our personal attachments, traditional beliefs and even wishful thinking also play an important part in the formation of choices. The rational choice model assumes that, even if human beings are rational 'minimaxers', they make choices with full and perfect knowledge of the possible end consequences of their decisions and of the various means for achieving the same results. It can be argued that all of these assumptions are unrealistic. For instance, the behaviour of stockbrokers during a crash in the investment markets does conform to the rational model in that they sell stocks and shares in order to avoid further loss of value. However, in conditions of normal trading this profession operates by rules of thumb, intuition and hunches even though their occupational description would suggest the purely rational pursuit of profit taking.

The philosopher and economist Friedrich Hayek began to address some of these difficulties and became deeply critical of attempts to develop purely rational accounts of social life. In particular, he argued that the social scientific method should take proper account of the complexity of social phenomena within open systems. For Hayek the problem is **scientism**, which involves any claim to know the most appropriate way of investigating a social phenomenon before considering it (Hayek, 1952). Hayek warns against obstacles to the further advance of modern science, such as:

- the belief that ideas of things, such as 'laws', 'causes' and 'social order', possess some reality (that by analysing ideas we learn about the attributes of reality);
- the tendency of human actors to interpret external events after their own images;
- the attribution of a designing mind to the objects in question.

He was particularly concerned to counter the belief that it was possible to reconstruct the real world in social scientific theories and use this knowledge rationally to reconstruct actual societies (which he associated with the social engineering of fascism and communism). Hayek suggests that it is impossible to comprehend collective entities such as 'capitalism', 'society' and the 'economy', for:

> The concrete knowledge which guides the action of any group of people never exists as a consistent and coherent body. It only exists in the dispersed, incomplete and inconsistent form in which it appears in many individual minds, and the dispersion and imperfection of all knowledge are two of the basic facts from which the social sciences have to start.

(Hayek, 1952, pp.49–50)

Hayek also starts from a position of **methodological individualism**. However, unlike in rational choice theory, people are not treated as discrete atoms but are seen as engaged in mutual discovery through relationships. The examples Hayek has in mind include the long-term evolution of a system of language or the emergence of a system of monetary exchange. These evolving systems are seen as the unintended and unanticipated consequences of all the shared experiences of exchange.

g

Methodological individualism breaks things down into their smallest components and uses this to reconstruct more complex relations.

> The way in which footpaths are formed in a wild broken country is just such an instance. At first everyone will seek for himself what seems to him the best path. But the fact that such a path has been used once is likely to make it easier to traverse and therefore more likely to be used again; and thus gradually more and more clearly defined tracks arise and come to be used to the exclusion of other possible ways. Human movements through the region come to conform to a definite pattern which, although the result of deliberate decisions of many people, has yet not been consciously designed by anyone.
>
> (Hayek, 1952, pp.70–1)

While the nomothetic method which identifies 'recurrent events of a particular kind' (Hayek, 1952, p.118) predominates in natural science in relation to social science, Hayek sees idiographic explanations of particular or unique situations as playing as important a role as that of generalization. He suggests that the role of theory is to constitute the wholes through recognizing the importance of the related parts and comprehending the intentions, shared experiences and tacit knowledge of subjective individuals. In the next section we turn to those approaches which focus upon the roles of tacit and subjective knowledge in social science.

Summary

Rational choice approaches resolve the problems of cultural values by focusing upon the 'subjective preferences' of rational individuals. In praxeology and game theory, the rationality of individuals is established at an abstract theoretical level prior to empirical research and typically adopts a 'minimaxing' approach to decision making.

The imaginative use of games to identify the process of decisions made by individuals in complex and unpredictable situations provides social scientists with a means of identifying the similarities in decision making in very different contexts, highlighting the rule-governed nature of social life.

The assumption of rationality in these approaches provides a useful indication of the problems created by wishful thinking in social scientific research. In such cases, social scientists imagine an object (such as society, the economy, the mind, or the polity), treat it as a thing in itself and neglect the very processes by which such objects are constructed in the first place.

5   Meaning and subjectivity

For neo-Kantian idealists, general explanations have a useful role in social science even if they are only part of the whole picture; rational choice theories raise the prospect of a purely rational or 'minimaxing' approach to human decision making. However, the third group of idealist approaches, which we examine now, embraces the subjective dimension of social life wholeheartedly. They regard the existence of objects of analysis that we think of as real, as the product of our interpretations. In addition, individuals are not viewed as atoms bouncing off each other, but as having a sense of the shared existence through which identities are constructed. This does not mean that such 'objective things' have no effect – if we believe something to be real, it is real enough in its consequences for we behave as if it does exist. This section is concerned with a variety of approaches which have come to be known as forms of hermeneutics or phenomenology and which contain some useful insights into the problems of social science. We focus upon the interpretive approaches and their exploration of the self, interaction and meanings. The aim of hermeneutics is to make the obscure clear and plain, by identifying the processes and context of all approaches which attempt to understand society and culture. To do this, we should place ourselves inside the mind of the author or the social actor under consideration. The concept of **subjectivity** used in this approach is not the calculating machine of rational choice theory but, instead, it involves the meaningful interpretation of unpredictable relationships in everyday life.

Hermeneutics and phenomenology seek to understand the subjective and meaningful construction of the complex social world.

The emergence of contemporary hermeneutics, defined as the theory of the interpretation of meaning, can be traced to Wilhelm Dilthey's *Introduction to the Human Sciences* (1883; for brief extracts see Rickman, 1976). Dilthey's main concern was to identify a distinctly 'human science' which did not treat the study of society and history as the automatic play of objective forms and processes. For Dilthey, the natural sciences presented an inappropriate analogue for social science because natural objects cannot meaningfully interpret and construct their own cultural environment, whereas human beings can. Therefore, the study of society and history involved very different ground rules from those of natural scientific research because all human values, ideas, concepts, purposes and desires are seen as an inescapable part of understanding social life. This means that while human beings acted *upon* the natural environment, they also acted *within* the social environment. So the social and cultural forms taken as the objects of the social sciences were the expressions of the mind rather than external to the mind. The 'lived experiences' of individuals are thus the source of understanding. To deal with this, Dilthey argued, we have to recognize the problem of the *hermeneutic circle*: 'The whole of a work must be understood from individual words and their combination but full understanding of an individual part presupposes understanding of the whole' (Dilthey, 1896, cited in Bryant, 1985, pp.66–7). A common metaphor for explaining this idea is the sentence analogue, whereby the meaning of a word is identified by reference to its place in a sentence and the meaning of the sentence is established through the meaning of the individual words. Thus all mental constructions are historically and socially specific and hence prone to change as part of the web of cultural forms. There is, therefore, a crucial

Hermeneutics focuses upon the lived experience of human beings in their social and historical context.

difference between the approaches here and all the other approaches considered so far in this chapter. Here, there is no 'knowing subject' above and beyond the experiences of those being studied. In the following sections we look at ways in which this approach has been developed in the social sciences, particularly psychology, sociology and geography.

5.1 The self-concept and social interaction

The approaches considered in this section start from the assumption that the 'real world' is actively constructed by human beings, even though social scientists tend to behave as if it is independent of our knowledge. The first grouping we should consider, interactionism, draws from the philosophy of **pragmatism**. This is concerned with the way in which meanings and interpretations are the product of the 'pragmatic concerns' of practical problems and purposes of social life. The mind is treated as a tool for solving problems encountered in everyday life. This problem-solving approach has had a profound impact upon the interactionist approach in psychology (sometimes labelled humanistic psychology or sociological social psychology) and in sociology.

Pragmatic approaches treat social inquiry as a form of problem solving closely related to the concerns of everyday life.

Interactionism treats social actors and their small face-to-face interactions as the basis of all social life, so that the meaning of any concept or idea (personal, political, philosophical or scientific) can only be located in the experiential consequences which it produces. On the basis of this, the pragmatist William James distinguished 'knowledge about' from 'knowledge of' (James, 1890). 'Knowledge about' – that which is acquired through textbooks – is conveyed in abstract general principles which can be learned and memorized. However, 'knowledge of' – practical knowledge acquired through experience in everyday life – is established through trial and error and can take an unconscious or tacit form. This treats the concept of the mind as a 'thinking process' always in development, rather than as a fixed thing. In this way, individuals can define objects and their context, identify sensible courses of action or modes of conduct, imagine the consequences of these choices and, finally, select an appropriate course of action.

Practically adequate knowledge is derived through a process of trial and error.

Other forms of interactionist thinking, like that of psychologist and sociologist George Herbert Mead, focused more upon the social context in the shaping of choices. For Mead, in *Mind, Self and Society* (1934), meaning can be identified in the actual behaviour of the actors and the development of the mind as an unfolding process can be seen in the activities of children. In the *play stage* children play out roles and characters in order to be someone else, such as cowboys and Indians, doctors and nurses, etc. In the more advanced *game stage* the child learns to develop an inner conversation with the 'generalized other', which enables the child to predict the behaviour of others. The prediction of the routine habitual practices of others and responding in similarly predictable ways enables the everyday social interaction of human beings to take place while avoiding conflict. In Mead's own words:

For Mead, the concept of self is not fixed but the changing product of an ongoing process of interaction.

> in a game where a number of individuals are involved, then
> the child taking one role must be ready to take the role of
> everyone else ... [and] must have the responses of each position
> involved in his [sic] own position. He must know what everyone

else is going to do in order to carry out his own play. He has to take all of these roles. They do not all have to be present in consciousness at the same time, but at some moments he has to have three or four individuals present in his own attitude, such as the one who is going to throw the ball, the one who is going to catch it and so on.

(Mead 1934, p.151)

Often the things we know about can help us understand situations of which we have little or no experience.

This can be demonstrated through the example of the metaphor of the *looking glass self*, whereby other people act like mirrors for an individual's imagination. This is based upon three steps: the individual imagining how he or she looks to others; the imagination of how others judge the individual; and the emotional reaction of the individual to the imagined judgement. In this way, we constantly monitor ourselves at the level of our own imagination and, consequently, an adequate social science should attempt to address the existence of these processes (Cooley, 1902). Social interaction can be seen as an ongoing process, rather like the changing patterns of a kaleidoscope, instead of following a definite fixed plan. The search for patterns can be seen in the identification of 'career' patterns in different situations. It is possible to identify similar patterns in occupational careers, criminal careers (Becker, 1963) and the moral career of a mental patient (Goffman, 1987, pp.117–56). In criminal and non-criminal career patterns we would expect the rewards and respect to fit their place in the career ladder; Goffman reminds us that careers can be brilliant but also disappointing. A career in this approach is defined by the relationship between the internal processes through which we define our concept of self and the external processes through which we understand our social positions, lifestyles and institutional locations. It also helps us to see that labelling someone as criminal, or as mentally ill, matters. Goffman suggests that these moral aspects of careers can help us understand the relationship between the self and social institutions in the treatment careers of 'mentally ill' patients. Nevertheless, this approach is limited to considering what we can empirically observe rather than attempting to identify the assumptions upon which these actions and interactions are based.

Activity 4.5

If we consider identities to be social locations, it is worthwhile thinking through what it means to ask yourself the question 'Who am I?' before engaging in social research. Various dimensions of your identity should come to mind, such as your age, gender, ethnicity, social class, marital status and so on. You will consider some of these to be more important than others.

- Make a list of the relevant dimensions for your own identity.
- Organize this list in terms of their importance.
- Which of these dimensions has changed in importance and why?
- Quickly list the areas of social science which really interest you. Are these related to the dimensions of your identity? If so, in what ways?

5.2 Phenomenology and intersubjective meaning

Phenomenology asks us to dig deeper than in previous approaches, in order to explore the taken-for-granted assumptions of social research. The German philosopher who established contemporary phenomenology, Edmund Husserl, asks us to reconsider the idea of the 'objective world', and the way that some approaches treat subjectivity as a pale reflection of some deeper or more authentic state of affairs. As you saw in Chapter 2, Descartes started with 'I think therefore I exist' as a foundational principle. However, for Husserl, the starting-point always involved an intention, 'I think something'. This means that the act of describing experience actually creates the object of analysis. Therefore, the distinction between 'surface appearances' and some 'underlying reality' is no more than a convenient fiction for positivist scientists. To get around this problem, Husserl argued, we have to 'bracket' the objective. This means that we should suspend our belief in the existence of the objective world and abstain from making judgements about whether the world does or does not exist. This process has been characterized as the peeling away of the layers of ideas to identify the pre-scientific forms of experience of the *Lebenswelt* (life-world), rather like peeling away the layers of an onion.

Phenomenology treats the distinction between surface appearances and reality as the product of the conscious mind.

Schütz developed this in a more practical way. In *The Phenomenology of the Social World* (1932/1967), he argued that it is through the condition of **intersubjectivity** that the individual actors involved are able to grasp each other's consciousness and construct their life-world. By sharing time and space, the two or more individual actors involved in communication could engage in a process of understanding which involves the discovery of what is going on in the other person's mind (Schütz, 1932/1967, pp.112–13). Although Weber had developed the use of ideal types as a theoretical tool against which empirical evidence could be compared, this still treated the evidence as factual even though it was open to various interpretations. Instead, Schütz argued that there were no hard facts, only interpretations – that facts are intersubjectively constructed. As you saw in Chapter 1, Schütz sought to establish connections between the second-order constructs of social science and the first-order constructs of everyday life (Schütz, 1953). At the heart of Schütz's approach is the sociological formulation often described as 'cookery-book' or 'recipe' knowledge, the notion that we do not need to understand the origins of a particular set of practices in order to select the ingredients, bake the cake and 'eat and enjoy it' (Schütz, 1943, p. 137).

Phenomenology sees consciousness as the product of the intersubjective relations between actors engaged in communication.

Schütz suggests that we need to identify the recipe knowledge of social scientists as well as everyday life.

Two points should be highlighted here. First, the social world is constructed by actors who possess free will and who can and will behave in spontaneous ways not anticipated by the 'fictitious consciousness' of the scientific model. Second, scientists employ the same procedures of typification as actors in everyday life. For Schütz, in the natural sciences it is plausible to collect 'facts and regularities', but, when faced with the problem of understanding social existence, we need to account for the motives, the means and ends, the shared relationships and the plans and expectations of human actors. In the next two sections we explore some of the ways in which this approach has been applied.

Social scientific practice should find ways to connect the 'first-order' constructs of everyday life and the 'second-order' constructs of social scientific knowledge.

5.3 Ethnomethodology and tacit knowledge

While phenomenology offers a useful philosophical critique of social scientific knowledge, the sociologist Harold Garfinkel developed this into a viable research programme which attempted to reconstruct the 'taken-for-granted' commonsense assumptions (tacit knowledge) of people in their everyday lives. This became known as ethnomethodology (literally, 'people-method'), combining Schütz's insights with the empirical research strategies of symbolic interactionists (Garfinkel, 1967). The interactionists used ethnographic research techniques, such as in-depth interviews and participant observation, to attempt to reconstruct social life in a way that was as true to life as possible. However, they limited their evidence to the relationships they could observe, even if they didn't see observation in quite the same way as empiricists did.

Garfinkel wanted to delve deeper into the lives of his subjects and aimed to reconstruct the tacit knowledge that they could not even express (which Schütz had labelled 'cookery-book' or recipe knowledge). For Garfinkel, human actors continually create and transform their social existence, so that the supposedly objective contexts in which we live are fragile and transitory. Garfinkel suggests that actors are constantly attempting to make sense of the mass of sensations they experience. To do this, actors draw upon their stock of stories and meaningful interpretations. The moment that the evidence seems to suggest the application of a particular story, the sensory evidence is transformed into a support for the story. Garfinkel labels this technique the 'documentary method', involving a constant reciprocal process of interaction between the story-lines and evidence. Consequently, the stock of stories itself undergoes renegotiation and transformation as identities are reinvented.

Ethnomethodology seeks to find ways of locating and reconstructing the taken-for-granted commonsense assumptions of social practices.

Some of Garfinkel's research strategies bordered on the unethical, for they deliberately disturbed 'normal' relationships to see what would happen. For example, he engaged in the disruption of conversations to identify how much the respondents would adapt. He would play chess in seminars with new students and, after a period of following the rules, would then violate minor rules to see how far his students would adapt. Taken by surprise in this way, the students would accommodate the rule changes in the game and play accordingly. More controversially, he trained a number of his students to pretend to be lodgers in their own homes when they left the university for the vacation. These students simply behaved politely at home as they would have done when visiting a distant relative, yet the minor changes in behaviour provoked considerable familial conflict and disorientation. In these ways, Garfinkel was able to identify the tacit assumptions of games, conversations and family life, and reconstruct the complex processes by which the 'objective world' only appears as such because we construct it in that way. Similar investigations have been carried out by Aaron Cicourel in *The Social Organisation of Juvenile Justice* (1976), which examined the taken-for-granted assumptions of the police and courts in defining and processing 'juvenile delinquents' in two comparable Californian cities. The differences in delinquency rates, Cicourel argued, were the product of the different judicial cultures in each city. In another example, Robert Bellah drew upon this strategy in his inves-

Ethnomethodologists demonstrate that the rules of social life are more flexible and fragile than is often assumed.

tigation of new religious movements. Bellah used a range of qualitative research techniques to identify the commonsense assumptions of religious people in their everyday lives to establish the intensity of belief and the extent of their commitment to religious values (Bellah, 1976). These different studies have different objects and are responding to very different debates; nevertheless, they all have a common concern to establish the taken-for-granted commonsense assumptions (or recipe knowledge) of the people involved.

Activity 4.6

Turn to Reading E from Roger Jeffery's 'Normal rubbish: deviant patients in casualty departments' (1979).

- Make notes on the forms of taken-for-granted typifications used in the treatment of patients in the casualty department and how they are used to place a value on the patients.

- Consider in which other ways you would engage in the study of casualty wards. In what ways would you say that Jeffery's approach has limits?

In this reading you should note the strengths and weaknesses of this kind of social scientific practice. Does Jeffery identify things that other social scientists overlook?

Summary

A common theme in hermeneutic and phenomenological accounts of social life is the identification of the meanings, intentions and context of the author of a text or the social actor in his or her natural setting. The focus of analysis is the social and historical conditions in which a specific set of ideas or actions is located.

Interactionist and ethnomethodological approaches sought to draw upon these insights in developing an active research programme into the self-concepts and/or tacit assumptions of everyday social life.

Schütz made a distinctive contribution to social scientific method by attempting to overcome the tendency towards detachment associated with the application of natural science methods to social objects. In order to prevent social scientists imposing their own typifications upon objects in social research, an adequate approach should seek to ensure that the concepts used are also intelligible in everyday life.

Positivism: The March of Science

MICHAEL CROTTY

Truth is truth
To the end of reckoning.

William Shakespeare, *Measure for Measure*

Inherent in the methodologies guiding research efforts are a number of theoretical perspectives, as the previous chapter has suggested and Table 1 has exemplified. Furthermore, there is a range of epistemological positions informing the theoretical perspectives. Each epistemological stance is an attempt to explain how we know what we know and to determine the status to be ascribed to the understandings we reach.

In Chapter 1 we tried our hand at establishing some relationships among these elements. We connected epistemologies to perspectives to methodologies to methods. In the history of the natural and social sciences, some connections of this kind occur more frequently than others. Certainly, as we look back over the last century-and-a-half, there is one very common string that emerges across our columns. It starts with objectivism (as epistemology), passes through positivism (as theoretical perspective), and is found, historically, informing many of the methodologies articulated within social research.

This positivist perspective encapsulates the spirit of the Enlightenment, the self-proclaimed Age of Reason that began in England in the seventeenth century and flourished in France in the century that followed. Like the Enlightenment that gave it birth, positivism offers assurance of unambiguous and accurate knowledge of the world. For all that, we find it adopting a number of guises. This chapter is concerned with the various meanings that positivism has assumed throughout the history of the concept and with the post-positivism that has emerged to attenuate its claims without rejecting its basic perspective.

Positivism

The coining of the word 'positivism' is often attributed to Auguste Comte. Unjustifiably, it seems. While he did make up the word 'sociology' (and its predecessor, 'social physics'), he cannot be credited with 'positivism'. We are on safer ground in seeing Comte as a populariser of the word, especially through the *Société Positiviste*, which he founded in 1848. Populariser is an apt term to use here, for positivism undoubtedly became a vogue word and soon replaced the earlier usages 'positive science' and 'positive philosophy'.

These latter terms were used by Comte himself, following his mentor Henri de Saint-Simon. One of Comte's major works is the six-volumed *Cours de philosophie positive,* which appeared between 1830 and 1842. However, by the time Comte began talking of positive philosophy and positive science, the terms already had a very long history. They can be found centuries earlier in the writings of Francis Bacon (1561–1626).

'Positive science' sounds strange to our ears. We may have to resist the temptation to ask what negative science would look like. Yet, if *positive* is not being used here in contradistinction to *negative,* in what sense is it being used? To answer that question, we need to look to the traditional use of the word in comparable terms such as 'positive religion' and 'positive law'. There the word serves to distinguish positive religion from natural religion and positive law from natural law.

Natural religion? This is religion that people reason their way to. They work out the existence of God (or of many gods), the duty of divine worship, and so on, by rational argument based on their knowledge of the world. It is styled 'natural' because it is seen to stem from the nature of things. Positive religion, to the contrary, is not the outcome of speculation. It is essentially *something that is posited.* What is posited, thereby forming the starting point and foundation for positive religion, is divinely revealed truth. Positive religion is not arrived at by reasoning. It is a 'given'.

Positive law, too, finds its basis in *something that is posited.* In this case, what has been posited is legislation enacted by a lawgiver. Drawing its authority from an existing code of prescriptions and proscriptions, positive law contrasts sharply with the traditional notion of natural law. While the concept of natural law has a long and ambiguous history, for our purposes here it can be seen as a complex of responsibilities and obligations that, starting from the nature of the world and human nature within the world, people reason their way to. Once again, it is 'natural' because it is seen to stem from the nature of things. Thus, actions seen as wrongful in terms of natural law are considered to be wrong by their very nature. As the old principle has it, such acts are 'prohibited because they are evil' (*prohibita quia mala*). On the other hand, an action considered wrongful in terms of positive law is not regarded as wrong in itself. It is wrong because it has been forbidden by a legislator. In other words, acts of that kind are 'evil because they are prohibited' (*mala quia prohibita*). The concept of positive law is very different. Here there is no cerebral process reasoning about nature or natures. Positive law, like positive religion, is founded on a 'given'.

What does all this have to do with science? Quite a lot, as it happens. Those speaking and writing of 'positive science' were using the word in the same vein. They were talking of a science—*scientia*, 'knowledge'— that is not arrived at speculatively (as in the metaphysics of philosophical schools) but is grounded firmly and exclusively in *something that is posited.* The basis of this kind of science is direct experience, not speculation. Rather than proceeding via some kind of abstract reasoning process, positive science proceeds by a study of the 'given' (in Latin *datum* or, in the plural, *data).*

For many adherents of positive science ('positivists', therefore), what is posited or given in direct experience is what is observed, the observation in question being scientific observation carried out by way of the scientific method. This is certainly the understanding of positivism that prevails today. Although this contemporary understanding assigns a quite definite meaning to positivism, it is not in itself a univocal concept. As many as twelve varieties of positivism have been distinguished by some authors. There is not scope here to deal with the whole bewildering array of positivisms, but we can perhaps touch on some important historical forms that positivism has assumed.

Comte's positivism

Auguste Comte (1798–1857) saw himself at all times as a scientist. A largely self-taught and independent scientist, to be sure, for his formal training was short-lived and he never held an academic post of any standing. In 1814 he began studies at France's leading scientific school, the *École Polytechnique* in Paris. Less than two years after his enrolment, student unrest led to the closure of the school and a far-reaching reorganisation of its program. When it opened its doors once more, Comte did not seek readmission but devoted himself instead to private tutoring in mathematics.

Much more influential than his year or two at the *École Polytechnique* was his association from 1817 to 1824 with Henri de Saint-Simon. A bizarre, yet fascinating, figure in French intellectual life around the turn of the nineteenth century, Saint-Simon had a long-standing concern for the reconstruction of society. He was convinced that no worthwhile social reorganisation could take place without the reconstruction of intellectual understanding. What Comte imbibed from Saint-Simon was, above all else, this concern for the emergence of a stable and equitable society—and therefore for the development of its *sine qua non*, a valid and comprehensive social science. Despite his bitter parting from Saint-Simon and a total rejection of his mentoring, this goal continued to inspire all of Comte's subsequent endeavours. To the positivism of his science he brought a passionate zeal for social reform. His dedication to society's wellbeing was as fervent as that of any religious zealot and led him in the end to promulgate an utterly secular Religion of Humanity, incorporating a priesthood and liturgical practice all its own. For all the disdain he evinced for the 'theological stage' of societal development and for the religious aspirations of Saint-Simon's latter days, and notwithstanding his eagerness for a thoroughly 'positive' science to replace the ratiocinations of the philosophers, there are metaphysical and quasi-religious assumptions aplenty in what Comte wrote and did. It was certainly on the basis of a well-elaborated worldview that he felt able to call upon all people to become positivists and thereby play their part in establishing the just society.

The kind of social reorganisation Comte envisages requires the human mind to function at its very best. This, he feels, can happen only when all have embraced one scientific method. True enough, there is no one general law obtaining in all the sciences to give them substantive unity. Comte is no reductionist. Nevertheless, there is a universality of method that can unify the practice of science. The scientific method he has in mind is the method emanating from positivism. Not that it is a uniform method to be woodenly applied. Rather, it is a flexible method that succeeds in remaining homogeneous in a multitude of contexts. It is this desire for unity-via-method that moves Comte to set all the sciences in a hierarchy, leading from the most basic science—mathematics—through astronomy, and then physics, to chemistry and biology, culminating in what he sees as the highest science of all, his beloved sociology. Hence Comte's belief that scientific method retains the same essential features whether one is speaking of the natural sciences or the human sciences.

What are these essential features of the scientific method?

Given the contemporary identification of positivism with quantitative methods of research, and in view of Comte's known skills in mathematics, one might be forgiven for expecting the essential features of his scientific method to be couched in mathematical terms. That would be a mistake, nonetheless.

> When Comte talks about positivism, it cannot too often be stressed that he means an attitude of mind towards science and the explanation of man, nature, and society, and not some predilection for mathematical precision, especially not in sociology. In fact, Comte expressly makes a distinction between the search for certainty in science and the mistaken search for numerical precision. (Simpson 1982, p. 69)

Comte, in fact, warns against the dangers of an overly mathematical approach. 'The most perfect methods may, however, be rendered deceptive by misuse and this we must bear in mind. We have seen that mathematical analysis itself may betray us into substituting signs for ideas, and that it conceals inanity of conception under an imposing verbiage' (in Simpson 1982, p. 80).

Nor is Comte to be linked to some crude kind of objectivism. For him, scientific knowledge is not a matter of grasping an objective meaning independent of social thought and social conditions. Comte recognised, like Marx (and like Hegel before Marx), that human consciousness is determined by 'the social'. There is an interdependence here, as Simpson points out in expounding Comte's thought on this matter:

> Only long struggles for positivistic ideology by men of foresight serve to achieve social conditions under which metaphysical propositions give way to positivistic ones. Conversely, the positivistic stage is reached in any science—and especially in sociology—through a continual reorganization of society made possible by the pursuit of sociology and its application to practical problems, particularly problems in the organization of knowledge, its propagation, and its being passed on from generation to generation. (1982, p. 70)

Comte's quarry is the order he believes can be found in the world. Not for him the quest for first causes and last ends so beloved of the metaphysicians. Whether one is focused on nature or society, his positive science bids us look instead to 'laws' that can be scientifically established; that is, to facts that regularly characterise particular types of beings and constant relationships that can be shown to obtain among various phenomena. The direct methods whereby these laws can be established scientifically are observation, experiment and comparison.

At long last! This is finally beginning to sound like what we have always known as positivism. Yet even here we find Comte warning us, 'No social fact can have any scientific meaning till it is connected with some other social fact; without such connection it remains a mere anecdote, involving no rational utility' (in Simpson 1982, p. 78). Nor by 'experiment' does he necessarily mean what we know today as controlled experimentation. He includes under this rubric the study of events that just happen to happen and over which the sociologist has no control. And the 'comparison' he suggests is multifaceted: it includes cross-cultural comparison and especially historical comparison. Comte is, in fact, eminently historical in his approach. As Raymond Aron puts it (1965, p. 70), Comte holds that 'the different phases of human history are characterized by their way of thinking, and the present and final stage will be marked by the universal triumph of positive thought'.

Auguste Comte is seen as the founder of positivism. He did not see himself in that light. As he understood his role, it was that of passing on a torch that had been lit centuries before his time. Certainly, what he had to say about observation and experiment and the establishment of scientific laws can be found centuries earlier in Bacon. Yet, whether we see Comte as the source or merely the channel, it appears clear enough that positivism has changed dramatically since he first appropriated the word. One of the factors in its evolution has been its passing from the hands of working scientists to those of theoretical scientists and philosophers. The former are anxious to determine whether they can use in the human sciences the methods that are being used in the natural sciences. The latter's concern is different. It has to do directly with epistemology and logic. It is a concern to determine what truth claims can be made about scientific findings—or, indeed, about anything.

The Vienna Circle and logical positivism
The roots of the Vienna Circle lie in discussions that began in the first decade of the twentieth century, involving social philosopher Otto Neurath, mathematician Hans Hahn and physicist

Philip Frank. The Circle came to prominence in the 1920s when Moritz Schlick assumed its leadership. Schlick, who had begun his academic life as a physicist, turned to philosophy and in 1922 was appointed to the chair of philosophy of the inductive sciences at the University of Vienna. It was the discussions that took place within the Vienna Circle, and between the Vienna Circle and its counterparts at Warsaw and Berlin, that gave birth to the philosophy of logical positivism.

The Vienna Circle flourished throughout the 1920s but the coming of Nazism spelled its doom, most of its members being Jewish or Marxist (or both). Many went abroad in the early 1930s, Schlick was assassinated on the steps of the University of Vienna in 1936, and the Circle was officially dissolved in 1938. Its voice was not stifled, however. In fact, the scattering of Circle members—Rudolf Carnap to Chicago, Kurt Godel to Princeton, Otto Neurath and Friedrich Waisman to Oxford, and so on—served to ensure that logical positivism had world-wide impact. Even before the demise of the Vienna Circle, its philosophy had been popularised in the English-speaking world by A.J. Ayer's *Language, Truth and Logic,* which appeared in 1936.

What was the Vienna Circle's focus of interest, then? As we have seen, Comte and his associates wanted to introduce the methods of the natural sciences to the practice of the social sciences. Now the Vienna Circle was seeking to introduce the methods and exactitude of mathematics to the study of philosophy (as had already happened in the field of symbolic logic).

The Circle certainly appeared to have the expertise it needed for this task. Within its membership, besides an array of empiricist philosophers, there were a number of individuals with outstanding expertise in the field of mathematics (Gödel, for one) and logic (Rudolf Carnap, for instance). There were also eminent scientists whose science was highly mathematical in character.

The work of Gottlob Frege, Bertrand Russell and Alfred North Whitehead provided the Vienna Circle with an infrastructure for their discussions in the field of logic. An even more important influence on its developing philosophy was the thought of Ludwig Wittgenstein (1889–1951). Wittgenstein, a native of Vienna, came into contact with the Circle in the late 1920s. His *Tractatus Logico-Philosophicus,* published in 1921, had been studied intensely by several members of the Vienna Circle and the Circle shared his interest in the logical analysis of propositions. Wittgenstein's thought was probably not fully understood within the Vienna Circle and, in any case, he went on to reverse his position quite radically, as his posthumous work *Philosophical Investigations* dramatically reveals. All this notwithstanding, the early Wittgensteinian position was a crucial influence in the development of the Circle's viewpoint. Its membership constructed from it a basis for linking truth to meaning in a way that allows no pathway to genuine knowledge other than that of science. Thereby they excluded metaphysics, theology and ethics from the domain of warrantable human knowledge.

One of the notions drawn from Wittgenstein was what came to be known as the verification principle' (or 'principle of verifiability'). Schlick and Ayer embraced this principle enthusiastically and made it a central tenet of logical positivism. According to the verification principle, no statement is meaningful unless it is capable of being verified.

How does one verify a statement, then? As logical positivism would have it, there are only two ways.

In some cases, a statement can be verified because what is predicated of the subject is nothing more than something included in the very definition of the subject. A very obvious instance of this would be the statement, 'A doe is a female deer'. This can be verified simply by examining the definition of a doe. Mathematical statements can also be seen in this light. Two-plus-two equals four', or 'three-plus-one equals four', is a statement in this category, since the term 'four' is one that we have created to stand for 'two-plus-two' and 'three-plus-one'. Following terminology that derives from Immanuel Kant, such statements are known as *analytic* statements. An analytic proposition is one whose ascription of a predicate to a subject can be verified, and its meaningfulness thereby established, simply via an analysis of what the subject is.

Analytic statements are far from earth-shattering. They do no more than spell out what is already contained, or not contained, in the definition of the subject. To say that 'A' is 'A', or that 'not-A' is not 'A' is hardly an almighty contribution to human knowledge. Logical positivists would agree. Analytic propositions are either tautologies or contradictions. Nothing more, nothing less. On this accounting, logic and mathematics are merely formal in character. They are quite empty of factual content. In the language of the early Wittgenstein, their content is 'senseless'.

'Senseless' does not mean 'nonsense'. The early Wittgenstein and the logical positivists reserve the latter epithet for non-analytic, or *synthetic,* statements that prove incapable of verification. As one would expect from what has been said already, synthetic statements are propositions in which what is predicated of the subject is *not* included in its definition. Something new is being said about the subject, therefore. Not surprisingly, it is in synthetic statements that logical positivism is primarily interested.

Can synthetic statements be verified and thereby rendered meaningful? If so, how? The logical positivists have a clear-cut answer. Synthetic propositions are verified by experience—and only by experience. Experience? Here too logical positivism is quite definite. Experience means sense-data. What we experience through our senses (immediately, or by way of the instruments of science that extend the operation of our senses) is verified knowledge. This knowledge is 'factual'—and facts are what logical positivism is concerned with before all and above all.

It is, of course, the role of science to establish facts. Philosophy has the task of clarifying and analysing propositions made in the wake of scientific findings.

This line of thought excludes metaphysics, ethics, aesthetics and religion from the purview of genuine philosophy. Metaphysical viewpoints, ethical values, aesthetic judgments and religious beliefs are, as such, unverifiable in the empirical manner demanded by logical positivism. They do not deal in facts and are therefore of no interest to logical positivism. Emotionally, perhaps even spiritually, they may be of great value to people, but cognitively they are meaningless—nonsense, even.

From the viewpoint of logical positivism, the philosopher and the scientist must remain ever alert to the cognitive meaninglessness of views and beliefs of this kind. A clear disjunction must be maintained at all times between fact and value. If we want to deal in human knowledge that has validated meaning, the pathway is that of observation and experiment invoking the evidence of the senses. We need to be thoroughgoing empiricists. (Logical positivism is also known as *logical empiricism,* although some reserve this latter term more strictly for the combination of traditional empiricism and symbolic logic, whether in logical positivism or elsewhere.)

Since physics is the science where such thoroughgoing empiricism is most obvious, we should not be surprised that logical positivism makes particular use of its language. It uses the language of physics both as a tool for analysing and clarifying philosophical issues and as a way to unify scientific terminology. This reflects a certain reductionism within logical positivism: the other disciplines or areas of study are considered to be built upon, and to derive their validity from, the findings of empirical science.

Positivism today

Quite clearly, the meaning of the term 'positivism' has changed and grown over time. So much so that, from the standpoint of the Vienna Circle and in terms of the contemporary understanding of positivism, its acknowledged founder, Auguste Comte, hardly makes the grade.

In the history of ideas, the pathway trodden by positivism turns out to be long, tortuous and complex. Logical positivism has obviously played a major role in developing the concept of positivism that obtains at the present time. For a while, logical positivism looked set not only to dominate the understanding of science but also, in some places at least, to occupy centre stage within the discipline of philosophy itself. Of course, there have been many other factors in the development of the contemporary understanding of positivism. Rather than tracing that development in close detail, we will have to be content to set down positivism's principal features as it is most generally understood today.

One thing is certain: positivism is linked to empirical science as closely as ever. The logical positivists have always been great lovers of science. It has been said of them that they are infatuated with science. Be that as it may, the positivist spirit at the present time continues to adhere to a philosophy of science that attributes a radical unity to all the sciences and sets few bounds to what science is capable of achieving.

Since the time of the Enlightenment, a melioristic spirit has been abroad. There is a widespread notion that we are on a path of inevitable progress. 'Every day, in every way, I'm getting better and better'—Émile Coué's famous dictum parallels a comparable optimism at the societal and even global level. Positivism not only shares this optimistic faith in progress but also presents scientific discovery, along with the technology it begets, as the instrument and driving force of the progress being achieved.

This supreme confidence in science stems from a conviction that scientific knowledge is both accurate and certain. In this respect scientific knowledge contrasts sharply with opinions, beliefs, feelings and assumptions that we gain in non-scientific ways. The principal point of difference is the alleged objectivity of scientific knowledge. It is unlike the subjective understandings we come to hold. Those subjective understandings may be of very great importance in our lives but they constitute an essentially different kind of knowledge from scientifically established facts. Whereas people ascribe subjective meanings to objects in their world, science really 'ascribes' no meanings at all. Instead, it *discovers* meaning, for it is able to grasp objective meaning, that is, meaning already inherent in the objects it considers. To say that objects have such meaning is, of course, to embrace the epistemology of objectivism. Positivism is objectivist through and through. From the positivist viewpoint, objects in the world have meaning prior to, and independently of, any consciousness of them.

From this same viewpoint, scientists are required to keep the distinction between objective, empirically verifiable knowledge and subjective, unverifiable knowledge very much in mind. It emerges as the distinction between fact and value and founds the goal of value-neutral science, which positivistically minded scientists tend to uphold with a significant degree of fervour.

What kind of world, then, is the world of the positivist? Were we to answer, 'A *mathematised* world', we would find ourselves in good company. We would be following the lead given by Edmund Husserl, the founder of phenomenology. Husserl (1970b) attributes this alleged mathematisation of the world to Galileo, in the first instance. He recalls how Galileo dealt with attributes in which there is a clearly subjective element. Such attributes (colour, taste and smell, for instance) he refused to accept as real properties, dismissing them instead as mere secondary properties and not the concern of the scientist. For Galileo, the primary properties of things— 'real' properties, therefore—are those that can be measured and counted and thereby quantified. Size, shape, position, number—only properties like these make the grade scientifically. The real world, for the Galilean scientist, is a quantifiable world.

This scientific world is not, of course, the everyday world that people experience. Not even scientists experience it that way in their everyday mode of being. Various authors have considered the example of Tycho Brahe and Johannes Kepler standing together on a hill at sunrise.

These two seventeenth-century astronomers held very different views. Brahe thought that the sun circles the earth; Kepler believed that the earth circles the sun. As they watch the sun appear at daybreak, what do they see? Does Brahe see the sun move above the earth's horizon, while Kepler sees the horizon dip below the sun? Norwood Russell Hanson (1972) makes a case for this being so. Others, such as Gerhart and Russell (1984) demur, asserting that, whatever the differences in their scientific stance, Brahe's and Kepler's human experience of a sunrise will be the same in this respect. Most would surely agree. We may believe that the earth is round, and 'Flat Earthers' may be our favourite epithet for people we judge to be behind the times—yet, unless we are doing something like buying a round-the-world air ticket, we do think and act as if the earth were flat. And we are expected to do so. In buying a road map for my trip from Adelaide to Cairns, I would be looked at askance were I to complain to the supplier that the map I am given is flat and not curved.

In other words, the world addressed by positivist science is not the everyday world we experience. As Husserl points out, the scientific world is an abstraction from the 'lived' world; it has been distilled from the world of our everyday experiences, distances us from the world of our everyday experiences, and takes us further still from the world of immediate experience lying behind our everyday experiences. Science imposes a very tight grid on the world it observes. The world perceived through the scientific grid is a highly systematic, well-organised world. It is a world of regularities, constancies, uniformities, iron-clad laws, absolute principles. As such, it stands in stark contrast with the uncertain, ambiguous, idiosyncratic, changeful world we know at first hand.

Making this scientific abstraction from lived reality is not to be criticised. It serves eminently useful purposes, as the history of science and the development of technology witness so forcefully. While there is a downside to the achievements of science and this needs to be kept in mind as well, most of us have abundant reason to be grateful to science.

If we want to quarrel with the positivist view, our quarrel will not be, in the first instance, with what positivist science does. Rather, it will have to do with the status positivism ascribes to scientific findings. Articulating scientific knowledge is one thing; claiming that scientific knowledge is utterly objective and that only scientific knowledge is valid, certain and accurate is another. Since the emergence of positivist science, there has never been a shortage of philosophers and social scientists calling upon it to rein in its excessive assumptions and claims. Many of these philosophers and social scientists have operated out of a quite different epistemology and worldview. As the twentieth century got underway, however, more and more scientists 'from within' added a chorus of their own. Without necessarily jettisoning the objectivism inherent in positivism, these insiders have challenged its claims to objectivity, precision and certitude, leading to an understanding of scientific knowledge whose claims are far more modest. This is a less arrogant form of positivism. It is one that talks of probability rather than certainty, claims a certain level of objectivity rather than absolute objectivity, and seeks to approximate the truth rather than aspiring to grasp it in its totality or essence.

This more or less attenuated form of positivism is known today as post-positivism.[3]

Post-positivism

Early inroads into the absoluteness and dogmatism of positivist science were made by a pair of eminent physicists, Werner Heisenberg (1901–76) and Niels Bohr (1885–1962).

Heisenberg, a German scientist, is one of the founders of 'quantum theory'. He articulates an 'uncertainty principle' which well and truly calls into question positivist science's claims to certitude and objectivity. According to Heisenberg's principle, it is impossible to determine both the position and momentum of a subatomic particle (an electron, for instance) with any real accuracy. Not only does this preclude the ability to predict a future state with certainty but it suggests that the observed particle is altered in the very act of its being observed, thus challenging the notion that observer and observed are independent. This principle has the effect of turning the laws of physics into relative statements and to some degree into subjective perceptions rather than an expression of objective certainties.

Bohr, a Dane, received the 1922 Nobel Prize in Physics for his work on the structure of the atom. Like Heisenberg, Bohr is concerned with uncertainty but he has a different view about the nature of the uncertainty in question. Heisenberg's argument is epistemological: in pointing to science's inability to determine subatomic dynamics with accuracy, he locates this limitation in the very way in which we humans know what we know. For Bohr, however, the limitation is ontological rather than epistemological: it is due not to how humans *know* but to how subatomic particles *are*. In fine, these particles need to be seen as a kind of reality different from the reality we are used to dealing with. In thinking or talking about them, we need a new set of concepts. We cannot simply take classical concepts like position and momentum and apply them with accuracy to particles. The traditional concepts may, of course, be the best we have, and we may have no alternative but to make do with them. Yet, we should not succumb too easily to the tyranny of prevailing concepts. Bohr urges us to complement their use with other kinds of description that offer a different frame for our considerations. However successful we may be in doing that, the essentially ambiguous character of human knowledge, including scientific knowledge, cannot be sidestepped, as Bohr's whole discussion underlines very cogently.

The impact of Heisenberg's and Bohr's thought has been far-reaching. These scientists sound a note of uncertainty within what has been a very self-confident philosophy of positivist science. That note comes to echo even more loudly as other thinkers begin to address similar issues within science.

One of the factors prompting this concern with epistemology and the philosophy of science has been the recognition that a contradiction exists in scientific practice. There is a chasm between what science purports to do and what it actually does. For all the positivist concern that statements be verified by observation before being accepted as meaningful, a host of elaborate scientific theories have emerged whose development clearly requires the acceptance of much more than direct conclusions from sense-data. Many of the so-called 'facts' that serve as elements of these theories are not directly observed at all. Instead, they have been quite purposefully contrived and introduced as mere heuristic and explanatory devices. This is true of alleged 'entities' such as particles, waves and fields. Scientists act as if these exist and function in the way they postulate and, in terms of their purposes, this may prove an effective way to proceed. In this situation, it is very easy to go on to reify[4] these presumptions. Yet, by positivism's own criteria, such reification is unjustified.

What is emerging in this line of thought is the picture of scientists actively constructing scientific knowledge rather than passively noting laws that are found in nature. This has clear implications for the status that scientific knowledge deserves to have ascribed to it. Many thinkers—philosophers or scientists, or both—have not been slow to point out these implications.

Popper's principle of falsification

Sir Karl Popper (1902–94) was born in Vienna. In the 1930s, like so many other figures we are considering here, he was forced by Nazism's advent to power to quit his native land. After a brief period in England, he spent the years of World War II in New Zealand, returning to England in 1946 and serving as a professor at the London School of Economics from 1949 to 1969.

Popper is interested in the philosophical and political implications of genuinely scientific work. He contrasts scientific work with what is done in the 'pseudo-sciences' and tries to draw a clear line of demarcation between the two. His early ideas are found in *The Logic of Scientific Discovery* and *The Open Society and Its Enemies.* Later works include *Objective Knowledge: An Evolutionary Approach* and *The Self and Its Brain,* the latter coauthored with J.C. Eccles.

Despite early association with the Vienna Circle, Popper offers a view of human knowledge very different from that of logical positivism. Not for him any limiting of valid knowledge to statements capable of empirical verification. How, then, does he see scientific knowledge being established? We find a clue to that in the title of yet another of his books, *Conjectures and Refutations: The Growth of Scientific Knowledge.* Instead of scientists proceeding by way of observation and experimentation, thereby pinpointing scientific laws evident in nature itself, Popper sees them engaging in a continual process of conjecture and falsification. An advance in science is not a matter of scientists making a discovery and then proving it to be right. It is a matter of scientists making a guess and then finding themselves unable to prove the guess wrong, despite strenuous efforts to do so.

In putting this position forward, Popper is taking issue with the scientific method as it has been traditionally understood. In fact, he is challenging one of its pivotal notions. He is confronting head on the role that scientific method ascribes to induction. Induction is the process whereby a general law is established by accumulating particular instances. For example, because scientists find time and time again that water boils at 100°C, at least under certain definable conditions, they have felt confident in ascribing to this 'fact' the status of a universal law of physics. Not everyone has shared their confidence. Eighteenth-century philosopher David Hume characterised that confidence as a matter of psychology but not an outcome of logic. We might boil water a thousand times and find in every case that it boils at 100°C; but in Hume's view this provides no *logical* justification for the belief that it must always boil at 100°C. To assume that it must is to assume a world in which the regularities we perceive today will remain unchanged in the future. That is an assumption, not an empirically established truth. A number of later philosophers, Bertrand Russell and C.D. Broad among them, side with Hume in this, seeing induction as very much the weak link in the chain of empiricist science. Scientists may be as empirical as they like in their observations and experiments; yet they must reckon with the consideration—an unpalatable consideration, perhaps—that a non-empirical logical principle remains intrinsic to scientific method.

Popper's solution to this impasse is to substitute falsification for verification at the heart of scientific method. No matter how many examples we muster in support of a general principle, we are unable, logically, to prove it true in absolute terms; yet it takes only one example at variance with a general law to prove, logically and in absolute terms, that it is false. So Popper believes that, in engaging in observation and experiment, scientists are called upon not to prove a theory (they can never do that) but to try to prove it wrong.

For the Baconian understanding of science as an inductive process Popper has substituted the idea of science as hypothetico-deductive. Scientific method is like this: (a) scientific theories are proposed hypothetically; (b) propositions are deduced from these theories; and (c) the propositions are then tested, that is, every effort is made to prove them false. It is this falsifiability that sets scientific claims apart from non-scientific or pseudo-scientific claims. A theory or hypothesis not open to refutation by observation and experiment cannot be regarded as scientific. With this goal of falsification in view, Popper recommends that all scientific theories be presented as clearly as possible so as to lay them wide open to refutation.

It is only when propositions deduced from scientific theory have survived every attempt to refute them that the theory can be provisionally accepted as true. Here the operative word is 'provisionally'. The conviction that no theory can ever be definitively accepted as true lies at the heart of Popper's philosophy. As he put it (1959, p. 280), 'every scientific statement must remain *tentative for ever'.*

All this evinces a very different picture of science, and of the scientist, from the one we find at large among the positivists.

First, in the search for scientific truth, there is a place for guesswork, intuition, the following up of 'hunches'. Not for Popper the image of the scientist as the detached observer of nature. In fact, he does not believe such disinterested observation is possible. Observation takes place within the context of theory and is always shaped by theory. All our observing is done within a horizon of expectations and is therefore necessarily selective.

Second, on Popper's accounting, what is put forward as scientific truth turns out to be, not something shown to be true, but simply something that scientists have so far been unable to prove false. This turns scientific truths into merely provisional statements. 'Our science', warns Popper (1959, p. 278), 'is not knowledge (*epistēmē*): it can never claim to have attained truth, or even a substitute for it, such as probability'.

> Science is not a system of certain, or well-established, statements; nor is it a system which steadily advances towards a state of finality . . .
>
> The old scientific ideal of *epistēmē*—of absolutely certain, demonstrable knowledge—has proved to be an idol ... It may indeed be corroborated, but every corroboration is relative to other statements which, again, are tentative. Only in our subjective experiences of conviction, in our subjective faith, can we be 'absolutely certain' . . .
>
> Science never pursues the illusory aim of making its answers final, or even probable. Its advance is, rather, towards the infinite yet attainable aim of ever discovering new, deeper, and more general problems, and of subjecting its ever tentative answers to ever renewed and ever more rigorous tests. (Popper 1959, pp. 278, 280, 281)

On that accounting, Olympian dogmatism would seem entirely out of place among Popperian scientists. One would expect of scientists, instead, a large measure of tentativeness, perhaps even a measure of humility.

Where does one find these Popperian scientists? There are humble scientists, to be sure, and scientists often put their hypotheses forward quite tentatively in the first place. Still, on the whole they do seem to be looking for verification rather than falsification, and the observer of the scientific scene is hard put to find any widespread and impassioned effort to prove scientific theories wrong. This is particularly true of the broader, more fundamental, realm of theory. This is rarely called into question. Even in the face of conflicting evidence scientists only too often cling to theory in a quite determined fashion. Obviously, and unsurprisingly, it takes more than falsification to break scientists loose from what they have known and experienced as the very matrix of their thought and practice. Achieving that, some would want to say, takes nothing short of revolution.

Kuhn's 'scientific revolutions'

Possibly the most influential book in modern-day philosophy of science is *The Structure of Scientific Revolutions*.

The ideas contained in this book were developed by Thomas Kuhn (1922–96) while he was a graduate student in theoretical physics at Harvard University. What provided the impetus and starting point for this work was an invitation Kuhn received from University President James B. Conant to do some lecturing in science. The course in question was for under-graduates majoring in the humanities and it was put to Kuhn that he should take an historical perspective. So he turned to the history of science to see what lessons it might hold for scientists today.

This is new territory for Kuhn and the lessons he comes to glean from history are not of the kind he has been anticipating. Led back to Aristotle's *Physics,* he is struck forcefully by what he sees as an utter disparity between Aristotelian physics and the physics of Newton. Not a difference of degree but a difference of kind. Not inchoate, less-formed notions in Aristotle that are later to be developed and brought to fruition in Newton. No, these two sets of ideas appear to him so different as to be incomparable. As Kuhn sees it, Aristotle and Newton do not stand at different points on a continuum; they are not even within the same spectrum.

Accordingly, Kuhn concludes, the thought of Newton cannot have grown and developed out of the thought of Aristotle. At some point, the basis and essential elements of Aristotelian physics must have been jettisoned and replaced by a whole new way of seeing things. There has to have been a revolution in scientific thinking.

It is this insight that leads Kuhn to the thesis he develops in *The Structure of Scientific Revolutions.* There, and elsewhere, he takes a much more historical and sociological perspective than philosophers of science before him. He begins by looking directly at scientists and what they do, whether they be scientists of the past or scientists of the present. Where Popper's philosophising and his focus on logic lead him to see scientists and the process of scientific research in terms of what they ought to be rather than what they are, Kuhn's starting point leads him at once to question the alleged objectivity and value-free neutrality of scientific discovery.

What Kuhn never ceases to emphasise is that scientists do their work in and out of a background of theory. This theory comprises a unitary package of beliefs about science and scientific knowledge. It is this set of beliefs that Kuhn calls a *paradigm.* It is an overarching conceptual construct, a particular way in which scientists make sense of the world or some segment of the world.

For scientists in general, the prevailing paradigm is the matrix that shapes the reality to be studied and legitimates the methodology and methods whereby it can be studied. More than that, the prevailing paradigm is quite simply taken for granted within the contemporary scientific ethos. Any challenges that are mounted tend, at the start at least, to be dismissed out of hand. Normal science, Kuhn says, 'often suppresses fundamental novelties because they are necessarily subversive of its basic commitments' (1970, p. 5). Thus, the paradigm establishes the parameters and sets the boundaries for scientific research and, in the ordinary course of events, scientific inquiry is carried out strictly in line with it. At most, scientists will attempt to solve problems in ways that refine the paradigm and extend its scope. Even Popperian science, fiercely focused as it is on refuting the alleged findings of science, takes place in accordance with the dictates of the ruling paradigm. Such science—science in keeping with the paradigm of the day—is what Kuhn is calling 'normal science'. He sees it as a 'sort of puzzle-solving activity in which . . . most physical scientists are normally engaged' (1977, pp. 221–2). As he puts it, 'normal research, even the best of it, is a highly convergent activity based firmly upon a settled consensus acquired from scientific education and reinforced by subsequent life in the profession' (1977, p. 227). Kuhn goes so far as to characterise normal science as 'a complex and consuming mopping up operation' (1977, p. 188). It 'aims to elucidate the scientific tradition in which [the scientist] was raised rather than to change it' (1977, p. 234).

There comes a time, however, when the paradigm proves inadequate. Findings are proposed that cannot be explained within the context of the paradigm that prevails. When anomalies like this arise, 'nature has somehow violated the paradigm-induced expectations that govern normal science' (Kuhn 1970, pp. 52–3). It is a time of crisis. New findings are being put forward in such cogent or widespread fashion, and theories espoused so fervently, that they succeed in calling the paradigm itself into question. The process is often helped on its way by the impact of a revolutionary scientist—usually, Kuhn thinks, a younger person not schooled so long or so deeply in the paradigm guiding current scientific inquiry. Through factors such as these, it comes to be accepted that a whole new way of viewing reality is called for. It is time for a 'paradigm shift'.

In this period of change, what emerges within science is a 'willingness to try anything, the expression of explicit discontent, the recourse to philosophy and to debate over fundamentals' (Kuhn 1970, p. 91). Normal science is being turned on its head and an era of 'extraordinary science' is being ushered in. It is this development that Kuhn styles a *scientific revolution.*

Once one begins to think in this fashion, it is not difficult to find revolutions enough in the history of science. Galileo (and the Leaning Tower of Pisa?) destroying forever the Aristotelian view that bodies fall at a speed proportional to their weight. Copernicus and his heliocentrism prevailing over earth-centred Ptolemeian astronomy. Lavoisier's oxygen theory of combustion replacing Becher's hypothesis of phlogiston. Darwin's theory of natural selection overthrowing forms of scientific theorising that base themselves on a world governed by design. Einstein's theory of relativity shaking the foundations of Newtonian physics. And so on. These are not mere changes *within* science that leave science itself very much as it was. These are changes *of* science. They alter forever the way scientists see the world they are trying to explain. For Kuhn, then, the history of science is not a story of steady advance through adding new data to those already in hand and gradually developing existing theory. Instead, the significant changes in science appear to have occurred through radical shifts in the way scientists view reality.

How have these shifts in perspective come about? Certainly, many non-scientific factors have played a part. Kuhn effectively relates the 'doing' of science to the broader sweep of history and to social factors and social change. Just as effectively, he links scientific effort to the interests, and the psychology, of both the scientific community and individual scientists. Because of this, his influential line of thought constitutes a further loosening of the hold positivism has taken on scientific thought and research. The picture Kuhn paints is not a picture of objective, valid, unchallengeable findings emerging from scientists working with detachment and in a spirit of unalloyed scientific dedication. To the contrary, scientific endeavour, as Kuhn conceives it, is a very human affair. Human interests, human values, human fallibility, human foibles—all play a part.

If one accepts Kuhn's picture of things, it becomes very hard to sustain an image of science as a 'garden enclosed'. Kuhn's arguments make it impossible to elevate the work of the scientist over that of other professionals. Science now appears as run of the mill as any other human activity. Seen in the light of his arguments, how can science remain on the pedestal where the logical positivists have enshrined it? Change in science, it would seem, takes place in very much the same way as it occurs elsewhere—in art, say, or politics. It certainly does not necessarily come about in a disciplined or orderly fashion. Often, it just seems to 'happen', coming about in makeshift and fortuitous ways. In 'anarchic' fashion, perhaps? Could one go so far as to say that? Yes, even that.

Feyerabend's 'farewell to reason'
It is Paul Feyerabend (1924–94) who describes scientific progress as 'anarchic'. Science, he tells us, 'is an essentially anarchic enterprise' (Feyerabend 1993, p. 9). This is not a criticism. For Feyerabend, working in anarchic fashion is simply the way things have to be. Rather than decrying scientific anarchism, we should embrace it warmly and celebrate it fervently, for it is necessary for the progress of science and the development of culture. Scientific progress may mean

different things to different people, but Feyerabend's thesis is *'that anarchism helps to achieve progress in any one of the senses one cares to choose'* (1993, p. 18). He goes on to outline for us 'an anarchistic methodology and a corresponding anarchistic science' (1993, p. 13). Already we may be glimpsing why Feyerabend has so often been referred to as the *enfant terrible* of late twentieth-century philosophy of science.

Feyerabend too was born in Vienna. He originally studied physics but, after working under Popper, he came to the fore as a philosopher of science in the 1960s. He spent several decades in Britain and the United States before becoming professor of the philosophy of science in Zürich, a post he filled for the last fifteen years of his life.

Feyerabend starts off reasonably close to the position of Popper, his one-time mentor and fellow Austrian. However, his forceful style of presentation provokes, even at the start, an accusation that has never been levelled at Popper—the charge of being an enemy of science. If Feyerabend's critics brand him anti-science on the basis of his early thought, they very soon find further and more explosive ammunition in what he goes on to say and write. He moves not only well beyond Popper but even beyond Kuhn. One way in which he does so is in his attitude to 'normal science'. For all his talk of normal science as a 'mopping up operation', and notwithstanding its failure to challenge the ruling paradigm, Kuhn never fails to uphold the importance of its problem-solving function. Feyerabend, on the contrary, is thoroughly suspicious of this unchallenged continuance of normal science, alleging that it is based on indoctrination and constitutes a threat to academic freedom.

While Feyerabend may not be anti-science, he leaves no doubt about how he views the adulation traditionally offered to science.

> On the other hand, we can agree that in a world full of scientific products scientists may be given a special status just as henchmen had a special status at times of social disorder or priests had when being a citizen coincided with being a member of a single universal Church. (Feyerabend 1993, p. 250)

In all this, Feyerabend insists that his quarry is positivism, not science as such. What he is questioning radically is the role of reason in science. He titles one of his books *Farewell to Reason.* Not that he is descending into wild irrationalism. He is querying the role of reason *as it is generally understood.* As he goes to some pains to emphasise in his posthumous autobiography, *Killing Time*, he is not denigrating reason as such but only attacking petrified and tyrannical versions of it. Feyerabend's basic position is that, since science cannot be grounded philosophically in any compelling way, scientific findings are no more than beliefs and we should not privilege them over other kinds of belief—even Voodoo! Voodoo, in fact, 'has a firm though still not sufficiently understood material basis', writes Feyerabend, as he calls for a 'pluralistic methodology' (1993, pp. 36, 38).

Science, then, is 'much more "sloppy" and "irrational" than its methodological image' and 'the attempt to make science more "rational" and more precise is bound to wipe it out' (Feyerabend 1993, p. 157). In Feyerabend's judgment, 'what appears as "sloppiness", "chaos" or "opportunism" . . . has a most important function in the development of those very theories which we today regard as essential parts of our knowledge of nature' (1993, pp. 157–8). Hence his likening of the scientific anarchist to 'an undercover agent who plays the game of Reason in order to undercut the authority of Reason' (Feyerabend 1993, p. 23). He is influenced here by the Austrian satirists Johann Nestroy and Karl Kraus and by Dadaism, that nihilistic movement earlier this century which stressed the absurd and the unpredictable in artistic creation. Feyerabend stresses the absurd and the unpredictable in scientific knowledge.

Anything goes, then? Feyerabend does boldly say as much. He even describes this as the only principle 'that can be defended under *all* circumstances and in all stages of human development' (Feyerabend 1993, pp. 18–19). Yet he has norms of his own. For one thing, he demands that scientists test out their perceptions. The willingness to do this constitutes the difference between science and non-science (or, in his more forthright terms, between the domains of the respectable thinker and the crank). Adopting a certain point of view means a starting point for research, not some kind of conclusion. Cranks will flatly deny that any issue exists or will be content to defend their position, but the respectable thinker thoroughly tests out the usefulness of the viewpoint, taking full account of factors that seem to favour its opponents. As one would expect from what has been said of Feyerabend already, he does not identify the respectable thinker simply with the person who is faithful to the accepted line in science. One example of this is his refusal to dismiss creationism out of hand as a crank viewpoint and his opposition to its exclusion from school curricula. If people are willing to test out their perceptions and have them tested out by others, they are respectable thinkers, no matter how unconventional their thinking, and they have a place in the generation of human knowledge.

How, then, should scientists test out their perceptions? By *counter-induction.* Counterinductive measures are not Popper-style attempts to falsify theories and hypotheses. 'Methodologists may point to the importance of falsifications', Feyerabend writes scathingly, 'but they blithely use falsified theories' (1993, p. 50). No, we need rules that will 'enable us to choose between theories which we have already tested *and which are falsified'* (Feyerabend 1993, p. 51). Counterinduction is just such a 'measuring-stick'. Rather than an attempt to prove something false, it is a calling of 'commonly-used concepts' into question by developing something with which they can be compared.

> Therefore, the first step in our criticism of customary concepts and customary reactions is to step outside the circle and either to invent a new conceptual system, for example, a new theory, that clashes with the most carefully established observational results and confounds the most plausible theoretical principles, or to import such a system from outside science, from religion, from mythology, from the ideas of incompetents, or the ramblings of madmen. (Feyerabend 1993, pp. 52–3)

Ideas of incompetents? Ramblings of madmen? Obviously, anything does go! Feyerabend's point, of course, is that, if we want to examine something we are using all the time, we cannot discover it from the inside. We need, he tells us, 'an *external* standard of criticism', 'a set of alternative assumptions' (Feyerabend 1993, p. 22). This is his strategy of counterinduction. Counterinduction is 'both a *fact*—science could not exist without it—and a legitimate and much needed *move* in the game of science' (Feyerabend 1993, p. 53).

Behind this stance is Feyerabend's recognition that scientific thinking, like all human thought, is historically conditioned through and through.

> However, the material which a scientist actually has at his disposal, his laws, his experimental results, his mathematical techniques, his epistemological prejudices, his attitude towards the absurd consequences of the theories which he accepts, is indeterminate in many ways, ambiguous, *and never fully separated from the historical background.* (Feyerabend 1993, p. 51)

Ideas being historically conditioned and never absolute, Paul Feyerabend believes in pushing them to their extremes. In *Three Dialogues on Knowledge,* a series of dialogues based on the Socratic model, he reveals that, when he comes across unusual ideas, he tries them out. His way of trying them out is to push them to the limit. 'There is', he tells us (1991, p. 50), 'not a single idea, no matter how absurd and repulsive, that has not a sensible aspect, and there is not a single view, no matter how plausible and humanitarian, that does not encourage and then conceal our stupidity and our criminal tendencies'. Many would be comfortable enough with this thought when it is applied to cultural understandings and socio-political stances. People find it far more challenging when applied, as Feyerabend intends it to be applied, to scientific 'truths'. The point is, of course, that Feyerabend refuses to accept the distinction. For him, scientific truths are no less cultural in character, and no less socio-political in origin, than any other of the beliefs we hold. He tells us, in fact, that 'rationalists clamouring for objectivity and rationality are just trying to sell a tribal creed of their own' (Feyerabend 1987, p. 301).

Feyerabend, along with Popper and Kuhn, has had an impact. Positivism, as we have seen, postulates the objective existence of meaningful reality. It considers such meaningful reality to be value-neutral, ahistorical and cross-cultural. It believes that, if one goes about it in the right way, one can identify such reality with certitude. What people like Popper, Kuhn and Feyerabend have done is to question one or other, or all, of these tenets in quite radical fashion.

In the wake of their considerations, some have come to reject positivism and the objectivism that informs it and to adopt a constructionist view of meaningful reality. Others remain within the positivist camp but temper very significantly the status they ascribe to their findings, the claims they make about them. It is not possible, they have come to recognise, to find some Archimedean point from which realities in the world can be viewed free from any influence of the observer's standpoint. They admit that, no matter how faithfully the scientist adheres to scientific method, research outcomes are neither totally objective nor unquestionably certain. They may claim a higher level of objectivity and certitude for scientific findings than for other opinions and beliefs, but the absoluteness has gone and claims to validity are tentative and qualified.

It is this humbler version of the scientific approach, one that no longer claims an epistemologically or metaphysically privileged position, that has come to be known as post-positivism.

Reporting our research requires us to set forth the research process we have engaged in and to do so faithfully and comprehensively. It is, after all, our account of the research process that establishes the credentials of our research. Why should anyone set store by what we are asserting as a result of our investigation? And what store should anyone set by it? The only satisfactory answer to these questions is, 'Look at the way we have gone about it'. The process itself is our only justification. For that reason, expounding our research process, including its more theoretical moorings (or, if you prefer, the assumptions we bring to our methodology and methods), assumes obvious and crucial importance.

What store should anyone set by our research findings? Even in putting the question, we sense another question coming to the fore—and a prior question, into the bargain. What store are we *asking* people to set by our research findings? After all, we may be presenting our findings as objective truths, claiming validity, perhaps generalisability, on their behalf. In that case, we are calling upon people to accept our findings as established fact, or at least as close to established fact as our research has enabled us to reach. On the other hand, we may be offering our findings as interpretation. It is a certain spin we have put on the data. In that case we are inviting people to weigh our interpretation, judge whether it has been soundly arrived at and is plausible (convincing, even?), and decide whether it has application to their interests and concerns.

In other words, we may be presenting our research in positivist terms or non-positivist terms. Let us say it again: it is a matter of positivism vs non-positivism, not a matter of quantitative vs qualitative. It is possible for a quantitative piece of work to be offered in non-positivist form. On the other hand, there is plenty of scope for qualitative research to be understood positivistically or situated in an overall positivist setting, and, therefore, for even self-professed qualitative researchers to be quite positivist in orientation and purpose. When investigators talk, as they often do, of exploring meanings by way of qualitative methods and then 'confirming' or 'validating' their findings by a quantitative study, they are privileging the latter in a thorough-going positivist manner. What turns their study into a positivist piece of work is not the use of quantitative methods but the attribution of objectivity, validity and generalisability to quantitative findings.

Accordingly, our consideration of positivism and post-positivism in this chapter turns out to be relevant enough. Called upon to set forth our research process incisively and unequivocally, we find ourselves unable to do that without, for a start, confronting the objectivist understanding of meaning and the positivist understanding of reality— and declaring our hand.

Interpretivism: For and Against Culture

MICHAEL CROTTY

We pass the word around; we ponder how the case is put by different people; we read the poetry; we meditate over the literature; we play the music; we change our minds; we reach an understanding.

Lewis Thomas, *The Medusa and the Snail*

In the schema presented in the Introduction, the first column is headed 'Epistemology'. Objectivism, which we have related to positivism and post-positivism, and constructionism, which we dealt with in the last chapter, are examples of epistemological positions encountered within the field of social research. As stated already, we shall encounter examples of a more subjectivist epistemology when we come to postmodernism. Now, however, we are returning to our second column, already visited in our discussion of positivism, and will concern ourselves with further theoretical perspectives embedded within research methodologies.

'Theoretical perspective' is being taken here to mean the philosophical stance lying behind a methodology. The theoretical perspective provides a context for the process involved and a basis for its logic and its criteria. Another way to put it is to say that, whenever one examines a particular methodology, one discovers a complexus of assumptions buried within it. It is these assumptions that constitute one's theoretical perspective and they largely have to do with the world that the methodology envisages. Different ways of viewing the world shape different ways of researching the world.

The theoretical perspective considered in this chapter—interpretivism—emerged in contradistinction to positivism in attempts to understand and explain human and social reality. As Thomas Schwandt puts it (1994, p. 125), 'interpretivism was conceived in reaction to the effort to develop a natural science of the social. Its foil was largely logical empiricist methodology and the bid to apply that framework to human inquiry'.

A positivist approach would follow the methods of the natural sciences and, by way of allegedly value-free, detached observation, seek to identify universal features of humanhood, society and history that offer explanation and hence control and predictability. The interpretivist approach, to the contrary, *looks for culturally derived and historically situated interpretations of the social life-world.*

Roots of interpretivism

Interpretivism is often linked to the thought of Max Weber (1864–1920), who suggests that in the human sciences we are concerned with *Verstehen* (understanding). This has been taken to mean that Weber is contrasting the interpretative approach (*Verstehen*, understanding) needed in the human and social sciences with the explicative approach (*Erklären*, explaining), focused on causality, that is found in the natural sciences. Hence the emphasis on the different methods employed in each, leading to the clear (though arguably exaggerated) distinction found in the textbooks between qualitative research methods and quantitative research methods. However, discussion of whether methods used in the human and social sciences ought to differ from those of the natural sciences predates Weber's concern with the issue.

Wilhelm Dilthey (1833–1911) does, indeed, contrast *Verstehen* and *Erklären*. He proposes that natural reality and social reality are in themselves different kinds of reality and their investigation therefore requires different methods.

Neo-Kantian philosophers Wilhelm Windelband (1848–1915) and Heinrich Rickert (1863–1936), while rejecting the notion that there is some kind of real distinction between natural reality and social reality, accept that there is a logical distinction, one posited by the mind, between the two. One implication this bears is that, in studying one and the other, we have different purposes in view. In the case of nature, science is looking for consistencies, regularities, the 'law' (*nomos*) that obtains. In the case of human affairs—in historical studies, for instance—we are concerned with the individual (*idios*) case. So Windelband talks of natural science seeking what is *nomothetic* and the human and social sciences seeking what is *idiographic*.

For his part, Rickert talks of a *generalising* method (in the natural sciences) over against an *individualising* method (in the human and social sciences). Thus, a distinction is made between the natural sciences, which seek to establish general laws, and the cultural sciences, which isolate individual phenomena in order to trace their unique development.

What about Weber, then? On the one hand, he agrees with Windelband and Rickert in rejecting Dilthey's real distinction between natural reality and social reality and positing only a logical distinction between them. On the other hand, Weber does not feel that this necessitates the use of different methods in researching these two realms of being.

As Weber sees it, both the natural sciences and the human and social sciences may be concerned at any given time with either the nomothetic or the idiographic. Uniqueness and historicity are manifest in nature as well as humanity, while general covering laws may explain human behaviour as well as natural phenomena. Sociology can be found to engage in empirical research to discover what regularly occurs, while biology or astronomy may sometimes study unique aspects of particular phenomena. Weber holds, then, that the one scientific method should apply to these two forms of science and should cater for both nomothetic and idiographic inquiry.

Admittedly, the natural sciences are primarily concerned with the nomothetic and the human or social sciences primarily with the idiographic. This establishes a different orientation in the one area and the other. Our interest in the social world tends to focus on exactly those aspects that are unique, individual and qualitative, whereas our interest in the natural world focuses on more abstract phenomena, that is, those exhibiting quantifiable, empirical regularities. This, however, is a matter of interest rather than something the nature of the science in question specifically calls for. For his part, Weber looks for empirical validation of any claims made in the social arena and spends the best part of a lifetime attempting to elaborate a methodology that will enable him to verify claims in this way.

To be sure, Weber's *Verstehen* sociology locates the study of society in the context of human beings acting and interacting.

Interpretative sociology considers the individual and his action as the basic unit, as its 'atom' ... In this approach the individual is also the upper limit; and the sole carrier of meaningful conduct ... In general, for sociology, such concepts as 'state', 'association', 'feudalism', and the like, designate certain categories of human interaction. Hence it is the task of sociology to reduce these concepts to 'under-standable' action, that is without exception, to the actions of participating men. (Weber 1970, p. 55)

Here Weber is expressing the need to focus social inquiry on the meanings and values of act-ing persons and therefore on their subjective 'meaning-complex of action'. Nevertheless, he defines sociology as 'a science which attempts the interpretive understanding of social action in order thereby to arrive at a causal explanation of its course and effects' (1968, p. 3). Sociology's 'concepts and generalizations are fashioned on the premise that it can claim to make a contribu-tion to the causal explanation of some historically and culturally important phenomenon' (Weber 1962, p. 51).

Causal! This hardly squares with the position of those who claim to stand in the line of Weber's *Verstehen* but take it to have no interest in causality and contrast it with the *Erklären* approach that does. 'Interpretivism', says Silverman (1990, p. 126), 'rests on the emphatic denial that we can understand cultural phenomena in causal terms'. If that is the case, the interpretivism Silverman is speaking of is far removed from Weber's. Weber certainly is interested in causes. He wants to explain as well as understand. He writes (1962, pp. 35, 40) of 'explanatory under-standing' and a 'correct causal interpretation of a concrete course of behavior'. Nowak, in fact, goes so far as to claim that, for Weber, '*Verstehen* is a method of explaining and of explaining only' (in Weiss 1986, p. 68).

Going so far may be going too far, all the same, and, in citing Nowak, Weiss feels the need for further distinction. 'Perhaps a better way of saying this would be that *Verstehen* is "for the purpose of explanation"' (Weiss 1986, p. 68). Certainly, Weiss's account accords better with Weber's own definition of sociology. For Weber, as far as human affairs are concerned, any understanding of causation comes through an interpretative understanding of social action and involves an explanation of relevant antecedent phenomena as meaning-complexes. This role ascribed to *Verstehen* implies a difference in outcome in comparison with the natural sciences. As Weber sees it, the causation that the social scientist seeks to clarify is at best 'adequate' rather than 'necessary'. He is ready to 'consider an interpretation of a sequence of events to be causally *adequate*, if on the basis of past experience it appears probable that it will always occur in the same way' (1962, p. 39).

As already suggested, it is Weber's contention that, in any scientific study of society, *Verstehen* has to be substantiated by empirical evidence. He has a passion for empirical knowledge and stresses the need for scientifically valid historical and social data. Weber's philosophy, Lewis assures us, is 'an empiricist venture'.

It was as strictly an empirical sociology as academic philosophy was speculative. For it attempted to establish a science of social fact, and to use an appropriate methodology devised for historico-political material rather than for the natural sciences, a methodology which would describe and classify his-torical and social facts schematically and deduce experimentally the laws-system of society. (Lewis 1975, p. 39)

Weber finds the centrepiece of this 'appropriate methodology' in what he calls the *ideal type*. This is his principal diagnostic tool, a heuristic device for the precise purpose of amassing empirical data. It seeks to subject social behaviour, for all its subjective dimension, to the scien-tific need for the empirical verification of all knowledge.

Using the word 'tool' to describe Weber's ideal type points up the important fact that it is something the social scientist makes up. It is not something found through an analysis of what is real. Weber (1949, pp. 90–4) calls his ideal types conceptual or mental constructs. They involve imagination, he tells us, and they are Utopian in nature. What the ideal type embodies is the 'pure case', with no admixture of fortuitous and confusing features. As such, it never exists in reality, but can serve as a useful model to guide the social inquirer in addressing real-life cases and discerning where and to what extent the real deviates from the ideal. It reveals, Weber tells us (1970, p. 323), what is 'possible and "adequate"'.

Weber sets strict limits to the use of his ideal types. He believes that ideal-type methodology is applicable only to social behaviour that can be described as 'rational goal-oriented conduct' and not to 'rational value-oriented conduct', 'affectual conduct', or 'traditionalist conduct'. What is being studied by way of the ideal type is the outcome of persons acting under a common motivation and choosing suitable means to the ends they have in view. It is only in regard to such rational goal-oriented conduct that we can take stock of empirical data according to preconceived rational criteria implicitly accepted by both actor and observer.

Alfred Schutz (1899–1959) is very taken with Weber's ideal-type methodology. Schutz attempts to ground it philosophically and develop it further by way of his own 'second-order' constructs, which he refers to as 'puppets' or *homunculi* (1973, p. 255). Like Weber, and the similarly minded scholars who preceded him from Dilthey on, Schutz strives to harmonise the idiographic with the nomothetic and make possible a study of human affairs that can be said to be rigorously scientific. It was this very concern that launched the *Verstehen* approach in the first place.

In more recent times, interpretivism seems to have largely cut itself loose from these traditional moorings. While continuing to trace its lineage back to Weber and his call for 'understanding' and 'interpretation', the *Verstehen* approach has not maintained his passion for empirical verification or his concern to explain in causal terms. In most instances, it has accepted what Weber refused to accept, that is, that the human and social sciences require methods essentially different from those of the natural sciences. It is usually not easy to discern the basis for this demand of different methods. Often without thematising the issue, interpretative researchers seem to evince either Dilthey's hard and fast distinction between the subject matter of these two areas of science or at least Windelband's and Rickert's 'distinction of reason' along with the nomothetic/idiographic divide to which these distinctions lead. Blaikie, for one, writes of the 'fundamental difference between the subject matters of the natural and social sciences' (1993, p. 36). Hence the widespread espousal of quantitative research methods in the one and very different qualitative research methods commonly found in the other.

For all that, studies of the natural world and the social world have come closer together. This has been largely due to the development pointed up in Chapter 2, namely, the recognition by many thinkers that positivist science's age-old claims to certitude and objectivity cannot be sustained and that the findings of natural science are themselves social constructions and human interpretations, albeit a particular form of such constructions and interpretations.

What we understand today as the *Verstehen* or interpretivist approach to human inquiry has appeared historically in many guises. It will be useful to consider three historical streams that have borne it along. In their historical order of appearance, these are hermeneutics, phenomenology, and symbolic interactionism. It will suit our purposes to reverse the order.

We will consider symbolic interactionism and phenomenology in the remainder of this chapter. These contrast with each other quite sharply in their attitude towards culture as our inherited meaning system. Symbolic interactionism explores the understandings abroad in culture as the meaningful matrix that guides our lives. Phenomenology, however, treats culture with a good measure of caution and suspicion. Our culture may be enabling but, paradoxically, it is also crippling. While it offers us entrée to a comprehensive set of meanings, it shuts us off from an abundant font of untapped significance.

For culture and against culture, then. Two very different traditions. As researchers, we learn from both.

Symbolic interactionism

Symbolic interactionism offers what is very much an American perspective on life, society and the world. As already noted when discussing constructionism, it stems from the thought of pragmatist philosopher and social psychologist George Herbert Mead. Mead's teaching, which extended over a period of almost 40 years, principally at the University of Chicago, is encapsulated in a posthumous work, *Mind, Self and Society* (1934). This book was compiled by grateful students from papers Mead had left and lecture notes they had accumulated. It is to one student in particular, Herbert Blumer, that most credit must go for the impact Mead's thought has had in the realm of sociology.

In a much-cited formulation, Blumer (1969, p. 2) enunciates three basic interactionist assumptions:

- 'that human beings act toward things on the basis of the meanings that these things have for them';
- 'that the meaning of such things is derived from, and arises out of, the social interaction that one has with one's fellows';
- 'that these meanings are handled in, and modified through, an interpretive process used by the person in dealing with the things he encounters'.

To do them justice, these tenets need to be set against the backdrop of pragmatist philosophy, for the pragmatism informing Mead's social psychology and Blumer's sociology remains a significant dimension of symbolic interactionism today.

Pragmatist philosophy

Within pragmatism, the quintessentially American philosophy, we find diverse streams. There are, one has to say, many pragmatisms. For all that, pragmatist approaches display a number of common characteristics, even if attempts to articulate these characteristics, as in Rescher's generalised account here, tend to reflect a popularised view of pragmatism rather than the careful nuances of its founders:

> The characteristic idea of philosophical pragmatism is that efficacy in practical application—the issue of 'which works out most effectively'—somehow provides a standard for the determination of truth in the case of statements, rightness in the case of actions, and value in the case of appraisals. (1995, p. 710)

Pragmatism derives, in the first instance, from the work of Charles Sanders Peirce. In launching his pragmatism, Peirce was seeking a critical philosophy. He insisted (1931–58, vol. 5, p. 9) that '*pragmatism* is not a *Weltanschauung* but it is a method of reflexion having for its purpose to render ideas clear'.[10] Peirce went on to develop his own version of phenomenology—'phaneroscopy' he came to call it in the end—independently of the acknowledged founder of phenomenology, Edmund Husserl. Peirce looked to determine the elemental categories present to the mind in their 'Firstness' or qualitative immediacy. In doing so, Peirce was, to a significant degree, paralleling the phenomenologists' efforts to delineate phenomena encountered in immediate experience (Spiegelberg 1981).

Peirce's work remained largely unknown, and certainly unacknowledged, until pragmatism became popular through the work of William James some years later. John Dewey had already been involved with pragmatism for many years and it was the James/Dewey version that now came to the fore. Peirce, unhappy with the turn pragmatism had taken, began to call his own approach 'pragmaticism' instead. This, he hoped, would prove sufficiently ugly a term to discourage any would-be kidnappers!

What had happened to the pragmatism launched by Peirce that led him to disown it? Well, for one thing, it was far less critical. As we have already seen in discussing constructionism, some have gone so far as to accuse James's and Dewey's versions of pragmatism of being totally uncritical. While, in the case of James and Dewey, this appears to rest on a gross misreading, the allegation can certainly be sustained when levelled at the pragmatism that developed later. Pragmatism did become essentially an uncritical exploration of cultural ideas and values in terms of their practical outcomes. Even in James and Dewey, the authentic meaning of ideas and values is linked to their outcomes and therefore to the practices in which they are embedded. Pragmatism, says William James (1950, p. 15), is the 'attitude of looking away from first things, principles, "categories", supposed necessities; and of looking towards last things, fruits, consequences, facts'.

> When it is maintained that conceptualization is purposive [Peirce], or that thought is teleological [James], or that ideas are instruments [Dewey], the methodological principle these doctrines suggest is that the analysis of meanings (of signs, i.e., ideas, concepts, statements) is an analysis of certain kinds of action in certain contexts . . . For the pragmatist, therefore, meaning has reference, if sometimes only remotely so, to the ordinary situations and conditions in which actions occur. (Thayer 1968, p. 429)

In this understanding of things, experience and culture come to be almost interchangeable terms. Seeking the meaning of experience becomes an exploration of culture. Dewey once remarked that he would have avoided many misunderstandings if he had used the word 'culture' instead of 'experience' (in Thayer 1968, p. 173, n.28).

The view of culture and society that pragmatism came to adopt is essentially optimistic and progressivist. The pragmatist world is a world to be explored and made the most of, not a world to be subjected to radical criticism. Horkheimer describes pragmatists as 'liberal, tolerant, optimistic' and believes, in fact, that pragmatists cannot deal with the possibility that, at a given historical moment, 'truth might . . . turn out to be completely shocking to humanity' (1974, p. 51). 'Increasingly', writes Horowitz (1966, p. 29), 'pragmatism came to stand for acquiescence in the social order'. Mary Rogers describes what emerged as a 'pragmatic-naturalist philosophy which focuses on the nature and genesis of a shared world, intersubjectivity, and communication' (1981, p. 140).

This, to be sure, is the focus found in the work of Dewey's associate, George Herbert Mead, through whose thought pragmatism enters sociology in the form of symbolic interactionism.

From Mead to ethnography

As we have noted, Mead attributes our very personhood to social forces that shape us and our behaviour. 'A person', Mead says (1934, p. 162), 'is a personality because he belongs to a community, because he takes over the institutions of that community into his own conduct'. This certainly puts the spotlight on the practices found in any given culture as the very source of personhood. For Mead (1934, p. 7), 'the whole (society) is prior to the part (the individual)'. We owe to society our very being as conscious and self-conscious entities, for that being arises from a process of symbolic interaction—interaction, that is to say, by way of significant gestures.

> Only in terms of gestures as significant symbols is the existence of mind or intelligence possible; for only in terms of gestures which are significant symbols can thinking—which is simply an internalized or implicit conversation of the individual with himself by means of such gestures—take place. (Mead 1934, p. 47)

To 'enter the attitudes of the community' and 'take over the institutions of the community', as Mead argues we inevitably do in our emergence into personhood, we must be able to *take the role of others*. We have to see ourselves as social objects and we can only do that through adopting the standpoint of others. The process begins in childhood, Mead teaches us. It starts with early imitative acts and proceeds via play (in which children act out the role of others) and games (in which children have to put themselves in the place of others and think about how others think and act). With games the child starts to think in terms of the 'generalised other'. Later this generalised other will be related to broader social institutions.

Here we find emerging a central notion of symbolic interactionism: the putting of oneself in the place of the other. Coser stresses this point:

Mead must be credited alongside Cooley and other pragmatists with having been instrumental in stressing the need for always considering situations from the point of view of the actor. For him, just as for Weber, when the sociologist refers to meaning, it is to the subjective meaning actors impute to their actions. (1971, p. 340)

In symbolic interactionism as a theoretical perspective informing methodologies for social research, this notion remains pivotal, as numerous commentators attest:

Methodologically, the implication of the symbolic interactionist perspective is that the actor's view of actions, objects, and society has to be studied seriously. The situation must be seen as the actor sees it, the meanings of objects and acts must be determined in terms of the actor's meanings, and the organization of a course of action must be understood as the actor organizes it. The role of the actor in the situation would have to be taken by the observer in order to see the social world from his perspective. (Psathas 1973, pp. 6–7)

Some interpretive sociologists—those identified as 'symbolic interactionists' for example—are content to operate with a relatively naive set of assumptions about how we come to know about social phenomena. They are prepared to accept the meanings that the actors attribute to social phenomena at face value, and proceed to erect their systematic interpretations on these foundations. This implies that the sociological observer must exercise sufficient discipline on himself to ensure that it is indeed the *actors* meanings that are recorded in his notebook and not merely his own. (Mitchell 1977, pp. 115–16)

Methodologically, symbolic interactionism directs the investigator to take, to the best of his ability, the standpoint of those studied. (Denzin 1978, p. 99)

This role taking is an *interaction*. It is *symbolic* interaction, for it is possible only because of the 'significant symbols'—that is, language and other symbolic tools—that we humans share and through which we communicate. Only through dialogue can one become aware of the perceptions, feelings and attitudes of others and interpret their meanings and intent. Hence the term 'symbolic interactionism' (though it is a term that Mead himself never used).

Given the emphasis on putting oneself in the place of the other and seeing things from the perspective of others, it is not surprising that symbolic interactionism should take to its bosom the research methodology developed within cultural anthropology, that is, ethnography. American cultural anthropology was shaped most decisively by Franz Boas, whose experience in studying Arctic Eskimos is said to have turned him from a scientist's view of cognition to an historian's view of culture. Cultures, as Boas comes to see them, are irreducible and incomparable. Through Boas's influence, cultural relativism succeeded in dominating American anthropology, accompanied by a strong rejection of all ethno-centrism (Bloch 1983, pp. 124–8). Culture is not to be called into question; it is not to be criticised, least of all by someone from another culture. Instead, one is to observe it as closely as possible, attempt to take the place of those within the culture, and search out the insider's perspective. Herein lies the origin of ethnography, born to anthropology but adopted (and adapted) by sociology.

For ethnography, then, as for the symbolic interactionism that now commonly forms its matrix, the notion of taking the place of the other is central.

> . . . ethnography is a form of research in which the social settings to be studied, however familiar to the researcher, must be treated as anthropologically strange; and the task is to document the culture—the perspectives and practices—of the people in these settings. The aim is to 'get inside' the way each group of people sees the world. (Hammersley 1985, p. 152)

Interactionist research

Ethnography undertaken from an interactionist perspective has been framed schematically in many ways.

One form in which it has emerged has been the *dramaturgical approach* associated especially with Erving Goffman. Research done in this vein draws on the familiar analogy between social life and the theatre. Actors on a stage form a cast. The cast teams with producer, director, choreographer, stage hands, and the like, to present a theatrical production. It is possible to view people interacting in a life situation (family, social club) or work setting (courtroom, operating theatre) in much the same light. In these settings we find people speaking, dressing and generally comporting themselves in certain ways; we find them displaying certain instruments or items of property; we find them moving, as it were, between 'front-stage' and 'back-stage'—all of this to convince others as to who they purport to be and what they purport to be doing. In this figurative sense, they have an audience and seek to influence the audience by way of roles and scripts and stage props. Who would deny that there are rituals in social life, some quite overt and others subtly disguised, which are very meaningful forms of interaction? Dramaturgy as a form of interactionist research identifies such rituals, examines their rubrical directives, and attempts to delineate their meanings and outcomes.

Game theory is not dissimilar. It analyses social interaction using the everyday concept of the game. The rules of a game define a team of players, specify a set of permissible manoeuvres, and construct a context ('match', 'set', 'bout', 'event' . . .) within which players can play. Viewing social life as a game, one can divide the broad array of social interactions into various events. Within the setting of a particular event, one can go on to distinguish the rules of the game. It is these rules that set boundaries and parameters, appoint players, govern what players are permitted and required to do, and determine the prize for success or the 'wooden spoon' for failure.

Another interactionist strategy takes the form of *negotiated-order theory*. There are many accounts of society that present social settings as definitively structured and offering social actors very clear-cut roles. Negotiated-order theory disputes this view. In this stream of interactionist inquiry, to the contrary, societal arrangements and procedures are considered to be constantly reworked by those who live and work within them. Work settings in which, sometimes on a day-to-day basis, tasks are reassigned, roles exchanged, responsibilities shouldered, and partnerships formed, typify this view of things. In such settings—and, indeed, quite broadly within society as a whole—there is an ongoing, albeit often tacit, process of negotiation and adjustment of action. Analysing this process in specific social situations has proved a useful avenue for interactionist inquiry. Anselm Strauss and his associates have been to the fore in exploring its potential.

Yet another form of interactionist inquiry has to do with the study of deviance. *Labelling theory* models itself on the everyday ways in which we categorise people and things. Society is quick to style certain individuals and groups 'deviant'. However, according to labelling theorists such as Howard Becker in his 1963 book *Outsiders*, while this says much about the society in question, it says little about the behaviour of the deviants. Deviance, from this perspective, is simply behaviour that people so label. Thus, in studying deviants, one is studying only those who have been labelled by society as having engaged in deviant behaviour. This being the case, searching for causes of deviant behaviour by, say, analysing the heredity and environment of so-called deviants, would appear a futile and misguided enterprise. Instead, symbolic interactionism directs us to a study of the labelling process itself. Why is it, we should ask ourselves, that society wants to exclude some members from full and free participation in its life? And what are the mechanisms it uses to do so? Symbolic interactionism s involvement in research of this kind has brought it an enviable reputation for being on the side of the 'underdog'.

Symbolic interactionism has also spawned the research methodology known as *grounded theory*. Grounded theory can be viewed as a specific form of ethnographic inquiry that, through a series of carefully planned steps, develops theoretical ideas. Throughout the process, it seeks to ensure that the theory emerging arises from the data and not from some other source. It is a process of inductive theory building based squarely on observation of the data themselves. Barney Glaser and Anselm Strauss launched this approach in *The Discovery of Grounded Theory* in 1967 and it has subsequently undergone a number of modifications and refinements and been issued in a number of variant forms.

For qualitative research, symbolic interactionism is a diversified and enriching matrix. Several streams have flowed from its headwaters in the thought of Mead. One stream has been the Chicago School with its emphasis on the origin and development of meaning. Another has been the Iowa School, which moved to a much more empirical and quantitative orientation. Then there are the role-theory interactionists, who tend to make social structures far more pivotal to their interactionism. Whatever the stream, the theoretical perspective of symbolic interactionism has clearly proved useful in identifying research questions and framing research processes for several generations of researchers.

Phenomenology

Phenomenology, in itself, is a simple enough concept. The phenomenological movement was launched under the battle cry of 'Back to the things themselves!'. The 'things themselves', as phenomenologists understand the phrase, are phenomena that present themselves immediately to us as conscious human beings. Phenomenology suggests that, if we lay aside, as best we can, the prevailing understandings of those phenomena and revisit our immediate experience of them, possibilities for new meaning emerge for us or we witness at least an authentication and enhancement of former meaning (Crotty 1996a).

This line of thought presumes that there *are* 'things themselves' to visit in our experience, that is, objects to which our understandings relate. That there are indeed such objects is what the notion of intentionality proclaims and it lies at the heart of phenomenology. Husserl (1931, p. 245) describes intentionality as 'a concept which at the threshold of phenomenology is quite indispensable as a starting-point and basis'. Natanson (1973, p. 103) calls it 'the axis of phenomenology'.

We have been introduced to intentionality in considering constructionism. It denotes the essential relationship between conscious subjects and their objects. Consciousness is always consciousness *of* something. An object is always an object *for* someone. The object, in other words, cannot be adequately described apart from the subject, nor can the subject be adequately described apart from the object. From a more existentialist viewpoint, intentionality bespeaks the relationship between us as human beings and our world. We are beings-in-the-world. Because of this, we cannot be described apart from our world, just as our world—always a human world—cannot be described apart from us.

We might recall at this point the distinction we made between constructivism and constructionism. Constructivism describes the individual human subject engaging with objects in the world and making sense of them. Constructionism, to the contrary, denies that this is what actually happens, at least in the first instance. Instead, each of us is introduced directly to a whole world of meaning. The *mélange* of cultures and sub-cultures into which we are born provides us with meanings. These meanings we are taught and we learn in a complex and subtle process of enculturation. They establish a tight grip upon us and, by and large, shape our thinking and behaviour throughout our lives.

Our cultural heritage can therefore be seen as pre-empting the task of meaning making so that, for the most part, we simply do not do what constructivism describes us as doing. Phenomenology, however, invites us to do it. It requires us to engage with phenomena in our world and make sense of them directly and immediately. What about the understandings we are already saddled with? These we have to 'bracket' to the best of our ability and let the experience of phenomena speak to us at first hand (Crotty 1996b). Thus, we find phenomenologists talking about 'primordial phenomena', the 'immediate, original data of our consciousness', the 'phenomena in their unmediated and originary manifestation to consciousness'. Big words, some of them, but they refer to *what we directly experience*; that is, the objects of our experience before we start thinking about them, interpreting them or attributing any meaning to them. These are the *things themselves*.

That phenomenology requires us to place our usual understandings in abeyance and have a fresh look at things has been driven home to us by phenomenologist after phenomenologist.

- Phenomenology invites us to 'set aside all previous habits of thought, see through and break down the mental barriers which these habits have set along the horizons of our thinking ... to learn to see what stands before our eyes' (Husserl 1931, p. 43).
- Phenomenology is 'a return to the unadulterated phenomena' and an 'unusually obstinate attempt to look at the phenomena and to remain faithful to them before even thinking of them' (Spiegelberg 1982, pp. 680, 717).
- Phenomenology 'exhorts a pristine acquaintance with phenomena unadulterated by preconceptions: it encourages the inquirer to sustain an intuitive grasp of what is there by "opening his eyes", "keeping them open", "looking and listening", "not getting blinded"' (Heron 1992, p. 164).
- 'Phenomenology asks us not to take our received notions for granted but . . . to call into question our whole culture, our manner of seeing the world and being in the world in the way we have learned it growing up' (Wolff 1984, p. 192).
- 'It is the task of phenomenology ... to make us conscious of what the world was like before we learned how to see it' (Marton 1986, p. 40).
- Phenomenology is an 'attempt to recover a fresh perception of existence, one unprejudiced by acculturation' (Sadler 1969, p. 377).

In this same vein, Merleau-Ponty tells us (1962, p. xiv) that 'in order to see the world and grasp it as paradoxical, we must break with our familiar acceptance of it'. The outcome, he assures us, is 'nothing but the unmotivated upsurge of the world'. It is as if Merleau-Ponty sees the world as a seething cauldron of potential meaning that is held down by our received notions. Once phenomenology 'slackens the intentional threads which attach us to the world', we experience the upsurge and can 'watch the forms of transcendence fly up like sparks from a fire' (1962,

p. xiii). Merleau-Ponty employs yet another metaphor—the blossoming of wild flowers. Our phenomenological endeavour to break with inherited understandings 'awakens a wild-flowering world and mind'. 'This renewal of the world', Merleau-Ponty assures us (1964, p. 181), 'is also mind's renewal, a rediscovery of that brute mind which, untamed by any culture, is asked to create culture anew'.

Lying behind this attempt to put our culturally derived meanings in abeyance and renew culture in this radical fashion is a deeply rooted suspicion of culture and the understandings it imposes on us. 'Phenomenology is much more than a suspension of assumptions. The phenomenological reduction is a change of attitude that throws suspicion on everyday experiences' (Armstrong 1976, p. 252).

Why be suspicious of culture? Surely we owe it our very humanness. Phenomenologists are happy to acknowledge that debt. They recognise that it is culture that allows us to emerge from our immediate environment and reflect upon it. They agree that it is because of culture—our symbols, our meaning systems—that we know our past and can plan our future. Yes, our culture is liberating. However, as we have already noted, in agreeing that culture is liberating, phenomenologists remain very aware that it is also limiting. It sets us free but at the same time it sets boundaries. It makes us human but in and through *this* particular culture, *this* special system of significant symbols, *these* meanings. This is circumscribing. In imposing these meanings, it is excluding others. And we should never lose sight of the fact that the particular set of meanings it imposes has come into being to serve particular interests and will harbour its own forms of oppression, manipulation and other forms of injustice.

Another way to look at this matter is to underline the difference between a reality and any concept we might have of it. Because we are the kind of beings we are, we rely on concepts. We have a need to define and classify. Unfortunately, our definitions and classifications displace what they stand for in our experience of them so that, rather than concepts pointing us to realities, realities are relegated to being mere exemplifications of concepts. Yet a concept is never able to exhaust the richness of a phenomenon. As many philosophers and social scientists have pointed out, there is always so much that the concept fails to express. It leaves so much behind. Adorno, for one, is most conscious of this. His reflections, Tertulian tells us (1985, p. 95), 'always gravitate around the ineluctable gap between the concept's inherent abstraction and the rich density of the web of phenomena'. Following Benjamin, Adorno wants attention paid to 'everything that has slipped through the conventional conceptual net' (1981, p. 240). John Dewey too talks of what is 'left over', seeing it 'excluded by definition from full reality' (1929, p. 48).

The need we experience to define and classify proves to be a two-edged sword, therefore. Giving ourselves over to it, Cioran emphasises (1976, p. 222), dries us out and renders us barren. 'Our inmost aridity results from our allegiance to the rule of the *definite*, from our plea in bar of imprecision, that innate chaos which by renewing our deliriums keeps us from sterility.'

There is still more. Not only is our symbol system limited and limiting; it is also a barrier. It stands *for* things but it also comes to stand *between* things and us, that is, between us and our immediate experience of objects. It tends to substitute itself for what we actually see, hear, feel, smell, taste or even imagine. We have already seen a number of thinkers describing cultural understandings as nothing less than masks, screens or blindfolds. Heidegger goes so far as to describe them as a seduction and a dictatorship (1962, pp. 164, 213).

Phenomenology is about saying 'No!' to the meaning system bequeathed to us. It is about setting that meaning system aside. Far from inviting us to explore our everyday meanings as they stand, it calls upon us to put them in abeyance and open ourselves to the phenomena in their stark immediacy to see what emerges for us. True enough, the phenomena in their stark immediacy—the 'things themselves'—will prove elusive. In describing what comes into view within immediate experience (or even in thinking about what comes into view), we necessarily draw on language, on culture. For that reason, we end, not with a presuppositionless description of phenomena, but with a reinterpretation. It will be as much a construction as the sense we have laid aside, but as reinterpretation—as new meaning, or fuller meaning, or renewed meaning—it is precisely what we as phenomenologists are after.

To take a fresh look at phenomena is, of course, to call into question the current meanings we attribute to phenomena. Phenomenology, it is often said, calls into question what is taken for granted. It is critique and grounds a critical methodology. This has been said many times over from the very beginning of the phenomenological movement:

> ... the science having the unique function of effecting the criticism of all others and, at the same time, of itself is none other than phenomenology. (Husserl 1970a, vol. 1, p. 45)

> Phenomenology is a reflective enterprise, and in its reflection it is critical. (Larrabee 1990, p. 201)

> Phenomenological philosophy is first of all philosophical criticism ... I disengage from a claim in order to criticise it ... in the systematically adopted attitude of disengagement. (Zaner 1970, pp. 79–80)

> The value of phenomenology from a critical point of view is evident. The programme of reflecting upon all knowledge and experience, with the ideal of the 'self-givenness' in experience of what is meant, may well have an emancipating effect. (Farber 1991, p. 234)

From what we have considered to this point, two clear characteristics of phenomenology emerge. First of all, it has a note of *objectivity* about it. It is in search of objects of experience rather than being content with a description of the experiencing subject. Second, it is an exercise in *critique*. It calls into question what we take for granted.

In both respects it contrasts sharply with what is usually presented today as phenomenology, at least in the English-speaking world. Here phenomenology is generally seen as a study of people's subjective and everyday experiences. For a start, researchers claiming to be phenomenological talk of studying experience from the 'point of view' or 'perspective' of the subject. What these researchers are interested in is 'everyday' experience, experience as people understand it in everyday terms. If they talk at all of 'phenomenon', it is either used interchangeably with 'experience' or presented as an essence distilled from everyday accounts of experience, a total picture synthesised from partial accounts.

The phenomenological method as understood by these researchers is geared towards collecting and analysing data in ways that do not prejudice their subjective character. It puts in place a number of procedures to prevent, or at least minimise, the imposition of the researcher's presuppositions and constructions on the data. For a start, in most cases the researcher's own knowledge and presuppositions are said to be 'bracketed' so as not to taint the data. ('Bracketing' is a term introduced by Husserl and used by later representatives of the phenomenological movement, but here it is being used in an essentially different sense.) To ensure that the subjective character of the experiences is not prejudiced, these researchers tend to gather data by way of unstructured interviews in which only open-ended questions, if any, are asked. The researchers also want to make sure that the themes pinpointed in the data do, in fact, arise out of the data and are not imposed on them. So they talk of 'intuiting' the data and invite others (often including the subjects) to support their claim that the themes they point to are genuinely to be found in the data.

What has emerged here under the rubric of 'phenomenology' is a quite single-minded effort to identify, understand, describe and maintain the subjective experiences of the respondents. It is self-professedly *subjectivist* in approach (in the sense of being in search of people's subjective experience) and expressly *uncritical*.

In this attempt to understand and describe people's subjective experience, there is much talk of *putting oneself in the place of the other*. This is sometimes styled 'the great phenomenological principle'. Even so, the emphasis typically remains on common understandings and the meanings of common practices, so that phenomenological research of this kind emerges as an exploration, via personal experiences, of prevailing cultural understandings.

This is a new understanding of phenomenology and one may well ask how it came to be. As argued elsewhere (Crotty 1995, 1996a), it is very much a North American development. When phenomenology arrived on the shores of that continent, it was slow to receive any kind of welcome at all. In the end, within philosophy and to some extent and for some time within sociology, it gained a measure of acceptance and a number of adherents, but overall the indigenous forms of philosophy (pragmatism) and sociology (symbolic interactionism) won out. In psychology there was even less acceptance. In the 1960s, when phenomenologists like van Kaam and Giorgi and Colaizzi began expounding their stepwise methodologies for phenomenological research, humanistic psychology was already at centre stage and not about to surrender its hold on the audience. What seems to have happened is that, instead of being genuinely transplanted west of the Atlantic, phenomenology was grafted onto local stock. It was not permitted to set down its own roots. Consequently, its fruit embodies the American intellectual tradition far more than any features of its parent plant. It has been assimilated to that tradition. Its 'foreignness' has been removed. It has been translated into something familiar.

For one thing, we have noted how central to symbolic interactionism is the notion of 'taking the place of the other'. It is not central to phenomenology. One can read Spiegelberg's massive history of the phenomenological movement (1982) from cover to cover but the so-called 'great phenomenological principle' is not to be found there. Why should it be there? The phenomenology of the phenomenological movement is a first-person exercise. Each of us must explore our own experience, not the experience of others, for no one can take that step 'back to the things themselves' on our behalf.

In all this transformation the vocabulary of phenomenology remains. There is still talk of 'experience' and 'phenomenon', of 'reduction' and 'bracketing'—of 'intentionality', even; yet the meaning of these terms is no longer the meaning they have borne within the phenomenological movement from which they have been taken.[11]

Does it matter that this new understanding of phenomenology has arisen? It would seem to matter a great deal. Not because a different methodology has emerged laying claim to the name of phenomenology. The phenomenological movement emanating from Husserl has no monopoly on that word. The word was used in different senses long before Husserl borrowed it from Brentano. It is used in different senses today. There is no place here for any kind of purism or the mounting of a defence of some alleged orthodoxy. Still, it is legitimate enough to lament what has been lost in the process. What has been lost is the objective character and critical spirit, so strong in the phenomenological tradition.

When the focus on the object is lost, inquiry readily becomes very subjectivist—even, at times, narcissistic. And, when the critical spirit is lost, there is at best a failure to capture new or fuller meanings or a loss of opportunities to renew the understandings that already possess us. At worst, it means that oppression, exploitation and unfreedom are permitted to persist without question. To use Walzer's words, 'the maxim holds here as elsewhere: Criticize the world; it needs it!' (1989, p. x) Walzer is not speaking of phenomenology. If he were, he might need to say that the maxim holds here more than elsewhere. As critique of the very notions to be used in any further critique, phenomenology is first critique, most basic critique, a radical and necessary element in all human inquiry.

To refer to phenomenology as 'first' critique is already to acknowledge that it is not the only critique. Husserl often states that he is concerned with 'beginnings', and phenomenology may be viewed as essentially a starting point. One may wish to argue that it is a most valuable starting point—an essential starting point, even—but it is by no means the be-all and end-all of social inquiry.

Nor is the initial attempt to contemplate the immediate phenomenon the last. The sociologist will lay the phenomenological mantle aside and move far afield, but needs to return to the starting point time and again. What phenomenology offers social inquiry is not only a beginning rooted in immediate social experience but also a methodology that requires a return to that experience at many points along the way. It is both starting point and touchstone.

Merleau-Ponty sounds this note for us. He warns us that, instead of attempting to establish in positivist fashion the things that 'build up the shape of the world', we need to recognise our *experience* 'as the source which stares us in the face and as the ultimate court of appeal in our knowledge of these things' (1962, p. 23). For Merleau-Ponty, the phenomenological return to experience is philosophy—not philosophy as a particular body of knowledge but philosophy as a vigilance that never lets us forget the origin of all our knowledge. Philosophy of this kind, he insists, is necessary to sociology 'as a constant reminder of its tasks'. Through it 'the sociologist returns to the living sources of his knowledge' (Merleau-Ponty 1964, p. 110).

> What, then, is the world as the phenomenologist sees it? Certainly a bountiful world, a world teeming with potential meaning.
>
> Our experience is no less than an existential encounter with a world which has a potentially infinite horizon. This human world is not predetermined, as common sense or physicalist language would indicate; it is a world that is open for the discovery and creation of ever-new directions for encounter, and hence open to the emergence of as yet undiscovered significance. (Sadler 1969, p. 20)

Yet the phenomenologist's world is also a world in which our received notions—the systems of significant symbols that make us human—are seen to hide that potential meaning from us and hold us back from bringing it to birth. Phenomenologists chafe under what they see to be a tyrannous culture. They long to smash the fetters and engage with the world in new ways to construct new understandings.

Research, for phenomenologists, is this very attempt to break free and see the world afresh.

20 Philosophical Disputes in Management Research

JOHN GILL and PHIL JOHNSON

Learning outcomes At the end of this chapter the reader should be able to:

- understand the different types of philosophical commitment available to the management researcher with regard to nature of human behaviour, epistemology and ontology;

- understand how these different philosophical commitments impact upon how management research is conceived and conducted;

- differentiate between mainstream positivism, qualitative positivism (sometimes called neo-empiricism); critical theory, pragmatism and postmodernism in terms of varying philosophical and methodological commitments;

- understand how shifts in philosophical stance impact upon methodologies such as ethnography and action research.

In the earlier chapters of this book we have tried to provide the aspiring researcher with an overview of several methodological approaches, or research strategies, widely used by management researchers. In undertaking a piece of research, inevitably any researcher must choose between a wide array of different approaches in making an area of interest researchable. The nature and content of the 'problem' or question to be investigated, as well as the extent of the available resources, clearly influence this choice. However, these decisions are much more complex than merely choosing a methodology that is thought to be practically viable in relation to a specific research context with its apparent constraints and opportunities. Inevitably when we try to conceptualize what it is we are trying to investigate, and most significantly here, how we are going to investigate it, we tacitly deploy philosophical assumptions that lead us to comprehend and construct these issues in particular ways.

In many respects any research method articulates, and is constituted by, philosophical commitments which are often sublimated if those methods are presented as mere tools for enabling us to collect particular types of data and to deal with particular research questions. As we have already suggested in earlier chapters, how different methodologies are variably constituted inevitably expresses the appropriation of often competing philosophical commitments. So far, our discussion of these issues has been purposefully limited to the choice between *erklaren* and *verstehen* by research-ers. However, let's take the decision to use hypothetico-deductive research meth-ods that are designed to test, and indeed try to falsify, previously formulated theory through confronting its predictions with empirical data, or facts, objectively gathered through observation of the social world. Clearly this decision draws upon an array of philosophical assumptions and commitments beyond the disputes between those who favour *erklaren* over *verstehen*. To many contemporary management researchers, these commitments are highly contestable yet so often remain uninterrogated by those using them. Indeed, the above sentence, that describes hypothetico-deductive research methodology, has embedded in it two particularly significant philosophical assumptions:

1 that it is possible to neutrally gather data without contaminating them through the very act of observation;
2 that there exists an independent social reality, out there, awaiting our inspec-tion, through the deployment of a suitable methodology;

However, whilst we cannot avoid making philosophical commitments in undertak-ing any research, any philosophical commitment can be simultaneously contested. This is because the philosophical commitments which are inevitably made in under-taking research always entail varying stances with regard to knowledge constituting assumptions about: the nature of truth; the nature of human behaviour; the pos-sibility of neutral representation of the facts; and the independent existence of the social reality we are supposed to be investigating. In other words, tacit answers to questions about *ontology* (what are we studying?) and *epistemology* (what is the basis of warranted knowledge about our chosen domains?) impact upon any methodologi-cal engagement.

The philosophical assumptions we make in dealing with these questions implic-itly present different normative definitions of management research along with particular justificatory logics which support the selection of particular methodolog-ical approaches. Moreover, as we shall explore in Chapter 9, these philosophical assumptions influence the criteria that are used to normatively evaluate the find-ings of management research. Even a cursory inspection of the management field would show that such methodological choices are common place yet, by default, also involve the decision not to engage through alternative means: alternatives that themselves articulate different philosophical commitments to varying degrees. For example, as we have already discussed in this book, philosophical assumptions about 'human nature' (that is the nature of the processes that influence human behaviour) impact upon to decision to build theory inductively out of observation of the empirical world using qualitative methods that enable *verstehen*, rather than deductively testing previously formulated theory by deploying quantitative meth-ods that enable *erklaren*.

Because methodological choices always entail taking a position upon the philo-sophical issues noted above, there is a need for any researcher to be aware of these often hidden and unnoticed aspects of management research so that they make their philosophical commitments not by default but through their conscious interrogation of the assumptions inevitably at play in undertaking any research. Such an orienta-tion to methodology supports some recent developments in management research. For instance, although initially inspired by Burrell and Morgan's work (Burrell and Morgan, 1979; Morgan, 1983, 1986, 1993) it is largely since the early 1990s that there has been much discussion of the notion that in order to understand ourselves as social science researchers we must reflexively engage with ourselves through thinking about our own beliefs and how those beliefs have repercussions for our engagements with our areas of interest. Although this 'new sensibility' (Willmott, 1998) has many implications for management research, several commentators have emphasized how it entails noticing, and being suspicious of, the relationship between the researcher and the substantive focus of his/her research. This involves reflecting upon how those often tacit, unacknowledged, pre-understandings impact upon: how those 'objects' of research are conceptually constituted by the researcher; what kinds of research question are then asked by the researcher; and how the results of research are arrived at, justified and presented to audiences for consumption (e.g. Chia, 1995; Holland, 1999; Alvesson and Deetz, 2000; Johnson and Duberley, 2003). Simultaneously, such increased vigilance might serve to broaden the philosophical repertoire available to management researchers so that alternatives to the current Positivist mainstream are also understood and not merely dismissed as bizarre, or even perverse, aberrations not worthy of serious consideration.

Thus, this chapter largely involves elucidation of the overarching structures of thought within management research so as to explore how divergent philosophical conventions inform different methodologies: the often subliminal a priori knowledge constituting assumptions which tacitly organize theoretical and methodological variation. It is thus about the choices management researchers always have to make in doing research and we hope that it will enable the reader to engage with a fuller consideration of the ever present alternatives rather than inadvertently limiting the focus of their decisions, by default, to that which is often presented as the 'normal' way of doing research in particular management disciplines.

So as Morgan (1983) has pointed out, decisions on methodological matters are largely determined by the philosophical assumptions researchers implicitly and explicitly make by adopting what he terms a 'mode of engagement' (see also Johnson and Duberley, 2000). We have deliberately used Morgan's terminology at this point since his use of this term is intended to indicate how empirical research is not simply a choice of method; rather, as he points out, research as a mode of engagement is part of a wider process ...

> ... that constitutes and renders a subject amenable to study in a distinctive way. The selection of method implies some view of the situation being studied, for any decision on how to study a phenomenon carries with it certain assumptions, or explicit answers to the question 'what is being studied?' (Morgan, 1983: 19)

It is to these wider, essentially philosophical questions and choices that we now turn. This will be facilitated by a discussion of some of the problems associated with the dominant philosophical position in management research: positivism. Here we will build upon the philosophical issues we first raised in Chapter 3 and subsequently developed in Chapter 7. In particular we will focus upon three key philosophical questions and debates – to which there are competing answers which directly impact upon our methodological choices:

1 What is the nature of human behaviour?
2 Epistemology – is it possible to neutrally observe social reality?
3 Ontology – does social reality exist independently of the cognitive processes through which we apprehend what we take to be "out-there"?

The nature of human behaviour

We argued, particularly in Chapters 3 and 7, that interpretative qualitative approaches to research, such as ethnography, arise out of a critique of positivism's tendency to reduce human action to the status of automatic responses excited by external stimuli (i.e. *erklaren*). Essentially we argued that this reduction was achieved by Positivists ignoring the subjective dimensions of human action, that is, the internal logic and interpretative processes by which action is created. Many Positivists (e.g. Neurath, 1959: 295) justify such an approach by being concerned to prevent a divorce of the social sciences from the natural sciences; attempts at such a severance being perceived as a result of the 'residues of theology' (Neurath, 1959: 295). Other Positivists, as Smart (1975) indicates, have justified their concern to follow what is assumed to be the approach of the natural sciences by expressing a desire to achieve in the social sciences the evident operational successes of the former. The result of the positivist's concern to emulate natural science methodology thus necessitates a denial of the importance of human subjective, or interpretive processes, because the physical objects that constitute the subject matter of natural science do not display such processes – their behaviours are merely responses elicited by causal stimuli. This denial of the relevance of the subjective in the explanation of human behaviour is usually supported by further methodological criteria. As Giddens points out,

the specific unreliability of the interpretation of consciousness, indeed whether by self or by an observer, has always been the principal rationale for the rejection of verstehen by such schools. The intuitive or empathetic grasp of consciousness is regarded by them merely as a possible source of hypotheses of human conduct. (1976: 19)

On the other hand, interpretative approaches such as ethnography reject what they perceive as the Positivist's over-deterministic orientation towards an understanding of human action and behaviour. Instead they argue that, unlike animals or physical objects, human beings are able to attach meaning to the events and phenomena that surround them, and from these interpretations and perceptions select courses of meaningful action which they are able to reflect upon and monitor. It is these subjective processes that provide the sources of explanation of human action and thereby constitute the rightful focus for social science research enabled through the deployment of qualitative research methodologies such as ethnography. Thus, the aim of such interpretative approaches is to understand (*verstehen*) how people make sense of their worlds, with human action being conceived as purposive and meaningful rather than externally determined by social structures, innate drives, the environment or economic stimuli and so on.

We are therefore confronted with a philosophical choice regarding the nature of human action and its explanation which has direct methodological implications. Which set of philosophical assumptions we implicitly or explicitly adopt regarding what Burrell and Morgan (1979: 6) have termed 'human nature' influences our subsequent choice of particular 'modes of engagement' and what we see as warranted in research. If we accept the philosophical assumptions of positivism and its consequent epistemological prescriptions, we are invariably drawn towards the exclusive utilization of deductive (i.e. nomothetic) methodologies. Conversely, if our philosophical orientation is interpretative the ensuing epistemological mandate impels us towards a more inductive (i.e. ideographic) methodology such as ethnography as it enables *verstehen* (see Burrell and Morgan, 1979: 1–37).

However, lurking here there are other important philosophical commitments which seem to moderate the apparent differences between the deductive and inductive methodologies we have considered so far in this book. For instance, most of the methodological approaches we have considered so far share the assumption that it is possible for researchers to neutrally research, through the observation and collection of data, without contaminating that data through the very process of researching. Thus, the dispute between many positivists who limit themselves to undertaking deductive research and many qualitative researchers, referred to above, is largely about whether or not human subjective processes are observable in a neutral, objective, fashion. Clearly many ethnographers think that it is possible to do this whereas the former reject ethnography and its basis in *verstehen* as being too subjective (see the quote from Giddens above) and hence not proper science. But ironically one can discern in this dispute a shared epistemological and ontological commitment expressed in terms of assumptions about being able to neutrally observe the world out there provided that the correct methodology is used by the researcher. It is this very commitment to objectivity that has been recently challenged by many management researchers: particularly those working in what we have broadly defined as qualitative management research and who have thereby added to the heterogeneity of management research (see Johnson et al., 2006). We shall now turn to this particular set of philosophical disputes, which have been articulated by a range of important alternatives to positivism, including postmodernism and critical theory.

Epistemology

The philosophical term epistemology ...

> *derives from two Greek words: 'episteme' which means 'knowledge' or 'science'; and 'logos' which means 'knowledge', 'information', 'theory' or 'account'. ... epistemology is usually understood as being concerned with knowledge about knowledge. In other words, epistemology is the study of the criteria by which we can know what does and does not constitute warranted, or scientific, knowledge. (Johnson and Duberley, 2000: 3)*

Epistemology is a pivotal issue in any form of research for it is about *how we know* whether or not any claim, including our own, made about the phenomena we are interested in, is warranted. That is, what do we mean by the concept 'truth' and how do we know whether or not some claim is true or false? In other words, what is our theory of truth? These are major epistemological issues and we can only introduce the reader to some of these debates and thereafter direct those interested to further reading.

Very often people think that such processes of justifying knowledge claims are in principle straightforward: in judging the truth or falsity of any such claim surely 'the facts speak for themselves'? All we need to do is look for the relevant evidence whose content will either support or refute any claim. Thus, it is often thought that what is true is something that corresponds with the given facts: the empirical evidence that we have collected by undertaking some form of empirical research. Whilst such a view of truth arose out of various attacks upon what was construed as religious dogma (see Johnson and Duberley, 2000: 12–13), today these views of warranted knowledge, at first sight seem apparently harmless and uncontentious. However, recently they have been subject to much dispute in both the natural and social sciences: a dispute which is now of direct concern to management researchers, and has had a direct influence on the evolution of an increasing philosophical diversity in management research wherein the positivist mainstream has come under considerable further attack.

Key methodological concept

Positivist epistemology

According to many commentators (for example, Keat and Urry, 1975; Giddens, 1979) two of the most significant characteristics of positivist epistemology contain the claims that warranted science is concerned with:

1 only directly observable phenomena, with any reference to the intangible or subjective being excluded as being meaningless; and
2 the testing of theories, in a hypothetico-deductive fashion, by their confrontation with the facts neutrally gathered from a readily observable external world.

However, as we imply above, even those who reject key aspects of positivist epistemology around the use of hypothetico-deductive methodology, and the exclusion of the subjective as meaningless, will sometimes retain a commitment to being able to inductively investigate human intersubjective cultural processes by gathering the facts from a readily observable external world. In a sense the result is a kind of 'qualitative positivism' (see Knights, 1992; Van Maanen, 1995b; Schwandt, 1996; Prasad and Prasad, 2002), which although different from mainstream Positivism shares its commitment to what is called a theory-neutral observational language (see Figure 9.1).

Stop and Think Exercise 8.1   How and to what extent do the qualitative methodologies illustrated in Chapter 7 involve a break with positivist philosophical commitments?

This attack has largely been driven by the view that it is not possible to neutrally apprehend the facts 'out there', regardless of the methodology used, in order to test the veracity of knowledge claims. Thus, the positivist philosophical commitment, that it is possible to objectively, or neutrally, observe the social world and thereby gather 'positively given' data in order to test theoretical predictions, has been considerably undermined by those who think that in observing the world we inevitably influence what we see. Indeed, as Willmott (1998) explains, there has been some erosion of the positivist consensus by scholars who have dismissed the possibility of what is called a neutral observational language and who argue that notions of truth and objectivity are merely the outcomes of prestigious discursive practices which mask rather than eliminate the researcher's partiality. For Willmott a key implication of this 'new sensibility' is the potential demise of managerialism. This is because any claim that management is founded upon a technical imperative to improve efficiency, justified and enabled by objective analyses of how things really are, epistemologically crumbles and along with it some elements of managerial authority. The latter become highly problematic because the idea that managers may govern because they have superior knowledge and expertise is simultaneously undermined. Below we shall trace in much more detail how this attack upon positivist epistemology has developed and where the alternative philosophical stance leads us in terms of management research.

Positivist epistemology limits its conception of valid or warranted knowledge (i.e. science) to what is taken to be unproblematically observable 'sense-data'. If a theory corresponds with a researcher's observations of these facts its truthfulness is taken to be established. If it fails to correspond, it is discarded as mistaken or false. Thus, the theory of truth that is proposed, implicitly and explicitly, is a correspondence theory of truth. Such a view of truth is made viable only through the prior assumption that it is possible to observe the facts of the external world neutrally and objectively by the application of rigorous methodological procedures and protocols aimed at testing the theory. This latter assumption is often called the assumption of a theory-neutral observational language. As Hindess (1977: 18) points out,

> it makes possible a very precise conception of the testing of theory against observation. The testing of theory against irreducible statements of observation is equivalent to a direct comparison between theory and the real world. If they fail to correspond then the theory is false and therefore may be rejected.

In this way doxa (what we believe to be true) becomes transformed into episteme (that which we know to be true), hence epistemology. At first sight, particularly from a standpoint imbued with Western cultural norms, this positivistic epistemology appears as eminently rational – indeed commonsensical. However, there seem to be major problems with this view of scientific endeavour:

1 it seems self-contradictory;
2 the possibility of directly and objectively observing phenomena, and thereby accumulating the 'facts' of the world so as to test the truthfulness of a theory, seems dubious.

We shall now proceed to discuss each of these problems in turn.

1 Positivist epistemological self-contradiction   In order to observe directly, and objectively, the phenomena in which they are interested, positivists must assume what is called a dualism between 'subject' and 'object'; that it is possible to separate the 'subject' (the knower, the observer, the researcher) from the 'object' (the known, the observed, what are taken to be the 'facts' of the world) by the application of scientific methodology. Therefore, by using rigorous methodology it is possible to have knowledge that is independent of the observer and uncontaminated by the very act of observation. As we noted previously, this idea is central to positivism. Indeed, it is embedded in the term 'positivism': for as Comte (1853) originally proposed, science could only progress by ridding itself of (e.g. religious) dogma through the examination of the 'positively given': those empirical data or objective facts which were cognitively accessible through sensory perception. Thus, explanations of the world which relied upon the claim that they were caused by God's will, or by the actions of supernatural beings such as demons etc., were dismissed from the realm of scientific explanation. This limitation of the scientific to phenomena that were empirically observable was the culmination of the social and philosophical upheaval called the Enlightenment (see Johnson and Duberley, 2000: 12–19).

In order to be pursue their research agenda, positivists have to assume the possibility of generating and/or testing theory by direct comparison to the real through

Figure 8.1 | Positivist dualism

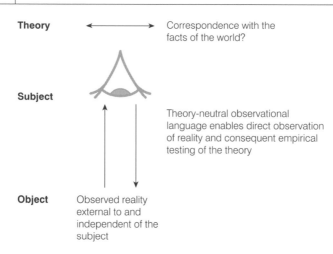

the deployment of a theory-neutral observational language. Thus, it is only through the prior assumption that a dualism between subject and object is possible, and consequently that a theory-neutral observational language is available, that the correspondence criteria of the positivist (i.e. his or her epistemology) becomes viable. This is illustrated by Figure 8.1.

According to both Hindess (1977) and Gorman (1977), however, the contention above about the nature of subject/object relations (i.e. a dualism) demonstrates the contradictory nature of positivism. As we have tried to show, many (but not all) positivists exclude from what is taken to be warranted knowledge, the metaphysical – that is to say the intangible, the subjective or abstract. These domains are ruled out because it is thought we cannot empirically observe them. Indeed, operationalization processes, so central to positivist methodology and discussed in Chapter 3, are about making the abstract observable in a valid and reliable manner. Whilst there are disputes about kinds of information, etc. this commitment excludes from scientific processes the problem of self-contradiction lies at the heart of this stance. This is because by rejecting the metaphysical it rejects as meaningless our knowledge of subject/object relationships (i.e. our own relationship as researchers to the phenomena we are trying to observe as illustrated in Figure 9.1) upon which any epistemology, including positivism's own, is ultimately grounded. There is therefore a potential contradiction since positivism seems to exclude from its conceptualization of warranted knowledge its own philosophical grounds for warranted knowledge (see Hindess, 1977: 135). Thus, it would appear that since positivism cannot account for itself on its own terms, it becomes indefensible in its own terms, and is thereby lapses into epistemological incoherence. Obviously such a contradiction applies less to what we have termed 'qualitative positivists' since they do not exclude human subjective processes from what they take to be a legitimate area for scientific inquiry. However, most of the contemporary attacks upon positivism tend to focus more upon our second problematic issue.

2 Is positivism's theory-neutral observational language possible? As we have shown, positivism, with its articulation of a subject-object dualism, assumes that there

Figure 8.2 | Science as a neutral endeavour

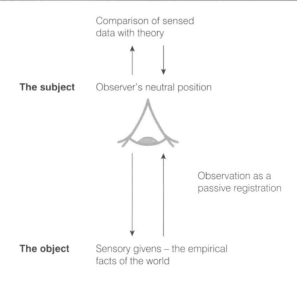

Comparison of sensed
data with theory

The subject   Observer's neutral position

Observation as a
passive registration

The object   Sensory givens – the empirical
facts of the world

is some neutral point from which the observer can stand back and observe the world objectively. That is, the observations that are registered are independent of the very process of the observer observing and thus 'truth' is to be found in the observer's passive registration of the 'sensory givens' (Mattick, 1986), or facts, that constitute reality. This philosophical commitment to objectivity and neutrality is illustrated by Figure 8.2.

As we have already suggested, and following Van Maanen (1995b), it is important to note here that some interpretive management researchers share this commitment to a theory-neutral observational language – save that this would be construed as a subject-subject dualism where the observer can stand back and neutrally apprehend what other knowers subjectively know. For instance, here it would be assumed that it is possible for organizational ethnographers to neutrally describe members' cultural attributes and how these subjective elements impel particular modes of organizational behaviour (see also Hammersley, 1992; Knights, 1992; Alvesson and Skoldberg, 2000; Prasad and Prasad, 2002).

Figure 8.2 illustrates the empiricist maxim that science should be, and can be, a neutral, value-free and disinterested endeavour. So as Rorty (1979: 46) argues, a correspondence theory of truth relies upon the received wisdom that the veracity of competing theories may be adjudicated through an appeal to their correspondence with the facts of an external objective reality that is 'mirrored' in the 'Glassy Essence' of the observer.

This is often labelled as an *objectivist epistemology* as it presupposes the possibility of a theory-neutral observational language where our sensory experience of the 'given' 'facts' of reality provides the only secure foundation for social scientific knowledge (e.g. Ayer, 1971). Located in this dualism, observers can 'picture' (Wittgenstein, 1922) the external world objectively and thereby deductively test, or inductively generate, theory in an objective fashion. Thus truth, as correspondence, is to be found through the observer's passive registration of the facts that constitute reality. Here we have indicated that two approaches to management research are evident – positivism and qualitative positivism: the latter is more commonly called neo-empiricism (see Alvesson and Deetz, 2000). Both share the empiricist commitment that our sensory experience provides the only secure foundation for management research. As we have argued, where they part company is over what they understand to be observable as opposed to metaphysical (see Lessnoff, 1974). Unlike the positivists, neo-empiricists argue that in order to understand human behaviour in organizations we must access their cultures through *verstehen* and the deployment of qualitative methods of data collection. So as to legitimate this interpretive methodological imperative, neo-empiricism questions the methodological unity of the sciences, grounded in *erklaren*, as proposed by positivists. Positivists have reciprocated by denying both the possibility and desirability of *verstehen* thereby restoring the methodological unity of natural and social sciences (e.g. Abel, 1958).

Because each of the dualisms noted above rest on a putative epistemic objectivity, which privileges the consciousness of the management researcher as capable of discovering the 'truth' about the world in a correspondence sense, regardless of the methodology used there is a constant concern with maintaining the objectivity of the researcher by ensuring the 'right' methodological moves: a critique and evaluation of the 'technical' aspects of the particular methodology deployed, rather than the underlying philosophical assumptions that justify that methodology in the first place, in order to nurture and sustain objective inquiry.

However, in assuming the possibility for an observer to register passively the facts of reality, this epistemological position ignores the possibility that the observer's perceptual apparatus does not provide mere reflections of what is out there, but is proactive and creative in influencing what we apprehend. As Habermas (1974b: 199), a famous Critical Theorist, contends,

> *even the simplest perception is not only performed pre-categorically by physiological apparatus – it is just as determined by previous experience through what has been handed down and through what has been learned as by what is anticipated through the horizons of expectations.*

Factors that might influence observation

It is now important to turn to considering how various factors might influence observation/sensory experience and thereby consider their implications for the possibility of a theory-neutral observational language. Once one rejects the possibility of a neutral observational language there occurs a move towards a much more *subjectivist epistemological* stance. Such a stance assumes that what we perceive is, at least in part, an outcome of how we engage with the world and the conceptual baggage that we bring to bear in order to make sense of what we experience. The origins of this baggage are usually assumed to be social in origin hence are encapsulated in the idea that we *socially construct* either versions of reality or indeed reality itself (see Burr, 1995). Thus, in order to explain this subjectivist stance we shall review the processes of perception and how many scholars argue that far from being theory-neutral, observation is inevitably 'theory-laden' and thereby pursue what amounts to a devastating critique of the objectivist epistemology shared by positivists and neo-empiricists and the assumption that observation can be a neutral, objective and unbiased endeavour.

The process of perception   As we have illustrated, for both positivists and neo-empiricists (i.e qualitative positivists), warranted knowledge about the world

Figure 8.3

emanates from social reality, that is an external world directly and objectively accessible through human sensory experience provided that the correct methodology is used to, in effect, polish Rorty's 'mirror in the mind': a possibility that Rorty disputes (1979). As such, warranted knowledge is that which has a correspondence with the world that has been established through our neutral and passive registration of various sensory inputs.

Stop and Think Exercise 8.2   What do you see?

Often the same event or identical set of sensations is perceived and experienced by people in different ways.

For instance, consider the two objects in Figures 8.3 and 8.4. How many women do you see in Figure 8.3? Do you see the object in Figure 8.4 in three dimensions? If so, how many cubes do you see? Can you also see it as one dimensional and composed of squares, triangles and parallelograms, etc.? People outside Western cultures may perceive this figure in only one dimension.

If the sensory process of perceiving even relatively simple objects was indeed merely a matter of the passive reception and registration of their evident characteristics, how is it that the same object can be apprehended so differently by people? This must surely imply that we are not passive receivers of external stimuli and data but rather that we apply various inferences and assumptions which mediate what we 'see'. Perhaps there is more to seeing than meets the eye-ball?

What are the implications of this for the claim that we can possess a neutral observation language as put forward by positivists and neo-empiricists?

It would seem from Exercise 8.2 that our interpretation of the relatively simple figures illustrated can vary considerably. This has led people to argue that whilst we

Figure 8.4

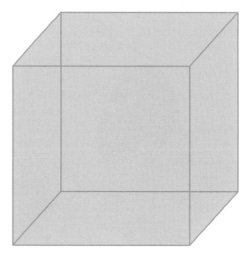

are continually bombarded by sensations and stimuli, we project on to those inputs a form and substance that derives from within, from our own 'cognitive processing mechanisms' (Unwin, 1986: 300). Such projection entails selection, as we choose what we sense by giving attention to particular stimuli while de-emphasizing, filtering out or ignoring others. The selected sensory stimulations are simultaneously organized and interpreted by being put into a coherent and meaningful whole. This organization, interpretation and consequent imposition of order may be highly influenced by the schemas built up from our previous experience, or received as stocks of knowledge, or *discourses*, through our social interaction in various cultural milieu. We usually do these things rapidly and automatically and often unconsciously. Although the result may appear objective and separate from ourselves – as 'out there' – in many respects perhaps we are actively creating, or at least influencing through interpretation, what we apprehend. So far from being a process that involves the *passive* registration of sensory 'givens' emanating from a reality separate from us, 'perception allows us to impose a logic and order on the chaos of the thousands of sensations that bombard our senses ... perception allows us to make sense out of all these sensations' (Spinelli, 1989: 38). In other words, it would seem that we are active participants in the process of perception as we experience an interpreted world and not one that is directly accessible through passive sensory capacities imprinting on our minds mere reflections of what is 'out there'. So what we perceive as being external to and separate from us is just as much an expression of our subjective processes as what is actually going on 'out there'.

The theory-laden nature of observation   The ways in which we make sense of the various sensations that bombard our senses also direct attention to the issue that has usually been termed the 'theory-laden' nature of observation. This term refers to the way in which prior theories influence what we take to be factual, given, observations. Hanson (1958) contends that, rather than a theory and the data accumulated to test that theory being separate elements, they are actually intimately linked.

To illustrate this point, Hanson asks the reader to imagine two famous sixteenth century astronomers, Tycho Brahe and Johannes Kepler observing the sun at dawn. He poses the question; what do they see? According to Hanson (ibid.: 23–24) Brahe, because he adheres to the (then) Catholic Church's officially sanctioned, geocentric Aristotlean cosmology, or theory of the universe, sees this apparently simple everyday event, quite differently from Kepler who adheres to Copernicus's alternative, and at the time heretical, cosmology. Brahe has previously imprinted on his mind the Church's Aristotlean theory that tells him that a static Earth is at the centre of the universe, around which all the planets and the stars, including the Sun, orbit. In contrast Kepler adheres the heliocentric theory that proposes that the planets, including the spinning Earth, orbit the Sun. The operation of rival theses theories lead Brahe and Kepler to interpret the same mundane event (dawn) in very different ways. According to Hanson (ibid.: 23–24) Brahe would 'see the sun beginning its journey from horizon to horizon. He sees that from some celestial vantage point the sun ... could be watched circling our fixed earth'. However, Kepler, due to his heliocentric theory, 'will see the horizon dipping, or turning, away from our local fixed star. The shift from sunrise to horizon ... turn is occasioned by *differences between what Tycho and Kepler think they know*' (our emphasis).

In other words, Hanson claims that observation is theory-laden in that our theories influence what we see, and hence there is no actual separation between theory, interpretation and data. If Hanson is correct, then there are devastating implications for positivism's epistemological claim to theory-neutrality in observation.

Implications

Our brief discussion of the various processes involved in perception and the theory-laden nature of observation casts doubt upon the possibility of there being a theory-neutral observational language that would enable theory to be tested directly against empirical reality. Thus, the assumption of a subject–object dualism, so necessary for epistemology based on a correspondence theory of truth, appears implausible. Advocates of such correspondence criteria fail to acknowledge what is known as the 'hermeneutic circle', that no 'pure' description of data free from interpretation based upon presuppositions is possible. As Spinelli (1989: 58) comments, 'the assumed separation between the data being analysed and the person who analyses them ... becomes questionable'. It seems that the possession of a theory-neutral observational language is impossible. Further, it implies that what we take to be warranted knowledge is not objective and independent but is imbued with the partiality and theoretical dispositions of the observer, through the action of our 'cognitive processing mechanisms' (Unwin, 1986: 300).

Thus, for a long time, many scholars have argued that any observer, explicitly or implicitly, projects a priori beliefs and sentiments upon sense-data and thereby moulds them through this imposition of common sense or theoretical (Hanson, 1958; Quine, 1960; Habermas, 1974a) or paradigmatic (Kuhn, 1970) or unconscious (Hunt, 1979) assumptions and background expectancies (Giddens, 1976). It may of course also be moulded by cognitive schemes to which researchers may be emotionally committed (Mitroff, 1974) and whose nature is highly influenced by social factors (D. Bloor, 1976; Barnes, 1974, 1977; Law and Lodge, 1984). Indeed, as Gadamer (1975) in his critique of Dilthey argues, the notion of a neutral, detached observer is a myth. Interpretations cannot escape background preconceptions embedded in the language and life of their authors. In other words, social intersubjective processes, to which we have been exposed, are at the heart of how we make sense of what we think is 'out there'.

The result is a subjectivist epistemological stance which implies that:

1 scientific claims cannot be seen as true descriptions, in a correspondence sense, of some external reality but are socially constructed creations of the scientist;
2 the acceptability of a scientific claim is not the outcome of the application of some universally valid evaluation criteria (see Chapter 9), rather, the product of the value-laden subjectivity of an individual scientist or a community of scientists;
3 the truth or falsity of statements is 'underdetermined' by empirical data in that observation cannot provide objective control over scientific claims.

So from the above philosophical stance, the notion of interpretation is not just applied to the meaningful behaviour of the organizational members we happen to be investigating; it equally must apply to the researcher him/herself. Hence, as we indicated earlier, while some ethnographers clearly attack positivism on the grounds that human action is interpretive and therefore, cannot be investigated using methods that derive from the investigation of non-sentient physical phenomena, simultaneously they may often tacitly share positivism's commitment to an epistemology that preserves a neutral observational language in the form of a subject–subject dualism (see Marcus, 1994). Obviously a key debate in social science generally, and increasingly in the management disciplines, is how the rejection of positivist notions of neutrality then impact upon our research and the methods we use.

So it follows that the processes described in the previous sections are not merely interesting curiosities that we should try to sublimate or ignore in considering the status of our research findings. Rather, their implications demand that we should attempt to develop epistemologies capable of coping with their burgeoning critique and which by implication have devastating consequences for how we undertake management research. It is precisely this issue which Willmott (1998) is referring to in his call for an increasing sensitivity in management research.

It is now therefore imperative to consider some of the methodological implications of this alternative epistemological stance, albeit briefly. However, before doing so we need to attend to one further area of philosophical controversy that has plagued management research. This is to do with what is called ontology.

Ontology – status of social reality

As we have tried to show, once we reject the possibility of neutral observation, we have to admit to dealing with a socially constructed reality. But this philosophical shift can, but not necessarily, entail a questioning of whether or not what we take to be reality actually exists 'out there' at all? This leads us to the philosophical issue that revolves around our ontological assumptions.

Like the term epistemology, the term ontology also is a combination of two Greek works – but in this case they are ontos and logos. The former refers to 'being' whilst the latter refers to theory or knowledge, etc. Ontology is a branch of philosophy dealing with the essence of phenomena and the nature of their existence. Hence, to ask about the ontological existence of something is often to ask whether or not it is real or illusory. Here ontological questions raise questions regarding whether or not some phenomenon that we are interested in actually exists independently of our knowing and perceiving it – or is what we see and usually take to be real, instead, an outcome, or creation, of these acts of knowing and perceiving? So we are primarily concerned with what is called the ontological status of social reality and the phenomena we take to constitute aspects of that reality. Importantly it is useful to differentiate between realist and subjectivist assumptions about the status of social reality.

- *Realist assumptions* about the ontological status of the phenomena we assume to constitute social reality entails the view that they exist, 'out there', independently of our perceptual or cognitive structures. We might not already know its characteristics, indeed it may be impossible for us to ever know those characteristics in a correspondence sense, but this reality exists, it is real, and it is there potentially awaiting inspection and discovery by us.
- *Subjectivist assumptions* about the ontological status of the social phenomena we deal with which, philosophically, entail the view that what we take to be social reality is a creation, or projection, of our consciousness and cognition. What we usually assume to be 'out there', has no real, independent, status separate from the act of knowing. In perceiving, or knowing, the social world we create it – we just probably are not usually aware of our role in these creative processes.

By combining the above ontological assumptions with the competing assumptions regarding epistemology we have already discussed, we can see three different philosophical positions which impact upon management research. These are illustrated in Figure 8.5. These philosophical assumptions about ontology and epistemology are always contentious and debatable, because that is all they are – assumptions. Indeed, we cannot operate without adopting some epistemological and ontological position: but we should be aware of them, be prepared to defend them, and consider their implications. The trouble may be that we don't always subject our particular philosophical choices to critical inspection and often make them by default. Major differences over these issues pervade areas like management research and in part account for the diversity illustrated by Figure 8.5.

Figure 8.5 | Epistemological and ontological assumptions: the constitution of different approaches to management research

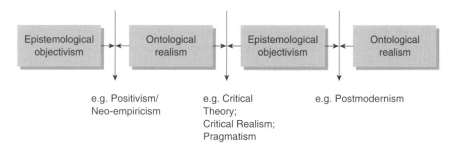

One response to the philosophical issues raised here appears to involve their suppression in undertaking research through the maintenance of what many management researchers would now consider to be a naive and unreflective empiricism that makes various research methods used appear as philosophically expurgated techniques and protocols. Obviously, this is a strategy with which we have little sympathy. We would particularly concur with Giddens's (1984: xviii) warning that 'the social sciences are lost if they are not directly related to philosophical problems by those who practise them'.

However, such attacks upon correspondence theory can have far more radical implications. Indeed, as Sayer (1981: 6) observed over 20 years ago, the 'shattering of innocence' that has arisen through the radical undermining of positivism by the rejection of the doctrine of the theory neutrality of observation has often produced much more critical approaches to management research. Whilst these approaches vary considerably, but are often given the umbrella label Critical Management Studies (see Forester et al., 2000; Fournier and Grey, 2000), they share Willmott's (1998) 'new sensibility' in part due to the subjectivist epistemological stance they articulate. Below we shall trace the development of some of these alternatives before moving on to how particular methodologies have been reconfigured in response to the shift in philosophical assumptions that drives these alternatives.

For instance, the positivist basis of a variety of management disciplines has increasingly been subject to various critiques – for example, accountancy (Tinker, 1985; Lehman, 1992; Johnson, 1995); corporate strategy (Knights and Morgan, 1991; Barry and Elmes, 1997; Darwin et al., 2002); human resource management (Townley, 1994; DuGay, 1996); and organization theory (Reed and Hughes, 1992; Hassard and Parker, 1993; Burrell, 1997; Hancock and Tyler, 2001; McAuley et al. 2007). Although substantively varied, epistemologically these critiques tend to share a desire to demystify those disciplines through a rebuttal of what is seen as the positivist, tendency to present those disciplines as objective, value-free and technical enterprises; to point to how such a perspective is grounded in an epistemological objectivism expressed in terms of the unreflexive application of a theory-neutral observational language; to reject the objectivist view that the essentials of the world are to be discovered through the exercise of managers' privileged reason (i.e. rationality); and to replace it with a social constructivist view of management knowledge which exposes and disrupts the partial taken-for-granted assumptions that underpin ostensibly neutral management practices.

Postmodernism

Of the approaches noted above, perhaps the most radical in its implications for management research is the postmodernist. In the last 20 years or so postmodernism has emerged and attracted considerable interest in most of the management disciplines. Largely these developments can be seen as an outcome of a growing disillusion with the positivistic assumptions which still dominate those disciplines and the apparent demise of traditional alternatives, such as Marxism. As we have suggested, postmodernism is characterized by a profound scepticism regarding the idea that language can neutrally represent reality. Rather, through what postmodernists call the 'linguistic turn' (Lyotard, 1984: 40) linguistic representations are thought to construct the objects which populate our realities. Thus, postmodernist research assumes that what we take to be reality is itself created and determined by our acts of cognition. Here the social world isn't there waiting for us to discover it, rather that act of knowing creates what we find. Whilst this philosophical stance also argues against the possibility of an objective empirical science of management, it is also a relativistic stance. For the postmodernist, efforts to develop theories that reveal causal relationships through accumulating objective empirical data are a forlorn hope. This is not just because knowledge is contaminated by the discourse of the social scientist, rather their theoretical stance, their norms, beliefs and values, etc. encoded into their academic disciplines act to constitute, or create, what we take to be social reality. The result is that what we take to be reality becomes a self-referential and arbitrary output of linguistic or discursive practices – which are potentially always open to revision. For Baudrillard (1983, 1993) such hyper-realities have no independent ontological status as they are divorced from extra-linguistic reference points, in which there is nothing to see save simulations which appear to be real. The result is 'you can never really go back to the source, you can never interrogate an event, a character, a discourse about its degree of original reality' (1993: 146).

Here the concept of discourse is pivotal. Discourses are subjective, linguistically formed, ways of experiencing and acting and constituting phenomena which we take to be 'out there'. As such they are expressed in all that can be thought, written or said about a particular phenomena which through creating the phenomena influence our behaviour. Therefore a discourse, for the postmodernist, stabilizes our subjectivity into a particular gaze by which we come to normally construe ourselves, others, and what we take to be social reality. A dominant discourse, which is taken for granted by people and hence is not challenged, thereby limits our knowledge and practices by dictating what is legitimate. Inevitably a dominant discourse excludes alternative ways of knowing and behaving – alternative discourses and their associated practices are always possible, they are just being suppressed. So here, social reality (which post-modernists often call hyper-reality) becomes a self-referential and arbitrary output of the researcher's, and other actors', discursive practices. However, there is a tendency to externalize, objectify and then forget built into how we are the source of what we assume to be 'out there'. The result is that discursively produced hyper-realities are mistaken for an independent external reality: a 'false concreteness' is accorded to these subjective linguistic outcomes which appear as being natural and out-there independent of us. Hence, the epistemological fulcrum provided by a commitment to reality as an independently existing reference point is erased since 'the world is not already there, waiting for us to reflect it' (Cooper and Burrell, 1988: 100). For Chia (1995, 1996) it follows that knowledge or truth has no secure vantage point outside, and is always relative to, socio-linguistic, or discursive, processes.

From this philosophical stance, the interrelated methodological tasks of the post-modernist are:

1 to describe these discursive forms often through a distinctive form of discourse analysis (e.g. Ball and Wilson, 2000);
2 to explore how they have developed and impact upon people, through gene-alogy and by examining discursive truth effects (e.g. Knights and Morgan, 1991);
3 to examining how discourses adapt and change by, for instance, deploying nar-rative theory (e.g. Barry and Elmes, 1997);
4 to destabilize dominant discourses so that alternative discourses, which are always possible, might then develop through the use of deconstruction (e.g. Calas and Smircich, 1991; Kilduff, 1993; Linstead, 1993b) or through a dis-tinctive form of action research (e.g. Barry, 1997; Treleaven, 2001).

Key methodological concept

Postmodern action research (Treleaven, 2001)

An example of postmodern action research is provided by Treleaven's account of a 'collaborative inquiry' that deconstructed the gender narratives at play in an Australian university. By integrating 'the turn to action with the linguistic turn' (ibid.: 261) Treleaven used a collaborative inquiry group to facilitate 11 female co-participants' deconstruction of critical incidents within their organizational experiences. This involved these co-participants reflecting upon the patterns of meanings they deployed in making sense of their various organizational experiences and reconstructing those meanings through the use of discourse analysis to foreground and inspect the taken-for-granted factors that shaped these processes of sense making. This served to unsettle the dominant discourses which were usually at play in their sense making and enabled the surfacing of alternatives which allowed for the production of new subjective interpretations of their experiences and the construction of alternative subjective identities for the participants themselves. This reinterpretation of experience opened up the possibility of change within and beyond their university workplace. For Treleaven, the various discourses surfaced and at play, offered the formation of new subjectivities based upon the liberation of multiple new understandings of their social experience by participants. However, these discourses were often contradictory and hence could provide sites for both ambivalence and resistance. So an outcome of this postmodernist deconstructive intervention through action research was not just to destabilize the hegemonic patriarchal discourse of gender but to 'highlight unsettling actions and points of contradiction as strategic opportunities for change in the workplace' (ibid., 266). Thus, through Treleaven's postmodern form of action research, participants became empowered to manipulate signifiers to create new discursive means of apprehension of themselves and their workplace thereby engendering discursive diversity rather than the discursive closure that the operation of dominant discourses can create.

However, while postmodernism poses an important challenge to positivist orthodoxy, it also has its own contradictions located in its apparent sanctioning of relativism.

First, relativism is riddled with fundamental contradictions. As Mannheim (1952: 130) has observed, 'the assertion of relativity itself claims absolute validity and hence its very form presupposes a principle which its manifest content rejects'. In other words, the emergent relativism of postmodernist views of management is incoherent in that it is unable to cope with its own critique of itself and thereby cannot justify its approach on its own grounds. If we take Townley's Foucauldian analysis (1994) as an example, she portrays human resources management as involving the social constitution of knowledge and order – a process of representation in which organizational worlds are rendered known, visible and potentially manageable (ibid., 144). Power is made invisible by the presentation of information as objective facts ostensibly independent of the interests of those who produce it (ibid., 145). But if we accept this postmodernist claim that all knowledge is the outcome of such partial and arbitrary linguistic processes, what therefore is the epistemological status of Townley's, and other postmodernists', own accounts? Is there a danger that they construct discourses about discourses that inadvertently assert an implicit claim to privilege for their own accounts through some epistemological backdoor?

Alternatively, if the above contradiction is avoided, postmodernism must adopt a relativistic argument that concludes that since all knowledge is discursively produced, there are no good reasons for any discursive closure: that is preferring one discursive representation over another – including their own. Indeed, it would seem that pivotal for many postmodernists is the preference-less toleration and promotion of the polyphonic (many voices) since any discursive closure must mean the arbitrary dominance of a particular discourse which merely serves to silence alternative voices and hence must be disrupted (see Gergen, 1992; Rosenau, 1992; Chia, 1995; Barry, 1997).

So despite the optimistic assertions of Bauman (1995) that relativism can provide a liberating potential it is also evident that it undermines the basis of critique. Indeed, relativism can also promote a disinterestedness that tacitly supports the status quo by engendering a conservative silence about current practices (see, for example, Neimark, 1990: 106). Thus, the naiveté of positivisms objectivism gives way to possibly more dangerous and contradictory views which promote the idea that knowledge is not subject to any extra-discursive checks.

However, perhaps some of the above criticism is unfair for, as illustrated by Treleaven's action research, the possibility of intervention is evident within a postmodern stance. However, this intervention is primarily about destabilising hegemonic discourses without being able to, as a researcher, put forward any alternative because of the perceived dangers of arbitrary discursive closure.

Critical realism and pragmatism

Sayer (1992) presents a Critical Realist stance which overtly attempts to avoid what he sees as the epistemological quagmires of both objectivism and relativism. In this he draws indirectly upon American pragmatism, and more directly upon Marxist traditions, by developing an alternative approach to truth which he calls practical adequacy.

> To be practically adequate knowledge must generate expectations about the world and about the results of our actions that are actually realised ... These expectations in turn are realised because of the nature of the associated material interventions ... and of their material contents. In other words, although the nature of objects and processes (including human behaviour) does not uniquely determine the content of human knowledge, it does determine their cognitive and practical possibilities for us. (Sayer, 1992: 69–70)

Here Sayer is in many respects following Kolakowski in differentiating between 'thought objects' and 'real objects'. Kolakowski (1969: 75) believes there is an external reality independent of and resistant to human activity; but this is a 'thing in itself' which remains unknowable. Such 'things in themselves' do not have conceptual counterparts; rather, our objects of knowledge – 'things for us' – are constituted by 'active contact with the resistance of nature [that] ... creates knowing man and nature as his object at one and the same time'. So as Kolakowski claims, while reality does exist, we can never ultimately know it because of our lack of a theory-neutral observational language; but this is not to say that our engagements with the external world are completely determined by us.

The implications of this combination of epistemological subjectivism and ontological realism are further elaborated by Arbib and Hesse (1986). As implied by Kolakowski (1969), they argue that the constraints and tolerance of spatio-temporal reality provide a feedback procedure that enables evaluation of the pragmatic success of our 'cognitive systems' and 'networks of schemata'. This pragmatic criterion prevents 'science' becoming purely an intersubjective representation of, and consensus about, social realities. These schemata allow people to make sense of the world – a world so complex that it is amenable to many interpretations.

For Arbib and Hesse (1986), while such schemata are not individualistic but socially shaped and constructed, they are not socially determined. Rather, since such schemata are guides for action, the pragmatic criterion operates consciously and unconsciously as people adjust and reject schemata when the expectations they support are violated (see also Barnes, 1977). Thus, schemata are ideological, pragmatic and interest laden in the sense that they are enmeshed with our knowledge of how to interact with the world, and such knowledge of 'how to' is 'intertwined with our knowledge (not necessarily conscious) of our goals and what we wish to achieve through our actions' (Arbib and Hesse, 1986: 129).

Law and Lodge (1984: 125) attempt to investigate further these social processes through the notion of 'workability', that is, truthfulness in a pragmatic sense. In this they argue that if a theory/network allows people to interact satisfactorily with their environment it is then reinforced, but if, from the stance of theory, their environments become unpredictable and uncontrollable the theory is undermined and is likely to change. Therefore, they argue that the workability of a theory is a function of the purposes for which it is used.

The importance of these issues lends force to Morgan's (1983: 393) consideration that since the pursuit of knowledge is a particular form of human action that has an essentially social nature, 'it must be understood as being an ethical, moral, ideological and political activity as it is an epistemological one'.

If, therefore, there are any criteria available for evaluating knowledge they do not relate to some quest for absolute knowledge; rather, they relate to 'the way knowledge serves to guide and shape ourselves as human beings – to the consequences of knowledge, in the sense of what knowledge does to and for humans' (Morgan, 1983: 393).

It follows that research embracing practical adequacy maintains the necessity for reflexivity on the part of the researcher. Knowledge, as such, is evaluated in terms of how successfully it may guide action towards the realization of particular objectives which are the expressions of particular interests or needs. This necessarily leads the researcher to reflect upon the partisan nature of his or her research with regard to its human consequences. As Carchedi (1983) argues, this inevitably involves questions such as: for whom and for what does the resultant construction of reality proffer aid? Management researchers should therefore accept their (albeit fallible) role as that of partisan participant in interest-laden dispute and divest themselves of allusions to the role of detached observer (Chubin and Restivo, 1983) occupying a neutral position.

Hence, according to the 'pragmatist' position, the 'truthfulness' of any methodologically corroborated explanation or account would be ultimately available, or testable, only through practice. This makes it incumbent upon the researcher to provide a clear guide to the practical ramifications of the theory and the subsequent practices that would pragmatically test that theory. Therefore, as Fay (1975: 94–5) comments, there would be an explicit recognition that social theory is interconnected with social practice such that what is to count as truth is partially determined by the specific ways in which scientific theory is supposed to relate to practical action. Thus, the theories of such a science will necessarily be composed of, among other things, an account of how such theories are translatable into action.

The processes by which our methodologically produced and corroborated accounts, or 'cognitive systems', might then be tested by these practical concerns are illustrated in Figure 8.6.

Figure 8.6 | The pragmatist position

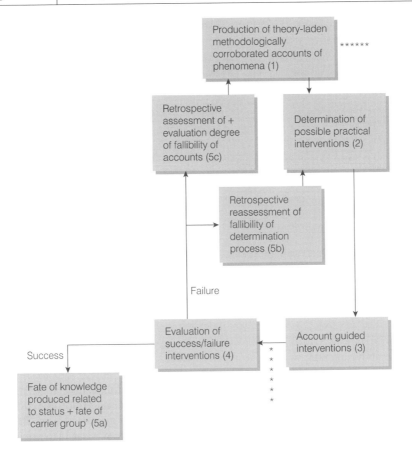

So, all these considerations regarding the 'truth' imply that research should not stop at the presentation of an account that has been produced and corroborated by the methodologies reviewed and evaluated in this text. Rather, research should proceed at least to identify the practical ramifications of that account and, ideally, should also proceed to test that account through practical interventions into our world so as to get feedback from that external reality. Indeed, inspired primarily by Critical Theory, some action researchers have integrated similar epistemological commitments into their work in a distinctive manner to produce coherent methodologies. As we shall illustrate, a key difference is how these action researchers produce its stage 1 in the first place.

Critical theory: reconfiguring action research and ethnography

Critical theorists (for example, Habermas, 1974a; Beck, 1992, 1996) deny the possibility of a theory-neutral observational language – what counts as warranted knowledge or truth is always conditioned by the operation inescapable socially established and linguistically based modes of engagement. The key epistemological question is how have these modes of engagement been socially established? Six key implications arise here for the critical theorist are illustrated below.

Given the above agenda, which is driven by Critical Theory's argument for a democratic epistemological standard for all knowledge, Critical Theorists seek to show the practical, moral and political significance of particular communicative actions. They also investigate how a particular social structure may produce and reinforce distorted communicative actions that practically and subtly shape its members' lives. Because they have not been developed in the democratic conditions of what Habermas calls the 'ideal speech act' (1974a, b), actors' culturally derived subjective apprehensions must in some sense be the outcome of asymmetrical power relations and hence are ideologically distorted.

Therefore, as Forrester argues, Critical Theory entails structural phenomenology which investigates the social construction of intersubjective meanings in a particular social and historical context – 'the objective social structure in which those actors work and live' (1983: 235). In order to accomplish structural phenomenologies Critical Theorists usually undertake a modified form of *verstehen* often called 'critical ethnography' (see Forrester, 1992, 2003; Putnam et al., 1993; Thomas, 1993; Morrow and Brown, 1994). The aim here is to investigate the nature of contemporary cultural forces and how these hegemonic regimes of truth impact upon the subjectivities and behaviour of the disempowered in contemporary organizational contexts. According to Thomas (1993: 2), what makes this ethnographic work *critical* is the attempt to 'describe, analyze and open to scrutiny otherwise hidden agendas, power centres and assumptions that inhibit, repress and constrain'. As Jermier observes (1998: 242), there is therefore a controversial commitment to attempting to access actors' culturally derived world views while revealing the socio-economic conditions which create and maintain asymmetrical power relations by ' ... the blending of informants' words, impressions and activities with an analysis of the historical and structural forces that shape the social world under investigation' (1998: 242).

Hence, the form that ethnography takes here moves beyond the description of actors' subjective worlds to considering the structural forces that have led to the development of these subjectivities and considers how these subjectivities entrap people in particular ways of understanding themselves and their worlds that serve particular interests at play in society. In other words, because those culturally derived views have most likely not been established under dialogical conditions, the subjective situation of the actors under investigation through conducting a critical ethnography is inevitably ideologically forced and distorted. Therefore, to this research agenda many critical theorists add (e.g. Freire, 1972a, b; Dryzek, 1995) a further important element. This involves both enabling the disempowered to become aware of the forces that have contributed to their oppression and through the establishment of a democratically grounded critical consciousness enable them to overcome these forces through promoting, for instance, organizational change through a distinctive form of action research often called critical-emancipatory action research.

For critical theorists, due to the problematic status of any epistemic authority not grounded in democratic relations, the role of the action researcher is fundamentally reconstructed to one of facilitating democratic agreement. For Freire, to avoid 'introjection by the dominated of the cultural myths of the dominator' (1972a: 59), action researchers must facilitate the development of a 'critical consciousness' (1972a: 46). He argues that the necessary prerequisites for the development of a critical consciousness, that dismantles the current hegemony, are not only the recognition by actors of their present oppression through that hegemony, but also the understanding that a critical consciousness is only constitutable through an authentic dialogue with the educator/action researcher where both are 'equally knowing subjects' (Freire, 1972b: 31).

By examining how particular interest-laden discursive practices sustain, for instance, particular strategic or operational preferences and change manoeuvres, Freire would see such a programme as an educative and therapeutic catalyst because the intent is to engender, through reflection, new (theory-laden) self-understandings. People should thereby begin to: understand those practices as social constructions; become aware of their own role in production and reproduction of those practices; construe those practices as mutable; identify how they might intervene in the evolution of their organizations and society. The result would be a challenge to traditional management prerogatives and the negotiation of alternative renditions of reality which create novel questions, inaugurate new problems and make new forms of organizational practice sensible and therefore possible (see, for example, Gaventa and Cornwall, 2006; Park, 2006).

Thus, a direct consequence of the epistemological ontological position taken by critical theory is a concern with organizational change – not just in the form of a distinctive analysis and critique of current management theory and practice but also in the form of a moral imperative to engender democratic social relations and thereby shift the balance of power to currently marginalized groups. For management researchers who ally themselves with critical theory, those individuals and groups whose perspectives are ordinarily silenced in organizations must be given voice. The demand is for members' conscious self-determination of social values and practices through participation and dialogue (e.g. Greenwood and Levin, 1998; Kemmis and McTaggart, 2000; Gustavsen, 2006; Kemmis, 2006). The epistemological demand is to mobilize and emancipate stakeholders usually silenced or duped by the status quo, through, for instance, 'co-operative inquiry' (Heron, 1996; Reason, 1999). Reason (1999) suggests that those who advocate co-operative inquiry focus on two

Figure 8.7 | Critical-emancipatory action research processes

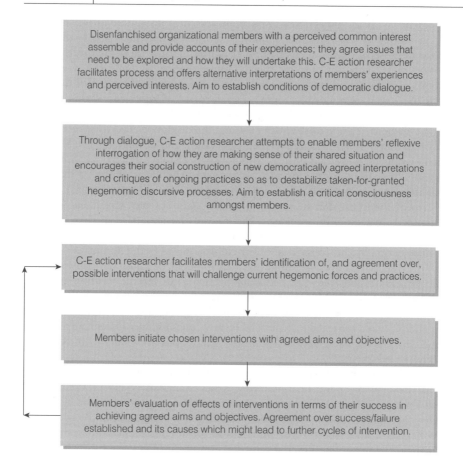

important purposes. The first is to 'articulate and offer democratic and emancipatory approaches to inquiry' (ibid.: 207). This suggests that in line with critical theory, those traditionally silenced in the academic research process are provided with some kind of voice in all aspects of the research endeavour, ranging from designing the research questions, to planning eventual action strategies. The second (ibid.: 208) purpose has a deliberate aim of critiquing the epistemology underlying the positivist view of the action researcher as a detached expert who exercises a legitimate role as architect of change as this is seen to be a process that disenfranchises the less powerful who have as much claim to epistemic authority as any other putative change-agent. Key elements in this critical-emancipatory action research process are illustrated by Figure 8.7.

Here it is important to note that pragmatist action researchers see themselves as complementing and extending the perspective and praxis of critical theorists. While admitting to the significance of social construction, pragmatists develop extra-discursive criteria of truth that complement and supplement the critical theorists' demand for democratic agreement (see Levin and Greenwood, 2001).

In Sayer's terms, these extra-discursive criteria are (1992: 69) in the form of the 'actual realization of expectations' through interventions which enable contact with the tolerance of reality. This epistemology has led some action researchers to argue that action research itself becomes a vehicle for judging ideas in terms of their efficacy in actual application (see Gustavsen, 2006; Park, 2006) while retaining democratic consensus as pivotal to generating the ideas in the first place (Levin and Greenwood, 2001).

In sum, the epistemological commitments of critical theory and pragmatism reconstitute action research. The intent is to engender new (socially constituted) self-understandings and simultaneously expose the interests which produce and disseminate knowledge which was taken to be authoritative and hence unchallangeable. In doing so, members democratically reclaim alternative accounts of phenomena – 'transformative' redefinitions which thereby become available to transformative interventions which can themselves be judged by the pragmatic criterion of 'what works' in terms of the pursuit of particular goals and interests.

Conclusions

In this chapter we have attempted to review several key philosophical disputes which influence how management research is both conceived and undertaken. Largely we have presented these disputes as revolving around different assumptions about the nature of human behaviour (i.e. *erklaren* vs *verstehen*); and different assumptions about whether or not we can neutrally engage with the social world as researchers (i.e. epistemology); and different assumptions about whether or not the social world exists independently of our cognitions (i.e. ontology). Often these contentious philosophical issues are ignored, or even suppressed, in management research leading, by default, to the preservation of what amounts to a positivist status quo – a point we shall take up further in the final chapter of this book. However, increasingly this status quo has been questioned by an array of management researchers who deploy philosophical assumptions that contest those embedded in the Positivist approach(es). As we have tried to illustrate these shifts in assumptions about epistemology and ontology drive various methodological reconfigurations in particular critical theory, postmodernism, critical realism and pragmatism. Although diverse, these alternatives to the positivist mainstream seem to shared an increasing commitment to philosophical introspection in that they require management researchers to be able to interrogate and contest the philosophical assumptions they inevitably make when engaging with research. One of the outcomes of this increasing sensitivity is that management researchers should be able to articulate, explain and defend the philosophical baggage they inevitably bring with them in and through their modes of engagement. The role this baggage plays in how we plan and undertake research is illustrated by Figure 8.8.

However, there is one further key implication of the various philosophical shifts we have described in this chapter. This is to do with how management research may be evaluated – a key concern for anyone undertaking management research and a further area that expresses philosophical disputes and differences. We turn to this area called Criteriology in our next and final chapter.

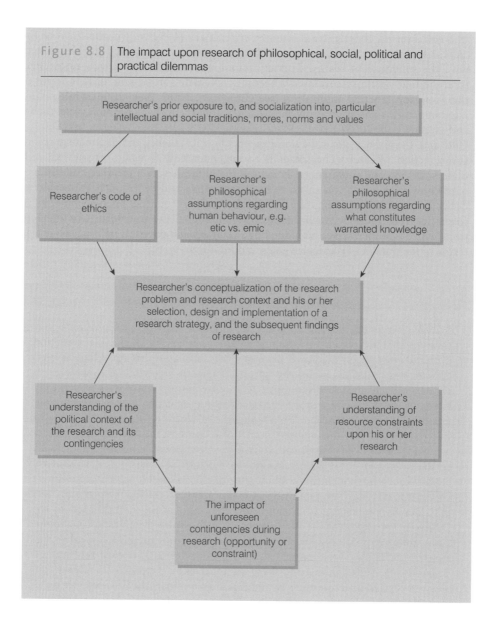

Figure 8.8 | The impact upon research of philosophical, social, political and practical dilemmas

Further reading

For an overview of the principal epistemological debates in management research we obviously recommend Johnson and Duberley (2000). This covers positivism, conventionalism, postmodernism, critical theory and critical realism and calls for more reflexive approaches to management research. Also Alvesson and Skoldberg (2000) provide an accessible guide to undertaking reflexive research which reviews how different epistemological commitments are expressed in various qualitative approaches including grounded theory, ethnography, critical theory, postmodernism and feminism. Meanwhile, Alvesson and Deetz (2000) contain a detailed discussion of how critical theory can inform organizational research and interventions. Postmodernist theory and research is incisively discussed and carefully evaluated in Hancock and Tyler (2001). We also recommend Law's (2004) fascinating critique of positivism and empiricism in social science methodology. His argument is that the research methods we use in social science do not merely describe social realities but actually help create them.

As we have indicated in this chapter postmodernists attempt to describe and deconstruct discursive forms, explore how they have developed and impact upon people, identify how they might change and then ultimately to destabilize them so that alternative discourses, which are always possible, might then develop. Interesting examples of the use of deconstruction are provided by Kilduff (1993) and Linstead (1993b) and discourse analysis by Ball and Wilson (2000). The examination of how discourses develop through using genealogy is provided by Knights and Morgan (1991) and how they adapt and change is provided by Barry and Elmes (1997). The use of a distinctive form of postmodern action research in order to destabilize the hegemonic patriarchal discourses of gender is provided by Treleaven (2001). The methodological implications of critical theory for ethnographic research, and the tensions it creates, are illustrated by Putnam et al. (1993). Critical theory's concern with forms of research aim to be both participative and emancipatory are also evident in feminist methodology. Here we recommend Mies' (1993) highly influential critique of positivism. With regard to critical theory's reconfiguration of ethnography and action research we recommend for the former Thomas (1993) and Jermier (1998) along with Kemmis (2006) and Gaventa and Cornwall (2006) for the latter. critical realism has significant implications for how both quantitative and qualitative methods are deployed and how the results of research are used and understood. These aspects are discussed by Mingers (2000) whilst critical realism's reconfiguration of ethnography may be found in Porter (1993).

These journal articles are freely available on the companion website (www.sagepub.co.uk/gillandjohnson):

Cooper, R. and Burrell, G. (1988) Modernism, postmodernism and organizational analysis: an introduction, *Organization Studies*, 9: 91–112.
Holland, R. (1999) Reflexivity, *Human Relations*, 52(4): 23–48.

Lecture 8

Philosophy of Social Sciences II

Paradigms, Conventions and Relativism

MARK J. SMITH

I   Introduction

In the earlier chapters we focused upon whether it is possible and desirable to apply the assumptions and methods of the natural sciences to study social objects of analysis. So far, these approaches have lined up either for or against **naturalism**. The positivist and empiricist answer to this issue is that we should adopt a naturalist position, while many idealists question whether we should study people in this way. Nevertheless, most of the idealist approaches considered in Chapter 4 tend to accept the positivist view of scientific method as an accurate description of natural science; they just do not see it as appropriate for studying social life. In contrast, many of the approaches considered in this chapter see natural scientific knowledge itself as situated in definite historical and social locations – as social products or conventions. For this reason, we use the label **conventionalism** to designate all of these views. These conventionalist approaches shook the foundations of natural scientific thinking, sometimes provoking considerable hostility. However, in addition to telling us more about natural science and natural scientists, they also opened up new possibilities for reinterpreting the history and the philosophy of the social sciences.

In the last chapter we saw how the same observations can be interpreted in various ways, whether we are observing natural or social things. So far you have worked through the debates on the relationship between interpretation and observation. These debates prepared the way for thinking through a new relationship between natural and social science. Rather than the social sciences trying to copy natural scientific methods, both have attempted to share their ideas about how knowledge works. The relationship is now two-way rather than one-way. Conventionalism raises important and difficult issues about the nature of the natural sciences themselves as well as the ways in which positivist or empiricist methods are applied to the study of social objects such as 'society', 'the economy', 'the state', 'the environment' and 'the mind'. These issues can be expressed in a series of closely related questions all of which are addressed in the following sections of this chapter.

- What is the relationship between approaches in the philosophy of science and the actual practices of both natural and social science? How realistic are these approaches in describing the scientific process of discovery?

- To what extent is scientific knowledge a social product or convention and what are the implications of this for the status of science? What is the role of the communities and institutions which produce scientific knowledge?

- Do accounts which portray the growth of scientific knowledge as a slow process of testing and accumulating evidence take adequate account of the role of hunches, guesswork and flashes of inspiration?

- If scientific knowledge changes periodically as scientific communities change, such that the status of science is *relative* to the cultures which produce it, is it possible to remain committed to the idea of progress in human knowledge?

- What are the implications of adopting either a relativist or a rationalist position in the social sciences?

- How are conventionalist accounts of scientific knowledge interpreted within the disciplines of the social sciences?

So, while in Chapter 3 we saw how there was already an increased resistance to the application of natural science methods to the social sciences, the studies raised in this chapter will actually challenge your understanding about what makes a natural science 'scientific'; that is, what makes it a true account of reality.

Before we address these questions, let's consider the structure of the present chapter (shown in Figure 5.1). In section 2 we focus upon the approaches which have generated an increased sense of doubt about empiricist accounts of knowledge. For empiricists, one of the key ways in which science is demarcated from non-science is whether it can be tested and falsified. However, we will explore how scientists build escape clauses into their theoretical constructs to avoid refutation. In section 3 we examine the arguments and evidence developed by Thomas Kuhn and others who, in their different ways, contributed to this crisis in the construction of knowledge. Kuhn was a historian of scientific thought and practice who initially set out to write about the unification of scientific method. In the course of his research, he became increasingly convinced that a universal and rational scientific method could not be established. In section 4 we return to the falsificationists to consider how they have responded to these arguments, focusing on the ideas of Imre Lakatos and how they have been applied. The empiricists suggested that conventionalism had given up on progress and offered no basis for making authoritative judgements about the world. Finally, section 5 explores the debate between empiricists and conventionalists in a little more detail by reassessing the relationship between rationality and relativism.

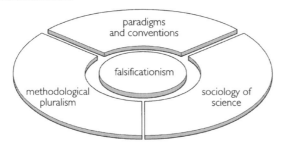

This sign will help you chart your way through the approaches in the chapter.

Figure 5.1 Conventionalist approaches in the social sciences: the chapter structure.

Before we address conventionalism, its applications and its critics, it is important to examine why empiricist theory and practice came to be questioned in the post-war debates on the philosophy of science. While the scientific method developed within empiricism offered a powerful rationale for conducting scientific research, by the 1960s it had become evident that there were serious problems with the falsificationist approach. In the social sciences, one of the main problems which emerged was the difficulty in disproving a proposition within the body of work from which it had been generated. In effect, it was possible in both the natural and the social sciences to build escape clauses from falsification into any scientific statement so that the critical edge of the approach was blunted.

We start off with Popper, but come back to falsificationism again in section 4.

2 Falsificationist escape clauses

One of the most important problems in empiricist accounts of the scientific method is that of identifying a set of circumstances in which a scientific statement can be falsified through the acquisition of new empirical evidence. Statements and propositions attempting to explain the workings of the 'real world' do not exist in isolation but within complex theoretical systems. To begin, it is useful to distinguish between two types of theoretical statement.

Elsewhere this sign *g* will direct you to the glossary, but revisit this section if you need to.

- **Bedrock assumptions** specify the underlying assumptions within a particular scientific approach. These can be formally defined but can also be tacit, taken-for-granted rules and procedures which are rarely questioned. In short, they act as the 'bedrock' for building contextual hypotheses.

- **Contextual hypotheses** are generated when these bedrock assumptions are used within a definite context, producing statements which take into account the complex conditions of the objects in question. Contextual hypotheses also convey the combined operation of established laws working together within these conditions.

Scientists are often so busy testing statements about definite situations that they rarely consider their bedrock assumptions.

It has become increasingly apparent in the history of the scientific method that theories, hypotheses and propositions can continue to exist for some time despite the existence of conclusive evidence for their refutation. A good example of bedrock assumptions in the natural sciences can be seen in Newton's 'laws of motion'. In a similar way, the assumption that human beings are 'rational calculating individuals' is adopted in some branches of the social sciences. If it can be demonstrated that scientists evade falsification by introducing qualifications or by restricting empirical tests to contextual hypotheses rather than their bedrock assumptions, then how viable are the approaches? It is these issues which we consider in section 2.1. A Popperian response might be to describe this as bad science – a violation of the spirit if not the letter of falsificationism. However, Popper's approach applies to the testing of singular conjectures or hypotheses. In practice, empirical tests are conducted in the context of complex configurations of principles, laws, theories and previous empirical tests. This means that the conclusive refutation of a specific hypothesis can take place only within a reassessment of the whole body of theory concerned. But scientists become attached to specific bodies of theory, so are empiricist accounts idealized reconstructions of scientific method rather than an accurate and useful account of actual practice? This important question will be addressed throughout the chapter.

2.1 Interpretation and observation in the natural sciences

While the following sections explore the attachments and practices of natural and social scientists engaged in organized communities, here we consider the relationship between testing hypotheses and the theoretical systems in which hypotheses make sense, particularly what has become known as the Duhem-Quine thesis. In *The Aim and Structure of Physical Theory* (1914/1962), Pierre Duhem, a French philosopher and historian of

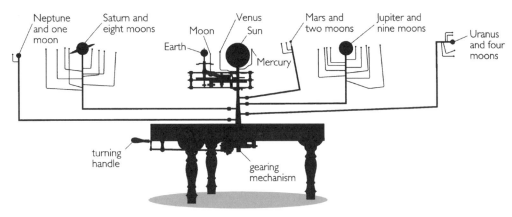

Figure 5.2   The orbital movements of the solar system: a clockwork model.

science, reassessed the history of physics from Newton onwards. He was concerned with the way scientific statements exist, not in isolation, but as part of complex hierarchies of theories and with reference to accumulated empirical evidence. So Duhem explored examples of situations where the available empirical evidence did not match the existing theories.

Astronomy provides a useful illustration of these problems. Until 1781 it had been assumed that the solar system consisted of six planets – Mercury, Venus, Earth, Mars, Jupiter and Saturn, ordered in terms of their distance from the Sun (see Figure 5.2). The discovery in that year of the planet Uranus, beyond Jupiter, created a new problem for astronomers. Using Newton's laws of motion and his law of gravity (as bedrock assumptions) in conjunction with a range of additional contextual hypotheses about the conditions within which the object existed (such as the various effects of other known planetary objects and taking into account their proximity and relative mass), astronomical scientists were able to plot a theoretical orbit for Uranus. For this example, it is important to note that planets exert gravitational pulls of varying strengths upon neighbouring planets. If we can estimate the gravitational effects of known planetary objects, then we should be able to plot their respective orbits around the Sun. However, the observational evidence of Uranus did not match the theoretical orbit established by the astronomers. This raised questions about the existing assumptions involved in the contemporary theories of astronomy. Two options exist in such a situation: either to question the bedrock assumptions and initiate a root-and-branch reassessment of the body of theory concerned, *or* to develop better contextual hypotheses but still founded upon existing bedrock assumptions.

New discoveries in scientific research often require a reappraisal of existing scientific theories.

In this example from natural science, the calculations of astronomers John Couch Adams and Urbain Leverrier (working independently in the mid 1840s) raised doubts about the contextual hypotheses developed on the orbit of Uranus; they raised the possibility of an additional planet orbiting beyond Uranus and exerting a gravitational effect on its orbit. The discrepancies between the theory and empirical evidence were, in this case, accurately explained in terms of their description of the mass and orbit of another planet (which was identified by telescope soon afterwards as the planet Neptune). So, in this example, by sticking to their bedrock assumptions and by making adjustments to the contextual hypotheses, Adams and Leverrier produced useful scientific knowledge. However, being loyal to your bedrock assumptions does not always work out so successfully. When attempting to explain unexpected features in the orbit of Mercury, Leverrier posed the existence of a planet closer to the Sun which was exerting a gravitational pull on Mercury. He labelled this planet Vulcan. This modification to contextual hypotheses was not to be so successful, for no such planet exists. This left an anomaly between theory and evidence which remained unresolved until the bedrock assumptions of Newtonian physics in astronomy were thrown into doubt eighty years later, when Einstein questioned these theories of gravitation.

Examples such as these led Duhem to question the standards of scientific theorizing. Francis Bacon had argued that 'true science' should involve the identification of all possible contending theories in the explanation of a specific phenomenon and the use of experimental tests to identify the inaccuracies and flaws in each theory until all but one of the contending theories had been eliminated and absolute certainty could be established. For Duhem, no such definitive test of a single hypothesis could be devised and applied. He suggested that it was possible only to examine **theoretical systems** against the available empirical evidence. When faced with a situation in which observations do not fit the existing theoretical framework, scientists must make a choice between the modification of bedrock assumptions and revision of contextual hypotheses. Whereas Duhem had related testing statements to theoretical systems, more recently Willard von Quine's essay 'Two Dogmas of Empiricism' (1953/1965) argued that such tests could throw whole **knowledge systems** into doubt. Rather than seeing scientific knowledge as just bundles of individual theories focused upon the same object of analysis and/or set of problems, Quine saw them as a 'sort of man-made fabric' woven together in complex ways. This means that when you start to unpick certain patterns in knowledge, the whole fabric can unravel. Therefore, empirical tests can also throw our view of reality into doubt. In Quine's account, it is the whole field of inquiry of human knowledge which is disturbed by the emergence of anomalies between empirical evidence and established theories, in much the same way as a stone can cause ripples on the surface of a pond. We see the full implications of this in section 4.

Quine's intervention is also important for highlighting the way in which scientists actually seek to avoid falsification by building escape clauses into their theories and explanations. They do this either by reformulating the contextual hypotheses or by making adjustments in the theoretical system in order to protect the bedrock assumptions from refutation (Quine, 1953/1965; Gillies, 1993). Such difficulties are not only a feature of natural science, they emerge in the social sciences as well. They exist regardless of the differences between the objects of analysis within the natural and the social sciences. In all areas where there is a fairly structured and extensive body of thought in a particular social science, we can witness a reluctance to question bedrock assumptions. In the next section we explore how these problems exist in the social sciences through two case studies, one drawn from political studies and the other from sociology.

Explaining new discoveries generates a choice between modifying existing theories or reassessing the foundations.

To revisit Bacon, see Chapter 2, section 3.1.

The Duhem thesis – an empirical test can never falsify an isolated hypothesis, it challenges the whole theoretical system of which it is a part.

The Quine thesis – an empirical test can never falsify an isolated hypothesis, it challenges the whole knowledge system of which it is a part.

Summary

The falsificationist method focuses upon the testing of single hypotheses. This runs into difficulty when put into practice in the natural sciences. Knowledge systems comprise different forms of theoretical statements which are defined in relationship to each other as well as in relation to empirical evidence.

Rather than reassessing the bedrock assumptions, scientists frequently test the contextual hypotheses generated from these bedrock assumptions. When these are found to be inadequate, then further contextual hypotheses are developed in the conduct of research without raising doubts about the underlying assumptions.

3 Paradigms and conventions: the end of progress?

In the middle sections of this chapter we explore approaches which consider scientific knowledge to be defined as a social product – as a convention which scientists and others hold to be true. As you saw in section 1, **conventionalism** has been used as a broad label to describe these approaches. To some extent, Popper's account of verisimilitude (that truth was a matter of degree, not an absolute) had prepared the way for this line of argument. However, with the conventionalists, this questioning of the foundations of knowledge was taken further to undermine the faith in 'rationality' and 'progress' as well. In *The Structure of Scientific Revolutions* (1962/1970), Kuhn developed an argument that is often identified as the cause of a 'crisis of rationality' in Western scientific thinking. He concluded that scientific knowledge does not produce an independently true account of the external world but reflects the organized activities of scientific communities. Kuhn was not the first conventionalist in the study of natural science, but his importance here is due to the role which his concept of **paradigm** has played in the social sciences since the 1960s. Now, before we consider how the idea of paradigm has been understood and applied in the social sciences, let's look at Kuhn's historical account of scientific change in a little more detail.

If you want to revisit Popper, see Chapter 3, section 5.1.

3.1 Kuhn's account of scientific change

The idea of paradigmatic change was a direct challenge to the idea of progress through the accumulation of knowledge.

Empiricist accounts of scientific knowledge had been committed to the idea of progress through the gradual accumulation of knowledge. Even though Popper had given up on the search for truth, the whole point of falsification was to build on existing knowledge in a cumulative way (rather like walking up a never-ending staircase). Kuhn's approach, however, suggested that it was not even possible to identify a progression in knowledge. Through a careful study of the ways in which natural science has developed and changed, Kuhn suggested that scientific knowledge went through long periods of stability interrupted by short periods of sudden transformation. In addition, instead of establishing a universal standard against which it was possible to compare all statements about the world, Kuhn argued that knowledge was a social product and, as such, changed as society changes. He described each phase of stability in the history of science as a period of **normal science**. This occurs when the rules of scientific method are well established and the role of scientists is limited to solving problems and puzzles without questioning the rules within which they work. These rules involve widely accepted **demarcation criteria** through which we can distinguish which forms of knowledge which are scientific and which are not. In the case of logical positivism, the demarcation criteria between science and non-science were such that if something could not be reduced to a simple observation statement and the theories could not be empirically verified, then it contained metaphysical components and was thus meaningless. These rules become part of the institutional life in which scientists work and their work is judged according to how closely they operate by the accepted principles of their disciplinary fields.

Kuhn developed the concept of 'paradigm' to characterize changes in the 'standards governing permissible problems, concepts and explanations' (Kuhn, 1970, p.106) within the context of a historical and sociological approach. The concept of paradigm is a matter of much dispute (which we come back to in section 3.2). However, the idea of paradigm in this context can be taken to mean the 'universally recognized scientific achievements that ... provide model problems and solutions to a community of practitioners' (Kuhn, 1970, p.viii) and therefore forms the implicit taken-for-granted commonsense assumptions of a scientific community. In this way, paradigms are more than sets of theories, they are scientific communities through which knowledge is produced and understood.

Each paradigm has its own demarcation criteria between which ideas and forms of evidence should or should not be taken seriously as scientific knowledge.

This historical account of scientific knowledge starts with a **pre-paradigmatic stage** in which a range of approaches compete for dominance although none is able to achieve it. Kuhn argued that the social sciences remain in this state, for they have not as yet achieved the maturity of one dominant set of rules. The natural sciences, he argued, have achieved this. For instance, the development of Newton's physics marked the emergence of a paradigm in physics, closely followed by paradigms in chemistry, biology and physiology. Kuhn described the dominance of normal science within which the activities of scientists can be characterized as puzzle solving within an established set of principles and methodological procedures. Newton's mechanics provided physics with just such a workable set of principles (rules of experimental inquiry and scientific laws of motion) for the development of further scientific laws and the identification of facts. However, by the middle of the nineteenth century a series of problems or anomalies emerged in the application of Newton's laws to astronomical objects which could not be adequately explained. By the 1890s these anomalies had accumulated to the point that physics was in a state of crisis and, with the emergence of an alternative set of principles, physics experienced a scientific revolution as a new paradigm emerged to replace the old one (see Figure 5.4).

This view of the history of science involving long periods of stability marked by sudden breaks draws from common narrative structure of historical storytelling.

Kuhn argues that a scientific revolution like the one from Newton's to Einstein's physics involves a 'gestalt shift'. This means that the scientists involved would have to go through a 'conversion experience' in order to move from the old paradigm to the new one. In the case of physics, Newton's mechanistic laws were replaced by Einstein's theory of relativity. However, many scientists were left behind in this process, unable to cope with the trauma of such a transformation. Kuhn agrees with Planck's view: 'a new scientific truth does not triumph by convincing its opponents and making them see the light, but rather because its opponents eventually die and a new generation grows up that is familiar with it' (Planck cited in Kuhn, 1970, p.151).

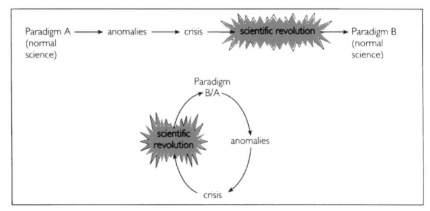

Figure 5.4 Kuhn's theory of scientific revolution.
The figure shows two ways of representing Kuhn's account of the transformations involved in a scientific revolution. Each representation tells a different story. In the linear one, the shift of paradigms implies a kind of progress (perhaps that Einstein's physics improves on Newton's). In the cyclical version, a paradigm shift sends us full circle – it implies that science changes but does not progress.

Paradigm shifts are intergenerational transformations in the bedrock assumptions of knowledge held to be true by scientific communities.

In practice, the shift takes place over a generation or even longer, for few of those who have worked their way up the academic career ladder are likely to question the theories upon which their research and careers are based. Each of these paradigms is mutually exclusive and the members of the scientific communities which construct each paradigm interpret their experiences so differently that they can be said to occupy 'different worlds'. In Chapter 3 you saw how experience could be interpreted in different ways, but nevertheless it was generally assumed that the interpreters had enough in common to communicate their interpretations effectively to each other. In Kuhn's account of paradigmatic differences, this would not be feasible. This can be seen when we look at examples of paradigm shifts. For instance, by the middle of the twentieth century, Einstein's theories provided the underlying rules for physics in the new normal science in much the same way as Newton's had in the previous paradigm. A physicist viewing the physical universe with the assumptions developed by Einstein would see a different universe from that of Newton. It is possible to see this as yet another addition to scientific knowledge, but the questions which Einstein raised struck right at the heart of the assumptions that had dominated physics for centuries.

Paradigms are incommensurable – the ideas generated by one paradigm cannot be used to judge the truth value of the ideas of another paradigm.

To suggest that members of different paradigms experience different worlds has further implications. Kuhn argued that each paradigm has its own way of demarcating science from non-science. Consequently, paradigms are **incommensurable**; in other words, it is impossible to use the criteria of one paradigm to judge the truthfulness of the theories of another. In effect, this means that there is no such thing as universally true knowledge, but it also means that paradigms do not progress, they merely change. Kuhn argued that because the standards of assessment are internal to each paradigm, then scientific revolutions involve a shift in the standards governing which explanations we can consider to be legitimate. Paradigms are seen as incommensurable, in that they involve mutually exclusive foundational assumptions. This is expressed in the different vocabularies of each paradigm.

During the tranquillity of periods of 'normal science', the scientific assumptions go unquestioned, with problems subject to the procedure of puzzle solving, whereby established theories are modified to maintain consistency with the evidence. Gradually, anomalies within a paradigm build up to the point of generating a crisis which precipitates a scientific revolution or paradigm shift, allowing a new paradigm to emerge through a form of conversion experience of gestalt shift (analogous to a religious conversion) rather than by a series of rational logical steps (see Figure 5.4).

Ian Hacking has written a useful summary of the key features of Kuhn's approach which helps us to differentiate the conventionalist position from the common foundations of empiricist approaches, and which relates closely to the conclusion of Chapter 3. You may recall that, for empiricists, theory and observation are distinct, science has a tight deductive structure, concepts should be precise, the sciences should be unified, the **context of discovery** is distinct from the **context of justification** and scientific knowledge provides, or should aspire to provide, universal explanations of things. Hacking highlights the way in which conventionalism provides a very different account of scientific knowledge because it disagrees with all the standpoints and assumptions on which empiricists are agreed. For Hacking:

You may find it useful to revisit section 7 of Chapter 3 where you met Hacking before.

> There is no sharp distinction between observation and theory.
> Science is not cumulative.
> A live science does not have a tight deductive structure.
> Living scientific concepts are not particularly precise.
> Methodological unity of science is false; there are lots of disconnected tools used for various forms of inquiry.
> The sciences themselves are disunified. They are composed of a large number of only loosely overlapping little disciplines many of which in the course of time cannot comprehend each other ...
> The context of justification cannot be separated from the context of discovery.
> Science is in time and is essentially historical.
>
> (Hacking, 1983, p.6)

However, this does not mean that Kuhn offered no basis for considering knowledge as good or bad. He became concerned that many portrayals of his ideas assumed that his account provided no basis for making judgements about knowledge. Consequently, he later identified five characteristics of good scientific theory, as a way of making these judgements:

Accuracy	that a theory should be accurate within its domain of inquiry
Consistency	that a theory should be internally consistent as well as consistent with other theories
Broad scope	that a theory should explain more than it set out to explain
Simplicity	that a theory provides a clear and simple account of complex objects
Fruitfulness	that a theory should identify new phenomena or previously unnoticed relationships between such phenomena

(adapted from Kuhn, 1977, pp.320–9)

The meaning of the concept of paradigm is open to question on two grounds. First, Kuhn himself was very imprecise as to how a paradigm

The imprecise definition of the idea of 'paradigm' has produced many and varied uses in the natural and social sciences.

could be defined. Margaret Masterman identified twenty-one different uses of the concept of paradigm in Kuhn's landmark text alone (Masterman, 1970). Kuhn responded in the second edition of his book with a sharper definition of paradigm as a 'disciplinary matrix' consisting of a strong network of commitments, theoretical, instrumental and methodological (Kuhn, 1970). Second, this conceptual confusion has led to different uses of the concept of paradigm between different disciplines and even different uses within each social science discipline. In the next section, we find it is often used loosely to mean a 'model' of the social world or to identify a school of thought, a tradition or a perspective. However, it is the many and varied uses of Kuhn's work which has made his approach so influential.

If we look at Kuhn's use of the term in his historical account of natural sciences, paradigms would have to dominate exclusively in a field of knowledge for a significant period of time. We can see something approaching this in sociology in the 1950s, when functionalism (considered in section 2.2) came close to exercising a dominance along these lines. Nevertheless, alternative approaches continued to coexist with functionalism in sociology and soon re-emerged in the 1960s. Actually, Kuhn only expected a paradigm to emerge in economics, so in terms of Kuhn's own use of the concept of paradigm the social sciences remain **pre-paradigmatic** (by which he understood them to occupy a pre-scientific phase of development). Kuhn's approach views scientific knowledge as a social product and the rules by which we judge knowledge to be scientific as merely conventions. Critics of Kuhn's approach, such as Karl Popper and Imre Lakatos, have argued that conventionalist approaches offer little hope for humanity. A defender of falsificationism, Lakatos suggested that, by giving up on the possibility of progress and by attributing scientific knowledge to the internal workings of communities of scientists, Kuhn's account was in fact the 'mob psychology' of scientific knowledge (Lakatos, 1970).

Summary

Thomas Kuhn situates scientific knowledge in the context of the historical and social practices which define natural science in a particular time and place. Consequently, the truth of a scientific statement is only relevant to those who share the belief system upon which such 'truths' are based.

Kuhn argues that each paradigm possesses its own demarcation criteria on what constitutes science and non-science. Paradigms replace one another through scientific revolutions and they are incommensurable. If one paradigm can never be used to judge another and the occupants of each paradigm are in 'different worlds', then progress is no longer a relevant term in the description of scientific knowledge.

If the way we think shapes the way we interpret evidence, we face substantial problems in distinguishing theories from observations and facts from values. This directly challenges the foundations of empiricist accounts of scientific knowledge.

3.2 Paradigms in the social sciences

How have these arguments been used to understand changes in the social sciences? Earlier it was argued that Kuhn's significance was a consequence of the widespread uses to which the concept of paradigm had been put in the social sciences. To make these changes comprehensible, these uses can be identified as falling into three broad categories.

- **Paradigm 1** – the strict sense identified by Kuhn in his account of the natural sciences, when a single dominant framework, disciplinary matrix or normal science exists and one demarcation criterion operates between science and non-science operates. In this case, paradigms are incommensurable and they are assumed to succeed one another rather than compete, although competition between alternatives may occur in the relatively short-lived periods of crisis and evolution.

- **Paradigm 2** – where the intellectual foundations of the community are such that to move from this paradigm to another would require reorientation of the type identified by Kuhn as a gestalt shift. In this case, we can identify a distinct scientific community with its own institutional foundation and academic career ladder existing within a particular field of knowledge. This use acknowledges the presence of competing paradigms in the same field of knowledge but requires them to be incommensurable.

  Elsewhere this sign **g** *will direct you to the glossary, but revisit this section if you need to.*

- **Paradigm 3** – used to designate a school of thought, theoretical perspective or set of problems. This is the loosest but most common use, in which the term paradigm is seen as synonymous with a 'model' of a particular aspect of social life. This use does not require incommensurability between different paradigms nor does it require a reasonably coherent scientific community with an institutional foundation in research and educational settings (although these features may be present and are usually necessary for the long-term survival of the approach).

We can explore the use of each of these conceptions of paradigm through two case studies, one from psychology and the other from economics. Within the social sciences, there are no perfect applications of Kuhn's original sense of **Paradigm 1**, where clearly identified foundational principles have replaced each other in quick succession, but we'll consider some examples which come pretty close. One of the nearest illustrations can be seen in psychology with the emergence of the behaviourist approach. Even here, the absolute dominance of one approach (of one world-view) implied by Kuhn is not apparent, for other approaches exist on the fringes of the discipline. However, behaviourism was influential in establishing psychology as a scientific discipline and, despite a great deal of self-criticism within the discipline, psychology is often identified as the closest of the social sciences to the natural sciences. This association of behaviourism with the dominant scientific method was also reinforced by the adoption of behaviourist approaches in sociology and 'political science' (including pluralism, identified earlier in section 2.2). The behaviourist approach focuses upon observable behaviour and specifically excludes any reference to inner states or intrinsic qualities which, by their character, cannot be observed.

Behaviourism is largely concerned with the relationship between individual human beings and their social and physical environment. This is partly a product of the origins of the behaviourist programme in the animal

See Chapter 4, section 3.1.

experimentation of John B. Watson. In his early studies of rat behaviour, Watson developed a theoretical framework which argued that consciousness was irrelevant to psychology and that, as a result, the introspective approach of Wundt, the dominant approach until the early twentieth century, was an inappropriate basis for establishing an objective science of behaviour (Watson, 1928). The rats in Watson's experiments were subjected to different environments within experimental conditions and to a range of rewards and punishments for their responses to various problems, such as finding food in a maze. (Figures 5.5 and 5.6 illustrate similar experimental work.)

Figure 5.5   Scientists monitoring the behaviour of rats in a maze experiment.

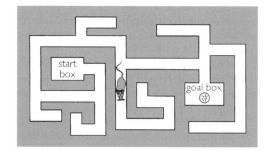

Figure 5.6   Diagram of the maze used in a behaviourist experiment.

The results of this experimentation established that rats could learn to respond to their environment and to various sanctions so establishing that their behaviour was not static but could be modified. Watson was at the forefront of arguing that the techniques developed in the objective study of animal behaviour could also be used within human psychology. This involved refocusing psychology towards the study of behaviour so that it could become a 'purely objective experimental branch of natural science'. Behaviourism required a move away from the study of the conscious mind, mental stages and images as subjectively defined. This challenged the existing approach of introspection which took subjective states as its starting-point. It is this difference in approach which marks off behaviourism from introspection and other earlier forms of experimental psychology, as a **Paradigm 1**. Since each approach operated through different demarcation criteria between science and non-science, there is no common basis for establishing objective knowledge or for judging between them. So introspection and behaviourism can be characterized as incommensurable.

In psychology, the shift from introspection to behaviourism is often seen as a paradigmatic shift.

It is worthwhile exploring this approach in a little more detail in order to highlight the ways in which psychologists have responded to behaviourism more recently. The central principle of behaviourist psychology is the explanation of the process of learning as one of **operant conditioning**. This assumes that behavioural modifications of individuals are a response to the consequences of their behaviour. The environment is assumed to react towards the individual in three ways – negative, neutral and positive – and that this reaction can act as a reinforcer (a reward) or as a punishment for the behaviour concerned. Of course, rewards and punishments can have a neutral effect, in that they may not alter behaviour. Nevertheless, there are four possible ways in which the modification of individual behaviour can take place.

Positive reinforcement – takes place when a particular form of behaviour produces pleasurable consequences for the individuals concerned and encourages similar behaviour in the future.	*Negative reinforcement* – takes place when an inhibiting or an aversive feature is removed, enabling the individual to carry out a particular form of behaviour and encouraging similar behaviour in the same circumstances.
Positive punishment – introducing (or the threat of introducing) an aversive stimulus in order to support or discourage particular forms of behaviour in the future.	*Negative punishment* – removing (or the threat of removing) a reward of entitlement which would otherwise provide pleasurable consequences in order to suppress or discourage particular forms of behaviour in the future.

Behaviourist psychologists have used this system of reinforcers and punishments to examine the processes of childhood socialization and to recommend therapeutic uses of behaviour modification where the behaviour of children was considered to be inappropriate or 'abnormal'. Similarly, in the treatment of criminality, solutions were sought in the modification of behavioural traits, rather than assuming that criminals would be deterred in future through the application of a particular standard form of punishment. If it were assumed that consciousness was not relevant to the study of behaviour then, when conducting research, it could be assumed that human beings are no different from non-human animals. All behaviour could be studied in experimental conditions, or through careful observation, in order to establish patterns of modification in learning behaviour. These studies could be replicated and the data verified to establish their authenticity, creating objective scientific accounts of human behaviour. The work of Watson became an important reference point for the generational shift from introspection to behaviourism in psychology. However, alternatives remained in existence, such as Gestalt psychology and psychoanalysis, although they remained marginalized in the discipline until the debates of the 1950s and 1960s which saw the reintroduction of the concept of the self as an intentional and purposeful social actor.

Introspection works from the subjective mental states of individuals, while behaviourism regards them as irrelevant for generating scientific knowledge.

In the behaviourist approach, a great deal of stress is placed upon the role of the stimulus–response relationship, whereby the behaviour of the individual is seen as an effect of external stimuli, with responses taking one of the four forms identified above. However, the same evidence can also be interpreted as an example of purposeful behaviour (or, if we are talking about animals, behaviour that appears to have a purpose) rather than as a conditioned reflex to a particular stimulus. The cognitive psychologist Edward C. Tolman (Tolman et al., 1946) argued that an alternative model of the learning process, whereby knowledge of past experiences is stored in a cognitive map of the environment, provided an account which could explain the variation of responses to the same stimuli in human and animal behaviour (in addition to the evidence explained by the behaviourist approach). Cognitive psychology assumes that the acquisition of information allows for 'rule-governed behaviour' but that these rules are flexible and adaptive in the light of subsequent experiences. There is some dispute as to whether cognitive psychology replaced the behaviourist approach in psychology as the most influential theory. In addition, Tolman's approach coexists with that of the later behaviourists, such as Burrhus F. Skinner, in a different disciplinary context where a range of new alternatives was also emerging. Human cultures are defined by Skinner as the composite of behaviours of the individuals who form a particular community. Skinner sought to purge any conception of individual autonomy and creativity. Like Watson, he was particularly concerned to challenge the conception of the 'autonomous man' within voluntarist approaches to social life (Skinner, 1953, 1971). For Skinner, it is not ideas, wants, values or desires which determine behaviour, for these can only be identified through the study of those aspects of social relationships and personal choices which, in a causal explanation, would be conventionally defined as effects (the dependent variables). In the field of social psychology, the emergence of a range of new approaches placed a greater emphasis upon the meaningful, personal and social aspects of the lived experience of social actors. Such humanistic and critical social psychologies focused on subjective experience as a foundation for knowledge and the role of social actors in actively constructing the social world, and moved beyond the experimental setting to draw upon a wider range of empirical research strategies.

Activity 5.2

Reading B includes three short extracts from *Theory and Social Psychology* (Sapsford *et al.*, eds, 1998): 'Experimental social psychology' by Patrick McGhee, 'Humanistic and experiental social psychology' by Richard Stevens and 'Critical social psychology' by Margaret Wetherell. Read these extracts now.

- Identify the differences between each approach and consider which of the three senses of paradigms adequately describes this area of social scientific knowledge.

You may also find it useful to think about how these different kinds of psychology lead to different approaches to research methods: defining the object of analysis differently may mean having to gather evidence in ways which match.

Psychology has now fragmented into those areas where one approach dominates in a paradigmatic way and those areas where contesting approaches coexist.

Cognitive psychology has, in time, become a scientific community in its own right with an institutional basis in research and teaching organizations separate from other approaches; in this context, it appears to exist in a paradigmatic way (in the sense of **Paradigm 2**) as a methodological framework in most of the areas of psychology, with the exception of social psychology. In social psychology, the influence of the cognitive framework is more limited. Here it has become known as psychological social psychology competing with a range of approaches from sociological social psychology. So, in the case of social psychology, the use of **Paradigm 3** would be more appropriate as a descriptive label for cognitive psychology (that is, psychological social psychology). The problems of applying the concept of paradigm to other social sciences are just as complex. In the case of economics, even Kuhn himself held out some hope of a singular mature science developing in the sense of **Paradigm 1**, although it should be added that his own perspective was coloured by the apparent success and widespread acceptance of Keynesian economic management strategies in the Western post-war boom from the 1950s to the early 1960s.

Activity 5.3

Turn to Reading C, 'Economic paradigms', on the Keynesian and monetarist approaches to the economy, from Vane and Thompson's *An Introduction to Macroeconomic Policy* (1982), and 'Economic crisis: the Marxist view' from Hunt and Sherman's *Economics: An Introduction to Traditional and Radical Views* (1981).

- Identify the key assumptions in each of the three approaches and consider whether these approaches are incommensurable.
- Identify which concept of paradigm best describes the differences between them.

As in the examples from psychology in Activity 5.2, you should look for clues as to the similarities and differences between these approaches.

In economics the contrast between Keynesian and monetarist approaches to the study of the economy has often been couched in Kuhnian terms. These economic theories represent opposing philosophies about the role of the state in the organization of production, distribution and exchange which are reflected in completely irreconcilable positions in policy terms. In substantive terms, Keynesianism presumes that the state can intervene in the free market in various ways with positive consequences in terms of employment, prices and growth. In this approach, the state ensures that the level of total aggregate demand is such that the economy does not fall into recession nor does it become overheated, causing inflationary pressure. This precarious state of affairs, where the state moderates the tendencies of the business cycle through fiscal and monetary fine-tuning, is achieved through the intervention of a benevolent state, which seeks to maximize the common good. This approach, then, assumes that the economy can be planned, or at least guided, towards certain common goals and that when the market fails (such as in the decline of an industrial sector) the state can intervene directly and take control of key sectors in the public interest.

Keynesianism and monetarism are often described as different paradigms in economics.

Monetarism, on the other hand, rejects the role of the state as a benevolent actor and assumes that an economy functions most efficiently when left to its own devices. The activity of the state is interpreted as a form of interference which damages exchange relations and diverts valuable and scarce resources from profitable uses (through taxation) by maintaining declining sectors of industry (through subsidies or state ownership). From the monetarist standpoint, the intervention of the state (by increasing the money supply) is the cause of both inflationary pressure and the perpetuation of inefficient sectors of the economy. In addition, the growth of state intervention creates a greater tax burden which further undermines incentives for wealth production more generally, as well as 'crowding out' private sector capital from the limited opportunities for investment.

With such well rehearsed arguments and the existence of institutional group-ings of Keynesian economists (for instance, at Cambridge University) and monetarist economists (for instance, at Liverpool University), it is easy to see how these two opposed approaches could be interpreted as different worlds. However, on closer examination the relationship between the two approaches is not so simple. The ideas of the economist John Maynard Keynes are often contrasted with the neo-classical economics which preceded them. Neo-classical economics assumed that the market would inevitably resolve any imbalances (slumps and booms) through the adjust-ments of the 'invisible hand' of the price mechanism whereby, according to Say's Law, the supply of goods will always find its own demand at a given price. The 'Keynesian revolution' was a revolution in the sense that it became possible to envisage the state adopting a proactive rather than a reactive relationship to the problems of the market. However, this is not the same thing as a scientific revolution, because the conceptual landscape remained much the same as before. Moreover, the object of analysis in both Keynesian and monetarist approaches remained the market, for it was de-fined as a set of exchange relations between firms, households and individ-uals. In addition, the values of commodities are identified in terms of exchange value. As to how they define their field of analysis, both approaches remain committed to identifying the same objects in the same way. Where these approaches disagree, then, is over the legitimate role of the state in the market as well as over the normative issue of whether it is poss-ible and desirable to create an egalitarian society.

Compared with the 'Marxist paradigm', Keynesian and monetarist economics have common foundations.

If, however, we contrast both of these approaches with Marxist economics, a different set of issues arises. For the Marxist economist, the object of analy-sis is not simply the exchange relations which characterize capitalist mar-kets but also the productive relations and the productive forces which together make up the economy. Exchange relations are treated as operating upon the level of surface appearances and present an 'ideological' obstacle to understanding the underlying real workings of the economy (preventing us from seeing the world as it really is). In the Marxist approach, the re-lations between capitalist and working classes are characterized by irrecon-cilable conflicts of interest which, at any given time, may or may not manifest themselves in visible social and political conflict. In addition, per-iodic economic crises are treated as the symptoms of underlying productive processes in a class-divided society. For Keynesians and monetarists, how-ever, 'capitalism' in the sense identified by Marxists cannot be observed and as such cannot be said to exist. Similarly, we can observe workers but not the proletariat, and individual businesses and firms but not capitalism. Clearly, different demarcation criteria are at work.

Now, let's see how these differences relate to the three senses of paradigm identified earlier. While the difference between Keynesianism and monetarism appears to illustrate **Paradigm 3**, the difference between both of these approaches and the Marxist theory of the capitalist economy seems closer to the meaning of **Paradigm 2**. The move from seeing the economy as a set of exchange relations to seeing the economy as constituted by definite productive relations could be seen as a movement between different worlds. Economics does not offer an example of **Paradigm 1**, and from this study we can see that a crisis in theorizing within a particular discipline does not constitute a revolution unless an alternative paradigm is emerging which is itself incommensurable with the paradigm it is replacing (Katouzian, 1987, pp.100–6).

The previous sections illustrated the ways in which definite approaches seem to emerge in the social sciences and can dominate in a particular discipline. However, the frequency of the turnover of theories and methods in the social sciences seems to ensure that such dominance is short-lived. One possible answer to the question of why this occurs could lie in the social conditions in which these dominant approaches in Western societies emerged during the 1950s (which produced behaviourist psychology, Keynesian economics, functionalist sociology, pluralist political science and quantitative geography). If scientific knowledge is a social product, it is interesting that periods of consensus within disciplines occurred simultaneously with greater social solidarity in the societies which produced this knowledge. This period witnessed a sustained period of economic growth, political stability and greater opportunities for wider sections of Western societies. Similarly, perhaps the social scientific discord which has occurred since is related to the decline of social cohesion in Western societies since the 1960s. If we take seriously the argument that knowledge is a social product, then it is possible to see Kuhn's work itself as a product of social conditions in the same way. In the following sections we focus upon the other main contributors to conventionalist interpretations from this period. These approaches raise important questions about Kuhn's description of the history of the scientific method.

> Dominant paradigms in the social sciences tend to coincide with periods of greater social stability and consensus in the lives of the scientific communities involved.

Summary

The application of Kuhn's concept of paradigm to the social sciences is common but inconsistent. Anything close to the strict use identified by Kuhn (**Paradigm 1**) has only been witnessed for brief periods where a particular approach has influenced a social scientific discipline (as in the case of behaviourism in psychology and functionalism in sociology).

The treatment of paradigms as incommensurable but not necessarily dominant (**Paradigm 2**) is particularly useful in identifying the bedrock assumptions of different theoretical systems in social science. This is often confused with the 'loose use' of paradigm as a particular 'model' or 'school of thought' in open competition with other models or schools (**Paradigm 3**).

3.3 Conventionalism beyond Kuhn I: question everything!

> An approach associated with conventionalism is methodological pluralism.

So far, we have concentrated upon one example of conventionalism, Thomas Kuhn's historical account of science. Other conventionalists, such as Paul Feyerabend, place less emphasis upon fairly well defined periods of stability and change in the history of scientific knowledge. Feyerabend, perhaps more than anyone else, has challenged the tendency to look for order in knowledge. In *Against Method* (1975), he argued that the most important characteristic of scientific knowledge is its messy, accidental and discontinuous nature. This was directed as much against Kuhn's concept of paradigm as a period of normal science as it was against positivism. Feyerabend developed a standpoint which suggested that science was not rational, that no knowledge rules had operated effectively in any case, and that scientific knowledge could be oppressive rather than an instrument of progress. Further than this, he argued that rival theories themselves (rather than paradigms) are incommensurable, so that it was impossible to identify a basis for defining one form of knowledge as superior to another form at any point in time. For Feyerabend, to treat science as a rational and objective enterprise was a myth (that is, folklore for scientists). In addition, he portrayed the pursuit of rational scientific explanations (running from the positivists through to Popper) as undesirable because it substituted the accumulation of knowledge for the goal of emancipating human beings.

'Anything goes' – Feyerabend's view that the only defensible position is the idea that all ideas are equally valid.

Feyerabend was concerned that no ideas should be rejected just because they did not conform to a particular standard of useful or true knowledge. This principle of 'anything goes' earned him the label of 'epistemological anarchist'. The anarchistic vision he held was a positive one (in the sense that it referred to the positive condition of freedom from authority rather than a condition of chaos). Here, though, it was applied to knowledge systems rather than political systems. He never saw himself as a political anarchist, but more of a Dadaist who questioned our expectations. Kuhn and Feyerabend seem to offer different ways of thinking about the limits of truth, progress and reason. Feyerabend's conception of knowledge is relativist; he holds that all views are equally privileged, true and valid (Harré and Krausz, 1996). He hoped that it would be possible to live in a situation where all views could be taken seriously, that no ideas should be disregarded in case they become useful in another time and place. Feyerabend questioned the key principles of science just when it was reeling from the impact of Kuhn's work. Instead, he advocated the **principle of proliferation** as the alternative strategy to the imposition of one dominant view. The challenge that Feyerabend's approach presents can be seen in his comparison of scientific textbooks from the 1950s and the handbook for the Witchfinder General dating from the fifteenth century.

g

> In 1484, the Roman Catholic Church published the *Malleus Maleficarum*, the outstanding textbook on Witchcraft. ... It has four parts: phenomena, aetiology, legal aspects, theological aspects of Witchcraft. ... The aetiology is pluralistic, there is not just the official explanation, there are other explanations as well, purely materialistic explanations included. Of course, in the end only one of the offered explanations is accepted, but the alternatives are discussed and so one can judge the arguments that lead to their elimination. This feature makes the *Malleus* superior to almost every physics, biology, chemistry textbook of today. Even the theology is pluralistic, heretical views are not passed over in silence, nor are they ridiculed; they are described, examined and removed by argument. The authors know the subject, they know ... the positions of their opponents, they argue against these positions and they use the best knowledge available at the time in their arguments.
>
> (Feyerabend, 1978, p.92)

Feyerabend explicitly ties this critical questioning of established conceptions of authoritative knowledge to the desire to maximize the freedom and realize the untapped potential of individual human beings. In terms of the circuit of knowledge established through modern scientific thinking (considered in Chapter 2), Feyerabend questions science, reason, truth and progress in order to emancipate humanity, breaking the circuit in the process (see Figure 5.7). The existence of a single orthodox account of what constitutes authoritative knowledge is portrayed as a form of oppression and he raises the ways in which science can involve an increasingly diverse range of theories with equal standing.

Feyerabend questions the circuit of modern scientific knowledge established in an integrated way since the Enlightenment.

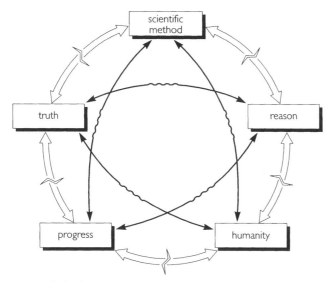

Figure 5.7 Breaking the circuit of modern scientific knowledge.

In a similar way, in *Deschooling Society* (1971) the radical social theorist and critic Ivan Illich has identified and criticized the use of knowledge as an instrument for promoting conformity and obedience. Illich distinguished 'education' (involving the process of learning and understanding) from 'schooling' which (through the practice of memorization and by instilling obedience) destroys human creativity. This draws from the distinction between 'knowledge about' and 'knowledge of' developed by William James. Illich suggested that the damaging effects of schooling on the realization of the full potential of individuals could be identified within all educational and academic institutions, ranging from the infant school to the university; such institutions were designed to reward those pupils and students who memorized and reproduced the authoritative knowledge rather than to encourage creative and free thinking. Illich's answer was to identify how a plurality of ways of thinking could be fostered and monolithic knowledge dislodged from its pre-eminence in the education system. This was to be achieved through learning webs, where tutors and students could come together around common interests and define their own curriculum, and through skill exchanges, which would enable the practitioners in a particular field to pass on their skills and experience through practical applied study.

See Chapter 4, section 5.1.

Science should help make human beings free and not enslave them within a dogmatic set of methodological rules. **g**

Feyerabend and others, in the late 1960s and early 1970s, offered a radical way of challenging established conventions about scientific knowledge. In particular, they challenged the assumption that this form of knowledge, by virtue of its ability to distinguish truth and falsehood, could lay claim to a superior status over other forms of knowledge. In the place of one way of seeing the world, they advocated **methodological pluralism**. This approach is based upon the philosophical position of **relativism**, the view that no form of knowledge is more valid than any other. However, two examples of inconsistency have been identified in Feyerabend's work. First, while he does not believe that reason can lead us to the truth (he adopts an anti-rationalist stance), he still argues for the use of 'rules of thumb' in research which does not exclude the use of 'rational standards' in explaining phenomena. Second, Feyerabend continues to accept the possibility of progress in the development of knowledge which the rejection of a universal rational standard would appear to preclude.

Activity 5.4

Turn to Reading D, 'Methodological pluralism', from Bruce Caldwell's *Beyond Positivism* (1994).

- Briefly identify the steps in establishing methodological pluralism raised by Caldwell.

This is a practical manifesto for raising questions about the way a discipline is organized. Think about any discipline with which you are familiar and try to identify the broad approaches within it. Now think about the strengths and weaknesses of these approaches.

g

Sympathizers with this critique of the claims associated with scientific knowledge in the social sciences have embraced the idea of methodological pluralism, whereas critics, such as the social anthropologist Ernest Gellner, have warned against the relativism that this view implies. For Gellner, this means that social scientists cannot support or condemn any theoretical position – they are merely left standing on the sidelines of serious discussion. In particular, Gellner criticized Feyerabend for leaving us in a position where, for example, it is impossible to condemn events such as the Holocaust. In effect, Gellner was asking what is the point of social science if it does not have an impact on the organization of social life. Feyerabend responded by arguing that his approach was not relativistic in that sense. Gellner is addressing the issue of moral relativism, whereas Feyerabend is concerned with **epistemological** questions. At this point it is important to separate questions of truth (addressed by Feyerabend) from questions of 'the good' (raised by Gellner). Actually, in *Science in a Free Society* (1978) Feyerabend advocated that all knowledge should contribute to human freedom and not oppression, so it is clear that his values did motivate his approach to knowledge construction – even Feyerabend, then, links questions of truth to questions about 'the good'. The problem of the relationship between rationality and relativism is addressed in more detail in the final section of this chapter, but first we shall consider the role of explanations which adopt the position of social constructionism in the study of natural science.

3.4 Conventionalism beyond Kuhn 2: the sociology of knowledge and science

In this section you have the opportunity to go back to the issue of scientific practice by exploring approaches which consider the practical experiences of scientists. A common strand throughout all conventionalist approaches is the emphasis placed upon the institutional and cultural context of knowledge production. In the field of the sociology of knowledge and science, Barry Barnes in *Interests and the Growth of Knowledge* (1977) and David Bloor in *Knowledge and Social Imagery* (1976) have developed what they call the 'strong programme' to explain how the social context of research affects the development of knowledge in both the natural and the social sciences. Barnes and Bloor point to the variation in knowledge between groups, the variations in different individual interpretations of the same experience, and the role of the interests of scientists and researchers in maintaining deference to their expertise and their own personal advancement. In particular, they identify the disjunction between the tentative character of the evidence upon which scientific knowledge is based and the strong degree of certainty which the use of the label 'scientific' presumes. In this approach, all knowledge is mediated through a culture and language which scientists themselves inhabit. The label of 'strong programme' reflects an attempt to adopt the relativist position more explicitly compared with the weaker versions in Kuhn's and Feyerabend's approaches. Barnes's and Bloor's research identified that scientific knowledge is the product of a range of social factors within the academic, professional and industrial contexts in which the knowledge was generated. This approach, sometimes loosely called 'social constructionism', draws upon the insights of hermeneutics, phenomenology, ethnomethodology and cultural anthropology, because of the way in which all these approaches focus upon the situatedness of human knowledge.

See Chapter 4, section 5 and Geographical Models 2.

Such studies ask whether the social sciences should follow the formal procedures of scientific method when natural scientists do not do so themselves. The history of science is littered with useful accidents, such as the discovery of penicillin, or with informed guesswork, such as the discovery of DNA. In such cases, progress in the accumulation of knowledge was not delivered by the careful and rigid application of a particular scientific method. Kaplan's work had already prepared the way for this by pointing to the difference between the 'reconstructed logics' favoured by philosophers of science (that all philosophies are idealized stories of what should be done) and the 'logics in use' in the everyday practices of scientists where hunches, guesswork, leaps of intuition and accidents play an important part in the construction of knowledge. Kaplan is, in effect, distinguishing between what scientists do and what they say they do (Kaplan, 1964). Textbooks from the philosophy of science tend to present a highly formal account of the scientific method and tend to avoid the complex settings in which research takes place. In particular, they often focus upon the most successful examples of research rather than the ambiguous evidence of the work of scientists in general.

The sociology of science considers what scientists do, not just what they say they do.

In 1994, at the British Association for the Advancement of Science, Harry Collins (Professor of Sociology of Science at the University of Bath)

Science is a social product – it conveys the authoritative knowledge of the social and historical context in which it was produced.

presented a case for questioning the status of science as a superior form of knowledge. He raised the extent to which a scientific community depends upon trust. In particular, Collins focused upon the ways in which the results of scientific investigations are more ambiguous, the scientific theories are more flexible and that progress is more uncertain than most theoretical accounts of science suggest. In his view, what is regarded as 'science' is the end product of a complex process of legitimation in the identification of authoritative knowledge and is dependent upon the social context in which such knowledge is produced. Collins argued that the designation of particular forms of knowledge as scientific is dependent upon the plausibility of this knowledge for the scientific community involved. (See Figure 5.8.) He went further to say that, in the light of this, knowledge should not be subject to any universal standard. Collins concluded that scientific knowledge is a social construct and that science is tied to definite social and historical conditions, so that when conditions change so too does knowledge (Collins, 1994).

Figure 5.8 The mechanics of celebrity can be seen in the academic performance.
Scientific knowledge is produced and communicated in organized communities ... some large, some small. Jacques Derrida addresses the assembled academic congregation at the University of Sussex (1 December 1997).

The identification of variations in the forms of knowledge as if they were matters of cultural difference was derived from interpretative sociology and anthropology. This involved the careful empirical study of communities of scientists through in-depth interviews and participant observation in order to identify the taken-for-granted assumptions of scientists and to reconstruct the processes through which scientific knowledge was made. The distinctive contribution of anthropological insights to a discussion of natural and social scientific method can be seen in the short story 'The Philosopher, the Scientist and the Anthropologist', related in Zygmunt Bauman's *Hermeneutics and Social Science* (1978):

> On one occasion Sir Karl Popper told his audience a story which had obviously shaken him. It concerned an anthropologist invited to join some other first-class brains in discussing an important matter in the methodology of science. At the end of long and heated arguments, to which the anthropologist listened in silence, he was asked to express his view. Much to the dismay of everybody present, the anthropologist replied that he paid little attention to the actual content of the dispute. The content was, he thought, the least interesting of what he saw and heard. Of incomparably greater interest were other things: how the debate was launched, how it developed, how one intervention triggered off another and how they fell into sequences, how the contributors determined whether they were in disagreement etc. Our anthropologist, presumably viewed the topic which aroused so much passion as just one of those 'native beliefs' whose truth or falsity is largely irrelevant for a scholarly study. This was why he was not particularly interested in the topic. Instead, he recorded with genuine interest the interaction in which the learned experts engaged. ... Sir Karl was, of course, indignant. For him statements are about something and are to be judged, in this way or another, by being tested against this something. ... He would try to extract from the sentence the message it contained, and then attempt to put the truth of the message to the test.
>
> (Bauman, 1978, p.172)

One way to try to understand what scientists (or even philosophers!) do is to observe them directly in their own environments, in the way that social scientists observe other small groups of people involved in communication and interaction.

Activity 5.5

Turn to Reading E, 'Two sociological perspectives on science', from Michael Mulkay's *Sociology of Science* (1991). Then consider the two journalistic extracts in Reading F: John Turney's 'Faking it to make it' (1989) and Stuart Sutherland's 'What if teacher is a cheat?' (1989).

• Identify which of the two approaches considered by Michael Mulkay is relevant for understanding the accounts of the practices of science given by Turney and Sutherland.

In this activity you should notice that each of the perspectives on science identified by Mulkay could be applied to the two journalistic accounts. However, you should also have noticed that the perspective adopted can lead you to look at them in very different ways and reach different conclusions. You may find it useful to to look back at Activity 3.3 in Chapter 3; again here the question is whether the research is evidence of 'bad science' or whether the way we see science itself needs to be rethought.

The scientific ethnographic studies of scientists, notably by Bruno Latour and Steve Woolgar (1979), Michael Mulkay (1972, 1991) and Karin Knorr-Cetina (1981), emphasize the differences between the informal and accidental dimensions of the research activity itself and the formal style of presenting results in scientific journals (Figure 5.9) and within the media as though a logical procedure had been followed from beginning to end of the research process. For sociologists of science, scientific communities are characterized by networks and forms of social interaction – like any other form of community. The interactions which take place are seen as governed by the same criteria of trust and credibility that obtain in other acts of exchange. In this case, the acts of exchange involve data, ideas and other forms of knowledge, whether the exchange is portrayed as an act of gift giving (Hagstrom, 1965) or as an investment in the collective body of knowledge which can be converted later into status, power and perhaps wealth by the investors (Bourdieu, 1975).

Figure 5.9 A measure of academic output.
The pressure to publish has become relentless – it's the only way in which academic work can be measured and performance compared. A snapshot of the *Economic Journal* in the 1940s and much more recently.

Scientific knowledge is the product of the complex social practices of scientific communities.

Latour and Woolgar compare scientific communities to markets in order to explain the social relationships and patterns involved. They are concerned to avoid general debates on whether science is a social construct and prefer to explore the process of research itself. They focus upon areas which they describe as 'hot' research, the cutting edge of research activity where scientists are more likely to meet unexpected problems and have to innovate to generate useful new knowledge. The research conducted by sociologists of science provides useful insights into the actual practices of scientists and the development of scientific communities. Such studies also focus upon the relations of communication and power which operate in scientific communities and the role of patronage and sponsorship (see Figure 5.10).

Figure 5.10 The master–disciple relationship in scientific work.
The recruitment process for joining an academic community is long, arduous and intensive (a doctoral student submits his research for scrutiny from his supervisor).

In a similar way, in the social sciences the success of a particular research approach is largely governed by social conditions such as:

- the compatibility of a research approach with existing evidence and research, or the extent to which the conclusions generated offer an 'acceptable' way of resolving an established problem;

- the support of academic colleagues who, through the process of peer review, can affect the reception of a particular piece of research (Figures 5.11 and 5.12);

- the relevance or usefulness of the social research in question for both the scientific community and wider society, particularly for the justification or questioning of policy making in a specific field of government;

- the contribution of the research to a currently exciting area of academic work rather than to a field of inquiry which is considered to be dormant or exhausted.

These four considerations have been portrayed in a favourable light. A critical interpretation would consider the success of a particular piece of research in the extent to which it does not challenge the orthodox interpretations of the field, and in the ways in which it attracts the patronage of established academics who sponsor or dismiss the work in question. Also important is the degree to which it serves the interests of those who control politics (and thus the financial basis for future research) and the extent to

Figure 5.11   Learning to use the tools of the trade.
A student tries to remember Kant's advice 'have courage in your own understanding' when presenting a paper in a seminar conducted by Professor William Outhwaite.

which the choice of research topic and method reflects fashion and fad rather than some other criteria for establishing the relevance and usefulness of research. This approach highlights the dangers involved when social research remains unquestioned, because it confirms the existing body of opinion in a particular field and simply reinforces what is already taken for granted.

Figure 5.12   Peer review: the exchange of ideas in an academic setting.
Contributing in a constructive way means that you stick your neck out and make your views heard. But you should also expect your colleagues to be critical as well as supportive.

Summary

Feyerabend presents a case for the acceptance of a proliferating diversity of competing scientific theories as a positive state for scientific and socially useful knowledge. This encourages greater tolerance and explicitly links the generation of knowledge to the development of human potential.

Sociologists of science identify the organization of knowledge in communities, the mechanics of celebrity and intellectual patronage and the relationship between knowledge and the interests of academic institutions as crucial factors in understanding the social construction of knowledge.

4   Rationality and relativism: keeping progress

The studies of scientific knowledge by Kuhn, Feyerabend and the sociologists of science provoked a crisis of rationality in the philosophy of science (particularly undermining the more positivistically inclined approaches). The sceptical treatment of truth by Popper and Lakatos ensured that supporters of **naturalism** and rational scientific methods in the social sciences could still draw upon a versatile approach. Lakatos usefully qualifies the Popperian approach and tries to draw some lessons from the work of the conventionalists. He draws upon the historical evidence produced by Kuhn on the ways in which knowledge is organized in communities of scientists and how academic and scientific organizations are as important as the methodologies adopted. However, his approach is committed to the principle that the gradual accumulation of knowledge should deliver progress. Popper and Lakatos are more often described as critical rationalists because they challenge empiricist assumptions about the role of ideas and theories. However, for both of them experience acts as the arbiter for testing scientific theories.

Through the work of Lakatos falsificationism learned something from its critics.

Lakatos, in his 1970 article 'Falsification and the Methodology of Scientific Research Programmes', argued that philosophers of science were faced with three alternatives: induction, conventionalism and falsificationism. He ruled out induction on the grounds that theories were not a direct reflection of experience. He rejected conventionalism for giving up on the accumulation of knowledge as a means of delivering progress, for this is the point of being a scientist in the first place. Regarding the last approach, he argued that it was important to distinguish various forms of falsificationist approaches. He gave the label **dogmatic falsificationism** to the scientists who interpreted Popper in too simplistic a way and immediately discarded any hypotheses which had been refuted. This position was to be distinguished from Popper's falsificationist approach, which accepted that a hypothesis, even if empirically refuted, may still be useful as a predictive statement in a different context. Such statements, Popper argued, should simply be shelved for the time being unless they had been comprehensively falsified. This was in part a recognition of the problems in conclusively falsifying scientific statements, which we explored when considering the Duhem-Quine thesis. However, because Popper's position remained

Defenders of falsificationism seek to draw upon the insights of conventionalism without losing the accumulation of knowledge as a source of 'progress'.

g

focused upon individual laws, theories and evidence on a particular problem, Lakatos labelled Popper's approach **naive methodological falsificationism.** Actually, it was Popper's focus upon individual theories and the importance of protecting individual freedom that prompted Lakatos to argue that Popper and Feyerabend had, in fact, a great deal in common.

g

In recognizing that theories do not exist in isolation, Lakatos addressed Kuhn's contributions on the way in which knowledge was culturally and historically located. However, unlike Kuhn, he argued that a viable methodology had to be both descriptively accurate and prescriptively useful (that is, it indicates what we 'should' do in scientific research). In developing **sophisticated methodological falsificationism,** Lakatos felt that he could account for the institutional life of scientists and offer a guide for further scientific research. Lakatos distinguished between the 'hard core' which held the key foundational assumptions of a scientific research programme, and the 'protective belt' of auxiliary hypotheses which could be tested and falsified at any point in time. This is very much the same distinction between bedrock assumptions and contextual hypotheses which we considered earlier in section 2.

Negative heuristic –
all theoretical
systems contain
assumptions about
what it is not
possible to study.

Lakatos suggested that a scientific research programme (his alternative to the concept of paradigm) is governed by two sets of methodological rules. First, the *negative heuristic* dictates which research pathways cannot be studied. This protects the hard core from criticism: anyone who does this is often treated as a heretic or dangerous to the programme. For instance, behaviourist approaches which focus upon human actions as a series of effects resulting from various stimuli (such as pluralism in political science and political sociology) could not accept the existence of human beings as creative and reflective beings. You may recall that behaviourists reject the existence of inner selves as speculative and hold that such considerations are not the concern of science.

Positive heuristic –
all theoretical
systems contain
assumptions about
which pathways of
research are
feasible and which
are likely to be
fruitful.

Now that we have established the grounds for excluding things from an inquiry, let's focus upon the second set of methodological rules, the *positive heuristic.* This indicates the research pathways which are legitimate and worthwhile. For instance, in the case of pluralism in political studies (considered earlier in the chapter) it is concrete decision-making situations which could be observed, measured and explained that are considered to be legitimate and worthwhile objects of analysis. For Lakatos, even if a set of theories and core assumptions has been falsified, as long as they continue to offer useful predictions, then it is worth keeping them. In addition, in the absence of a more adequate alternative, Lakatos suggests that it is better to hang on to a bad theory than to have no theory at all. He also makes a plea for tolerance with the emergence of budding research programmes. Overall, scientific research programmes, even if inadequate, can be identified as progressive or degenerating in the long term. This is a considerable way from Popper's falsificationism, yet it retains his commitment towards progress and the accumulation of knowledge. For instance, many sociological perspectives would fit this description. For instance, both functionalism and Marxism have encountered severe problems in explaining social life and have for a time appeared to degenerate. Nevertheless, with a reworking of their protective belt, both have bounced back at different times as neo-functionalism and neo-Marxism, taking into account some of the criticisms launched against them. In each case, the bedrock assumptions of both the old and new versions remain consistent. Neo-Marxism, for instance, retains its commitment towards defining the economy in terms of class structure and gives the economy a determinate role, in the long term, in explaining the development of capitalist societies.

In the social sciences, this defence of the idea of 'progress' developed by Lakatos continues to offer an attractive alternative to the relativistic assumptions of conventionalism. However, one of the difficulties in applying this approach is the problem of clearly identifying the hard core of bedrock assumptions which are taken for granted by the participants in a research programme. Another problem emerges when we attempt to find a means of distinguishing a progressive from a degenerating research programme. For Lakatos, a progressive problem shift takes place when the newly emergent theory accounts for the successes of the previous theory, contains a greater empirical content than the existing approaches, and has been subject to attempts at falsification and has been corroborated.

Scientists are usually considering the protective belt of the research programme, not the hard core of bedrock assumptions.

Activity 5.6

Now read the extract 'The schizophrenia research programme' by Mary Boyle (Reading G).

• Identify the hard core and the protective belt in this example of social scientific research. What is the evidence that the research programme is either progressing or degenerating?

Think about the issues which you explored in section 2 when you considered the differences between assumptions and contextual hypotheses. You should remember the ways in which scientists and social scientists, when they find their assumptions are challenged, dodge difficult questions simply by modifying the contextual hypotheses. Is the distinction between the hard core and the protective belt any different? In particular, ask yourself whether Boyle's evidence on the schizophrenia research programme leads you to question this as a particular example of a 'failed' programme. The survival of the schizophrenia research programme and its search for a biological explanation started in the early part of the twentieth century – perhaps even Lakatos is too optimistic about the capacities of scientists to discard ideas which have been repeatedly found wanting.

The Methodology of Scientific Research Programmes (MSRP) is particularly important in social scientific disciplines which retain a commitment to falsificationism and the application of the assumptions and methods of the natural sciences to social objects. While Lakatos draws upon Kuhn's account of the collective dimension of research, he does not reject the possibility of progress through the accumulation of knowledge in particular disciplines. He argues that it is rational to use some criterion to demarcate scientific knowledge from other forms of knowledge. However, the distinction between the hard core and the protective belt allows for the existence of unfalsifiable (that is, metaphysical) claims at the heart of the research programme. So, in some respects, his approach is at odds with empiricism as it is generally understood. Nevertheless, Lakatos found a way of maintaining a commitment to the accumulation of knowledge and progress while addressing the concerns originally identified by Duhem and Quine.

See section 2.1 of this chapter.

Summary

Lakatos establishes a compromise between the goals of progress that lie at the heart of the rational scientific method and the actual practices of scientists. This approach acknowledges the importance of studies of scientific communities, but also argues that the relativism and the treatment of scientific knowledge as a social product offer an inadequate foundation for identifying useful knowledge and for making progress.

5   Reassessing rationality and relativism: towards a conclusion

There is a tendency for critical rationalists (such as Popper and Lakatos) to be presented in complete opposition to relativists (such as Kuhn, Feyerabend and Collins). However, as we discussed in the last section, this oversimplifies the differences and similarities between their approaches to science. Consider Figure 5.13. All of the philosophers represented below disagree with each other about what science involves and what knowledge

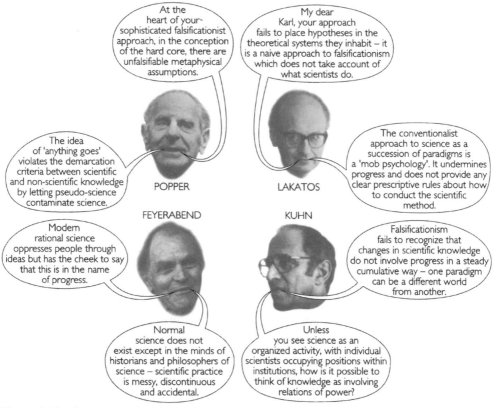

Figure 5.13   Philosophers like to argue a great deal ...

should be about. They disagree, in particular, on the role of falsification, whether progress is possible, the relationship between theory and observation, the role of scientific communities, and the relationship between science and freedom. Now consider Figure 5.14 on the connections between these positions. Actually, the disagreements only make sense when we consider the common terrain on which they stand (in other words, they agree on a great deal). Perhaps we need to reconsider the tendency to think of simple oppositional debates between rational science and relativism.

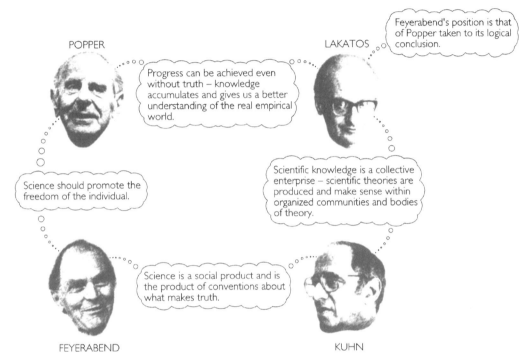

POPPER

LAKATOS

Feyerabend's position is that of Popper taken to its logical conclusion.

Progress can be achieved even without truth – knowledge accumulates and gives us a better understanding of the real empirical world.

Science should promote the freedom of the individual.

Scientific knowledge is a collective enterprise – scientific theories are produced and make sense within organized communities and bodies of theory.

Science is a social product and is the product of conventions about what makes truth.

FEYERABEND

KUHN

Figure 5.14   ... but we sometimes forget how much they agree.

So you can see that the tendency to set up Popper and Lakatos against Kuhn and Feyerabend misses a great deal. Rom Harré and Michael Krausz provide a useful alternative to the tendency to treat the difference between rationality and relativism as one of irreconcilable opposition. In *Varieties of Relativism* (1996), Harré and Krausz ask the question: is knowledge accepted as universal, objective and having definite foundations, *or* is it tied to particular social contexts, subjectively constructed and without firm foundations? For our purposes, let's accept the claim that there are no firm foundations to knowledge and that science is constructed within definite historically located cultures. Let's also accept the bold relativist view that this is a universal claim which applies to all forms of knowledge. We are still making a bold universal claim about science (the opposition doesn't work!). Once we have suspended our belief in the high status of scientific knowledge in Western culture, this leads us to question what social scientists have attempted to do. In particular, if natural scientists fail to live up to the standards of science, then why should social scientists try to copy them?

You can see how knowledge is situated by looking back at the examples of the scientific racist approach and positivist criminology in Chapter 3.

Conclusions: Evaluating Management Research

22

JOHN GILL and PHIL JOHNSON

Learning outcomes At the end of this chapter the reader should be able to:

- define the different evaluation criteria available for assessing management research;

- understand how many of the methods used in management research have distinctive strengths and weaknesses when evaluated using evaluation criteria such as validity and reliability;

- appreciate how case study research is an expression of methodological pluralism by combining different methods of data collection in a single piece of research;

- understand how the different types of evaluation criteria that may be used to evaluate management research articulate varying philosophical commitments regarding ontology and epistemology;

- distinguish between the various criteria used to assess research inspired by positivism, neo-empiricism, critical theory, and affirmative forms of postmodernism as examples of very different kinds of management research inspired by varying philosophical commitments;

- understand why there is no one best way of evaluating management research and appreciate that what is appropriate depends upon the philosophical assumptions at play in any given piece of research.

In this final chapter we turn to considering the complex issues that surround the evaluation of the quality of any findings when we complete a piece of management research. Inevitably, when we try to undertake any evaluation of research we have to deploy evaluation criteria that allow us to assess whether or not the research meets particular benchmarks, which are deemed important, and thus come to some judgement about whether or not the research is any 'good' or not. Clearly such processes of evaluation are very important for all management researchers, whether they are students undertaking various kinds of dissertation or experienced researchers submitting work for publication in prestigious academic journals: all are subject to such assessments undertaken by other people which directly affect their careers. Simultaneously management researchers regularly have to assess the work of others either informally when we read and try to make sense of others' published research or when we get involved in more formal peer review and student examination processes. However, as we shall try to show in this chapter, such evaluation is not a straightforward process – even though it may often be presented as such. This is because considerable confusion seems to permeate this area especially because, very often, the evaluation criteria that express particular underlying philosophical assumptions may be unintentionally applied as if they are the only means of assessing all research rather than being specific to only particular sets of philosophical commitments which we discussed in Chapter 8 of this book. Therefore, as Bochner forcefully observes (2000: 267), there is a danger of the widespread misappropriation of evaluation criteria and hence the unfair assessment of research findings. As he argues, this is because evaluation criteria constituted by particular philosophical conventions may be universally applied, as if they were 'culture-free' and hence indisputable, to what is a heterogeneous field inspired by a number of different epistemological and ontological dispositions which thereby justify a range of competing possible means of evaluation.

For example, this evaluation problem is sometimes fuelled by rather philosophically parochial reviews of evaluation criteria and policy statements in prestigious management journals (e.g. Behling, 1980; Mitchell, 1985; Scandura and Williams, 2000) which present specific criteria, that tacitly articulate positivistic philosophical assumptions, as if they were indeed universally applicable and thereby serve to exclude and undermine research inspired by the alternative philosophical stances discussed in Chapter 8. Given that the field of management research has been getting more philosophically diverse in recent years this issue of misappropriation has taken on an even greater importance as it may have created significant barriers to the use and publication of research outside the positivist mainstream (see Symon et al., 2000). Hence, one of the aims of this chapter is to demonstrate that there is no one universally applicable way of undertaking the evaluation of research: rather, what is appropriate depends upon the nature of the philosophical assumptions embedded in the research that is being assessed. The investigation of the varying ways in which research evaluation can, and indeed should, be undertaken is often called *criteriology*. We shall begin this investigation of these criteriological issues by looking at the most commonly used assessment criteria which operationalize positivist philosophical assumptions before moving onto the alternatives using neo-empiricism, critical theory, and affirmative forms of postmodernism as examples of criteriological diversity.

Positivist evaluation criteria

Here we shall first consider some of the most important criteria that are widely used to assess the quality of management research. However as we shall show, these criteria emerge out of positivist philosophical commitments and therefore are inappropriate to the evaluation of other types of management research. Nevertheless, they provide important insights into the inherent strengths and weaknesses embedded into some of the methodological research designs we have considered in this book. We shall therefore also consider these strengths and weaknesses in the light of these criteria. Whilst we have already touched upon some of these criteria in previous chapters it is worth elaborating them here by listing the most prominent criteria together.

1 *Internal validity* This criterion refers to whether or not what is identified as the 'cause(s)' or 'stimuli' actually produce what have been interpreted as the 'effects' or 'responses'. In other words, it refers to the issue of whether of not what has been defined as the independent variable actually is responsible for any identified variation in what has been defined as the dependent variable. It thus refers to the extent to which any research design allows the researcher to rule out alternative explanations, deriving from what we have defined as extraneous variables, of any observed variance in the dependent variable. Ideally the research design should also involve the use of procedures to gather data that allow the researcher to demonstrate that the action of the independent variable temporally precedes identified changes in the dependent variable. In other words, the research design should enable the researcher to tell if variation of the independent variable precedes that of the dependent variable thereby allowing him/her to elucidate the direction of causation between those variables.

2 *External validity* Generally, this criterion refers to the extent to which any research findings can be generalized, or extrapolated, beyond the immediate sample of people from whom data has been collected and/or the social setting in which the research took place. Therefore, the matter of external validity is often subdivided into the following two criteria.

   (a) Population validity – this criterion concerns the extent to which it is possible to generalize from the sample of people involved in the research to a wider population. In other words, it refers to how representative those people, from whom data has been collected in a piece of research, are of a defined larger population to which research findings are intended to be generalized.

   (b) Ecological validity – this criterion is concerned with the extent to which it is possible to generalize from the actual social context in which the research has taken place, and data thereby gathered, to other social contexts and settings. This is also related to the issue of how artificial or atypical the research setting is relative to 'natural' contexts typical of normal, everyday life.

3 *Measurement validity* This criterion refers to the operationalization processes discussed in Chapter 3 whereby abstract concepts are translated into a series of measures which tell the researcher whether of not instances of the abstract concept have empirically occurred and to what extent they have occurred. In other words, it is to do with whether or not the measures of independent, dependent and extraneous variables used in a research design faithfully measure those variables they claim to measure through the operationalization process.

4 *Reliability* This criterion basically refers to the consistency of results obtained in research. To satisfy this criterion it should be possible for another researcher to replicate the original research using the same, or equivalent, people and the same research design under the same, or equivalent, conditions in order to see whether of not the same results are then found. Hence, the assessment of reliability requires the use of clear methodological protocols so that regulation by

peers in the scientific community, through replication, would be possible in principle. For Merton (1938: 259) such processes are a vital aspect of scientific work as they involve a key aspect of what he called the 'scientific ethos': an 'organized scepticism' regarding any research findings and therefore the need for any findings to be checked by peers in the wider scientific community in order to guard against fraudulent, or mistaken, contributions.

It is important to emphasize here that the role of the above criteria, and their formulation, derive largely from positivist philosophical commitments. As we have seen in previous chapters, all positivist methodology emphasizes objective data collection in management research so as to test hypotheses by having built in 'extensive means for protecting against personal biases' (Behling, 1980: 489) which thereby afford some protection against 'fanciful theorizing' (Donaldson, 1996: 164). Here progress in management research entails a 'pursuit of "truth" that is a closer and closer fitting of our theories to the one objective reality we presume exists' (Mitroff and Pondy, 1978: 146). In order to preserve a theory-neutral observational language during data collection so as to enable this pursuit of a correspondence theory of truth, positivists try to methodologically ensure distance between the researcher and the researched so that research processes and findings are not contaminated by the actions of the researcher. Here positivists try to ensure this view of scientific rigour by deploying these particular conceptions of validity and reliability – evaluative criteria which assume that findings can be independent of the researcher, and the methodology used, provided that the 'correct' procedures are followed. Moreover, these criteria, especially reliability, express an important ontological commitment: that there is a "real" social world "out there", which is stable thereby allowing replication tests.

As Scandura and Williams (2000) argue with regard to management research, the deployment of the above criteria are seen to be pivotal to enabling progress through the assessment of the various methods used by management researchers. However, ecological validity is not usually considered in this specification of validities which researchers should pursue. This apparent oversight seems to largely derive from the implicit emphasis upon *erklaren* rather than *verstehen* in these list of criteria. Instead greater emphasis is given to the other types of validity and to the reliability of findings. Even some qualitative researchers have maintained this emphasis. For instance, Lecomte and Goetz have just slightly modified these positivist criteria and retained reliability in the sense that different researchers, or the same researcher on different occasions, would 'discover the same phenomena or generate the same constructs in the same or similar settings' (1982: 32) – something, as we shall see, some qualitative methodologies may have great difficulty in ensuring.

Stop and Think Exercise 9.1   The aim of this exercise is to evaluate the inherent strengths and weaknesses of some of the research methodologies we have discussed in this book when they are designed and used in the most appropriate manner according to the various methodological protocols and rules devised by researchers.

With these issues in mind, evaluate the six methods listed below in the table with reference to how potentially strong or weak they are, relative to one another, in terms of the evaluation criteria discussed above.

You should be able to discern a pattern in the relative strengths and weaknesses of these methods – as you gain something under these criteria something else is lost: what are these trade-offs?

	Internal Validity	Population Validity	Measurement Validity	Ecological Validity	Reliability
1 Laboratory experiment					
2 Quasi-experiment					
3 Positivist action research					
4 Analytical survey					
5 Ethnography					

Now read below where, armed with these criteria, we use them to evaluate each of the methodologies listed above to elucidate their potential strengths and weaknesses.

The application of positivist criteria to evaluating research methodologies

Ideal or laboratory experiments

As we demonstrated in Chapter 4, the highly structured nature of experimental research designs, with their identification and manipulation of independent and dependent variables with assignation of subjects to control and experimental groups, endows this approach with significant strengths of internal validity and reliability. Being highly structured, with clear protocols to follow, it is comparatively easy to replicate many aspects of an experimental research design. Moreover, its utilization of matched control and experimental groups enables observation of the effects of manipulating an independent variable while providing a high degree of confidence that the effects of any potential extraneous variables have been ruled out, or controlled, thus allowing the establishment of causal connections. This issue of internal validity may be further enhanced because the temporal ordering of cause and effect should be discernible through the manipulation of the independent variable, through experimental treatments, by the researcher. Simultaneously, experimental researchers can use a battery of measures to monitor changes in the dependent variable to, in principle, ensure measurement validity.

However, the ideal experiment, in gaining these strengths through its high degree of structure, loses or 'trades off' naturalism: experiments are low in ecological validity because of the artificial nature of the research process and context created by their very structure. Such weaknesses raise the issue of the extent to which any conclusions from ideal experiments are mere artefacts of the research process and context and thus inapplicable to social contexts outside those in which data have been collected (see Introna and Whitley, 2000). A further significant weakness in much experimental research is that it is often low in population validity since it may involve small numbers of subjects, who may often be unrepresentative volunteers. Researchers using experiments can, however, increase population validity by giving greater attention to the random sampling of subjects.

Quasi-experiments and positivistic forms of action research

Quasi-experiments and positivistic forms of action research attempt to take the research design of the ideal experiment out of the laboratory and into the field (see Chapters 4 and 5). As in the ideal experiment there is a concentration on measuring changes in the dependent variable often using a battery of measures so as to enhance measurement validity. By attempting to undertake research in relatively natural, non-artificial settings both are seen to gain naturalism and therefore are relatively higher in ecological validity. But here we confront the paradoxical relationship which exists between control and naturalism in research design. Through venturing into the field, naturalism may be gained, but only at the expense of losing the ability to manipulate the incidence of independent variables and control the incidence of extraneous variables. Except on rare occasions, in positivistic action research it is usually much more difficult for a researcher to manipulate the independent variable and assign subjects to matched and experimental groups. Indeed, to attempt to create such groups often disturbs the normal lives of subjects and so reduces naturalism. For quasi-experimental research it is very difficult to match naturally occurring control and experimental groups – that lack of match inevitably reduces internal validity. So, by increasing ecological validity quasi-experiments and action research trade off internal validity when compared with the ideal experiment. With regard to reliability, the socially specific context in which action research is undertaken, will frequently result in a relative decline in reliability as it becomes more difficult to replicate. In the case of quasi-experimentation, with its precise protocols and methods of measuring change in the dependent variable, replication in principle becomes much easier.

As with the ideal experiment, it is often the case that researchers using either a quasi-experimental design or action research fail to give sufficient attention to sampling. This causes problems regarding population validity. While this may be understandable given the difficulties of gaining access in the field, it is not necessarily an intrinsic weakness of these research approaches as methodological steps can be taken to improve it.

Analytical surveys

It should now be apparent that the qualities displayed in analytical survey research give it much strength in population validity and reliability (see Chapter 6). Such surveys usually entail the careful random selection of samples that enable results to be generalized to wider populations with a high degree of confidence. Concurrently, by using highly structured questionnaires to gather data in a form that is quantitatively analysable survey-based research is usually regarded as easily replicable and hence potentially reliable. In principle the questions on the questionnaire attempt to operationalize independent, dependent, and extraneous variables and measure their variation in a valid manner. However, the resultant high degree of structure, although conferring strengths, appears to create a relative lack of naturalism. For instance, the context in which data collection takes place will not usually be as artificial as the context of the ideal experiment. Nevertheless, respondents might often be constrained or impelled by the prompts of an interviewer or the rubric of a self-completion questionnaire. This may lead them to make statements which, although fitting into the conceptual and theoretical pro forma of the research, give little opportunity for the respondent to articulate the ways in which he or she personally conceptualizes and understands the matters of interest. It is usually for these reasons that survey research is often considered to be relatively low in ecological validity.

Analytical surveys are also considered to be relatively weak in internal validity as compared with experiments; that is, they have certain difficulties with regard to their control of rival hypotheses. For instance, analytic surveys rely on the use of the statistical controls of multivariate analysis to control extraneous variables, and this potentially weakens any causal conclusions arrived at. This is because correlation does not necessarily signify the presence of a causal relationship. Rather the presence of a correlation is taken to be necessary but not sufficient proof of a causal relationship whilst conversely its absence enables falsification of the hypothesis under test. Moreover, the presence of a correlation gives little indication of the direction of causation between independent and dependent variables unless some temporal ordering is simultaneously evident – something which very often is difficult to discern.

Ethnography

As we have attempted to make clear in earlier chapters, the more research is structured the more easily it can be replicated. Ethnography, with its commitment to induction and relatively unstructured qualitative methods of data collection, creates severe problems regarding replicability, and consequently reliability also appears problematic. Moreover, as we have seen in Chapter 7, since ethnography usually entails the intensive study of a small number of cases, its claims to population validity are usually considered to be limited to the actual phenomena in a specific social context under investigation during fieldwork. Although this apparent limitation regarding population validity has been thoroughly disputed by Mitchell (1983) (see also Bloor, 1976, 1978) in his discussion of the use of analytic induction and grounded theory, the main strength of ethnography is generally considered to be ecological validity.

It is often considered that ethnography has inherent advantages over other research methodologies (e.g. laboratory experiments and surveys) that suffer from deficiencies in ecological validity (Brunswick, 1956; Bracht and Glass, 1968). That is, ethnographic research (unlike many other research methodologies) takes place in the natural setting of the everyday activities of the subjects under investigation. This, and the research procedures used, ostensibly reduce contamination of the subject's behaviour by the researchers themselves and the methods they use for collecting data. However, few ethnographers would claim that it is possible completely to eliminate subjects' reactivity to the researchers' personal qualities or techniques of data collection. As we have already discussed, the ethnographer instead attempts to use a particular form of reflexivity; that is to say, an attempt is made by the researcher to understand his or her own effect upon, and role in, the research setting and to utilize this knowledge to elicit data.

Where ethnographers are concerned with inductively generating grounded theory, their commitment to naturalism may often obstruct their establishment of control and experimental groups and hinder their ability to manipulate independent variables. As such, ethnography is often considered to have difficulties regarding the clear establishment of cause-and-effect relationships and consequently is taken to be low in internal validity. This claim is, however, problematic for several reasons.

Because ethnographers can produce large amounts of qualitative data in an inductive fashion it is perhaps the most likely of all the methodologies indicated above to identify and include all the relevant variables in any subsequent theoretical analysis. In contrast, the experimental and survey approaches entail the formulation of theory prior to data collection through operationalization and instrumentation. At each stage of this process the deductive researcher is, in effect, excluding variables from consideration and limiting the extent and form that data take in an a priori fashion. To put it crudely, the researcher's deductive research strategy leads them to throw information away! – or at least not collect it in the first place.

Despite the ethnographer's inevitable selection of relevant aspects to study, he or she is more likely than deductive researchers to become aware of important factors that did not form part of his or her preconceived notion of the situation. This is particularly so when this process is combined with forms of analytic induction and grounded theory, which can enable the establishment of what are in effect control and experimental groups. In this way the criticism that ethnography is inevitably low in internal validity is open to question. Moreover, since ethnographers usually have a commitment to naturalism, they have the scope to rule out some of the threats to internal validity that stem from the artificiality of the research context and procedures; something to which the more structured research styles are evidently victims. Thus, it seems that the internal validity of ethnography can be problematic in some circumstances as it depends largely upon rigorousness and the specific concerns of the ethnographer. When those concerns entail analytic induction, and/or grounded theory, as well as reflexivity, the internal validity of the ethnographer's theoretical conclusions may well be very high in comparison to many of the deductive approaches.

However, the point is, that save for ecological validity it is probably inappropriate to use positivistic versions of reliability and validity to assess ethnographic research which has key philosophical differences in that the emphasis is upon *verstehen* rather than *erklaren*. This is a point which we shall return to when we discuss the evaluation criteria associated with what is called neo-empiricism.

Multi-methods: the criteriological justification

We are really like blind men led into an arena and asked to identify an entity (say an elephant) by touching one part of that entity (say a leg). Certainly we might make better guesses if we could pool the information of all the blind men, each of whom has touched a different part of the elephant. (Smith, 1975: 273)

The perceived need for what is often called methodological triangulation is illustrated by the above quotation from Smith (1975). Here he tried to metaphorically capture the idea that different kinds of complementary data about a 'problem' may be acquired by using different research techniques in the same empirical study. Such 'methodological triangulation' is thought to overcome the bias inherent in any single-method approach by advocating the use of multiple methods to address the same problems and research questions, on the basis that in this way different methodological strengths will be enhanced, and inherent weaknesses will be cancelled out, to produce more convincing findings.

Indeed, from the previous evaluation of some of the different methodologies we have considered in this book, it would seem that each approach has distinctive strengths and weaknesses. Hence, it would seem to make sense to combine the different methodologies in the same study to enhance the findings in terms of the evaluation criteria put forward earlier. This suggestion has long been discussed by methodologists who often have put forward the idea that we should combine quantitative and qualitative methods as it will provide opportunities for methodological triangulation.

For example, Denzin (1970: 297) defined triangulation, a term derived from surveying, as 'the combination of methodologies in the study of the same phenomenon'. Multiple and independent methods, especially if undertaken by different research

workers investigating the same problem, should (he argued), if reaching the same conclusions, have greater validity and reliability than a single methodological approach
to a problem. Elsewhere such triangulation is also described as the multimethod/
multitrait approach (Campbell and Fiske, 1959), and for the most part presents the
idea that complementary qualitative and quantitative methodologies can complement
one another rather than constituting competing approaches (Jick, 1979a; Fielding and
Fielding, 1986). This is illustrated by Jick's work summarized in the case study below.

Case Study 9.1   Methodological triangulation in action

Jick (1979a) describes his doctoral project (Jick, 1979b) to study the effects of a merger
of hospitals on their employees as an example of triangulation. As is usual in merger
cases there was high employee anxiety and one of the main purposes of the research
was to discover the sources and symptoms of this stress and its impact on the operation of the newly created organization.

On the basis of a review of research methods, especially those designed to collect data on the complex topic of employee stress, Jick decided that there was no
ideal, sole method of collecting such data. There were a number of possibilities. He
decided he might interview employees; use some indirect form of projective test; ask
those interacting with the focal person; systematically observe the person's behaviour;
measure physiological symptoms, and so on. Clearly all these strategies had strengths
and weaknesses which suggested some form of triangulation, and a design accordingly
emerged using a combination of methods. Methods eventually used in practice were
surveys distributed to a random sample of the population, followed by semi-structured,
probing interviews; interviews were also conducted with supervisors and co-workers to
ascertain their observation of particular employees.

In addition, and particularly fruitful, were data based upon unobtrusive measures (Webb
et al., 1969) and non-participant observation as well as archival materials. For example,
what is described as an 'anxiety thermometer' was developed from an observation by
the archivist in one of the organizations that employees frequently used comprehensive
newspaper files to compare recent reports of the organization's future with those in the
past. Employees were evidently seeking information to relieve their anxieties, and it was
hypothesized that the more people visited the archives the higher their level of anxiety.
Such data were compared with those derived from other data sources such as interviews
and surveys and the hypothesis for the most part confirmed.

Quantitative data sources were used largely to supplement qualitative data but, as
Jick observes, 'it is a delicate exercise to decide whether or not results have converged
… should all components of a multimethod approach be weighted equally? … there are
no formal tests to discriminate methods to judge their applicability' (Jick, 1979a: 607).

Nevertheless, in Jick's judgement the various methods taken together produced convergent findings. There were some discrepant findings, but data sources (whether divergent or discrepant) may of course be equally valuable, and discrepant findings are likely
to enrich explanations. In this particular case, for example, some employees, known to
be highly stressed on the basis of surveys of self-reports, were apparently least likely to
visit the archive files. The discrepancy was investigated by conducting further interviews
and observations, which helped to reconcile the apparently conflicting data by suggesting that poorly educated employees tended to rely more on oral communications than
written documents.

Methodological pluralism

The advocation of the use of multiple methods in the same study, in order to enable methodological triangulation suggests that these advocates do not perceive there to be any fundamental irreconcilable conflicts between quantitative and qualitative methods and thereby justifies what is seen as the adoption of what may be termed a *'methodologically pluralist'* position (see McLennan, 1995).

This position implies the possibility of rapprochement between quantitative and qualitative research methodologies, as articulated, for example, by McCall and Simmons (1969), McCall and Bobko (1990) and Cresswell (1994). From this stance the difference between the methods of the social scientist are perceived as being ones of trade-off around reliability, internal and external validity, etc. A slightly different argument is put forward by Currall et al. (1999) where they support pluralism on the grounds that qualitative ethnographic data can be used to discover or develop theory whilst quantification of that data using content analysis and statistical techniques enables theory testing and evaluation. Other methodologists have tended to emphasize instead that it is their appropriateness to the research topic that should decide which methodologies to use. One of the first to put forward this idea was Trow (1957: 33) when he proposed that 'different kinds of information about man (sic) and society are gathered most fully and economically in different ways, and the problem under investigation properly dictates the methods of investigation ... the methods and techniques most useful to the problems at hand'.

However, any pluralistic *rapprochement* is usually only tenable within philosophical assumptions which recognize the importance of actors' intersubjectivity and the consequent need for, and possibility of, *verstehen* whilst simultaneously recognizing the influence of external causal variables upon behaviour (see McLennan, 1995). For example, many pluralists would perceive qualitative methods as the most appropriate for fulfilling a commitment to an exploration of actors' intersubjective worlds whilst quantitative methods are deployed in order to explore the external causal forces that are presumed to impact upon actors' and are mediated by their intersubjective (that is, culturally derived) interpretations.

Moreover, it appears that such 'pluralism' is founded upon 'realist' assumptions about the ontological status of social reality, 'which postulate that the world is a real world made up of hard, tangible and relatively immutable structures' (Burrell and Morgan, 1979: 4). As we have seen in Chapter 8, this assumption considers that social reality has a concrete existence independent of human consciousness and cognition, which is, within this pluralist stance, empirically identifiable and presumably measurable in some way. Therefore, experimental or analytical survey researchers may legitimately impose their operationalizations of social reality upon their subjects, which become measured stimuli to which subjects' responses are also measured in some valid manner. Indeed, operationalization and measurement of social reality (stimuli) and action (responses) become the key activity in scientific inquiry and are clearly underpinned by the assumption that we all live in the same independent and external social world which we can neutrally access provided that the 'right' methodology is used in an appropriate fashion. In other words, positivist ontological and epistemological assumptions remain largely unchallenged. However, such methodological pluralists would also follow Laing (1967) in attacking the contention that social phenomena are analogous to the 'it-beings' or 'things' of nature and are thereby amenable to a type of causal analysis in which human beings are reduced to entities that automatically react to external stimuli in the same fashion as inanimate phenomena behave.

In the methodological pluralist position outlined here, human action is assumed to have an internal logic, for human beings have been freed from the 'reflexive arc' (Mead, 1934). It therefore creates a perceived necessity to explore the meanings people attach to that all-embracing, identifiable, concrete social reality – meanings integral to the construction of responses, i.e. action. Qualitative methods that enable *verstehen*, such as ethnography, are for the pluralist the methods appropriate for fulfilling their commitment to exploration of actors' phenomenological worlds. Therefore, as we have indicated above, in the methodological pluralist's web of what are essentially philosophical choices, ethnography takes its place within a version of 'variable analysis' (Blumer, 1967). This position is often promulgated through attempts at providing what Fay (1975: 84) has termed 'quasi-causal' accounts. In clarifying what he means by this term, Fay states that, 'in these sorts of conditionship relations, consciousness functions as a mediator between the determining antecedent factors and the subsequent actions, in other words, men act in terms of their external conditions, rather than being governed directly by them (sic)' (Fay, 1975: 84–5). In this, stimuli (social reality as measured and defined by the social scientist) and responses (human actions as measured and defined by the social scientist) are mediated by the actors' subjective processes of attaching meaning to and interpreting stimuli.

For example, within this epistemological stance, the experimental and survey researchers can legitimately follow their 'crafts' by imposing operationalizations of their versions of social reality upon subjects and subsequent data, through highly structured research strategies. The relationship between stimuli and responses may often be investigated while taking into account (or controlling for) the creative processes of interpretation and meaning construction by subjects with some kind of qualitative analysis aimed at ruling out competing hypotheses. In other words, pluralists would attempt to increase the internal and ecological validity of their findings by attempting to 'control' for the indexicality of their experiment or survey by using the research methods most suitable for that purpose. However, as we have tried to show, within this pluralist position qualitative methodology is not used purely within a hypothetico-deductive framework to control extraneous variables deriving from indexicality. Alternatively, methodological pluralism may arise from a commitment to linking micro-analyses of individual or group action(s) with a macro-structural analysis of society.

So in summary, the methodological pluralist position suggests that not only are different quantitative and qualitative methodologies suitable for different kinds of problem (e.g. Trow, 1957) but they also complement one another in a variety of ways that add to the credibility of a study by providing an internal cross-checking or monitoring device during the research process (e.g. McCall and Simmons, 1969; Denzin, 1970; H. W. Smith, 1975), as well as constituting aids for spanning the micro–macro divide (Godsland and Fielding, 1985; Fielding, 1988). It is now appropriate to turn looking at methodological pluralism in action and the most common vehicle for this in management research: the case study.

Mixing methods: case study research

There is a growing importance in the management field of what is often termed a mixed methods approach: research that may integrate quantitative and qualitative methods of data collection within a single project. As we have seen above, the use of different methods of data collection in the same study is presumed to have considerable benefits since any method has distinctive strengths and weaknesses and therefore research designs may benefit from counter-balancing strengths of one method with the weakness of others and vice versa. Within the area of management the most significant means of doing this is the case study. Now we need to be careful here since one could argue that much ethnographic research and action research could, for instance, also be categorized as case study research, and in many respects they are. However, here, following Yin (2003), we are only looking at case studies that purposefully mix quantitative and qualitative methods in data collection for the pluralistic epistemological reasons outlined previously in this chapter (see also case study 9.1). Based upon the concerns about triangulation referred to earlier in this chapter, case studies usually use a variety of methods to access different sources of evidence, amongst which the most commonly used are interviews, direct and participant observation, documentation and archival records. For Yin (2003), no single source has a complete advantage over the other sources, and that as the sources may be seen as complementary, a good case study will use as many different sources as possible collected via different appropriate means.

Despite some ambiguity concerning its status as either being a method in its own right or a research strategy that combines methods, the case study is being increasingly employed in organizational research and in the field of social sciences in general (Hartley, 2004). Indeed, the use of case studies has grown in importance over the past two decades and is often the preferred label for exploratory and evaluative research that is conducted by many research students in the management disciplines, often in organizations where they are employed. But we must be careful about using this catch-all phrase.

Whilst different writers define the case study in different ways, most seem to agree that a case study entails empirical research that focuses on understanding and investigating particular phenomena and their dynamics, within the context of a naturally occurring real life single setting, that uses multiple sources of evidence, usually using an array of quantitative and qualitative methods to collect that data (e.g. Eisenhardt, 1989; Yin, 2003; Hartley, 2004). In other words, a case study can be an intensive study of an individual, a group, an organization or a specific process. Basically the unit of analysis varies according to the interests and aims of the researcher: hence what constitutes a 'case' inevitably varies. Rather than following a fixed research design (as in the case of experiments and surveys) to examine a limited number of variables, the case study involves an in-depth examination of a single instance. The case is the situation, which is the focus of interest. So, with regard to management research, a case study can involve a detailed investigation, of one or more organizations, groups within an organization, or individuals therein, with the aim of providing some type of analysis of the context and processes involved in affecting the incidence and form taken by the phenomena of interest. Hence, case studies are a very flexible approach to research in the sense that the form they take, the methods used, and what they try to do, varies considerably according to the aims of the researcher.

For instance, a case study can be used to either inductively generate, or deductively test, theory. Alternatively they might be used to conduct merely exploratory pilot studies or descriptive research (see Yin, 2003). However, what is important here is that the purposes to which the case study is being put has an important bearing upon how the case study is, or the case studies are, selected by the researcher at the outset of the research, and in particular, how far the researcher wants to be able to generalize, if at all, any findings beyond the case(s) investigated. In other words, whilst case studies through various forms of triangulation may enhance our understanding of what is going on in a particular case, is there any means of being able to theorize from that case to other cases not investigated by the research? Within the pluralist epistemological stance there appears to be several strategies which may be viable for enabling such types of generalization.

One of the key weaknesses in much case study research is sometimes the lack of a coherent rationale for case study selection. Now often this may be because of the difficulty of getting access to organizational sites in management research. The practicalities of the situation may go against developing a thorough reasoning beyond some attempt at after the fact justification. Nevertheless it is always worth considering some of the strategies for selection available to researchers. For instance, as Flyvbjerg (2006) notes, there are a variety of possible rationales that might be used, in principle, in the selection of cases for investigation. Unlike with the random sampling strategies used in survey design, where generalization is based on the representativeness of the sample with regard to a specified population, case study selection should attempt to maximize the utility and richness of the information content provided by a small sample and single cases.

For instance the researcher may select what is called a 'critical case' where the phenomenon of interest is most likely or least likely to occur (Flyvbjerg, 2006: 231) because the information then gathered from that case is more likely to either support or falsify more general propositions and hypotheses, the rationale being: 'If this is (not) valid for this case then it applies to all (no) cases'. The example that Flyvbjerg uses is particularly apposite Robert Michel's work on oligarchy. As Flyvbjerg notes 'By choosing a horizontally structured grass roots organization with strong democratic ideals – that is a type of organization with an especially low probability of being oligarchical – Michels could test the universality of the oligarchy thesis; that is, "If this organization is oligarchical, so are most others"' (ibid.). An alternative strategy for selecting cases is termed 'maximum variation' (ibid.: 230–2). This is where the cases selected vary in terms of particular chosen dimensions so as to provide specific comparisons and contrasts. For instance, one might wish to investigate the impact of different forms of organizational governance structure upon feelings of job satisfaction by choosing several organizations that varied in terms of how bureaucratic or mechanistic they were in terms of organization structure and then measure variations in job satisfaction in each organization to provide important comparisons. This strategy of maximum variation could lend itself either to the falsification of a priori hypotheses, or could be part of theoretical sampling during the inductive development of grounded theory through the constant comparative method (see Chapter 7 of this book).

In sum, case study design involves the same attempt at answering the following interrelated questions usually prior to fieldwork:

- What are the aims and objectives of this research?
- Which processes and phenomena are to be investigated in their everyday social context?
- How are cases going to be conceptualized, in other words, what is the unit of analysis?
- What is the conceptual framework (this covers the main features aspects, dimensions, issues, variables) of a case study and their presumed relationship?
- What are the initial research questions (what, how, why, where, when)?
- Is the approach going to be inductive or deductive?
- What is the sampling strategy both within any case (who, where, when, what is going to be investigated) and what is the rationale for selecting these particular cases given the aims of the research?

- What are the key sources of primary and secondary data necessary to access during fieldwork?
- How is secondary data going to be accessed?
- Which different methods of primary data collection are to be used and for what purposes and why?
- How is primary and secondary data going to be analysed?

In sum, a case study is an example of the use of multiple methods of data collection to investigate specific phenomena in their natural settings. Sometimes the case study can almost reflect aspects of quasi-experimental research through attempts at identifying critical contrasts and comparisons that enable theory testing through the selection of specific cases. Alternatively the logic of grounded theory may be used in the selection of cases in order to develop theory across and within cases. Within cases, multiple sources of primary and secondary data are used with both quantitative and qualitative methods being used to collect that data where appropriate to ensure triangulation. Thus, methodological pluralism, in the form of the case study, considers that combining quantitative and qualitative methods is not only viable, it actually would significantly improve management research in terms of mainstream positivist criteria. However, such a stance can only be maintained by accepting the relevance of both *verstehen* and *erklaren* to social science and by assuming that there are no significant philosophical differences at play – something which not all researchers are prepared to agree with. It should be remembered that within the above ensemble of philosophical assumptions, once the role of human intersubjectivity (for whatever reason) is understood as irrelevant to the explanation of social phenomena, increasingly qualitative methods will be dismissed as irrelevant to management research. This, implicitly or explicitly, re-establishes a dichotomy between the quantitative and the qualitative by dismissing the latter as irrelevant to social science research. Conversely, other researchers may dismiss quantitative approaches as overly deterministic and as undermining their commitment to what we have called naturalism (see Chapters 3 and 7) and hence limit their work to the deployment of qualitative methods. This has led some of these researchers to overtly re-evaluate positivistic evaluation criteria and develop alternatives. It is to these alternative forms of evaluation that we now turn.

Re-evaluating evaluation criteria

In Chapter 7 we reviewed certain ethnographic research practices as examples of management research which were influenced by the epistemological assumption that it is possible to collect qualitative empirical data in an unbiased and objective fashion and simultaneously reject hypothetico-deductive falsificationism in favour of induction. This type of management research is an example of has been more generally called 'qualitative positivism' (see Prasad and Prasad, 2002: 6) or neo-empiricism (see Alvesson and Deetz, 2000: 60–74) because researchers use non-quantitative methods within largely positivistic assumptions (see also Chapter 8). For example, within an interpretive agenda, these researchers deploy what Schwandt (1996: 62) calls a 'third-person point of view' that privileges the consciousness of the management researcher (see also Knights, 1992; Van Maanen, 1995b) by retaining the key positivist assumption that there is a social world out there, awaiting to be discovered and explored in an objective manner provided that the correct methods are used to collect data.

In doing so, neo-empiricists rely upon an array of qualitative methods to inductively develop thick descriptions of the patterns in the intersubjective meanings that
actors use to make sense of their everyday worlds and investigate the implications
of those interpretations for social interaction usually in organizational settings (see
Prasad and Prasad, 2002). Often these data are used to generate grounded theory that
can explain and predict behaviour through the deployment of Glaser and Strauss'
(1967; see also Strauss and Corbin, 1990; Locke, 2000; Partington, 2000) constant
comparative method (see Chapter 7). Thus, the key differences with mainstream positivism, and its largely quantitative methodologies, are primarily about what is open to
direct, neutral, observation through sensory experience and the continuing relevance of
induction in the social sciences.

For some people these apparent philosophical differences with mainstream positivism are not very significant and therefore they argue that it is legitimate to directly
apply the positivist evaluation criteria (e.g. Lecompte and Goetz, 1982; Kirk and
Miller, 1986), illustrated earlier in this chapter, in the assessment of all qualitative
research. According to others these differences with quantitative research are philosophically significant and it is therefore inappropriate to attempt to evaluate qualitative research by applying unreconstructed criteria such as reliability and validity.
Therefore, they have attempted to revise those positivist evaluation criteria to both
reflect their inductive agenda and attempt to devise alternative ways of demonstrating the qualitative researcher's objectivity and rigour.

For instance, in some early work, Lincoln and Guba (1985: 290) argued that 'conventional' (i.e. mainstream positivist) evaluation criteria have evolved in response to
some important questions regarding the determination of any findings' truth, applicability, consistency and neutrality. In doing so they argue that these conventional
criteria need to be revised for what they call naturalist inquirers. In doing so they
emphasized the need for qualitative researchers to provide various audit trails, in a
self-critical fashion, that allow audiences to make judgements for themselves as to its
rigour. In specifying the need for an audit trail they also suggested the following four
general principles for assessing the quality of qualitative research, which combine to
enable the assessment of what they call the *trustworthiness* of the research. Each of
these criteria, they argued, should replace an equivalent criterion deriving from the
assessment of quantitative research.

1 Internal validity is replaced by *credibility*: the provision of authentic representations of the cultural worlds of the people who are being investigated. This is
  primarily established by what they call 'member checks' (1985: 314): feeding
  back to those members the researcher's account of their worlds so as to assess
  the extent to which they recognize and give assent to those representations.
  This allows evaluation of the extent to which an account is corroborated by
  accurately representing members' subjective dispositions.
2 External validity is replaced by *transferability*: the extent of applicability of
  the findings both within the social context situation under investigation and
  to other social contexts. With regard to the former, this is established by sampling different aspects of the social setting under investigation. By producing
  in-depth accounts of that setting and cultural phenomena Lincoln and Guba
  (ibid.: 316) argue that the researcher provides other researchers with a database
  which allows them to judge the extent to which the findings are transferable
  to other social settings with which they are familiar. Here, there has to be '...
  enough "thick description" ... available about both "sending" and "receiving"

contexts to make a reasoned judgement about the degree of transferability possible' (ibid.: 247).

3 Reliability is replaced with *dependability*: the minimization of researcher idio-syncrasies. This criterion is mainly met through the provision of the audit trails mentioned above. An audit trail involves documentation of all stages of the research, and the choices made by the researcher, from inception to comple-tion: detailed evidence that would enable other researchers to reconstruct the processes by which the researcher came to any findings. In particular it should provide information upon the conceptual development of the research so that the theoretical inferences made by the researcher are justified and thereby open up those processes to critical scrutiny and assessment.

4 Objectivity is replaced by *confirmability*: researcher self-criticism and the demonstration that the researcher's analysis is 'grounded in the data' (ibid.: 323). This too is largely established by the provision of an audit trail where the researcher provides a self-critical account of key research processes and the methodological decisions they have made.

In contrast to Lincoln and Guba's approach, Morse (1994) focuses more specifi-cally upon the inductive analysis of qualitative data in establishing not so much evalu-ation criteria *per se* but conventions, or guidelines, which make explicit the processes of theory construction and which researchers ought to follow. In this respect she adds to and complements key aspects of Lincoln and Guba's approach.

1 Morse begins with what she calls *comprehending* and learning about a setting prior to any fieldwork. Here she argues that it is important for researchers to be familiar with any relevant literature but they simultaneously need to distance themselves from it to avoid the contamination of the setting by any precon-ceptions deriving from that literature. Thus, her stance is similar to that of Blumer (1954), which we discussed in Chapter 7, where sensitizing concepts are derived from the literature in order to give directions in which to look, rather than theoretical preconceptions.

2 This first stage is followed by *synthesizing* where the researcher sifts the data collected during their fieldwork to identify different themes and concepts in order to construct patterns in the data and produce categories and initial explanations.

3 This is closely related to the next stage that involves *theorizing* to produce explanations that fit the data in the most coherent and parsimonious manner. Here data are confronted with various possible theoretical schemes which pro-vide alternative explanations. The sources of these theoretical schemes entail both the use of those deriving from other settings and the use of induction to construct theory from the data collected in the setting. The causal linkages sug-gested by different theoretical schemes are tested upon different informants to enable corroboration of the explanation that best fits the data.

4 The final stage involves *recontextualizing* – the development of the emerging theory so that it is applicable to new settings. This involves abstracting the emerging theory to new settings and populations as well as by relating it to established knowledge to assess its contribution.

Throughout, a significant issue for Morse is that the qualitative researcher must provide an account of how the inductive analysis of the organizational settings under investigation was accomplished by demonstrating how concepts were derived and applied as well as showing how and why alternative theoretical explanations have been considered but rejected (see also Adler and Adler, 1994; Miles and Huberman, 1994; Locke, 1996). Morse's approach therefore further reinforces the importance of the audit trail in the evaluation of qualitative research.

As Seale (1999a: 45) notes, auditing 'is an exercise in reflexivity, which provides a self-sustaining critical account of how the research was done, and can also involve the use of triangulation exercises'. Here Seale is referring to a particular form of triangulation rather unlike those referred to earlier in this chapter. It entails the contingent use of multiple researchers and/or multiple data sources, sometimes accessed by using different qualitative methods, to cross reference and compare data pertaining to the same phenomenon to substantiate the objectivity of findings by demonstrating their convergence and consistency of meaning (see Leininger, 1994; Miles and Huberman, 1994; Lowe et al., 2000).

For other commentators, usually with reference primarily to ethnographic research (see Chapter 7), an important aspect of the audit trail's reflexivity is the researcher's critical scrutinization of the impact of their field roles upon the research setting and findings, so as to reduce and evaluate sources of contamination and disturbance, thereby enhancing naturalism or ecological validity whilst demonstrating how the researcher has avoided 'over rapport' with those members and 'going native' (see Brunswick, 1956; Bracht and Glass, 1968; Cicourel, 1982; Pollner and Emerson, 1983; Hammersley, 1989, 1990, 1992). Here the ethnographer has to maintain a balance, and demonstrate this balance in the audit trail, that involves trying

> to be both insider and outsider, staying on the margins of the group both socially and intellectually ... For this reason it is sometimes emphasised that, besides seeking to 'understand', the ethnographer must also try to see settings as 'anthropologically strange', as they would be seen from another society, adopting what we might call the Martian perspective. (Hammersley, 1990: 16)

Hence, a further key aspect of the audit trail is for the researcher to demonstrate how they have also maintained 'social and intellectual distance' and preserved 'analytical space' for themselves (Hammersley and Atkinson, 1995: 115) whilst simultaneously gaining access to what is going on. So, as Seale notes (1999a: 161), through revealing aspects of themselves and the research process, again as a crucial aspect of a traceable audit trail, these concerns stress how researchers must demonstrate their 'hard won objectivity' thereby establishing the credibility, dependability and confirmability of findings: key aspects of Lincoln and Guba's trustworthiness criterion (1985) illustrated previously.

In sum, neo-empiricist evaluation criteria express an interpretive stance that has an interest in building theories out of accessing organizational actor's subjective, cultural, meanings in order to explain their actions in varying organizational contexts that maintains a commitment to objectivity and neutrality albeit with particular nuances. Their dispute with mainstream positivists who reject *verstehen* in favour of *erklaren* is therefore more about *what* is important in understanding human behaviour, what is *directly* observable in a neutral fashion, and how this may be accomplished. In other words, it is the source of this data that is different from mainstream positivism (see also Knights, 1992; Van Maanen, 1995a, b) in that they argue that they can neutrally access actors' subjective understandings by using particular methodologies. Hence, they share mainstream positivism's ontological idea that there is a world out there that awaits discovery and epistemological exploration in an objective manner by collecting data – the ostensibly 'positively' given. Nevertheless, as we have tried to explain, the above differences have often led to the articulation of alternative evaluation criteria to those usually deployed to assess the outputs of mainstream positivism.

However, within neo-empiricism there lurks a tension between their objectiv- ist epistemological impulse that emphasizes how inductive descriptions of cultures should correspond with members' intersubjectivity and an interpretive impulse that suggests that people socially construct the versions of reality that drive their mean- ingful behaviour – culturally derived processes which somehow do not extend to the neo-empiricist's own research processes (see Hammersley, 1992). It is this epistemo- logical assumption that is questioned by social constructionists through their claim that interpretation applies to both researchers and the researched. As Van Maanen (1995b: 74) argues, social constructionism dismisses the possibility of a neutral observational language because such a possibility can only be sustained through the (illegitimate) deployment of a rhetoric of objectivity that privileges the subjective consciousness of the researcher over that of the researched.

Social constructionist evaluation criteria

As we demonstrated in Chapter 8, the argument here is that when we engage with phenomena we inevitably interpret them using different cultural and linguistic tools that carry social bias emanating from our own cultural backgrounds. These ways of engaging influence everyone's perception of what we often take to be 'out there': including the researcher, no matter how well they may have been methodologically trained. The idea here is that we are not, and cannot be, passive receivers of sensory data no matter what methodology we might use to enable this in developing our theories. Hence, the positivist ideal of a neutral detached observer is a myth – and probably a dangerous one because it allows people to claim objectivity when none exists. Rather, according to this subjectivist epistemological challenge to positivism, we inevitably apply various inferences and assumptions which:

1 either mediate and shape what we see like a set of filters, or lens, which lead us to interpret the external social world in particular ways (a stance typical of critical theory): the social world might be 'out there' but we can never know it as we are stuck in socially constructed versions of reality;
2 or, we create what we see, in and through the very act of perception itself (a stance typical of a type of postmodernism often called 'affirmative' postmod- ernism): what we take to be the social world 'out there', is a projection of the discourses that are socially produced and reproduced in and through everyday social interaction.

Hence, the questioning of the researcher's ability to be a neutral conduit and pre- senter of actors' intersubjectivity creates a point of departure of two competing social constructionist approaches to qualitative management research that themselves have some degree of departure over ontological issues. These philosophical disputes have important implications for processes of research evaluation and the criteria that may be deployed. As examples of this variation within social constructionism, we shall now consider criteriological issues in critical theory and postmodernism.

Critical theory

In some cases, methodologists whose early criteriological work may be classified as neo-empiricist seem to articulate key social constructionist philosophical assumptions. For instance, in their original work, at one point Lincoln and Guba reject what they term 'naive realism' (1985: 293) in favour of 'multiple constructed realities' (ibid.: 295). However, such an enisteuological and ontological shift, as Seale (1999a) points out, seems at odds with their proposed evaluation criteria that try to judge the 'trustworthiness' of research because the social constructionist impulse is not simultaneously applied to research processes and outputs by being limited to the interpretive processes occurring in the people being investigated. Likewise Hammersley also argues for 'subtle realism' which ...

> *... retains from naive realism the idea that the researcher investigates independent, knowable phenomena. But it breaks with it in denying that we have direct access to those phenomena, in accepting that we must always rely on cultural assumptions ... Obversely, subtle realism shares with relativism a recognition that all knowledge is based upon assumptions and purposes and is a human construction, but rejects ... abandonment of the regulative ideal of independent and knowable phenomena ... subtle realism is distinct ... in its rejection of the notion that knowledge must be defined as beliefs whose validity is known with certainty. (Hammersley, 1992: 52)*

In talking about the implications of this philosophical position, Hammersley, like Lincoln and Guba in their early work (1985), seems to underestimate the epistemological implications of his argument for evaluating research. Indeed, these writers fail to systematically translate this apparent philosophical shift towards social constructionism into a congruent set of evaluation criteria: the criteria they proposed still rely upon privileging the consciousness of the researcher relative to the researched.

In response to similar criticisms of their early work (1985), Guba and Lincoln (1989, 1994) seem to replace their earlier neo-empiricist evaluation criteria with ones that they claim overlap those of critical theory's social constructionism. In commenting upon the reasons for this development Guba and Lincoln (1994: 114) argue that their previous work represented 'an early effort to resolve the quality issue for constructivism; although these criteria have been well received, their parallelism to positivist criteria makes them suspect'. Elsewhere the critical theory origins of this epistemological shift are made more explicit by the expression of a commitment to the 'belief that a politics of liberation must always begin with the perspectives, desires, and dreams of those individuals who have been oppressed by the larger ideological, economic and political forces of a society, or a historical moment' (Lincoln and Denzin, 1994: 575). This stance is articulated alongside an appeal to what amounts to a consensus view of truth and is expressed through new criteria of different types of 'authenticity' wherein a key issue is that research findings should represent an agreement about what is considered to be true.

Hence, they argue that in order to demonstrate authenticity (1994: 114) researchers must show how in any social setting:

1 different members' realities have been included and represented in any account (fairness);
2 they have helped those members to develop a range of understandings of the phenomenon being investigated thereby enlarging their personal constructions (ontological authenticity);

3 they have helped those members appreciate and understand the constructions of others (educative authenticity);
4 they have helped to stimulate action on the part of those members to change their situation based upon their new understandings (catalytic authenticity);
5 they have helped members to undertake those actions to change their circumstances through their research empowering them (tactical authenticity).

Thus, as Guba and Lincoln seem to admit, their social constructionist criteriology has a parallel with the development of critical theory, inspired by the Frankfurt School, in management research. As we illustrated in Chapter 8, critical theory has grown out of an overt rejection of positivist philosophical assumptions and by implication a critique of management prerogative, to articulate a consensus theory of truth intimately linked to highly participatory approaches to management research where the aim is the empowerment and emancipation of the disenfranchised through facilitating their development of a critical consciousness to transform organizational relationships and practices. Here an array of different critical theorists have attempted to specify evaluation criteria that may be seen as further elaborating those put forward by Guba and Lincoln above.

In outlining these criteria it is firstly useful to note the problem posed for critical theorists by their philosophical stance. Here Kincheloe and McLaren pose the problem ...

How do you determine the validity of information if you reject the notion of methodological correctness and your purpose is to free men and women from sources of oppression and domination? Where traditional verifiability rests on a rational proof built upon literal intended meaning, a critical qualitative perspective always involves a less certain approach characterized by participant reaction and emotional involvement ... Trustworthiness, many have argued, is a more appropriate word to use in the context of critical research. It is helpful because it signifies a different set of assumptions about research purposes than does validity. (1998: 287)

In developing the notion of what they seem to call *'critical trustworthiness'* (ibid.: 288) which is significantly different from Lincoln and Guba's original formulation of 'trustworthiness' (1985) and is much closer to their later specification of 'authenticity' (1989, 1994), Kincheloe and McLaren outline several key criteria that may be used to assess the critical trustworthiness of research inspired by critical theory and some associated forms of postmodernism. These centre on five interrelated issues:

1 Because there is no such thing as a neutral observational language, and thus all knowledge is a product of particular values and interests, researchers must 'enter into an investigation with their assumptions on the table so no one is confused concerning the epistemological and political baggage they bring with them' (Kincheloe and McLaren, 1998: 265). So, for instance, critical theorists need to be self-consciously critical of the philosophical assumptions they are making, reflexively interrogate those assumptions and present and justify those assumptions to others in their dissemination of any findings: to do otherwise is an abdication of intellectual responsibility (see also Johnson and Duberley, 2003).
2 Through 'critical interpretation' (Denzin, 1998: 332) and what amounts to a structural phenomenology (Forrester, 1993) or 'critical ethnography' (Thomas,

1993; Morrow and Brown, 1994), researchers attempt to sensitize themselves and participants to how hegemonic regimes of truth impact upon the subjectivities of the disadvantaged (Marcus and Fisher, 1986; Putnam et al., 1993). Thus, for Kincheloe and McLaren researchers must 'struggle to expose the way ideology constrains the desire for self-direction, and ... confront the way power reproduces itself in the construction of human consciousness' (1998: 288) in doing so they 'undermine what appears natural, and open to question what appears obvious' (ibid.: 293).

3 Here positivist conceptions of validity are overtly rejected and replaced by democratic research designs to generate conditions that approximate Habermas's ideal speech situation (e.g. Broadbent and Laughlin, 1997) and are dialogical (Schwandt, 1996: 66–7). Here what is important is what is termed the 'credibility' of the constructed realities to those who have participated in their development. However this, and consequently the critical trustworthiness of research, can be difficult to establish. As Kincheloe and McLaren observe, 'critical researchers award credibility only when the constructions are plausible to those who constructed them, and even then there may be disagreement, for the researcher may see effects of oppression in the constructs of those researched – effects that those researched may not see' (ibid.: 288).

4 Fourth, positivist concerns with generalizability are rejected in favour of what Kincheloe and McLaren (ibid.: 288) call 'anticipatory accommodation' where 'through their knowledge of a variety of comparable contexts, researchers begin to learn their similarities and differences – they learn from their comparisons of different contexts'.

5 Fifth is what Kincheloe and McLaren (ibid.: 289) call 'catalytic validity'. This is the extent to which 'research moves those it studies so that they understand the world and the way it is shaped in order to transform it'. Hence, catalytic validity refers to the way in which research processes enable the researched to understand themselves and their experiences in new ways and based upon that new understanding, challenge previously taken-for-granted discourse and practices (see also Freire, 1972a, b; Schwandt, 1996: 67).

In sum, it is evident that the evaluation criteria deriving from Kincheloe and McLaren's and supported by an array of critical theorists, closely parallel Guba and Lincoln's (1989, 1994) own increasing emphasis on authenticity. Here a social constructionist stance redirects management research into a more processual form that emphasizes researchers' encouragement in the researched of reflexive and dialogical interrogation of their own understandings to produce new democratically grounded self-understandings to challenge that which was previously taken to be unchallengeable thereby reclaiming the possibility of transformative organizational change (see also Unger, 1987; Beck, 1992; Alvesson, 1996; Gaventa and Cornwall, 2006; Park, 2006).

In their work, Kincheloe and McLaren claim that their evaluation criteria are equally suitable to both critical theory and postmodernism. However, as they explain in some detail, the type of postmodernism they refer to is commensurable with critical theory because it shares a realist ontology where discourse are played out and 'politicized by being situated in real social and historical conditions' (ibid.: 272). This 'resistant' (ibid.) form of postmodernism shares with critical theory a concern with an 'interventionist and transformative critique of Western culture' (ibid.). Thus, it is quite different from what might be termed labelled 'hard', 'affirmative' or 'reactionary' postmodernism (Rosenau, 1992; Tsoukas, 1992; Alvesson and Deetz, 1996, 2000; Kilduff and Mehra, 1997) which we described in Chapter 8.

According to Alvesson and Deetz (1996, 2000) both critical theory and resistant postmodernism, through critique and reflexivity, seek to denaturalize and challenge repressive discursive practices whilst avoiding relativism through using democracy as an epistemic standard. However, this is not the case with 'hard', 'affirmative' or 'reactionary' postmodernism where a subjectivist ontology comes to the fore and a demarcation with critical theory becomes clearer (see Alvesson and Deetz, 1996: 210). It is to this form of postmodernism and the possibility of its evaluation we now turn.

Affirmative postmodernism

As we have indicated, affirmative postmodernists think that discourses actively create and naturalize, rather than discover, the objects (i.e. simulacra) which seem to populate our (hyper) realities (Baudrillard, 1983). The result is that knowledge, truth and reality become construed as discursive productions potentially always open to revision but which are often stabilized through scientists', and other actors', 'performative' ability that persuades others to accept those renditions, as objective, as truthful, as normal, as therefore unchallengeable (Lyotard, 1984) and thereby accomplish what is called discursive closure. However, given this subjectivist ontological and epistemological stance, the affirmative postmodernist must accept that there are no good reasons for preferring one intersubjectively accomplished discursive representation over any other – including those that have been ostensibly democratically formulated. However, alternative discursive productions to those that have been stabilized are always possible and may always be immanent in any situation. Indeed, encouraging those silent but immanent potential 'voices' without specifying them, in order avoid discursive closure, wherein lies what amounts to evaluation criteria particular to affirmative postmodernism.

For some affirmative postmodernists (e.g. Smith, 1990; Mulkay, 1991; Smith and Deemer, 2000), a commitment to avoiding discursive closure means that the development of specific evaluative criteria should not be pursued since such criteria can only be rhetorical devices which operate to performatively hide the precarious subjectivity of both the researcher and the evaluator. Hence, any evaluation criteria are themselves merely discursively constituted regimes of power that produce truth-effects and must therefore be subverted by ending criteriological debate. Nevertheless, there is some irony here for there seems to be a largely tacit evaluative agenda embedded within affirmative postmodernists' own stance that promotes research practices aimed at understanding the ways in which discourses are sustained and undermined, in order to encourage discursive plurality and indeterminacy, rather than making claims about a reality independent of human cognition (see, for example, Edwards et al., 1995). These evaluative issues seem to be concerned with how this form of research unsettles those dominant discourses that have become more privileged than others by helping people to think about their own and others' thinking so as to question the familiar and taken-for-granted and thereby encouraging resistance and space for alternative discourses without advocating any preference which might impose discursive closure (see, for example, Gergen and Thatchenkerry, 1996; Barry, 1997; Barry and Elmes, 1997; Ford, 1999; Boje, 2001; Treleaven, 2001; Currie and Brown, 2003). In other words, these criteria may well be about how to establish, maintain and encourage relativism through methodologically avoiding the perceived anathema of discursive closure.

If a key aim of affirmative postmodernists is to open up any attempted dis-cursive closure to a multiplicity of divergent possibilities that are thought to be always potentially present (see Baudrillard, 1983, 1993; Jeffcutt, 1994; Chia, 1995) by subverting established discourses, affirmative postmodernists must con-sistently deny that any linguistic construction, including their own (see Clifford and Marcus, 1986), produced in any social setting, can be ever settled or stable. Any discourse can be reflexively questioned as layers of meaning are removed to reveal those meanings which have been suppressed, sublimated or forgotten (Chia, 1995) in the act of speaking or writing. Therefore, a key task is to display and unsettle the discursive 'rules of the game' through deconstruction: the dis-mantling of such texts so as to reveal their internal contradictions, assumptions and different layers of meaning, which are hidden from the naive reader/listener and unrecognized by the author/speaker as they strive to maintain unity and con-sistency (see also Cooper, 1990; Martin, 1990; Kilduff, 1993; Linstead, 1993a; Czarniawaska-Joerges, 1996; Boje, 2001). However, at most, such deconstruc-tion can only invoke alternative discursive social constructions of reality which are themselves amenable to further interrogation so as to expose their underlying narrative logic – and so on. In other words, any deconstruction is itself a dis-cursive product that can be deconstructed – and presumably should be in order to promote plurality and instability and to simultaneously avoid the dangers of discursive closure.

One key means of destabilizing their own narratives used by some postmodernists is to avoid the dominant conventions of writing academic texts by purposefully pro-moting an awareness of the author(s) behind the text thereby undermining what they see as the asymmetrical authority relations between author and reader promoted by conventional forms of writing which create a illusion of objectivity on the part of the author. According to Putnam (1996: 386) the aim here is to encourage multiple read-ings 'to decentre authors as authority figures; and to involve participants, readers and audiences in the production of research'. For Ashmore (1989; Ashmore et al., 1995) these decentring processes involve hyper-reflexivity: the deconstruction of decon-structions and the development of new literary forms which repudiate any claim to textual and authorial authority. Here the conventional mode of writing, exemplified by the authoritative monologue of the single official writer, is abandoned. Instead a number of different voices appear, disappear and reappear in the text, interrupting and disrupting each other by debating each other in a potentially endless series of introspective iterations which purposefully surface various discursive possibilities in any social context. Alternatively researchers may articulate key aspects of themselves in the texts to display how they have personally influenced the presentation of their work by demonstrating 'their historical and geographical situatedness, their personal investments in the research, various biases they bring' (Gergen and Gergen, 2000: 1027). In this manner the author's authority is undermined and how the account they present is merely just one amongst many different possibilities is illustrated to avoid discursive closure. Indeed, the resultant unsettling, or paralogy (see Lyotard, 1984), is pivotal since it avoids the authorial privileging upon which any discursive closure depends (Ashmore et al., 1995) and encourages the proliferation of discur-sive practices which postmodernists call heteroglossia (see Gergen, 1992). Therefore, a further key evaluation criterion for this type of research relates to how the author is decentred, through hyper-reflexivity, to avoid any authorial privileging which would result in discursive closure.

Conclusions

At the beginning of this chapter we used several widely used evaluation criteria to identify the varying strengths and weaknesses of the different methods we have reviewed in this book. We used this to illustrate how the making of methodological choices involves a consideration of the inevitable trade-offs that occur when issues such as internal validity, measurement validity, ecological validity, population validity and reliability are considered. As we have seen, such trade-offs occur because of the various strengths and weaknesses the different approaches have built into them. While we were trying to make a serious point it was also slightly mischievous since the evaluation criteria deployed, save perhaps for ecological validity (and even that might be suspect), are legitimated by an underlying positivist epistemology. Hopefully it should be evident now that the use of such criteria may be appropriate when it comes to hypothetico-deductive research but it would be completely inappropriate to extend their usage, say to neo-empiricism, or affirmative postmodernist research, or action research that is inspired by critical theory and so on. These alternatives to the positivist mainstream philosophically vary and thus have different modes of evaluation which are appropriate. These different modes of evaluation are primarily relevant to qualitative management research which does not possess the relative philosophical homogeneity evident in quantitative management research where a tacit consensus has enabled the development of explicit evaluative criteria and has largely limited any controversy to debates about how to most effectively meet those benchmarks (Schwandt, 1996; Scheurich, 1997): a veritable discursive closure! Nevertheless, different evaluation criteria need to be used within different epistemological approaches and it is crucial that management researchers develop the skills to be able to assess the quality of management research using the appropriate criteria in a self-conscious manner. Unfortunately this 'contingent' approach to research evaluation, based upon the idea that 'it all depends', is not always used in practice and we must be alert to the dangers of criteriological misappropriation which are often present. So whilst the different approaches to management research that we have illustrated in this book all have something to offer, the point is that what that 'something' is, and how it is valued and evaluated, varies considerably according to the underlying philosophical dispositions that lead us to engage with our areas of interest in different ways.

Methodological differences and controversies continue to pervade management research – issues that tacitly influence how management research is variably constituted and evaluated by its own practitioners. As Kuhn (1970) noted, scientists will often first learn their trade by examining and copying how exemplars of their discipline went about research. Here Kuhn was referring to the security afforded by the protocols and 'puzzle-solving' of 'normal science' practice within a well established paradigm where philosophical questions were not open to dispute by practitioners. Instead they were largely accepted without question. However such consensus about how to do management research is not so evident, for as with the rest of social sciences, it remains a philosophically contested terrain. Therefore who to turn to for guidance and inspiration always is a somewhat problematic issue, for the direction provided by established scholars will send any aspirant researcher upon different trajectories which articulate different sets of philosophical assumptions.

Therefore, in this book we have included an array of exemplars of different management research approaches. Although we have largely concentrated upon mainstream positivist methodologies, we have tried to use this as an heuristic foil to illustrate how, in recent years, an increasing diversity has become evident amongst management researchers which, in different ways, has challenged the established positivistic mainstream. Nevertheless, positivism remains pivotal to many researchers especially since its philosophical stance supports the possibility of managerial prerogative and moral authority through presenting a persuasive claim to expertise grounded in objective knowledge. Of course it is precisely this claim that is undermined by the development of various social constructionist stances, such as postmodernism and critical theory, since the possibility of neutral apprehension of reality is dismissed as naive and quixotic (see Thomas, 1997; Fournier and Grey, 2000; Grey and Willmott, 2002). From the philosophical stances of these alternatives to positivism, notions of truth and objectivity are dismissed as being outcomes of prestigious discursive practices which mask an inevitable partiality that must always operate. The result is not only the evolution of different methodologies and criteriologies but also the constitution of different research questions about the management terrain.

Despite the above developments, the role of philosophy in constituting how we do things and how we ask questions often remains unnoticed especially from the orientation of those who occupy the positivist mainstream. Philosophical introspection does not usually sit easily with the technical imperative that tends to dominate positivist research to improve the efficiency and effectiveness of management (see Grey and Mitev, 1995). However philosophical assumptions are always present in, and articulated by, any mode of engagement. Adopting a philosophical stance, no matter how tacitly, is always unavoidable: some philosophical position always guides what we do in research yet it is always contestable. So in understanding management research methodologies the issue is not about whether or not our research should be philosophically informed, it is about how well we reflexively interrogate our inevitable philosophical choices and are able to defend them in relation to their ever-present alternatives. This applies as much to positivists as it does to neo-empiricists, critical theorists, postmodernists and so on: – so dear reader – read carefully!

Further reading

Bochner (2000) lays out some of the problems inherent in criteriology. In doing so he argues that the philosophical diversity evident in the social sciences suggests a need for caution since there may be a tendency to universally apply evaluation criteria constituted by particular philosophical conventions. In contrast, Scandura and Williams (2000) provide an interesting review of research in three top-tier American business and management journals and examine changing practices in the triangulation of methods and how different forms of validity have been addressed. Their research suggests that business and management research may be 'moving even further away from rigour' (2000: 1259) by failing to methodologically triangulate findings – something which has resulted in a decrease in the internal, external and construct validity of studies. Whilst the evaluation criteria they propose are appropriate to positivist hypothetico-deductive research, they could be inadvertently applied in a universalistic manner and thereby would be open to the charge of being philosophically parochial. Lecompte and Goetz (1982) provide a good example of the idea that qualitative research is not philosophically distinct from quantitative research and apply relatively unreconstructed positivist evaluation criteria to ethnographic research whilst identifying some methodological strategies qualitative researchers could use to ameliorate possible weaknesses. In contrast, Seale (1999b) considers how philosophical differences are significant and therefore he traces the evolution and proliferation of various alternative sets of evaluation criteria with regard to different forms of qualitative research and their underlying philosophical commitments. However Seale is not content to just review others' work, therefore he develops his own ideas around criteriology to present a form of triangulation as a pragmatic device to ensure quality in qualitative research which seems to articulate a form of methodological pluralism. The theme that qualitative research is philosophically different to quantitative research is also evident in the work of Guba and Lincoln (1989, 1994) where they interrogate the philosophical underpinnings of both quantitative and qualitative approaches to undertaking research and propose that different evaluation criteria must be deployed depending on the paradigmatic location of the researcher whose research is being evaluated. This philosophical shift away from neo-empiricist assumptions is also provided by Kichenloe and McLarens' (1998) consideration of evaluation criteria appropriate to critical theory. Within this mode of engagement they argue that critical trustworthiness is a more appropriate concept to use to evaluate research since it signifies very different philosophical assumptions about the research process in comparison to positivist approaches. They proceed to identify how trustworthiness may be assessed and produce three key criteria which fit the critical theory's emancipatory agenda: the credibility of the portrayals of constructed realities; anticipatory accommodation; and catalytic validity. This can be compared with Schwandt's (1996) attempt to redefine social inquiry as a practical philosophy, with a post-foundationalist epistemology that derives also from critical theory. This project entails dialogue, critique and democracy, without recourse to criteriology as it abandons 'any indisputable criteria for distinguishing legitimate from not so legitimate scientific knowledge' (ibid.: 70). Although not specifically concerned with criteriology *per se*, Mabry (2002) is concerned with the possibilities and problems of evaluation from what she considers to be two different postmodern stances – a rupture primarily due to the different ontologies she sees to be at play.

These journal articles are freely available on the companion website (www.sagepub.co.uk/gillandjohnson):

Schwandt, T.A. (1996) Farewell to criteriology, *Qualitative Inquiry*, 2(1): 58–72.
Seale, C. (1999) Quality in qualitative research, *Qualitative Inquiry*, 5(4): 465–78.

23 Appendix, References and Glossary

INGEMAN ARBNOR and BJORN BJERKE

INTRODUCTION

This Appendix introduces briefly into the discourse *some* philosophical/methodological orientations and their *relationships* to the *methodological grammar* and the three *methodological views* presented in this book. Methodology alone is indeed in itself an immense and complicated topic and we are in no way pretending that in this relatively short Appendix we can give more than a rough summary of its main points. We have selected, for the purpose of the book, some philosophical/methodological orientations and our selection is based on the following:

- They have had some, direct or indirect, influence on our own methodological thinking.
- They are frequently referred to and/or used in business research settings.

This Appendix will be divided into nine sections:

The Appendix concludes with a list of proposals of texts for further reading for anyone who wants to deepen his/her knowledge.

A1 SOME ONTOLOGICAL AND EPISTEMOLOGICAL PERSPECTIVES

Empiricism (from Greek *empeiria*, experience) is an epistemological perspective, which claims that all knowledge of reality is derived from our *sensory* impressions (compare *induction* in Figure 4.3).

Rationalism (from Latin *ratio*, reason) claims, on the other hand, that it is possible to reach knowledge of reality or to justify it by our *reason* only. That is a kind of deductive methodological reasoning (compare relations to *deduction* in Figure 4.3).

It is, however, a great oversimplification to claim that these two concepts of epistemology are mutually exclusive. In a way, we could claim that they rather illustrate good points of departure in a methodology of complementarity where the *analytical view* is the transformative operator.

Pragmatism (from Greek *pragma*, act, deed) is a philosophical stream with great variety, primarily as a sociology toward the approach to find criteria of meaning and truth by practical consequences. A scientific result is thus judged by its usefulness and workability when applied in the *empirical* world. Hereby pragmatism rejects the opinions of *empiricism* and *rationalism* that knowledge can have a positive fundament. The concept of pragmatism is mainly rooted in our *systems view,* but can also be regarded as a weak undertone to our *actors view.*

Idealism (from Greek *idea*, appearance, state, art) is a collective term for a number of epistemological and metaphysical perspectives, which all stress that reality is shaped and constituted by knowledge and thinking such that no reality can exist which is independent of human consciousness or thinking. Our *actors view* has to a certain extent some of its roots in this kind of thought.

Traditional oppositions to idealism are *realism* (there is a world, independent of human consciousness) and *materialism*. Materialism (from Latin *materia*, stuff, material, matter) is a long tradition in European philosophy, which claims that all that exists in reality are things and processes and that they only have physical characteristics. It is, however, no exaggeration to claim that our two other views (*analytical* and *systems*) have to a certain degree some of their roots in this kind of thought.

Such branches as those mentioned above form a kind of historical undercurrent to our methodological views/approaches, and that's the reason why we have mentioned them here. They may possibly enter the methodological process when the meaning and content of various research results are discussed. It is true that the *start* of the analytical view, i.e. *positivism* (see below), stood on a firm *empirical* ground, but positivism as a clear-cut movement does not exist in business research today (even if it is true that its influences linger on with varying degrees of strength), and there exists elements of all the above branches in our three methodological views today.

A2 SOME PHILOSOPHERS ON PARADIGM

Philosophies as well as philosophers and other schools of thought and thinkers will appear in this Appendix in the order in which they would come in this book. This means that we start with some philosophers who are of interest to the concept of *paradigm* (see Box 1.6) after which come research and researchers whose goal is to *explain* and then research and researchers whose ambition is to *understand* (see Figure 3.1). The Appendix will finish with some further notions of the positions of our three methodological views in all this.

A2.1 Kuhn

The concept of *paradigm* (paradigm = model, pattern) was given a central place in the history of science by Kuhn (1922–1996). A paradigm can, as illustrated in Chapter 1, be seen as a set of assumptions, values and practices that forms a way of conceptualizing reality. According to Kuhn, major changes in scientific thinking (scientific revolutions) involve a change (a shift) in paradigm and such changes are rare. Kuhn's thesis is that when scientists work under a paradigm, they take part in what he calls *normal science*, trying to solve the problems thrown up by the theories they hold. This science then becomes a kind of puzzle solving.

Every so often, however, a scientific revolution occurs when the existing paradigm proves unable to cope with what appears to be *anomalous* situations (deviations from the normal or common order in the frame of a paradigm). Existing assumptions become so inadequate that they collapse and are replaced by a new set of assumptions. A new paradigm is then in a process of development. Such shifts of paradigms cannot occur within a normal – puzzle solving – science itself. That's why Kuhn talks about "scientific revolutions". One such example of how different assumptions pave the way for a new paradigm was illustrated in the beginning of Chapter 1, with the discovery of DNA.

In consequence, scientists working under different paradigms possess different concepts and make different observations. They cannot appeal to any theory-neutral observation and Kuhn considers the introduction of a neutral language of observation hopeless. In relation to this, we have in this book tried to realize a *thematic language* of methodology (see the

Glossary) to bridge some of the problems of language confusion between our three views/approaches.

A2.2 Feyerabend

Feyerabend (1924–1994) goes even further than does Kuhn in his anti-empiricism. In contrast to Kuhn, he is dealing much more with questions of epistemology and methodology. Kuhn primarily illustrates the development of science by historical narratives in an ambition to better understand the shifts.

According to Feyerabend, there should not be any generally valid norms or rules for science. Science should instead be an essentially anarchistic operation. As a research strategy, therefore, he recommends an extreme form of *methodological pluralism*, according to which the researcher must always be prepared to break with existing norms in order to be open to new types of research.

His central theme is that the *positivists* and the *rationalists* (see above) have misunderstood science as a process of rationality on its way to the idea of the "wholly true", where the right *method* should be the way. He also meant that science couldn't reasonably be the only way for developing knowledge with high credibility.

As a philosopher he was also concerned with the concept of *freedom* in relation to truth. For example: if science says that it has found some final truth, must we then give up our freedom to be sceptical?

In the development of our methodological grammar, certain clues from Feyerabend have had some impact on us. Our concept of *knowledge creator* (see Box 3.2) can be seen as an answer to his point of departure that not only science can be a part in creating reliable knowledge, especially in a business society based on knowledge, as can also our development of *crealiability*, as an extended concept of excellence in this domain. Our *actors view* has been influenced by Feyerabend too, especially by his creative research strategy, mentioned above, and his concept of freedom. Even our *methodology of complementarity* contains certain seeds from Feyerabend's thoughts. Apart from this we do not side with his, as we see it, pronounced relativism.

A2.3 Törnebohm

Törnebohm (b. 1919) was a professor of the theory of science. His works are mainly in the theory of physical science, influenced by, among others, Kuhn, but he has developed the theories of paradigms further, inspired by social science.

This book is in its entirety influenced by paradigmatic thinking. However, we prefer, in the main, Törnebohm's evolutionary theory over Kuhn's revolutionary one for three reasons:

1. Kuhn's discussions are exclusively devoted to physical science.
2. Scientific revolutions rarely, if ever, take place in social sciences. Paradigms there live together side-by-side and many social science methodologies do not deserve to be called developed and mature paradigms.
3. In our opinion, Törnebohm's theories fit better with the social sciences than do Kuhn's.

A2.4 Classifications of paradigms

We have *ontologically* and *epistemologically* classified various ultimate presumptions in relation to *methodology* and by that derived and developed three *methodological views*:

- the analytical view
- the systems view
- the actors view

We came up with this *classification* in the first edition of this book and we think it is still, together with our new developed principle of complementarity, quite complete and that every kind of methodological idea or action intended to deal with a problem of business can be related to it. We have also found it to be clear and useful worldwide. We continue therefore to use it in this third edition of our book.

There are other proposals for classifying paradigms, of course. Two quite recognized such classifications, also using the concepts of ontology, epistemology and methodology to classify, are by Burrell & Morgan (1985) and by Guba (1990). Burrell & Morgan talk about

- Functionalist paradigm
- Interpretive paradigm
- Radical humanist paradigm
- Radical structuralist paradigm

Guba talks about

- Post-positivism
- Critical science
- Constructivism

There are similarities between both these classifications and our own. One *important difference*, however, is that we do not find any of the two alternatives "complete". Burrell & Morgan assert that three of their paradigms (all but interpretive) are influenced by Marx. We do not find Marx that important and influential in business paradigms and methodological views. Furthermore, Guba is classifying paradigms for so-called qualitative research only. We also see much relevant quantitative research around in business.

A3 EXPLAINING AND UNDERSTANDING

To claim a clear difference between "explaining" and "understanding" may seem of little interest to some. However, it has become customary, *though by no means universal*, to distinguish between trying to describe *events* and trying to describe *actions*. It has also been suggested that the term *understanding*, in contrast to *explaining*, ought to be reserved for the latter. Let us look at this discussion in some historical light. We will see that there are variations on this theme today.

Since the inception of the discipline of social science, lines of controversy have been drawn between those who do and those who do not make a principal distinction between two presumed alternative modes of thought, that is, *natural* sciences and *social* sciences. Theorists rejecting any fundamental distinction between those modes have traditionally been called *positivists*. We may call them *knowledge creators solely interested in explaining*. They assume that the methods which historically have proved their value in the analysis of the physical world are applicable to the materials of social sciences, and that while these methods may have to be adapted to a special subject matter, *the logic of explanation* in physical and social sciences is the same.

Theorists who draw a distinction between "explaining" and "understanding" have been labelled *anti-positivists* or *hermeneuticians*. We may call them *knowledge creators solely interested in understanding*. The critical element in anti-positivism was that the methods of physical sciences, however modified, are intrinsically inadequate to the subject matter of social sciences; in the physical world man's knowledge, they insist, is *external* and empirical, while social sciences are concerned with knowledge which is *internal* to man and with various kind of experience.

The controversy between explaining and understanding is deeply rooted in Western thought. In its most elementary sense it is based on a presumed intrinsic difference between mind and all that is non-mind. The controversy cannot be eliminated by choosing between explaining and understanding, because, basically, they cannot be compared. Most researchers interested in *explaining*, for instance, claim that everything, in the natural world as well as in the human world, can be explained, at least in principle; while researchers interested in *understanding* claim that understanding is only for humans. Furthermore, there is no neutral position where you can choose between explaining and understanding in a businesslike or impartial way. One has to "choose" at the same time as, by necessity, being positioned in either the explaining or the understanding camp. Which is really no choice at all!

Furthermore: the purpose of explanations is to depict a *factive* (objective and/or subjective) reality in order to better predict its course from *outside*; the purpose of understanding is to develop *means* in order to better manage human existence from *within*. One explanation can replace another explanation; one understanding can replace another understanding. However, an explanation cannot (according to knowledge creators interested in understanding) replace an understanding (which it can according to knowledge creators interested in explaining).

According to von Wright (1971) and Apel (1984), the German philosopher of history Droysen (1808–1884) was the first, within science, to introduce the difference between "to explain" and "to understand" (in German, *erklären* and *verstehen* respectively), to ground historical sciences methodologically and to distinguish them from natural sciences. He did this in *Grundrisse der Historik*, which was published in 1858:

> According to the object and nature of human thought there are three possible scientific methods: the speculative (formulated in philosophy and theology), the mathematical or physical, and the historical. Their respective essences are to know, to explain, and to understand. (Droysen, 1858: 13)

Droysen's term "verstehen" can be traced back to the modern founders of hermeneutics, Schleiermacher (1768–1834) and Boeckh (1785–1867), among others, and was made more generally known through Weber (1852–1931). A historically significant form of the debate between understanding and explanation began with Dilthey (1833–1911).

Initially understanding gained a psychological character, which explanations lacked. This psychological element was emphasized by several of the nineteenth-century anti-positivist methodologists, perhaps above all by Simmel (1858–1918), who thought that understanding, as a method characteristic of the humanities, is a form of *empathy* (von Wright, 1971). But empathy is not a modern way of separating understanding from explanation. Understanding can today be associated with *intentionality*, for instance, in a way which explanation cannot. We will come back to this concept a little later.

Generally we can say that natural sciences, according to Fay (1996), require concepts that "permit the formation of testable laws and theories". Other issues, for instance, those deriving from ordinary language, are of less interest. "But in the human sciences another set of considerations exists as well: the concepts used to describe and explain human activity must be drawn at least in part *from the social life being studied*, not only from the scientists' theories." (Fay 1996: 114) (emphasis in original)

Scientific concepts then, according to Fay, "bear a fundamentally different relationship to social phenomena from that which they bear to natural phenomena. In the social sciences, concepts partially constitute the reality being studied while in the latter case they merely serve to describe and explain it" (1996: 114).

> It is possible to explain human behaviour. We do not try to understand an area of low pressure because it has no meaning. On the other hand we try to understand human beings because they are of the same kind as we are. (Liedman, 2002: 280; our translation)

The descriptions as far as explaining and understanding are concerned are, as we regard it, more mixed today than was historically the case. There is research aimed at explaining as well as at understanding in both scientific camps. Furthermore, as we will see later, explaining is no longer solely associated with positivism and understanding is no longer something done only by hermeneuticians.

Generally, we want to distinguish between two kinds of explanations:

⇨ explaining by causality ("because of" explanations)
⇨ explaining by finality ("in order to" explanations)

So, for instance, to explain why a company has a budget can be explained either by the fact that its senior management had previously introduced the procedure in that company ("because of") or explained by the fact that its senior management wants to control its economy better ("in order to").

We also want to distinguish between two kinds of understanding:

⇨ understanding by significance
⇨ understanding by intentionality

The first is based on the *understanding* by the knowledge creator of the study area, what he/she thinks is significant there. The second is based on the actors' understanding of themselves in everyday reality.

So, in general, the difference between explaining and understanding is that *explanation* provides a description, a *representation,* of a situation or a phenomenon. *Understanding* is a description that has a *meaning* to somebody, to the researcher or to the actors in the study area or to both. Another way to phrase it is to say that an explanation is *depicting* reality, while an understanding is *constituting* reality. We will see later that understanding by significance is associated with hermeneutics and understanding by intentionality is associated with phenomenology.

Some researchers talk about understanding also by knowing the reasons or motives behind somebody's behaviour. This, to us, is however, to explain something by bringing up subjective aspects of factive reality.

It is not unusual to say that researchers that are interested in explaining are building *models* and that researchers that are interested in understanding come up with *metaphorical interpretations*. However, one has to be careful with this terminology. Understanding can also mean to come up with models, but then as part of constituting reality (see Box 3.3 and Figure 3.14).

By studying Figure 3.1, the relevance of this illustration for our three methodological views/approaches can easily be seen.

A4 EXPLAINING THINKERS AND THEORIES

A4.1 Positivism

It was Comte (1789–1857) who gave the concept of *positivism* a prominent place in the history of philosophy. At the beginning of the nineteenth century, many academicians and philosophers had an unwavering faith in the possibilities of the natural sciences and claimed that they should be the foundation of what was then modern philosophy. This could also be seen, for instance, among the utilitarians Bentham (1748–1832) and Mill (1773–1836). By the mid-1900s, positivism had a revival in what became known as the *Vienna circle* with leading figures like Carnap (1891–1970) and Neurath (1882–1945). The preferred term was then *logical positivism* (later *logical empiricism*).

The following three statements, as far as the social sciences are concerned, can characterize the *positivist* movement:

- Explanations in social sciences should be of the same type as explanations in natural sciences, that is, statements expressed in the form "X causes Y".
- Social sciences should use the same methods as natural sciences when constructing and testing such explanations (*the unity of sciences*).
- Metaphysics does not belong to science.

Logical positivism (or logical empiricism) is today seen mainly as an abandoned direction in the Anglo-Saxon, so-called, *analytical philosophy,* and from around 1950 ceased to exist as an independent philosophical movement.

Even if logical positivism has ceased to exist as an independent movement, its influence still looms over many analytical creators of knowledge. We can therefore not neglect positivism in its different and later versions when we discuss the *analytical view*.

A4.2 Analytical philosophy

Analytical philosophy is a twentieth-century movement. *Conceptual analysis* was its central theme. Conceptual analysis was by analytical philosophy also made into a *logical analysis* (called a *conceptually* logical analysis unlike a *formally* logical analysis) and it was stated that it had to be so in order to be *objective*.

Moore (1873–1950) and Russell (1872–1970) turned logical analysis into a *definition process*. They wanted to come up with a definition of what is a "fact" and came to the conclusion that if the statement "knowledge is well established truth" is true, then it is an *analytical fact*.

Analytical philosophy is a name covering a number of directions in twentieth-century philosophy, mainly in the English-speaking world. In spite of large differences in theory as well as in practice, the various directions agree on some main points and basic ideas:

- They are based on a clearly averse attitude to metaphysical constructions.
- They build on the opinion that traditional philosophical problems only can be (dis)solved through a *clarification* of the content of those expressions that are central to the formulation of problems.
- A basic *empiristical* point of departure.

Analytical philosophy is the foundation of the *analytical view* in this our book. In spite of this very short illustration we can easily discover the roots for the analytical view's emphasis on definitions and focusing on problems and problem clarifications.

A4.3 Holism

According to the *Oxford English Dictionary*, the term *holism* was introduced by the South African statesman Smuts (1870–1950). He defined it as "The tendency in nature to form wholes that are greater than the sum of the parts through evolution". Holism comes from a Greek word *holos*, which means "all", "entire", "total".

Holism is, together with concepts such as determinism and individualism, one of different epistemological perspectives, and as such concerns central questions of *explanation* in the social sciences. Holism is, in this regard, the opposite of the idea of coming to the truth via a number of mere descriptive factors of something instead of a consideration of its totality (holism).

According to the *Encyclopedia Britannica*, Methodological holism

> maintains that at least some social phenomena must be studied at their own autonomous, macroscopic level of analysis, that at least some social "wholes" are not reducible to or completely explicable in terms of individuals' behaviour. ... Semantic holism denies the claim that all meaningful statements about large-scale social phenomena (e.g., "The industrial revolution resulted in urbanization") can be translated without residue into statements about the actions, attitudes, relations, and circumstances of individuals.

Many thinkers have been classified as holists, for instance, the economist Schumpeter (1883–1950) in his evolutionary approach, the philosopher Morin (b. 1921) due to the transdisciplinary nature of his work, the sociologist Durkheim (1858–1917), when he opposed the notion that a society was nothing more than a simple collection of individuals and the psychologist Adler (1870–1937), claiming that the individual must be understood within the larger whole of society.

Our *systems view* is based on holistic thinking according to our first guiding principle of the view (see Figure 5.5).

A4.4 Structuralism

Structuralism generally means theories and methods within different scientific subjects which assert that individual elements cannot be analysed in isolation as they are determined by broader regularities and patterns; reality is *structured*. Only when the *determining* structures – the relationship between elements – have been uncovered, can individual elements be explained.

Structuralism can also mean, more specifically, that perspective which has been developed within *linguistics* starting from de Saussure (1857–1913). The term "structuralism" appeared in this perspective in the works of the anthropologist Lévi-Strauss (b. 1908). He aims at finding those universal structures which are behind all human conceptions. Along the same lines, the psychologist Piaget (1896–1980) studied those cognitive development stages that every human being, according to him, must pass in childhood.

Today, pure structuralism is less popular. It has often been criticized for being ahistorical and for favoring structural forces, as a kind of determinism, over the ability of individual people to act (we hear the same criticism from our *actors view* – see Chapter 13).

Structuralism has developed into perspectives like *post-structuralism* and *deconstructionism* (see "Recommended further reading: structuralism" at the end of this Appendix to explore further these two perspectives). However, the search is still for underlying structures in language. The claim is, that true and full knowledge of language cannot be reached at the individual level, only at a systems level. Therefore, we maintain that structuralism (with or without developments) is an important part of our *systems view*, as it supports our systems view in several fundamental aspects:

- A close connection between thought and language is pointed out, but the latter explains the former. So, for instance, if you talk about systems, you *think* systems and you *see* systems!
- We must look at the existence of language as a system rather than as the thoughts or activities of individuals. Not only are there systems, there is also a language *of* systems for us to take part in.
- Language exists independently of single individuals and cannot be completely described only at the level of single individuals. To think of language in terms of human systems is natural because it is something we share.

A4.5 Marxism and critical theory

Marxism is a political philosophy and practice derived from Marx (1818–1883) and Engels (1820–1895). Marx points out that philosophy is possible only as a critical analysis which has as its purpose to change praxis. In order to lay the foundation for this change of praxis, Marx introduces a new meaning of the term *materialism*, where materialism looks at man as an active creature, a creature who is able to put him/herself above nature and tries to rule it by realizing his/her human purposes and becoming free and able to determine him/herself. Man is creating *history*, but this possibility can be obscured and man may become a stranger to a him/herself, become *alienated*.

Engels supports Marx by adding among other things the term *dialectical* to *materialism*. *Historical materialism* is one part of this dialectical materialism. It has to do with the historical development of, for example, workers, social classes and societies. According to historical materialism, historical studies should have the *material* development of the societies as a starting point, and above all the different forms of production there.

The *Frankfurt School* (critical theory) attempts to develop a materialistic philosophy, which to some extent opposes dialectical materialism. The school generally claims that it is useless to speak of things or facts as independent of those *concepts* by which these things or facts are described.

The main proponents of the Frankfurt School are Horkheimer (1895–1973), Adorno (1903–1969), Fromm (1900–1980), Marcuse (1898–1979) and Habermas (b. 1929).

We claim that Marxism is closest to our *systems view* among our three methodological views/approaches due to its holistic orientation towards facts and reality and the risk of alienation (which in turn must be based on the belief of a factive self). The *critical theory* of the Frankfurt School has, to some extent, had an impact on us in our overarching notion of what it means to be a knowledge creator, whatever methodological view. Our actors view has also been influenced by *critical theory*, especially Fromm's humanistic approach to social science and to business as well.

A4.6 Systems thinking

There is really no philosophy that could be labelled *systems thinking*. However, there are some systems theories presented in the 1900s which have had an influence on the beginning of the development of our *systems view*:

- *Cybernetics* (from Greek *kybernetike*, the art of steermanship) is a scientific theory of control, established in 1948 by Wiener (1894–1964), which refers to studies of mathematical models for control systems. Cybernetics is researching communication technology problems related to control and internal information flow in complicated, preferably self-regulating, systems. Wiener's original definition of cybernetics pointed out similarities between biological, mechanical and electronic systems, but the cybernetic thought was later applied to economic, administrative and social systems as well.

- von Bertalanffy (1901–1972) was originally a biologist, and developed what he referred to a "holistic theory of life and nature". This was launched as a *general systems theory*. He saw in such a theory the possibility of developing principles and models applicable to all systems, regardless of their nature and organizational level. Von Bertalanffy claimed, therefore, that he was using more "organic" and "humanistic" opinions about human nature than the "mechanistic" and "robot-like" theories that were common at the time.
- Churchman (1913–2004) was a professor of Business Administration. He published in a number of different subjects, including ethics and value sciences. He is best known among business scholars for having launched, what he referred to as *the systems approach* in the 1960s as a framework for a further analysis of business problems. Churchman's interests can be seen as an extension of operations research and traditional decision theory.

A4.7 Symbolic interactionism

Mead (1863–1931) is a philosopher of the *pragmatic* school. He studied how our consciousness and the self are created in the social communication process. For pragmatists, meaning is primarily a property of *behaviour* and only secondarily a property of objects themselves. Meaning is seen as *stable* relations between a subject and a class of objects, defined in a way in which the latter is *typically* handled. Physical attributes are important, however, because they set limitations on what can be done. Meaning is also normally subject to social control in that the anticipated reactions of other people place additional restrictions on its usage.

Mead sets himself the task of formulating a scientific and empirical social psychology. Starting from situations of evolutionary biology he tries to *explain* how the human mind, the self, and self-consciousness come into existence.

Blumer (1900–1987) was a student of Mead and the sociologist who coined the term "symbolic interactionism". According to him this perspective rests on three "simple premises" (1986: p. 2):

1. Human beings act toward things on the basis of the meanings that the things have for them.
2. The meaning of such things is derived from, or arises out of, the social interaction that one has with one's fellows.
3. These meanings are handled in, and modified through, an interpretative process used by the person in dealing with the things he encounters.

Blumer looks upon the symbolic interactionism as an empirical social science. He asserts that: "its methodological principles have to meet the fundamental requirements of empirical science. … an empirical science presupposes the existence of an empirical world. Such an empirical world exists as something available for observation, study, and analysis" (1986: 21).

Among Blumer's students we can find Strauss who is the co-founder of "Grounded theory" (see A4.8 below).

Social creators of knowledge who build on Mead's and Blumer's ideas are often called *symbolic interactionists*. They try to avoid the dilemma that behaviour is *caused* either by forces *internal* to the individual, such as instincts, or by social forces impinging from *outside*, by stressing the interaction of the two.

Our opinion is that symbolic interactionism may have an important part to play in the frame of our *systems view* due to its empirical and factive base. George Mead also claimed that he was a kind of social behaviourist.

A4.8 Grounded theory

Glaser (b. 1930) and Strauss (1916–1996) first developed grounded theory in their book *The Discovery of Grounded Theory* (1967). Glaser and Strauss emphasize *generation* of theory rather than its verification. They aim at formulating a number of more cogent and coherent collections of methodological rules to generate theory from empirical data. Glaser and Strauss originally presented their grounded theory as clearly influenced by positivism.

Grounded theory is based on the idea of systematically collecting and analysing data using an *iterative* process of considering and comparing earlier literature, its data and theories that emerge as the research process goes on (Glaser & Strauss, 1967; Strauss & Corbin, 1998).

The grounded theory research process starts with formulating the research question and defining some early concepts. References to existing earlier results of relevance can be made here. Thereafter, cases and groups are sampled in a theoretical manner, which means that the researcher does not look for representativity but for variations in key variables and other theoretically interesting characteristics of the units of analysis.

Researchers then move on to collection of data. When doing the data collection fieldwork or other forms of data collection, this is supposed to be done concurrently with analysis so as to be flexible to accommodate possible changes of plans in order to discover better theory.

Grounded theory researchers may, according to Mäkelä and Turcan (2007), benefit from triangulation of data collection methods, data types (for instance, along the quantitative-qualitative dimension) or investigators. If findings converge, this will enhance confidence in the quality of the study. If, on the other hand, findings are in conflict with each other, this will help prevent the premature closure of data collection or analysis.

We place grounded theory on the explaining side of our methodologies (see Figure 3.1). Even if Strauss himself considered grounded theory as qualitative research, this does not prevent it from being used in the name of explaining, as we know. A study based on this theory can develop into an *analytical approach* or a *systems approach* depending on the desirable outcome of the study. The result may become sets of cause–effect relations or systems structures.

A4.9 Sensemaking

Sensemaking is often associated with Weick (b. 1936). Weick's ideas can be summarized in the following points:

- Most of sensemaking is concerned with *recreating* and *confirming* those opinions we already hold about our reality.
- Sometimes, however, we stop and ask ourselves the question: "How can this make sense?" This takes place above all when we want to make *new* and *unknown* situations meaningful.
- This can be done by retrospectively selecting those aspects of these situations, which suit our opinion about what a reality is and should be. We may construct a *narrative*.
- In this way we *enact* another aspect of our perceived reality.
- This could *explain* why two persons may *experience* the same situation so differently.

Weick's sensemaking does not cover all aspects of life, but it fits, by and large, primarily those rare situations when we stop and think about the meaning of what we are doing and what is going on. It is generally understood that people handle their ordinary days with a fairly low degree of conscious thinking.

However, it sometimes seems like non-reflective scripts are controlling our behaviour. The basic idea of Weick's sensemaking is that cognition lies in the path of action. Action precedes cognition and focuses cognition. It has been pointed out that Weick's retrospective perspective is passive and lacks the proactive position of an organization, which includes creative chaos. Sensemaking, some claim, may also take place proactively.

Sensemaking is a process where people try to *make sensible explanations* of experienced situations. It is concerned with the future, but is retrospective in nature, and is based on earlier sensemaking in an *ongoing flow*.

Weick's version of it is definitely part of what we, in this book, refer to as the *systems view*. However, there are versions of sensemaking which are closer to our *actors view*, or rather to our *methodology of complementarity* with the actors view as a transformative operator.

A5 UNDERSTANDING THINKERS AND THEORIES

A5.1 Hermeneutics

Hermeneutics began as a discipline attempting to interpret biblical and legal texts. Now, however, it has been given a much wider application, so that the problem of *interpretation* is seen by many as being of central importance in the social sciences.

The main emphasis in hermeneutics is on *understanding* and *communication*. It aims to arrive through language at a common understanding or shared vision. Gadamer (1900–2002), who is regarded as one of the great authorities in social science hermeneutics, was of the opinion that "the world" is in language, rather than constituting its foundation. As a consequence he rejected all notions of a "world in itself" against which different conceptions of the world can be positioned.

According to Trigg (2000), philosophical presuppositions (compare our ultimate presumptions) are a necessary point of departure for social science. He writes in relation to Gadamer:

> When language creates the categories with which we think, any attempt to understand those writing and acts at a different time and/or in a different language is fraught with difficulty. Their thoughts must be conditioned by their social situation, just as ours is by ours. Again and again, Gadamer emphasizes the primacy of language. Tradition is, he says, "linguistic in character", and he stresses, in a manner reminiscent of Wittgenstein, that "all forms of human community of life are forms of linguistic community". (2000: 220)

Several of Gadamer's influences can be traced in our methodological views. Gadamar's theories of hermeneutics – about language and interpretation – have been of great importance in the development of the *actors view*. However, in the respect that Gadamer stresses the importance of the interpretation made by the creator of knowledge, when he/she tries to come up with what is significant in the study area (even if only one interpretation among many) in the process of coming up with new knowledge, he has also influenced our *systems view* (in understanding mode).

A5.2 Phenomenology

The father of modern phenomenology is Husserl (1859–1938). Husserl's opinion about philosophy changed more than once, but he never wavered in his conviction concerning his indisputable demands of philosophers: they must look for complete clarity.

Husserl wanted in the beginning to understand the *essence* of things which consciousness has produced. This led to his *phenomenological method*, through which he hoped that the universal nature of things might be grasped. Husserl introduced, therefore, the concept of *transcendental-phenomenological reduction*. Roughly, this is a transition from an ordinary, natural, unconscious attitude toward the world and its objects to a position of oneself in a (transformatively creative) reflecting attitude (*free imaginative variation*). This process, which aims at discovering the essences in the world, starts by "bracketing" existence (Husserl called it *Epoché*), which does not mean the deny the world or question its existence, but methodologically to impose a limitation that permits one to make only judgements that do not depend on the world in time or space for validation.

Husserl claimed that when we perform this reduction we will discover what he called our "transcendental ego" or "pure consciousness". He was then interested in exploring and describing *the definite foundation of the experienced world*, a foundation that furthermore is not available to empirical observation but only to something Husserl called *eidetic intuition*.

Husserl held for a long time that the transcendental ego exists "absolutely" and that everything else exists "relative" to it. But toward the end of his life he changed his opinion about phenomenology one more time (including abandoning his belief in transcendental-phenomenological reduction as a progressive way to go in philosophizing):

- He now asserted that the transcendental ego was "correlated" to the world. It had lost its absolute status.
- He no longer claimed that the world had to be described starting from what it is to a transcendental individual but from an inter-subjective community of individuals.

- He made a sharp distinction between the world as known to science and the every-day reality in which we live, *der Lebenswelt*. Husserl was now of the opinion that scientific knowledge is only understandable if we understand this latter reality.

Husserl's phenomenology thereby acquired clear *dialectic* undercurrents.

A central concept to Husserl all along was *intentionality*, a concept which means that our consciousness is not fed by passive impressions but instead is always actively directed to *form* and *interpret* things around us, trying to make them meaningful; we are not referring here to objects as things in the outer world by themselves, but to things *intended*.

One can say that Husserl's final opinion is that phenomenology is not a description of a separate realm of experience but rather a reflection, and description, of *the ways in which our common experience comes to be and what the criteria are for different sorts of experiences and their adequacy*.

Husserl's later ideas were continued by one of his students, Schutz (1899–1959). He soon became one of the most recognized proponents in the field of *social phenomenology*. Standing with his feet in both the camps of philosophy and sociology, he developed a critical synthesis of Husserl's thinking and Weber's ideas about understanding. Schutz suggests that our experience of the world is directed by *the natural attitude*, where we take for granted that the world is built up by assumptions about groups of events in our language, so-called *typifications*, assumptions that we rarely question. For Schutz, it was always a matter of retracing and reconstructing the basis on which the construction of the life-world rests. In his *Collected Papers*, Vol. I, he developed such a base for a methodology of the social sciences.

Another person who ought to be named with respect to social phenomenology is Gurwitsch (1901–1973). His primary interest was the relation between phenomenology and Gestalt psychology.

Possibly the best-known social phenomenological publication known to business scholars is *The Social Construction of Reality*. This was published in 1966 by the sociologists Berger (b. 1929) and Luckmann (b. 1927). This book is based on Schutz's theories and even dedicated to him. This book is an attempt to answer the question: "What makes us produce the kinds of society that we do?"

Social phenomenology is the cornerstones for our *actors view*. The models of *typified cases* and the models of *constitutional ideals* (see Figure 6.11) and the construction of *ideal types* in the actors approach (see the end of Case III, Chapter 14) have, to a great extent, been inspired by the phenomenological idea of "free imaginative variation". These models are ideal states that can "imaginatively" reflect human freedom and the potential of life/business, and thereby engage various actors in procreating dialogues in which the potential will be transformed into the factual, that is, into a new social reality.

A5.3 Ethnomethodology

The ethnomethodological project focuses on the common-sense methods that we use to make sense of our experiences and constitute social reality. This project was started by Harold Garfinkel (b. 1917). The methods of special interest to ethnomethodologists are the various interpretive procedures that we routinely use to classify aspects of our experience and to establish connections between them. (Silverman, 1997: 28)

To put this social science movement in relation to other movements we can refer to Garfinkel himself and those persons he names that have influenced him most. Here we find name such as Husserl, Gurwitsch and Schutz (see A5.2 above).

Ethnomethodology can be seen as a branch of social phenomenology. As in phenomenology in general the development and the maintenance of our life-world is studied here. Criticism of traditional social science is strong.

Ethnomethodology is concerned with unconsidered and unquestioned background expectations and implicit rules that govern action in the quotidian world. Its method is to focus on micro processes that make it possible for the life-world to develop and to be maintained. Ethnomethodology has been criticized for studying the consequences of our everyday conventions, while ignoring the sources of these conventions.

In spite of being a branch of social phenomenology and in spite of the fact that Garfinkel denies the concept of social facts as having a reality of their own, it has only indirect bearing on the methodological treatments of our *actors view*.

A5.4 Social constructionism

There are a number of variations of social constructionism. They include elements of social phenomenology, ethnomethodology, discourse perspectives, semiotics and some varieties of post-structuralism, cultural concepts and gender perspectives.

There are, however, a number of similarities among all of the social constructionist movement:

- Person and reality are inseparable.
- Language produces and reproduces reality instead of being a result of reality.
- Knowledge is socially constructed, not objectively given.

Also, there are four basic working assumptions, emanating from Gergen, among social constructionist researchers to assure that the branch not merge into total relativism (Gergen, 1999):

1. Those terms by which we understand our world and ourselves are neither required nor demanded by "what there is". This has to do with the failure of language to map or picture an independent world. Another way of stating this assumption is to say that there are a potentially unlimited number of possible descriptions of "the situation in question" – and none of these descriptions can be ruled superior in terms of its capacity to map, picture or capture its features.
2. Our modes of description, understanding and/or representation are derived from relationship. Language and all other forms of representation are meaningful only in their relationships with people. Meaning and significance are born of coordination

between individuals – agreements, negotiations and affirmations. Nothing exists for us intelligible people before there are relationships.
3. As we describe or otherwise represent our reality, so do we fashion our future. Language is a major ingredient of our worlds of actions and therefore a part of building futures either as continuations of what already exists or as part of what will be new.
4. Reflection on our forms of understanding is vital to our future well-being. What shall we save, what shall we resist and destroy, what shall we create? There are no universal answers, only socially constructed ones.

We can say that our *actors view* is one variant of social constructionism. However, there are several differences, but one very important one is that the actors view illustrated in this book assumes that reality has an essence; most variations of social constructionism do not.

A5.5 Metaphorical thinking

A metaphor is in everyday life for most of us a figure of speech where things are compared in a symbolic way, as in "she is a dolphin" about a swimmer. Or, as the *Encyclopedia Britannica* describes it, a "figure of speech that implies comparison between two unlike entities, as distinguished from *simile,* an explicit comparison signalled by the words 'like' or 'as'". A metaphor may therefore in knowledge-creating pave the way for new perspectives. Some of the qualities of the intrinsic image of a metaphor are thus transferred to the idea or object in question. By using metaphors, the knowledge creator can also gain deeper insights into complex situations.

Metaphorical thinking provides us with effective means of dealing with complexity. It shows us how we can open our thought processes so that we can read one situation from multiple perspectives in a critical and informed way. But the opposite may also be the case.

In organizational theory, interpretations using metaphors are quite common (sometimes referred to as *poetic hermeneutics*). They often refer to Morgan (b. 1943). His argument is that researchers use metaphors, which are *taken for granted* and which are influencing their efforts. In order to get rid of their own implicit thoughts, it is important for them to become aware of the metaphors they use in their daily work. Those communities of theorists subscribe to relatively coherent perspectives (sometimes called *root metaphors or pre-scientific concepts* – see Chapter 2), which are based upon the acceptance and use of different kinds of metaphors as a foundation for inquiry.

Morgan does not, however, stop at pointing out the necessity for researchers to reflect on the metaphorical character of their knowledge. He also indicates a "method" of creating knowledge, which is based on the possibility of knowledge creators using different metaphors in their work, thus disclosing interesting aspects of the complex phenomenon of an organization. One interpretation of Morgan is that the researcher, if he/she is aware of the existence of different metaphors, can always consciously choose one or more metaphors to make his/her research a creative process. Examples of such metaphors could be: machine, organism, culture and psychic prison.

There are many ways to read what metaphors are and how they are used. In this book, we use it in the *systems view/approach* as a way to gain further insight into a factive reality, that is, when trying to come up with understanding in this approach, not only explanations. In the *actors view/approach*, however, it is especially common to make use of metaphors, from the very beginning of a knowledge-creating process to the procreative report. But the influence of Morgan is not very great, rather the actors view employs a real variety of influences from science to philosophy, from everyday language to poetry.

A6 CAN BE SEEN AS EITHER EXPLAINING OR UNDERSTANDING

A6.1 Ethnography

Ethnography is the study of people in their own naturally occurring settings or 'fields' by using methods of data collection which capture their social meanings and ordinary activities, involving the researcher participating him/herself directly in the setting, if not also in the activities, in order to come up with results in a systematic manner but without meaning being imposed on them externally. (Brewer, 2000: 6)

The following five features identify ethnographic research (Hammersley, 1990):

1 Behaviour is studied in everyday contexts. The researcher is not to impose any unnatural or experimental circumstances.
2 Observation is the primary means of data collection. However, other techniques can be used as well.
3 Data collection is flexible and unstructured in order to avoid imposing categories on what people say and do.
4 Focus is normally on a single setting or group.
5 The data are analysed by attributing meanings to the human actions described.

The word ethnography often refers to research methods used in cultural anthropology or to written text produced by such efforts. In this respect ethnography has also influenced, and been influenced by, literary theory.

Similarly to how we later in this Appendix will talk about narratives, there are, in a broad sense, two kinds of ethnography. One could be called ethnographical *realism* and the other could be called ethnographical *constructionism* (or constitutive ethnography; partly related to ethnomethodology, see A5.3). In the first case, the knowledge creators try, in an *explaining* mode, to depict people in their natural settings "*as they are*". This can be associated with our *analytical* or our *systems view*. The other takes a more *understanding* position in the sense of our *actors view*.

A6.2 Cultural studies

Culture can be seen in many different ways. In its widest sense one can say that culture is everything not given to man by nature, but produced by man himself. However, one can see culture either as something that exists as a *fact* (as a factive reality) or something which is *constituted* only *between* human beings (as a factified reality), something which is triggered only when people meet, people who have some cultural aspects in common, and is not something which is stored as objects in people's minds. In such a case, we can compare it with the modern concept of memory. Memory exists only as dispositions in people's brains. Every time we remember something, we are reconstructing what we believe we remember. It is not like the computer, where all retrieved documents are exactly the same as when they were last stored, or like a book, which when once again is picked off the bookshelf contains the same text and the same pictures as before. The brain must create anew every time we "remember".

Further aspects of culture can be picked up from Geertz (1926–2006), a cultural anthropologist and a researcher more interested in understanding than in explaining. (We discussed Geertz in Chapter 5.) Our interpretation of him is that he is looking for systems *results*. However, he often uses concepts that seem to be very *actors view* oriented, but when doing so, he always uses, in our methodological language, the *systems view* as a *transformative operator*.

- There is a difference between "thin" and "thick" descriptions. In the former case we can read what an actor is doing; in the latter case we can read what meaning underlies the action. The latter is the object of *ethnography*, according to Geertz.
- Culture is public because meaning is. The cognitivist fallacy – that culture consists of mental phenomena, which can be analysed by formal methods similar to those of mathematics and logic – is as destructive for an effective use of the concept, according to Geertz, as are the behaviourist and idealist fallacies to which it is a "misdrawn correction".
- A human being not influenced by his//her environment does not exist, has never existed, and most important, could not in the very nature of the case exist.
- To draw a line between what is natural, universal and constant is extraordinarily difficult. To draw such a line may even be seen as falsifying the human situation.
- Language and culture are intimately related. One can say that they mirror each other.

Explaining and *understanding* provide different perspectives of what culture is (the same way as we earlier saw alternative perspectives behind doing ethnographic research). *Explaining* looks at culture as an aspect of a firm alongside other aspects such as strategy and structure (compare Figure 5.2, where "shared values" can be seen as culture), while *understanding* can envisage the whole situation *as* culture being socially constructed. Research in the first case could be associated with our *systems view*; research in the second case with our *actors view*.

A6.3 Narratives

To construct a narrative is to reconstruct experience in a story. An issue discussed among social scientists (similar to the discussion we have had in the case of ethnographic research and cultural studies) is whether narratives are useful as a tool for researchers to get a new kind of order into what they are studying, or whether reality, as we approach it and try to understand it as human beings, means constructing our own narratives in our life-world. According to Fay (1996), the first we may call *narrative realism*, the second *narrative constructionism*. He asserts that narrative realism presumes that narratives *exist* in our human world and the mission for a creator of knowledge is to *depict* them, that is, to have people in the study area to tell them. Narrative constructionism presumes that we *impose* stories on our lives to make them more meaningful. In other words, in the latter case, narratives are *constructed*, not discovered.

So, as in the case of ethnography and cultural studies, (see above), we have *explaining* as well as *understanding* modes of researching narratives. In this sense we may say that *narrative realism* can be seen as related to our *systems view* and *narrative constructionism* as related to our *actors view*.

A7 TWO UNIQUE PERSONALITIES

There are two philosophers/thinkers that are particularly difficult to position in our *methodological views*, i.e. Foucault and Wittgenstein. In spite of that, they have influenced our work, alongside the others, with respect to the three views/approaches presented in the book.

A7.1 Michel Foucault

The strength of the work of Foucault (1926–1984) lies not so much in the problems he treats, but in the particular kind of analyses he performs. They all concern the modern organization of theoretical and practical knowledge and their relation to certain practices and forms of social organization. As a philosopher, sociologist and historian he has been named as a "structuralist" as well as a "post-structuralist", and also described as "postmodernist", labels he himself has rejected.

Foucault's radical/critical intellection has powerful implications for theoretical work within the social sciences. This should be taken in two senses. First, his particular analyses of the relation between forms of knowledge and social practices implicated in psychiatry or criminology throw into question a number of widespread epistemological and sociological assumptions, which govern conventional analyses. Second, he provides an analysis of the human sciences themselves, together with the ancillary fields of criminology and psychiatry. If Foucault's analyses are accepted it is clear that many a conventional position in the social sciences could be questioned.

The analyses of Foucault are in the most obvious sense historical. He believed that the large question he posed regarding the meaning of human existence today could be answered only within the context of humanity's understanding of the past. The changing order of knowledge and power is historically conditioned and our ignorance of these conditions leads us to believe that our present state of existence is the epitome of humanity. The theoretical disciplines that Foucault's reflection incorporates, according to Kendall and Wickham, 1999, are *genealogy* – the theory of power practice – and *archaeology* – the theory of discourse and knowledge.

Foucault is probably best known for his analyses of power. It is his conviction that power is the principle of development and integration within our society. If this assertion is accepted as a general rule, then power, as a practical principle must also apply as a principle for a theoretical system of knowledge. In fact, power and knowledge are the main themes of Foucault's work. What Foucault calls the *episteme* are the conditions of knowledge within which organized knowledge is structured. He has developed this in *Power/Knowledge* (Foucault, 1980).

Foucault uses the term *discourse* here to analyse diverse configurations of assumptions, categories, logics, claims and modes of orientation. The configurations provide persons with coherent interpretive frameworks and discursive practice for bringing up different realities, within which particular kinds of people reside, relationships prevail and opportunities are likely to emerge. According to Foucault, the production of discourses in any society is controlled, selected, organized and redistributed by certain procedures.

Foucault is also working with the history of ideas and he is using unconventional methods while doing so. But, basically, his working hypothesis is that underlying structures control different products within a given epoch. There is a system of concepts or a code which determines what can be thought within the epoch.

Foucault refused, as mentioned above, to accept any kind of scientific label on his thoughts. It is our opinion that, among our three views, we are closest to his intellection with our *systems view*. For most of his life he talks about necessary and "hidden" structures influencing our possibility to know and learn and to exert power. It is not until late in life that he is discusses how men can get around these structures and release their free will. This later train of thought turns him partly, as we regard it, towards what we refer to as the *actors view*.

A7.2 Ludwig Wittgenstein

Wittgenstein (1889–1951) is one of the most influential and most widely discussed philosopher of the twentieth century. One of those rare human beings who radically differs from the mainstream, but still remains relevant and of his time, he is also rare in another sense. He really knows the meaning of a paradigmatic shift (see A2.1 above). He made one himself.

Wittgenstein is mainly a language philosopher and he was a professor at the University of Cambridge. It is common to speak of his two periods. The first preceded his doctoral theses *Tractactus Logico-Philosophicus*. The second began around 1930 and continued to his death. In this period he rejected practically every aspect of his conceptions of language as presented in his thesis. It is these later radical thoughts on how to learn a language, on meaning in language and on language itself, which are of interest here. According to Pears (1971), this is also normally the case in most other contexts.

As Wittgenstein looks at it in his second period, language is something we do. To understand a language is not, according to him, a matter of grasping some inner essence of meaning, but rather of knowing how to perform. The emphasis falls on the "functions" of words rather than their "content". Wittgenstein refers to this as *language games*.

If language is seen as human *activity* rather than a collection of labels for categories of phenomena, then we will not be surprised to find systematic inconsistencies in it – not as a fault or as problems, but as essential to its function. Further, if language is seen as human activity, that activity may be carried out in quite different ways, depending on what the talking human beings are up to. Furthermore, if words need not be used for referring and their meaning is not their reference, and if concepts may be internally inconsistent, then many of our traditional and common-sense assumptions about the relationship between language and reality are called into question. The way Ziff (1960) looks at it, one could, according to Wittgenstein, say that the essential language function is *not to comment on factual circumstances but to be together*. We can say that Wittgenstein's opinion of the meaning of "understanding" is related to action:

> Try not to think of understanding as a 'mental process' at all. For *that* is the expression which confuses you. But ask yourself: in what sort of case, in what kind of circumstances, do we say: "Now I know how to go on". (Wittgenstein, 1953: 61)

Wittgenstein calls the regularities of our life in language "forms of life". In other words, human life as we live and observe it is not just a random, continuous flow, but displays recurrent patterns, regularities, characteristic ways of doing and being, of feeling and acting, of speaking and interacting. Because they are patterns, regularities, configuration, Wittgenstein calls them "forms", and because they are patterns in the fabric of human existence and activity on earth, he describes them as "of life". The idea is clearly related to the idea of language games, and more generally to Wittgenstein's action-oriented perspective of language as Pitkin (1972) has pointed out. "The speaking of language", Wittgenstein says, "is a part of an activity, or a form of life" (Wittgenstein, 1953: 23).

Wittgenstein talks much about rules and patterns, but he never leaves the level of humans as actors. He also stresses the *constituting* rather than the *depicting* purpose of language. In the language of this book, we could, with the greatest humility, say that Wittgenstein is using systems concepts in an *actors view*.

A8 A SUMMARY

It isn't an easy task to relate philosophical thoughts and concepts to each other and to different philosophical branches. It's a slightly hazardous business, where you continuously risk treading on somebody's toes. In this Appendix we have made our descriptions only in respect to how various branches, movements, perspectives, thinkers, etc. have influenced the development of our three methodological views. To summarize this briefly:

- The *analytical* view is still today influenced by positivism, but its modern foundation is analytical philosophy. We have adapted the analytical view to business by giving subjective facts the same methodological status as objective facts, in the frame of the ultimate presumption of a factive reality. We have illustrated the ontological and epistemological roots of the view, from empiricism to rationalism, and related it to such branches as grounded theory and ethnography in the senses of explanation.
- The *systems* view is our name for all sorts of research/consulting/investigating based on systemic, holistic and structuralistic thinking either as explaining or as understanding. In the latter case, hermeneutics, symbolic interactionism, sensemaking, metaphorical thinking, etc. enter the picture.
- The *actors* view is based on social phenomenology and has a social constructionist aspect. However, as a methodological view/approach, as presented in this book, it is a genuine development by us, especially by Arbnor. Phenomenological thinkers rarely concern themselves with concrete research methodology, even less with creating business knowledge. Furthermore, the actors view is, besides the above-mentioned philosophers/thinkers, also influenced by figures like Bergson (1859–1941), Heidegger (1889–1976), Habermas (b. 1929), Sartre (1905–1980) and Ricoeur (1913–2005) and has therefore an orientation to the philosophy of human life itself, which the other two methodological views have not.

What makes this book unique, on top of its combining of philosophy of science, methodology and business, is that we have developed a *methodology of complementarity*, which means that the book is a complete package of methodology for creating business knowledge.

A9 RECOMMENDED FURTHER READING

(Visit: www.knowledge-creator.com)

Theory of science

Fay, B. (1996), *Contemporary Philosophy of Social Science*. Oxford: Blackwell Publishers.
Potter, E. (2006), *Feminism and Philosophy of Science*. London: Taylor & Francis Ltd.
Rosenberg, A. (2007), *Philosophy of Social Science*. Boulder: The Perseus Books Group.

Paradigms

Burrell, G. & Morgan, G. (1985), *Sociological Paradigms and Organizational Analysis – Elements of the Sociology of Corporate Life*. Aldershot: Ashgate Publishing Group.
Guba, E.G. (ed.) (1990), *The Paradigm Dialog*. Newbury Park: Sage.
Kuhn, T. (1996), *The Structure of Scientific Revolution*. Chicago: The University of Chicago Press.

Explaining and understanding

Apel, K.O. (1984), *Understanding and Explanation*. Cambridge, MA: The MIT Press.
Manicas, P.T. (2006) *A Realist Philosophy of Social Science: Explanation and Understanding*.
    Cambridge: Cambridge University Press.
von Wright, G.H. (1971), *Explanation and Understanding*. London: Routledge.

Positivism

Friedman, M. (1999), *Reconsidering Logical Positivism*. Cambridge: Cambridge University
    Press.
Richardson, A. & Uebel, T. (2007), *The Cambridge Companion to Logical Empiricism*.
    Cambridge: Cambridge University Press.

Analytical philosophy

Austin, J.L. (1979), *Philosophical Papers*. Oxford: Clarendon Press.
Martinick, A. & Soza, E.D. (2001), *Analytical Philosophy: An Anthology*. Oxford: Blackwell
    Publishers.
Stroll. A. (2007), *Twentieth-Century Analytical Philosophy*. Dehli: Motilal Banarsidass.

Systems thinking

Bertalanffy, L. (1973), *General Systems Theory* (rev. edn.). New York: Brazilier.
Buckley, W. (ed.) (1968), *Modern Systems Research for the Behavioural Scientist*. Hawthorne,
    NY: Aldine.
Jackson, M.C. (2003), *Systems Thinking: Creative Holism for Managers*. Chichester: John
    Wiley and Sons Ltd.
Skyttner, L. (2001), *General Systems Theory*. Singapore: World Scientific Publishing Co. Pte Ltd.

Holism

James, S. (1984), *The Content of Social Explanation*. Cambridge: Cambridge University
    Press.
Laszlo, E. (1996), *Systems View of the World: A Holistic Vision for Our Time*. Cress Kill, NJ:
    Hampton Press.
Phillips, D.C. (1976), *Holistic Thought in Social Science*. Stanford: Stanford University Press.

Structuralism

Dosse, F. (1998), *History of Structuralism* (two volumes). Minneapolis, MI. University of
    Minnesota Press.
Hawkes, T. (2003), *Structuralism and Semiotics*. London: Taylor & Francis Ltd.
Norris, C. (2002), *Deconstruction: Theory and Practice*. London: Taylor & Francis Ltd.
Sturroch, J. & Rabaté, J.M. (2003), *Structuralism*. Malden: Blackwell Publishing Ltd.
Williams, J. (2005), *Understanding Poststructuralism*. London: Acumen Publishing.

Marxism

D'Amato, P. (2006), *The Meaning of Marxism*. Chicago, IL: Haymarket Books.
Therborn, G. (2008), *From Marxism to Post-Marxism*. New York: Verso.

Grounded theory

Charmaz, K. (2006), *Constructing Grounded Theory. A Practical Guide Through Qualitative Analysis*. London: Sage.
Glaser, B.G. (1992), *Basics of Grounded Theory Research*. Mill Valley, CA: Sociology Press.
Glaser, B.G. & Strauss, A.L. (1967/1999), *The Discovery of Grounded Theory*. Edison: Transaction Publishers.

Sensemaking

Weick, K.E. (1995), *Sensemaking in Organizations*. Thousand Oaks, CA: Sage.
Weick, K.E. (2000), *Making Sense of the Organization*. Malden, MA: Blackwell Publishing Ltd.

Symbolic interactionism

Blumer, H. (1986), *Symbolic Interactionism: Perspective and Method*. Berkeley: University of California Press.
Charon, J.M. (2006), *Symbolic Interactionism: An Introduction, An Interpretation*. Englewood Cliffs, NJ: Prentice-Hall.

Metaphorical thinking

Morgan, G. (ed.) (1983), *Beyond Method*. Newbury Park: Sage.
Pugh, S.L., Hicks, J.W., Davis, M. & Ventra, T. (1992), *Briding: A Teacher's Guide to Metaphorical Thinking*. Urbana, IL: National Council of Teachers.

Hermeneutics

Bauman, Z. (1978), *Hermeneutics and Social Science. Approaches to Understanding*. London: Hutchinson and Sons.
Gadamer, H.G. (2004), *Truth and Method*. London: Continuum International Publishing Group Ltd.
Jasper, D. (2004), *A Short Introduction to Hermeneutics*. Louisville: Westminster John Knox Press.

Phenomenology

Husserl, E. (1931/2002), *Ideas: General Introduction to Pure Phenomenology*. London: Allen & Unwin.
Moran, D. (2000), *Introduction to Phenomenology*. London: Routledge.
Sokolowski, R. (1999), *Introduction to Phenomenology*. Cambridge, Cambridge University Press.

Social Phenomenology

Schutz, A. (1962–1970), *Collected Papers Vol. I: The Problem of Social Reality, Vol. II: Studies in Social Theory, Vol. III: Studies in Phenomenological Philosophy*. Leiden: Martinus Nijhoff Publishers.
Schutz, A. (1967), *The Phenomenology of the Social World*. Evanston: Northwestern University Press.

Ethnomethodology

Garfinkel, H. (1984), *Studies in Ethnomethodology*. Oxford: Blackwell Publishers.

Social constructionism

Burr, V. (2003), *Social Constructionism,* London: Routledge.
Gergen, K.J. (1999), *An Invitation to Social Construction*. London: Sage.

Ethnography

Atkinson, P. & Hammersley, M. (2007) *Ethnography: Principles in Practice*. London: Taylor & Francis Ltd.
Madison, D.S. (2005), *Critical Ethnography*. London: Sage.
Rose, D. (1990), *Living the Ethnographic Life*. Newbury Park: Sage.

Cultural studies

Alvesson, M. (1993), *Cultural Perspectives on Organizations*. Cambridge: Cambridge University Press.
Bjerke, B. (1999), *Business Leadership and Culture*. Cheltenham: Edward Elgar.
Geertz, C. (1983), *Local Knowledge*. New York: Basic Books.

Narratives

Czarniawska, B. (1998), *A Narrative Approach to Organization Studies*. Thousand Oaks, CA: Sage.
Mitchell, W.J.T. (ed.) (1981), *On Narrative*. Chicago: University of Chicago Press.

Michel Foucault

Foucault, M. (2002), *The Archeology of Knowledge*. London: Taylor & Francis Ltd.
Foucault, M. (1988), *Power/Knowledge*. New York: Random House.
Hoy, D. (ed.) (1986), *Foucault. A Critical Reader*. Oxford: Blackwell Publishers.

Ludwig Wittgenstein

Pears, D. (1997), *Wittgenstein*. London: Fontana Press.
Pitkin, H.F. (1976), *Wittgenstein and Justice*. Los Angeles: University of California Press.
Wittgenstein, L. (1967/2001), *Philosophical Investigations*. Oxford: Blackwell Publishers.

GLOSSARY

Each word in italics in the Glossary is possible to find as a cross-reference. We strongly recommend going further with such references if they are not already familiar to the reader.

ABC • IC The Arbnor Business Creating • Intelligence Cycle (see Figure 15.2).

abduction To place a single case (the result) from the *study area* in a *hypothetical* pattern to be confirmed by *theoretical* "rules" and/or new observations; a kind of combination of *induction* and *deduction*; associated with the *analytical view*.

actors approach *Actors view* in application.

actors view A *methodology* for creating knowledge devoted to *understanding*, creating and *vivifying meaning* in reality, where this reality is presumed to be *socially constructed*.

analysis An analysis can be made within all three of the *methodological views*. An analysis, according to the *analytical view*, consists of dissecting an object into its parts. An analysis in the *systems view* consists of *explaining* and/or *understanding* the relations of an object's parts to each other, to the *totality*. The analysis concept is also used in the *actors view* (however, more common is *diagnosis*) in order to emphasize an interest in looking at different parts and their *dialectic* relations to each other.

analytical approach *Analytical view* in application.

analytical philosophy A generic term for a philosophical movement, which has made the *methodological* use of conceptual *analysis* and formal logic its central theme; associated with the *analytical view*.

analytical view A *methodology* for creating knowledge devoted to *explain causality* in reality, where this reality is presumed to be *factive* and built up *summatively*.

anomaly A deviation from the normal or common order in the frame of a *paradigm*.

antithesis A *dialectical* element of a process, where this second (*antithesis*) is the contrasting part of the first (*thesis*), with the first inherent in itself; associated with the *actors view*.

approach See *methodological approach*.

Arbnor/Bjerke Methodological Principle of Complementarity The potential interdependency in opposite methodological opinions of similar problems is to be used for excellent explanations and/or understanding of them. The principle implies that there are many such problems with this kind of inherent interdependency, which cannot fully be treated by only one of the approaches, in question. Therefore, it is possible and desirable to use complementarity in studies faced with multifaced problems.

Arbnor Uncertainty Principle "The more precisely you determine isolated characteristics of a human being and her activities, quantitatively and statistically, the less you understand of her as a whole. And the better you understand her as a whole, the more uncertain the quantitative/statistic aspects become."

artistics The way in which the actors *creator of knowledge* expresses his/her knowledge-creating as a *procreative* language of description. Also, the final expression format of this interpretive pictorial language creating meaning and new prespectives (opposite: statistics).

atomism A philosophical/scientific perspective, presuming that aspects of a given situation can be determined or *explained summatively* by its parts (opposite: *holism*).

base view/approach A denotation of a *methodological view/approach* when used as a *transformative operator* in a *methodology of complementarity*.

causality A presumed relationship between an explaining factor (*cause*) and a factor being explained (*effect*); associated with the *analytical view*.

cause See *causality*.

ceteris paribus "Everything else being equal"; circumstances presumed to be *valid* for *explanations* in the *analytical view*.

complementarity A concept describing how a potential interdependency in opposite *methodological* opinions of similar problems can be used in a *reconciliation* for excellent *explanations* and/or *understanding* of them.

complementary procedure A *transformative operation*, where a *technique/method/theory* from one *methodological view* is being brought into another *methodological view* and inevitably transformed by being so (opposite: *primary procedure*). Compare *methodical procedure*.

consistency A concept of quality assurance, according to knowledge creating. Degree of methodological syntactical match in relation to *ultimate presumptions* of a *methodological view*. The concept is an essential core element of the overall scientific concept, *crealiability*, for excellence in knowledge creating work.

consistency of complementarity A concept of quality assurance, according to knowledge creating of complementarity. Degree of methodological syntactical match of complementarity in relation to the ultimate presumptions of the *transformative operator*. The concept is an essential core element of the overall scientific concept, *crealiability* of *complementarity*, for excellence in knowledge creating work.

constitutional factors Factors, which are *socially constructed*, by which reality is built up socially; associated with the *actors view*.

constitutional ideal A more "general" principle for how reality is *socially constructed* and how it could be if the potential in what is *factual* was delivered; associated with the *actors view*.

constitutive interpretive procedures "Rules" by which creators of knowledge *interpret/understand* the reality which the actors and the *creators of knowledge* are part of *socially constructing* themselves; associated with the *actors view*.

constitutive understanding *Understanding* which is seen as an inevitable part of reality, where this reality is presumed to be *socially constructed*; associated with the *actors view* (opposite: *representative understanding*).

constructionism See the Appendix.

constructivism See *constructionism*.

crealiability The concept is a compound of creativity and liability and the prefix "crea" denotes, in scientific contexts, to be creative, to have imagination and ingenuity, this connected to the suffix "liability" in the sense of responsibility, obligation and duty. Crealiability is our concept for excellence in knowledge-creating work and consists of the four core elements: creativity, *objectivity* (*validity*/*reliability*), *stringency* and *consistency*.

creator of knowledge (also *knowledge creator*) A conscious researcher, consultant and/or investigator who has the will to apply curiosity and imagination, has the insight that knowledge also contains manifestations of *ultimate presumptions,* and uses his/her training in the concrete handicraft to develop knowledge, and to present new knowledge to others and be accountable for it.

culture Fundamental values, assumptions and beliefs associated with members of a social group (can also be seen as, or including, how a social group manifests itself in various artifacts, including language).

cybernetics A generic term, taken from Wiener around 1950, to describe *teleological* structures, interactions, responses, feedbacks, etc. in complex systems. The "art of steering and control" of multifaceted systems structures, especially communication processes.

deduction Inference of specific forecasts/conclusions from general *theories*/premises; associated with the *analytical view* (compare: *induction* and *abduction*).

denotation of conceptual meaning A fundamental ambition of *the actors view*, that is, to come up with pictures/descriptions/*metaphors* of how actors attach *meaning* to their language and actions.

depiction A "map" of reality, where this reality is presumed to be *factive*; associated with the *analytical view* and the *systems view* in the *explanatory* mode.

determinism A philosophical concept, presuming that every phenomenon or event, including human acts and behaviour, has a cause – is *causally* determined by a link of previous occurrences; partly associated with the *analytical view* and the *systems view*.

diagnosis A way to interactively *interpret* and *understand* actors in situations of *everyday* life through deeper insight and broadened perspectives; associated with the *actors view*.

dialectics The process of *thesis, antithesis* and *synthesis*, that is, relationships and situations where people constantly reinterpret and give different meaning value. This is also the process where the knowledge-creator gives scientific meaning to his/her interactive *diagnosis*; associated with the *actors view*.

dialogue The interplay between "talking" and "listening" that takes place on equal terms for the participants. A dialogue is to clarify differences in order to transgress them toward something new, in a deepened *understanding* and *meaning* of life, that is, the parties of the dialogues are looking for an agreement through what is different; associated with the *actors view*.

discourse A praxis in communication, governed by (often implicit) rules. In social science applications it involves concepts, methods and skills with specific purposes. This means, in general, that the chosen discourse delivers a way of thinking and a style of communicating. The concept is mostly connected with the work of Foucault (see the Appendix).

eclectic maze A jumbled mixture of what appear to be best *techniques*, *theories*, and so on, without any reflection in relation to *ultimate presumptions* on the various *methodological views*.

effect See *causality*.

egological sphere The internal logic of an actor that constitutes his/her *finite province of meaning*, and by which he/she orients him/herself; associated with the *actors view*.

emancipative understanding Come to an *understanding* that one's reality is seen through the "lenses" of a language and that those lenses can be shifted, thereby providing another *understanding*; associated with the *actors view*.

emancipatory interactive action Action taken by the *creator of knowledge* together with other actors in the *study area*, aiming at providing *emancipative understanding* by delivering the potential in what is factual; associated with the *actors view*.

empirical Pertaining to human experience.

empiricism A philosophical movement, presuming that all knowledge of reality, seen as *factive*, is derived from our sensory impressions (opposite: *rationalism*).

epistemology A set of philosophical presumptions concerning human knowledge and learning. The philosophical *"theory"* of the nature and grounds of knowledge.

ethnography See the Appendix.

ethnomethodology See the Appendix.

everyday reality See *life-world*.

explaining Providing objective and/or subjective reasons for phenomena or events, presumed to be independent of us as *creators of knowledge*; associated with the *analytical view* and the *systems view* in the explanatory mode.

externalization The process by which we make our subjectivity available to others ("society is a human result"); associated with the *actors view*.

factified reality See *factual reality*.

factive reality A reality presumed to be built of by objective and/or subjective facts and independent of us as *creators of knowledge*; associated with the *analytical view* and the *systems view*.

factual reality A reality presumed to be *socially constructed* but treated as a fact without being one in the sense of the *analytical view* and the *systems view* (can also be called *factified reality*); associated with the *actors view*.

falsification If a theory is to be regarded as scientific, according to the concept of falsification, it has also to specify results that, if found, would disprove the theory. Falsification means therefore to direct the researcher's attention to look for refuting or counter instances as well. Conclusions in the theoretical reality for prediction are open for falsification, that is denial in empirical reality that some conclusion derived in the theoretical reality is valid; associated with the *analytical view* (opposite: *verification*). The concept is connected with the work of Popper.

finality A presumed relationship between an *explaining* factor (*producer*) and a factor being explained (*product*), that is, to *explain* by the purpose they serve rather than by postulated previous *causes* (see *causality*); associated with the *systems view*.

finite province of meaning An actor's picture/concept of reality – the actor's subjective reality in its entirety – more or less socially shared by a larger or a smaller number of other actors (includes also parts of which are not shared with anybody else); associated with the *actors view*.

functionalism A philosophical/scientific thought, having made the relationship between patterns and their *factive* consequences a central theme; associated with the *systems view*.

General Systems Theory A scientific attempt to come up with a *holistic theory* of life and nature, based on systems principles; a forerunner to the *systems view*.

grounded theory A scientific branch, based on the idea of systematically collecting and *analyzing* data from the study area instead of starting from "grand theories", mainly associated with the *analytical view* or the *systems view*.

hermeneutics See the Appendix.

holism A philosophical/scientific perspective, presuming that all aspects of a given situation cannot be determined or *explained* by its parts only; associated with the *systems view* (opposite: *atomism* or *reductionism*).

hypothesis In a strict sense: a *cause–effect* (see *causality*) relationship proposal, not yet verified or falsified; associated with the *analytical view*. In a loose sense: supposition, idea, point of departure, etc.; mainly associated with the *systems view* and the *actors view*.

idealism See the Appendix.

ideal-typified language A more "general" language constituted by *typified cases* and the *constitutional ideal*; associated with the *actors view*.

induction Generation of general *theories* from individual facts in the *empirical (factive)* reality; associated with the *analytical view* (compare: *deduction* and *abduction*).

institutions An institution emerges according to the *actors view* when common *typifications* of habitual acts are established. By "institution" can be meant everything from established concepts of description – lingoes/clichés – to different public authorities; associated with the *actors view*.

institutionalization The process of establishing values, norms, routines, etc. as *institutions* in the *socially constructed reality*; associated with the *actors view*.

internalization The process by which we take over the world in which others already live ("humans are a societal result"); associated with the *actors view*.

interpretation To decode something contextually and through that coming up with an *understanding*, either by a *metaphor* provided by the *creator of knowledge* in the *understanding* mode of the *systems view*, or by a denotation of conceptual *meaning* in the *actors view*.

intentionality The dimension, process and structure behind intention that gives a *meaning* to experience; associated with the *actors view*.

intersubjectivity Agreement between results from *creators of knowledge*, working independently of each other; mainly associated with the *analytical view*.

knowledge creator See *creator of knowledge*.

legitimization The process of the justification of *institutions* in *socially constructed reality*; associated with the *actors view*.

life-world (also called *everyday reality*) The world regarded as the one immediately given to us in everyday life and not imposed by any scientific models or one's own interpretations. In a society where scientific results continuously influence us, this is a crucial concept (compare: *self-reference*); associated with the *actors view*.

magnifying level Degree of details contained in systems models or systems *interpretations*; associated with the *systems view*.

materialism See the Appendix.

meaning Significant sense-quality (value and importance) that actors attached to their situation; associated with the *actors view*.

meaning structure A more "complete" built-up of *meaning* relations in a group of actors; associated with the *actors view*.

metaphor In everyday life for most of us, a figure of speech where things are compared in a symbolic way, as in "she is a dolphin" about a swimmer. In science, a concept, an abstraction or image placed by the creator of knowledge on one situation in the study area, taken from another and different situation, where the qualities of the intrinsic sense of the metaphor thus are transferred to the object in question in the first situation. A metaphor may therefore in knowledge-creating pave the way for new perspectives; associated with the *systems view* and the *actors view*.

metaphysics Branch of philosophy that deals with "being" (*ontology*) and "knowing" (*epistemology*), that is, the ultimate nature of reality. These kinds of studies have been subjected to many criticisms regarded as too subtle and theoretical. Since the middle of the nineteenth century the predominant social science course has been *positivism*, which denies the value of any metaphysical assertion.

metatheories The background theories in the conception of science that are held by *creators of knowledge* and that, in general terms, guide their practical knowledge-creating. More fundamental "theories of theories", which inevitably include the people using them; associated with the *actors view*.

method Guiding principle for creation of knowledge and choosing among *techniques*.

methodical procedure The way the *creator of knowledge* incorporates, develops and/or modifies a technique or a previous result and/or theory in a *methodological view*; can be of a *primary* or a *complementary* type.

methodics Applying *methodical procedures* in a plan and/or in an implementation of a study.

methodological approach A *methodological view* in application.

methodological view A consistent set-up of *ultimate presumptions*, concepts and principles guiding creation of knowledge. Three such *views* are: the *analytical view*, the *systems view* and the *actors view*.

methodology A *theory* and a grammar of the modes of thinking and acting for knowledge creating.

methodology of complementarity A complete grammar for creating knowledge containing *primary* as well as *complementary procedures* open for all kinds of *transformative operations* within the three *base views/approaches*.

model A deliberately simplified picture of the *factive reality*; mainly associated with the *analytical view* and the *systems view* in *explanatory* mode. The concept may also be used by the *actors view* in "painting" the *socially constructed reality*, both in the sense of visualizing aspects of it and *vivifying* the potential in what is *factual*, but, of course, then with a totally different meaning of the concept than with the two other views.

narrative A story guided by specific rules, either seen as a part of the *factive reality* in the *systems view* (narrative *realism*) or as told by actors as part of the *factified reality* (narrative *constructionism*).

objectification The process by which an *externalized* human thought and/or act might attain the characteristics of a *socially constructed objectivity* ("society is an objective reality"); associated with the *actors view*.

objectified Something seen as *objective* in the *actors view* without being so in the sense of the other two *views*; this means that this *objectivity* of reality can be questioned and changed in the logic of delivering what is potential in what is *factual*.

objective Characteristic of the non-subjective part of the *factive reality*, presumed to be general and independent of any single individual; mainly associated with the *analytical view*.

objectivity See *objectified* and *objective*. As a concept of quality assurance in *knowledge creating* and as a core element of *crealiability* it will signify different substances in relation to the various *methodological views*. (See "The problem of objectivity" in Chapter 7.)

ontology A set of philosophical thoughts and presumptions concerning the set-up and constitution of all reality and the problems/opportunities of existence. (See *metaphysics*.)

operative paradigm A consistent arrangement of *methodical procedures* and *methodics* as a bridge between a *methodological view/approach* and a *study area*.

paradigm A philosophical and *theoretical* framework of presumptive and guiding principles which are governing knowledge and the creation of knowledge, but which cannot be *empirically* or logically tested.

phenomenology A philosophical branch, which has made the study of human consciousness or subjective experience, neglecting questions of truth in the sense of traditional *analytical philosophy*, a central theme. The *intentional diagnosis* of *everyday* life from the point of departure of the actors who are living it, is a central theme; associated with the *actors view*.

positivism A philosophical/scientific branch presuming that classic natural sciences are the path to true knowledge. By using the *methods* of these sciences, suggesting that human behaviour is an *effect* of social, economic, biological, etc. *causes,* the truth of the *factive reality* will be mapped; mainly associated with the *analytical view*.

pragmatism A school of philosophy, based on the principle that a scientific result is judged by its usefulness, workability, etc. when applied in the *empirical* world; mainly associated with the *systems view*.

pre-scientific concept A concept that will be taken for granted when conducting a study, because of its belonging to the special subject, the lingo of the profession, the study area, etc. in question.

primary procedure The term for a *methodical procedure* when applied in a *methodology of complementarity* (opposite, in this frame of methodology: *complementary procedure*).

problematization To make what is common uncommon – to question what is taken for granted. To pave the way for new points of departure for orientation and by this discover new aspects. Problematization is therefore intimately connected to both the act of knowing and the concrete situations in the *study area*, as well as the act of creativity.

producer–product relationship Same as *finality* relationship; associated with the *systems view*.

procreative report A written report with ambitions to communicate *procreative understanding*; associated with the *actors view*.

procreative understanding A kind of higher form of consciousness that fertilizes the mental power to create, to transform, to *vivify* and to change in uniquely and desirable directions; associated with the *actors view*.

procreative word Concept in language development that is "loaded" by the right kind of fertilizing energy for the *study area* and for the *knowledge creator's* own development *of procreative understanding:* associated with the *actors view.*

rationalism See the Appendix.

realism A philosophical perspective, regarding reality as independent of human consciousness (opposite: *idealism*).

reconciliation A process of getting two opposite thoughts/things to correspond in a knowledge-creating mode. Compare: *complementarity* and *methodology of complementarity.*

reductionism A philosophical/scientific thought presuming that events and circumstances at a given level of nature or society can be *explained* at a lower level of nature or society, for instance, providing psychological *explanations* to sociological phenomena (opposite: *holism*).

reification Looking at immaterial concepts such as being, having soul, etc. as concrete objects, that is, humans giving them characteristics as "mechanical" components and as such neglecting the fact that meanings and actions are made by people, mainly associated with the *actors view.*

relativism A philosophical branch presuming that there are different, possibly self-contained, traditions, ethics, knowledge and ways of life, each to be judged only in accordance with its own arbitrary standard, dependent upon circumstances.

reliability As a concept of quality assurance in *knowledge creating* and as a subcore element of *crealiability* it will signify different substances in relation to the various *methodological views.* (See "Measurement techniques and techniques for controlling reliability" in Chapter 7.)

representative understanding Understanding, which is seen as a *depiction* (map) of reality, where this reality is presumed to be *factive*; associated with the *systems view* (opposite: *constitutive understanding*).

self-reference A phenomenon, according to the *actors view*, that exists between scientific results and the development of society. The social scientist will therefore always, when doing research, also research the influence of his/her own earlier results, without any possibility of clear-cut results. The existing social science knowledge representation of generality, normality, clichés, uniformity, etc. in individual human beings will always be there as an *everyday reality*.

sensemaking See the Appendix.

social construction (of reality) A reality, which is built and rebuilt by its members in a *dialectical* process and does not exist independently of, or beyond, these members, including its *knowledge creators*; associated with the *actors view.*

social phenomenology A critical *synthesis*, created by Schutz, of Husserl's *phenomenology* and Weber's thoughts about *understanding;* associated with the *actors view.*

stringency A concept of quality assurance, according to knowledge-creating, including a degree of rigorous performance and standard of attainments. The quality of being stringent in the frame of a *methodological view*. The concept is an essential core element of the overall scientific concept, *crealiability,* for excellence in knowledge-creating work.

stringency of complementarity A concept of quality assurance, according to knowledge creating of complementarity, including a degree of rigorous performance and standard of attainments. The quality of being stringent in the frame of the *complementarity* in question. The concept is an essential core element of the overall scientific concept, *crealiability* of *complementarity,* for excellence in knowledge-creating work.

structuralism A philosophical branch, generally looking at the study area as patterned or, more specifically, derived from linguistics and applied to other fields, presuming that phenomena should be *explained* or *understood* in terms of invariant underlying structures of organization; associated with the *systems view*.

study area The field of focus and interest in an effort to create knowledge.

subjectification The process of consciousness by which we create and constitute ourselves as *intentional* subjects ("humans are a subjective reality"); associated with the *actors view*.

summative Built up *ceteris paribus*, that is, the belief that any new finding when creating knowledge can be added to a previous finding without any complications or additions for the latter one; associated with the *analytical view*.

synergy A principle that *totality* is presumed to be more or less than the sum of its parts; mainly associated with the *systems view*.

synthesis The *dialectical* "end" of a process, where the first (*thesis*) has been contrasted by the second (*antithesis*), with the first inherent in itself, and at the "end" both the *thesis* and the *antithesis* have been moved up into a higher form, the synthesis; associated with the *actors view*.

systems approach *Systems view* in application.

systems view A *methodology* for creating knowledge, devoted to *explaining* and/or *understanding* reality, presumed to be built up *holistically*.

technique Rules given a priori for using various tools to create knowledge in practice.

teleology See *finality*.

theory A word with an unambiguous sense as well as an ambiguous one, depending on in which *methodological view* it appears and under which circumstances. In the former sense, for example: empirical (experiential) laws *explaining* regularities existing in objects and events of a *study area;* associated with the *analytical view*. In the latter sense: A set of assertions or main beliefs devised to *explain* and/or *understand* a set of facts or phenomena; associated with the *systems view* and the *actors view*.

thesis The first *dialectical* element of a process, where this first (*thesis*) is going to be contrasted by the second (*antithesis*); associated with the *actors view*.

thematic language of methodology A "neutral" language, developed in this book to bridge the problems of knowledge creation and knowledge quality between various contexts of research, consultation and/or investigation, containing: *paradigm, ultimate presumption, factive reality, factified reality, methodological view/approach, operative paradigm, methodical procedure, methodics, method, technique, reconciliation, methodology of complementarity, base view, transformative operator, primary procedure, complementary procedure, study area, crealiability, and crealiability of complementarity.*

totality A world, presumed to be an entity, where the parts are more or less dependent on each other; mainly associated with the first guiding principle of the *systems view*.

transformative operation The total amount of *methodical procedures, primary* as well as *complementary*, in connection with the *methodics* will form the *operative paradigm*, and the overall concept for all these operations in a *methodology of complementary* is thus transformative operations.

transformative operator The concept for a *methodological approach* when acting as a base of *complementarity* for *transformative operations*.

typification Describing our way of attaching various labels and typical designations to – and having different understandings of – the people and things around us. We expect, and then take for granted, that what is typified behaves according to the understanding mediated by the typification; associated with the *actors view*.

typified cases Knowledge-illustrations with an ideal character describing various ideal states that "imaginatively" can reflect the potential, and thereby engage various actors in *procreating dialogues* in which the potential will be transformed into the *factual*, that is, into a new *social reality*. Typified cases, in spite of being ideal, have a strong connection to the "living" social reality.

ultimate presumption Fundamental belief of reality and life (same as normative thesis), which cannot be empirically or logically tested, but which influences and steers each and every one of us when acting as *knowledge creators*.

understanding Providing knowledge based on the creator of knowledge, attempting to gain a "deeper" knowledge of his/her *study area*, associated with the *systems view* in an understanding mode, or knowledge based on the actors *denotation of conceptual meaning*, associated with the *actors view*.

validity As a concept of quality assurance in *knowledge-creating* and as a subcore element of *crealiability*, it will signify different substances in relation to the various *methodological views*. (See "Validation techniques" in Chapter 7).

verification Confirmation in *empirical* reality of some conclusion derived in the *theoretical* reality; associated with the *analytical view* (opposite: falsification).

verstehen See the Appendix.

view See *methodological view*.

vivify To give new energy to life, ennoble the values of life, provide reinforcement to what is unique; associated with the *actors view*.

24 Reviewing Existing Literature

IAN LINGS

SUPERVISOR'S VIEW: DR ANNE SOUCHON

Many research students approach their study with some degree of anxiety over data collection and/or analysis, blissfully unaware that what will cause them grief is, in fact, the rather innocuous-sounding '*literature review*'. There are two reasons why the literature review is often a major stumbling block.

First, it is a common belief that the literature should be thoroughly reviewed in a bid to identify a suitable topic (and by suitable, of course, I mean one which will make a contribution to knowledge and be deserving of a Ph.D.). Your supervisor may insist on it, even if this process takes you well over a year; even if it delays your study so much that your funding runs out before you've completed your thesis; even if after reviewing 'your' literature, you decide that there is no theoretical gap there after all, and want to start reviewing an entirely different research stream.

Second, intimate knowledge of the literature is essential in order to position the study within its broader area (otherwise, researchers would forever be reinventing the wheel), develop propositions or hypotheses if this is what the study requires, and explain the findings uncovered in the empirical phase of the project. Thus, as Ian Lings explains below, the literature review is the backbone of the project; it supports the entire study. Its importance is so ingrained that I battle on a daily basis with Doctoral students who are so paralysed by the fear of not knowing the literature well enough that they are stuck at reviewing literature and refuse to move on.

So, here are a few hints to reduce your literature review stress:

(A) Choose a *supervisor*, not a topic. A good supervisor will know the literature already and could (I want to say should) steer you towards a worthy topic.
(B) Learn to let go of the literature. Do not get trapped into thinking that you need to keep collecting/reading/assimilating more and more papers *before* you start conceptualising and/or collecting data yourself. If you do, you are simply procrastinating and using the literature as a security blanket,

not as a means-to-an-end. And you run the risk of losing focus and getting lost.

(C) Start multi-tasking: keep abreast of new papers coming out *as you embark on other stages of your research.*

And remember that the literature review is an ongoing activity. It is only finished when the thesis has been successfully defended, hard leather-bound (at some considerable expense), and distributed (for free) to friends and family who will never read it!

VIEW FROM THE TRENCHES: JOOBEE YEOW

If there are two words that would appear in the worst nightmares of the perfectionists of this world, especially the perfectionist researchers, they would be *literature review!* I am in the third year of my Ph.D. and even now one of my greatest fears is that I do not know anything and everything regarding my research topic. What if my supervisors ask me this? Or what if my peers ask me that? Or worse, what if someone in the audience when I am presenting my research asks me: 'Why is the moon round in shape'? Shouldn't I know that too? My research is supposed to earth-shattering, it is supposed to solve all the problems of the world! With this in mind, at the start of my research, I combed through every journal paper and book – in fact, anything that was readable, anything that bore even the slightest resemblance to the keywords of my topic. To my bitter discovery, it was not only resource inefficient, but I ended up *lost in reviewing,* torn in all directions.

If I were to offer some advice from my own experience; first and foremost, structure is *very important* in literature review. Secondly, a crucial point is to have structure, and thirdly, you must have guessed, is **structure**. Start by identifying the most relevant authors, journals, databases and other sources that publish work that is most relevant to your topic. By doing this groundwork, you begin to create a boundary in your mind for your literature review, preventing the temptation to go astray – bear in mind that one needs to actually *complete* the Ph.D. at some stage!

Imagine the literature review is in the shape of a diamond. You start at the tip, broaden your knowledge of the topic and eventually come back again to the tip, where now you have gained your focus and pinpointed the gap in the literature. To know when to stop, when you have exhausted most of the literature relevant to your research, is vital as one needs eventually to derive hypotheses and collect data to be able to produce a piece of work to advance knowledge or inform practice. I am not suggesting that you should limit your literature review, but it is impossible for one to know absolutely everything, thus it is important to know in *depth* what you are doing and in *breath* what is relevant to what you are doing.

Last, but not least, a piece of advice from my supervisor at the beginning of my Ph.D. that I still find very useful: 'Your Ph.D. is not supposed to solve the problems of the world, but to make enough of a significant contribution (even as small as it is in the vast sea of knowledge) that you or future researchers will continue and snowball from it to make greater contributions and *eventually*, change the world of knowledge.'

Many beginning researchers have significant problems with reviewing the literature. This might be due to the fact that there just isn't much information out there on how to do it. In fact, many research students are simply given the instruction to 'go away and review the literature on topic x', closely followed by 'see me in a few months'. Learning how to do a good literature review is therefore often done via trial and error. However, it doesn't have to be that way, and in this chapter I hope to give you a good head-start on doing your literature review, and ensuring you end up with a solid piece of work.

The aims of your literature review are to show that you have studied existing work in your field and to provide insights into this work. An effective review critically analyses material, synthesises it, and will be relevant, appropriate, and useful for the reader. Your literature review presents the case and context for the rest of your thesis. For this reason it is important to demonstrate the relationship of your work to previous research in the area. This chapter is written from a deductive perspective; recommending that you should review the literature *before* starting your project. You will probably have an idea of the domain of the literature that you wish to examine and possibly even a more specific and focused area, however, I am assuming that one of your aims in reviewing the literature is to decide on the specific research that you will undertake. An alternative to this view is presented in Alternative View 9.3 which presents a 'grounded' approach in which the literature is not reviewed until after the project has started.

At the end of this chapter I really hope you have come to terms with these key ideas:

* What literature is.
* Where you can find it.
* What a literature review is, and what it does.

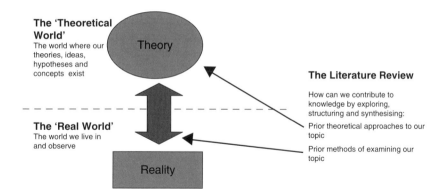

The 'Theoretical World'
The world where our theories, ideas, hypotheses and concepts exist

Theory

The Literature Review

How can we contribute to knowledge by exploring, structuring and synthesising:

Prior theoretical approaches to our topic

Prior methods of examining our topic

The 'Real World'
The world we live in and observe

Reality

Figure 4.1   The place of literature reviewing

- What critiquing the literature means.
- How you can organise your thoughts.
- How you can structure your literature review.
- How you can organise your sources.

Why is it Important to Know This Stuff?

Understanding the basics of reviewing the literature is essential for anyone who wishes to undertake research and contribute to an existing body of knowledge. It's really about uncovering and exploring how prior researchers have explored the theoretical issues in your topic, and also to some extent which methods they have used to collect data and examine those theories, as shown in Figure 4.1. Becoming comfortable with how to locate, understand and critically analyse literature is necessary for you to build your work on top of that which has been done previously. A thorough review of the literature serves several purposes; it helps you to better understand the field in which you are working, it identifies work that has already been conducted and knowledge that has already been developed, it helps you to identify, and often explicitly suggests, areas in which new contributions can be made, and it will illustrate methodologies that have been applied to your particular field of research. In short, the literature review helps you to ensure that you do not simply repeat what has already been done, and to have more confidence that the contribution to knowledge that you wish to make is *indeed* a contribution.

Familiarity with the literature is essential if you are to be able to defend your ideas and arguments in peer-reviewed written work, or even more daunting, when you are standing in front of your peers, be it in front of a class, at a degree viva or at a conference. However, familiarity is not sufficient for a successful literature review, *critical appraisal* is also necessary. Critical evaluation of others' work is a particularly difficult task for many researchers, especially those who feel relatively junior or who are not yet qualified. I have often heard research students and new colleagues comment 'How can I criticise Professor X's work, she is a famous professor and knows so much more than me'. While this is undoubtedly true (professors do usually know more than those just embarking on a research career) the art of the literature review is in the **critique** (not the criticism), and *all work is open to critique.*

As you will see in the following chapters, there are many different ways to approach a given research question. Previous literature will perhaps indicate that different philosophies have been followed, different conceptualisations constructed and different models created. Each of the approaches that you find in published works will present some benefits to answering a particular research question and some inherent limitations to answering the question. It is a discussion of these philosophies, conceptualisations, methods and findings, and their benefits and limitations that forms the basis of the critique of the literature.

Of course, you will also come across some research that is just weak, and can be criticised as being so (sometimes even in the best journals). In order to criticise research as weak, you will need to not only understand how to conduct your review and critique of the literature, you will also need to know about the research designs, methods and analytical techniques discussed in the later chapters of this book.

What is a 'literature review'?

The literature review is literally that, a *re-view* (or look again) at what has already been written about a topic. The literature review is where you demonstrate that you *understand* that which has been done before, and can point to where this existing research is *deficient* in some way. It's important to realise that you are not trying to 'insult' prior research and researchers here, but to point out where existing work needs some supplementing, which maybe because the world has changed since prior work was conducted, or maybe because such work doesn't address important issues that are now relevant – in fact often the authors will indicate this themselves. Further, you need to explain how your work adds to existing knowledge, by overcoming the problems with the existing literature, maybe by bringing together disparate fields of research and extending them, or developing new theory. You also have to show why your work is *important, relevant* and *interesting*. Unfortunately, none of these tasks is easy.

As I mentioned earlier, if you are a research student, it's very likely that one of the first things you will be asked to do on commencing your research degree will be something like 'go away and read the literature' that is relevant to your topic (assuming that you know what your topic will be in more specific terms than just something like 'consumer behaviour' or 'motivation'). Now, it's not that your supervisor doesn't like you and wants to avoid you – although I guess sometimes that's the case. No; at this stage you are actually trying to achieve two simultaneous aims with your reading. You will almost certainly still be trying to tightly define your research problem or thesis (something that you will probably be doing for quite some time in an iterative fashion) and, at the same time, you will be trying to identify, read, understand and assimilate every source of information relevant to your thesis. Therein lies the difficulty. Essentially, you don't know exactly *what* you are going to research until you have read the relevant literature (so everything seems relevant) and you don't know if what you are reading is really relevant until you have decided exactly what you are going to research (which could be many things, as there is more that we don't know than which we do).

If you are in this situation, try to take comfort in two pieces of advice: 'all reading is good',[1] and 'everyone is in the same boat at this stage of their research'. This advice I offer readily, in the knowledge it failed to impress me, assuage my fears and insecurities, or in fact comfort me in any way at all when offered to me by my thesis supervisor. Typically, subsequent experience has shown that he was absolutely right (don't you just hate it when that happens?).

Whatever your situation, one thing is for certain, you have to start somewhere, and, believe it or not, many potential researchers fall at this first hurdle; deciding to start (not deciding *where to* start but just deciding to start *somewhere*). Many of you will have a research topic which is relatively tightly defined. If this is so you will know pretty specifically what you are looking for in relation to unexplained phenomena or theory that is in need of updating or re-examining in the light of a changed world. A **directed** literature review strategy is appropriate in such circumstances. You should write out the research question(s) and analyse it for assumptions (these are what questions you must also answer in order to answer the research question). Write out all of these associated research questions and direct your reading to be able to answers these. IDE 4.1 shows how a research question has assumptions on which it is based, and how further assumptions are made at other stages of the research process. Most often these are not explicitly stated by researchers, but it is useful for you to be aware of the assumptions that you are making in developing your research question and the associated research methods that you wish to adopt to explore your question.

---

[1] Well, this is not strictly always true, but at this point it is a useful rule to live by.

IDE 4.1: Assumptions of a Research Question

A research question is a statement that identifies the phenomenon to be studied. For example, 'What influence do performance bonuses have on employee behaviour?' There are several assumptions that underlie this research question. Firstly, this research question assumes that employee behaviour is something that can be observed by you as a researcher. Underlying this assumption is a realist view of the world, i.e. that there is an observable world to be researched. Depending on the approach that you wish to adopt and the theory on which you base your research, you may have to make further assumptions. If you decide that performance bonuses are one facet of a person's job, along with many other facets, you may wish to adopt a utility framework to analyse the research question. This would require an assumption of 'rational behaviour' and possibly an assumption of utility maximisation by the employee. The question could also be approached using a psychology framework such as the theory of planned behaviour, which also assumes rational behaviour but does not assume utility maximising. Both of these frameworks could direct you to collect quantitative data, which in turn would be based on an assumption that there is a 'real' world and that this can be measured. Further assumptions would then be made in the development of the questionnaire (if one were used) and these will be discussed later in the book. If you were to conduct observational research, then you would make assumptions about the validity and meaning of the observations. You would need to assume that you are observing real behaviour and that your observation is an accurate reflection of what is happening; that you are attributing the correct meaning to the behaviour that you are observing.

If you do not have a very specific research topic, your very first aim should be to try to tightly define your thesis or research question. Most likely, this task will involve coming up with a tentative, working definition. But how on earth do you do this? In this case, an **emergent** literature review strategy works best. Such a strategy involves reading everything, and looking for similarities and contradictions in ideas, methods, theories, assumptions and definitions. From this you can identify interesting research topics that you wish to explore. With the emergent approach, you have the benefit of being able to define the scope of your topic for yourself. Although on the surface this can seem daunting, it has the advantage of allowing you more opportunity to bring your experiences, beliefs and interests to bear on your research. For example, if you are interested in researching 'branding', one starting point is to think about what it is about 'branding' that particularly interests you, and which is not already explained in the literature? Of course, at this point, you don't know if it has already been explained in the literature until you look, but at least you know where to start looking.

Another useful starting point is to think about your observations of the world that suggest to you that existing theory isn't up to explaining the nuances of what you see in the real world. For example, can existing theory explain the fine details of your own experiences of human behaviour, concerning individuals such as customers, employees or managers, or groups such as segments, organisations, industries, or countries? This approach may seem rather 'unscientific' to many (although I hope that reading Chapters 2 and 3 should have given you some pointers on that issue), but it is not a bad place to start developing your research question, provided that you are aware of the purely natural tendency of human beings to confirm our beliefs rather than challenge them; try not to let this bias your readings of the literature.

Furthermore, it is important to remember that you are almost certainly not going to provide a general theory of your field, solve all of the problems that organisations or institutions face and explain all of employee/customer/government or other entities' behaviour (or whatever it is you are interested in). Your research problem will need to be much more focused on a specific issue. Until you have tightly defined your topic, hundreds of sources will seem relevant. However, you cannot define your topic until you read around your research area. Consequently, defining your research question (or thesis) is an iterative process; as you read you refine your thesis, and as you refine your thesis you can decide more easily on what to read and what to ignore.

Finally – and this can be a long and involving process for many – after defining the topic (however tentatively) you are in the position of being able to commence your **directed** reading. But be aware that *directed* is the important adjective here, if you are not directed in your reading you run the risk of becoming lost in the literature, constantly finding exciting avenues to follow but never actually doing anything. You will never complete your research unless you do something. Research requires both *thought* and *action*. Just thinking about your research will not get your thesis written. Please remember that!

Deciding what 'literature' is

It is very common for research students to ask me questions concerning exactly 'what' is literature. It's hard to answer this conclusively, but there are some basic pointers which can help. In general, information for your literature review may be gathered from many sources, and the basic term 'literature' here means the works that you consult to investigate your research problem. That said, while there are many sources of information available, the merits of each must be considered very carefully, and you need to decide how much confidence you wish to place in the information that you find in each of the sources. Should you judge an article from the top journal in your field to be as valuable as one from the local newspaper, or a company report? How do you decide which information is appropriate to include in your literature review? To my mind, there are four main questions that need to be answered for all information in your literature review:

- Is it relevant?
- Does it come from a reputable source?
- Does it present a compelling theoretical argument, and/or rigorous empirical results (i.e. is it any good?)
- What were the motives of the author?

I'll deal with the last question later in the chapter, because it is more concerned with analysing literature, and what you include when you write up your literature review. However, the first two issues are concerned with deciding what types of information to gather for review. To address the question of relevance; there are several decisions that need to be made. Your literature review will need to be sufficiently broad to explain your research area in the context of other research, perhaps in other areas of interest or even other disciplines. Simultaneously, it will have to be focused on your particular research topic, and comprehensive within your own field of enquiry. This means that you will need to be very clear about the definition of your *field* of research; for example, are you doing research in 'marketing' or 'organisational psychology'? Your field should be closely related to your research question or thesis. However, it should not be too close and restrictive, or you run the risk of missing other important literature from adjacent fields, and other disciplines. Actually, you should be adventurous in deciding where contributions to your understanding may come from. Many projects do not restrict themselves to just one body of knowledge, such as marketing, or economics. In fact, some of the best advances in thinking have been as a result of bringing together two or more, apparently disparate, bodies of knowledge to advance in our understanding of the world – which could be termed 'horizontal thinking', as I'll talk about in IDE 4.2.

IDE 4.2: 'Horizontal Thinking'

Horizontal thinking is an interesting term I came across recently when I was reading about creativity, and interestingly enough it recalls a conversation I had with Nick when we were thinking about this book. The idea of horizontal thinking is simply taking ideas and concepts from other fields and disciplines and applying them to your own research problem. It is another great example of how it is useful to read widely and be interested in many different fields. In fact, it's amazing how many ideas you can get from areas which might seem totally unrelated to your own. If you never venture outside your own discipline, you will never be exposed to this kind of thing. There are all kinds of examples of this happening in research, but some of the clearest are the use of Darwinian evolution theory in the social and applied business disciplines, for instance: 'Which automobiles will be here tomorrow?' by Robert J. Holloway, in the *Journal of Marketing*, Vol. 25, Issue 3, p. 35; 'Social Darwinism and the Taylor system: A missing link in the evolution of management?' by Roland E. Kidwell Jr, in the *International Journal of Public Administration*, Vol. 18, Issue 5, p. 767; 'It's Darwinism – survival of the fittest: How markets and reputations shape the ways in which plaintiffs' lawyers obtain clients' by Stephen Daniels and Joanne Martin, in *Law & Policy*, Vol. 21, Issue 4.

Having decided on your topic, and set the scope of your literature search, it is time to start looking for appropriate sources of information. This addresses the second of the two main questions about the confidence of the information and the quality of the source. Where should you get your information about theories, concepts, methods and philosophies that you are interested in? Different types of literature can be grouped in various ways, but for our purposes it is useful to group things according to their intended audience.

Academic literature

Academic (also called 'scholarly') literature can be thought of as work that is written and reported primarily for an academic audience, i.e. scholars who will be using this published work to inform future research in this area. As such, academic literature has certain requirements that are sometimes not met in other types of literature. Academic work should be reported in a scientific manner, such that it is possible for someone reading it to be able to evaluate the theories on which is it based, the research methods used, analyses conducted and conclusions drawn. The need to include lots of information in a very exact manner has the advantage that exactly what the researcher(s) has done should be clear and unambiguous. This means it is easier to identify the limitations of the work, and often this is done for you. However, it can also make academic work dry and tedious to read. The flowery and descriptive language, by its nature often imprecise, which makes normal prose quite interesting to read, often has to be removed to fit to publishing page limits and to make the reporting of the research exact and the work undertaken replicable. Despite the challenge of staying awake while reading academic literature, this is generally the most relevant type of literature for your review. The main sources of academic literature are detailed below, along with some discussion of the usefulness in the critical literature review.

Peer Reviewed Journal articles are works that have been 'refereed' or 'quality assured' by scholars working in the field of inquiry discussed in the paper. If the article is published, then these 'peers' and the journal editor consider that the article has advanced the body of knowledge in some way. In other words, the arguments presented should be well researched and discussed, the research undertaken should have been done in an appropriate manner, the data analysed correctly, and any results should follow logically from the information presented in the article.

As a general rule, peer reviewed articles should be the main source of information for your literature review. Journal articles provide concise information regarding theories, methodologies, applications and interpretations relevant to your thesis. However, not all journals have the same academic standing and it is important to have a feel for the relative importance of each journal in your own field. This is not to say that top-quality work does not appear in lower-standing journals, nor that sometimes average or (frankly) poor work does not appear in top journals. Nevertheless, many people do use the idea of 'journal standing' as a guide to the quality of articles in those journals. Those journals that are the most important tend to have the highest reputation and standing in your field (often called the 'A list'). Many universities have rankings of journals and, although they rarely agree completely, these can be useful in deciding which journals are the most important in your field of study. Table 4.1 is an excerpt from a report which discussed perceptions of different marketing journals, and gives a good example of how different journals are ranked within a field. The *social science citation index* (SSCI) can also be a guide, but not all journals within many fields are ranked by SSCI.

Table 4.1 Example journal quality rankings

Rank	Quality	Name of journal
1	1.867	Journal of Marketing
2	1.837	Journal of Marketing Research
3	1.753	Journal of Consumer Research
4	1.749	Journal of the Academy of Marketing Science
5	1.729	Marketing Science
6	1.608	Journal of Retailing
7	1.587	Journal of Business Research
8	1.544	Journal of Consumer Psychology
9	1.540	International Journal of Research in Marketing
10	1.493	Journal of Advertising
11	1.461	Journal of Advertising Research
12	1.457	European Journal of Marketing
13	1.424	Journal of Service Research
14	1.423	Psychology and Marketing
15	1.380	Marketing Letters

Source: From an unpublished (to date) ranking study, Jordan Louviere, Siggi Gudergan and Ian Lings (University of Technology Sydney).
Note: Quality rankings were determined through a study of marketing academics.

Top-ranking journals can, generally, be thought of as having the most impact in your field, and therefore you can generally have more confidence in the results and findings of any study reported in them. Having said this, it is important not to restrict yourself to just those journals with high quality rankings. There is a whole range of research that is reported in other journals, some are specialist journals and do not always appear high on the list of journal rankings because of their specialist nature, some are journals targeting audiences other than academics. This does not mean that these journals are irrelevant or 'low' quality, just that in the general scheme of things they do not have as much overall impact as others. As Webster and Watson (2002, pp. xiii) report in their discussion of writing a literature review:

> Studies ... have consistently been limited by drawing from a small sample of journals. Even though the [ones] investigated here may have reputations as our top journals, this does not excuse an author from investigating 'all' published articles in a field.

As a final note on journal articles, it is extremely important not to assume that 'just because it is in the journal it must be perfect'. There are many examples of work that has some pretty significant flaws appearing even in top journals. Be aware that time moves on, research standards change, and articles may be published which fall short on some criteria because they are very strong in another. In particular, articles which deal with 'hot topics' may get published even though they are not as strong as they might be. So be careful not to simply assume the quality of the literature, wherever it may appear!

Conference proceedings are articles or abstracts that are published by the organisers of the many academic conferences that occur annually in each field and specialist area. In case you didn't know, academics are always attending conferences (especially those in far-flung locations), and these conferences are ostensibly aimed at disseminating leading-edge research as quickly as possible. They are definitely *not* excuses to visit exotic places and have fun – honest! Many of those who attend conferences go to present their work in front of peers and colleagues, and this work is also generally published in the 'proceedings' of the conference. A lot of conference proceedings are also peer reviewed and have to meet minimum standards of scientific rigour. The main strength of conference proceedings as opposed to peer-reviewed journal articles is that they are often the first place that research is published and tested in front of peer audiences. For this reason, conference proceedings are useful in providing information about the latest research, which often has not yet been published in peer reviewed journals. Conference proceedings are also a useful source of information about who is working in a particular research area, and what they are doing. You can then search to find out what else they have published in other outlets.

Conference proceedings tend not to be a main source of information for a literature review for many reasons. Firstly, there is a general perception in some fields that they are of a 'lower' quality than peer-reviewed journals (although this is not always the case, and not for all conferences in a field either). Further, there is also the idea that most of the high-quality work will eventually reach the journals (academics are rarely happy with 'just' a conference paper). That is not to say that good quality work cannot be expected in a conference paper. Sometimes, conference proceedings can be the only place to get really radical, new, or esoteric work. However, one of the major drawbacks of conference proceedings is the increasing tendency of conference organisers to restrict the size of conference papers to just a few pages. This means that, often, the paper does not provide as rich an indication of the background and scope of the research. Similarly, conference proceedings are often hard to locate and gain access to, unless you know someone who has attended the conference and has the proceedings. Nevertheless, they are a useful resource and are worth pursuing.

Previous research theses and dissertations are also a possible source of information. All UK Ph.D. theses should be published in the British Library and can be requested by inter-library loan. In other countries Ph.Ds may or may not be published; it is often necessary to contact the author to request a copy of their work. However, it is important to remember that they are of uncertain quality (yes, even including mine and Nick's!).[2] For example, you do not know if the student who wrote the thesis did a good job or not; after all, you don't get the examiner's reports on it. Also, most research degrees are seen as an apprenticeship piece, they will often contain mistakes that the researcher would be expected to rectify in subsequent work. As a consequence, you should treat the contents of student theses with some caution. Furthermore, it can be a big task to search through the huge store of theses without any direction. Nevertheless, it's important to realise that they are available to those who are interested.

As a final note, you should be careful about drawing too much from other theses – it can be tempting to use them too much, especially if they are in similar areas. This would seem an opportune moment to mention **plagiarism**: something that should be avoided at all costs. If you don't know what plagiarism is, ask your supervisor or any other academic. They will explain to you what it is, why it is bad and what happens if you get caught[3] – probably at great length.

Teaching literature

Teaching literature is also a type of academic literature; however, its primary purpose is usually to provide a general description of a field, rather than a detailed and scientific description of specific theories and models. This type of literature is generally aimed at students and lecturers who teach or take courses in a field. Teaching literature has many advantages over the academic literature described previously. It is usually much more accessible in

---

[2] Actually, if he ever reads that he might have something to say!
[3] Hint: it's not good!

terms of being easy to read and understand. This makes it a great resource for learning about ideas that are new to you. This accessibility of teaching literature comes at a price though; this type of literature is generally much less comprehensive in its discussion of all aspects of the scientific investigation that underpins what is discussed. This makes it virtually impossible to critique teaching literature in a scientific manner, because essentially what is being presented is '*the accepted wisdom of the day*'. Although teaching literature is a very useful resource to you as a researcher, it should not form a major part of your critical literature review. Two types of teaching literature are discussed below. Hopefully, you will see the merits of both, and also their limitations for inclusion in your literature review.

Textbooks are generally less detailed and less up-to-date than journal articles. By the time that a model or theory has entered the pages of a textbook it is generally seen as the 'accepted wisdom' in a field. This is why it has been included in a book designed for teaching rather than research. Consequently, textbooks are less useful for including in your literature review. But, this does not mean that they are less useful to you. Quite the contrary; as the content of a textbook has been well examined, often simplified and is generally presented in such a way as to facilitate understanding, they make an excellent place to start. This is especially true if the scope of your research takes you into new and unfamiliar disciplines. Textbooks are useful to bring you up to speed on the basic theories quickly and effectively. However, they will not generally provide you with cutting-edge research findings. One thing textbooks are very useful for, though, is for methodology and research techniques (just like this one in fact). The peer-reviewed journal literature on methodology can be a pretty scary place. To write about leading-edge developments in methodology requires that the authors assume those reading the article already know the basics, and often more advanced theories, up to the point at which the paper makes contribution. This may not be the case. It often takes book authors to integrate such material in such a way as to reach a more general research audience.

Finally, as I am becoming aware, the textbook is often the place where authors are able to put down their thoughts without too much censure from reviewers, so you should be aware that not all textbooks have had the same rigorous reviewing as a typical scholarly journal article. Of course, this particular one has.

Case studies

There are two common types of case study that you will come across. These are: (1) Journal articles that describe and report on 'case study research' and which belong in the academic literature category; and (2) Case studies used in teaching, that describe a company situation and provide (or require) some degree of analysis and interpretation.

Adopting a scientific view, the case study can be thought of as a neutral description of a situation, subject to objective analysis. From an artistic perspective, it can be viewed as an incomplete narrative, open to multiple interpretations. Whichever view is adopted, teaching case studies aim for students to gain depth in both problem-solving and problem-posing skills. Most commonly, the scientific view leads you to analyse the facts and to propose a specific answer to a real business problem. The literary view leads you to consider the interpretation of words, to select evidence based on values, and to reflect on the case as a parable. Both of these are laudable aims but they do not address the needs of your research literature review.

Practitioner-oriented literature

We use the term 'practitioner-oriented' to refer to literature who's primary target is those who actually have 'real' jobs in the field you study, if you see what I mean. For example, if you are a marketing researcher, 'practitioner-oriented' literature includes trade journals aimed at retail store managers, advertising executives, human resource managers, rather than journals aimed at academics studying those fields. Several types of practitioner oriented journals are available and some are discussed below.

Magazines and trade journals. The definition of magazines for our purposes is somewhat ambiguous. The Oxford Dictionary lists a magazine as 'a periodical publication containing articles and illustrations'. However, it should be clear at this point that we do not mean magazines like *Woman's Weekly, Hot Celebrity Gossip*, or the *NME* (although we know many academics who do read such august publications[4] for non-research purposes in general). We are assuming that the type of magazine you may consider reading for your research would address issues relevant to your research. Among academic circles I have heard the term *'magazine'* used to describe non-peer-reviewed publications and publications intended for a more managerial audience. These could be quite specialist, such as *The Economist, Marketing Week* or *New Scientist;* or they may be more general in nature, such as *Newsweek, National Interest* or *Time.* These publications can also provide a good starting point for justifying your research and demonstrating that it is both current and topical. General information about new discoveries, policies, etc. can provide a useful way to explain to your reader the impact of your work on the business environment.

As are textbooks, magazines are unlikely to be useful for inclusion in your literature review. However, like textbooks they can be a great resource to help you to understand your research domain. They can also be brilliant to 'set the scene' of your research in the real world, and give it a nice foundation. Typically, articles written in this type of publication are less technically difficult than peer reviewed articles and so can aid in developing your understanding of a particular area, prior to getting into more technical content in peer reviewed journal. It is worth remembering, though, that these articles are often journalistic and may be politically motivated, so it is always worth taking the time to try to understand the motives of the author before using information from them.

---

[4]And many others far too embarrassing to list here!

Government reports and business reports are also a good source of general information. The government and many businesses undertake research into areas of particular importance for them. These published reports can be a useful source of secondary information, depending on your field of study. However, many business reports are confidential, or at least embargoed for a period of time, so those that paid for them can get the best advantage. If you are lucky enough to get hold of one of these before it is released to the public domain, you should be careful about how you use it – or you could get someone (including yourself) into a lot of trouble. However, all publicly listed companies have to produce a public report at the end of each financial year, and these can be very useful for research purposes. A cautionary note with government reports is to remember that there is the potential for them to contain political bias, which may result in reporting of selective 'facts' to support a particular view; they should be interpreted with care!

Newspapers are not usually that useful. Information in newspapers is often only of note as 'background'. For example you may want to refer to particular pieces to illustrate trends, discoveries or changes, in much the same way as you might refer to general magazines, discussed above. Nevertheless, they can give an indication of what the public considers important at the time, which in some fields (especially those which are policy-related) is very important. As with magazines, trade journals, government and business reports, newspaper articles are subject to bias, both from the journalistic nature of the piece and the political affiliations of the source. Depending on the publication, they may also only have a passing acquaintance with the truth, and so caution is advised when using them.

The Internet

The Internet is the fastest-growing source of information on the planet, and it has revolutionised the life of an academic. For example I can't even imagine what it must have been like to have to physically search through hard copies of journals to find an article of use. But while the Internet is a great resource to connect you directly to the sources of literature I have just talked about, what about the information you can also get from the Internet such as on websites and the like? Do not be fooled into thinking that just because information is available on the Internet that it will be useful to you, or should be included in your research. My personal feeling is that you should avoid using the Internet as a direct source of information about theories, models, methodologies and such like. This information will also be available in peer reviewed journals and this should be your first port of call. Anyone with access to a computer can post information on the Internet (I could give you some examples, but the Internet changes so fast that they would be out-of-date immediately).

When you find information on the Internet, you have no way of knowing if this information is true, scientific or motivated by things other than the advancement of knowledge. For example, many individuals have grudges against some corporations, and they have Internet sites as a forum for their bitterness.

If you do search the Internet and find useful models and theories, try to confirm what you have found in scientific publications to see if the theory has been tested. As a great professor (who shall remain anonymous) once said to me 'theory without evidence is just opinion, and opinions are like a★★★holes,[5] everybody has one'.

As a general rule, if you find useful information on the Internet, make sure a reputable source is cited, and then find that study for yourself. If you intend to cite this source, make sure that you have, and can, read the original source yourself.

In suggesting that you avoid using information from the Internet I do not mean avoiding accessing peer reviewed journals available on, or via the Internet. Most academic libraries now have fantastic sets of electronic resources, and there are many databases which collate and index journal articles. These databases are constantly growing, and it is good advice to consult with your librarians to see what you have access to. You may even be able to help out your supervisor – who, if they are anything like me, have no idea of the full range of resources! Furthermore, some academic journals are what can be called 'e-journals', meaning they are published solely on the Internet, and not in hard copy at all. If an e-journal is peer reviewed the quality should be just as rigorous as a typical 'off-line' peer-reviewed journal (depending on the reputation of the journal).

Evaluating the 'quality' of literature

Once you have found the literature, you need to make some kind of 'first-cut' to work out what is worth spending more time on, and what can be discarded immediately. As shown above, there are many different sources of literature and it is easy to get overwhelmed and confused. The following checklist can be used to help you to decide the 'quality' of the research that you have found:

- *Provenance:* What are the author's credentials, qualifications and affiliations? Affiliations can point to alternative motives and so are important. Are the author's arguments supported by some kind of evidence?
- *Objectivity:* Is the author's perspective unbiased or prejudiced? Are contrary views and data considered in the piece or is certain pertinent information ignored to prove the author's point? Typically, journalistic reports do not consider alternative perspectives; often government reports also fail to incorporate alternative views.
- *Persuasiveness:* Which of the author's arguments are the most and least compelling? The peer review process should identify incorrect arguments, but subsequent work may challenge some assumptions and may invalidate the arguments on which the work is based.
- *Value:* Are the author's conclusions convincing? Does the work ultimately contribute in any significant way to an understanding of the subject? Many papers present replications of previous work in new contexts; although this is important to establish the generalisability of a theory, many

---

[5] If you're American, please remove one star.

journals will not publish straight-forward replications. This has the disadvantage that theories may go unchallenged or unconfirmed as replication studies may not get published.

However, remember that there is far more to analysing and reviewing a piece of work than just these few pointers (I'll discuss this soon). In particular, the last two points can be quite a difficult task, and if you are unsure of them at this early stage, it's best to keep the literature for now and make your mind up later, when you come back to read it again (which you will do many times).

Remember that when you are conducting your literature search, you have access to some great resources. Most librarians are also skilled researchers; they can help you identify reputable sources. They have more experience of searching for, and within, these sources and so can save you a lot of time by showing you how it is done most effectively. Your supervisor should be able to guide you towards journal rankings and provide you with a feeling for which are the better journals in your field of enquiry, other research students will have developed research strategies that you could consider adopting, they may have accessed journal databases that you are unaware of, and will almost certainly have made many of the mistakes that you are about to make. Try to minimise your effort by learning from their experiences.

How do you turn 'literature' into a 'literature review'?

As stated earlier, the aims of the literature review are to demonstrate that you understand that which has been done before, explain why your work is important, relevant and interesting, and how it adds to existing knowledge, either by bringing together disparate fields of research and extending them or developing new theory. Before describing what a literature review is, it is worth mentioning the most commonly encountered examples of what a literature review is *not*. The following issues are all very common with new researchers, so you shouldn't feel bad about them. However, if you do find yourself prone to these problems, you should make strenuous efforts to overcome them – and the best way of doing this is to write, write, and write some more. Then get your supervisor to read it. Then write again (and so on …). If you are a research student, one point worth making here is that your supervisor is a useful resource for you,[6] but one which may quickly wear out. Supervisors have many conflicting demands on their time; teaching, writing and reviewing articles and books, administration, supervising other research students. If you put poor work to your supervisors they will be unhappy, and may well tell you so (never a nice experience). If you ask your supervisor to comment on your work, please make sure that it is as good as you can make it. Most importantly, don't be afraid to get feedback, but also please

---

[6]If you are not a research student, your academic colleagues can often perform the same function.

do your utmost to *learn* from that feedback for next time. Most supervisors don't expect fantastic work at first, but it rapidly grates when students repeat the same mistakes over and over.

How not to do it

First, a literature review is not a list or summary of one piece of literature followed by another. It's usually a bad sign to find a series of paragraphs beginning with the name of a researcher, describing what they did and then moving on to the next researcher on the list. The aim of the literature review is not to simply list all the material published, without any consideration regarding how it fits together and how it can be synthesised into your research question. If all you are providing is a list of information then the reader has to do all the work. They have to interpret, synthesise and come to a conclusion about what they have read. They will soon tire and – worse – may come to a conclusion different from the one you hold. After putting in all that mental effort to come to their own conclusions they are unlikely to change their mind just because you wish them to, and you may then experience resistance to your views, making it harder to convince the reader of the 'worth' of your work. IDE 4.3 presents a *laundry list* of relevant facts regarding strategy, resources and capabilities. This example (and IDE 4.4) are not meant to reflect the work of the authors cited, just some inappropriate ways of presenting their work in the context of a literature review. Although the information itself is OK, there is no attempt to *interpret* the information presented and the reader is left to work out for themselves what is important and what is not; also the reader has to try to work out how these different pieces of information fit together. This is really the job of the author, not the reader.

IDE 4.3: A 'Laundry List'

Topic: 'Dynamic capabilities and organisational strategy'
Strategy is a pattern in a stream of decisions that gives guidance to organisations when dealing with its environment, it shapes internal policies and procedures (Hambrick, 1983; Mintzberg, 1978). It is a relative phenomenon; business level strategy can only be analysed substantively in relation to competitors' strategies (Hambrick, 1983).

Porter (1985) states that there are two main strategies that companies can follow in order to increase performance and gain competitive advantage: cost leadership or differentiation. Both strategic options are applicable to a mass market or segmented market approach. In an alternative framework, Miles and Snow (1986) identify four strategic types: Prospectors, defenders, analysers, and reactors.

Gruber and Harhoff (2001) consider resources to be the starting point of strategic deliberations and argue that resources are the main drivers of organisational performance. This view can be traced back to Penrose (1959) who stated that 'The business firm [...] is both an administrative organisation and a collection of productive resources; its general purpose is to organise the use of its "own" resources together with other resources acquired from outside the firm.'

Organisational capabilities are intangible assets or resources, based on skills, learning, and knowledge in deploying resources (Amit and Schoemaker, 1993; Combe and Greenley, 2004). Helfat and Peteraf (2003) differentiate between operational and dynamic capabilities. Operational capabilities are high-level routines (or collections of routines) that offer management a set of decision alternatives for the production of significant outputs. Routines represent repetitive patterns of activities (Nelson and Winter, 1982). Dynamic capabilities do not directly aim at the production of a product or a service (Helfat and Peteraf, 2003; Teece *et al.*, 1997); they build, integrate, or reconfigure operational capabilities and concern change (Helfat *et al.*, 2007).

Eisenhardt and Martin (2000) describe dynamic capabilities as specific organisational and strategic processes that contribute to the value creation of the organisation. They define dynamic capabilities as: 'The firm's processes that use resources – specifically the processes to integrate, reconfigure, gain and release resources – to match and even create market change. Dynamic capabilities thus are the organisational and strategic routines by which firms achieve new resource configurations as markets emerge, collide, split, evolve, and die' (p. 1107).

Teece *et al.*(1997) emphasise the development of management capabilities and combinations of organisational, functional, and technological resources, and define dynamic capabilities as 'the firm's ability to integrate, build, and reconfigure internal and external competences to address rapidly changing environments. Dynamic capabilities thus reflect an organisation's ability to achieve new and innovative forms of competitive advantage given path dependencies and market positions' (p. 516).

Secondly, a literature review is not the same as a *literary* review. The purpose of your review is not to identify the merits and weaknesses of the literary style of the article (whatever you may think about how well it is written or otherwise). Unlike a literary review, which is typically concerned with poems, plays, short stories, novels, or books as a finished piece of writing, a literature review is an extensive search of the information available on a topic and its evaluation. IDE 4.4 shows how a literary review of the literature may look, based on similar content to that in the previous example. You can see that, although a conclusion is

---

IDE 4.4: A 'Literary Review'

Topic: Dynamic capabilities and organisational strategy

Mintzberg (1978) discussed strategy as a pattern in a stream of decisions that gives guidance to organisations when dealing with its environment, it shapes internal policies and procedures. The article is somewhat technical and the logic of the conclusions was not clear to me, consequently, it is difficult to establish if the definition of strategy is appropriate or not. In contrast, the work of Hambrick (1983) is much easier to read and the suggestion that strategy is a relative phenomenon because any strategy at the business level can only be analysed in relation to competitors' strategies seems reasonable based on the information in the article.

When looking at different types of strategy two main views were available via ABI Inform. One article by Porter (1985) discusses the possibility of two main strategies that companies can follow in order to increase performance and gain competitive advantage. These are cost leadership and differentiation. Porter's suggestion that these options are equally applicable to segmented or mass markets is an elegant solution to the generalisability problem that plagues so much work of this type. An alternative view is discussed by Miles and Snow (1986), but this article was much more technical and did not communicate the basic ideas as well as Porter's work. Consequently, the dual strategy framework proposed by Porter will be used in my study.

---

presented about the best framework to use, this is based on the literary merit of the article and not the theoretical soundness of the work.

Reading the literature

Let's not make any bones about this, reading academic articles, especially when you are starting your research career, and the area is new to you, is difficult. Not only is it difficult, it's boring a lot of the time. Space in academic publications is expensive, so journal articles have to make maximum contribution for minimum words. This, and the need to be clear and unambiguous, gives rise to a dense, and very exact writing style, with much of the padding which we take for granted removed. This style can be difficult to read because it is generally not entertaining; every sentence contains relevant information that should be important. Don't worry though, reading academic writings should become easier the more you read in your area. From the outset it is worth being purposeful in your reading (and writing).

This will help you to avoid becoming too bogged down with trivia, or by being distracted by new 'shiny' ideas that you will regularly come across.

1. In your reading, remember that you want to précis the work you read, but you have to decide: (a) what information is important to your research, and emphasise it, and (b) what is peripheral, and can be omitted from your review. One way of doing this is to focus on the major concepts, conclusions, theories, arguments, etc. in the article you are reading and look for similarities and differences with other related work, including your own. Before you can do this though, you need to know exactly what problem or research question you are looking at. Try asking yourself: 'What is the *specific thesis, problem, or research question* that my literature review helps to define?' Can you answer it? Once you can, you can then work out which parts of the papers you are reading are important and which are peripheral to your literature review.

2. Related to deciding what is important or not are questions regarding the area of your literature review that you are focusing on. It is unlikely that you will read the papers that form your literature only once; typically, you will need to read them many times, each time looking for something specific and different. Your literature review may have sections looking at issues of theory, methodological issues, quantitative studies and evidence, qualitative studies and evidence, and more. In most cases it is not possible to examine all of these issues at once. Typically at the start of a research project or degree, you don't have the know-how in the area to analyse the literature for methodological issues. If you are a student, training in philosophy and methodology will help you to develop these skills, but you will probably have to wait until you have completed these classes before you can fully analyse the literature for these issues. Try not to worry about this; most people are in the same boat, and don't let them tell you that they are not.

3. Initially you will probably want to review the literature to identify themes, theories, patterns and ideas related to your central thesis. There are many ways of organising information that you find in the literature to help you to identify patterns that arise. For a thematic structure (which is one of the most common structures found in academic wiring of this type) I prefer to use a kind of mind map (see Figure 4.2 overleaf).

Other people use different techniques to organise their thinking; there is no right and wrong way, just the one that suits you the best. Some other techniques for organising information include spider maps, clustering organisers, interaction outline organisers and Venn diagrams. There is some quite sophisticated software available to help you to do this, but I have always found that a piece of flip chart paper and some coloured pens work just as well (but perhaps this is a function of my age and technological ability).

Structure and synthesis: Adding something to what's there

It's important to realise that the literature review should have its own value and intellectual contribution to your research project. As I have already stated, simply listing something does not provide anything that the reader could not do themselves, if they could be bothered. You need to provide some kind of added value to the literature, which proves you know

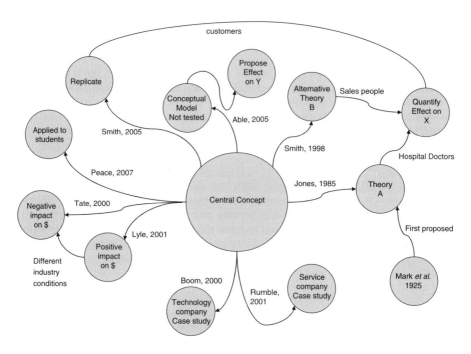

Figure 4.2 A mind map of literature
Note: References are fictitious

the field, as well as have added something. I find that considering the literature review as another component of your theoretical contribution really helps you clarify what you need to do. There are two main ways which a literature review could contribute to our existing knowledge. First is by organising the wide-ranging body of literature in such a way that new perspectives are given, leading to your own research questions. Second is by synthesising and drawing from the literature to create a new and original theory about your topic area. I'll discuss both of these as the chapter moves on.

Structuring your literature review

Rather than simply listing works that have been conducted in your research area, as shown in IDE 4.4, your literature review should be structured around your thesis or research question. The literature should be evaluated and its contribution to your research identified. You will need to consolidate this literature into meaningful 'themes', explaining what is known and what is not, what is controversial and what has already been identified as interesting areas for future research. You will then need to synthesise all this into a new/advanced/modified theory, which I'll discuss in Chapter 5.

Chronological structure: For some studies, organising your literature review chronologically is an appropriate structure. Such chronological literature reviews may be useful if you wish to explore the evolution of a particular theory or body of knowledge. Typically though, a purely chorological structure to your literature review is not appropriate. It is more commonly used to structure sections of the literature review that are organised along other lines. An example of a chronological structure is given in Table 4.2.

Table 4.2   Example of chronological structure

Time period 1	Time period 2	Time period 3
Concepts discussed in this time period.	Concepts discussed in this time period – how they evolved from those in the previous time period.	Concepts discussed in this time period – how they evolved from those in the previous time period.
Qualitative work regarding these concepts.	Qualitative work regarding these concepts – how does it confirm or challenge previous work?	Qualitative work regarding these concepts – how does it confirm or challenge previous work?
Quantitative work examining constructs and their nomological network.	Quantitative work examining constructs and their nomological network – how does it confirm or challenge previous work?	Quantitative work examining constructs and their nomological network – how does it confirm or challenge previous work?

Conceptual and thematic structures: Many literature reviews are organised by the concepts studied. This can be a useful way to organise your writing. Once this broad structure has been adopted, a different structure can be adopted for the discussion of each of the concepts in your review (such as chronological, methodological or contextual.) Organising your literature into meaningful 'themes', and developing an appropriate structure for your literature review can be achieved in many ways. Thematic reviews of the literature are organised around the topic under investigation, rather than chronologically, although the chronology of the literature may also be important. The choice of how to organise your literature review will ultimately depend on your preference, the literature that you are reviewing and the research question that you are addressing. Whatever the structure of your literature review, you will have to illustrate how previous research relates to your research question and how it relates to other works which you include in your review. (Remember, these must also be clearly relevant to your research question.) An example of a thematic structure is given in Table 4.3.

Methodological structure: A methodological review of the literature differs from the above in that the focus usually is not the content of the material; rather it is the 'methods' of the researcher. Typically for first research projects a methodological literature review is not appropriate, as the aim here is generally to understand the concepts, models and

Table 4.3 Example of thematic structure

Construct 1	Construct 2	Construct 3
Definitions of the construct, commonalities and differences in conceptualisations.	Definitions of the construct, commonalities and differences in conceptualisations.	Definitions of the construct, commonalities and differences in conceptualisations.
How it evolved and how it has been applied.	How it is related to Construct 1.	How it is related to Construct 1 and 2.
Empirical studies (qualitative and quantitative) explaining the role of the construct in a nomological network.	Theories that explain these relationships.	Theories that explain these relationships.
Operationalisations of the construct in previous work, strengths and weaknesses of these, etc.	Empirical studies (qualitative and quantitative) examining the relationships between Construct 1 and 2.	Empirical studies (qualitative and quantitative) examining the relationships between Construct 1, 2 and 3.
	Operationalisations of Construct 2 in previous work, strengths and weaknesses of these, etc.	Operationalisations of Construct 3 in previous work, strengths and weaknesses of these, etc.

frameworks used to describe and explore your area of interests. A methodological review of the literature may come later in your project, when you better understand and can critique the methods used by various researchers. At this stage you may wish to revisit your draft literature review and discuss methodology in more detail. This will be dealt with later in the book when methods are discussed. Unless absolutely necessary for your research, I would recommend using a methodological structure only as a sub-structure for a conceptual or thematically organised literature review. In this way, previous research examining the concepts in your conceptual model can be organised according to the methods that were used to conduct the research, but the overall arguments in your literature review remain centred around the relationships between the constructs of interest to you.

Writing within your structure

Once you've decided on how to organise your review, the sections you need to include in the chapter should be easy to figure out. They should arise out of your organisation. In other words, a chronological review would have subsections for each vital time period. A thematic review would have subtopics based upon factors that relate to the theme or issue and a methodological review would have sections reviewing the various methods. However, other sections may be necessary for your literature review but may not fit in the organisation of your work. You will have to decide what other sections to include in your literature review, but remember, put in *only what is necessary*.

In the following discussion, I am assuming a conceptual or thematic structure as this appears to be the most prevalent in social science research. When examining your concepts, you will need to address some common areas that an informed reader will be looking for:

- What do we know about the key concepts or variables?
- What are their characteristics?
- What are the potential relationships between concepts (researchable hypotheses)?
- What existing theories explain the relationships between these key concepts or variables?
- What research has been conducted to explore all of the above?
- Where is this research inconsistent, are variables always viewed as the same thing, or do some authors call different things by the same name, or the same thing by different names?
- What are the overriding characteristics of the concepts?
- Is empirical evidence available to confirm the existence of the concepts, and the relationships between them? If so, how have researchers defined and measured key concepts?
- Is the empirical evidence consistent, inconclusive, contradictory or limited in some way? If so, Why?
- What methodologies have been used?
- Where have data been collected?
- Are these satisfactory?
- How are they similar to what you propose? How are they different?
- Are there views in the literature that need to be examined in more detail?
- Why study (further) the research problem?
- What contribution can the present study be expected to make?

Once you have decided your central research question or thesis, and have identified appropriate sources of information and have started to organise the ideas in these sources of information into some coherent structure, you can start to communicate your *story*.

Remember (and this is a hugely important point), *you are not writing a literature review just to tell your reader what other researchers have done.* Your aim should be to show why your research needs to be carried out, how you came to choose certain methodologies or theories to work with, how your work adds to the research already carried out, and that sort of thing. I always say to students that the literature review is not a history of everything they read, it is an argument.

This raises another, and often painful, point. You have to *edit out information that is not relevant to your argument.* I know that this may be painful for you. After all, you have read the information, internalised it, made notes on it, typed it up and incorporated it into your document – it must be relevant, you took weeks to do all that! Don't delude yourself, examine every sentence critically and ask yourself how does it contribute to the argument that you literature review presents. If it doesn't then cut it out, be ruthless and your review will be much more focused and relevant.

Some final thoughts and tips

Your literature review should aim to critically evaluate previous research, comparing and contrasting what has been done and what hasn't, showing relationships between published works (e.g. is Smith's theory more convincing than Jones'? Why? Did Smith build on the work of Jones?), and demonstrating how this relates to your research. Some tips to help you achieve this are:

- Follow through a set of concepts and questions, comparing papers to each other in the ways they deal with these concepts and questions.
- Among other things you can look at are:
  - What research questions do the authors pose?
  - Do authors define the concepts in the same way?
  - Do they use the same underlying rationale or theory to discuss the concepts? (The next chapter may help you to decide this.)
  - If comparing quantitative research papers; do different authors operationalise constructs in the same way?
  - Are data drawn from similar or different contexts?
  - How are the data analysed?
  - Are the data and analysis appropriate for the study? Can they answer the research question?
  - What are the major conclusions made by the authors in terms of the research questions that the authors pose?
  - Are the data sufficient to draw the conclusions that the authors present?
  - Do authors come to similar conclusions about the nature and impact of the constructs that you are interested in?
  - If not, why not? (The previous questions should allow you to answer this.)
  - What limitations does each of these authors present about their own work?
  - Do they also give you insights into the limitations of previous work? (Often this forms part of the justification that is presented for their work.)

Also, it is vitally important to *keep all your bibliographic information* in an easily retrievable format. One day, possibly quite a long way into in the future, you will have to write your references pages (whether you are writing a thesis, or an article). You do not want to find that you didn't keep the information you need to do this, and consequently have to spend days or weeks finding the references for the citations in your thesis.[7] You will spend a lot of time in the library or on the Internet tracking down the sources that you read, going through your writing to find which information came from which source. Most likely, you will not be able to find all your sources and will then have to remove the ones that you can't find, hoping that they are not critical to your argument. If they are, there is nothing for it but to continue to search for them or a replacement. It is far better to avoid this by keeping

---

[7] As Nick did, and still does! In fact, I bet he is doing it when writing this very book!

this information in your notes from the outset. Always put citations into your writing and immediately into the reference list for your work. Software packages such as Endnote and ProCite can help greatly in this process. However, they don't do it for you; you will have to develop the discipline to remember for each citation to make sure there is a reference. Do you have a piece of work that you are writing at the moment? How many times have you written 'insert ref here' or something similar? If you have, make sure you go back now to find out and insert that reference, you will thank me later (well actually if you do it you will probably not even think about it, if you don't, you may just remember me telling you to and regret ignoring me).

Some things to avoid

Perhaps just as important as the tips about things you need to *do* to help you be successful, are the things you need to *avoid* in order to make a good job of the literature review. So here are a few which may help your cause when you are conducting your review.

Using only those papers that support your view: A common weakness of a literature review is one-sided reporting. It is tempting to report only those studies that support your view of the world and how the constructs within it should relate to each other. This is unscientific and should be avoided. You need to ensure that you review and present papers that both support your view and contradict it (if they exist).

Trying to read everything: If you try this you will never be able to finish reading. The idea of the literature review is to provide a survey of the most relevant and significant work, not to provide a census of all the published work that relates even in the tiniest way to your research. There will also come a time when you have to **stop reading**. This does not mean stop completely but stop for the moment and consolidate your knowledge. Typically, once you have conceptualised your theoretical framework, tested it mentally against your peers, supervisors and perhaps at a presentation, the time has come to nail your colours to the mast and adopt your model as the one that you will use and test further. Stop adding new information from more extensive reading, this will just continue to confuse you and prevent you from progressing. It's time to move on the next stage of your research.

Reading without writing: Even given the often intractable nature of academic journals, it's much easier to read than to write. Not writing is one of the most common mistakes that research students fall into. Many excuses abound, and I have heard a lot of them: 'It's all in my head and I am sorting it out before writing it down', 'I don't need to write because I am much more of a thinker than a writer', 'I'm going to write it all down when I have finished reviewing the relevant literature'. Interestingly enough, Nick used all of these, and still does in fact.

It's all just excuses for putting off what we don't want to do. As a supervisor, no matter how inventive the excuse, I can generally tell when a student is procrastinating for some reason, maybe because they do not understand what they are doing, and are avoiding challenging their understanding by refusing to commit what they know to paper. The discipline of writing helps you to understand what you have read, and highlights what you do and don't know for you and your supervisor. It will help you to identify relationships between the works that you have reviewed, and highlight inconsistencies in the literature and a whole range of other important stuff. By refusing to write you are denying yourself the chance to learn what you know and what you don't. In my experience, persistent refusal to write generally leads to disaster. The student either does not progress their thinking, or the supervisor gives up and decides that the student is not working and cannot meet the research deadlines imposed on them. Either way, a common consequence of failure to write regularly is failure to complete the research project.

It's very important to recognise that what you write will *not* be a final or near-final version, and you should not expect it to be. It will evolve and change as your understanding grows, as you discover new things, as your writing style becomes more 'academic' and as you incorporate your methodology, results and conclusions. Writing is a way of thinking, so allow yourself to write as many drafts as you need, change your ideas and information as you learn more about your research problem. If you are passing these drafts to a supervisor, or colleague, remember my earlier comments and please make sure you don't wear out your supervisors' patience by passing interminable rough drafts to them for comment.

Summary

Remember that the aim of your literature review is to show that you have studied existing work in your field and provide insights into this work. An effective review analyses and synthesises material, and will be relevant, appropriate, and useful for the reader. Your literature review presents the case and context for the rest of your research. For this reason it is important to demonstrate the relationship of your work to previous research in the area. Without a good literature review, your work will never be able to assure the reader that it makes a solid contribution to knowledge, so you should *never* ignore the importance of the literature review stage. Key points to take from this chapter:

- The most important stage in a literature review is **starting**. Do not spend an age agonising over *where* to start, just start somewhere. The path will become clear after a while.
- The second most important stage of the literature review is **stopping**. Eventually you will need to decide that it is time to move onto the next stage of your research, even though you may have missed one or two articles that may be relevant to your research question. If you don't stop you won't progress and consequently won't finish. Don't worry about the one or two articles that you may have missed. If you have conducted a thorough review, there is a vanishing small chance that one or two missed articles will answer your research question for you and spoil your thesis.
- The aims of your research and the research question are important; they help to focus and direct your reading.
- Reviewing academic literature is an iterative process; you will need to read papers several times, each time focusing on different aspects of the paper.

- You will use the literature to explain what is known in the field in which you are working and what is not known.
- What is not known forms part of the rationale for your thesis and motivates the work that you will be doing in your research project.
- Critiquing literature is not the same as criticising it, and in fact authors often critique their own work when they discuss the limitations of their research.
- Your literature can be organised in several different ways, although thematic organisation is often used.

Further reading

There aren't too many sources for information on reviewing the literature, but in more recent times a few interesting pieces of work have arrived.

- *Doing a Literature Review: Releasing the Social Science Research Imagination* by Chris Hart: One of the very few books entirely dedicated to the literature review. As such it is a vital source of information for beginning researchers, and even those more experienced are likely to pick up a few useful tips.
- *Critical Reading and Writing for Postgraduates* by Mike Wallace and Alison Wray: A good introduction for the actual process of reading and critiquing academic literature.
- *Doing Your Research Project: A Guide for First-Time Researchers in Education, Health and Social Science* by Judith Bell: This book is highly rated by many of my students, and gives some good information on how to get out there and review the literature.

Recent work on systematic literature reviewing in the social sciences (drawing from evidence-based medical research) also provides a useful starting point. For an introduction you can check out a 2003 paper in the *British Journal of Management* by David Tranfield *et al.* entitled 'Towards a methodology for developing evidence-informed management knowledge by means of systematic review'.

1. Write down your area or field of research.
   - Is it too broad? Can you narrow it down?
   - What *specifically* do you want to look at?
2. List the constructs that you are interested in.
   - Which of these is the central construct of your thesis?
3. Create a mind map with your central construct taking the dominant position and other constructs surrounding it.
   - What does the literature tell you about the relationships between your central construct and the other constructs in your mind map?
   - Does the literature tell you anything about relationships among the other constructs in you mind map?

EXERCISES

4. Look in your literature and identify several different definitions for each of your constructs. (There will be more than one, even if they are somewhat similar.)
    -   How do these definitions differ? Are the differences important?
5. For each of the definitions can you identify different operationalisations of the construct?
    -   If you identified three different definitions in Q4 and three different operationalisations for these definitions in Q5 you now have nine operationalisations of the same thing. This is where it gets interesting. Now you can start to put together a bit of a critique of the literature.
6. How have these operationalisations (or operational definitions) been used? Are they applied qualitatively or quantitatively? Why were they applied in this way and what has the author used them for?
7. Comment on the suitability of the research using the information that you have collected in the previous exercises.
8. Do you have a bibliographic database? If not, set one up today. Go on, just do it. If you already have one, is it up to date?

25 Writing up the Research

DAVID E. GRAY

CHAPTER OBJECTIVES

After reading this chapter you will be able to:

- Write a report that matches your original or evolving research objectives.
- Plan and resource the report writing process.
- Select from a number of different report formats.
- Present your findings in a written style, format and structure that is accessible to your intended audience.

You have planned your research project, adopted an appropriate research methodology, designed valid and reliable data gathering tools and collected and analysed the data. What could be easier than writing up the research report? Actually, it is not as easy as many would imagine. The most carefully planned and skilfully implemented research study will be doomed if you are incapable of presenting the findings in a manner that is engaging, coherent and accessible for your intended audience. As Murray (1994) warns, reports are too often written in a private language that excludes the very people who may have responsibility for actually implementing or assessing the research. One of the keys, therefore, is to keep it simple.

Timing is also important. Most people assume that reports are written at the end of a research project. This is not necessarily the case. Indeed, the more time you can devote to writing sections or chapters of the report during the research process itself, the better. This is because the process of writing is extremely valuable in clarifying your own thoughts, and in finding where gaps and inconsistencies may be emerging in the research. It is better to discover these problems well before the end of the research project so that they can be rectified.

Another concern is that of objectivity. It is likely that you are tackling a research project because you are interested in the subject, or have been asked to do it by a sponsor. Either way, even though at the start of the project you do not see yourself as an expert, it is probable that you have some interest or connection with the topic. The key here, then, is adopting and maintaining an objective 'distance' from the subject and not getting dragged into some sort of polemical argument. Failure to maintain an objective stance will not only cloud and obscure your writing, it may alienate your audience.

Report writing is (or should be) a creative process. Even using the same sets of data, two researchers will not produce reports that are identical. But report writing is also a skill and, like any skill, it must be learned through practice. It must also be based upon sound principles. Presented in this chapter, then, are some basic approaches to producing a research report that will hopefully complement rather than hinder the research effort that has preceded it. Note that the term 'report' is used here to mean actual reports produced in an organizational context, but many of the principles discussed apply equally to academic dissertations, theses and articles written for the academic literature. These are also discussed with reference to their own specific requirements.

THE REPORT WRITING PROCESS

You will recall that in Chapter 3 and, indeed, throughout this book, the importance of writing clear and unambiguous research objectives has been stressed. It would certainly be a pity if, at the final hour, these objectives were ignored and the report aimed at a completely different set of goals! Of course, it is possible that your objectives may have shifted or even radically changed during the research process itself. This is entirely acceptable, as long as you have clearly articulated what these new objectives are going to be. Even in the most heuristic research approach, the researcher sets off with an intended goal – even though this may become modified through the process of inquiry itself.

PLANNING THE REPORT

Some writers prefer to launch themselves immediately into the writing process, but it is usually prudent to start with at least a draft plan for the report, even if the plan may change during the writing itself. The plan can initially be sketched out on paper or typed straight into a word processed document. The plan might contain the main headings and sub-headings of the report, and references to where notes, files or data sets can be found for when the actual writing process starts. It is nearly always sensible to get this plan evaluated by a reviewer. This person might be your supervisor or tutor if you are undertaking an academic course of study, a peer or co-worker or even the report's organizational sponsor. In seeking this review, make it clear that you want critical feedback. Eliciting the views of managers or sponsors is always useful because it enables you to gain some assurance that the report meets with their interests and needs.

In some cases, the planning of the report may be assisted by terms of reference that describe the purposes of the report, its scope, type and readership. Sometimes these terms of reference may be given to you by whoever is commissioning you to carry out the research. Wainwright (1990) suggests that if you have not been given any terms of reference, you should write your own.

Knowing the purpose of the report

Before starting, as Turk and Kirkman (1989) warn, you must begin with a clear idea of what it is you want to achieve. This is not the same as your subject. By focusing on the aim of your report, you are considering what it is that the readers want to know, so that it is relevant, interesting and usable for them. Failure to think clearly about the needs, interests and motivations of the target audience is one of the most common reasons why reports fail to fulfil their potential. It often helps to think what it is you expect readers to actually do after they have read the report. For example, do you expect them to:

- Request a presentation.
- File the report.
- Pass the report on to another individual or committee.
- Send an email.
- Arrange a meeting.
- Sign a cheque.

Activity 19.1

Examine each of the following words, and select one or more that describe the purpose of your report: describe, explain, instruct, specify, evaluate and recommend, provoke debate but does not seem to lead, persuade, concede and apologize, protest, reject.

Knowing your audience

You also need to remember that the report may be read by a variety of people, each of whom has a different interest or motivation for reading it. If it is, say, a technical report, those with technical expertise in this field may be interested in issues of how and why. Senior managers in an organization, however, may have less time to read all the technical details, but want to get quickly to the issue of what is the purpose, what is the cost, and where are the resources? Writing for an academic audience will require a style of writing that includes a strong engagement with the academic literature. So you will need to think of how the report can be written in a way that is accessible to a diverse audience, at least some of whom will not want to read it in its entirety.

Turk and Kirkman (1989) suggest that, before you start, you ask yourself each of the following questions:

* Are all the readers alike?

* What do they already know about the subject?

* What do they need to know?

* What are their attitudes to the subject, to the writer, and to the writer's objectives?

* What are the psychological and physical contexts within which the report will be received?

Booth (1991) also suggests that the writer needs to decide whether the message to be delivered is going to be made explicit or implicit in the report. She argues that it is often better to make the argument implicit, and to lead the reader towards the appropriate conclusion.

Activity 19.2

Taking a report that you intend to write, now add a description of your audience using the bullet points above.

Getting started with the report

Even if it may seem logical to start writing with an Introduction, this is probably not the best place – indeed, it could be argued that it is easier to write this at the very end (when the whole 'story' of the project is clear). Most researchers find it easiest to begin with the literature review (if the report requires one). There are a number of reasons for this:

- The review will normally have been conducted at an early stage of the research and so can be attempted well before the final phases.

- The process of writing the literature review helps to articulate the objectives, focus and direction of the research.

- The literature review, of course, can always be updated and improved at a later stage, but writing a first draft early in the research can provide a solid theoretical and directional underpinning to the entire project. Where you start is obviously up to you. The only point to emphasize is that you should get started on the writing process as soon as possible!

Many researchers have difficulty in making the transition between reading books and articles and constructing a literature review. If they find the writing up stage challenging, they may indulge in 'displacement' activities which comprise endless reading but no writing! To avoid this, the best strategy is to:

- Read books, academic articles, conference papers, etc. Make notes and/or summaries.

- From the ideas generated by the literature (using notes/summaries), identify some main themes; type these into a document.

- Organize the themes into a logical structure; add sub-themes if possible.

- As themes are added, note the author/source; build up a number of authors/sources for each theme or sub-theme.

- Read more sources if necessary, make notes and summaries and add the source to existing themes or if necessary start a new theme.

- Once the structure is complete, flesh out each theme into an argument, supporting each argument with reference to the sources identified.

MAKING AND USING TIME

In writing a report, time is one of the most precious, but probably least available, commodities you have at your disposal. It is important, then, to use it wisely and to make as much time available to writing the report as possible. Good project management is the key. At the very start of the research process, you should have allocated a block of time (days, weeks or even months, depending on the scale of the project), for the report writing process. Within this elapsed time schedule, you should also have planned for the writing sessions you need in order to complete the report. If your research and data gathering efforts have overlapped into the report writing phase, then you need to evaluate whether you can complete the report in the planned time, or whether you need to negotiate an extension. What is vital here is that you take some control of decisions, and do not leave requests for extensions until the last minute.

As far as the report writing process is concerned, people tackle this in different ways. According to Saunders et al. (2007), most people can write about 2,000 words in a day, but this will depend on their experience, confidence and the complexity of the subject. Some people prefer to devote large blocks of time to writing and to keep going into the night until exhaustion overwhelms them. Others prefer to allocate discrete blocks, spread across a time period. What is important is that, whatever your preferred style, the time resource you allocate yourself is sufficient to get the job done. Whatever time you have planned for yourself, you obviously want to make the best use of it. In doing this you might want to:

- Find a place to work where distractions are minimized and where you can think clearly.

- Write at a time of day when you are physically and mentally fresh. Take regular breaks.

- Have access to all the resources you are going to need (a computer for word processing, keeping notes, files, data, and for data analysis, etc.).

- Set yourself challenging but realistic goals for each writing session. This might be a word count – in which case, you could keep a record of your production achievements.

Of course, the report writing process is made more complicated if it is a team effort. The general principles, however, are the same. Plan for the writing of the report and allocate roles and responsibilities. Set deadlines and meet or communicate regularly to see if all team members are on track. Since the timing of the report is now dependent on the speed of the slowest member, it is often prudent to have contingency plans in case the process is held up. For example, can another member of the team or additional staff resources be drafted in to write some more sections or to provide assistance?

TOP TIP 19.1

In preparing to write the report, consider how you are going to reward yourself as you write it. We all need incentives. For some people, merely keeping a word count of how they are progressing is enough. Others require more tangible incentives such as chocolate, or going out for a meal as key sections or chapters are completed!

GETTING DOWN TO WRITING THE REPORT

Some people like to leave the report writing phase to a time when they have amassed all their data. This, however, can be a mistake partly because it is leaving the most vital phase right until the end. A better approach is to start the writing from day one. This will give you the satisfaction of achieving some 'output' and, even more importantly, will provide you with practice at writing skills. Writing up chapters or at least sections as you go along will both develop your writing style, and also allow you to elicit feedback from your supervisor.

TOP TIP 19.2

A useful tip is to keep a research diary to note ideas as they crop up, to keep notes of your meetings with your supervisor and to provide a reminder of which sources (books, academic articles) you have ordered and when.

Students often find structuring their report or thesis difficult, often because they find themselves immersed and drowning in detail. A useful approach is to reorganize material by creating mind-maps, diagrams that illustrate how concepts and ideas relate to one another (see On the Web 19.1 below). Using mind-maps can be particularly useful when trying to understand and describe the interrelationships between a large number of concepts or theoretical models. In dissertations or theses, then, mind-maps can be particularly useful when structuring and writing up the literature stage.

ON THE WEB 19.1

Take a look at the Inspiration software at the website:

http://www.inspiration.com/productinfo/

Download a trial copy and experiment mind-mapping your study outline.

Using a supervisor

If you are studying for an academic qualification it is likely that you will have a tutor or supervisor to guide you, especially at the writing-up stage. Supervisors are a vital resource of knowledge, wisdom and experience, but are not always used well by students, partly because we find it hard to accept critical feedback. Yet such feedback is essential if the research output is to reach the necessary standard. When being given feedback, either face-to-face or through written comments, try to resist the temptation to be defensive and start justifying yourself. Any critique your supervisor offers is designed to help you and should be taken as such.

THE REPORT STRUCTURE

The structure of the report will very much depend on what type of report you are producing and for whom. There are, essentially, two kinds of readers: those who commissioned or who are expecting the report, and those who are not expecting the report but who may, none the less, be interested in it. The commissioning group will want to know if this is the report they were waiting for and whether it contains the information they need. The second group will want to know if the report has any relevance to them, and whether it contains any new information. Therefore, for both groups, you need to give the audience information quickly and in an accessible way. It must compete for their limited time and attention. The kinds of criteria readers might apply in deciding whether they read the report or not might include:

- The title – does this sound relevant or interesting to me?

- Do the contents of the report actually match the title?

- How long is the report – what is my investment of time going to be and is it worthwhile?

- How well presented is the report – how confident am I in the abilities of the writer?

The structure of a report is made clear when some of the principals of typography are applied for heading structures. Many students simply use the same font type and size for all headings, but this can be confusing. Table 19.1 shows how typography (the size and style of fonts) can be used to illustrate to the reader where they are in the structure of the piece. These styles can be set up in Word quite easily by clicking on [Format] and then [Styles and Formatting]. Click on the small downward arrow on the style you want to set up and click on [Modify] then [Format].

TYPOGRAPHIC STYLE	FONT DESCRIPTION
HEADING 1	12 point font, capitals and bold
Heading 2	12 point font, lower case, bold
Heading 3	12 point font, lower case, bold italics
Heading 4	12 point, lower case

WRITING ORGANIZATIONAL AND TECHNICAL REPORTS

A business report is taken to mean any report written for the purposes of general management or organization, whereas a technical report has, obviously, a more specifically technical focus. Of course, organizational research can often involve the need to understand and act upon technical issues. Some business and technical reports may be written for publication in an academic journal, and so will tend to follow the structure discussed later. Technical reports may be written for organizational purposes and be commissioned or sponsored by an individual or committee within the organization. When undertaking reports of this kind, both you and the sponsor need to be clear about:

• The objectives of the report.

• Access to resources needed to complete it.

• Timescales for delivery.

• The extent to which the report is purely descriptive or analytical. If the latter, are recommendations required?

• The importance, or otherwise, of theoretical underpinning. This, of course, is essential for academic journal articles but may be irrelevant for some kinds of technical report.

• The final intended audience for the report (which may not actually be the initial sponsor) and the style, tone and structure that the report should adopt.

In contrast to academic articles, business and technical reports tend to be much more utilitarian and 'to the point'. White (1997) suggests the following typical structure, but this should not be adhered to rigidly – select sections according to your needs.

Cover: A well-designed cover can help to attract a reader's attention and give a positive impression about the report before it is even read. White (1997) recommends that a cover should include at least four elements: a descriptive title of the report; the names of the report's principle authors, investigators and editors, if applicable; publication number, if the organization requires a record of this; and the publication date.

Title page: This is the first page of the report and repeats some of the cover content. For example, it contains a descriptive title of the report, the author's name and the organization's name and address. This page can also include the name of the person who commissioned the report.

Abstract/executive summary: This is designed for busy people who do not usually have the time to read a report in its entirety, and may be between 200 and 500 words long. This summary, then, has to be both comprehensive in its coverage but also very succinct. It should present a short description of the project, plus findings and recommendations. Figures, illustrations and tables are not used.

Table of contents: White (1997) recommends that a table of contents should be used for reports that are over 10 pages long. The table of contents shows all main headings and even sub-headings. Since all headings should fully describe each section, the table of contents not only provides a guide to finding sections, it can actually help to describe what a document is about. Most word processing application programmes will generate a table of contents automatically, but only if you have formatted your report by allocating a style (for example, Heading 1, Heading 2, etc.) to your headings.

List of symbols, abbreviations, definitions: If your report contains complex terms, abbreviations or definitions, then it is helpful to provide an explanation at the beginning. Of course, you will still be required to explain each new term or abbreviation in the main body of your text as it occurs. For example, you will write 'Human Resource Management (HRM)' before alluding to HRM in the remainder of the report.

Introductory material: This might include any of the following:

- The nature of the problem being addressed.

- Why the research was undertaken.

- Any limitations on resources, materials or time in undertaking the research.

- The scope of the research (for example, did the study look at the problem from the perspective of individual employees, departments, sites or the entire organization?)

- An outline of previous work on this topic.

Report of work done: This will probably be the longest section and will, obviously, be determined by your subject, which might be:

- A new product or service. Readers may be interested in its potential uses, the risks involved, and its technical, financial and material requirements. They may also be interested in the life cycle of the product or service, its potential competitors and plans for its development.

- Technical or managerial problems. Readers may be interested in the origins and nature of the problem, whether it is temporary or permanent, options for solving the problem, and which option is selected and why. They may also want to know how and when the recommendations are going to be implemented, and what the outcomes are likely to be.

One of the weaknesses of many reports is that the main findings are buried in the middle or end of the document. Hence, busy managers will have to spend time delving for the nub of the argument. But this is not just an issue of time, it is also one of cognition and understanding. By presenting the important findings or arguments first, subsequent information can then be used to supplement and support them. Readers find it easier to process and assimilate detailed information if they are first given a general framework to work with. This is not to argue that there may not be reports where the argument proceeds like a detective story with the 'solution' arriving at the end, but most readers of business reports will be both irritated and confused by this approach and will want you to get to the point! Herbert (1990) offers a helpful suggestion here: imagine that you have been asked to appear on a serious radio programme to explain your report. Think of how you would have to quickly and succinctly explain what you have been investigating, how, why and with what results.

Turk and Kirkman (1989) suggest that reports should be written using a pyramid structure (see Figure 19.1). Since only the first few pages of the report will be read by most readers in an organization, this should contain an accurate summary of the main substance of the report (see *Abstract/executive summary*, above). The most detailed information, including appendices, will be included at the end of the document.

The main aim of the business report should be to put over the information needed, to those that require it, so that something can be done. It is not an exercise in writing down everything you have learned about the subject, no matter how interesting (to you) this may be. It is worth, however, just qualifying this last statement. It might be worthwhile noting problems encountered in undertaking the research, the false starts made and negative findings recorded, so that other researchers may learn from your experience. Managers who delve this far may also note some of the 'side issues' you were not able to pursue, so that further research might be commissioned. But, overall, try to maintain the focus of the report – keep to the point!

Results/findings: This section should not be a 'dumping ground' for all your research data. Most of the data sets will probably be presented in the appendices. The results section should contain summaries of the data that focus on

Figure 19.1
Pyramid of evidence
model for report
design (adapted
from Turk and
Kirkman, 1989)

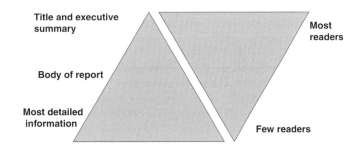

Title and executive summary

Most readers

Body of report

Most detailed information

Few readers

the main findings of the research. For clarity, it helps if data can be presented in the form of tables or graphs (recall Chapter 17). Note that the Results section should concentrate precisely on this and not discuss the findings. The Discussion section comes next.

Discussion and analysis: This section is where you have an opportunity to draw inferences from the results (what do the data mean?), look at relationships between sets of data and also differences. What was unexpected? What were the causes and what are the likely effects. What do the results mean in terms of options for action? It must be stressed that the Discussion is not an opportunity merely to repeat the results, although reference may need to be made to the findings in drawing out the threads of the analysis. Remember, the Results tell you what has happened, the Discussion/Analysis section aims to understand how and why it happened.

Conclusions: Conclusion could be merely a number of remarks that 'round off' the report, or it could mean a 'logical outcome' of the report's arguments. The latter is probably preferable in most cases. A conclusion should not be used to repeat findings or facts – it should contain a series of statements that bring together, in a succinct format, what the study has discovered. Berry (2004) warns that Conclusions should not present new evidence, but should relate back to the original purpose and focus of the report.

Recommendations: These should flow logically from the evidence presented by the report, so that there should be no sudden surprises for the reader. This section should also focus completely on these recommendations and not contain other material such as data or discussion that has already been presented. Recommendations are usually presented in a concise format, so the use of a list is entirely appropriate. White (1997) advises that a recommendations section is only relevant if the author has been commissioned to make such recommendations.

Acknowledgements: Turk and Kirkman (1989) recommend limiting acknowledgements to those outside the organization that have provided you with help, and only if this assistance is beyond what one would normally expect from someone in their position. This section should not be used to flatter those who are acknowledged, but to provide the reader with a sense of where some of the information originated.

References: This will be used for citing all the books, journal articles, reports, websites and internal organizational documents used in the study. Only those sources that are actually referenced in the report should be cited, not all those that you read but did not necessarily use. If you want to refer to documents that you are not referencing but which readers might find useful, then place these in a Bibliography section. You might also want to indicate why these sources might be useful.

Appendix for tables, figures and graphs: Some of these tables and figures will probably appear in the main body of the report. Ensure that they are not gratuitous, that is, they should be there for a purpose. Also make sure that they are referred to and described in the body of the text (and not just dumped to stand on their own), and that they appear as close to this description as possible. The citation 'Table' should appear above the table to which it refers, while the citation 'Figure' should appear below the figure. This is the convention. More detailed data can be summarized in tables, figures and graphs in the appendix.

Other appendices: These should include any research instruments you have used, such as questionnaires, interview or observation schedules, and any accompanying documentation such as letters sent to survey participants. They might also include copies of emails or other communications generated during the process of the research (but remember not to breach confidentiality by revealing the names of research subjects without their permission). Whatever topic is covered in an appendix, it is important that there is a reference to the appendix and its purpose in the main body of the report.

WRITING ACADEMIC THESES AND DISSERTATIONS

An academic thesis or dissertation is very different to an organizational or technical report in that it is usually more comprehensive and expansive. It seeks to marshal all the relevant information that relates to the topic or problem, and to support all data and arguments with sources of evidence, so that the way in which a case is built up can be judged (Halpenny, 2003). It also seeks to be original. According to Phillips and Pugh (2000), this could include:

- Carrying out empirical work that has not been done before.

- Using already known material but with a new interpretation.

- Replicating a study that has been done in another country or context.

- Bringing new evidence to bear on an old issue.

How a thesis or dissertation is structured will partly depend on the nature of the research itself, but it is sound advice to sketch out an intended outline at as early a stage as possible. Clearly, this tentative outline may change during the research or writing up process, but it does give the writer a sense of structure and direction (Teitelbaum, 1998). The usual convention for the layout is as follows:

- Title page (which should contain the title, the name of the author and qualifications, a statement of the degree for which the document is being presented, the names of the academic School or Department of the University or college and the date of submission).

- The Abstract (a summary – usually of not more than 300 words – of the content of the thesis).

- Contents page (a listing, giving precise headings for each section and their page numbers).

- Acknowledgements (thanking people and organizations that have assisted in the work).

- The main body of the thesis. This could comprise an Introduction, several chapters dealing with a review of the literature and comprising theoretical issues and arguments (recall Chapter 3), Research Methodology, plus Findings, Analysis and Conclusion and/or Recommendations.

- Appendices (if any).

- References (a complete listing of all works cited).

It could be argued that, in some ways, the first and last chapters are the most important as these are what readers tend to remember. The Introduction chapter (often just a few pages in length) will usually be written after the completion of the research and will often contain:

- A broad review, putting the work within a wider context.

- A coherent argument for the significance of the problem being considered.

- An outline of the thesis, showing how the problem was approached.

The final chapter may contain:

- A brief restatement of the problem, now seen from the perspective of what has been learned.

- A clear outline of what has been achieved.

- A discussion of the main recommendations for work in the future.

Between these chapters, of course, we have the all-important literature review. This provides a context for the proposed study and demonstrates why it is important and timely. In order to do this, it sets out to clarify the relationship between the study and previous research on the topic.

TOP TIP 19.4

A very common mistake is that this part of the dissertation reads like a 'laundry list of previous studies' (Rudestam and Newton, 2007: 46). Hence, every paragraph begins, 'Brown found that...', or 'Fletcher argues...'. Recall Figure 5.1 in Chapter 5 and the advice that you should gradually synthesize and focus your ideas, so that all material is linked to the central direction of the study. By the time the reader reaches the Methodology section, he or she should be saying to themselves: 'Yes, these are the questions I too am asking myself and this is what the study should focus on so that knowledge in the field can move forward.'

WRITING FOR ACADEMIC JOURNALS

You may undertake research with the specific intention of submitting the outcome for publication to an academic journal, or you may have written a thesis and want to see an edited version of it published. Berry (2004) warns that editors and publishers loath theses. This is because they are written in a cumbersome academic style where length is relatively unrestricted. For a professional reading public, the material will have to be completely reworked, with a succinct and taut prose.

Selecting the right journal

It is also not enough just to decide that you want to publish an article in a journal. The question is: which journal? All journals require contributors to adhere to a specific format. This is usually stated within the journal itself, and normally gives guidance on the structure of articles, writing style, reference system, length and so on. Obviously, this is the first place to look if your report is being written for publication. But you will also find it useful to go beyond this formal outline and in particular to look at:

- The types of articles that have been recently published. What kinds of subjects are of interest to the readers of this journal? Are the research approaches mainly quantitative, qualitative or a mixture of the two, and what epistemological traditions do they follow?

- The formality, or otherwise, of the academic style. In most journals, you should expect a very formal style to be adopted, using the past tense and the passive voice (for example, 'Fieldwork was undertaken using a structured observation schedule. It was then decided to...').

- The depth and content of the academic underpinning. Review the reference section of a number of articles. How lengthy is the typical reference section? Is any particular research paradigm favoured?

As Berry (2004) notes, it is usually better to have details of your selected journal's format before writing the article rather than after. The following Case Study provides an example of what to look out for.

CASE STUDY 19.1   TYPICAL STRUCTURE FOR AN ACADEMIC JOURNAL ARTICLE (ABRIDGED)

Aims and Scope

The *International Journal of Human Resource Management* is the forum for HRM scholars and professionals worldwide. Concerned with the expanding role of strategic human resource management in a fast-changing global environment, the journal focuses on future trends in HRM, drawing

(Cont'd)

on empirical research in the areas of strategic management, international business, organizational, personnel management and industrial relations.

The *International Journal of Human Resource Management* encourages strategically focused articles on a wide range of issues including employee participation, human resource flow, reward systems and high commitment work systems. The journal aims to address major issues arising from:

- internationalization of market integration
- increased competition
- technological change
- new concepts of line management
- changing corporate climates

Notes for Contributors

By submitting a manuscript, the authors agree that the exclusive rights to reproduce and distribute the article have been given to the Publishers, including reprints, photographic reproduction, microfilm, or any other reproduction of a similar nature, and translations. Submissions should be in English, typed in double spacing with wide margins, on one side only of the paper, preferably of A4 size. The title, but not the authors name, should appear on the first page of the manuscript. The publishers encourage submission on disk; however, please ensure that the typescript is exactly the same as the version of the article on disk. Articles should normally be between 7,000 and 8,000 words in length.

Source: Adapted and abridged from the *International Journal of Human Resource Management* (2008)

Activity 19.3

Locate at least two academic journals that cover issues within the subject field of your report or thesis. Looking at both the 'Notes for Contributors' and the kinds of articles published, are there any significant differences between the journals in terms of:

- Subject areas.
- Emphasis on approaches to research (qualitative/quantitative) and epistemology.
- Theoretical underpinning in the articles.
- Emphasis on original, empirical work as against descriptions of other people's research.

You will note from Case Study 19.1 that the journal editors have made it as transparent as possible as to what they are looking for. Note also that they want empirical research, not a reworking of past articles or reports. They also provide a list of the kinds of articles they are looking for.

You might want to select a journal that focuses on the subject of your report. On the other hand, you might argue that the journal has failed to publish anything on your subject and that your article would make a vital contribution. This may be so, but do check that the subject is one that is covered in the general rubric of subjects of interest. If you are in doubt about whether a journal might publish your work, you can send an abstract to the journal editor asking if the subject would be worthy of consideration.

Article submission and outcomes

In submitting an article, it is advisable to include a short covering letter. This is not an opportunity to recapitulate the rationale, objectives and research methodology and results of the research. The editor will see these clearly from the actual article. The purpose of your letter is simply to offer the article for consideration and to thank the editor for his or her time.

Once you have submitted an article to an academic journal make sure that the editor acknowledges that it has been received. You can then sit back for weeks, and probably months, before you hear whether it is to be published. This is because the article first of all has to be accepted by the editor as worthy of further consideration, after which it will usually be sent to two or perhaps three peer reviewers. The review process is 'blind', that is, your name will not be divulged to the reviewers, who will work completely independently on their evaluations. The reviewers will recommend one of the following:

1. Publish with no revisions.

2. Publish with minor revisions.

3. Publish with major revisions.

4. Revise and resubmit.

5. Reject.

While 1 or 2 are obviously what all writers want to hear, responses 3 and 4 should be treated as a success because this means that the reviewers consider the article as interesting and relevant to the journal. It frequently happens that one reviewer likes the article and recommends publication and another rejects it. The editor then has to either make a casting decision, or may send the article out for further review. Not surprisingly all this takes time. You are entitled to make the occasional inquiry as to how the review process is going (just in case the busy editor has forgotten about you!), but it is best not to pester editors too much.

They have a difficult and often thankless, unpaid task. If making revisions, help the reviewers by constructing a two column table, with the left hand column listing the reviewers comments and recommendations and the right hand column what you have done and where the changes can be found. If there are recommendations you do not want to make, say so and explain your reasons.

Typical outline for an academic article

It would be wrong to be dogmatic about this, but presented below is a typical structure.

Title page: This includes the title itself, that should neatly summarize the main focus of the article. The title page should also include the name of the author and her/his institution, and acknowledgements (especially if the research has received external funding or assistance). The actual title itself should be short, and should specify exactly what the article is about. If the title is rather long, you could consider using the less significant element of it as a 'strap line'. For example:

> The influence of improved process control systems and resource allocation on widget production through the use of a case study.

This could read:

> Case study: widget production improvement – process control systems and resource allocation.

Abstract: The abstract provides a concise summary of the article (often between 150 and 200 words). The actual length of the abstract will usually be specified by the journal's Notes for Contributors. This is a very important section because it may be the only part of the article that some people read. Herbert (1990) suggests that the abstract should contain:

- The main hypothesis.
- A synopsis of the methods used.
- A summary of the major findings.
- A brief mention of subjects and materials.
- The conclusions based on the results.
- Design procedures.

In addition to the abstract, and perhaps adjacent to it, some journals ask for a list of keywords. In paper-based versions of the journal, these can provide readers with an indication of whether they want to read the article or not. For

Web-based abstracting services, typing in one of these keywords will link another researcher to a list of articles containing this keyword, including your article.

Introduction: This explains the purpose of the study, the rationale for undertaking it and some background information. The Introduction also provides an opportunity to outline the main research questions and hypotheses (if any). If the research is based on findings in an organization, it is useful to provide the reader with some additional details on, say, the history of the organization, its size, products or services, mission, etc.

Literature review: After reading the literature review, the reader should understand why the study is being undertaken and how and why it is adding to the store of knowledge. A literature review written for an academic journal will usually be shorter than the kind of very comprehensive review that would be written for an academic thesis or dissertation. It should be self-evident after reading the literature review as to why the study's research questions (and hypotheses, if any) have been selected. Take care, however, not to merely label this section 'Literature review' even though this is what it is. Help and inspire the reader by choosing a title that reflects what the section is really about. If several themes or issues are being addressed, it may be necessary to write a number of literature sections, each with an appropriate heading.

Methodology: This is a key section and will be evaluated meticulously by reviewers and readers, and, of course, by anyone seeking to replicate the findings. The methodology should follow the principles outlined in many chapters in this book, including:

- A description of the research context: what kind of organization or setting, what were the original specifications for the study, what practical or ethical considerations were evident?

- The processes of sample selection: how was the sample selected? When was it selected: at the commencement of the study, or iteratively during it?

- A description of, and justification for, the sample: how many participants were there, what were their characteristics and how representative were they of the population?

- The research procedure, including the kinds of research methodology (experimental, survey, grounded study, etc.), research tools used and evidence for the validity, reliability and credibility of these tools.

- The duration, number and timing of the data gathering sessions: if used, how were interviewers or observers trained, what instructions were given to respondents?

- How were the data analysed?

Results: As the title suggests, this is the section in which you report on your findings. This may be in the form of descriptive text, tables and figures (recall Chapter 17) or through selected quotations. The key word here is 'selected'. Quotations should only be used where the comments themselves are revealing or interesting – they should not be used to carry the main burden of a description or argument. Quotations should also be used sparingly; try to avoid the phenomenon of 'death by quotation'.

Ensure that the results section is precisely this and not a discussion or commentary (which comes in the following section). The easiest way of differentiating between the two sections is that the Results should deal with what happened, while the Discussion section should deal with why (that is, the analysis). Make sure that you do not mix the two.

Discussion: The Discussion section, using the data (Results), presents answers to the original research questions and/or hypotheses. In doing this, it is particularly important to refer back to the literature review section, so that comparisons and contrasts can be drawn out between what your research found and what the literature suggested you might expect. In some cases you may be confirming the theoretical propositions from the literature, but within new (say, organizational) contexts. In other cases you may be finding relationships between variables that few studies have explored. Remember, all research does not have to be so original or unique that it puts you in line for a Nobel Prize. Nevertheless, unless it has something to add to knowledge, it is unlikely to be considered worthy of publication.

References: There are several types of referencing convention, one of the most widely used being the Harvard or author–date system, as used in this book.

Of course, what we have just discussed is quite a conventional format. Journals that take a more inductive, qualitative or ethnographic stance may discourage such a structured approach. The key, as has been suggested, is to look at these journals to see what approach they take.

ETHICAL AND LEGAL CONSIDERATIONS

We have dealt with ethical issues in a number of previous chapters, but it is worth exploring some of them here in the context of writing up the research as well as looking at legal and copyright implications.

THE ETHICS OF REPORT WRITING

Researchers have a responsibility for reporting their findings in a way that matches the data and which upholds the reputation of the researcher and the research community. However, as Table 19.2 shows, there is a spectrum of unethical behaviour in reporting research ranging from speculation to fabrication, the latter, of course, being the most serious. For example, it is important not to make interpretations that are inconsistent with the data or to make claims for the validity and generalizability of research that are exaggerated. Not only is it important that researchers do not make false claims, they have a duty to speak out when clients or organizations in which they have conducted the research

Table 19.2 Unethical reporting of results *Source*: Adapted from Blumberg et al., 2005		
Speculation	Expanding answers beyond what was required by the original research question.
Exaggeration	Making claims for the data that cannot be supported.
Neglect	Failing to acknowledge the limitations of the study and/or results.
Fabrication	Deleting data, modifying answers of respondents, faking results of analyses.
Plagiarism	Copying the work of others.

make such claims in public. Especially in cases where a research report is going to be presented to the organization in which the research was conducted, the limitations of the research must be clearly in evidence so that the organization is not misled. Polonsky (1998), for example, suggests that the research report should contain a section in which the potential problems and limitations of the research are explained. Academic supervisors could also append their comments regarding the limitations of the final report.

AVOIDING PLAGIARISM

Plagiarism is becoming of increasing concern in the research community, partly because the growth of the Internet has made it easier. Plagiarism has many meanings, and is still the subject of much debate, but essentially refers to the submission of the words, ideas, images, or data of another person as one's own. Researchers can be confused about this, because they have to use the work of previous researchers to identify the kinds of questions that are worthy of research and the designs and methodologies needed to find the answers. According to Higher Education and Research in the UK (HERO) (2007), plagiarism takes several forms, including:

- Using published ideas as one's own.
- Representing images from books, journals or information published on the Web as one's own.
- Copying the work of another student or another person and presenting it as one's own.
- Collaborating inappropriately with another student when the assignment or report requires individual work.
- Resubmitting substantive excerpts of your own work from other assignments as a new piece of work.

Whether the plagiarism is unintentional or deliberate it still constitutes a serious offence, attracting sanctions depending on the institution, ranging from grading the paper at zero marks, or being dismissed from a course. Perpetrators of plagiarism are also now more likely to be caught, thanks largely to the heightened vigilance of academic institutions and the use of innovative computer software. So, how can it be avoided? HERO (2007) suggests that when reading, you keep a notebook handy so that you can note down the name of the author, date and place of publication, page numbers, etc. You can also minimize the risk of plagiarism by:

- Quoting directly from the source (but making sure, of course, that you cite the name of the author and date of publication).

- Paraphrasing the author's text but in your own words.

- Summarizing the text.

> ## TOP TIP 19.5
>
> Never be tempted to cut and paste passages from the Internet into your own work. This may appear at first sight to be a speedy way of accessing information, but it is plagiarism. If you do find a passage that is relevant, print out a 'hard' copy, read it through, and then paraphrase the content in your own words as you type your ideas into your assignment or dissertation.

LEGAL ISSUES

Legal issues might arise through the process of conducting your research, and also at the report writing stage, for example, where you:

- Reveal your sources of information and use statements made by individuals – are they defamatory, libellous or in breach of sex discrimination laws?

- Present material – has it been published elsewhere and is it copyright? (See next section.)

- Make recommendations – do they infringe the law?

Common sense suggests that whenever you are in doubt about whether anything you have written contravenes a legal provision, you should consult a legal expert.

INTELLECTUAL PROPERTY AND COPYRIGHT ISSUES

Intellectual property (IP) refers to creations of the mind and includes: inventions, literary and artistic works, names, images, symbols and designs. The four main types of IP are:

- Patents for inventions – new and improved products and processes that are capable of industrial application.

- Trade marks for brand identity – of goods and services, allowing distinctions to be made between different traders.

- Designs for product appearance.

- Copyright for material including literary and artistic material, sound recordings, films, etc.

Copyright laws were first introduced in England in 1710 and now exist in most countries. While the precise nature of national copyright laws varies, the basic premise is that authors need to obtain permission before using another author's document, and must give the author appropriate acknowledgement. Take particular care when tempted to copy material from the Web. While websites are in the 'public domain', this does not mean that they are not protected by copyright laws. It is only safe to copy Web material when the author has abandoned copyright ownership, it is clear that the copyright has expired, or if it is a site owned by the government.

In many countries, what is written by a person while at work, automatically, in most circumstances, becomes the property of their employer. This may well apply to the research report itself.

ON THE WEB 19.2

For more details on copyright laws see the following website:

http://whatiscopyright.org/

In particular take a look at the section of 'Fair Use'.

DEVELOPING A WRITING STYLE AND TONE

It is difficult to exaggerate the importance of developing and using a fluent, concise and engaging writing style when writing up research. Put yourself, for a moment, in the place of someone who has to read your research, often having to wade through a long, detailed document containing complex arguments. A writing style that is laborious, repetitive, or simply ungrammatical, can not only make it hard for the reader to understand the work, but even make that person hostile to it.

Activity 19.4

Read through the dissertations or theses of previous students to recognize the different 'voices' used. Decide on the voice or style that is most appropriate to you. Write up a chapter or section of a chapter using this voice and ask your supervisor to comment on its style.

The appropriateness of a particular writing style can only be measured in the context of who the report is being written for. Hence, a style that is designed to inspire or enthuse will be very different from one that is meant to criticize or warn. Since the purpose of most reports is functional rather than imaginative, it has been suggested that this style of writing 'should be unobtrusive, an invisible medium, like a window pane through which the information can be clearly seen' (Turk and Kirkman, 1989: 90). Too many writers (particularly those writing scientific or technical documents) use leaden prose, and a stiff, formal style, failing to instill variety into their language.

One of the keys to good style is readability, a factor determined by:

• The writer, through the careful selection of material, by signposting, and by using a variety of emphasis.

• The text, in terms of language (structures and vocabulary) and layout (e.g., headings).

• Readers, particularly their motivation and attitudes, and their overall interest in the report.

Presented next are a number of important areas where writing style can be improved.

WORDINESS

Procter (2007) argues that one of the best ways of improving writing style is to be concise – that is, avoiding 'wordiness'. A wordy style not only adds unnecessary length to a proposal, thesis, or dissertation, but can give the writing a sense of pomposity. Table 19.3 presents some examples of wordiness and some more succinct alternatives.

UNBIASED LANGUAGE

Sexist, racist and ageist language must also be avoided, of course, and reference made to particular genders, races or ages only when they are relevant to the subject of the report. Procter (2007) warns against what she calls the 'Man trap', that is, the use of standard words that seem to assume that the subject is male. This can be avoided by using phrases such as 'him and her' or 'he or she' but this becomes clumsy. Better is to find a gender-neutral word. For example, rather than say: 'Every novelist has learned from those that came before him or her', you could say: 'Every artist has learned from previous artists'. Proctor also advises that feminine forms of words such as 'policewoman', 'women doctors' are becoming outdated, especially since there are neutral terms available such as 'police officer' and simply 'doctor'. In academic writing, titles such as Dr or Professor are rarely used. So, rather than refer to a source by saying 'Professor Brown argues', it is sufficient (and correct) to say, 'Brown (2008) argues…'

Table 19.3
Examples of
wordiness and
how to avoid it

Source: Adapted
from Procter, 2007

CATEGORY	WORDY EXAMPLE	SUCCINCT ALTERNATIVE
Doubling of words	Mutual agreement Reconsider again	Agreement Reconsider
Intensifiers/qualifiers	Very Extremely To a certain extent	Either omit, or give specific details of what you are trying to say.
Formulaic phrases	At this moment in time With regard to In view of the fact that	Now About Because
Catch-all terms	Aspect Quality Fact Feature Problem A surprising aspect of most coaching relationships is their friendly quality.	 These words can sometimes be omitted Most coaching relationships are surprisingly friendly
Padded verbs	To develop an understanding To have an expectation To formulate a plan	To understand To expect To plan

SENTENCE CONSTRUCTION

At a practical level, readability is aided by generating a balance between the use of long and short sentences. A report that contains just long, verbose sentences will be difficult to cognitively process and understand; conversely, a report based just on short, staccato sentences will appear disjointed and monotonous. Using sentences that vary in length will aid the reader's attention, concentration and, therefore, understanding. The readability of text can be measured by a variety of indices, one of the most common of which is the Flesch index.

Activity 19.5

You can measure the readability of the text you are producing using one of a number of alternative measuring indices. Microsoft Word, for example, can be used to give you both a Flesch Reading Ease score and a Flesch–Kincaid Grade Level score. For the Flesch readability score, text is rated on a 100-point scale.

(Cont'd)

The higher the score, the easier the text is to understand. Most documents aim for a score of at least 60–70.

Perform a Flesch readability score on your own report. If this is not already set up in your program, go to the Help facility in Word and type in 'readability'. Follow the instructions to set up the readability statistics tool.

VOCABULARY

The use of long, technical or unfamiliar words also affects readability. But, it is not the length in itself that is the problem. For example, the word 'organization' has many syllables, but would not cause the average reader any problems. As Turk and Kirkman (1989) warn, it is the combination of unfamiliarity with length that can inhibit readability. Unfamiliarity itself is linked to the frequency with which a word appears. Technical terms, in particular, will only be familiar to an audience that is also knowledgeable and competent in this field. So, in writing technical reports, you need to be particularly careful that either the terms you use are clearly explained, or that they are likely to be well known to your audience. Jargon can be useful because it can be used as a short and convenient way to name new ideas and concepts. Technical reports would be lost without it. But it must also be used with care since, if it is overused, or used in an attempt to give an air of importance, it can obscure the central message of the report.

NOMINALIZATION

Turk and Kirkman (1989) warn against the use of nominalization, that is, the habit of turning verbs into nouns. Take, for example, a perfectly good sentence:

The survey collected data on customer attitudes, showing that …

Nominalizing the verb in this sentence, 'collected', gives us the following nominalized sentence:

Collection of the data through the survey revealed customer attitudes, which showed that …

Nominalization reduces the effectiveness of the written style because it produces a passive sentence and also forces the writer to insert an additional verb, 'revealed'. While it is tempting to use passive forms of writing because they add a sense of detachment and perhaps spurious objectivity to the report, they also make it longer, more complex and lacking in dynamism.

WRITING TONE

The tone of a report relates to the general mood of the finished text. It is important, for example, not to betray personal feelings such as anger, frustration, jealously, resentment or anxiety in the report, even if you are feeling these emotions. The overall tone of a report should reflect the nature of its message.

UNDERTAKING A REVIEW PROCESS

It is difficult to overstate the importance of a review process. After 'completing' the report, always regard this as merely the first draft. Leave the document for a few days (if this is possible) before you return to it, so that you will have forgotten the thoughts behind the report and will read what you actually said! You will almost certainly find not only typing and grammatical mistakes, but also gaps, inconsistencies and errors. Turk and Kirkman (1989) suggest first reading the draft without stopping, but noting problem passages or words so that you can return to them later. This top-level overview allows you to evaluate the general flow of information and ideas and to see if the structure 'hangs together'. In conducting this review, Potter (2006) also suggests that you take regular breaks so that you are always fresh and alert. If the report is for an important piece of assessment or intended for a very senior audience, then you will need to go through a number of iterations, ideally using a number of experienced and expert reviewers (see Top Tip 19.6 below).

In terms of content, Potter (2006) suggests that the review task should carefully check on:

- *Content*: Check that the main ideas are clear and of relevance for the reader.

- *Argument*: Check that the main line of argument is transparent, that alternative positions have been considered and that evidence and citations are provided to support arguments.

- *Organization*: Check that the headings describe the content beneath them and chapters and sections are in the right order. Ensure that there is progression from familiar to unfamiliar topics, and that different issues are dealt with in different paragraphs. Ensure that links are made between sections and topics.

- *Language*: Check that the style is appropriate to the intended audience and that meanings are clear.

Also ensure that tables and figures are described and numbered correctly and sources properly referenced.

TOP TIP 19.6

If you are submitting a dissertation or thesis, or an important report, then it is useful getting two quite different kinds of people to act as reviewers. Subject matter experts can tell you whether the content is accurate and whether there are any important gaps. You should also elicit review help from someone totally unfamiliar with the subject area, who can read the work with a detached eye. Try to use the services of someone who is experienced and proficient at report writing and who has a good working knowledge of English grammar. Before submitting a final version of the thesis, you might also consider paying for the services of a professional proof reader.

SUMMARY

- Understand the needs and interests of your intended audience and write for them.

- Plan the report writing process, allowing yourself sufficient time to write the report and resources to aid its completion.

- Different structures are required for case study reports, organizational and technical reports and academic dissertations and journal articles.

- A common structure for an organizational report is one that presents the substantive arguments and findings at the beginning, using the rest of the report to support them.

- Dissertations and theses usually contain an Abstract, an Introduction, several theoretical chapters, plus chapters on Research Methodology, Findings, Analysis and a Conclusion and/or Recommendations.

- The precise structure of journal articles is determined by the journal in question, but such articles will usually contain, amongst other sections, a strong, theoretical underpinning.

- Some of the main ethical considerations to think about when writing up research include maintaining confidentiality and taking care not to breach copyright laws. Be particularly careful when copying material from the Web.

- Style and presentation are important for the impact of a research report and are improved through practice and redrafting. Expert reviewers are of value in this process.

_____ ː // SUMMARY OF WEB LINKS /_____

http://www.inspiration.com/productinfo/

http://whatiscopyright.org/

FURTHER READING

Rudestam, K.E. and Newton, R.R. (2007) *Surviving your Dissertation: A Comprehensive Guide to Content and Process,* 3rd edn. Newbury Park, CA: Sage. Provides practical guidance on selecting topics, and what the literature review, methods and results chapters should contain.

Berry, R. (2004) *The Research Project: How to Write it,* 5th edn. Oxford: Routledge. Covers themes such as choosing a topic, shaping and composing a project and avoiding common pitfalls. Includes an example of a well written paper along with notes and bibliography.

McCarthy, P. and Hatcher, C. (2002) *Presentation Skills: The Essential Guide for Students.* London: Sage. Practical and constructive advice for students that includes, but goes well beyond, how to use technology in making presentations.